The Fat Studies Reader

The Fat Studies Reader

EDITED BY

Esther Rothblum and Sondra Solovay

FOREWORD BY

Marilyn Wann

NEW YORK UNIVERSITY PRESS

NEW YORK AND LONDON

NEW YORK UNIVERSITY PRESS
New York and London
www.nyupress.org

Library of Congress Cataloging-in-Publication Data

The fat studies reader /
edited by Esther Rothblum and Sondra Solovay;
foreword by Marilyn Wann.
p. cm.
Includes bibliographical references and index.
ISBN-13: 978-0-8147-7630-8 (cl : alk. paper)
ISBN-10: 0-8147-7630-2 (cl : alk. paper)
ISBN-13: 978-0-8147-7631-5 (pb : alk. paper)
ISBN-10: 0-8147-7631-0 (pb : alk. paper)
1. Obesity—Social aspects. 2. Overweight persons.
I. Rothblum, Esther D. II. Solovay, Sondra, 1970–
RA645.O23F55   2009
362.196'398—dc22   2009017385

New York University Press books are printed on acid-free paper,
and their binding materials are chosen for strength and durability.
We strive to use environmentally responsible suppliers and materials
to the greatest extent possible in publishing our books.

Manufactured in the United States of America
c   10 9 8 7 6 5 4 3 2 1
p   10 9 8 7 6 5 4 3 2 1

Contents

Foreword: Fat Studies: An Invitation to Revolution   xi
    Marilyn Wann

Acknowledgments   xxvii

Introduction   1
    Sondra Solovay and Esther Rothblum

PART I WHAT IS FAT STUDIES? THE SOCIAL AND
          HISTORICAL CONSTRUCTION OF FATNESS

1. The Inner Corset: A Brief History of Fat in the United States   11
    Laura Fraser

2. Fattening Queer History: Where Does Fat History Go from Here?   15
    Elena Levy-Navarro

PART II FAT STUDIES IN HEALTH AND MEDICINE

3. Does Social Class Explain the Connection   25
    Between Weight and Health?
    Paul Ernsberger

4. Is "Permanent Weight Loss" an Oxymoron? The Statistics   37
    on Weight Loss and the National Weight Control Registry
    Glenn Gaesser

5. What Is "Health at Every Size"?   41
    Deb Burgard

6. Widening the Dialogue to Narrow the Gap in Health   54
    Disparities: Approaches to Fat Black Lesbian and
    Bisexual Women's Health Promotion
    Bianca D. M. Wilson

7. Quest for a Cause: The Fat Gene, the Gay Gene, and the New Eugenics 65
    Kathleen LeBesco

8.   Prescription for Harm: Diet Industry Influence,   75
     Public Health Policy, and the "Obesity Epidemic"
     Pat Lyons

9.   Public Fat: Canadian Provincial Governments and Fat on the Web   88
     Laura Jennings

10. That Remains to Be Said: Disappeared Feminist Discourses   97
     on Fat in Dietetic Theory and Practice
     Lucy Aphramor and Jacqui Gingras

11. Fatness (In)visible: Polycystic Ovarian Syndrome and   106
     the Rhetoric of Normative Femininity
     Christina Fisanick

PART III FATNESS AS SOCIAL INEQUALITY

12. Fat Kids, Working Moms, and the "Epidemic of Obesity":   113
     Race, Class, and Mother Blame
     Natalie Boero

13. Fat Youth as Common Targets for Bullying   120
     Jacqueline Weinstock and Michelle Krehbiel

14. Bon Bon Fatty Girl: 127
     A Qualitative Exploration of Weight Bias in Singapore
     Maho Isono, Patti Lou Watkins, and Lee Ee Lian

15. Part-Time Fatso   139
     S. Bear Bergman

16. Double Stigma: Fat Men and Their Male Admirers   143
     Nathaniel C. Pyle and Michael I. Loewy

17. The Shape of Abuse: Fat Oppression as a   151
     Form of Violence Against Women
     Tracy Royce

18. Fat Women as "Easy Targets":   158
     Achieving Masculinity Through Hogging
     Ariane Prohaska and Jeannine Gailey

19. No Apology: Shared Struggles in Fat and Transgender Law   167
     Dylan Vade and Sondra Solovay

20. Access to the Sky: Airplane Seats and Fat Bodies as Contested Spaces   176
     Joyce L. Huff

21. Neoliberalism and the Constitution of Contemporary Bodies   187
     Julie Guthman

22. Sitting Pretty: Fat Bodies, Classroom Desks, and Academic Excess   197
    Ashley Hetrick and Derek Attig

23. Stigma Threat and the Fat Professor: 205
    Reducing Student Prejudice in the Classroom
    Elena Andrea Escalera

24. Fat Stories in the Classroom: What and How Are They Teaching About Us?   213
    Susan Koppelman

PART IV SIZE-ISM IN POPULAR CULTURE AND LITERATURE

25. Fat Girls and Size Queens: Alternative Publications and   223
    the Visualizing of Fat and Queer Eroto-politics in
    Contemporary American Culture
    Stefanie Snider

26. Fat Girls Need Fiction   231
    Susan Stinson

27. Fat Heroines in Chick-Lit: Gateway to Acceptance in the Mainstream?   235
    Lara Frater

28. The Fat of the (Border)land: Food, Flesh, and Hispanic   241
    Masculinity in Willa Cather's *Death Comes for the Archbishop*
    Julia McCrossin

29. Placing Fat Women on Center Stage   249
    JuliaGrace Jester

30. "The White Man's Burden": Female Sexuality, Tourist Postcards, and   256
    the Place of the Fat Woman in Early 20th-Century U.S. Culture
    Amy Farrell

31. The Roseanne Benedict Arnolds: How Fat Women Are   263
    Betrayed by Their Celebrity Icons
    Beth Bernstein and Matilda St. John

32. Jiggle in My Walk: The Iconic Power of the "Big Butt"   271
    in American Pop Culture
    Wendy A. Burns-Ardolino

33. Seeing Through the Layers: Fat Suits and Thin Bodies   280
    in *The Nutty Professor* and *Shallow Hal*
    Katharina R. Mendoza

34. Controlling the Body: Media Representations,   289
    Body Size, and Self-Discipline
    Dina Giovanelli and Stephen Ostertag

PART V   EMBODYING AND EMBRACING FATNESS

35.   "I'm Allowed to Be a Sexual Being":   299
      The Distinctive Social Conditions of the Fat Burlesque Stage
         D. Lacy Asbill

36.   Embodying Fat Liberation   305
         Heather McAllister

37.   Not Jane Fonda: Aerobics for Fat Women Only   312
         Jenny Ellison

38.   Exorcising the Exercise Myth: Creating Women of Substance   320
         Dana Schuster and Lisa Tealer

PART VI   STARTING THE REVOLUTION

39.   Maybe It Should Be Called Fat American Studies   327
         Charlotte Cooper

40.   Are We Ready to Throw Our Weight Around?   334
      Fat Studies and Political Activism
         Deb Burgard, Elana Dykewomon, Esther Rothblum, and Pattie Thomas

      Appendix A: Fat Liberation Manifesto, November 1973   341
         Judy Freespirit and Aldebaran

      Appendix B: Legal Briefs   343

      About the Contributors   351

      Index   359

Foreword

Fat Studies: An Invitation to Revolution

Marilyn Wann

> You'll learn things you never knew you never knew.
> —Lyrics from *Pocahontas*, an anticolonialist movie that contains
> unexamined colonialism (Menken & Schwartz, 1995)

As a new, interdisciplinary field of intellectual inquiry, fat studies is defined in part by what it is not.

For example, if you believe that fat people could (and should) lose weight, then you are not doing fat studies—you are part of the $58.6 billion-per-year weight-loss industry or its vast customer base (Marketdata Enterprises, 2007).

If you believe that being fat is a disease and that fat people cannot possibly enjoy good health or long life, then you are not doing fat studies. Instead, your approach is aligned with "obesity" researchers, bariatric surgeons, public health officials who declare "war on obesity" (Koop, 1997), and the medico-pharmaceutical industrial complex that profits from dangerous attempts to "cure" people of bodily difference (more on "obesity" later).

If you believe that thin is inherently beautiful and fat is obviously ugly, then you are not doing fat studies work either. You are instead in the realm of advertising, popular media, or the more derivative types of visual art—in other words, propaganda.

Fat studies is a radical field, in the sense that it goes to the root of weight-related belief systems.

The contrasting endeavors mentioned above are prescriptive in nature. They assume that human weight is mutable and negotiable, assumptions that are informed by current social bias and stigma against fatness and fat people. On this point, fat studies is—in strong contrast—descriptive. Weight, like height, is a human characteristic that varies across any population in a bell curve (Flegal, 2006). An individual person's weight also varies over the course of a lifetime, influenced largely by inherited predisposition and only marginally by environmental factors like eating and exercise patterns (Hainer, Stunkard, Kunesova, Parizkova, Stich, & Allison, 2001). Most people naturally occupy a middle range of weights (and heights), whereas some people naturally weigh less and some people naturally weigh more (just as some people are naturally tall or short). Heights and weights also vary between populations and time periods, due in large part to levels of economic development, access to food, advances in medicine and immunization, and other large-scale factors (Kolata, 2006). There have always been and will always be people of different heights. There have also always been and there will also always be people of different weights. Unlike traditional approaches to weight, a fat studies approach offers no opposition to the simple fact of human weight diversity, but instead looks at what people and societies make of this reality.

The field of fat studies requires skepticism about weight-related beliefs that are popular, powerful, and prejudicial. This skepticism is currently rare, even taboo. Questioning the received knowledge on weight is socially risky. American culture is engaged in a pervasive witch hunt targeting fatness and fat people (a project that is rapidly being exported worldwide). Although this urge to eradicate fat people continues, it is not only challenging to be fat, but also especially challenging to question any aspect of the witch hunt on fat people (not that it is so very comfortable to be thin during a weight-based witch hunt). Whenever members of a society have recourse to only one opinion on a basic human experience, that is precisely the discourse and the experience that should attract intellectual curiosity.

Social Justice and Fat Studies

Historically, liberation movements have preceded the establishment of related fields of academic or theoretical inquiry. The Stonewall riots took place years before the first queer theory conference. Women were fighting for the right to vote at least 150 years before professors started getting tenure in women's studies departments. African Americans won freedom from slavery and began to found traditionally black colleges and universities long before being granted full civic equality. In 1935, people with physical disabilities held a sit-in to protest their automatic exclusion from WPA jobs during the Great Depression, but a deaf person was not president of a major U.S. university (Gallaudet) until 1988. And transgender people resisted police brutality during the Compton's Cafeteria riot in San Francisco long before gender theorists considered a nonbinary approach.

Fat pride community, often called the size acceptance movement, began in the United States with the National Association to Advance Fat Acceptance in 1969 and the powerful work of the Fat Underground in the 1970s. Since then, grassroots groups have built resources for self-esteem, fitness, fashion, socializing, medical advocacy, and defense from discrimination, while creating theater, dance, music, poetry, fiction, magazines, film, and art. Weight prejudice is a U.S. export that activists overseas are starting to resist. The field of fat studies offers a crucial corollary to fat pride community and fat civil rights activism. Fat studies has the potential to make a unique contribution as a theoretical and analytic undertaking, and also to provide much-needed momentum and moral suasion for social justice for people of all sizes.

For many years, fat studies was not a field but an individual endeavor taken up by isolated scholars. Esther Rothblum has a career-long commitment to exploring weight stigma. Anthropologist Margaret Mackenzie conducted important research on fat acceptance in Pacific Island cultures (1986). Medical anthropologist Jeffrey So-bal's work on the social meanings of weight include coediting two anthologies with Donna Maurer, *Interpreting Weight: The Social Management of Fatness and Thinness* (1999a), and *Weighty Issues: Fatness and Thinness as Social Problems* (1999b). Sondra Solovay surveyed the diverse fields of law where weight had become a courtroom topic in *Tipping the Scales of Justice: Fighting Weight-Based Discrimination* (2000). Kathleen LeBesco coedited the anthology of thoughtful essays *Bodies Out of Bounds: Fatness and Transgression* (Braziel & Lebesco, 2001) and later wrote her own impor-tant analysis in *Revolting Bodies? The Struggle to Redefine Fat Identity* (2004). In the last decade, people have written enough dissertations, journal articles, and books to begin to fill a fat studies bookshelf. A small yet worthy footnote family has devel-oped. I locate the beginnings of the fat studies field with the conference at Columbia University Teachers College in the spring of 2004 titled "Fat Attitudes: An Examina-tion of an American Subculture and the Representation of the Female Body," and the accompanying art show titled "Fat Attitudes: A Celebration of Large Women." Both events were organized by then–graduate student Lori Don Levan, PhD, who is now a professor of arts education and crafts at Kutztown University. In the next two years, fat studies expanded via panels at regional and national conferences of the Popular Culture Association/American Culture Association, thanks in large part to the vision of Susan Koppelman, editor of a short-fiction anthology *The Strange History of Su-zanne LaFleshe, and Other Stories of Women and Fatness* (2003). In spring of 2006, Sheana Director and other members of the Smith College anti-sizism student orga-nization Size Matters hosted another landmark conference titled "Fat and the Acad-emy." At the time of this writing, several hundred fat activists and people working in the field of fat studies are discussing issues and supporting each other's work on the fat studies e-mail list (http://www.groups.yahoo.com/group/fatstudies) that I founded in June 2004 and continue to moderate. In 2006, the *New York Times*, the *Chronicle of Higher Education*, and the National Women's Studies Association newsletter *NWS-Action* covered the nascent field of fat studies. This book, *The Fat Studies Reader*—not to mention the scholarship and course offerings that it will inspire—represents a big step toward establishing fat studies as a field.

Before Starting Any Fat Studies Program, Consult Your . . .

In the opening of this essay, three examples are offered in contradistinction to fat studies. They are written in the second person for this reason: If you participate in the field of fat studies, you must be willing to examine not just the broader social forces related to weight but also your own involvement with these structures. If you do fat studies work, you yourself are always already part of the topic. Every person who lives in a fat-hating culture inevitably absorbs anti-fat beliefs, assumptions, and stereotypes, and also inevitably comes to occupy a position in relation to power arrangements that are based on weight. None of us can ever hope to be completely free of such train-ing or completely disentangled from the power grid. None of us is responsible for the whole belief system. But if you undertake to do fat studies work without also acknowledging and addressing your own position in relation to weight-based privilege and oppression, you risk undermining your ostensible efforts with your own unexamined and counterproductive assumptions. Your relationship to weight-based privilege and oppression is both internalized (the beliefs that we carry with us and impose on ourselves and others) and external (our interactions with people, institutions, and social and material conditions that are affected by weight). Acknowledging one side (internal or external) without acknowledging the other leaves you vulnerable to fat hatred and is unlikely to be fully effective. Addressing internalized attitudes supports your ability to address external power dynamics, and vice versa, in a positive feedback loop that can benefit both your work and your life. You will inevitably encounter personal and conceptual blind spots in the process of understanding and refining your own position. These interruptions in awareness are remediable; they come into view more readily if you keep shaking your head at the absurdity of any of us being made to explain or defend the basic fact of our embodiment.

What Do You Say?

Word choice is a good place to begin to examine assumptions. How do you refer to people at the heavier-than-average end of the weight bell curve? Currently, in mainstream U.S. society, the O-words, "overweight" and "obese," are considered more acceptable, even more polite, than the F-word, "fat." In the field of fat studies, there is agreement that the O-words are neither neutral nor benign. (The editors and contributors of this *Reader* have chosen to surround the O-words with scare quotes to indicate their compromised status.) In fat studies, there is respect for the political project of reclaiming the word *fat*, both as the preferred neutral adjective (i.e., short/tall, young/old, fat/thin) and also as a preferred term of political identity. There is nothing negative or rude in the word *fat* unless someone makes the effort to put it there; using the word *fat* as a descriptor (not a discriminator) can help dispel prejudice. Seemingly well-meaning euphemisms like "heavy," "plump," "husky," and so forth put a falsely positive spin on a negative view of fatness.

Over What Weight?

"Overweight" is inherently anti-fat. It implies an extreme goal: instead of a bell curve distribution of human weights, it calls for a lone, towering, unlikely bar graph with everyone occupying the same (thin) weights. If a word like "overweight" is acceptable and even preferable, then weight prejudice becomes accepted and preferred. (The population is getting taller, but we do not bemoan *overheight* or warn people to keep below, say, five feet eight. Being tall is valued. For an important introduction to height prejudice, see Ellen Frankel's book *Beyond Measure: A Memoir About Short Stature and Inner Growth*, 2006).

In related terminology, it is not meaningful to call weights "normal" or "abnormal." (Although mathematically, "average" weights certainly exist in any population.) The body shape that is normal for tall and thin Broadway choreographer Tommy Tune is not the weight that is normal for short and fat movie and television actor/producer Danny DeVito. Expecting either of these entertainers to look like the other would not be healthy, nor would it increase their box-office value. There would also be no benefit if Olympic weightlifter Cheryl Haworth and tennis champion Maria Sharapova were expected to trade weights.

Similarly, health is a problematic concept when linked with weight. Health is not a number, but rather a subjective experience with many influences. Stepping onto a scale cannot prove a person healthy or unhealthy. In Health at Every Size (HAES), people discuss weight in health-neutral ways and discuss health in weight-neutral ways. (Readers may refer to Deb Burgard's excellent introductory chapter, "What Is Health at Every Size?" in this volume. As a field, Health at Every Size joins fat studies and fat pride community in creating a sturdy tripod of support for the larger project of questioning and undoing weight prejudice.) Weight is an inaccurate basis for predicting individual health or longevity, much less someone's eating or exercise habits. For example, the majority of people categorized as "obese"—seven out of eight—are not diabetic (National Center for Health Statistics, 2006). "Health" can be used to police body conformity and can be code for weight-related judgments that are socially, not scientifically, driven. "Health" can also cover a whole range of beliefs and behaviors (eating disorders, moralizing about food or fitness, alienation from one's own body) that reinforce social control around weight and can be very damaging to well-being. Like the F-word, health is a term that calls for a conscious project of reclamation.

The Epidemic of the Word "Obesity"

It will require the work of many fat studies scholars to fully trace all the harm caused by use of the term "obesity" (including belittling assumptions, internalized oppression, discriminatory consequences, and more). As shorthand for this litany, many people doing fat studies quarantine "obesity" inside scare quotes. It is also common to begin presentations with a disclaimer that the term "obesity" is, at best, contested. Others use qualifiers, referring to alleged or so-called obesity. In sum, "obesity" is sic [sic].

Calling fat people "obese" medicalizes human diversity. Medicalizing diversity inspires a misplaced search for a "cure" for naturally occurring difference. Far from generating sympathy for fat people, medicalization of weight fuels anti-fat prejudice and discrimination in all areas of society. People think: If fat people need to be cured, there must be something wrong with them. Cures should work; if they do not, it is the fat person's fault and a license not to employ, date, educate, rent to, sell clothes to, give a medical exam to, see on television, respect, or welcome such fat people in society. Such hateful attitudes are acceptable because no one really believes that being fat is any kind of disease. If fat people suffered from a real illness, our detractors' attitudes would be unacceptably cruel. The pretense of concern for fat people's health wards anti-fat attitudes against exposure as simple hatred. Belief in a "cure" also masks that hatred. It is not possible to hate a group of people for our own good. Medicalization actually helps categorize fat people as social untouchables. It is little surprise, then, that when fat people do fall ill, we get blame, not compassion. We receive punishment, not help. Medical cures are inappropriate when applied to social ills. Such a misdiagnosis can be very dangerous. Ascribing illness to everyone whose weight falls above an arbitrary cutoff inevitably yields mistakes—when I give weight diversity talks, I say, "The only thing that anyone can diagnose, with any certainty, by looking at a fat person, is their own level of stereotype and prejudice toward fat people."

Who Is Fat?

In the United States, any number of self-appointed authorities are eager to designate who is fat and who is not. The federal government, health insurers, medical doctors, school nurses, popular media, advertising, the fashion industry, strangers, acquaintances, friends, family members, romantic partners, and, of course, the bathroom scale—each alleged authority draws its own line between fat and thin, does so at different weights, and may redraw the line at any time. For example, a Blue Cross of California health insurance underwriter admitted to me in 2003 that the company's weight limit for people it deems "morbidly obese" (and thus uninsurable) had changed six times in the preceding decade. I replied, "Those lines sure are infallible!" Such intermittent feedback can be very disorienting. When being thin or fat in our society confers privilege or oppression, the stakes are high.

The federal government has used a variety of "ideal" weight charts, most recently switching to Body Mass Index (BMI, a way to collapse height and weight into one number). (It is no more meaningful to know that I have a BMI of 49 than it is to know that I'm five feet four inches and weigh 285 pounds.) In 1998, the BMI cutoff points that define "overweight" and "obese" categories were lowered; with that change, millions of people became fat overnight. The "obesity" researchers who lobbied for this redefinition argued that the new lines were evidence-based: the "overweight" line was supposed to indicate the weight at which people face increased risk of disease (morbidity), and the "obese" line was supposed to indicate the weight at which people face increased risk of death (mortality). Morbidity/mortality correlations with weight are often contradictory. Sometimes being fat protects against disease. Sometimes fatter people live longer (Andres, 1980; Flegal, Graubard, Williamson, & Gail, 2005). The federal government still draws lines at the conveniently memorable BMIs of 25 and 30. People with a BMI under 18.5 are labeled "underweight." People whose BMI falls between 18.5. and 25 are labeled "healthy weight." People with a BMI of 25 and up are labeled "overweight." And people with a BMI of 30 and up are labeled "obese." (The term "morbidly obese" refers to BMI 40 and up, but is not used as a major reporting category; mostly it is used to sell stomach amputations.) In *Health, United States, 2006* (National Center for Health Statistics, 2006), a publication of the National Center for Health Statistics, part of the Centers for Disease Control, results from the National Health and Nutrition Examination Survey for 2001 to 2004 indicate that 1.7 percent of Americans between the ages of 20 and 74 fell into the "underweight" category, 32.2 percent fell into the "healthy" weight category, 34 percent fell into the "overweight" category, and 32.1 percent fell into the "obese" category.

The weight divide is not just a fat/thin binary. In *The Culture of Conformism: Understanding Social Consent*, Patrick Colm Hogan (2001) describes microhierarchization, a process that certainly applies to weight-based attitudes. People feel superiority or self-loathing based on each calorie or gram of food consumed or not consumed, in each belt notch, pound, or inch gained or lost, in each clothing size smaller or larger. Each micro-rung on the weight-based hierarchy exerts pressure to covet the next increment thinner and regret the next increment fatter, leaving little room for people to recognize and revolt against the overall system that alienates us from our own bodies.

Power lies both in naming and in rejecting naming. The federal government categorizes me as "morbidly obese"; I identify as fat. Is it self-contradictory to claim membership in the fat club when I seek to disrupt belief in the meaningfulness or usefulness of weight categories? No, it's just ironic. Claiming one's embodiment (whatever one weighs) is a form of political resistance, a way to undo alienation. A fat-hating society asks fearfully, "Do I look fat?" I respond, "I am Fatacus!" Just as Kurt Cobain of Nirvana (1993) sang, "Everyone is gay," in a fat-hating society everyone is fat. Fat functions as a floating signifier, attaching to individuals based on a power relationship, not a physical measurement. People all along the weight spectrum may experience fat oppression. A young woman who weighs eighty-seven pounds because of her anorexia knows something about fat oppression. So does a fat person who is expected to pay double for the privilege of sitting down during an airplane flight. Each person brings useful leverage to help shift attitudes. I welcome thin people not as allies but as colleagues. If we imagine that the conflict is between fat and thin, weight prejudice continues. Instead, the conflict is between all of us against a system that would weigh our value as people. If we cannot feel at home in our own skins, where else are we supposed to go?

The field of fat studies is not concerned with a small subgroup of people. U.S. government health officials designate two-thirds of people as over the line for "ideal," "healthy," or "normal" weight. The remaining third are encouraged to live in fear of getting fat. Frustrated by a failed, forty-year effort to cut adults down to cookie-cutter size, hysteria mongers have shifted their aim to children. One scare tactic involves schools alerting parents their children have fallen into the nonsensical category "at risk of becoming overweight." Yet Americans are fatter and taller and healthier and longer-lived than ever before in human history (Kolata, 2006). Nonetheless, its public policy to aggressively export fear of the fat menace—"globesity"—even to places where people go hungry (World Health Organization, 2006). Fat or not, everybody has a stake in the findings of scholars who advance the new field of fat studies.

Three Hundred Thousand Fat Deaths?
Do I Hear Four Hundred Thousand?

For a decade, fat people have been hearing more frequent and more insistent death threats. The threats first became popular when Interneuron Pharmaceuticals and Wyeth-Ayerst sought FDA approval for Redux in 1997. (Redux produced six pounds of weight loss compared to placebo. It was recalled when users developed serious illness and even died.) "Obesity" researchers who testified in support of Redux claimed that three hundred thousand people die annually from being fat. University of California, Davis, nutrition professor Judith Stern testified that things were dire, and that anyone who did not vote to approve Redux should be shot (McAfee, 1994). The three hundred thousand claim was based on an estimate of extra deaths due to poor nutrition and lack of exercise. The original study, by McGinnis and Foege (1998), included no weight data. Its authors took the unusual step of publishing an open letter in the *New England Journal of Medicine* in April 1998 asking people to stop misusing their results. By that point, however, the FDA had already responded to the threats by approving Redux.

Although journalists continue to cite the debunked three hundred thousand figure, "obesity" researchers invented a new, improved version—four hundred thousand fat deaths per year. They developed this number by applying estimates of how many fat people *should* be dying to the current number of fat people and the current number of deaths. In comparison, Katherine Flegal, PhD, a researcher for the National Center for Health Statistics at the Centers for Disease Control, published a methodologically unassailable study of actual deaths in various weight categories and found a much lower figure—111,900 more deaths—among the alleged "obese" than in the "normal" weight category (Flegal, 2006; Flegal et al., 2005). She also found 86,000 *fewer* deaths among people whom the government labels "overweight," and 33,746 *more* deaths among "underweight" people. In an editorial, she admonished, "We thought it important to clarify in our article that any associations of weight with mortality were not necessarily causal but might be due, wholly or in part, to other factors, such as activity, diet, body composition or fat distribution, that were associated both with weight and with mortality" (Flegal, 2006, p. 1171).

One need not quote Mark Twain regarding exaggerated predictions of our demise to note that most of the experts who influence federal "obesity" policy fantasize about fat people dying in droves. To put these fantasies in harsh perspective, consider that in the twenty-five-year history of the HIV/AIDS epidemic in the United States, more than 529,000 people have died from AIDS. At its worst, in 1995, more than 50,000 people died from this infectious disease (Centers for Disease Control, 2004). If fat deaths truly were sixfold or eightfold compared to AIDS deaths, I think we would have noticed. There'd be an outcry. Lynn McAfee, the medical liaison for the Council on Size and Weight Discrimination, would not be the only self-identified fat person to attend CDC and FDA meetings to ask the government to check its facts on "obesity." With no giant pile of dead fat bodies, death threats about fatness sound like wishful thinking. During the last quarter century, while Americans have gained on average twenty or so pounds, the mainstream media has gone from mentioning the term "obesity" only sixty times per year in the early 1980s to five hundred times per year in 1990, to one thousand mentions in 1995, three thousand mentions in 2000, and seven thousand panic-stricken mentions of "obesity" in 2003 (Saguy & Riley, 2005). When Flegal significantly lowered estimates of fat deaths, none of the "obesity" researchers were glad.

Only sturdy people could endure the kind of neglect and endangerment that fat people often experience at the hands of the medical establishment and continue to live as long as we do.

You Cannot Simultaneously Prevent and Prepare for War

Overt prejudice and discrimination may be less of a hindrance to social justice for fat people than projects that claim to offer help but nonetheless rely on—and promote— fat hatred. Echoing the quotation attributed to Albert Einstein that provides the title for this section, several institutions offer examples of this disturbing oil-and-water mix of politics and prejudice: the American "Obesity" Association (AOA), the "Obesity" Law and Advocacy Center, and Yale University's Rudd Center on Food Policy and "Obesity," for example (I have added the scare quotes to their names). The AOA is a group made up of "obesity" researchers and weight-loss physicians who seem to believe that the interests of fat people are completely subsumed in the interests of professionals whose careers profit only if fat is a disease. A visitor to attorney Walter Lindstrom's "Obesity" Law and Advocacy Center Web site might imagine that fat people's civil rights reside in our gastrointestinal tracts, as the preponderance of his materials concern making insurers pay for digestive mutilations, with only a few brief mentions of the phenomenon of weight discrimination. For example, twenty-six of the Web site's thirty-one Frequently Asked Questions are about gastric bonsai, yet none addresses weight discrimination. A Resources section has only surgical listings. In Lindstrom's eStore, which sells numerous nutritional supplements for surgery survivors, twenty-eight of thirty-one books for sale proselytize so-called weight-loss surgery, whereas no titles address weight discrimination (Lindstrom, 2007). As a vehicle for social change, Yale's Rudd Center manages to stomp on both the accelerator and the brake pedal. According to Rudd's mission statement, its goals are to "improve the world's diet, prevent obesity, and reduce weight stigma" (Rudd Center, 2006). With its first two goals, Rudd actually increases weight stigma, thereby undermining its third goal. There is no nice, unstigmatizing way to wish that fat people did not eat or exist. Besides, "obesity" prevention is a fallback position, a tacit admission that experts hope the same tips that have failed to produce weight loss will somehow prevent weight gain. Why should good nutrition not concern thin people? Why advance a food-policy agenda on the backs of fat people? When HAES psychologist Deb Burgard asked Brownell just that question at the International Conference on Eating Disorders in Montreal in spring of 2005, he said, "The reason that in terms of testifying before Congress and giving a talk like this, I use 'obesity' so much, is it has political currency these days" (Brownell, 2005). The dubious goal of "obesity" prevention gets funding, yet ending weight discrimination does not. Al Gore quotes Upton Sinclair in the global warming film *An Inconvenient Truth* as having written, "It is difficult to get a man to understand something when his job depends upon his not understanding it." Weight discrimination will continue to thrive so long as efforts to end it focus on changing people's bodies rather than changing people's minds.

This chapter serves as an introduction to concepts necessary for a field of fat studies. Such a field is an intellectual endeavor, but it is also inevitably involved with how individuals and institutions in our world relate to weight. Insofar as fat studies work reinforces or revolutionizes attitudes about weight, it is political.

Fat Studies and Fat Realities

In 1974, not long after the Fat Underground staged a takeover of the stage at a major women's rally to protest ugly rumors about popular singer (and fat woman) Cass Elliot's death, this quote appeared in the majority finding of the California Court of Appeal, Third Appellate District, case involving the Black Panthers: "Textual analysis is not enough" (Black Panther Party v. Kehoe, 1974, p. 651). Fat studies texts need to connect with the reality of weight discrimination. Claims of neutrality or objectivity in fat studies risk making analyses less credible, not more so. Critical race theory offers an excellent example of engaged academia, but fat studies need not adopt the label of critical weight theory to prove the point—as long as fat prejudice exists, fat studies will have a crucial impact.

I pass along the reminder from Paul Campos (law professor, fat studies author, and public denouncer of weight-related irrationality) that Rabbi Tarfon cautions us in Pirke Avot 2:21 that "it is not your obligation to complete the task . . . but neither are you free to desist." Although the essays in this *Reader* investigate specific topics related to weight, each one may also serve as a kind of lever, prying against a way of thinking. This *Reader* both explores a cultural construct and wields leverage on a power dynamic. The field of fat studies as a whole does not just map the contours of the vexing boulder of weight-based oppression; it also helps move that obstacle from our shared path, freeing us to enjoy authentic—rather than alienated—embodiment. This political project might matter to you because you see that people encounter extreme cruelty due to weight stigma. Better that fat studies should matter to you for your own, selfish reasons—because you are willing to recognize how weight-based attitudes needlessly constrain you, whatever you weigh.

Reasons for Revolution

In the hope of offering a partial indication of what may be at stake when we confront attitudes about weight, here is a review of some of the data documenting the impact of weight-based prejudice and discrimination in the United States.

Weight-based discrimination is a cradle-to-grave phenomenon. Fat people are officially barred from adopting babies from China. In Britain, health clinics may refuse in vitro fertilization to fat women, and the British Fertility Society has recommended a general ban (BBC News, 2006). In the United States, public health departments advertise that parents should prevent childhood "obesity." They even encourage breast-feeding, with its many benefits, as a means to this end. Girls as young as five fear gaining weight (Davison & Birch, 2001; Irvine, 2001; Richardson, 1971) At age ten, fat children are chosen last as friends by peers (Latner & Stunkard, 2003). (This survey compares the fat child only to children with visible disabilities, a poor study design; I wish to note the extent of fat children's unpopularity without reinforcing ableism.) Fatter children are far more likely to be bullied or teased (see chap. 13 by Weinstock & Krehbiel, this volume). After years of ostracism, fat teens may bully or tease others (Janssen, Craig, Boyce, & Pickett, 2004).

The National Education Association reports, "For fat students the school experience is one of ongoing prejudice, unnoticed discrimination, and almost constant harassment. From nursery school through college, fat students experience ostracism, discouragement, sometimes violence. Often ridiculed by their peers and discouraged by even well-meaning education employees, fat students develop low self-esteem and have limited horizons. They are deprived of places on honor rolls, sports teams, and cheerleading squads and are denied letters of recommendation" (1994, p. 1).

Fatter children are sadder, lonelier, more worried about school and their futures, and face greater ridicule from gym teachers (Rimm & Rimm, 2004). Average-weight children who fear becoming fat may eat too little, thereby slowing growth and delaying puberty (Pugliese, Lifshitz, Grad, Ford, & Marks-Katz, 1983). Fatter teens are more likely to face humiliating or shaming experiences that can lead to depression (Sjöberg, Nilsson, & Leppert, 2005). Teens who think that they're not the "right" weight are more likely to contemplate or attempt suicide (Eaton, Lowry, Brener, Galuska, & Crosby, 2005). A disordered relationship with food is standard among young women (Polivy & Herman, 1987). Boys are not immune. After playing with GI Joe dolls, they are more likely to starve themselves, lift weights compulsively, or take steroids (Pope, Olivardia, Gruber, & Borowiecki, 1999).

High school counselors are less likely to encourage fat students to apply for college, colleges are less likely to admit equally qualified fat applicants, and parents are less likely to pay a fat daughter's college tuition (Crandall, 1995). Colleges are typically unaware of fat students' seating needs.

Adulthood is no escape from mistreatment. In the workplace, 93 percent of human resources professionals said that they would hire a "normal weight" applicant over a fat applicant with the same qualifications. Fifteen percent would not promote a fat employee. One in ten think it is acceptable to fire an employee for being fat (Fattism Rife in Business, 2005). There is little stigma attached to discriminating against fat people (Crandall, 1994). Fat women earn nearly seven thousand dollars less in annual household income than thinner women (Gortmaker, Must, Perrin, Sobol, & Dietz, 1993). Fat workers are paid less, for no other documentable reason than weight; over a forty-year career, the disparity can total one hundred thousand dollars less in pretax earnings (Ford & Baum, 2004). In a review of twenty-nine weight discrimination studies, the fattest women earned one-fourth less than thinner workers. Women who weighed sixty-five pounds more than average-weight women received 7 percent less in salary. Employers admitted routinely turning down promising fat applicants for not "fitting the corporate image" (Cawley, 2000; Roehling, 1999, p. 969). Weight may outweigh other characteristics in influencing hiring and other employment decisions (Larkin & Pines, 1979). Fat employees are denied health insurance benefits and are pressured to resign or are fired for being fat (Rothblum, Brand, Miller, & Oetjen, 1990). People who are considered beautiful enjoy a 5 percent salary bonus, whereas people who are considered ugly earn 5 to 10 percent less (Hamermesh & Biddle, 1994). College and university professors receive higher ratings in student evaluations if they also rank high for attractiveness (Hamermesh & Parker, 2003).

In retail settings, fat people get less respect. When fat people engage in diet talk around shop clerks, however, we are treated better than if we talk about our bodies with pride (King, Shapiro, Singletary, Turner, & Hebl, 2006). It is not just harder for fat people to work or shop; it is also harder to find housing—landlords are 50 percent less likely to rent to an equally qualified fat person (Karris, 1977).

Fat prejudice has a profound impact on social life. Fat men are 11 percent less likely to be married, and fat women are 20 percent less likely to be married (Gortmaker et al., 1993). Just being seen with a fat person can affect the social status of an average-weight person (Gallagher, Tate, McCologan, Dovey, & Halford, 2003). In that study, people described a thin man with a fat woman as "miserable, self-indulgent, passive, shapeless, depressed, weak, insignificant, and insecure" (p. A119). Internalized fat oppression is so intense that fat people hold harsher judgments upon viewing a thin man with a fat woman than average-weight people do (Gallagher, Tate, McCologan, Dovey, & Halford, 2003). Social isolation is a serious concern, not just because it is emotionally painful, but also because it can affect health. Men who have numerous friends and close friendships are half as likely to develop heart disease (Rosengren, Wilhelmsena, & Orth-Gomérb, 2004).

Fat people are at risk in the medical setting itself. Imaging equipment like MRIs or CT scans often have weight limits. Finding machines that accommodate higher weights is left to patients, who may face life-or-death consequences from the result of their search (and information about accessible imaging devices is not reliably available from providers, accrediting bodies, or device manufacturers). The fatter a patient is, the more likely a surgeon is to leave sponges or even surgical instruments behind, an error that necessitates further surgery for 70 percent of such cases (Gawande, Studdert, Orav, Brenner, & Zinner, 2002).

The biased attitudes of health-care providers also put fat patients at risk (O'Neil & Rogers, 1998). Physicians view fat patients negatively and avoid spending time with us (Hebl & Xu, 2001). Even doctors and researchers who specialize in "obesity" harbor stereotypes of fat people as lazy, stupid, and worthless (Schwartz, Chambliss, Brownell, Blair, & Billington, 2003; Teachman & Brownell, 2001) (the Rudd Center scholars who authored these studies also specialize in "obesity," but do not disclose their own levels of weight bias). Nurses hold negative views of fat patients (Brown, 2006; Maroney &

Golub, 1992). Students of exercise science see fat people as bad and lazy (Chambliss, Finley & Blair, 2004). Mental health professionals are more likely to evaluate fat people negatively (Agell & Rothblum, 1991; Young & Powell, 1985). Fat people who need organ transplants may be told to lose weight to be eligible (Hasse, 1997).

Fat women are a third less likely to receive breast exams, Pap smears, or gynecologic exams, but are no less likely to receive mammograms, which may indicate obstetric/gynecology physicians' hesitation to touch fat patients. Researchers admitted that weight-based barriers to care "may exacerbate or even account for some of the increased health risks correlated with higher weights" (Fontaine, Faith, Allison, & Chetkin, 1998, p. 383). Twelve percent of well-educated women reported delaying or canceling physician appointments because they knew that they would be weighed. Olson, Schumaker, and Yawn (1994, p. 891) wrote, "If we are to reach our goal of health maintenance, we must work to remove the barriers that keep obese patients out of their physicians' offices." Even when fat women have health insurance, we avoid doctors because of "disrespectful treatment, embarrassment at being weighed, negative attitudes of providers, unsolicited advice to lose weight, and medical equipment that was too small to be functional" (Amy, Aalborg, Lyons, & Keranen, 2006, p. 147). Given the intensity of fat stigma, especially in the medical setting, it is no surprise that a third of "obese" people would risk death or trade five years of life to lose even 10 percent of their weight. The more we weigh, the more willing we are to risk our lives to lose weight (Wee, Hamel, Davis, & Phillips, 2004; these findings explain, to some extent, why fat people consent to life-threatening stomach amputations). If fat people believe the lie that our lives are not worth living, we are unlikely to hold our health-care providers to a high standard of safety or efficacy for our care.

The anti-fat bias of health-care providers leads to improper diagnoses. For example, physicians told a fat man in London for an entire decade that his abdominal pain was due to his "obesity." Finally, he received a scan and surgeons removed a fifty-five-pound malignant tumor ("Overweight" Man, 2005).

Anti-fat attitudes are rigged to be impervious. Anti-fat attitudes increase when weight is explained by overeating and lack of exercise, but do not decrease with a genetic explanation. Stories of weight discrimination (like the above litany) reduce anti-fat attitudes only in people who are fat (Teachman, Gapinski, Brownell, Rawlings, & Jeyaram, 2003). Fat studies can challenge this ingrown thinking.

Conclusion

Every major industry and institution has some level of monetary stake in perpetuating weight-based stereotypes, prejudice, and discrimination. A billboard advertising the MINI Cooper automobile showed the car with the slogan "100% fat free." Fear and hatred sell, and people are buying megadoses. Yet anti-fat attitudes impose a huge personal and financial cost to society. Amid such crushing social coercion and control, the field of fat studies can offer a revelatory new lens on the central human question of embodiment, a theoretical approach that will have direct political and social effects. Like feminist studies, queer studies, and disability studies, which consider gender, sexuality, or functional difference, fat studies can show us who we are via the lens of weight. Fat studies can offer an analysis that is in solidarity with resistance to other forms of oppression by offering a new and unique view of alienation. I would have stopped my work after publishing one issue of the *FAT!SO?* zine if I had not received letters from people who said, "This is the first thing that ever made me feel okay." Until the fat studies bookshelf is longer than the diet book shelf, people will find their first contact with self-respect via the writing in this field. There is more than enough fat studies work for all of us to do: connections to make, freedom to envision, liberation to embody, and implications to comprehend. As disability theory scholar Lennard Davis (2002, p. 26) wrote, "Difference is what we all have in common." Welcome to the revolution!

REFERENCES

Agell, G., & Rothblum, E.D. (1991). Effects of Clients' Obesity and Gender on the Therapy Judgments of Psychologists, *Professional Psychology: Theory and Practice, 22*, 223–229.

Amy, N.K., Aalborg, A., Lyons, P., & Keranen, L. (2006). Barriers to Routine Gynecological Cancer Screening for White and African-American Obese Women, *International Journal of Obesity, 30(1)*, 147–155.

Andres, R. (1980). Effect of Obesity on Total Mortality, *International Journal of Obesity, 4(4)*, 381–386.

Baum, C.L., & Ford, F.F. (2004). The Wage Effects of Obesity: A Longitudinal Study, *Health Economics, 13(9)*, 885–899.

BBC News. (2006, August 30). Call for Fertility Ban for Obese. Retrieved February 28, 2007, from http://news.bbc.co.uk/2/hi/health/5296200.stm.

Black Panther Party v. Kehoe (1974). 42 Cal. App. 3d 645, 652–656. 117 Cal. Rptr. 106; Civ. No. 13961.

Braziel, J.E., & Lebesco, K. (2001). *Bodies Out of Bounds: Fatness and Transgression.* Berkeley, CA: University of California Press.

Brown, I. (2006). Nurses' Attitudes Towards Adult Patients Who Are Obese, *Journal of Advanced Nursing, 53(2)*, 221–232.

Brownell, K. (2005, April 28). Correcting the Toxic Food Environment: Real Change Requires Real Change. Academy for Eating Disorders, International Conference on Eating Disorders. Tape K1. Retrieved September, 20, 2006, from http://www.conferencemediagroup.com.

Cawley, J. (2000, August). Body Weight and Women's Labor Market Outcomes, National Bureau of Economic Research, Working Paper W7841.

Centers for Disease Control and Prevention (2004). *HIV/AIDS Surveillance Report, 16.* Retrieved April 3, 2009, from http://www.cdc.gov/hiv/topics/surveillance/resources/reports/2004report/pdf/2004SurveillanceReport.pdf.

Chambliss, H.O., Finley, C.E., & Blair, S.N. (2004). Attitudes Toward Obese Individuals Among Exercise Science Students, *Medical Science of Sports Exercise, 36(3)*, 468–474.

Crandall, C.S. (1994). Prejudice Against Fat People: Ideology and Self-Interest, *Journal of Personality and Social Psychology, 66(5)*, 882–894.

Crandall, C.S. (1995). Do Parents Discriminate Against their Heavyweight Daughters? *Personality and Social Psychology Bulletin, 21(7)*, 724–735.

Davis, L.J. (2002). *Bending Over Backwards: Disability, Dismodernism, and Other Difficult Positions.* New York: New York University Press.

Davison, K.K., & Birch, L.L. (2001). Weight Status, Parent Reaction, and Self-Concept in Five-Year-Old Girls, *Pediatrics, 107(1)*, 46–53.

Eaton, D.K., Lowry, R., Brener, N.D., Galuska, D.A., & Crosby, A.E. (2005). Associations of Body Mass Index and Perceived Weight with Suicide Ideation and Suicide Attempts Among US High School Students, *Archives of Pediatric Adolescent Medicine, 159*, 513–519.

Fattism Rife in Business (2005, October 25). Retrieved January 26, 2009, from http://www.personneltoday.com/articles/2005/10/25/32212/fattism-rife-in-business.html.

Flegal, K.M., Graubard, B.I., Williamson, D.F., & Gail, M.H. (2005). Excess Deaths Associated with Underweight, Overweight, and Obesity, *Journal of the American Medical Association, 293*, 1861–1867.

Flegal, K. (2006). Excess Deaths Associated with Obesity: Cause and Effect, *International Journal of Obesity, 30*, 1171–1172.

Fontaine K.R., Faith, M.S., Allison, D.B., & Cheskin, L.J. (1998, July–August). Body Weight and Health Care Among Women in the General Population, *Archives of Family Medicine, 7*, 381–384.

Frankel, E. (2006). *Beyond Measure: A Memoir About Short Stature and Inner Growth.* Nashville, TN: Pearlsong Press.

Gallagher, S., Tate, T.J., McColgan, B., Dovey, T.M., & Halford, J.C.G. (2003) Negative Judgments About Male Associates of Obese Females, *Obesity Research, 11(s)*, A118–119.

Gawande, A. Studdert, D.M., Orav, E.J., Brenna, T.A., & Zinner, M.J. (2002). Risk Factors for Retained Instruments and Sponges After Surgery, *New England Journal of Medicine, 348*, 229–235.

Gortmaker, S.L., Must, A., Perrin, J.M., Sobol, A.M., & Dietz, W.H. (1993). Social and Economic Consequences of Overweight in Adolescence and Young Adulthood, *New England Journal of Medicine, 329(14)*, 1008–1012.

Hainer, V. Stunkard, A., Kunesova, M., Parizkova, J., Stich, V., & Allison, D.B. (2001). A Twin Study of Weight Loss and Metabolic Efficiency, *International Journal of Obesity Related Metabolic Disorders, 25(4)*, 533–537.

Hamermesh, D., & Biddle, J. (1994). Beauty and the Labor Market, *American Economic Review, 84*, 1174–1194.

Hamermesh, D., & Parker, A. (2003, July). Beauty in the Classroom: Professors' Pulchritude and Putative Pedagogical Productivity, National Bureau of Economic Research, Working Paper 9853.

Hasse, J. (1997). Is Obesity an Independent Risk Factor for Transplantation? *New Developments in Transplantation Medicine, 4*, 1.

Hebl, M.R., & Xu, J. (2001, August) Weighing the Care: Physicians' Reactions to the Size of a Patient. *International Journal of Obesity, 25(8)*, 1246–1252.

Hogan, P.C. (2001) *The Culture of Conformism: Understanding Social Consent.* Durham, NC: Duke University Press.

Irvine, M. (2001, July 22). Experts: Kids Worried About Weight, Associated Press.

Janssen, I., Craig, W.M., Boyce, W., & Pickett, W. (2004). Associations Between Overweight and Obesity with Bullying Behaviors in School-Aged Children, *Pediatrics, 113(5)*, 1187–1194.

Karris, L. (1977). Prejudice Against Obese Renters, *Journal of Social Psychology, 101*, 159–160.

King, E., Shapiro, J, Singletary, S., Turner, S., & Hebl, M. (2006, May) The Stigma of Obesity in Customer Service: A Mechanism for Remediation and Bottom-Line Consequences of Interpersonal Discrimination, *Journal of Applied Psychology, 91(3)*, 579–593.

Kolata, G. (2006, July 30). The New Age: So Big and Healthy Grandpa Wouldn't Even Know You, *New York Times*. Retrieved April 3, 2009, from http://www.nytimes.com/2006/07/30/health/30age.html.

Koop, C.E. (1997, September). In Spite of Diet Drug Withdrawal, the War on Obesity Must Continue Says Dr. C. Everett Koop, Shape Up America! press release. Retrieved September 30, 2006, from http://www.shapeup.org/about/arch_pr/091997.php.

Koppelman, S. (Ed.). (2003). *The Strange History of Suzanne LaFleshe, and Other Stories of Women and Fatness.* New York: Feminist Press of CUNY.

Larkin, J.C., & Pines, H.A. (1979). No Fat Persons Need Apply. *Sociology of Work and Occupations, 6,* 312–327.

Latner, J.D., & Stunkard, A.J. (2003). The Stigmatization of Obese Children, *Obesity Research, 11,* 342–456.

LeBesco, K. (2004). *Revolting Bodies: The Struggle to Redefine Fat Identity.* Amherst: University of Massachusetts Press.

Lindstrom, W. (2007). Obesity Law and Advocacy Center. Retrieved February 28, 2007, from http://www.obesitylaw.com.

Mackenzie, M. (1986). Making Morals out of Biology: an Anthropologist Looks at Cultural Values About Body Size, *Radiance Magazine, 3(2),* 10–12.

Marketdata Enterprises (2007, April 19). U.S. Weight Loss Market To Reach $58 Billion in 2007. Retrieved January 26, 2009, from http://www.prwebdirect.com/releases/2007/4/prweb520127.php.

Maroney, D., & Golub, S. (1992). Nurses' Attitudes Toward Obese Persons and Certain Ethnic Groups, *Perceptual and Motor Skills, 75(2),* 387–391.

McAfee, Lynn (1994, April). Personal communication to author by McAfee, who attended FDA hearings on approval of Redux.

McGinnis, J.M., & Foege, W.H. (1998). The Obesity Problem, *New England Journal of Medicine, 338(16),* 1157–1158.

Menken, A., & Schwartz, S. (1995). Colors of the Wind, *Pocahontas,* Walt Disney Studios.

National Center for Health Statistics (2006). *Health, United States, 2006: With Chartbook on Trends in the Health of Americans.* Retrieved November 27, 2006, from http://www.cdc.gov/nchs/hus.htm.

National Education Association (1994, October 7). Report on Discrimination Due to Physical Size. Retrieved September 30, 2006, from http://www.lectlaw.com/files/con28.htm.

Nirvana (1993). All Apologies, *In Utero,* Geffen Records.

Olson, C.L., Schumaker, H.D., & Yawn, B.P. (1994). Overweight Women Delay Medical Care, *Archives of Family Medicine, 3(10),* 888–892.

O'Neil, P.M., & Rogers, R. (1998). Health Care Providers' Unhealthy Attitudes Towards Obese People, *Weight Control Digest, 8,* 765–767.

"Overweight" Man Had 55lb Tumour. (2005, March 14). *The Evening Standard.* Retrieved September 30, 2006, from http://www.thisislondon.co.uk/news/articles/17257602?source=PA.

Polivy, J, & Herman, C.P. (1987). Diagnosis and Treatment of Normal Eating, *Journal of Consulting and Clinical Psychology, 5(1),* 635–644.

Pope, H.G., Olivardia, R., Gruber, A., & Borowiecki, J. (1999). Evolving Ideals of Male Body Image as Seen Through Action Toys, *International Journal of Eating Disorders, 26(1),* 65–72.

Pugliese M.T., Lifshitz F., Grad G., Fort P., & Marks-Katz M. (1983). Fear of Obesity. A Cause of Short Stature and Delayed Puberty, *New England Journal of Medicine, 309(9),* 513–518.

Richardson, S.A. (1971). Research Report: Handicap, Appearance, and Stigma. *Social Science and Medicine, 5,* 621–628.

Rimm, S., & Rimm, E. (2004). *Rescuing the Emotional Lives of Overweight Children.* New York: Rodale.

Roehling, M. (1999). Weight-Based Discrimination in Employment: Psychological and Legal Aspects, *Personnel Psychology, 52,* 969–1016.

Rosengren, A., Wilhelmsena, L., & Orth-Gomérb, K. (2004). Coronary Disease in Relation to Social Support and Social Class in Swedish Men, *European Heart Journal, 25(1),* 56–63.

Rothblum, E.D., Brand, P.A., Miller, C.T., & Oetjen, H.A. (1990). The Relationship Between Obesity, Employment Discrimination, and Employment-Related Victimization, *Journal of Vocational Behavior, 37,* 251–266.

Rudd Center on Food Policy and Obesity (2006). Who We Are: Rudd Center Mission. Retrieved September 30, 2006, from http://www.yaleruddcenter.org/default.aspx?id=29.

Saguy, A.C. & Riley, K.W. (2005) Weighing Both Sides: Morality, Mortality, and Framing Contests over Obesity, *Journal of Health Politics, Policy, and Law, 30(5),* 869–921.

Schwartz M.B., Chambliss, H.O., Brownell, K.D., Blair, S.N., & Billington, C. (2003). Weight Bias Among Health Professionals Specializing in Obesity, *Obesity Research, 11(9),* 1033–1039.

Sjöberg, R.L., Nilsson, K.W., & Leppert, J. (2005). Obesity, Shame, and Depression in School-Age Children: A Population-Based Study, *Pediatrics, 116(3),* e389–e393.

Sobal, J., & Maurer, D. (1999a). *Interpreting Weight: The Social Management of Fatness and Thinness.* New York: De Gruyter.

Sobal, J., & Maurer, D. (1999b). *Weighty Issues: Fatness and Thinness as Social Problems.* New York: De Gruyter.

Solovay, S. (2000). *Tipping the Scales of Justice: Fighting Weight-Based Discrimination.* Amherst, NY: Prometheus.

Teachman, B.A., & Brownell, K.D. (2001). Implicit Anti-fat Bias Among Health Professionals: Is Anyone Immune? *International Journal of Obesity, 25(10),* 1525–1531.

Teachman, B.A., Gapinski, K.D., Brownell, K.D., Rawlins, M., & Jeyaram, S. (2003). Demonstrations of Implicit Anti-fat Bias: The Impact of Providing Causal Information and Evoking Empathy, *Health Psychology, 22(1),* 68–78.

Wee, C.C., Hamel, M.B., Davis, R.B., & Phillips, R.S. (2004). Assessing the Value of Weight Loss Among Primary Care Patients, *Journal of General Internal Medicine, 19,* 1206–1211.

World Health Organization (2006) Controlling the Global Obesity Epidemic. Retrieved November 27, 2006, from http://www.who.int/nutrition/topics/obesity/en/index.html.

Young, L. & Powell, B. (1985). The Effects of Obesity on the Clinical Judgments of Mental Health Professionals, *Journal of Health and Social Behavior, 26(3),* 233–246.

Acknowledgments

We, the editors, would like to thank Marilyn Wann for her leadership in the field of fat studies, and the members of the Fat Studies Listserv for their dedication. In addition, we had an amazing literary agent in Ellen Geiger of the Frances Goldin Literary Agency. We thank our tremendous trio at New York University Press for their enthusiasm about this book project: assistant director and editor-in-chief Eric Zinner, assistant editor Ciara McLaughlin, and managing editor Despina Papazoglou Gimbel. Also special thanks to our ace copyeditor, Nicholas P. Taylor. Both Sheana Director and Josie Leimbach, graduate students in Women's Studies at San Diego State University, assisted with the editorial work of this book.

Sondra is greatly appreciative of the work of the National Association to Advance Fat Acceptance, NoLose, the Council on Size and Weight Discrimination, the International Size Acceptance Association, the Southern Poverty Law Center, and the National Organization for Women. Thanks to the following for bravery in the quest to make the world a better place: Larry Brinkin, Claudia Center, Kim Gandy, Mo Kalman, Elizabeth Kristen, Lynn Lieber, Debrenia Madison, and the students of New College of California School of Law. For supporting and inspiring Sondra in so many ways over the years, her profound appreciation goes to: Carole Cullum, Jennifer Portnick, her darling Joe, Nancy Dunbar, Kathy Solovay, and Marilyn Wann. Deep gratitude goes to: Audey, Beth, Charlotte, Chris, Christie, Cian, David, Deva, Dylan, Ed, Elena, Esther, Frances, Giorgio, Jake, Jim, Judy, Julie, Kathy, Ky, Leah, Linda, Mary, Matthew, Max, Nomy, Ora, Pat, Rae, Sabrina, Sharon, Tanisha, and all the LoveTroopers. Also, thanks go to Deb Burgard and Lene Whitley-Putz, who helped vision this project. Most important, this project would not have happened without the influence of Sondra's mother, Alice Solovay, a superb motivator and an incredible writer who graduated from law school, passed the bar, and turned fifty all in the same year. This book is in memory of Sondra's father and grandfather, both of whom saw the start, but not the end, of *The Fat Studies Reader*.

Esther would like to credit the Fat Lip Readers Theatre for a mind-altering performance in 1983 in Seattle that inspired her to begin research on weight and stigma. The Fat Think Tank of the Bay Area, the ShowMeTheData Listserv, and the FatStudies Listserv provided a supportive background at a time when it was hard to get fat-affirmative research published. Most of all, she would like to thank the following friends for inspiring conversations and creative ideas about fat studies: Laura Brown, Deb Burgard, Elana Dykewomon, Judy Freespirit, Nanette Gartrell, Marny Hall, Marcia Hill, Beth Mintz, and Penny Sablove.

Introduction

Sondra Solovay and Esther Rothblum

Fat Is Bad

Isn't it odd that people deeply divided on almost every important topic can so easily and seemingly organically agree on the above assertion? Isn't it similarly strange that countries significantly divergent in culture, attitudes, and approaches apparently share the fat-is-bad sentiment? In fact, according to the popular media, one of the few disagreements that exists is which country is hardest hit by the so called "obesity epidemic."

Consider the following contradictory statements:

"Somewhere along the way, [Americans have] supersized ourselves into becoming the fattest nation on earth" (MSNBC, 2003).

"Australia has become the fattest nation in the world, with more than 9 million adults now rated as obese or overweight, according to an alarming new report" (Stark, 2008).

"Canadian adults, both men and women, are the most obese in a survey of 63 nations that raises new health warnings for our country." (Spears, 2007).

"Fat German citizens—the fattest in the European Union?" (Müller-Nothmann, 2008).

"Now heavyweight Brits are the fattest people in Europe" (Macrae, 2008).

Regardless of which country is actually the "fattest nation on earth," the United States quickly declared a "war on fat" with the support of former U.S. surgeon general C. Everett Koop (Koop, 1997). The World Health Organization (O'Hara, 2006) data on "obesity" in adults indicate that the United States ranks twentieth, Australia thirty-fifth, and Canada thirty-seventh in global rates of "obesity." Ranking ahead in weight are a number of nations in the Pacific (e.g., Fiji, Samoa) and the Middle East (e.g., Kuwait, Jordan). Countries that have the greatest number of "obese" children include a number of nations in eastern Europe (e.g., Albania, Armenia) and some African nations (e.g., Algeria, Lesotho; see O'Hara & Gregg, 2006.)

What Is Fat Studies?

Fat studies scholars found the opinions about fat suspicious and began conducting research to examine these claims. Building on this foundation, a few decades later the field of fat studies emerged. In the tradition of critical race studies, queer studies, and women's studies, fat studies is an interdisciplinary field of scholarship marked by an aggressive, consistent, rigorous critique of the negative assumptions, stereotypes, and stigma placed on fat and the fat body. The field of fat studies invites scholars to pause, interrupt the everyday thinking about fat (or failure to think), and do something daring and bold. Learners must move beyond challenging assumptions; they must question the very questions that surround fatness and fat people. They must not be satisfied by noting that people diet and asking why—they must ask why we continue to expect people to diet. Who is oppressed by that pattern? To whom, and to which industries and organizations, do the resulting privileges flow? Fat studies requires approaching the construction of fat and fatness with a critical methodology—the same sort of progressive, systematic academic rigor with which we approach negative attitudes and stereotypes about women, queer people, and racial groups.

Fat studies scholars can begin to explore the relevant categories and construction via three crucial intellectual steps. Examples related to children, the most innocent victims of the war on fat and the U.S. export of anti-fat sentiment, are listed below, though the steps work equally well for all affected groups.

First, be suspicious of any non-neutral policy, attitude, or procedure where a line is drawn between fat and thin. Be especially skeptical when people are treated differently, rights are denied, or an action is motivated by the desire to "help" a group that falls on either side of the line. (For example, be suspicious of school-based exercise programs that are mandatory for fat children, or cheerleading or dance programs where fat students are categorically excluded.)

Second, be aware of and alert to seemingly neutral policies that have different effects on groups based on their weight. (For example, a policy requiring BMI [body mass index] to be listed on report cards, or a science teacher who weighs all children during class and has them calculate their BMI as an assignment, is neutral but will have a different impact on fat children than thin children.)

Third, keep the actual lives of fat people at the heart of the analysis. (For example, fat children in the United States have repeatedly been taken out of loving homes and away from caring, capable parents based on nothing but the child's weight, yet no general civil rights agency has provided legal assistance when asked to, let alone created a task force to focus on this discrimination. When policies are made to help fat people, are they addressing the issues that affect fat people? If not, how is the agenda being set?)

Some readers may find their critical inquiry interrupted by a rush to frame the weight discussion through the health discourse that dominates popular culture (where there is nothing to be gained from any fat endeavor except when the goal is fighting fat); they should consider where we stand with regard to unpacking "obesity" in comparison to the critical theory more established in academia. For example, today we do not stop our analysis after noting that people are treated differently based on race, nor do we stop after asking what race is. The field is well established and the deeper questions about the social construction of race come reasonably naturally—for example, how and why did we establish categories of race as known today, how have they changed, and why do we continue to use them? But in earlier stages of the field's development those questions were likely to be buried behind the distracting public discourse of the time. This moment in fat studies provides us with the rare chance to experience the development of a critical studies field while propaganda is at its peak; we must make our own paths. This is quite a reward—one that only scholars studying at a particular crossroads can experience—and one that provides a unique window into our own ability not just to see outside the box, but also to first see and experience the box for ourselves.

The assumption that fat people are unhealthy is so ingrained in western society that it is hard to get people to face the facts. The research on weight and health is vast, and merits an entire *Fat Studies Reader* itself. For readers needing to tame the pressure of the current public health view of fat to open themselves to the social and historic construction of fat and fatness, start with Marilyn Wann's preface and then turn immediately to part 2, "Fat Studies in Health and Medicine." Pay special attention to Glenn Gaesser's chapter (which addresses the long-term failure of weight loss) and Deb Burgard's chapter, which explains the Health at Every Size model (HAES) and its focus on current best practices regarding weight-neutral approaches to health. It will also be of interest to realize that weight in North America is strongly related to income. Fat people are poorer than thin people, and this is especially true for women. The general public usually assumes that *poverty causes fatness* (for example, they will point out that poor people cannot afford "healthy" foods such as fruits or vegetables, or that health clubs are expensive and thus out of reach to poor people). Paul Ernsberger makes the groundbreaking case that *fatness causes poverty* due to discrimination, and Bianca Wilson in "Widening the Dialogue to Narrow the Gap in Health Disparities" explains how the U.S. obsession with weight affects Black lesbian and bisexual women; these chapters help transition from the health-concern framing of fatness to the deeper intersectional issues.

Why The Fat Studies Reader? And Why Now?

The Fat Studies Reader is the first comprehensive anthology that maps the contours of this emerging field. The *Reader* brings together essays that identify key issues in the field, including intersectionality (the intersection of oppressions), health, and international and legal issues, as well as history, literature, and popular culture. After decades of independent study focused on the body, weight, and fat, the past few years have seen an exponential growth in the organization, communication, and focus of professionals and academics working and researching in fat studies. Multiple fat studies courses have been offered in numerous universities for several years. The year 2006 marked the tipping point—it was the first time that *three national conferences* were held to address fat studies! Undergraduate students at Smith College hosted "Fat and the Academy," focusing on the experiences of fatness and academia for college students, faculty, and staff. Later in the year, the Popular Culture Association and the American Culture Association joint conference featured a separate area in the field of fat studies. Finally, the Association for Size Diversity and Health Conference promoted the critical analysis of weight-related health matters for, and with an emphasis on the needs of, professionals.

It may come as a surprise, but questioning the appropriateness of discrimination based on height and weight was actually on the national radar in the United States, at least to a minor degree, during the 1960s. That period of time was profoundly important for the U.S. civil rights movement. Central to the movement was the passage of the Civil Rights Act of 1964, and the U.S. Congress vigorously debated that legislation; Senator Hubert Humphrey's remarks during those debates demonstrate awareness of body size discrimination even during that time: "[If] we started to treat Americans as Americans, not as fat ones, thin ones, short ones, tall ones, brown ones, green ones, yellow ones, or white ones, but as Americans. If we did that we would not need to worry about discrimination" (110 *Cong. Rec.* 5866, 1964). Several years later, a few courageous individuals began to protest the inhumane treatment of fat people and fat bodies. In 1969 William Fabrey founded NAAFA, the National Association to Advance Fat Acceptance (it was originally called the National Association to Aid Fat Americans). NAAFA continues to be a major source of fat advocacy cited in U.S. and international media. It has established a Declaration of Health Rights for Fat People, works to dispel myths about fat people, publishes a newsletter, and holds an annual convention (see http://www.naafa.org).

From 1973 to 1977 in Los Angeles, the Fat Underground group asserted that fat women are powerful, take up space, and are feared for their strength and sensuality (Fishman, 2001). Members included Aldebaran (Sara Fishman), Reanne Fagan, Sheri Fram, Gudrun Fonfa, Judy Freespirit, Lynn Mabel-Lois (Lynn McAfee), and Ariana Manow, among others. They viewed the effort to eradicate fat people via weight loss as a form of genocide perpetrated by the medical profession. The Fat Underground was influenced both by feminism and by radical therapy, a type of treatment that put the focus of change on society, not on individuals. In the words of Gudrun Fonfa, "By refuting the dogma of the diet industry and rejecting the aesthetics of the patriarchal culture, [we made] activists out of each individual fat woman who liberated herself from a lifetime of humiliation" (Fishman, 2008).

The early 1970s was a time of liberation movements, such as the women's liberation movement, the gay liberation movement, and the Gray Panthers. In 1973 two members of the Fat Underground, Judy Freespirit and Aldebaran, wrote "The Fat Liberation Manifesto." In that work, they stated that fat people are fully deserving of human respect, demanded equal rights for fat people, and viewed the struggle to end fat oppression "as allied with the struggles of other oppressed groups against classism, racism, sexism, ageism, financial exploitation, imperialism and the like" (Freespirit & Aldebaran, 1973). It specifically mentioned the diet industries as harmful to the health of fat people, and ended with the following statement in all capital letters: "FAT PEOPLE OF THE WORLD, UNITE! YOU HAVE NOTHING TO LOSE."

The Fat Studies Reader—Approach and Organization

Parts I and II

In keeping with the goal of introducing the broad scope of the field of fat studies in a manner that facilitates the reader's ability to suspend the dominant conception of fat to see the full picture, and recognizing fat as the historically dependent social construction that it is, the *Reader* is divided into six sections. As mentioned earlier, *The Fat Studies Reader* begins with descriptions of the social and historical construction of fatness via the preface and part 1, and then continues by promptly providing the fat studies take on the dominant public health discourse in part 2.

Part III: Fatness as Social Inequality

Most recently, fatness is framed as a health problem, yet it is stigma and prejudice (and their consequences) that inspire much of the extensive research in the field of fat studies. Consequently a number of chapters focus on fatness as social inequality. Topics highlighted in the *Reader* include mother blaming, race/class and the "epidemic of childhood obesity," bullying, mandatory weight reduction for children in Singapore, personal "choice" and responsibility as the focus of a neoliberal interpretation of fatness, gender privilege relating to size, fatness in gay male communities, violence against women, and "hogging."

As of publication time, only five locations in the United States had laws that prohibit weight-based discrimination; as a result, fat people often rely on disability law and the premise of "accommodation." Sondra Solovay, Dylan Vade, and Joyce Huff incorporate the idea of accommodation in their chapters on fat and transgender law and the debate on airplane seats as contested spaces. Ashley Hetrick and Derek Attig continue the seating discussion in the education context by examining the discomfort of classroom desks for fat students. Additional chapters focus on education, showing how fat becomes a topic in the literature classroom (Koppelman) and how fat educators face stigma that carries consequences for their careers (Escalera).

Part IV: Size-ism in Popular Culture and Literature

The fat studies discipline has spread to all genres in literature, poetry, theatre, popular culture, and performance. The *Reader* contributors write about fat fiction (Stinson), "chick-lit" (Frater), fat queer zines (Snider), representations of fat and Hispanic masculinity (McCrossin), fat female characters on television (Giovanelli and Ostertag), and fat women in theater (Jester). Fat studies has also exploded in its focus on the visual. Amy Farrell looks at the way that tourist postcards portrayed fat women in the early twentieth century. Beth Bernstein and Matilda St. John describe the phenomenon of fat female television celebrities losing weight as they achieve success. Wendy Burns-Ardolino's chapter is about the "big butt" in American popular culture, and Katharina Mendoza describes the occurrence of "fat suits" in the movies.

Parts V and VI: Fat People on the Move and Starting the Revolution

Ironically, fat people are urged to exercise but then hindered due to lack of available exercise clothing, ill-fitting exercise equipment, or degrading responses from exercise staff and others. Nevertheless, fat people have always been and continue to be physically active. The *Reader* includes coverage of fat people moving, dancing, and engaging in physical exercise.

Lacy Asbill observed fat burlesque dancers and audience members. Heather McAllister, founder of the all-fat burlesque troupe Big Burlesque, writes about fat embodiment: "The fastest way to fat liberation is physical. We will never have our freedom if we live only 'from the neck up,' yet that is the way many fat people live, even, or especially, the activists and academics among us." Jenny Ellison describes aerobics for fat women, and Dana Schuster and Lisa Tealer share their experiences creating the Women of Substance Health Spa, a health club for fat women. The *Reader* concludes by reiterating the call to revolution and challenging whether that revolution is uniquely a U.S. phenomenon or can truly be an international effort.

Getting Respect

The Fat Studies Reader contributors include established professors, writers, researchers, and activists, as well as rising stars. Many of the leaders in the field have encountered significant obstacles and academic disapproval for focusing on this topic of inquiry. When Sondra, studying law at a "top ten" law school, attempted to find an adviser for her project on weight discrimination and the law, she was forced to petition the school to allow an adjunct faculty member to supervise her—only her "Sexual Orientation and the Law" professor understood the importance of this critical legal inquiry and would agree to sponsor the project. Years later, with her book *Tipping the Scales of Justice* (the first book to thoroughly document weight discrimination as a civil rights issue in several legal fields) firmly in hand, Sondra attended a conference addressing the lack of "women and minorities" in legal academia. She recalls the easy dismissal of her work by a key conference speaker as "not a *real* topic."

When Esther submitted her research about weight and stigma to academic journals in psychology, the reviewers were often dieting researchers. For example, one reviewer commented, "I do have several suggestions for improving this paper. First, the tone is a bit strident and accusatory. The field of obesity research is cast as sexist, short-sighted and misdirected. There are, of course, flaws in some of the research and the public view of obesity is often not supported by the evidence, but I do feel the paper would profit from more objectivity and from using a less angry tone." Another wrote, "One concern I have with this paper is that some of the myths it debunks (such as the notion that dieting is ineffective) are not views currently held by psychologists. These views may be held by nonpsychologists; however, even the popular press has challenged them. For example see, 'Why smart women don't diet' (*Glamour* Magazine, November, 1987) and 'A woman's body in a man's world' (*Shape*, October,

1987)." The phrase "strident and accusatory" is reminiscent of critiques of research done by feminists not too many years earlier, and it is highly unusual for an academic colleague to cite popular magazines such as *Glamour* or *Shape*!

Despite intense community and even public support for the *Reader*, along the way we encountered significant institutional resistance. Most notable was the response from Harvard University Press. The senior editor for behavioral sciences and law rejected the *Reader*, explaining, "I think I'd have trouble at various stages of the review process with a book that discounted, or seemed to discount, the health risks of obesity." According to Harvard, not only can we not question research about the "health risks of obesity," but we must avoid even the *appearance* of such an inquiry! In a world where appearances matter, we are proud to present a fat book about fat issues! Welcome to the field of fat studies.

REFERENCES

Fishman, S. (January 30, 2001). Life in the Fat Underground, retrieved June 30, 2008, from http://www.largesse.net/Archives/FU/Life%20In%20The%20Fat%20Underground%20 by%20Sara%20Fishman.html.

Freespirit, J., & Aldebaran (1973). The Fat Liberation Manifesto, retrieved June 30, 2008, from http://www.largesse.net/Archives/FU/manifesto.html.

Koop, C.E. (1997, September). In Spite of Diet Drug Withdrawal, The War on Obesity Must Continue Says Dr. C. Everett Koop, Shape Up America! press release, retrieved September 30, 2006, from http://www.shapeup.org/about/arch_pr/091997.php.

Macrae, F. (July 1, 2008). Now Heavyweight Brits Are the Fattest People in Europe. *Mail Online*, retrieved January 27, 2009, from http://www.dailymail.co.uk/health/article-566473/ Now-heavyweight-Brits-fattest-people-Europe.html.

MSNBC (November 13, 2003). Survival of the Fittest: America's War on Weight, retrieved January 27, 2009, from http://www.msnbc.msn.com/id/3079856/.

Müller-Nothmann, S. (2008). Dicke Deutsche Bürger—die dicksten in der EU? retrieved June 30, 2008, from http://www.helloarticle.com/de/dicke-deutsche-buerger-die-dicksten-in-der-eu-r2415.htm.

O'Hara, L. (2006). Australians to Become the Biggest Within the World in Ten Years. *Health at Every Size, 19*, 235–247.

O'Hara, L., & Gregg, J. (2006). Are Weight-Centred Public Health and Health Promotion Policies and Programs Consistent with a Human Rights Approach to Health? Unpublished Manuscript, University of the Sunshine Coast, Australia.

Spears, T. (October 23, 2007). We're the Fattest Nation of Them All. *Vancouver Sun*, retrieved March 4, 2009, from http://www2.canada.com/vancouversun/news/story. html?id=e9aa812a-be66-4fc2-9e54-08a9cc366e69&k=6473.

Stark, J. (June 20, 2008). Australia Now World's Fattest Nation. *The Age*, retrieved January 27, 2009, from http://www.theage.com.au/news/health/australia-now-worlds-fattest-nation/2008/06/19/1213770886872.html.

Part I

⁞⁞⁞

What Is Fat Studies?
The Social and Historical Construction of Fatness

Welcome to Part I of The Fat Studies Reader

What Is Fat Studies? The Social and Historical Construction of Fatness

This section serves as an invitation to think about the framing of fatness in its historical context and to understand the central tenets of the field of fat studies. The authors pose challenges regarding approaching this field with the needed rigor despite vehement anti-fat attitudes and indoctrination.

After reading these chapters consider the following discussion questions:

What is the field of fat studies?

Why does this area of academic inquiry exist?

How have mainstream attitudes toward fat changed over the last fifty years? Over the last ten years?

How have mainstream attitudes toward fat people changed over the last fifty years? Over the last ten years?

What, if anything, is wrong with the mainstream approach to fatness?

What market forces have shaped societal attitudes regarding fat and fat people?

Who is privileged by the current construction of fatness?

Who is disadvantaged by the current construction of fatness?

Is a person's weight, generally, within the control of the individual? What relevance does this question have for the social construction of fatness?

Identify a significant experience in your life (or in the life of a friend or loved one) and explain how it would have been different if the mainstream attitude toward fat was one of acceptance.

||||||||||||||||||||||||||||||||||||||||||||||||||||||||||||||||||||||||||||

The Inner Corset

A Brief History of Fat in the United States

Laura Fraser

Once upon a time, a man with a thick gold watch swaying from a big, round paunch was the very picture of American prosperity and vigor. Accordingly, a hundred years ago, a beautiful woman had plump cheeks and arms, and she wore a corset and even a bustle to emphasize her full, substantial hips. Women were *sexy* if they were heavy. In those days, Americans knew that a layer of fat was a sign that you could afford to eat well and that you stood a better chance of fighting off infectious diseases than most people. If you were a woman, having that extra adipose blanket also meant that you were probably fertile, and warm to cuddle up next to on chilly nights.

Between the 1880s and 1920s, that pleasant image of fat thoroughly changed in the United States. Some began early on to hint that fat was a health risk. In 1894, Woods Hutchinson, a medical professor who wrote for women's magazines, defended fat against this new point of view. "Adipose," he wrote, "while often pictured as a veritable Frankenstein, born of and breeding disease, sure to ride its possessor to death sooner or later, is really a most harmless, healthful, innocent tissue" (Hutchinson, 1894, p. 395). Hutchinson reassured his *Cosmopolitan* readers that fat was not only benign, but also attractive, and that if a poll of beautiful women were taken in any city, there would be at least three times as many plump ones as slender ones. He advised them that no amount of starving or exercise—which were just becoming popular as means of weight control—would change more than 10 percent of a person's body size anyway. "The fat man tends to remain fat, the thin woman to stay thin—and both in perfect health—in spite of everything they can do," he said in that article.

But by 1926, Hutchinson, who was by then a past president of the American Academy of Medicine, had to defend fat against fashion, too, and he was showing signs of strain. "In this present onslaught upon one of the most peaceable, useful and law-abiding of all our tissues," he told readers of the *Saturday Evening Post*, "fashion has apparently the backing of grave physicians, of food reformers and physical trainers, and even of great insurance companies, all chanting in unison the new commandment of fashion: 'Thou shalt be thin!'" (Hutchinson, 1926, p. 60).

Hutchinson mourned this trend, and was dismayed that young girls were ridding themselves of their roundness and plumpness of figure. He tried to understand the new view that people took toward fat: "It is an outward and visible sign of an inward and spiritual disgrace, of laziness, of self-indulgence," he explained in that article, but he remained unconvinced. Instead, he longed for a more cheerful period in the not-so-distant past when a little fat never hurt anyone, and he darkly warned that some physicians were deliberately underfeeding girls and young women solely for the purpose of giving them a more svelte figure. "The longed-for slender and boyish figure is becoming a menace," Hutchinson (1926, p. 60) wrote, "not only to the present, but also the future generations."

And so it would. But why did the fashion for plumpness change so dramatically during those years? What happened that caused Americans to alter their tastes, not only to admire thinner figures for a time, but for the next century, culminating in fin de siècle extremes of thinness, where women's magazines in the 1990s would print ads featuring gaunt models side-by-side with photo essays on anorexia?

Many things were happening at once, and with dizzying speed. Foremost was a changing economy: In the late 1800s, for the first time, ample amounts of food were available to more and more people who had to do less and less work to eat. The agricultural economy, based on family farms and home workshops, shifted to an industrial one. A huge influx of immigrants—many of them genetically shorter and rounder than the earlier American settlers—fueled the industrial machine. People moved to cities to do factory work and service jobs, stopped growing their own food, and relied more on store-bought goods. Large companies began to process food products, distribute them via railroads, and use refrigeration to keep perishables fresh. Food became more accessible and convenient to all but the poorest families. People who once had too little to eat now had plenty, and those who had a tendency to put on weight began to do so. When it became possible for people of modest means to become plump, being fat no longer was a sign of prestige. Well-to-do Americans of northern European extraction wanted to be able to distinguish themselves, physically and racially, from stockier immigrants. As anthropologist Margaret Mackenzie notes, the status symbols flipped: it became chic to be thin and all too ordinary to be overweight (personal communication, June 12, 1996).

In this new environment, older cultural undercurrents suspicious of fat began to surface. Europeans had long considered slenderness a sign of class distinction and finer sensibilities, and Americans began to follow suit. In Europe, during the late 18th and early 19th centuries, many artists and writers—the poets John Keats and Percy Bysshe Shelley, and authors Emily Brontë, Edgar Allan Poe, and Anton Chekhov—had tuberculosis, which made them sickly thin. Members of the upper classes believed that having tuberculosis, and being slender itself, were signs that one possessed a delicate, intellectual, and superior nature. "For snobs and parvenus and social climbers, TB was the one index of being genteel, delicate, [and] sensitive," writes essayist Susan Sontag in *Illness as Metaphor* (1977, p. 28). "It was glamorous to look sickly." So interested was the poet Lord Byron in looking as fashionably ill as the other Romantic poets that he embarked on a series of obsessive diets, consuming only biscuits and water, or vinegar and potatoes, and succeeded in becoming quite thin. Byron—who, at five feet six inches tall, with a clubfoot that prevented him from walking much, weighed over two hundred pounds in his youth—disdained fat in others. "A woman," he wrote, "should never be seen eating or drinking, unless it be *lobster salad* and *champagne*, the only truly feminine and becoming viands" (quoted in Schwartz, 1986, p. 38). Aristocratic European women, thrilled with the romantic figure that Byron cut, took his diet advice and despaired of appearing fat. Aristocratic Americans, trying to imitate Europeans, adopted their enthusiasm for champagne and slenderness.

Americans believed that it was not only a sign of class to be thin, but also a sign of morality. There was a long tradition in American culture that suggested that indulging the body and its appetites was immoral, and that denying the flesh was a sure way to become closer to God. Puritans such as the minister Cotton Mather frequently fasted to prove their worthiness and to cleanse themselves of their sins. Benjamin Franklin, in his *Poor Richard's Almanack*, chided his readers to eat lightly to please not only God, but also a new divinity, Reason: "Wouldst thou enjoy a long life, a healthy Body, and a Vigorous Mind, and be acquainted also with the wonderful works of God? Labour in the first place to bring thy Appetite into Subjection to Reason" (Franklin, 1970, p. 238). Franklin's attitude toward food not only reveals a puritanical distrust of appetite as overly sensual, but also presaged diets that would attempt to bring eating in line with rational, scientific calculations. "The Difficulty lies, in finding out an exact Measure;" he wrote, "but eat for Necessity, not Pleasure, for Lust knows not where Necessity ends" (p. 238).

At the end of the 19th century, as Hutchinson observed, science was also helping to shape the new slender ideal. Physicians came to believe that they were able to arrive at an exact measure of human beings; they could count calories, weigh people on scales, calculate "ideal" weights, and advise those who deviated from that ideal that they could change themselves. Physicians were both following and encouraging the trend for thinness. In the 1870s, after all, when plumpness was in vogue, physicians had encouraged people to *gain* weight. Two of the most distinguished doctors of the age, George Beard and S. Weir Mitchell, believed that excessive thinness caused American women to succumb to a wide variety nervous disorders, and that a large number of fat cells was absolutely necessary to achieve a balanced personality (Banner, 1983, p. 113). But when the plump figure fell from favor, physicians found new theories to support the new fashion. They hastily developed treatments—such as thyroid, arsenic, and strychnine—to prescribe to their increasing numbers of weight loss patients, many of whom were not exactly corpulent, but who were more than willing to part with their pennies along with their pounds.

As the 20th century got underway, other cultural changes made slenderness seem desirable. When many women ventured out of their homes and away from their strict roles as mothers, they left behind the plump and reproductive physique, which began to seem old-fashioned next to a thinner, freer, more modern body. The new consumer culture encouraged the trend toward thinness with fashion illustrations and ads featuring slim models; advertisers learned early to offer women an unattainable dream of thinness and beauty to sell more products. In short, a cultural obsession with weight became firmly established in the United States when several disparate factors that favored a desire for thinness—economic status symbols, morality, medicine, modernity, changing women's roles, and consumerism—all collided at once.

Thinness is, at its heart, a peculiarly American preoccupation. Europeans admire slenderness, but without our Puritanism they have more relaxed and moderate attitudes about food, eating, and body size (the British are most like us in both being heavy and fixating on weight loss schemes). In countries where people do not have quite enough to eat, and where women remain in traditional roles, plumpness is still widely admired. Other westernized countries have developed a slender ideal, but for the most part they have imported it from the United States. No other culture suffers from the same wild anxieties about weight, dieting, and exercise as we do because they do not share our history.

The thin ideal that developed in the United States from the 1880s to 1920s was not just a momentary shift in fashion; it was a monumental turning point in the way that women's bodies were appraised by men and experienced by women. The change can be traced through the evolution of three ideal types: the plump Victorian woman, the athletic but curvaceous Gibson Girl, and the boyishly straight-bodied flapper. By 1930, American women knew how very important it was for them to be thin. From then on, despite moments when voluptuousness was admired again (e.g., Marilyn Monroe), American women could never be too thin.

NOTE

This chapter is adapted from the book *Losing It: America's Obsession with Weight and the Industry That Feeds on It* (New York: Dutton, 1997). © Laura Fraser. Hillel Schwartz's *Never Satisfied* provided a good deal of background material for this chapter, and is an excellent resources on the history of dieting. Lois Banner's meticulously researched *American Beauty* traces American beauty ideals, and was also very helpful in preparing this chapter.

REFERENCES

Banner, L. (1983). *American Beauty*. Chicago: University of Chicago Press.

Franklin, B. (1970). *The Complete Poor Richard Almanacks*, Vol. 1: *1733–1747*. Barre, MA: Imprint Society.

Hutchinson, W. (1894, June). "Fat and Its Follies." *Cosmopolitan*. 395.

Hutchinson, W. (1926, August 21). "Fat and Fashion." *The Saturday Evening Post*. 60.

Schwartz, H. (1986). *Never Satisfied: A Cultural History of Diets, Fantasies, and Fat*. New York: The Free Press.

Sontag, S. (1977). *Illness as Metaphor*. New York: Farrar, Straus and Giroux.

ıı

Fattening Queer History
Where Does Fat History Go from Here?

Elena Levy-Navarro

Until recently, fat studies has been largely dominated by an interest in contemporary politics of fatness. Although such work has been and continues to be important, other social justice movements teach us that we need to turn to history as well. The turn to history, if performed in a self-conscious way, can sustain a fat-positive movement even as it helps us to imagine, and thus to create, alternatives to what sometimes seems like an all-too-oppressive present. In this chapter, I draw on the field of queer historiography to suggest some of the ways that histories can work with fat activism to intervene constructively in our own historical moment. I realize that the gay and lesbian community is not free from fat-phobia; indeed, those especially interested in assimilation are often even vociferously fat-phobic. The queer historiography that I discuss here embraces a more expansive definition of "queer" that is more expressly inclusive of all who challenge normativity, including fat people. In what follows, I consider what I believe should be the two main tasks of fat histories. First, we need fat histories to look to the past in order to critique the constructs that oppress us now. We should, for example, give "obesity" a history so that we make it clear that the category currently applied to our bodies is not natural or "real." Second, we need more creative historical interventions to complement such genealogical ones because only the latter can help us imagine new relationships with our bodies and the bodies of others.

I can begin to reflect on the role that history can play in creating fat-positive communities because there already exist a significant body of fat histories, including constructionist fat histories. Recent interest in the subject in the United States is fueled by the contemporary fat-panic that has taken hold, especially since the terrorist attacks of 9/11. Bureaucrats and public officials draw on our own generalized fear and anxiety, warning us that the "obesity epidemic" poses the greatest threat to the national security of the United States. U.S. Surgeon General Koop has repeatedly called it the "terror within" (Carmona, 2003).

Within this atmosphere, fat histories have proliferated: *Bodies Out of Bounds*, a collection of essays that includes some on historical topics, edited by Jana Evans Braziel and Kathleen LeBesco (2001); Peter Stearns's *Fat History* (1997), Sander Gilman's

Fat Boys (2004); and Christopher E. Forth's and Ana Carden-Coyne's *Cultures of the Abdomen* (2005). Despite their methodological diversity, these works cumulatively expose the extent to which "obesity" is a cultural construction. As a whole, they constitute the beginnings of what must be a larger project to provide a genealogical history of oppressive concepts, especially biomedical ones like "obesity." Just as the queer-inflected studies in the history of sexuality have given a history to concepts, like "homosexuality" and "heterosexuality," that are oppressive insofar as they are taken to be universal and transhistorical, so too fat histories must give a history to oppressive constructs such as "obesity" and the broader construct of "health." To give such concepts a history is to consider when they were invented, when they began to have broad appeal, and how they have changed through the years.

A fat history should explore the reasons why these categories are emotionally appealing to many in our culture. The category "obesity" is appealing because from its inception it has played a central role in reinforcing hegemonic power relations. More particularly, "obesity" has helped to define what it was and is to be "white" or "American," just as it helped to define what it was to be nonwhite or ethnic. This area has yet to be explored, although several histories touch briefly on the way that "obesity" has helped to define the nonwhite, the non-western, and the non-American. As Sander Gilman explains, nineteenth-century racialized discourse distinguished between the type of the Jew and non-Jew by the "fact" that the former was fat (Gilman, 2004, p. 49). Hillel Schwartz suggests a similar relationship in *Never Satisfied: A Cultural History of Diets, Fantasies, and Fat* (1986). Widespread fear of "obesity" coincided in the United States with a cultural anxiety over the influx of immigrant groups, especially Italians and Jews (Schwartz, 1986, p. 143). We need more fat histories to explore the way in which the category "obesity," and its invisible, unmarked counterpart, "thin," serve to secure certain oppressive power relations. What role do they play in defining what it is to be nonwhite, poor, and foreign, on the one hand, and white, upper-class, and native, on the other.

I hope that eventually the category "obesity" will be seen as questionable in and of itself. Until then, an understanding of the misuses to which this category has been used can help sustain us in this fat-hating, dominant culture. Our histories, however, must never allow this dominant culture to define us. As such, we also need more histories that consider the experiences of the defiantly and happily fat in our culture. As one Latina writer observes, she lives in two worlds with two very different understandings of her "fat" body. Where the one would insist that she is "obese," the other understands her to be "bien cuidada" or well-cared for (Haubegger, 2000, p. 242; Levy-Navarro, 2005). In her experiences, she defies a culture that would insist she is unhealthy and unlovely because she is "obese." Fat histories must also work to explore alternative realities, which they can do in part by exploring the very different way that the fat body can be understood by nondominant cultures in the West as well as by non-western cultures worldwide.

To explore alternatives to our all-too-oppressive reality, we must also learn to write fat histories that are more imaginative and playful in nature. In this, our histories would queer a certain regulatory form of history—History—that has been and is used to exclude the nonnormative as that which is of inconsequence. One of the reasons that I believe we need a historical turn in fat studies is because a certain form of History is used to debase the nonnormative, including the transgendered, the lesbian, the queer, *and* the fat. In contemporary western culture, History has a regulatory function that is all-too-often invisible precisely because it has come to seem natural. Queer theorist Eve Sedgwick makes this point when she speaks about the way in which History and heterosexuality are imbricated. History secures heterosexuality as the norm because it moves toward an inevitable end—the happily ever after of Romance. For this reason, the history of heterosexuality is difficult to write because "it [heterosexuality] masquerades so readily as History itself" (Sedgwick, 1993, p. 111). In contemporary western culture, History is as an organizing principle that privileges certain normative identities at the expense of others. Indeed, by its logic, certain nonnormative identities become passé (Jagose, 2002; Halberstam, 2005; Traub, 2002). To resist such a history, we need to develop alternative histories that follow a very different, queer logic.

To queer History is, in particular, to begin to discover different relationships between the past and the present. Queer scholars readily acknowledge that it is the linear nature of modern time that makes the lesbian, the queer, the transgendered, and, I'd add, the fat an afterthought. Annamarie Jagose and Valerie Traub describe the way that modern linear time always sees the lesbian identity as literally of inconsequence because she is positioned outside this sequential ordering. The lesbian is placed in the position of the "before" that is superseded for the much desired, (hetero)normative "after" to be achieved. As the use of these terms suggests, the very same temporal logic is used to oppress us.

History that would make certain nonnormative identities inconsequential, including the fat, follows a certain modern logic of temporality in which time is conceptualized as that which follows a neat, linear chain of cause and effect. For this reason, scholars of queer studies have recently realized that their histories need to take a form that queers that oppressive, modern temporal logic. Lee Edelman (2004) and Judith Halberstam (2005) understand that such a temporal logic is itself destructive of queer lives, including fat ones. Such logic demands that we bow down to an elusive, utopian future and thus dismiss our pasts as over and done with. According to Edelman (2004), contemporary American culture is obsessed with what he calls "reproductive futurism": we are enjoined to make all our own pleasures and commitments secondary to a future that never comes. Edelman and Halberstam develop a definition of queer that would include all those who refuse to bow down to this reproductive futurism. For Halberstam, all are queer who live according to a "queer time" that does not privilege the future at the expense of the present and past (Halberstam, 2005, pp. 6–7). The fat would implicitly fit this group precisely because they are seen as refusing to live their life according to the imperative of "health." In this sense, the fat are queer in our culture exactly because they are seen as living a life that is "unhealthy," and thus a life that is *presumably* defying the imperative to cultivate maximum longevity.

That such a temporal logic is all-pervasive in contemporary western culture is evident in the ubiquitous diet discourse. Diet advertisements, for example, often focus on the way that the "successful" dieter has now achieved maximum longevity, which had hitherto eluded her. Mothers report that their newly thin bodies make them more vibrant and young; they beam as they announce that they will now live their lives well into the future. In a related way, dieters often describe themselves as having nearly escaped almost inevitable death. Often they quote their physicians as assuring them that they would have died unless they slimmed down. Such commonplaces suggest the degree to which the fat, like the queer, are seen as those who disrupt the temporal logic of History. They are seen by our culture as refusing to place the past as secondary to the present, and the present as secondary to the future. The fat are history itself—that is, they are the past that must be dispensed with as we move toward our seemingly inevitable future progress.

We can respond to this cultural reality in many ways. Some can insist, as the Health at Every Size movement does, that fat can be healthy. Others might want to participate in a broader cultural project of queering the straight, temporal logics of History. Such a fat history would cultivate a very different relationship to the past, one in which it is no longer taken to be a mere "before" that is assumed to be over and done with. Only with a creative engagement with the past can we sustain ourselves in our emotional and political commitments of the present. Queer historian Carla Freccero begins her book by insisting that she will not follow the "presumed logic of cause and effect, anticipation and result" or the "presumed logic of 'doneness' of the past" (Freccero, 2006, p. 5). Her project instead embraces a queer time that defies the temporal logic of modern, sequential History. As she explains, "Queer time is haunted by the persistence of affect and ethical imperative in and across time" (Freccero, 2006, p. 5). Her history enacts a respect for the past that the imperative of straight History would deny. In so doing, it uses the past to sustain people in the present. A writer of imaginative histories will not see the past as over and done with, nor will she see it as something that must be rendered serviceable to a future that never comes (pun intended). Instead, she will see how histories can engage with the past to reshape our present in ways that are more fat- and queer-positive.

The book *Taking Up Space* offers us a useful example of the way in which we should play with time (Thomas & Wilkerson, 2005). This book—importantly a pastiche that is part self-help book, part memoir, part cultural analysis—begins with an exorcism of the modern, regulatory History. Thomas writes in defiance of a temporal logic that would relegate her body to a "before" that is over and done with. As Thomas tells her life story, she carefully avoids reinscribing the modern logic of temporality that is used to degrade her into silence. She does so significantly in a poem that queers the straight temporal relationship of "before" to "after." I say *significantly* because it suggests the degree to which we need to use our imaginations to create a very different history. In our culture, Thomas acknowledges, "Only *afters* can tell this tale / And I am a *before* / Because I take up space" (Thomas & Wilkerson, 2005, p. 30). She defies such a logic in the simple but courageous act of speaking, and more specifically from the location of a "before." She is, in some senses, what our culture says cannot be: a "before" speaking powerfully and defiantly to the present. Simply by speaking from her position as a "before," she transforms the present. After all, she is defying the temporal logic that says that the past must always remain the before to an "after" or a future that we are all supposed to desire. As Thomas announces, "The space a body occupies / has nothing to do with the knowledge the body has to offer / *Befores* can tell this tale / And I am a *before*" (p. 31). Only someone who has been insistently made into a "before" could tell the tale that she is about to tell.

Thomas queers this modern form of time itself. Notably, she does this in her parenthetical expressions, as if to say that what happens in the interstices of modern time is what matters. She employs numerous befores and afters, which suggests that our lives comprise multiple befores and afters that can never make a neat line of cause and effect. Her own existence makes a lie of this temporal logic because she is, from the perspective of the modern temporal logic, a "before" in a culture that insists that "only afters can tell this tale." In speaking, she queers the logic that would silence her:

> (Never mind that I have been an *after*
> And a before
> And another after
> And another before
> And a *during*.) (p. 30)

Straight temporal logic, Thomas exposes, is simply mistaken. It would narrow her life down to one oppressively restrictive, normative reality. Her life, she says, is composed of multiple befores and afters that are themselves more complex than most would imagine.

In her next parenthetical, Thomas more powerfully queers this temporal logic in a way that offers us a model of the power that a playful history can have in discovering alternative relationships to the past. Not only does my life simultaneously consist of a number of befores and afters that encompass "real" events, but my life also consists of numerous befores and afters that encompass everything that I can imagine. Our imagination, in shaping our lives, can never be confined to a singular, straight line. We always experience multiple befores and afters simultaneously because we can always imagine other pasts and presents. Thomas writes, then,

> (Never mind that it is *after* my graduation
> And *before* I see Antarctica
> And *after* I learned to love my own skin
> And *before* I take my first hot balloon ride,
> And *during* my adventure called living.) (p. 31)

The imagination creates multiple times, and in so doing, offers multiple, queer relations between the supposed past and the present. Neither the present nor the past can ever be singularly or only an "after" or a "before" because we continue to forge new relations between the past and the present. Our fat histories need to occupy times that go athwart of or across the linear time of cause and effect that is currently used to oppress us.

To offer an example of just such a creative history, I now want to consider Ben Jonson (Herford, Simpson, & Simpson, 1925), a famous poet and playwright from the early seventeenth century. From the perspective of History, Jonson is a "before" that has little or nothing to teach us. A fat history would cultivate a very different relationship to this "before." In his defiance, Jonson speaks directly to us in ways that can help sustain the fat community.

In his own day, Ben Jonson was ridiculed by some because he was fat, which then was just beginning to be understood in moralistic terms. To be fat was to the ruling elite to be vicious, common, and unlearned. A contemporary piece of doggerel dismisses Jonson as a "big fat man that spake in rhyme," thereby insisting that he was not the learned man he was widely reputed to be (Herford et al., 1925, vol. 11: p. 288 modernized). Other doggerel was even more vicious, as when one writer imagined Jonson as being hung "like a nasty boar from behind" (11: pp. 411–12 modernized). I could say more about the moralized sensibility here, but for our purposes we should observe that his fat is seen as making him a dead hog, meat "hung" from a hook thrust into his anus. Jonson is important for fat studies precisely because he confronted such developing prejudices in his day.

Jonson does not ask that we ignore his corpulence, but instead demands that we reconceptualize it in more positive terms. Insofar as he does the latter, he speaks powerfully to us in late modernity. In fact, he counters a dehumanizing discourse that is, if anything, more oppressive to the present-day reader than to his early modern one. In his late poetry, collected in his posthumously published volume *Underwood* (1640), Jonson writes readily of his corpulence. Jonson tells us frankly that he has a "rocky face," a "mountain belly," and even such details as he "doth hardly approach / His friends, but to break chairs, or crack a coach" (Jonson & Donaldson, 1975, *Und.* 9.17, 56.9–10). The first to describe his corpulence in terms of "weight," Jonson understands how the numerical figure is used to dehumanize the fat person. To many a scholars' dismay, Jonson confesses ironically that "his weight is twenty stone within two pounds," or that he is a "full twenty stone; of which I lack two pound" (*Und.* 56.11, 54.12). How should we take such seeming confessions?

We come to an example of how fat histories should cultivate a more playful engagement with the past. In particular, we should come to see how figures who are defiantly fat speak directly to the present in ways that can sustain us. We, after all, are in more need of calling into question the numbers that seem to proliferate daily in late modern western culture. To us much more than to the early modern person, such vital statistics have come to what one scholar calls "damning enumerations" saying something supposedly essential about us (Van den Berg, 1987, p. 31). We, after all, are called on to render up these numbers almost daily whenever we are required to give our age, height, and weight to this or that government office. Increasingly, in the United States we find ourselves being measured, our weight recorded, our body mass index calculated, by our physicians, who pass those numbers along to our HMOs, and increasingly by our public schools, which can even send them home in health report cards. We, more than Jonson, understand how damning some numbers can be, especially if we were once rejected for health insurance because we were above a magical number.

Jonson can only speak to us directly if we respect the past and believe that it has something to tell us. We cannot, as many scholars have done, simply impose on such figures our presentist constructions. Jonson's own constructionist engagement has been largely ignored and underappreciated because scholars either wanted to ignore his corpulence or to see it through modern, pathologized constructions like "obesity." A strain of psycho-biographical criticism diagnoses Jonson through the latter and assumes that he has an "obese personality." Such a pathologized, psychological conception assumes that the fat person is the immature one. We know by his fat that Jonson did not develop into a fully mature adult; he is, after all, a victim of an insatiable appetite that is associated with an infantile oral phase. As Joseph Loewenstein diagnoses, "It may be that for Jonson, as for many people, eating is a defense of the ego, an attempt to shore up a fugitive being within a bulwark of flesh" (Loewenstein, 1986, p. 510). In imposing such a pathologized construction on Jonson, our past merely confirms our present, even as it serves to legitimize those oppressive ways of being that make certain nonnormative identities an all-too-dangerous "before." Scholars cite his weight again and again as proof that he is a dangerous "before," stuck in an immature stage of development that we are all supposed to leave behind.

A fat history needs to queer that modern temporal relationship between the past and the present by allowing the past to speak to the present. I have already suggested that Jonson speaks directly to us in anticipating many of the types of fat-phobia oppressing us even more strongly in this late modern bureaucratic society. I can only here suggest some of the ways that he does so. To offer just one example, I would insist that Jonson uses his late poetry to offer us another, more humanizing way to understand "weight." In the two poems that he writes to his friend Sir Arthur Squib, teller of the king's Exchequer, he urges him to understand "weighty" in a whole different sense from the developing modern one. Jonson's weight has nothing to do with the number on the scale; he has weight to the extent to which his friends love him. For precisely this reason, he urges his friend and reader to "weigh" him not by looking at his mere dead weight, quantified by the scale, but by appreciating his weighty animated presence. As he advises, "First weigh a friend, then touch, and try him too" (Jonson & Donaldson, 1975, 45: l.16). This line, and the poems in general, suggest that a more humanizing "weight" comes from a friend's active engagement with him. Weight will be understood and appreciated in a whole different sense when it is viewed in a more engaged, humanistic way.

Jonson offers us a model of how a fat history can use the past to help speak to the predicament of the present. That is, the past can be used to change the present, where we understand our fat bodies outside the terms dictated by the dehumanizing, objective, pathologized categories like "obesity." The past helps us reinterpret our fat in ways that are transformative. We are only stuck in an all-too-oppressive present if we impose on ourselves the modern temporal logic in which the past is supposedly over and done with, in which justice and joy can only be achieved in some utopian future. There is justice and joy enough right now, if we only use our imaginations to write histories that move across the conventional logic of time. We can enter into relationships across time with figures like fat Jonson, and in so doing we create communities based on an imagination that are as large and fat as any body. In this, we create communities that can sustain us—communities that are not merely fat-positive but also creatively queer.

REFERENCES

Braziel, J.E., & LeBesco, K. (Eds.). (2001). *Bodies Out of Bounds: Fatness and Transgression.* Berkeley: University of California Press.

Carmona, R. (2003, November 23). Interview. *Morning Edition.* [Radio broadcast]. Washington, DC: National Public Radio.

Edelman, L. (2004). *No Future: Queer Theory and the Death Drive.* Series Q. Durham: Duke University Press.

Forth, C.E., & Carden-Coyne, A. (Eds.). (2005). *Cultures of the Abdomen: Diet, Digestion, and Fat in the Modern World.* New York: Palgrave Macmillan, 2005.

Freccero, C. (2006). *Queer/Early/Modern.* Series Q. Durham: Duke University Press.

Gilman, S.L. (2004). *Fat Boys: A Slim Book.* Lincoln: University of Nebraska Press.

Halberstam, J. (2005). *In a Queer Time and Place: Transgender Bodies, Subcultural Lives.* Sexual Cultures. New York: New York University Press.

Haubegger, C. (2000). I'm not fat, I'm Latina. In Maurianne Adams et al. (Eds.), *Readings for Diversity and Social Justice.* New York: Routledge.

Herford, C.H., Simpson, P., & Simpson, E.M.S. (Eds.). (1925). *Ben Jonson.* 11 vols. Oxford: Clarendon Press.

Jagose, A. (2002). *Inconsequence: Lesbian Representation and the Logic of Sexual Sequence.* Ithaca: Cornell University Press.

Jonson, B., & Donaldson, I. (Ed.). (1975). *Poems.* Oxford Standard Authors. London: Oxford University Press.

Levy-Navarro, E. (2005). "So much meat": Gloria Anzaldúa, the mind/body split, and exerting control over my fat body. In AnaLouise Keating (Ed.), *Entre Mundos/Among Worlds: New Perspectives on Gloria E. Anzaldúa.* New York: Palgrave Macmillan.

Loewenstein, J. (1986). The Jonsonian corpulence: Or, the poet as mouthpiece. *ELH* 53, 491–518.

Schwartz, H. (1986). *Never Satisfied: A Cultural History of Diets, Fantasies, and Fat.* New York: Free Press.

Sedgwick, E.K. (1993). Jane Austen and the masturbating girl. In Eve Kosofsky Sedgwick, *Tendencies.* Series Q. Durham. Duke University Press.

Stearns, P.N. (1997). *Fat History: Bodies and Beauty in the Modern West.* New York: New York University Press.

Thomas, P., & Wilkerson, C. (2005). *Taking Up Space: How Eating Well and Exercising Regularly Changed My Life.* Nashville: Pearlsong Press.

Traub, V. (2002). *The Renaissance of Lesbianism in Early Modern England.* Cambridge Studies in Renaissance Literature and Culture. Cambridge: Cambridge University Press.

Van den Berg, S.J. (1987). *The Action of Ben Jonson's Poetry.* Newark: University of Delaware Press.

Part II

||||||||||||||||||||||||||||||||||||||||||||||||||||||||||||||||||||||||||||||

Fat Studies in Health and Medicine

Welcome to Part II of The Fat Studies Reader

Fat Studies in Health and Medicine

Much of the justification for the negative treatment of fatness and fat people rests on arguments related to health and medicine. Exploring the research on health and weight in detail is a project much larger than the scope of this section of *The Fat Studies Reader*. Instead, part 2 presents a fat studies perspective on the intersections between weight and class, race, sexual orientation, and gender; the implications of the search for the "fat gene"; and a solid introduction to Health at Every Size as an alternative to contemporary discourse regarding weight and health.

After reading these chapters consider the following discussion questions:

How does social class relate to weight and what relevance does that have for the pursuit of public health?

What are the benefits of a Health at Every Size (HAES) model?

What are the dangers of rejecting the HAES approach?

How do current attitudes toward weight and health disproportionately affect people who are members of one or more racial and other minority groups?

Is permanent weight loss achievable for the average person? Is this an important question? What difference should the answer make, if any, in public health policy?

How does governmental Web presence influence attitudes toward weight?

Does the Canadian approach to weight and health differ from other countries? If so, how?

What challenges are faced by HAES professionals who want to incorporate HAES perspectives into their respective fields?

What challenges are faced by individuals who want their health-care provider to adopt an HAES approach?

Does Social Class Explain the Connection Between Weight and Health?

Paul Ernsberger

SES and Weight

Adiposity is strongly related to socioeconomic status (SES) in modern Western societies (Sobal, 1991; Sobal & Stunkard, 1989). SES is usually measured by household income or years of education, although these two measures are clearly different and have many limitations as indices of social standing. In their seminal review in 1989, Sobal and Stunkard showed strong links between low social status and high body weight. This relationship only applied consistently to adult women in developed nations. For adult men, half the surveys showed the same trend as for women, but the remainder showed no relationship between SES and weight; in fact, some demonstrated the opposite relation, with high status males being heavier. Sobol and Stunkard offered one explanation for this gender difference: smoking. Tobacco consumption falls with rising SES, especially for men, and body weight is lower for smokers. But higher rates of smoking among low status males are probably not enough to explain such a fundamental difference, as Sobol and Stunkard admit. Reevaluating their summary of previous studies, there is a striking trend over time toward stronger links between SES and weight in men. For surveys dating from 1949 to 1967, five linked high SES with high weight and only one linked poverty to fatness. For surveys between 1968 and 1988, twenty-one linked poverty to fatness in men, whereas only three linked high SES with high weight. More recent surveys have shown increasingly strong relationships of poverty to high body weight (Banks, Marmot, Oldfield, & Smith, 2006). Thus, the link between adiposity and poverty, always strong for women, has been getting progressively stronger for men since the 1960s.

Surveys of children and adolescents did not show a consistent relationship between their body weight and the social status of their parents, at least in the seventy published reports that existed in 1988 (Sobal & Stunkard, 1989). This was true for both girls and boys. Sobol and Stunkard concluded that whatever process links fatness and SES must begin in early adulthood. Their conclusion, however, must now be revised. Nearly all the surveys reported since 1988 show a strong inverse correlation between children's body weights and the SES of their parents (Gortmaker, Must, Perrin, Sobol, & Dietz, 1993). The process that concentrates fatness in the lowest strata of society now appears to operate as early as kindergarten. A shift in society seems to have taken place in the last twenty years.

What Is Behind the Link Between Weight and SES?

Why are the poor so fat? The typical assumption made by experts in many different fields is that poverty is fattening. Living in poor neighborhoods with high levels of crime and pollution can limit the opportunities for leisure-time physical activity. Also, foods that are high in nutrients and relatively low in calories, such as fresh fruits and vegetables and lean meats, are difficult to come by in poor neighborhoods. Processed or fast foods may be the only alternative, especially because many of the working poor hold more than one job and have child-care duties.

What is the critical aspect of poverty that is most closely linked to body weight? More than income or education, it is the status of the neighborhood that people live in (Barry & Breen, 2005; Schrijvers, Stronks, van de Mheen, & Mackenbach, 1999; Yen & Kaplan, 1999). Thus, people living in the same poor neighborhood will all have higher body weights, whereas people living in affluent areas are thinner. Neighborhood of residence is more important than individual income or other characteristics. Thus, it appears to be a true environmental effect and not the result of limited income or education. Another significant risk factor is financial problems. Economic difficulties are associated with a doubling of the risk of heart attack, and this applies across the spectrum of income and education (Ferrie, Martiekainen, Shipley, & Marmot, 2005).Thus, disposable income is probably a key factor relating socioeconomic well-being with health.

Poverty has been strongly linked to low-quality nutrition, which can result in weight gain because excess calories must be consumed to maintain adequate intake of vital nutrients. Household income is highly correlated with diet quality as judged against a reference such as the Healthy Eating Index (Drewnowski & Specter, 2004). This may partly be driven by economics, because the price of food on a per-calorie basis is much higher for nutrient-dense foods, and thus recommended dietary patterns are much more expensive than the average diet. Persons of low SES have increased intakes of dietary fat and get less exercise, both of which can promote weight gain (Jeffery, French, Forster, & Spry, 1991). Both fatness and low SES are associated with low self-esteem, high job stress, and a lack of self-care (Wamala, Wolk, & Orth-Gomér, 1997). A loss of employment often precedes a significant (10% or more) gain in body weight (Morris, Cook, & Shaper, 1992), so it is also possible that a decline in SES can precede weight gain. Job loss did not lead to more alcohol consumption, so the weight gain was not result of extra calories from alcohol.

Although there is some evidence that poverty is fattening, a stronger case can be made for converse: fatness is impoverishing (Sorensen, 1995). Discrimination and stigma can result in unemployment or low-paying work. One key study looked at fat and thin teenagers and followed up on their life circumstances seven years later (Gortmaker et al., 1993). Fat young women were much less likely to be married (28% versus 56% of the thin women), their household income was a third lower, they were three times more likely to live in poverty, and they were half as likely to have finished college. This was not related to self-esteem, because levels of self-esteem according psychological testing on the Rosenberg Scale were the same in fat and thin women. All these same findings applied to men as well, although the effects were less pronounced in each instance. One exception to this was college completion, which was reduced by one-half for fat men relative to thin men, the same proportion found for women. The young men and women were also given an intelligence test, the Armed Forces Qualification Test. Intelligence scores are in general a good predictor for success in life. For the fat young women and men, however, it made no difference. Fat and thin young people scored equally on the test, but intelligent fat people were far more likely to end up living in poverty than intelligent thin people.

Is fatness impoverishing because it causes chronically poor health? This was also looked at by Gortmaker and colleagues. They found that fat young people were no more likely than others to have chronic health conditions. Moreover, when they looked at young people who really did have chronic health problems like asthma, diabetes, or epilepsy, the rates of marriage and college completion and levels of income were completely unaffected (Gortmaker et al., 1993). This means that it cannot be health conditions that hold fat young people back, but only prejudice. Further, health problems are not the cause of this prejudice, because people with health problems do not suffer the same discrimination.

Fatness is also linked to social mobility—if you are living as an adult in a lower social class than your parents, then you are twice as likely to be heavy as someone upwardly mobile (Stunkard & Sorensen, 1993). Thus, it seems that adiposity arises first, and then low SES results through societal discrimination and stigma. High adiposity is more common among minority groups, including Native Americans, Blacks, Hispanics, and Jews, further magnifying discrimination.

SES and Health

Low SES is a powerful predictor of death due to cardiovascular disease (Banks, Marmot, Oldfield, & Smith, 2006; Marmot, 2003). In a representative U.S. sample, low income was associated with relative risks of 3.9 in women and 3.3 in men (Lantz et al. 1998). These estimates were not changed by statistical adjustment for cigarette smoking, alcohol intake, exercise level, and body weight. Thus, known risk factors accounted for only a small portion of the mortality risk of low SES. Importantly, the risks of low SES apply across the weight spectrum. This has been found consistently in many different epidemiological studies (Marmot, 2003). Nonetheless, many experts persist in the assumption that poor people are often unhealthy because they are often fat. Instead, fat people might be often unhealthy because they are often poor.

Evidence points to psychological stress and limited access to health care as the primary sources of the high risk of premature death in the lower social classes. Low SES is an especially strong predictor of early death in diabetics, presumably because of impaired delivery of necessary medical care (Rosengren, Welin, Tsipogianni, & Wilhelmsen, 1989). Living in a poor neighborhood is associated with diagnosis of cancer at a later stage (Barry & Breen, 2005). In other words, if you are poor your cancer is less likely to be caught earlier, and you are more likely to die a preventable death. This reflects limited access to health care for the poor.

A demographer at the Congressional Budget Office (Gronniger, 2005) took a very clever approach to the question of the contribution of social factors to the apparent health risk of adiposity. The demographer looked at the effect on risk of death of having a fat person in your household. Obviously, there is no biological reason for a thin person living with a fat person to have an increased risk of illness and death. But there are social reasons: the thin person is sharing the social and physical environment with a fat person. The result was that it was just as hazardous to live with a fat person as to actually be a fat person. The author concludes that unmeasured factors such as genetics and the physical and social environment may be responsible for the increased death rate in fat people.

After controlling for SES in the American's Changing Lives study, the relative risk from low body weight was 2.03, whereas the relative risk for high weight was 0.94 (Lantz et al., 1998). Thus, for individuals with equivalent social status, there is no significant increase in risk of death from high body mass (a relative risk of 1.00 indicates an unchanged probability of dying). In the National Health Examination Follow-Up Survey, poverty had a major impact on mortality rates for people who were fat (BMI > 30) but less so for leaner persons (Tayback, Kumanyika, & Chee, 1990). Similarly, a study in Finland found high risks of fatness (BMI > 34) in the upper classes (relative risk of 1.4 to 1.7) but not in lower social classes (relative risk of only 1.2) (Rissanen et al., 1989). Also, low weight (BMI < 19) was not a hazard in the upper classes (relative risk of 1.1) but was a strong risk in lower classes (relative risk of 1.9). Thus, if you are rich it is dangerous to be fat (but being thin is fine); if you are poor it is much more dangerous to be thin than to be fat. The contrasting effects of weight on health risks in different socioeconomic groups might account for some of the discrepancies between epidemiological studies in different types of populations, as discussed below.

Influence of Group SES on the Relationship Between Weight and Health

The relationship between body weight and morality has been reviewed many times, often with strikingly different conclusions (Andres, 1980; Bray, 1987; Gaesser, 1999; Keys, 1981). One consistent conclusion is that different longitudinal studies have conflicting results. Different authors have focused their arguments on which of the studies were best or largest or took the most factors into account. In this review, we will compare different long-term follow-up studies not by their alleged strengths and weaknesses but by the SES of the study group (table 3.1). This comparison reveals that much of the disagreement between different longitudinal studies can be explained by differences in SES of the

TABLE 1
Population characteristics and outcome of epidemiological studies of fatness and total mortality

Study population	Relative hazard of adiposity	Likely prevalence of weight loss practices and stigma	Reference
Young nurses	Exceptionally high	Very high	(Manson et al., 1995)
Holders of individual life insurance policies	Very high	Very high	(Lew et al., 1979)
Harvard alumni	Very high	High	(Lee et al., 1993)
Health professionals	High	Very high	(Baik et al., 2000)
Residents of affluent Boston suburb (Framingham, Mass.)	High	High	(Garrison et al., 1983)
Neighbors and relatives of American Cancer Society volunteers	High	High	(Lew & Garfinkel, 1979)
Residents of Finland	Moderate	Moderate	(Rissanen et al., 1989; Rissanen et al., 1991)
White women in Charleston, S.C.	Moderate	Moderate	(Stevens et al., 1992)
Black women in Charleston, S.C.	None	Low	(Stevens et al., 1992)
Civil servants of rural eastern Finland	None (Women) Low (Men)	Low	(Tuomilehto et al., 1987)
British civil servants	U-shaped	Low	(Jarrett et al., 1982)
German construction workers	Inverse	Low	(Brenner et al., 1997)
Dutch civil servants	None (Women) Low (Men)	Low	(Schuit et al., 1993)
Paris civil servants	Inverse	Low	(Filipovsky et al., 1993)
Black Kaiser Permanente subscribers	None (Women) U-shaped* (Men)	Low	(Wienpahl et al., 1990)
Residents of villages in rural Italy	None	Very low	(Anon., 1982)
Residents of villages in rural Scotland	Inverse relation	Very low	(Garn et al., 1983)
San Francisco longshoremen	Inverse	Low	(Borhani et al., 1963)
People's Gas employees	Inverse	Low	(Dyer et al., 1975)
Elderly populations	Inverse relation	Very low	(Andres, 1980)
Residents of American Samoa	None	Very low	(Crews, 1989)
Residents of Micronesia	Inverse relation	Very low	(Vandenbroucke et al., 1984)
Residents of Fiji	Inverse relation	Very low	(Collins et al., 1998; Hodge et al., 1996)
New Zealand Maori	None	Very low	(Salmond et al., 1985)
Native Americans of the Pima tribe	Inverse relation (women) Inverse up to BMI of 40 (men)	Very low	(Hanson et al., 1995)

*Highest mortality at BMI < 20. Risk increased only for BMI > 40.

Note: Studies are ranked according to the degree of relative risk associated with adiposity. The incidence of weight loss behavior is based either on direct report or on the characteristics of populations known to be associated with a high prevalence of dieting practices.

participants. In general, studies of high-SES groups such as physicians, nurses, and suburbanites show a positive relationship between weight and mortality risk, whereas studies of lower-SES groups show much more mixed results; in fact, they sometimes show an inverse relationship, where higher weights are associated with lower death rates.

Several epidemiological studies were controlled for SES because they used defined occupational groups (table 1). The ten-year San Francisco longshoremen study, for example, showed lower mortality in nonsmokers who were heavy (BMI > 29; 6.0% died) than in those who were what was then called "ideal weight" (BMI < 22; 10.2% died) (Borhani, Hechter, & Breslow, 1963). Almost identical results were obtained for nonsmoking employees of People's Gas in Chicago: in fourteen years, 20.4% of the "ideal weight" (BMI < 23.5) workers died, whereas 16.9% of the heavy men died (BMI > 29) (Dyer, Stamler, Berkson, & Lindberg, 1975). The Whitehall Study in England also showed a protective effect of being moderately overweight on mortality in British civil servants (Jarrett, Shipley, & Rose, 1982; Jarrett, 1986). A comparable study of Paris civil servants showed highest mortality in those that conform to the latest weight standards (BMI < 24.4), whereas mortality was 34% lower in those who were "overweight" (BMI of 24.4 to 27) and 31% lower in the heaviest group (BMI > 30) (Filipovsky, Ducimetière, Darné, & Richard, 1993). These relative risks are adjusted for smoking; removing the deaths in the first five or ten years of follow-up did not remove the protective effect of fatness. In each of these studies of employment groups, the low body weights associated with increased death rates were not emaciated by any means, but were at or even slightly above the recommendations of the life insurance tables. The inescapable conclusion is that once SES has been taken in to account, being underweight is a significant contributor to excess mortality.

The studies of body mass and mortality listed in table 1 are arranged roughly in order of the degree of hazard found to be associated with rising BMI. A striking relationship, which has not been commented on in any previous review, is that the five studies showing a high hazard of adiposity have subjects drawn from the highest SES. This includes suburban nurses, Harvard alumni, persons who can afford individual life insurance policies, residents of an affluent suburb (Framingham, Mass.), and others. These are social groups enforcing the strongest stigma against body fat. Nurses, in particular, are under strong pressure to lose weight as a healthful example to their patients. In contrast, study populations showing no risk of high body weight, or even an inverse relationship between body weight and mortality, tend to be of low SES and belong to non-Western cultures that do not value thinness as strongly as affluent Americans. The incidence of high body weight was very low in the Harvard alumni, nurses, and insurance policyholders. The average BMI of each of these groups were well below the U.S. average. In contrast, fatness is more prevalent in the populations where its health effects are diminished. The world's highest rates of adiposity are found in the South Pacific and in Native American groups. Yet in these non-Western cultures there is no increased risk of cardiovascular disease even at the highest weights (BMI of up to 40). This raises the possibility that the stigma, discrimination, and stress faced by obese persons of high SES in Western cultures may be a major contributor to their excess of cardiovascular mortality.

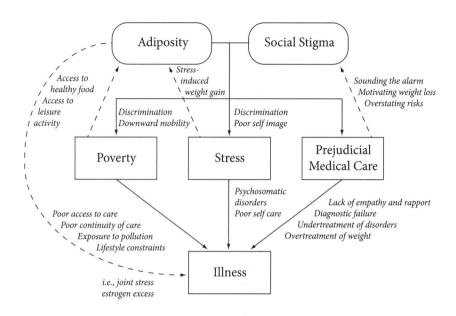

3.1. Hypothetical model for the relationship between SES, adiposity, and adverse health outcomes. The junction of adiposity and social stigma leads to poverty (low SES), individual and social stress, and prejudicial medical care. These three factors directly bear on the onset and exacerbation of medical illnesses. In addition, poverty may itself contribute to fatness, and stress can also facilitate further weight gain, leading to a positive feedback system. Prejudice on the part of health professionals also contributes to overall societal stigma against fatness. Finally, adiposity can directly contribute to disease, although this causal pathway has been greatly overemphasized in the medical literature. See text for further discussion.

Proposed Model for Interrelationship of SES, Weight, and Health

The possible relationships among adiposity, SES, and health are schematized in figure 1. Social stigma against fat people leads to diminished social status and ultimately poverty through discrimination in education and employment. Social stigma also restricts choices in a life partner, leading to downward mobility through marriage. Stigma, discrimination, and the resulting negative self-image and poverty are powerful stressors on the individual. The stigmatization of fat people extends to health professionals, leading to prejudicial medical care.

Poverty, stress, and prejudicial medical care, the three factors in rectangles in the middle of figure 1, in turn are all potential contributors to poor health outcomes. The relationship of low SES to illness and premature death is very well documented, and the adverse effects of poverty are independent of body weight. Poverty prevents access to quality health care, and the health care received lacks continuity as it often provided in emergency rooms rather than through a primary care office. Residents in poor neighborhoods are exposed to much more pollution from the air and land than residents of affluent areas, and exposure to toxins in the work environment is much more common in low-status occupations. Poverty also constrains lifestyle choices by limiting opportunities for safe outdoor activities or gym memberships, or access to fresh, whole foods. Stress is also a well-known cause of illness through the mechanisms of psychosomatic disorders, probably linked to excess levels of stress hormones and overactivity of the sympathetic nervous system (Ernsberger, Koletsky, & Friedman, 1998). Internalization of societal discrimination leads to poor body image, which can diminish self-care activities that maintain and promote health. Prejudicial medical care is a major factor leading to ill health among fat people. Physicians are less likely to perform preventative and screening measures on their fat patients (Adams, Smith, Wilbur, & Grady, 1993; Ostbye, Taylor, Yancy, & Krause, 2005). Also, a significant number of fat people avoid doctors altogether because of consistently negative experiences (Anon., 2002; Drury & Louis, 2002; Fontaine, Faith, Allison, & Cheskin, 1998; Olson, Schumaker, & Yawn, 1994). The heavier an adolescent patient is, the less likely they are to be satisfied by a medical encounter (Cohen, Tanofsky-Kraff, Young-Hyman, & Yanovski, 2005).

Several secondary relationships are shown in figure 1. Poverty can occasionally lead to increased adiposity, as discussed above. Stress can also lead to weight gain though biological and behavioral processes (Ernsberger et al., 1998). Prejudice on the part of health professionals plays a major role in sustaining and intensifying social stigma. Lay people commonly cite health concerns as the primary justification for discrimination and stigmatization of fat people (Ernsberger & Koletsky, 1999). Physicians may unwittingly promote stigmatization of fatness by sounding the alarm over the associated health hazards, and seeking to motivate weight loss by overstating the risks of high weight. Finally, in some circumstances there are direct relationships of adiposity to illness, although the importance of this process is probably overstated in the current medical literature. Well-established examples include wear and tear on weight-bearing joints (which also occurs in athletes of all weights, such as runners), and the effects of estrogen produced by fat cells. Excess estrogen increases the risk of uterine cancer, but only if appropriate gynecological care is not given (Barry & Breen, 2005).

Summary

SES is inversely related to adiposity in developed nations, meaning that people at the bottom of the ladder for income, education, wealth, and status are much more likely to be fat than the upper classes. This relationship is much stronger for adult women than for men, and is weaker in children than in adults. Although there is some evidence that poverty is fattening, there is much stronger evidence that fatness is impoverishing. Thin people from lower-class backgrounds are more likely to be upwardly mobile, and fat people from upper-class backgrounds are more likely to be downwardly mobile. The driving force behind the concentration of fatness among the poor is social stigma and systematic discrimination, which deprives fat people of the opportunity to move up the social ladder.

SES is also strongly related to health and longevity. Many of the diseases linked to adiposity are also linked to poverty and minority status, including high blood pressure, heart disease, and diabetes. These conditions are also related to individual and social stressors. Although most experts simply assume that the ill health of poor people is the result of their higher body weights, the evidence favors the converse explanation: that the ill health associated with adiposity is partly due to poverty. The association between high weight and ill health is much stronger for people in the higher social strata than for working class or poor people. This may reflect more stigma and discrimination among the educated classes, or more intense efforts at weight loss (which ultimately harm health).

Efforts to erase the stigma of fatness are not only of social benefit, but will also have multiple health benefits. The delivery of effective health care to fat people would be greatly enhanced by a lessening of stigmatization by the health professions.

REFERENCES

Adams, C.H., Smith, N.J., Wilbur, D.C., & Grady, K.E. (1993). The relationship of obesity to the frequency of pelvic examinations: do physician and patient attitudes make a difference? *Women's Health, 20*(2), 45–57.

Andres, R. (1980). Effect of obesity on total mortality. *International Journal of Obesity, 4*(4), 381–386.

Anon. (1982). Incidence and prediction of coronary heart disease in two Italian rural population samples followed-up for 20 years. *Acta Cardiologia, 37*(2), 129–145.

Anon. (2002). Medical care for obese patients: advice for health care professionals. *American Family Physician, 65*(1), 81–88.

Baik, I., Ascherio, A., Rimm, E.B., Giovannucci, E., Spiegelman, D., Stampfer, M.J., & Willett, W.C. (2000). Adiposity and mortality in men. *American Journal of Epidemiology, 152*(3), 264–271.

Banks, J., Marmot, M., Oldfield, Z., & Smith, J.P. (2006). Disease and disadvantage in the United States and in England. *Journal of the American Medical Association, 295*(17), 2037–2045.

Barry, J., & Breen, N. (2005). The importance of place of residence in predicting late-stage diagnosis of breast or cervical cancer. *Health and Place, 11*(1), 15–29.

Borhani, N.O., Hechter, H.H., & Breslow, L. (1963). Report of a 10-year follow-up study of the San Francisco longshoremen. *Journal of Chronic Diseases, 16* 1251–1266.

Bray, G.A. (1987). Overweight is risking fate: definition, classification, prevalence, and risks. *Annals of the New York Academy of Science, 499* 14–28.

Brenner, H., Arndt, V., Rothenbacher, D., Schuberth, S., Fraisse, E., & Fliedner, T.M. (1997). Body weight, pre-existing disease, and all-cause mortality in a cohort of male employees in the German construction industry. *Journal of Clinical Epidemiology, 50*(10), 1099–1106.

Cohen, M.L., Tanofsky-Kraff, M., Young-Hyman, D., & Yanovski, J.A. (2005). Weight and its relationship to adolescent perceptions of their providers (WRAP): a qualitative and quantitative assessment of teen weight-related preferences and concerns. *Journal of Adolescent Health, 37*(2), 163.

Collins, V.R., Dowse, G.K., Cabealawa, S., Ram, P., & Zimmet, P.Z. (1998). High mortality from cardiovascular disease and analysis of risk factors in Indian and Melanesian Fijians. *International Journal of Epidemiology, 25* 59–69.

Crews, D.E. (1989). Multivariate prediction of total and cardiovascular mortality in an obese Polynesian population. *American Journal of Public Health, 79*(8), 982–986.

Drewnowski, A., & Specter, S.E. (2004). Poverty and obesity: the role of energy density and energy costs. *American Journal of Clinical Nutrition, 79*(1), 6–16.

Drury, C.A., & Louis, M. (2002). Exploring the association between body weight, stigma of obesity, and health care avoidance. *Journal of the American Academy of Nurse Practicioners, 14*(12), 554–561.

Dyer, A.R., Stamler, J., Berkson, D.M., & Lindberg, H.A. (1975). Relationship of relative weight and body mass index to 14-year mortality in the Chicago Peoples Gas Company study. *Journal of Chronic Diseases, 28*(2), 109–123.

Ernsberger, P., & Koletsky, R.J. (1999). Biomedical rationale for a wellness approach to obesity: an alternative to a focus on weight loss. *Journal of Social Issues, 55*(2), 221–259.

Ernsberger, P., Koletsky, R.J., & Friedman, J.E. (1998). Contribution of sympathetic nervous system overactivity to cardiovascular and metabolic disease. *Reviews in Contemporary Pharmacotherapy, 9* 411–428.

Ferrie, J.E., Martikainen, P., Shipley, M.J., & Marmot, M.G. (2005). Self-reported economic difficulties and coronary events in men: evidence from the Whitehall II study. *International Journal of Epidemiology, 34*(3), 640–648.

Filipovsky, J., Ducimetière, P., Darné, B., & Richard, J.L. (1993). Abdominal body mass distribution and elevated blood pressure are associated with increased risk of death from cardiovascular diseases and cancer in middle-aged men: the results of a 15- to 20-year follow-up in the Paris prospective study I. *International Journal of Obesity, 17* 197–203.

Fontaine, K.R., Faith, M.S., Allison, D.B., & Cheskin, L.J. (1998). Body weight and health care among women in the general population. *Archives of Family Medicine, 7*(4), 381–384.

Gaesser, G.A. (1999). Thinness and weight loss: beneficial or detrimental to longevity? *Medicine and Science in Sports and Exercise, 31*(8), 1118–1128.

Garn, S.M., Hawthorne, V.M., Pilkington, J.J., & Pesick, S.D. (1983). Fatness and mortality in the West of Scotland. *American Journal of Clinical Nutrition, 38*(2), 313–319.

Garrison, R.J., Feinleib, M., Castelli, W.P., & McNamara, P.M. (1983). Cigarette smoking as a confounder of the relationship between relative weight and long-term mortality: the Framingham Heart Study. *Journal of the American Medical Association, 249*(16), 2199–2203.

Gortmaker, S.L., Must, A., Perrin, J.M., Sobol, A.M., & Dietz, W.H. (1993). Social and economic consequences of overweight in adolescence and young adulthood. *New England Journal of Medicine, 329*(14), 1008–1012.

Gronniger, J.T. (2005). Familial obesity as a proxy for omitted variables in the obesity-mortality relationship. *Demography, 42*(4), 719–735.

Hanson, R.L., McCance, D.R., Jacobsson, L.T.H., Narayan, K.M.V., Nelson, R.G., Pettitt, D.J., Bennett, P.H., & Knowler, W.C. (1995). The U-shaped association between body mass index and mortality: relationship with weight gain in a native American population. *Journal of Clinical Epidemiology, 48* 903–916.

Hodge, A.M., Dowse, G.K., Collins, V.R., & Zimmet, P.Z. (1996). Mortality in Micronesian Nauruans and Melanesian and Indian Fijians is not associated with obesity. *American Journal of Epidemiology, 143* 442–455.

Jarrett, R.J. (1986). Is there an ideal body weight? *British Medical Journal, 293*(6545), 493–495.

Jarrett, R.J., Shipley, M.J., & Rose, G. (1982). Weight and mortality in the Whitehall Study. *British Medical Journal, 285*(6341), 535–537.

Jeffery, R.W., French, S.A., Forster, J.L., & Spry, V.M. (1991). Socioeconomic status differences in health behaviors related to obesity: the Healthy Worker Project. *International Journal of Obesity, 15* 689–696.

Keys, A. (1981). Overweight, obesity, coronary heart disease, and mortality: the W.O. Atwater Memorial Lecture, 1980. *Progress in Clinical and Biological Research, 67* 31–46.

Lantz, P.M., House, J.S., Lepkowski, J.M., Williams, D.R., Mero, R.P., & Chen, J. (1998). Socioeconomic factors, health behaviors, and mortality: results from a nationally representative prospective study of US adults. *Journal of the American Medical Association, 279*(21), 1703–1708.

Lee, I.M., Manson, J.E., Hennekens, C.H., & Paffenbarger, R.S. (1993). Body weight and mortality: a 27-year follow-up of middle-aged men. *Journal of the American Medical Association, 270*(23), 2823–2828.

Lew, E., End, J.A., & Wilber, J.A. (1979). The new build and blood pressure study. *Transactions of the Association of Life Insurance Medical Directors of America, 62* 154–174.

Lew, E.A., & Garfinkel, L. (1979). Variations in mortality by weight among 750,000 men and women. *Journal of Chronic Diseases, 32*(8), 563–576.

Manson, J.E., Willett, W.C., Stampfer, M.J., Colditz, G.A., Hunter, D.J., Hankinson, S.E., Hennekens, C.H., & Speizer, F.E. (1995). Body weight and mortality among women. *New England Journal of Medicine, 333* 677–685.

Marmot, M.G. (2003). Understanding social inequalities in health. *Perspectives in Biology and Medicine, 46*(3 Suppl.), S9–S23.

Morris, J.K., Cook, D.G., & Shaper, A.G. (1992). Non-employment and changes in smoking, drinking, and body weight. *British Medical Journal, 304* 536–541.

Olson, C.L., Schumaker, H.D., & Yawn, B.P. (1994). Overweight women delay medical care. *Archives of Family Medicine, 3*(10), 888–892.

Ostbye, T., Taylor, D.H., Jr., Yancy, W.S., Jr., & Krause, K.M. (2005). Associations between obesity and receipt of screening mammography, Papanicolaou tests, and influenza vaccination: results from the Health and Retirement Study (HRS) and the Asset and Health Dynamics Among the Oldest Old (AHEAD) Study. *American Journal of Public Health, 95*(9), 1623–1630.

Rissanen, A., Heliovaara, M., Knekt, P., Aromaa, A., Reunanen, A., & Maatela, J. (1989). Weight and mortality in Finnish men. *Journal of Clinical Epidemiology, 42*(8), 781–789.

Rissanen, A., Knekt, P., Heliovaara, M., Aromaa, A., Reunanen, A., & Maatela, J. (1991). Weight and mortality in Finnish women. *Journal of Clinical Epidemiology, 44*(8), 787–795.

Rosengren, A., Welin, L., Tsipogianni, A., & Wilhelmsen, L. (1989). Impact of cardiovascular risk factors on coronary heart disease and mortality among middle aged diabetic men: a general population study. *British Medical Journal, 299*(6708), 1127–1131.

Salmond, C.E., Beaglehole, R., & Prior, I.A. (1985). Are low cholesterol values associated with excess mortality? *British Medical Journal, 290*(6466), 422–424.

Schrijvers, C.T., Stronks, K., van de Mheen, H.D., & Mackenbach, J.P. (1999). Explaining educational differences in mortality: the role of behavioral and material factors. *American Journal of Public Health, 89*(4), 535–540.

Schuit, A.J., Van Dijk, C.E., Dekker, J.M., Schouten, E.G., & Kok, F.J. (1993). Inverse association between serum total cholesterol and cancer mortality in Dutch civil servants. *American Journal of Epidemiology, 137*(9), 966–976.

Sobal, J. (1991). Obesity and socioeconomic status: a framework for examining relationships between physical and social variables. *Medical Anthropology, 13*(3), 231–247.

Sobal, J., & Stunkard, A.J. (1989). Socioeconomic status and obesity: a review of the literature. *Psychological Bulletin, 105*(2), 260–275.

Sorensen, T.I.A. (1995). Socio-economic aspects of obesity: Causes or effects. *International Journal of Obesity, 19*(Suppl. 6), S6–S8.

Stevens, J., Keil, J.E., Rust, P.F., Tyroler, H.A., Davis, C.E., & Gazes, P.C. (1992). Body mass index and body girths as predictors of mortality in black and white women. *Archives of Internal Medicine, 152* 1257–1262.

Stunkard, A.J., & Sorensen, T.I.A. (1993). Obesity and socioeconomic status—a complex relation. *New England Journal of Medicine, 329* 1036–1037.

Tayback, M., Kumanyika, S., & Chee, E. (1990). Body weight as a risk factor in the elderly. *Archives of Internal Medicine, 150*(5), 1065–1072.

Tuomilehto, J., Salonen, J.T., Marti, B., Jalkanen, L., Puska, P., Nissinen, A., & Wolf, E. (1987). Body weight and risk of myocardial infarction and death in the adult population of eastern Finland. *British Medical Journal, 295*(6599), 623–627.

Vandenbroucke, J.P., Mauritz, B.J., de Bruin, A., Verheesen, J.H., van der Heide-Wessel, C., & van der Heide, R.M. (1984). Weight, smoking, and mortality. *Journal of the American Medical Association, 252*(20), 2859–2860.

Wamala, S.P., Wolk, A., & Orth-Gomér, K. (1997). Determinants of obesity in relation to socioeconomic status among middle-aged Swedish women. *Preventive Medicine, 26*(5 pt. 1), 734–744.

Wienpahl, J., Ragland, D.R., & Sidney, S. (1990). Body mass index and 15-year mortality in a cohort of black men and women. *Journal of Clinical Epidemiology, 43*(9), 949–960.

Yen, I.H., & Kaplan, G.A. (1999). Neighborhood social environment and risk of death: multilevel evidence from the Alameda County Study. *American Journal of Epidemiology, 149*(10), 898–907.

Is "Permanent Weight Loss" an Oxymoron?

The Statistics on Weight Loss and the National Weight Control Registry

Glenn Gaesser

In view of the statistics on "obesity" and dieting in the United States, "permanent weight loss" might seem oxymoronic. Despite our collective efforts to lose weight, the average American continues to gain. For example, in 1991, the average U.S. man weighed 179 pounds, and the average woman weighed 143 pounds. In 1998, average weights for U.S. men and women were 186 pounds and 151 pounds, respectively (Mokdad et al., 1999). Prevalence of "obesity" among U.S. adults increased during the 1990s from approximately 23 percent at the beginning of the decade to 31 percent in 2000 (Flegal, Carroll, Ogden, & Johnson, 2003). The most recent data from the National Health and Nutrition Examination Surveys indicate that between 1999 and 2004 the prevalence of "obesity" continued to increase slightly for men, although no overall increases in prevalence rates for women were observed during this six-year period (Ogden et al., 2006).

During much of the time period covered by these studies of the national prevalence of weight gain and "obesity," large-scale surveys also indicated a high prevalence of weight loss attempts by Americans. In the early 1990s, 33–40 percent of U.S. women and 20–24 percent of men reported that they were trying to lose weight (NIH Technology Assessment Conference Panel, 1993). In 1998, approximately 44 percent of U.S. women and 28 percent of U.S. men indicated that they were trying to lose weight (Serdula et al., 1999). The 2000 Behavioral Risk Factor Surveillance System Survey (BRFSSS) revealed that these numbers increased further by the end of the decade, to 46.3 percent of women and 32.8 percent of men trying to lose weight (Bish et al., 2005). Additionally, the data indicate that the prevalence of weight loss attempts increased directly with body mass index (BMI), such that the prevalence of trying to lose weight among women with BMIs between 25 and 29.9 was 60 percent, and among women with BMIs greater than 30 it was 70 percent. Similar trends were observed for men. The fact that average body weights and "obesity" prevalence were increasing at a time of increased weight loss attempts suggests that weight loss was not successful.

Poor Long-Term Weight Loss Maintenance Statistics

These observations are consistent with the conclusions of experts regarding the efficacy of weight loss attempts. Success rates for long-term weight loss are not good: of those who intentionally lose weight, most will regain about one-third of their weight within the first year, and virtually all will return to their baseline weight within five years (NIH Technology Assessment Conference Panel, 1993). A more recent meta-analysis of U.S. weight loss studies suggests that success in weight loss maintenance has improved, but that most people regain a considerable amount of their initial weight loss after four or five years (Anderson, Konz, Frederich, & Wood, 2001). Based on data from twenty-nine reports, weight loss maintenance four to five years after participation in a structured weight loss program averaged only three kilograms, or about 23 percent of initial weight loss (meaning that participants had gained back approximately 77 percent of what they had initially lost).

Given these statistics, one must wonder why millions of Americans continue to go on any number of weight loss programs each year. One obvious reason is the anecdotal evidence, or testimonials, from the person (or, sometimes, persons) who provide the "living proof" that the program (or product, or diet) works. The power of the testimonial cannot be underestimated. In fact, the testimonial has always been the hallmark of the weight loss industry—mainly because no commercial weight loss program has ever published its "success" rates, which says a lot.

A Look at the National Weight Control Registry

But what of these anecdotal cases of alleged "permanent" weight loss? Do they exist? And if so, what can we learn from them? Until 1993, no study of people who claimed to be successful at maintaining a significant weight loss had been undertaken. In 1993, researchers at the University of Pittsburgh and the University of Colorado Health Sciences Center initiated the National Weight Control Registry (NWCR) in an effort to obtain information on men and women who apparently had been successful at maintaining a significant weight loss (see, for example, Hill, Wyatt, Phelan, & Wing, 2005; Wing & Hill, 2001; Klem, Wing, McGuire, Seagle, & Hill, 1997; Shick et al., 1998). The researchers who started the NWCR consider it the largest study of individuals "successful" at long-term maintenance of weight loss. Since its inception, more than twenty NWCR reports have appeared in the scientific literature.

To be eligible, participants had to be at least eighteen years old and have maintained a weight loss of thirty pounds for at least one year. In the initial reports from the NWCR, data on 784 (Klem et al., 1997) and 438 (Shick et al., 1998) individuals (approximately 80 percent women) were reported. It should be mentioned that the participants highlighted in these two initial publications reported having maintained an average weight loss of sixty-six pounds for 5.1 years. As for method of weight loss, most (especially women) received some assistance, either from a commercial program, self-help group, dietitian, physician, nurse, psychologist, or exercise club. On the other hand, 36 percent of women and 55 percent of men reported that they lost weight on their own (see Shick et al., 1998).

Food frequency questionnaires indicated that they consumed a diet adequate in minerals and vitamins, but low in calories (1,306 kcal/day for women; 1,685 kcal/day for men), averaging about 23–25 percent fat, 55–56 percent carbohydrate, and 18–19 percent protein. Participants were also very physically active, expending an average of about 2,800 kcal/week, or approximately 400 kcal/day (i.e., roughly equal to walking four to five miles per day, which might be expected to take between sixty and ninety minutes).

One obvious problem with the eligibility requirements for the NWCR is that one year is by no means sufficient to qualify as "permanent," or even "long-term," even though the initial enrollees used for both the Klem and Shick reports apparently maintained their weight loss for an average of about five years. Another limitation is that the weight loss/maintenance is self-reported, as are dietary intake and physical activity data. In fact, there is really no documented evidence (i.e., weigh-ins monitored by the NWCR researchers) of the weight lost by the participants and whether they have actually maintained that weight loss.

What can we learn from the NWCR? The registry promotes the notion that there are persons who have been successful at maintaining large weight losses for extended periods of time. But this must be considered in the context of the numbers of people in the United States currently trying to lose weight.

Using data from the 2000 Behavioral Risk Factor Surveillance System Survey cited above (Bish et al., 2005), and data from the 2000 U.S. census, approximately eighty million U.S. adults are currently trying to lose weight (if population estimates for 2005 are used, this number increases to about eighty-five million—again, using the 2000 BRFSSS survey data, published in 2005). The initial reports from the NWCR represent data on fewer than one thousand men and women (some of the subjects appear in both reports), or approximately one out of every eighty thousand Americans trying to lose weight. The current enrollment in the NWCR is approximately five thousand (Hill et al., 2005). This corresponds to roughly one out of sixteen thousand adults attempting weight loss—not exactly what one might consider representative.

What Is the Real Success Rate for Weight Loss Maintenance?

No one knows the true success, or failure, rates for long-term weight loss. The ubiquitous "90–95 percent failure rate" stems from a 1959 report (Stunkard & McLauren-Hume, 1959). Despite alleged improvements in weight loss maintenance techniques over the years (Anderson et al., 2001; Hill et al., 2005), published reports both on weight loss maintenance and on the increasing prevalence of weight gain and "obesity" in the face of increasing prevalence of weight loss attempts (Anderson et al., 2001; Bish et al., 2005; Mokdad et al., 1999; NIH Technology Assessment Conference Panel, 1993; Ogden et al., 2006), suggest that the "90–95 percent failure rate" may not be far from the truth.

In spite of the empirical evidence, researchers associated with the NWCR have suggested that the success rate for maintaining weight loss might be approximately 20 percent (Wing & Hill, 2001; Hill et al., 2005; McGuire, Wing, & Hill, 1999). This "success" rate is, however, defined as an intentional weight loss of at least 10 percent of body weight that is kept off for at least one year (Wing & Hill, 2001). The NWCR researchers argue that a one-year standard is consistent with the recommendations of the Institute of Medicine definition (Wing & Hill, 2001). In view of the time course of weight regain after weight loss (Anderson et al., 2001; NIH Technology Assessment Conference Panel, 1993), one year is arbitrary and likely to lead to an overly optimistic picture of weight loss maintenance.

The National Weight Control Registry May Need Another Forty Thousand Years

So what can be made of the approximately five thousand people currently in the NWCR, and the more than twenty reports using the NWCR registry as an example of weight loss success? Is this a meaningful sample of the U.S. population, or just a relative handful of anecdotal testimonials? Although the initial data from the NWCR may seem "encouraging" to the authors of the reports, if one uses the NWCR researchers' own assertions that the success rate for weight loss maintenance may be about 20 percent, the registry needs to enroll another 15,995,000 U.S. adults to reflect approximately 20 percent of the U.S. adult population trying to lose weight (i.e., 20 percent of 80,000,000 = 16,000,000; the NWCR already has enrolled 5,000). The registry currently enrolls about four hundred people per year (Hill et al., 2005). You do not need to be gifted at math to realize the NWCR has quite a ways to go before it can be considered anything more than just a collection of anecdotal testimonials. (At their current enrollment pace, the NWCR will reach sixteen million in another forty thousand years. Don't hold your breath.)

NOTE

This chapter was previously published in the *Health At Every Size Journal*, 2006, 20(2), pp. 91–95. Reprinted with permission, Gurze Books, http://www.gurze.com.

REFERENCES

Anderson, J.W., Konz, E.C., Frederich, R.C., & Wood CL. (2001). Long-term weight-maintenance: a meta-analysis of US studies. *American Journal of Clinical Nutrition, 74*, 579–584.

Bish, C.L., Blanck, H.M., Serdula, M.K., Marcus, M., Kohl, H.W., & Khan, L.K. (2000). Diet and physical activity behaviors among Americans trying to lose weight: 2000 Behavioral Risk Factor Surveillance System. *Obesity Research, 13*, 596–607.

Flegal, K.M., Carroll, M.D., Ogden, C.L., & Johnson, C.L. (2003). Prevalence and trends in obesity among U.S. adults, 1999–2000. *Journal of the American Medical Association 289,* 1747–1750.

Hill, J.O., Wyatt, H., Phelan, S., & Wing, R. (2005). The National Weight Control Registry: is it useful in helping deal with our obesity epidemic? *Journal of Nutrition Education and Behavior, 37,* 206–210.

Klem, M.L., Wing, R.R., McGuire, M.T., Seagle, H.M., & Hill, J.O. (1997). A descriptive study of individuals successful at long-term maintenance of substantial weight loss. *American Journal of Clinical Nutrition, 66,* 239–246.

McGuire, M.T., Wing, R.R., & Hill, J.O. (1999). The prevalence of weight loss maintenance among American adults. *International Journal of Obesity, 23,* 1314–1319.

Mokdad , A.H., Serdula, M.K., Deitz, W.H., Bowman, B.A., Marks, J.S., & Koplan, J.P. (1999). The spread of the obesity epidemic in the United States, 1991–1998. *Journal of the American Medical Association, 282,* 1519–1522.

NIH Technology Assessment Conference Panel (1993). Methods for voluntary weight loss and control. *Annals of Internal Medicine, 119,* 764–770.

Ogden, C.L., Carroll, M.D., Curtin, L.R., McDowell, M.A., Tabak, C.J., & Flegal, K.M. (2006). Prevalence of overweight and obesity in the United States, 1999–2004. *Journal of the American Medical Association, 295,* 1549–1555.

Serdula, M.K., Mokdad, A.H., Williamson, D.F., Galuska, D.A., Mendlein, J.M., & Health, G.W. (1999). Prevalence of attempting weight loss and strategies for controlling weight. *Journal of the American Medical Association, 282,* 1353–1358.

Shick, S.M., Wing, R.R., Klem, M.L., McGuire, M.T., Hill, J.O., & Seagle, H.M. (1998). Persons successful at long-term weight loss and maintenance continue to consume a low-energy, low-fat diet. *Journal of the American Dietetic Association, 98,* 408–413.

Stunkard, A, & McLauren-Hume, M. (1959). The results of treatment for obesity: a review of the literature and report of a series. *Archives of Internal Medicine, 103,* 79–85.

Wing, R.R., & Hill, J.O. (2001). Successful weight loss maintenance. *Annual Review of Nutrition, 21,* 323–341.

|||||||||||||||||||||||||||||||||||||||||||||||||||||||||||||||||||||||||||||||||

5

What Is "Health at Every Size"?

Deb Burgard

One of the most important inquiries within the new field of fat studies is the examination of the way that health issues have been used to oppress people of size. In a culture where there is at least some self-consciousness about the impoliteness of expressing blatant revulsion about fat, most people are quite willing to support the stereotype of fatness signifying ill health. Moreover, in contrast to other health concerns like cancer or flu epidemics, fat people are blamed for their health problems. The use of health concerns to convey disapproval and censure is a fascinating and disturbing phenomenon in the stigmatization of fat people.

It is also fascinating that there is a grassroots movement opposing this oppression among healthcare workers and health researchers, the very people who might be considered the "army" in the "War on Obesity." These people, in collaboration with activists and consumers, have been evolving an alternative public health model for people of all sizes called Health at Every Size (HAES).

The HAES approach differs from a conventional treatment model in its emphasis on self-acceptance and healthy day-to-day practices, regardless of whether a person's weight changes. Letting go of the goal of weight loss has made HAES controversial in a society where the pursuit of thinness is an unquestioned prescription for health and happiness. But many of the clinicians who have evolved the HAES approach have seen the devastating consequences of pursuing weight loss, in either the nearly universal failure of weight loss dieting (Mann et al., 2007), or the pursuit of thinness in individuals with eating disorders (Neumark-Sztainer, 2006). We find it hypocritical to prescribe practices for heavier people that we would diagnose as eating disordered in thin ones.

What Does Health at Every Size Stand For?

1. *Enhancing health*—attending to emotional, physical and spiritual well-being, without focusing on weight loss or achieving a specific "ideal weight."
2. *Size and self-acceptance*—respecting and appreciating the wonderful diversity of body shapes, sizes, and features (including one's own!), rather than pursuing an idealized weight, shape, or physical feature.

3. *The pleasure of eating well*—eating based on internal cues of hunger, satiety, and appetite; individual nutritional needs; and enjoyment, rather than on external food plans or diets.

4. *The joy of movement*—encouraging all physical activities for the associated pleasure and health benefits, rather than following a specific routine of regimented exercise for the primary purpose of weight loss or management.

5. *An end to weight bias*—recognizing that body shape, size, or weight are not evidence of any particular way of eating, level of physical activity, personality, psychological issue, or moral character; and confirming that there is beauty and worth in EVERY body. (written by Ellen Shuman and Karin Kratina)

The Link Between Health and Weight

Weight loss advocates who use body mass index (BMI) to determine healthy and unhealthy weights feel that dropping the goal of a particular weight endpoint is sidestepping the problem. These people cite numerous studies linking obesity with various health concerns, such as hypertension, diabetes, and cardiovascular disorders (see Gaesser, 2002, for a review). When examined in more detail, however, the same studies show that correlations between health problems and BMI are typically at most $r = .3$. A correlational statistic is squared to give the variation in outcomes due to that variable; this means that about 9% of the outcome of whether someone has a health problem or not is somehow related to BMI (correlated to it but not necessarily caused by it). In other words, 91% of what accounts for a health outcome has *nothing to do with BMI*. HAES practitioners advocate putting more effort into explaining the factors making up that 91% not related to weight. Some of these other factors might make a bigger impact on health than weight, and might be easier to implement as well. Moreover, because so few people change their weight for more than one to two years, we do not know whether weight loss would in fact change people's health outcomes. The "risk factor" of higher BMI comes from a comparison of always-been-thinner people to fatter people, and we do not know whether "reduced" fat people would have the same risk profile as always-been-thinner people because so few people change their weight for more than a brief period. We do not know that weight loss would improve long-term health, and we do not have a treatment to produce lasting weight loss for the vast majority of people.

Because these limitations are inherent in the traditional weight loss model, many health-care workers find the HAES approach more realistic and satisfying. The focus is on the day-to-day activities that help individuals of any size to flourish. When these activities are uncoupled from a weight loss goal, they can be assessed for their sustainability over a lifetime. The goal becomes helping individuals to make these healthy practices a lifelong investment in their own well-being. Because people are not doing the practices for the purpose of losing weight, weight fluctuations have less impact on motivation.

A weight-neutral approach focuses on loving self-care and the decisions that people can make on a day-to-day basis that are sustainable for a lifetime. HAES is not against weight loss; it is against the pursuit of weight loss. The task is to care for the body you have, and will continue to have, whether it gains or loses weight or ages or gets cancer or runs a marathon.

Determining a Healthy Weight

The HAES model does not suggest that anyone of any weight must by definition be healthy. It does not suggest that anyone must by definition be at their own healthy weight. HAES defines health by the process of daily life rather than the outcome of weight. If people have to do things in their day-to-day life to achieve a particular weight that a study says would be healthier—and the things that they have to do (like stomach surgery, starving, or exercising four hours a day) are not compatible with loving self-care—then, by definition, that is not a "healthy" weight for that individual. It would be like starving a St. Bernard because a study of dogs shows that greyhounds live longer. We are genetically like different breeds of dogs, but we can't tell what breed we are by sight. You have to tell your "breed" by the weight that you turn out to be when you are living a good life. HAES points out that when people are doing this they come in a great variety of natural weights; therefore, deeming any particular BMI pathological is a political rather than a scientific act.

This sort of argument is easiest to accept when considering people who have closer-to-average BMIs. But what about the largest members of our community? What does HAES say about people who have very high BMIs or health conditions that correlate with higher weight?

The problem with picking a dividing line between "acceptable" and "unacceptable" degrees of fatness is that it cannot be applied to individuals. For any given weight, there are people who are healthy and people who are not. Every health condition linked to higher BMI is found in thin people as well. There are lower risks of some health conditions with higher BMI that are given scant attention; after the age of seventy, higher BMI becomes a protective factor. The link between health and weight is understood only to the extent that we can say, "In a large and varied population, BMI may be correlated to some extent with the risk of certain health conditions, and that risk does seem to climb at higher BMI for reasons that we do not understand." The link between mortality and weight is understood to the extent that we can say, "In a large and varied population, BMI may be correlated to some extent with the risk of an earlier death, for the very low and very high ends of the BMI spectrum, for reasons that we do not understand." When it comes to applying this information, health-care workers who have thought critically about the conventional approaches have asked the following questions:

- How do we guess which patients are going to be the ones who will have health issues and who will not?

- If we knew which people would have problems, what would we suggest they do about changing their BMI when there are no safe and effective interventions to permanently change BMI for the majority of people?
- If fatness causes health problems, why does it not show up in all fat people? Why do those same health problems show up in thin people? Why do the diseases attributed to higher BMI seem to also be characterizable as diseases of aging or chronic stress?
- Is higher BMI measuring more body fat or more lean body mass? If we cannot isolate the variable we are trying to measure, what do the data using BMI mean?
- If we did have a way to change people's weight permanently, would their risk-factor profile as a starved fat person be the same as an always-thinner person?
- If we do not have a way to change a person's BMI permanently, is it better for their health to have them try to lose and then regain weight or to remain at a stable weight? Given the considerable evidence that people are harmed by weight cycling, both physiologically and psychologically, what circumstances could possibly justify such an intervention? Even when people have BMI-correlated health conditions, if there is no safe way to change their BMI, how can we justify trying to? Could our "treatments" be making people sicker? Is the prescription of weight loss dieting one of the biggest iatrogenic disasters of our time?
- If we are not going to intervene around weight, what else can we offer? Everything that we would offer to a thin person who did not trigger our weight bias: support in caring for one's needs for good nutrition, lively physical activity, social support, safety, a clean environment, meaning and satisfaction, freedom from oppression, and so forth.
- What about weight discrimination and stigma—what is our responsibility as health-care workers in addressing what may be the primary health threat to fat people?

- In the absence of causal mechanisms of illness that reliably operate at a given weight, and because there is so much evidence of ways to improve health regardless of weight, HAES advocates have adopted a commitment to assessing clients and patients on an individual basis, and rejecting the conventional assumption that arbitrary BMI dividing lines ("overweight," "obese") are indications of pathology in individuals.

HAES asserts that the medical pathologizing of the majority of the U.S. population harms people's health by stigmatizing them and causing discrimination in insurance, jobs, social relationships, and medical care (Brownell, Puhl, Schwartz, & Rudd, 2005). HAES directs medical researchers to investigate the health consequences of stigma and discrimination based on weight, including social and job discrimination, barriers to insurance and medical care, biased medical care, prescription of weight loss dieting, the effects of stigma on people who are vulnerable to developing eating disorders, and the health consequences of weight dissatisfaction on people across the weight spectrum (Muennig, Jia, Lee, & Lubetkin, 2008). In this way HAES includes a focus on social justice as an integral aspect of public health.

Challenging the Practice of Prescribing Weight Loss

If we follow the normal procedures of science, we need to show that there is evidence for our hypothesis before assuming it is true. But in real life, scientific consensus also occurs because a priori assumptions are so seamless that they are not questioned.

One of the a priori assumptions that does not seem to require evidence is the idea that being fat is unhealthy. Variations on this idea include the assumption that fat itself causes the disorders with which it is often associated, the assumption that one can tell by looking at a person's weight what they must be eating or how much exercise they get, the assumption that losing weight will improve health, and the assumption that successful and lasting weight loss is possible.

Because people in our culture, including physicians, subscribe so religiously to these assumptions, they have not been subjected to adequate scientific testing. In fact, in a bizarre twist, people who have pointed out that there is not adequate evidence for these assumptions are asked to "prove that they aren't true." How does one "disprove" a matter of faith, especially when people do not recognize it as such?

"It's scientifically proven that if you're overweight you have an increased risk of coming down with numerous medical conditions," said Dr. Howard Shapiro, a New York weight loss specialist and author of the *Picture Perfect Weight Loss* books. "It's a no brainer, and anyone who says that it's discriminatory is just trying to protect themselves" (Ellin, 2006, sec. 9, pp. 1, 6). Indeed, the "no brainer" part seems to be all too apt a description of the way that some medical professionals have lost their ability to think critically in the face of lucrative weight loss opportunities, the assumption that fat people are looking for excuses, and the medical training conditions that intensify physicians' revulsion to fatness.

Methodological Critiques of the Research on High BMI and Health

- The diseases that are associated with higher BMI also occur at low BMI. If fatness causes these diseases, why do they exist across the weight spectrum?
- The studies that show correlations between higher BMI and ill health fail to control for important variables known to mediate this relationship, including SES, physical activity levels, nutritional quality, sleep quality, access to quality medical care, exposure to weight-based stigma, or even trying to lose weight (weight cycling) itself.
- The studies that find pathology in higher-BMI participants are usually investigating a clinical population (e.g., patients in a weight loss clinic, cardiac patients, patients seeking help with eating disorders, etc.) but the findings are generalized to the normal population.

- Most studies of weight loss are limited to a six month to one year snapshot and are assumed to represent the outcome "happily ever after." Studies of improved health after weight loss have investigated at most two-year outcomes, before most people have regained weight or the initial health gains have reverted back to baseline.
- Health improvements attributed to weight loss occur without any weight loss when research participants improve their health practices. There is no dose-response relationship between the degree of weight loss and the degree of health benefits, which is what we would expect if weight loss was causing the health benefit. Also, weight loss in the absence of improved health practices, like liposuction, has not been demonstrated to correlate with health improvements.
- Weight cycling, which is the overwhelming outcome of attempting to lose weight, is correlated with hypertension and adverse body fat distribution.
- There is plenty of data, but inadequate attention, on the risks of having a low BMI, making the hysteria about high-BMI particularly suspect.
- The financial and political stakes in demonizing "obesity" are profound. It is rare to find researchers who are not paid consultants to the weight loss industry.

If we start from a position of neutrality, and do not make an a priori assumption that higher BMI is unhealthy, we are left with numerous studies showing health benefits based on quality nutrition, regular physical activity, social support, restful sleep, freedom from violence and stigma, abstention from smoking and excessive alcohol and drug use, access to quality medical care, and so on. Health at Every Size practitioners base their interventions on these empirically tested findings.

Assumptions That We Make Based on Weight

Are we prescribing for heavier people what we diagnose as eating disorders in thinner people? Read the following vignette with the assumption that the young woman, "Julie," is 105 pounds, 5' 5" tall. What do you see as problematic? How do you think health professionals would diagnose and treat Julie?

J. is a seventeen-year-old white female with concerns about her weight and loathing of her thighs. She feels hopeless about dating until she can lose weight, which she feels holds the promise of making her life "perfect." She has lost twenty-five pounds in the last five months, but in the last two weeks she has regained five pounds and is feeling panicky. Her mood on any given day depends on whether she has lost or gained weight. She is preoccupied with what food she will be eating that day, has "healthy" and "unhealthy" food categories, and does not trust her body's hunger and satiety cues. She keeps a log of everything she eats, is currently restricting her intake to about one thousand calories per day, and is particularly averse to eating dietary fat and carbohydrates. She is finding it difficult to focus mental energy on issues that are unrelated to food and weight. She avoids activities such as being seen in a swimsuit, going out with friends, and applying

*to be a camp counselor, postponing them until she feels that her body is more "accept-
able." She has been unable to maintain the restrictive intake recently and has "bingeing"
episodes in which she feels out of control, eats more than she feels she should, and does
not feel sated even when feeling over-full. J. saw herself as a "chubby" child, and experiencing teasing about her body. Her weight has been unstable since puberty, and there
have been two times in addition to the present when she has not had menstrual periods.
Repeated cycles of weight loss and regain have depleted her lean body mass to some degree, and she states that she finds exercising miserable.*

Now read the same vignette with the assumption that the young woman, "Jody," is
195 pounds and 5' 5" tall. What do you see as problematic? How do you think health
professionals would diagnose and treat Jodie?

Most traditional clinicians would view Julie's restrictive intake, rigidity about food,
and avoidance of daily activities as evidence of an eating disorder. They might even
see her binges as her body's healthy attempt to restore its natural weight. They would
be pleasantly surprised to see that Julie is not a compulsive exerciser and probably
would not encourage her to move more because they want her to gain weight. On the
other hand, most clinicians would view Jody's dieting and cognitive monitoring as
desirable, and her avoidance of daily activities as understandable. They would most
likely view her avoidance of exercise and her bingeing as typical problem behaviors
of fatter people.

Focusing on Behavior, Not Weight

The HAES model tries to untangle the effects of weight stereotyping. It asks us all to
focus on the day-to-day self-nurturing behaviors that result in physical and mental
health improvements, and to challenge the pursuit of weight loss so that our bodies
can settle at the weight they do when we are living in a healthy way. HAES is weight-
neutral. We ask the individual with anorexia to trust her body to find its healthy
weight when she is eating enough fuel to function well, and we ask the average- and
above average–weight women to do the same.

Myths and Realities of Health at Every Size

Myth: The HAES model ignores health.
Reality: HAES argues that giving up the pursuit of weight loss and focusing on the
daily practices that are empirically supported to enhance health are more likely to
result in better long-term health for more people.

Myth: The HAES model argues that people of every size must be healthy.
Reality: HAES recognizes that people may be at, below, or above the weight that
their bodies would settle at if they were consistently practicing body-nurturing

behaviors. HAES argues, however, that no one can or should assume by BMI alone what a person's health practices must be. HAES also advocates an end to arbitrary BMI "dividing lines" between good and ill health for use with individuals, as BMI is a poor predictor of the current or future health of individuals. Finally, HAES encourages a health perspective focusing on what is controllable, and on process rather than outcome. HAES advocates an end to public policies that use health *outcomes* as a basis for rewards or penalties, including job or insurance discrimination.

Myth: The HAES model ignores research showing that BMI is a risk factor for ill health.

Reality: HAES recognizes that many population studies show a correlation between higher BMI and various health problems, and insists that such research be reported accurately. HAES often critiques aspects of these studies or their coverage in the press that imply conclusions that are not supported by the reported data. HAES argues that the "fat = unhealthy" stereotype, undisclosed financial conflicts of interest, and the widespread lack of understanding about research methods and statistics often lower the quality and accuracy of reporting on health and weight.

Myth: The HAES model is anti–weight loss.

Reality: HAES challenges *the pursuit of* weight loss as a goal, not the result of weight loss. HAES is "weight-neutral": whether someone gains, loses, or stabilizes weight is of less interest than their adoption of long-term health-enhancing behaviors. HAES also recognizes that adopting sustainable health practices will not necessarily result in weight loss.

Myth: The HAES model is cruel because it says that fat people should have to settle for their lot.

Reality: HAES offers people who have been betrayed by empty promises of weight loss a more reliable definition of success, and a dependable pathway to improved health. Its practitioners are leaders in the fight against weight bias and are active in the effort to expand fitness, social, and occupational opportunities for people of all sizes. HAES does not ask people to solve the problem of stigma by urging them to escape from the stigmatized group.

Myth: The HAES model has no empirical support.

Reality: HAES is based on a critical, informed reading of thousands of existing research studies that show:

- high BMI has been exaggerated as a risk factor and inaccurately portrayed as a causal agent in ill health and premature death (Campos, Saguy, Ernsberger, Oliver, & Gaesser., 2006);
- health risks are lowered by physical activity, social support, good nutrition, access to medical care, and so forth, regardless of whether weight loss occurs (Lamarche et al., 1992; Bjorntorp, De Jounge, Sjorstorm, & Sullivan, 1970);

- ineffective weight loss interventions cause physical and psychological damage (Garner & Wooley, 1991; Neumark-Sztainer, 2006):
- a vacuum of long-term data showing empirical support for the safety or effectiveness of any current weight loss intervention (Mann et al., 2007); and
- a growing body of experimental studies showing that a HAES approach results in lasting beneficial health improvements because it supports sustainable day-to-day self-care (Bacon, Stern, Van Loan, & Keim, 2005).

The HAES model may be seen as a conservative approach that demands empirical data before recommending weight loss interventions, while also acknowledging the need for much more study of neglected topics such as factors influencing the adoption of long-term health-enhancing behaviors.

Myth: The HAES model is overly influenced by the politics of the size acceptance movement.

Reality: HAES evolved from the frustrations of actual clinical practice, by a cohort of health-care workers, fitness professionals, nutritionists, coaches, and therapists, who may or may not have been aware of the size acceptance movement but whose clinical practice showed them the futility or even harm of pursuing weight loss. It has evolved with the welcome input of higher-BMI people who have been on the forefront of the size acceptance movement, and is the stronger for it, as any model addressing the needs of a community is bolstered when it involves input from that community.

HAES shares many values with the size acceptance movement, including that: the diversity of body sizes, like many other biological traits, is a natural phenomenon to be valued; individuals should not be stigmatized based on weight, and stigma is itself a health risk for people of various sizes; and the research on "obesity" and medical practice are tainted by social prejudice against fat people. Although the size acceptance movement advocates for the rights of all individuals regardless of health practices, the HAES model attempts to define health in the absence of weight prejudice, and on an empirical basis. HAES takes a position advocating empirically defined practices that improve health for people of all sizes. Although deploring the use of health as a weapon for discrimination, HAES also takes a position on defining health. This advocacy includes supporting individual efforts to nurture one's body, even when it has been stigmatized, as well as demanding environmental, legislative, community, medical, and workplace policy support for sustaining these practices. Ending weight-related stigma is a common goal for both the size acceptance movement and HAES.

Myth: The HAES model perpetuates the oppression of fat people by defining healthier people or people who exercise as the "good" fat people while still condemning people who are sedentary or in poorer health.

Reality: The HAES model critiques the use of "health" as a moral assessment of worth. For example, instead of seeing exercise as a moral imperative for fat people, HAES demands equal *opportunities* for pleasurable, safe activity for people of all sizes. As health workers, we do take a stand on what we define as health, and what we take as the goal of our interventions with patients. In this regard, we try to rely on empirical data showing the practices associated with health and well-being at any size. HAES practitioners consider social justice issues essential for addressing public health. Individual choices are important, but they are not the only factors in determining health; it is imperative to change the discrimination and stigma facing fat people to improve their health.

Myth: The HAES model is only for people with high BMI.

Reality: HAES is for people across the weight spectrum. The needs of lower-BMI people are often overlooked in the "War on Obesity" (e.g., nutritional quality in school meals is just as important for thinner children as fatter children). The HAES model recognizes that weight stigma affects people across the weight spectrum, instilling in people of lower-BMI the fear of being stigmatized.

Implications for Illness Prevention: The HAES Model . . .

- De-emphasizes weight (while focusing on controllable choices) in health/medical communications, eliminating a source of stigma and anxiety for people of any weight.
- Does not ask people to control what may not be controllable. This prevents damaging cycles of body loathing, weight loss and regain, and feelings of ineffectiveness.
- Does not try to prevent "obesity," but rather body neglect and abuse.
- Offers a comprehensive approach to valuing and caring for our beloved human bodies for people of every size.

Directions for Research

HAES builds on existing research, but more research is needed to confirm initial experimental studies (Bacon et al., 2005) showing that a focus on nurturing practices leads to better long-term health than pursuing weight loss. It is odd that there is so little research on what has helped people achieve sustainable self-nurturing practices, yet such a glut of weight loss studies that amount to little more than academic versions of "before" and "after" snapshots. We are beginning to see empirical documentation of medical bias and barriers to care for higher-BMI people (Schwartz, O'Neal, Brownell, Blair, & Billington, 2003), as well as investigations of the effects of stigma and discrimination on health (Amy, Aalborg, Lyons & Keranen, 2006). Perhaps someday we will have evidence of the factors driving our current climate of hysteria, the strange use of health as a moral judgment, and the reasons that even well-trained researchers and statisticians seem to take leave of their senses when discussing "obesity."

In a more positive vein, HAES directs us to study resilience in fat people and identify the skills that we are using to craft satisfying lives in the face of oppression. Such lessons would take their place alongside the life experiences of people of many other stigmatized groups, giving all of us hope for living well in an imperfect world.

At its core, HAES is a model that reclaims the worth of our stigmatized bodies and encourages subversive acts of self-care. We take it as self-evident that people take better care of the body that they accept and love *now* than one that they are punishing for being the source of their ill treatment at the hands of other people. HAES takes the conventional demand for a "correct lifestyle" to be worthy and turns it on its head, demanding *access* to movement opportunities, compassionate medical care, delicious and nutritious food, stigma-free environments, and the right to show up as the unique individuals we are.

NOTES

This chapter was previously published in the *Newsletter of the National Eating Disorder Information Centre* (2005). Reprinted with permission.

REFERENCES

Amy, N.K., Aalborg, A., Lyons, P., & Keranen, K. (2006). Barriers to routine gynecological cancer screening for White and African-American obese women. *International Journal of Obesity, 30,* 147–155.

Bacon, L., Stern, J., Van Loan, M., & Keim, N. (2005). Size acceptance and intuitive eating improve health for obese, female chronic dieters. *Journal of American Dietetic Association, 109,* 929–936.

Bjorntorp, P., De Jounge, K., Sjorstorm, L., & Sullivan, L. (1970). The effect of physical training on insulin production in obesity. *Metabolism, 19,* 631–638.

Brownell, K.D., Puhl, R., Schwartz, M.D., & Rudd, L. (2005) (Eds.). *Weight Bias: Nature, Consequences, and Remedies.* New York: Guilford Publications.

Campos, P., Saguy, A., Ernsberger, P., Oliver, E., & Gaesser, G. (2006). The epidemiology of overweight and obesity: public health crisis or moral panic? *International Journal of Epidemiology, 35,* 55–60.

Ellin, A. (2006, November 26). Big people on campus. *New York Times,* sec. 9, pp. 1, 6.

Gaesser, G. (2002). *Big Fat Lies.* Carlsbad, CA: Gurze Books.

Garner, D., & Wooley, S. (1991). Confronting the failure of behavioral and dietary treatments for obesity. *Clinical Psychology Review, 11,* 729–780.

Lamarche, B., Després, J.P., Pouliot, M.C., Moorjani, S., Lupien, P.J., Thériault, G., Tremblay, A., Nadeau, A., & Bouchard, C. (1992). Is body fat loss a determinant factor in the improvement of carbohydrate and lipid metabolism following aerobic exercise training in obese women? *Metabolism, 41,* 1249–1256.

Mann, T., Tomiyama, A., Westling, E., Lew, A., Samuels, B., & Chatman, J., (2007). Medicare's search for effective obesity treatments: diets are not the answer. *American Psychologist, 62* (3), 220–233.

Muennig, P., Jia, H., Lee, R., & Lubetkin, E. (2008). I think therefore I am: perceived ideal weight as a determinant of health. *American Journal of Public Health, 98*(3), 501–506

Neumark-Sztainer, D. (2006). Obesity, disordered eating, and eating disorders in a longitudinal study of adolescents: how do dieters fare 5 years later? *Journal of the American Dietetic Association, 106* (4), 559–568.

Schwartz, M.B., O'Neal, H., Brownell, K.D., Blair, S., & Billington, C. (2003). Weight bias among health professionals specializing in obesity. *Obesity Research, 11*, 1033–1039.

|||||||||||||||||||||||||||||||||||||||||||||||||||||||||||||||||||||||||||||||

6

Widening the Dialogue to Narrow the Gap in Health Disparities

Approaches to Fat Black Lesbian and Bisexual Women's Health Promotion

Bianca D. M. Wilson

> . . . perhaps you question the size of my hips—
> the second largest continent in the world sired these hips
> of course they would be as large—
> the oldest civilization on earth gave birth to these hips
> of course they would be as wide—
> . . . make you release before you were ready to hips—
> when you want to hold a woman's hips
> when you want to feel the difference between you and my hips
> when hard hips want to be soothed by charmine hips
> these are my hips—so let the legacy live on
> —C.C. Carter, "Herstory of My Hips"

This poem, written by C.C. Carter, a contemporary Afro-Latina lesbian artist, deeply resonates with me. My personal experiences as a fat woman who participates in Black lesbian and bisexual women's communities have shown me an appreciation for body diversity that is atypical of mainstream American culture. I use the term fat to refer to anyone who sees themselves as larger, heavier, or rounder than average, as well as to refer to the population of people who are categorized as "overweight" or "obese" according to medical guidelines (which change periodically). In a Black lesbian and bisexual women's cultural context, we see evidence through Web sites, photos, and poetry that there is a consciousness that women of all sizes need to be valued and respected, and that larger women can represent ideals of beauty, health, and spiritual-physical balance. My empirical research on Black lesbian sexual culture has also echoed these sentiments, as I have found desire and attraction to larger body sizes as a key domain of Black lesbian sexual life (Wilson, 2006). As such, it is not surprising that I experience a stark contrast between my life and work in Black lesbian and bisexual women's communities and that of my professional life within health behavior and health promotion research. The dominant perspective within my professional settings would suggest that the deterioration of health among women in ethnic minority and lesbian communities is in large part due to their being fatter than other communities. That I reside at the intersection of these two worlds informs my attempt to craft a response to public health institutions' efforts to address the "obesity epidemic" in the various communities to which African American lesbian and bisexual women belong.

Introduction: Personal, Political, and Scientific Arenas Converge

As a health researcher working both in academia and community-based health settings, I am frequently informed of the high rates of "obesity" in the United States, and the even higher rates within African American and lesbian communities. Indeed, it has been reported that African American women as compared to European American women (Flegal, Carroll, Ogden, & Johnson, 2002), and that lesbians as compared to heterosexual women (Aaron et al., 2001; Cochran et al., 2001; Dibble, Roberts, Robertson, & Paul, 2002; Mays, Yancey, Cochran, Weber, & Fielding, 2002; Valanis et al., 2000), are heavier and more likely to be categorized as "overweight" and "obese" when using standardized measurements such as the body mass index (BMI). Further, a few studies have also reported higher weights among African American lesbians as compared to lesbians of other ethnic groups (Cochran et al., 2001; Mays et al., 2002). The simple reporting of these demographics is not problematic. My concern is the tone, language, and content of scholars' presentations that use these data as a starting point for their collection of "fat-is-bad" statements. Many public health scholars routinely provide an oversimplified message regarding the relationship between weight and health, clearly communicating the idea that to be overweight or obese inherently translates to being ill or on the verge of illness.

When these statements about weight and health are made, I often find myself reacting viscerally. I look around and am reminded that, at this level of education and profession, I am often the only large person in a given room, and am typically the only Black or gay person of any gender or size. Immediately my awareness of the differences between me and my colleagues is heightened, and I am reminded that I belong to the "target populations" of fat Black or lesbian people being discussed. I try my best to appear unaffected, but I am affected. Their talk about my impending early death due to my body size is juxtaposed with my experiences and work in Black gay communities, which demonstrate that there are far greater enemies to the health and well-being of Black lesbian and bisexual women than the fat on our bodies, such as violence, poverty, and psychological oppression. I acknowledge and embrace the emotionality behind this reaction. Such emotions have been a catalyst to considering alternative ways to view the issues of weight and health in Black lesbian and bisexual women's communities.

Reshaping the Problem: A Black Feminist Ecological Framework for Examining Health Among Fat Black Lesbian and Bisexual Women

My position on how to approach health promotion among fat Black lesbian and bisexual women is informed by Black feminist theory and is complemented by my training in community and cultural health psychology. Although typical scholarship informed by these theories have not applied a critical perspective to the dominant fat-is-bad health research paradigm, their major tenets have been useful for my own translation of a fat positive perspective into health research and practice. A Black feminist framework is broadly characterized by one that is asserted through the lived experiences of Black women, but which also seeks to understand and dismantle the power of interlocking oppressive systems (Combahee River Collective Statement, 1977; hooks, 1984). Synthesizing Black feminist thought as expressed through writing, activism, academic scholarship, and art, Patricia Hill Collins (1986; 2000) highlights the importance of both acknowledging the intersections of multiple oppressions and respecting and valuing the existence of Black women's culture as key dimensions. I apply this to Black lesbian and bisexual women's health work by privileging a "bottom-up" over a "top-down" approach to health promotion in which Black sexual minority women are active leaders in determining needed paths to maintain or improve their communities' health. Additionally, the oppression that Black lesbian and bisexual women face as a result of fat hatred, racism, sexism, heterosexism, and classism within and outside of the medical industries must be dismantled as an integral component to health promotion within fat Black lesbian and bisexual women's communities.

These domains of Black feminist thought are congruent with the salient components of my approach to health research rooted in theories of community psychology and cultural health psychology. Community psychology emphasizes the importance of collaborative approaches to research and the significance of developing applied research programs that account for the full ecology of human well-being (Wilson, Hayes, Greene, Kelly, & Iscoe, 2003). Within an ecological approach to health, there is an emphasis on both understanding the social processes that promote wellness and maintaining features of community settings, such as community norms and institutions, that serve as resources for healthy development. Cultural health psychology uses an integrated approach to health that seeks a balance of emotional, mental, and physical health, and specifically views cultural values and norms as a major factor in how health is constructed and practiced (Kazarian & Evans, 2001). A key feature of both of these areas of psychology is the view that individual and community wellness, rather than the absence of disease and dysfunction, is the ultimate goal,

Weaving these perspectives together, I advocate for approaches to Black lesbian and bisexual women's health that respect the self-definition and lived experiences of Black women. Additionally, I aim to apply frameworks for health research and practice that define health holistically, integrating our mental, emotional, and physical well-being. When we examine fat Black lesbian and bisexual women's health from this perspective, several directions for health research and practice become illuminated. Namely, we should attend more to the direct and indirect effects of oppression due to size, race, gender, and sexuality on the health of fat Black lesbian and bisexual women. Examining the full ecology of fat Black lesbian and bisexual women's health, we ought to study and address the physiological and psychological effects of oppression on the body. At the interpersonal levels, we could examine the impact of interactions within a health care system that is generally anti-fat. Finally, at the intersection between individual and cultural levels, I argue for an approach to healthy lifestyles that is respectful of existing cultural values for size diversity in Black lesbian and bisexual women's communities.

Oppression in the Lives and Deaths of
Fat Black Lesbian and Bisexual Women

A contemporary perspective on public health research posits that empirical and intervention endeavors ought to examine factors affecting health at multiple levels of the ecology (Laverack & Labonte, 2000). Examples of current efforts to think ecologically with regard to health among fat people include those who have turned their attention to structural factors that they believe affect weight levels among members of certain communities (particularly those who are African American or Latino and poor). These structural factors include lack of access to open, safe space for exercise, and over-access to high-fat, high-caloric food chains (Hill, Wyatt, Reed, & Peters, 2003), as well as the negative effects of experiences with oppression on eating behaviors among African American women (Lovejoy, 2001; Thompson, 1994).

Though ecological and anti-oppression thinking is evident in these scholars' important efforts to account for the interaction between individual behavior and structural systems, this line of research tends to focus on weight or BMI as the final health outcome of interest. This is a limited framework; examining and eliminating structural barriers to better foods and creating opportunities for movement ought to be seen as independent healthful goals regardless of impact on weight. In this way, much of the previous research examining structural barriers to healthy foods and activity perpetuate a simplistic fat-is-bad health model and assume without strong evidence that body weights categorized as "overweight or obese" are highly predictive of poor health outcomes. Further, they tend to assume that weight loss (or prevention of weight gain) is key to maintaining health across all populations. Detailing research that points to problems within the traditional paradigm for studying weight as a predictor of mortality and morbidity, however, is not the focus of this chapter. But there is a growing body of research highlighting the limitations of a simplistic "fat-is-bad" and "weight loss-is-good" approach to health research and practice that indicates that weight is not an ideal outcome for testing the effectiveness of health promotion programs (see, e.g., Campos, Saguy, Ernsberger, Oliver, & Gaesser, 2006; Ernsberger & Koletsky, 1999; Miller, 1999, for empirical reviews documenting that the relationship between weight and health is not causal, and is in fact more complex than typically reported; see Mann et al., 2007, for a review demonstrating that calorie-restrictive dieting is not effective for weight loss; and see Stevens et al. 1992; 1998, for studies illustrating that weight is not a significant predictor of African American women's cardiovascular health).

Although the relationships between weight and health are unclear, major systemic factors experienced by many Black lesbians and bisexual women, such as racism, anti-fat discrimination, sexism, poverty, violence, and heterosexism, are powerful detractors from health (physical, emotional, and mental) and should be considered in a meaningful way as targets for public health intervention. The health consequences of various intersecting oppressions on the lives of Black lesbians and bisexual women can be understood and addressed at individual, interpersonal, and systemic levels. At the individual level, it may be fruitful to examine empirically the moderating effects of psychological stress due to the experience of intersecting forms of oppression on the physiological health of fat Black lesbian and bisexual women. That is, what are the psychologically mediated health effects of discrimination due to being a fat, Black, sexual minority woman? Drawing from the broader research on the psychophysiological effects of stress, Black scholars have studied the direct relationships between racism and various indicators of health among African Americans (see Bowen-Reid & Harrell, 2002, for review; see also Clark, Anderson, Clark, & Williams, 1999). Through these studies, they have illustrated that in addition to genetics and behavior, structural forces such as discrimination and systemic oppression affect health, potentially through the physiological effects of stress (McEwen & Seeman, 1999). An ecologically valid approach to fat Black lesbian and bisexual women's health would avoid a narrow focus on weight loss and expand the levels of analysis to identify additional important factors affecting health within this community. Once we commit to studying the effects of contextual factors on health in African American and lesbian/bisexual women's communities, thereby expanding a medical model that is currently neither focused on nor equipped to address systemic factors associated with health, we will increase our capacity to develop effective health promotion programs. Public health researchers and interventionists can work with community, health, and social psychologists, as well as community organizers, to promote oppression coping and resistance strategies that optimize our chances of buffering the physiological effects of systemic discrimination due to size, sexuality, race, and gender.

Research that accounts for the effects of oppression on the lives of fat Black lesbian and bisexual women through physiological responses would then hopefully also lead to contextually focused interventions that directly target structural roots of oppression that serve as barriers to those women's wellness. Such interventions may be in the form of legislative and political action, such as targeting discriminatory health insurance company policies that deny insurance to people who are categorized as overweight or obese regardless of other markers of health. These policies leave many fat Black lesbian and bisexual women un- or underinsured (which is particularly troubling because these individuals are already at high risk for being underinsured as Blacks, sexual minorities, and women). Other forms of structural interventions include culture work through the arts to raise awareness and encourage critical dialogue about the ways that fat Black lesbian and bisexual women exhibit health in their everyday resistance to oppression.

Although suggesting these strategies for social change is not in and of itself innovative on my part (as I have borrowed these ideas from the many activists in my life), it would require a radical shift in current public health strategies to view environmental, power structure, and cultural change as equally, if not more, important work than discrete health behavior change. For example, over twelve years ago Angela Davis (1994), in her essay "Sick and Tired of Being Sick and Tired: The Politics of Black Women's Health," advocated for structural health interventions that increased access to health care and opportunities for overall well-being, such as the eradication of poverty and the creation of a universal health care system. Specific to the effects of racism on health, but relevant to the study of the effects of multiple forms of oppression on Black lesbian and bisexual women's health, Krieger (2003, p. 197) similarly argued, "The point is that neglecting study of the health impact of racism means that explanations for and interventions to alter population distributions of health, disease, and well-being will be incomplete and potentially misleading, if not outright harmful."

For fat Black lesbian and bisexual women, it is important to note that in addition to racism, we must also negotiate the realities of heterosexism (Eliason & Schope, 2001), sexism (Krieger & Fee, 1994), and anti-fat bias (Harvey & Hill, 2001) within the health care system. The fact that fat Black lesbian and bisexual women sit at the intersections of all these marginalized identities cannot be overlooked in our efforts to acknowledge the ecology of our health care experiences. Typically, however, larger-than-average weight among Black women is viewed as a symptom of the deleterious effects of other forms of oppression, and the effects of anti-fat bias within society (including within the health professions) on Black women's health are often ignored. I have heard numerous fat Black lesbian and bisexual women say that health providers willingly ignore their reported symptoms and concerns, choosing instead to reduce all health complaints to symptoms of their weight or a combination of being Black and fat. Anecdotally, this type of dismissive and frustrating experience that fat patients have with their health providers appears to lead to poor care, and in many cases patients eventually choose to stop accessing the health care system altogether. Research claiming that weight is highly predictive of the health statuses of people of any group systematically discriminated against by health providers is incomplete without an analysis of the confounding effects of low-quality healthcare. To what extent does poor treatment in health care systems due to size, race, gender, or sexuality account for previously identified correlations among weight, disease, and death for fat women? How do problematic, as well as positive, experiences with health care providers affect health care access rates among fat Black lesbian and bisexual women? In turn, do limited health care access behaviors in response to negative experiences with providers predict future health problems? These are some of the questions that researchers would be asking if they approached the study of health among fat people without an anti-fat bias and if they considered the full ecology of fat Black sexual minority women's health care. Research addressing questions like these can also help inform health provider–focused interventions designed to reduce negative biases against any and all of the communities to which fat Black lesbian and bisexual women belong.

Currently, there are various forms of cultural competency trainings that have been designed to address heterosexist, racist, and sexist policies and procedures in the health care system. A next step would be to develop and disseminate trainings that also address the stigma experienced by fat people, particularly because contemporary fat prejudice is partially justified through medically based arguments (Campos, 2004). With adequate health care and freedom from oppression, what would fat Black sexual minority women's health look like? A paradigm shift whereby health is truly constructed as a sociocultural phenomenon as much as a physiological one would lead to systemic-level interventions in which social justice work becomes a viable form of public health intervention.

Neither Placating nor Destroying Black Lesbian Women's Culture

Though moving toward a social change paradigm in public health is an ideal that I hold, I recognize that this may be, at the least, a slow-moving shift. Given this, we still must determine appropriate ways to pursue various forms of individual-level interventions that promote health and well-being in Black women's communities. I argue that our efforts to target health behaviors, however, should be grounded in the cultural values of Black sexual minority communities. Research suggests that both African American and lesbian communities, separately and at their intersections, have greater appreciation for women of larger-than-average sizes than that of the dominant, patriarchal, Euro-centered, heterosexist society. African American women have been found to exhibit lesser levels of body dissatisfaction as compared to White women, despite being generally heavier than White women (Celio, Zabinski, & Wilfley, 2002; see also Lovejoy 2001, for review). Also complementing the perspective that "big" is or can be beautiful, my own anecdotal experiences in Black communities have illustrated that heavier women have often been noted to be associated with health by the use of the term "healthy" to describe larger-than-average, attractive women. Similarly, lesbian participants in body image research have reported lower levels of body dissatisfaction as compared to heterosexual females (Owens, Hughes, & Owens-Nicholson, 2003; Rothblum, 2002). Although these studies' representations of African American and lesbian communities as accepting of large body sizes may not fully capture the complexity of esteem and body image among these groups, the empirical literature does suggest that there may be existing cultural values among these minority groups that support a higher value of body size diversity than found in mainstream U.S. culture.

As such, the relationship between the public health industry and African American and lesbian communities' culturally based values regarding body image is at a contentious place. Although many African American lesbians may appreciate body diversity and even view larger bodies as healthy, we are constantly confronted with the medical industry's view of our large bodies as inherently diseased and problematic. Several researchers examining weight among African American women and lesbians have called for culturally specific approaches to health promotion efforts that take this tension into account, but their intent appears to be to identify ways to *sensitively* get Black women to be *thinner* (Lovejoy, 2001; Yancey, Leslie, & Abel, 2006). Yet scholars have not adequately provided evidence that smaller bodies will equal greater health among African American or sexual minority women, which would justify the risk of changing a community's healthy norms toward body diversity. Though the practice of culturally grounding health promotion work may involve challenging cultural norms and values that promote illness and disease transmission (Wilson & Miller, 2003), the goal of public health work should not be to convince a group of people that their sense of themselves is inherently unhealthy and problematic. Rather than a focus on weight loss, an approach that balances cultural beliefs of beauty and health with well-intended health promotion messages to encourage healthy nutrition intake and physical activity would be most appropriate. For example, health promotion programs that facilitate all Black lesbian and bisexual women, not just those who are fat, to maintain physically active lives and to eat foods that help them maintain that lifestyle would be a start in the right direction. This type of program communicates the importance of nutrition and activity in the lives of all people, and does not make erroneous assumptions of health status based on weight, categorizing fat women as "needing" healthy foods and exercise while categorizing thin women as "fine the way they are."

Health programs may consider encouraging healthy behaviors and viewing actual health status, not weight, as markers of success. I view approaches such as these as commensurate with two of the main themes of Black feminist thought proposed by Patricia Hill Collins (1986; 2000)—respecting Black women's right to define and value ourselves, and acknowledging the existence of a Black women's cultural experience. At this time in public health research, however, the dominant paradigm consists of an externally defined health problem that produces an image of health and wellness for Black women that reduces the possible variations in healthy body sizes. Further, it focuses almost entirely on the reduction of weight as a remedy to disease. It would be more ethical to improve the scientific knowledge base regarding factors associated with health within the communities in which African American lesbians and bisexual women participate, than to find culturally "palpable" intervention strategies based on skewed interpretations of problematic data. Interventions focused on physical activity independent from weight loss as a means of achieving health have a stronger scientific evidence base (Miller, 1999) than interventions focused on weight reduction (see, e.g., Mann et al., 2007). Therefore, efforts aimed at balancing the cultural milieu of African American lesbian and bisexual women's communities, as well as the separate African American and lesbian communities in which they may participate, with the commitment to health promotion may do this best by targeting the ecological factors described above as well as individual barriers to physical activity and well-rounded nutrition. An example of such an intervention that has been found effective is Health at Every Size (Bacon, Stern, Van Loan, & Keim, 2005), which promotes body acceptance and healthy eating and activity without the goal of weight loss.

Conclusion

Looking ahead to future research, a more nuanced and ecologically valid examination of fat Black lesbian and bisexual women's health is required for the development of culturally grounded health programs intended for this community. Yet, given the data available today, it appears well advised to move away from approaches that seek to change the body sizes of Black women as a means of health promotion. As a fat woman who works in and is a part of Black lesbian and bisexual women's communities, I hope to never see the beautiful respect for body diversity that exists among many of us destroyed by the public health industry in the name of an uncritical acceptance of research that uses a problematic and oppressive "fat-is-bad" bias as its starting point. In the face of multiple forms of oppression that attack our sexuality, size, skin color, race, and femininity, the reality that even some of us have maintained at least small amounts of love for our bodies is an amazing act of resilience that should be cherished. A health movement in Black women's communities that prioritizes respecting internally defined conceptualizations of health and quality of life, improving access to nutrition and physical activity for all individuals, and eradicating our subjugation to oppression at structural levels would be an exciting and liberating next step.

REFERENCES

Aaron, D., Markovic, N., Danielson, M., Honnold, J., Janosky, J., & Schmidt, M. (2001). Behavioral risk factors for disease and preventive health practices among lesbians. *American Journal of Public Health, 91*, 972–975.

Bacon, L., Stern, J.S., Van Loan, M.D., & Keim, N.L. (2005). Size acceptance and intuitive eating improve health for obese, female chronic dieters. *Journal of American Diet Association, 105*, 929–936.

Bowen-Reid, T., & Harrell, J.P. (2002). Racist experiences and health outcomes: An examination of spirituality as a buffer. *Journal of Black Psychology, 28*, 18–36.

Campos, P. (2004). *The Obesity Myth: Why America's Obsession with Weight Is Hazardous to Your Health*. Gotham Books: New York.

Campos, P., Saguy, A., Ernsberger, P., Oliver, E., & Gaesser, G. (2006). The epidemiology of overweight and obesity: Public health crisis or moral panic? *International Journal of Epidemiology, 35*, 55–60.

Carter, C.C. (2003). Herstory of my hips. *Body Language* (pp. 84–85). Kings Crossing Publishing: Atlanta.

Celio, A.A., Zabinski, M.F., & Wilfley, D.E. (2002). African American body images. In T.F. Cash & T. Pruzinsky (Eds.), *Body Image: A Handbook of Theory, Research, and Clinical Practice* (pp. 234–242). Guilford Press: New York.

Clark, R., Anderson, N., Clark, V., & Williams, D. (1999). Racism as a stressor for African Americans: A biopsychosocial model. *American Psychologist, 54*, 805–816.

Cochran, S., Mays, V., Bowen, D., Gage, S., Bybee, D., Roberts, S., et al. (2001). Cancer-related risk indicators and preventive screening behaviors among lesbian and bisexual women. *American Journal of Public Health, 91*, 591–597.

Collins, P.H. (1986). Learning from the outsider within: The sociological significance of Black feminist thought. *Social Problems, 33,* 14–32

Collins, P.H. (2000). *Black Feminist Thought: Knowledge, Consciousness, and the Politics of Empowerment.* Routledge: New York.

Combahee River Collective Statement (1977). In B. Smith (Ed.), *Home Girls: A Black Feminist Anthology* (pp. 272–282). Kitchen Table Women of Color Press: New York.

Davis, A. (1994). "Sick and tired of being sick and tired: The politics of Black women's health. In E.C. White (Ed.), *The Black Women's Health Book: Speaking for Ourselves* (pp. 18–26). Seal Press: Seattle.

Dibble, S.L., Roberts, S.A., Robertson, P.A., & Paul, S.M. (2002). Risk factors for ovarian cancer: Lesbian and heterosexual women. *Oncology Nursing Forum, 29,* E1–7.

Eliason, M.J., & Schope, R. (2001). Does "don't ask don't tell" apply to health care? Lesbian, gay, and bisexual people's disclosure to health care providers. *Journal of Gay and Lesbian Medical Association, 5,* 125–134.

Ernsberger, P., & Koletsky, R.J. (1999). Biomedical rationale for a wellness approach to obesity: An alternative to a focus on weight loss. *Journal of Social Issues, 55,* 221–259.

Flegal, K.M., Carroll, M.D., Ogden, C.L., & Johnson, C.L. (2002). Prevalence and trends in obesity among US adults, 1999–2000. *JAMA, 288,* 1723–1727.

Harvey, E.L., & Hill, A.J. (2001). Health professionals' views of overweight people and smokers. *International Journal of Obesity, 25,* 1253–1261.

Hill, J.O., Wyatt, H.R., Reed, G.W., & Peters, J.C. (2003). Obesity and the environment: Where do we go from here? *Science, 299,* 853–855.

hooks, b. (1984). *Feminist Theory: From Margin to Center.* South End Press: Boston.

Kazarian, S., & Evans, D. (2001). *Handbook of Cultural Health Psychology.* Academic Press: San Diego.

Krieger, N. (2003). Does racism harm health? Did child abuse exist before 1962? On explicit questions; critical science; and current controversies: An ecosocial perspective. *American Journal of Public Health, 93,* 194–199.

Krieger, N., & Fee, E. (Eds.). (1994). *Women's Health, Politics, and Power: Essays on Sex/Gender, Medicine, and Public Health.* Baywood Publishing: New York.

Laverack, G., & Labonte, R. (2000). A planning framework for the accommodation of community empowerment goals within health promotion programming. *Health, Policy, and Planning, 15,* 255–262.

Lovejoy, M. (2001). Disturbances in the social body: Differences in body image and eating problems among African American and White women. *Gender & Society, 15,* 239–261.

Mann, T., Tomiyama, A., Westling, E., Lew, A., Samuels, B., & Chatman, J. (2007). Medicare's search for effective obesity treatments: Diets are not the answer. *American Psychologist, 62,* 220–233.

Mays V, Yancey A, Cochran S, Weber, M, & Fielding, J. (2002). Heterogeneity of health disparities among African American, Latina/Hispanic, and Asian American women: Unrecognized influences of sexual orientation. *American Journal of Public Health, 92,* 632–639.

McEwen, B.S., & Seeman, T. (1999). Protective and damaging effects of mediators of stress: Elaborating and testing the concepts of allostasis and allostatic load. In Adler, N.E., Marmot, M., McEwen, B.S., & Stewart, J. (Eds.), *Socioeconomic Status and Health in Industrial Nations: Social, Psychological, and Biological Pathways* (pp. 30–47). Academy Sciences: New York.

Miller, W.C. (1999). Fitness and fatness in relation to health: Implications for a paradigm shift. *Journal of Social Issues, 55,* 207–219.

Owens, L., Hughes, T., & Owens-Nicholson, D. (2003). The effects of sexual orientation on body image and attitudes about eating and weight. *Journal of Lesbian Studies, 7,* 15–33.

Rothblum, E. (2002). Gay and lesbian body images. In T.F. Cash & T. Pruzinsky (Eds.), *Body Image: A Handbook of Theory, Research, and Clinical Practice* (pp. 257–265). Guilford Press: New York.

Stevens, J., Keil, J.E., Rust, P.F., Tyroler, H.A., Davis, C.E., & Gazes, P.C. (1992). Body mass index and body girths as predictors of mortality in black and white women. *Archives of Internal Medicine, 152,* 1257–1262.

Stevens, J., Plankey, M.W., Williamson, D.F., Thun, M.J., Rust, P.F., Palesch, Y., & O'Neil, P.M. (1998). The body mass index-mortality relationship in white and African American women. *Obesity Research, 6,* 268–277.

Thompson, B.W. (1994). *A Hunger So Wide and So Deep: American Women Speak Out on Eating Problems.* University of Minnesota Press: Minneapolis.

Wilson, B.D.M (2006). African American lesbian sexual culture: Exploring components and contradictions. *Dissertation Abstracts International: Section B: The Sciences and Engineering, 66,* 4003.

Wilson, B.D.M., & Miller, R. L. (2003). Examining strategies for culturally grounding HIV prevention: A review. *AIDS Education and Prevention, 15,* 184–202.

Wilson, B., Hayes, E., Greene, G., Kelly, J., & Iscoe, I. (2003). Community psychology. In D. K. Freedheim (Ed.), *Comprehensive Handbook of Psychology,* Vol. 1: *The History of Psychology* (pp. 431–449). Wiley Publishers: New York.

Valanis, B., Bowen, D., Bassford T., Whitlock E., Charney P., & Carter R.A. (2000). Sexual orientation and health: Comparisons in the Women's Health Initiative sample. *Archives of Family Medicine, 9,* 843—853.

Yancey, A., Leslie J., & Abel, E. (2006). Obesity at the crossroads: Feminist and public health perspectives. *Signs, 31,* 425–443.

‖‖‖

7

Quest for a Cause
The Fat Gene, the Gay Gene, and the New Eugenics

Kathleen LeBesco

Science is a tricky political weapon; at best, it is a double-edged sword.
—Edward Stein

In the mid-1990s, newspaper headlines trumpeted research advances in discovering both a "gay gene" and a "fat gene." Now, over ten years later, despite considerable progress in scientific quarters, it is unclear what causes people to be fat or gay, and debates continue to be waged about whether the quest for a cause is even a desirable endeavor. Still, public imagination about the existence of these dictator genes, as prompted by media sources, suggests that the possibility of a genetic "cause" for fatness and homosexuality factors heavily in discourse about public policy, legal protection, civil rights, and social movement rhetoric.

I want to trace the rise of public discourse about the search for the fat gene and the gay gene, and to consider the ways in which these discussions are implicated in a new consumer eugenics movement aimed at abolishing aberrations seemed socially or aesthetically undesirable (but far from life threatening).[1] I will analyze the attitudes toward fatness and homosexuality prevalent among early twentieth-century eugenicists (notably Charles Davenport), consider cultural prejudices against homosexuality and fatness/gluttony in the United States, and examine late twentieth-century media discourse about the quest for genetic explanations for fatness and homosexuality in the guise of "cure" rhetoric. This will necessitate an investigation of several issues: How does the potential for prenatal genetic diagnosis of obesity or homosexuality raise the specter of consumer eugenics within our normalizing sociocultural environment? How have concepts of normalcy been deployed to underline the need for a "cure" (or, eventually, *prevention*) for fatness or gayness? and What is at stake, and who are the winners and losers?

Obesity and Homosexuality for Early Eugenicists: A Primer

A scientific zealot with plans for a racial purity crusade, zoologist Charles Davenport was the founder of the American eugenics movement around the turn of the twentieth century. He fathered the movement that would emphasize negative and positive eugenics—campaigns to restrict "the unfit" from procreating, and drives to urge the "fit" to reproduce more frequently. Davenport challenged the value of enriched social conditions for those he deemed genetically inferior, arguing that although it might do some immediate good to an individual, such improvements were evolutionarily useless and could not be passed to the next generation (Black, 2003, p. 38). For Davenport, selective breeding was the answer to the problem posed by the genetically unfit.

Davenport's particular interest was in racial hygiene; other eugenicists of his era focused on the genetic causes of disability, crime, and poverty. There was generally little attention paid to homosexuality or fatness among eugenicists obsessed with these "more pressing" problems (Allen, 1997, p. 245). I undertook an examination of Davenport's personal papers, housed at the American Philosophical Society, to see what precursors I could find to the present genetic quests for the fat gene and the gay gene. Although there was little on these topics relative to what one might expect, it was clear that Davenport was interested in obesity and homosexuality, especially as they related to race. His notes suggest his belief that obesity is hereditary. In responding to an 1875 article by L.S. Worthington about the etiology, therapy, and hygiene of obesity, Davenport challenges Worthington's presumption that "the tendency to obesity is more often acquired by the habits of life of the obese, for example, by copious nourishment, rich and succulent, sedentary life, much sleep, complete tranquility of spirit, warm baths, etc." (Davenport papers, MS Coll 077, Worthington entry, p. 1) than by a deterministic genetic predisposition. Davenport's tone in describing Worthington's attention to habits rather than heredity is damning: "The writer persists in considering excess of food and drink, inactive life, as of the first importance in causing obesity. . . . Three of the patient's [sic] had voracious appetite which could not be checked. However, it is not always the largest eaters who become obese" (pp. 3–4). Davenport clearly wants a genetic cause for obesity, and finds the behavioral explanation unsatisfying.

A later (1917) study summarized in Davenport's file charts the genetic effects of obesity over several generations. The picture is not rosy. By the fourth generation:

> there is no longer, even during youth, the appearance of health which distinguished the second and even the third generation. Many of the nurslings even are puny, pale, weak of frame. Later the stature will be below normal, chest narrow, the lymphoid system exaggerated. Often, also, malformations are accentuated, such as myopia, astigmatism, daltonism. The individuals are "diminues." Not infrequently in adult life there will be defects of balance in the affective or intellectual qualities. One or the other may be exaggerated or diminished, and to the detriment of the other. Good sense will be lacking. (Davenport papers, Ms Coll 077, Richardiere & Sicard entry, p. 3)

By the fifth generation, the outlook is bleak: "There will be a larger number of the puny, of the malformed, of abortions, of underdeveloped individuals, with retarded nutrition, dyspeptic and neuropathic. Almost the whole of this generation will be made up of imperfectly constituted individuals; of valetudinarians. Many of them will be sterile, a means of defense employed by nature against the evil consequences to the race of degeneration aggravated by inheritance" (Davenport papers, Ms Coll 077, Richardiere & Sicard entry, p. 3). Davenport does not quibble with this characterization the way he does with other authors who primarily blame habit rather than heredity for obesity.

Davenport's papers also suggest his belief in a hereditary cause for homosexuality. He understood to be genetic such characteristics as (for men) weak and irresolute manner, preponderance of artificial inclinations, lack of domestic independence, shyness, unpreparedness to deal with life, excessive elegance, and physical vanity; and (for women) sharpness, hardness, unadorned dress style, dominance in marriage, and predilection for weak, effeminate characters. Agreeing with the 1925 work of W. Wolf on sex perversion, Davenport noted that "homosexuality, an extreme variation of sex inclination, comes about through the accidentally determined combination of less marked variations" (Davenport papers, Ms Coll 077, Wolf entry, p. 4). Although neither homosexuality nor obesity were Davenport's primary concern, and neither were they the chief concerns of his peers and successors in the American eugenics movement, it is easy to see the seeds of contemporary quests to eradicate fatness and queerness in the perspectives that he articulated nearly one hundred years ago.

An undated booklet produced by the American Eugenics Society (AES) outlines plans for the U.S. eugenics movement, founded mostly on encouraging the fit to reproduce more and the unfit to reproduce less. There is no mention of fat people or queer people specifically, but one of the latter sections of the booklet should set off alarms for anyone familiar with how the current rhetoric of genetic diagnosis for obesity and homosexuality—as well as other forms of difference—is used as a political weapon. Called "Preventing Reproduction by Defectives and Subnormals," this section generously explains the reasons for the crusade: "In the first place, the perpetuation of a defective strain of human beings tends to thwart all future progress, and cannot be defended by either reason or charity. Secondary reasons are the need for reducing the enormous public expense as present involved in the care of defectives" (*A Eugenics Program for the United States*, n.d., p. 14).

The AES recommended both segregation and sterilization to combat this problem of expense: "In California recent experience with sterilization indicates the possibilities of combining effective control with great savings in cost, and a lessening of hardship among these unfortunates" (*A Eugenics Program for the United States*, n.d., p. 15). Any clamor over sterilization as a technique for preventing homosexuality or obesity remains well muffled (though it still rears its head as a strategy of race- and class-based oppression). These days, though, we hear a lot about the costs of obesity and homosexuality—escalating health insurance expenses and income penalties due to fatness, and the social costs of queerness, not to mention the mistaken collapse between queer practices and AIDS expenses. We also hear, from those in favor of eugenic "enhancement," that prenatal testing, abortion, or gene therapy are the sane things to do in a world where being different (disabled or diseased, in particular) is a hardship. In a society marked by vast advances in the explanatory power of science, not everything has changed since the height of the eugenics movement in the United States.

Wendy Kline contends that Americans are eager to dismiss eugenics as a momentary cultural lapse of reason—and to fob responsibility for it primarily (and incorrectly) on barbaric Nazis—but warns that "if we continue to approach eugenics as merely an embarrassing mistake with little historical significance, we will never understand the movement's powerful appeal to generations of Americans concerned about the future of morality and civilization" (Kline, 2001, p. 1). Eugenics was a particularly attractive resolution to the problem of moral disorder; in an era in which both fatness and queerness have been associated with such moral disorder, the promises of biotechnology rear their heads as updated solutions with eugenic roots. Fatness and queerness disrupt U.S. social and economic hierarchies—both cross class and race lines to interrupt privilege (whereas fatness once conferred privilege). The application of eugenic principles might be imagined as a "sensible" solution to counter this decline. Segregation and sterilization are no longer the chief weapons in an arsenal stocked with the ability to prevent (through prenatal testing and abortion) or change (through gene therapy) many aberrant conditions of a fetus. Before thinking through the frighteningly homogenizing future that this presents, we must turn our attention to the key moments in the scientific quest for the very genes that would allow such work to be done: the gay gene and the fat gene.

Gay Gene, Fat Gene: Quest for a Cause

I am particularly interested in thinking about the gay gene and the fat gene together, rather than in isolation, because the coupling illuminates the extent to which socially "troubling" body situations have provided fodder for scientific solutions in postmodern times. By the early to mid-1990s, when news of both a gay gene and a fat gene erupted in the headlines, obesity and homosexuality had come to be understood in the public imagination as undesirable conditions with no transparent etiology. Debates about whether both conditions were biologically determined or the result of lifestyle choices have raged on. Despite qualifications from the scientific community about the unpredictable and complex manner in which genes express themselves (Kevles, 1985) (for instance, someone with the so-called fat gene may not be fat, whereas another person without it very well may be fat), the enthusiasm of the general public, and specifically *members of the effected populations* (fat and queer folks), for such biologically determinist explanations needs to be dissected for its political ramifications.

In the last twenty years, much energy and brainpower has been devoted to the search for a biological cause of homosexuality. Simon LeVay's (1996) work in neuroendocrinology has been influential, as have Richard Pillard and J. Michael Bailey's (1995) twin studies, in building the case. No work has set the public imagination afire, however, as much as Dean Hamer's 1993 "discovery of the gay gene" (however unreplicable his work turned out to be). In his popular book about his research, Hamer's claims are muted: "The most important limitation of our research was that we didn't isolate a 'gay gene'; we only detected its presence through linkage. We narrowed the search to the neighborhood, the X chromosome—and even the block, Xq28—but we didn't find the house" (Hamer & Copeland, 1994, p. 147). A linkage is not a gene, but scientific illiteracy on the part of media professionals and the reading public effectively collapsed this distinction.

Just a few years after Hamer announced his findings, the U.S. media took notice of research advances on what we understand as "the fat gene." An obese gene (later renamed Ob[Lep]) was discovered in mice in 1995. A mutation in this gene produced an uninhibited appetite in mice; thus, mice with this genetic mutation that were injected with protein hormone leptin slimmed down considerably (Shell, 2002, p. 101). In the late 1990s, testing for this genetic variation among subjects revealed that the blood of several super-sized children revealed an absence of leptin. British researchers examined genes cloned from the children's fat tissue and discovered that their Ob(Lep) genes had the same defect. Thus, with no satiety signal in the form of the leptin hormone, the researchers concluded that the children's fatness was due to miscommunication between their bodies and their brains about them starving (Shell, 2002, p. 113).

Great excitement about the discovery of the "fat gene," however, was tempered in the scientific community by a few factors. First, the genetic mutation was extremely rare, and was found only in the research subjects who were the product of consanguineal marriage—thus the "fat gene" did not account for obesity on a large scale. Indeed, in the five years after the discovery of the leptin mutation, only about twelve people worldwide were found with it (Shell, 2002, p. 115). Most people who are fat do *not* have this genetic mutation (the absence of guanine in the part of the gene that normally codes for leptin) (Shell, 2002, p. 113). More recent research has focused on leptin sensitivity rather than its utter absence.

Cultural critic Robert Brookey (2002) has pointed out that discourse about choice in homosexuality is promoted by the religious right, which wants to argue that we all have inclinations, which themselves are not sinful; what *is* sinful is acting on them. I can make a similar case for fatness—we all have urges toward "overindulgence," or gluttony, but only those who act on them and (importantly) bear the stigma of the fat body are those who have committed sin. It is in this climate that biological research on homosexuality and obesity becomes more high stakes; if one can indeed locate these conditions as biologically intrinsic, it seems that rights will follow (although there are other more foreboding uses of such research). Nonetheless, the Human Rights Campaign Fund has jumped on the bandwagon for gay gene research (Brookey, 2002, p. 5). Fat folks nationwide have also been tantalized by the prospect of finding a gene that, if manipulated, might allow them to be slim. Merely by virtue of existing, the "fat gene" might also alleviate some of the burden of immorality that they carry. Freedom from blame for allegedly immoral choices, however, does not necessarily entail freedom from discrimination or the receipt of special rights; unfortunately, this distinction gets lost in the bandwagon approach to genetic research (Stein, 1994, p. 282).

That fat and queer people would heartily embrace science and medicine as a solution to their socially constructed problems is redolent of Stockholm syndrome—after all, science and medicine have long been instrumental in oppressing fat and queer people, providing argument after argument that pathologize the homosexual or "obese" individual (whether the mind or the body). Michel Foucault's work (1980) has shown us that placing bodies under the microscope of science, in the name of liberal projects of self-improvement, in fact reinscribes their deviance and increases their oppression. Jennifer Terry (1997, p. 288) muses that perhaps "biology is a more comforting way to narrate their desires than to make sense of them in terms of cultural and historical contradictions, conflicts, and contingencies."

This form of narration is particularly dangerous, however, in that the uses of biological research can cut both ways: science might be used as the basis for legal protection and moral respectability just as easily as it might be used as the proof of pathology and the justification for eradication (Allen, 1997; Ordover, 2003; Schmidt, 1984; Terry, 1997). Visions of a pluralistic society accepting of corporeal diversity might become quickly clouded by a return to the sharp realities of castration, lobotomies, psychotherapy, shock treatments, gastric bypass, jaw wiring, and stomach stapling, or, more frightening still, a future where fat or queer people do not even get the chance to exist at all.

The quest for a cause is not just a preoccupation of members of the tribe (fat or queer), but is an appealing sport for liberals of many stripes. The question of rights (of lesbians and gays to marry, for instance, or of fat people against employment discrimination) functions unfortunately as a distraction from the underlying conservative agenda of gay gene and fat gene discourse. Brookey (2002, p. 132) reminds us that "liberals have resisted biological arguments about women and racial minorities, and suspending their suspicion of such claims for the sake of gay rights puts them in a tenuous position." It would serve us well to remember that pleas for justice predicated on biology are unnecessary and wrongheaded (although appealing in the short term). The civil rights movement of the 1960s recognized biological essentialism as a tool of oppression and steadfastly refused to engage with that discourse, in favor of a mission rooted in visibility and demands for social and political change. It is, to parse Gar Allen, "in the streets, not the laboratory, that the struggle for social justice is ultimately waged" (Allen, 1997, p. 264; see also Terry, 1999).

All this is not to say that fat and queer people should deny the prospect that biology plays some role in their situations; to do so, in fact, would be ignorant. But it is equally important to remember that genes and biology are not the only game in town (Brookey, 2002, p. 147); scientific knowledge doesn't reveal all there is to know—or even very much—about how body size and sexuality are socialized and politicized. It is, I contend, *these* processes that must be transformed to alleviate the heavy burdens carried by fat and queer folks in a homophobic and fat-hating culture.

An Ounce of Prevention and a Pound of Cure:
An Eye on the New Eugenics

Scientists like Dean Hamer and Jeffrey Friedman—who have worked, respectively, on finding the gay gene and the fat gene—recognize the power of their research to shape the future. Hamer suggests that even when a gay gene is isolated, it will be impossible to test for present or future sexual orientation, because genes are only one part of the picture. Social, cultural, environmental, and other biological factors cannot be easily predicted. Even with prenatal testing, parents would only have a weak probability statistic on which to base decisions about the continued existence of their would-be child (Hamer & Copeland, 1994, p. 218). This seems reassuring; surely no one would make rash decisions about terminating a pregnancy based on such sketchy data, right? Alas, the statistics associated with prenatal testing and abortion for non-life-threatening disabilities (around 60 percent for positive Down syndrome results, for instance) show us that the very *probability* of deviance is often enough to scare away many otherwise–emotionally intrepid would-be parents.

Disability scholars and activists have created a compelling body of work on the politics of biotechnologies, particularly prenatal testing, that when coupled with abortion can effectively prevent a large number of people with disabilities from existing (Parens & Asch, 2000; Powell, 2000); I believe that the conversations in these areas can help to illuminate what is at stake in the quest for genetic explanations for fatness and queerness.

Americans tend to shudder at the thought of using prenatal testing and abortion to select against superficial traits like eye color; at the other end of the spectrum, even many people who are morally opposed to abortion in general cases find it morally permissible to terminate a pregnancy where the fetus has tested positive for a severe disease such as Tay-Sachs or Lesch-Nylan syndrome that would make for a short and intensely pain-filled life. The most ambiguous zone comes in the "in-between" cases where the condition is not life threatening but is undesirable. Many ethicists reject testing for "non-health-related traits" (Parens & Asch, 2000, p. 29), which does little to clarify our cultural position on obesity. (Homosexuality, removed from the DSM-III around thirty years ago, is no longer considered a mental illness.) Escalating levels of hype about the "obesity epidemic" are apparent in medicalized rhetoric about body size as first and foremost a health issue (conveniently obscuring the moral and aesthetic objections that fuel the demonization of fat bodies). Prenatal diagnosis would reinforce the primacy of the individual body as problematic (rather than socio-cultural attitudes toward that body). The problem to be solved (via abortion) is the body, not the prejudice (Parens & Asch, 2000, p. 13). A chief concern among disability scholars is the extent to which prenatal testing enables one trait to eclipse the total potential of personhood.

Concurring with critics of eugenics like Philip Kitcher and Allan Buchanan, "liberal eugenics" proponent Nicholas Agar concludes that biotechnology should not be used to alleviate the problems of living in a morally defective social environment

(Agar, 2004). Agar distinguishes between being disabled, which he believes means limited opportunities even in the context of no discrimination, and (for instance) being black or gay, where he thinks the limitations are purely based on discrimination. In these cases, he suggests that we change the discriminatory attitudes, not the genome. I am uncomfortable with Agar's splitting of hairs here: he ignores the powerful social model of disability in favor of a troublesome medical model, and he neglects the polysemic nature of the concept of inherent "limited opportunities." What happens to fatness? I would argue that it compels intense discrimination, but others might argue that it presents limited opportunities (increased morbidity and mortality rates, correlation with health problems, etc.). Agar's perspective, which generally favors the extension of reproductive choice at the individual level and sees the chief problem as equal access to these choices, does not provide a satisfactory consideration of the future of fat eugenics.

Prenatal testing for a genetic propensity toward homosexuality or "obesity" is not yet available. Professor of medicine Cynthia Powell, however, remarks that with the gene map complete, not only disease-causing genes but "also those affecting complex traits, such as obesity, intelligence, and sexual orientation" (Powell, 2000, p. 50) will be testable. As argued previously, this is problematic because genes are committees (working in concert with social and environmental factors) rather than dictators (Shell, 2002); their forms of expression are unpredictable. But even if genes *were* dictators, the problem of letting the prejudices of the moment (homophobia, fat hatred, and a panoply of other forms of bigotry) hold sway over reproductive decisions seems even more troubling.

One of the most compelling arguments against widespread gene therapy and prenatal testing coupled with abortion emerges from scientific quarters. Scientists Pillard and Bailey contend that a variety of sexual orientations evidences the "biologic diversity of human beings, a diversity with a genetic basis. Like all genetically influenced traits, this one will prove to have advantages and disadvantages depending upon the selection pressures in the environment" (Pillard & Bailey, 1995, p. 82–83). Given our own ignorance about the long-term significance of these variations, it would be foolhardy to pursue a eugenic project that effectively breeds them out. Pillard (1997, p. 238) concludes that "genetic variability is the substrate of adaptation and conversely, genetic homogeneity is a ticket to extinction. . . . Therefore, our present understanding of genetics suggests this axiom: Preserve genetic diversity wherever we can. The hope is that this point of view will take root before the exploitation of gene technology plunges us into an orgy of unthinking destruction of genetic potential." To preserve valuable genetic diversity, "society's collective interests might legitimately require regulating some individual preferences, at least until 'market' forces can produce a corrective change in individual values" (Pernick, 1996, p. 173). In other words, when dominant values (influenced by pervasive cultural messages in support of cults of thinness and heteronormativity) threaten to undermine our capacity to remain a genetically diverse population, we might all be better served by providing a check on the power of these values to shape our practices and policies surrounding gene therapy and prenatal testing. If one *must* engage with the terms of the current gay and fat gene discourses, this might be the most effective refrain. It may well buy us the time that we need to transform the social and political meanings of fatness and queerness.

NOTE

1. This chapter confines itself to discussion of the how the eugenic impulse is manifest in prenatal testing and abortion practices; however, the politics of selection, in terms of who is allowed to become a parent, are also fascinating and worth fuller investigation elsewhere. Policy decisions to exclude fat women from infertility coverage, to prevent fat men from donating sperm, and even to restrict the ability of fat would-be parents to adopt (as is the case presently with international adoptions of Chinese babies) reveal other tactics employed in an effort to keep fatness from reproducing itself.

REFERENCES

Agar, N. (2004). *Liberal Eugenics: In Defence of Human Enhancement*. Malden, MA: Blackwell.

Allen, G.E. (1997). The double-edged sword of genetic determinism: Social and political agendas in genetic studies of homosexuality, 1940–1994. In V. Rosario (Ed.), *Science and Homosexualities*, pp. 242–270. New York: Routledge.

Black, E. (2003). *War Against the Weak: Eugenics and America's Campaign to Create a Master Race*. New York: Four Walls Eight Windows.

Brookey, R.A. (2002). *Reinventing the Male Homosexual: The Rhetoric and Power of the Gay Gene*. Bloomington: Indiana University Press.

Davenport Papers. Eugenics Record Office, 1670–1964, Ms Coll 077. Accessed at the American Philosophical Society Library, Philadelphia, PA, April 2005.

A Eugenics Program for the United States. [Booklet]. Printed by the American Eugenics Society Inc. In the Frederick Osborn papers, folder #3. Accessed at the American Philosophical Society Library, Philadelphia, PA, April 2005.

Foucault, M. (1980). *The History of Sexuality, Volume I*. New York: Vintage.

Friedman, J. (2002). Diabetes—Fat in all the wrong places. *Nature* 415 (6869), 268–269.

Hamer, D., & P. Copeland. (1994). *The Science of Desire: The Search for the Gay Gene and the Biology of Behavior*. New York: Simon and Schuster.

Kevles, D.J. (1985). *In the Name of Eugenics: Genetics and the Uses of Human Heredity*. Berkeley: University of California Press.

Kline, W. (2001). *Building a Better Race: Gender, Sexuality, and Eugenics from the Turn of the Century to the Baby Boom*. Berkeley: University of California Press.

LeVay, S. (1996). *Queer Science: The Use and Abuse of Research Into Homosexuality*. Cambridge, MA: MIT Press.

Ordover, N. (2003). *American Eugenics: Race, Queer Anatomy, and the Science of Nationalism*. Minneapolis: University of Minnesota Press.

Parens, E., & A. Asch. (2000). The disability rights critique of prenatal genetic testing: Reflections and recommendations. In E. Parens and A. Asch (Ed.), *Prenatal Testing and Disability Rights*, pp. 3–43. Washington, DC: Georgetown University Press.

Pernick, M.S. (1996). *The Black Stork: Eugenics and the Death of "Defective" Babies in American Medicine and Motion Pictures Since 1915*. New York: Oxford University Press.

Pillard, R.C. (1997). The search for a genetic influence on sexual orientation. In V. Rosario (Ed.), *Science and Homosexualities*, pp. 226–241. New York: Routledge.

Pillard, R.C., & J.M. Bailey. (1995). A biologic perspective on sexual orientation. *The Psychiatric Clinics of North America: Clinical Sexuality 18*, 71–84.

Powell, C.M. (2000). The current state of prenatal genetic testing in the United States. In E. Parens and A. Asch (Ed.) *Prenatal Testing and Disability Rights*, pp. 44–53. Washington, DC: Georgetown University Press.

Schmidt, G. (1984). Allies and persecutors: Science and medicine in the homosexuality issue. *Journal of Homosexuality 10*, 127–140.

Shell, E.R. (2002). *The Hungry Gene: The Science of Fat and the Future of Thin*. New York: Atlantic Monthly Press.

Stein, E. (1994). The relevance of scientific research about sexual orientation to lesbian and gay rights. *Journal of Homosexuality 27*, 269–308.

Terry, J. (1997). The seductive power of science in the making of deviant subjectivity. In V. Rosario (Ed.), *Science and Homosexualities*, pp. 271–295. New York: Routledge.

Terry, J. (1999). *An American Obsession: Science, Medicine, and Homosexuality in Modern Society*. Chicago: University of Chicago Press.

||||||||||||||||||||||||||||||||||||||||||||||||||||||||||||||||||||||||||||||||

8

Prescription for Harm
Diet Industry Influence, Public Health Policy, and the "Obesity Epidemic"

Pat Lyons

Introduction

The girth of Americans is increasing . . . clothing dealers show that the average American of 1889 was easily fitted with a waistband of 46 inches. In 1899 he requires one of 47 ½ inches. At this rate of increase he will reach in 1909 a circumference of 49 or 50 inches . . . The dairy counters (and) labor-saving inventions, the elevators, telephones and other contrivances supposed to make people indolent and fat, have their part in producing this result.
—*JAMA*, June 28, 1899 (quoted in Reiling, 1999, p. 1502).

Messages of alarm about Americans' weight gain due to fast food and sedentary living that fill the pages of newspapers and public health policy forums today are eerily similar to the concerns voiced over one hundred years ago. Fear of fat is not new, nor is the promotion of pills, potions, surgery, and other "cures." What is new in the last fifty years, most especially since 1994, is the extent to which the diet and weight loss industry has moved from the sidelines to the center of American life, managing to dramatically increase its influence and profits without ever increasing product effectiveness. The failure rate for sustained weight loss has remained constant at 90–95% (National Institutes of Health Technology Assessment Conference Panel, 1992).

Despite this failure, bariatric medicine—diet doctors and weight loss surgeons—has become very influential in the federal government's public health decision making. Drug company money funds research, public health education, and policy forums; former drug company consultants hold key federal positions and fan the flames of fear over an "obesity epidemic" (Moynihan, 2006). With the National Institutes of Health leading the charge by defining over 60% of Americans as "overweight or obese," the majority of the population is now at risk for the negative health consequences of weight stigma. Because no effective weight loss treatment exists to allow escape from this stigma, just how is the public to protect itself?

The goal of this chapter is to provide insight into the history of corporate influence on current weight-related health policies and to challenge the ethics of such influence as a threat to public health and safety. It is intended to inform and mobilize educators and health advocates to challenge outrageous statements like those of U.S. Surgeon General Koop—that "obesity" is a greater threat to the nation's health than terrorists (Carmona, 2003)—and to call for a moratorium on weight reduction messages, programs, and policies (which have not only been woefully ineffective, but have resulted in increasing stigma against fat people). A strong public health effort must be launched to reduce weight bias and social stigma, and to ensure equal access to unbiased health information and services for people of all sizes. Principles and practices of the Health at Every Size model will be presented to guide such efforts while honoring the dictum, "First, do no harm."

History and Background

From a medical ethics standpoint, the diet and weight loss industry has quite a history—from outright fraud and diet scams to expensive programs developed at leading medical centers that resulted in patient deaths (Fraser, 1997; Moore, 1993). "Buyer beware" should be a warning label on all weight loss drugs, products, and programs. Enormous corporate profits are at stake, and maintaining public distress and biased attitudes about weight ensures the continued production of those profits.

Several excellent books have detailed the shifts in public attitudes and medical practices related to weight, dieting, and the increases in the stigma against fatness over the past one hundred years. As Seid (1989) points out, although products to lose weight have been promoted to consumers since the 1800's, it wasn't until the 1950 and 60's that weight loss products and programs really moved to center stage, becoming a national preoccupation (especially for women). During the 1950's, amphetamines, diuretics, and other drugs began being prescribed to both children and adults; profits for Metrecal and other weight loss drinks soared. In 1962, 40% of American families were using "low-cal" products; by 1970, 70% were. By 1971, government officials estimate diet product profits at somewhere between $250 million and $1 billion a year. Weight Watchers profits jumped from $160,000 in 1964 to $8 million in 1970 (Seid, 1989). Diet books by Dr. Stillman, Dr. Atkins, and others topped the charts and made those authors millionaires.

The 1970's also produced protein-sparing fasting programs at medical centers, which dramatically increased industry profits—but at the high cost of patient deaths, resulting in the eventual withdrawal of these programs from the market (Moore, 1993). "New and improved liquid diets" like Optifast appeared most prominently after the 1985 NIH Consensus Conference on Obesity; again profits grew exponentially, particularly after Oprah Winfrey hauled her famous wagon across the stage to show an equivalent of how much "ugly fat" she had lost. (Sadly, Oprah's continuing quest to be thin has overshadowed her many other accomplishments.)

By 1990 nearly one in four hospitals had opened a diet center. Phen-Fen and Redux, promoted in 1996 as "miracle diet pills," boosted weight loss industry profits to more than thirty billion dollars per year. The safety recall of these drugs in 1997 was perhaps one factor in desperate dieters returning to fad diets of the past. Dr. Atkins returned to the top of the heap, and these same old diets spawned entirely new lines of low-carbohydrate foods. In 2005, with the bankruptcy of the Atkins empire, such foods began being dumped at food pantries (Hirsch, 2005). That some health professionals could promote bacon, pork rinds, and sustained ketosis as a method to improve health still boggles the mind. But weight reduction by any means still seems to trump common sense.

By 2004, forty-six billion dollars was being spent annually on weight loss products and programs, not including weight loss surgery (Gibbs, 2005). Aggressive advertising of weight loss surgery now mirrors that of diet drugs. Dramatically increasing diet industry profits coincided with increasing ties between weight loss/drug industry corporations and obesity researchers. This interlocking web has heavily influenced social attitudes, medical practice, and public health policy. What is most remarkable is that all this has occurred despite the consistent failure of all weight loss treatments to demonstrate long-term success. If dieting was a drug to improve health, no doctor would prescribe it given its high failure rate.

Although there is no question that the number of adults and children at higher weight has increased, what it means and what should be done is still not clear. Simply because the population's weight has increased does not mean that the public's health has necessarily diminished. Increasing weight of the population since the 1970's has occurred at exactly the same time that life expectancy has increased and death rates from cancer and heart disease have decreased (Gregg et al., 2005). Considering that bias against fat children has increased 40% since the 1960's (Latner & Stunkard, 2003), and that so little is known about appropriate interventions for children, additional caution is needed to protect them from wildly misplaced efforts, like putting body mass index (BMI) on report cards (Lyons, 2003). There is no evidence that the advice to "eat less, exercise more, lose weight" works, yet it remains the central focus of public health recommendations.

Diets Still Don't Work

Although patterns of food consumption and physical activity have changed, some things have not changed in the past fifty years. In 1958, researcher Albert Stunkard, MD, concluded: "Of those who enter obesity treatment, most will drop out. Of those who stay in treatment, most will not lose weight. Of those who do lose weight, most will regain it" (Stunkard & Hume, 1959, p. 79). This landmark quote sums up data published almost twenty-five years later by Garner and Wooley (1991) in their exhaustive review of the failure of behavioral treatment for obesity, which was published just prior to the convening of the 1992 NIH Technology Assessment Conference on Voluntary Methods of Weight Loss and Control. It was at this NIH conference that researchers affirmed Stunkard's earlier findings that 90–95% of participants in all weight loss programs failed to attain and sustain weight loss beyond two to five years.

Research was also presented that highlighted the negative effects of failed weight loss attempts and challenged the long-held assumption that weight loss improves mortality. A key recommendation at the conclusion of the NIH conference offered a way out, encouraging "a focus on approaches that can produce health benefits independently of weight loss may be the best way to improve the physical and psychological health of Americans seeking to lose weight" (National Institutes of Health Technology Assessment Conference Panel, 1992, p. 947). Although many physicians and health advocates found this recommendation to be both sound and necessary—and some went on to develop the Health at Every Size approach to weight as an alternative—mainstream obesity researchers and public health officials completely ignored it. They continued with their diet industry partners to focus research and medical practice on designating obesity as a serious disease needing weight loss treatment—and they did so by virtually any means necessary.

By 1996 this line of thinking led to the epidemic of prescriptions for the diet drugs Phen-Fen and Redux, although these were eventually withdrawn as the result of primary pulmonary hypertension deaths and disability caused by the drugs. Investigative reporter Alicia Mundy provides a chilling account of the Phen-Fen/Redux/Wyeth-Aeryst diet pill debacle (2001). Mundy cites documentation of the highly questionable process of drug approval at the FDA, as well as the drug companies' funding of marketing and physician education campaigns that dwarfed drug safety monitoring budgets. Driven by the huge profit potential in keeping risks of the drugs concealed, drug company documents subpoenaed in court actions detailed the interlocking relationships of physicians and obesity researchers that Mundy dubbed "Obesity Inc." Even after reports of illness and death resulting from diet drug use began to emerge, the blatant disregard for the public's health could be summed up in one Wyeth-Ayerst Laboratories memo regarding an FDA proposal to issue a "black box" warning on the package: "A weight-maintenance positioning strategy is still possible with a primary pulmonary hypertension warning, because physicians may overlook the warning as they currently do with other drugs" (Mundy, 2001, p. 252). Counting on physicians to overlook warnings can hardly be viewed as protecting consumers. That the drugs were eventually removed from the market was a victory for health consumers. If it had been left to Obesity Inc. to advocate for removing these drugs, however, we would still be waiting.

It will also be a long wait for Obesity Inc. to acknowledge any failure of their weight loss focus, such as that evidenced by recent research. The studies included data from Weight Watchers, which is likely recommended by thousands of medical providers as the "best program out there." One study funded by Weight Watchers defined weight loss success as a loss of 2.7 kilograms (5.9 pounds) after two years (Heshka et al., 2003). One of the researchers, Thomas Wadden, has long-time weight loss industry ties. The research conclusion offered the standard spin: "After reviewing this article, some health care providers may conclude that evidence is inadequate to recommend commercial or self-help programs. The evidence is clearly modest. However, such an assessment would not relieve providers of the need to assist patients with weight control. Neither practitioners nor their patients can afford to overlook the epidemic of obesity, with its profound health and economic consequences" (Tsai & Wadden, 2005, p. 65). In other words, although patients are highly likely to fail, doctors are being told to keep the pressure on them to lose weight despite hypertension, depression, weight gain over time, and the other risks associated with weight cycling (Stice, Cameron, Killen, Hayward, & Taylor, 1999). How can this be construed as a science-based medical practice designed to improve health? On the other hand, it does protect industry profits.

Obesity Inc.: The Players, the Process, the Problems

It is difficult to get a man to understand something when his salary depends upon his not understanding it.

—Upton Sinclair

Widespread promotion of Redux was only one of most visible of the ongoing efforts of "obesity experts" and federal health officials to define obesity as a disease and recommend medical treatment regardless of the lack of safety or effectiveness data. Their first widespread effort to define obesity as a "killer disease" occurred at the conclusion of the 1985 NIH Consensus Conference on Obesity. This conference established the foundation for their clear goal of getting insurance coverage for weight loss treatment. It solidified the pattern that continues today: the same "Obesity Inc. experts" who run weight loss clinics are on the faculty of medical institutions; they serve on NIH panels that define research and public health priorities; they obtain millions in NIH research grants; and they review research papers for publication in medical journals. These same researchers have long-standing relationships as paid consultants and board members of weight loss and drug companies, and speak at medical conferences sponsored by those same companies (Fraser, 1997; Moore, 1993; Mundy, 2001; Oliver, 2006). Exaggerating the health consequences of higher weight while downplaying treatment failure has been their consistent approach, fostering the idea that any effort to reduce weight is worth any risk. No one on a federal public health level has voiced any concern about this issue. In fact, former federal employees are in drug company leadership positions, and former drug company consultants are now in powerful federal positions. To cite just a few examples:

1. Former U.S. surgeon general C. Everett Koop, MD, declared a public health "war on obesity" and initiated the Shape Up America! (SUA!) campaign in 1995 with over one million dollars in funding from Weight Watchers, Jenny Craig, and Slim-Fast (Fraser, 1997). His photo appeared in magazine ads promoting these products as the "safe way to lose weight." With Wyeth-Ayerst a key supporter of SUA!, a SUA! press release declared that "the war on obesity must continue" when Redux and Fenfluramine were recalled (PR Newswire, 1998).
2. William Dietz, MD, formerly from Tufts University School of Medicine, was a consultant to Hoffman–La Roche and Knoll Pharmaceuticals before taking his

current position as head of federal Centers for Disease Control nutrition and weight related programs (MacPherson & Silverman, 1997). His slideshow on the increasing "obesity epidemic" was delivered at public health meetings nation-wide and was pivotal in raising public fears (Oliver, 2006). Dietz leads efforts to define children as "overweight or obese" by BMI, which will greatly raise stigma directed toward them (Moynihan, 2006).

3. James Hill, PhD, is a primary spokesperson for community coalitions "fighting obesity"; he was being paid as a consultant to Hoffman–La Roche, Knoll Pharmaceuticals, and several other companies developing weight loss drugs while he was a member of the NIH Task Force on Obesity Prevention and Treatment, which was also declaring obesity a national emergency (MacPherson & Silverman, 1997; Oliver, 2006).

4. Richard Atkinson, MD, was a major spokesperson for Wyeth-Ayerst and numerous other drug companies; he joined Judith Stern, DSc (a consultant to Knoll, Wyeth-Ayerst, and Weight Watchers), to found the American Obesity Association with funding from Knoll and other drug companies to "advocate for obese people." The focus of their advocacy is for federal and private insurance coverage for weight loss treatment (Hall, 1998; MacPherson & Silverman, 1997); Atkinson is also the current editor of the *International Journal of Obesity Research.*

5. Xavier Pi-Sunyer, MD, has been a long-time consultant to Hoffman–La Roche, Knoll, Eli Lilly, and Weight Watchers, and is a member of the advisory board of Knoll Pharmaceuticals and Wyeth-Ayerst Laboratories (MacPherson & Silverman, 1997). At the same time that Pi-Sunyer was chairing the NIH Task Force on Obesity Treatment and Prevention, he was also identified as one of several researchers offered payment by Wyeth-Ayerst to put their name on research papers favorable to Phen-Fen that had been written by the drug company (Birmingham, 1999).

These are only a few of the known relationships between some of the most visible public health officials and the weight loss industry (Fraser, 1997; Oliver, 2006). An in-depth, detailed chart of these relationships was published in the *Newark Star-Ledger* (MacPherson & Silverman, 1997). Key articles have also appeared prominently in the *Wall Street Journal* (Johannes & Stecklow, 1998; McKay, 2002) and the *New York Times* (Kolata, 2005). Media stories about the conflicts of interest inherent in these relationships continue to be of critical importance to educate the public.

Since the 1970's, health professionals have consistently challenged obesity researchers, but no challenge to the status quo carried as much weight as a January 1998 *New England Journal of Medicine (NEJM)* editorial, "Losing Weight: An Ill Fated New Year's Resolution" (Kassirer & Angell, 1998), which reviewed the "dark side" of America's preoccupation with weight. Citing the failure and risks of dieting and weight loss, as well as the vast amounts of money wasted on such efforts, the *NEJM* editors also called into question the sacred cows of Obesity Inc.: "The data linking overweight and death, as well as the data showing the beneficial effects of weight loss, are limited, fragmentary and often ambiguous. We simply do not know whether a person who loses 20 lbs will thereby acquire the same reduced risk as a person who started out 20 lb lighter. The few studies of mortality among people who voluntarily lost weight produced inconsistent results; some even suggested that weight loss increased mortality" (Kassirer & Angell, 1998, p. 52). They also called on doctors to do what they could to "end discrimination against overweight people in schools and workplaces" (p. 53). To date, no physician organization has taken up the cause of reducing weight bias.

The editorial resulted in positive responses, but a much larger barrage of outrage was expressed in Obesity, Inc.'s follow-up letters to the editors. The *NEJM* editors held their ground, responded to critics, and summarized by saying, "We continue to believe that when doctors emphasize body weight and fail to consider the efficacy and risks of available treatments, the cure can be worse than the disease" (Letters, *NEJM*, 1998).

It is important to note that weight loss treatment cannot be considered harmless simply because it fails in the long run (Wooley & Garner, 1991). Chronic dieting and weight cycling have been linked to medical problems of increased blood pressure, depression, and eating disorders. Repeated losing and regaining of weight (weight cycling) has also been cited as one cause of dieters ending up at a higher weight over time (Blair, Shaten, Brownell, Collings, & Lissner, 1993; Garner & Wooley, 1991; National Institutes of Health Technology Assessment Conference Panel, 1992; Stice et al., 1999). This means that dieting itself is part of the problem that must be addressed if we are to get to the truth of what constitutes causal factors in the number of people at higher weights today.

Repeated weight loss failure can also be a contributing factor in delaying or avoiding medical care. In a study of barriers to gynecological cancer screening reported by large women (BMI 25–122), those who had tried to lose weight more than five times in the past ten years were most likely to delay care. The largest women had the lowest rates of Pap smears (Amy, Aalborg, Lyons & Keranen, 2006). Another study on first dieting experiences of women over two hundred pounds found that those who began dieting before age fourteen were at the highest adult weights. The reported memories of early dieting experiences recount feelings of constant hunger and deprivation, shame at being fat and not being able to keep weight off, and lifelong parental disappointment in these failed weight loss attempts. Women believed that repeated dieting had resulted in their present high weight and contributed to lowered self-esteem (Ikeda, Lyons, Schwartzman, & Mitchell, 2004).

Media attention and the public health frenzy surrounding the "childhood obesity epidemic" have produced new diet and weight programs that seem to be springing up on almost every street corner—even in churches, schools, and after-school programs. Although many of these programs are being developed under the banner of "long-term lifestyle change," the measure of success most valued is still weight loss. Public agencies and private foundations rarely fund proposals that do not include a goal of reducing weight. But maintaining this position, particularly with a goal of "preventing overweight and obesity" is not only likely to fail, but also holds the potential for additional harm in the future.

The 1991 warning of eating-disorders specialist Susan Wooley is still critical to acknowledge today: "Weight loss treatments provide patients with failure experiences, expose them to professionals who hold them in low regard, cause them to see themselves as deviant and flawed, confuse their perceptions of hunger and satiety, and divert their attention away from other problems" (quoted in Wooley & Garner, 1991, p. 1250). In the same way that millions play the lottery because they dream of redemption when they see the winner on television, people will likely keep trying to attain their own weight loss miracle, especially when urged on by all the forces of mainstream medicine. But genetics researcher and leptin discoverer professor Jeffrey Friedman says that genetics may account for as much as 70% of factors contributing to weight; additionally, he points out that "trying to lose weight is a battle against biology, a battle that only the intrepid take on and one in which only a few prevail" (Friedman, 2003, p. 856). As long as "obesity" is categorized as a "killer disease," such wisdom will continue to be ignored. But what if researchers found that, rather than being a killer disease, mortality figures for people considered "overweight" are much lower than previously reported? Would this be enough for "Obesity Inc." to reconsider its stance?

What About Those "Three Hundred Thousand Deaths Caused by Obesity"?

No matter how cynical you get, it's hard to keep up.

—Lily Tomlin

In 1993, McGinnis and Foege published the study most often cited as justification for launching the "war on obesity." In analyzing all causes of death in the United States, they found that "dietary factors and activity patterns that are too sedentary are associated with 300K deaths per year" (McGinnis & Foege, 1993, p. 2208). This figure began to appear in both media and research articles as "three hundred thousand deaths caused by obesity." It was this number that was misused at the FDA hearings to approve Redux, despite strong safety concerns that had been raised. And it was this number that was used repeatedly in press releases by the Shape Up America! campaign to prove the "dangerous epidemic of obesity, second only to tobacco as the leading cause of preventable death" (Johannes & Stecklow, 1998, p. B1). McGinnis and Foege—and others who read their actual research—kept trying to point out the gross misuse of their data. In 1998, McGinnis and Foege reaffirmed that the link with obesity deaths was not what they had claimed: "Instead, the figure . . . applies broadly to the combined effects of various dietary factors and activity patterns . . . [and] we noted explicitly the difficulty in sorting out the independent contribution of any one factor" (Letters, 1998, p. 1157). Predictably, rather than acknowledging that the figure was inaccurate, Obesity Inc. kept using it. In 1999 David Allison and colleagues published another data analysis trying to maintain the accuracy of the three hundred thousand figure (Allison, Fontaine, Manson, Stevens, & VanItalie, 1999). In 2005, Allison reported having received funding from 148 drug and diet industry sponsors (Gibbs, 2005).

The April 2005 publication of a paper by Flegal, Graubard, Williamson, and Gail should have put the three hundred thousand death figure to rest once and for all. Pointing out the methodological flaws in the Allison article, and using more recent national data sets of measured, rather than self-reported, heights and weights, Dr. Flegal and three other highly respected colleagues from the Centers for Disease Control and the National Cancer Institute soundly challenged the contested figure. They estimated the associated deaths to be far lower—112,000 for those with BMI over 35. What created even greater headlines and controversy—and predictable outrage from Obesity Inc.—was their finding that slightly "overweight" people had lower mortality rates than people at recommended weights (Flegal, Graubard, Williamson, & Gail, 2005). But rather than see these data as a reflection of better treatment of medical problems in people at higher weights—which is one explanation that Flegal and colleagues posed as a potential factor in the lower numbers—members of Obesity Inc. attacked the data as "flawed." NIH Obesity Task Force member Jim Hill, in his role of editor in chief of *Obesity Management*, decried the Flegal data and subsequent media coverage as damaging to the "war on obesity." Hill described media coverage as biased, and urged colleagues to try to get the media "on our side . . . write a letter to your local newspaper stating your views" (Hill, 2005, p. 86). Not surprisingly, he also took the opportunity to attack as "biased coverage" any media references to potential conflicts of interest among obesity research (p. 85).

It is time for health advocates to become much more knowledgeable about the full picture provided by multiple sources of research, as well as about the backroom nature of public health policy development related to weight and health. Public health professionals not involved in the size acceptance movement have even begun to challenge the focus on "obesity" as harmful to the public's health by increasing stigma and undermining efforts to access the benefits of healthy lifestyle independent of weight (Cohen, Perales, & Steadman, 2005). There has never been a better time for health advocates to learn more about a new paradigm, one that had its beginnings in the early 1970's and has existed side by side with the traditional paradigm, albeit without the billions of dollars of resources of the weight loss industry. This new paradigm, mentioned earlier—called Health at Every Size (HAES)—provides a framework for improving health, nutrition, and physical activity practices independent of weight loss.

A Public Health Paradigm for Success: Health at Every Size

My grandmother died at 85. They put "obesity" as her cause of death. Just how old does a fat person have to get to die of old age?
—Fat Lip Readers Theatre performance, 1985

In 1969, as a natural outgrowth of the civil rights movement, activists gathered under a banner of fair treatment for fat people and founded an education and advocacy group now called the National Association to Advance Fat Acceptance. In the early 1970's a group of women reclaimed the word "fat" as a political term, declared themselves the Fat Underground, and posed the idea that dieting not only failed to make people thinner, but also contributed to poor health, lowered self-esteem, and higher weight over time. They said that it was the cultural prejudice against fat people, combined with repeated failed attempts at weight loss, that were the source of greater health problems than weight itself. In 1982, Harvard physician William Bennett and coauthor Joel Gurin added further support to challenge traditional medical thinking in the book *Dieter's Dilemma*, which cited research on "set point" genetic theory, detailed the failure of dieting, challenged the exaggerated claims of the harm of higher weight, and advocated an end to weight prejudice (Bennett & Gurin, 1982).

The groundbreaking work of many health professionals, backed up by the claims of fat activists, has formed the basis for development of the HAES approach. The focus of the HAES paradigm is to create an environment of respect for body size diversity and to support lifestyle behaviors and attitudes that can improve health and well-being for people of all sizes, rather than focusing on weight loss. HAES promotes a holistic philosophy that acknowledges the harmful effects of stigma against fat people as a social justice issue, and aims to reduce barriers to participation in nutrition, physical activity, positive body esteem, social support, and community connection activities for people of all sizes. In this new paradigm, a "healthy weight" is not determined by a number on a chart or scale, but rather is "the weight at which a person settles as they move towards a more fulfilling and meaningful lifestyle" (Robison, 2003, p. 1). Fat people are not singled out as "the problem"; they are not used as a bad example of what everyone else should avoid becoming; they are not told that losing weight is the only way to improve health. Positive images of people of all sizes, including large sizes, are used to promote the idea that healthy living is for everybody. People of all sizes are encouraged to work together to reduce fat bias and social prejudice.

Several research studies support this new approach, including the latest published study by Bacon, Stern, Van Loan, and Keim (2005), which compared outcomes of a traditional diet/weight loss program to a HAES program. After two years, the HAES group enabled participants to maintain long-term behavior change; the diet approach did not. HAES participants had a lower attrition rate, and maintained weight and all improved outcome variables (blood pressure, lipids, eating restraint/ eating disorders pathology, self-esteem, depression, and body image); dieters did not.

Given all the factors discussed thus far, it is clear that the NIH should devote significant research dollars to this new paradigm; state, federal, and private foundation funding should also be devoted to interventions conceived from this stance. Much more effort should be focused on reducing the impact of stigma and weight discrimination on health. Furthermore, until there is long-term safety and efficacy data to support focusing on weight loss, it should probably not be recommended to anyone, let alone to someone whose health is already compromised. It certainly should not be recommended to the population as a whole.

Conclusion

> Follow the money.
>
> —"Deep Throat"

When issues raised here have been discussed with those in key health policy positions, one usually hears something like, "Well, you may be right, but now there is finally money available for nutrition and exercise programs and we don't want to jeopardize that." But why should fat people bear the burden of increasing stigmatization as a result of such decisions? It is important to realize that were it not for weight bias, weight loss programs would wither and die because they consistently fail to produce lasting weight loss. If concern for health is truly the primary motivator, then reducing fat stigma would be at the top of the list for health activism. Instead, research has identified weight bias in virtually all health professionals—physicians, nurses, dietitians, and therapists—including those who specialize in obesity treatment (Schwartz et al., 2003). Thus weight bias has been a cornerstone of public health policies so far, and drug industry profits have been inflaming these efforts. It is time to denounce the "war on obesity" and declare a peaceful approach to improving health for people of all sizes. The HAES model can guide individuals, activists, and public health policy leaders in such efforts.

NOTE

This chapter is based on an unpublished policy opinion by the author that was requested by the Bay Area Media Studies Group/Public Health Institute, Berkeley, California.

REFERENCES

Allison, D.B., Fontaine, K.R., Manson, J.E., Stevens, J., & VanItallie, T.B. (1999). Annual Deaths Attributable to Obesity in the United States. *JAMA: Journal of the American Medical Association, 282,* 1530–1538.

Amy, N., Aalborg, A., Lyons, P., & Keranen, L. (2006). Barriers to Routine Gynecological Cancer Screening for Obese White and African American Obese Women. *International Journal of Obesity (London), 30 (1),* 147–155.

Bacon, L., Stern, J.S., Van Loan, M.D., & Keim, N.L. (2005). Size Acceptance and Intuitive Eating Improve Health for Obese, Female Chronic Dieters. *Journal of the American Dietetic Association, 105 (6),* 929–936.

Bennett, W., & Gurin, J. (1982). *Dieter's Dilemma.* New York: Basic Books.

Birmingham, K. (1999) Lawsuit Reveals Academic Conflict-of-Interest. *Nature Medicine, 5,* 717.

Blair, S.N., Shaten, J., Brownell, K., Collins, G., & Lissner, L. (October 1, 1993). Body Weight Change, All-Cause Mortality, and Cause-Specific Mortality in the Multiple Risk Factor Intervention Trial. *Annals of Internal Medicine, 119 (7),* 749–757.

Carmona R. (November 23, 2003). Interview. *Morning Edition* [Radio broadcast]. Washington, D.C.: National Public Radio.

Cohen, L., Perales, D.P., & Steadman, C. (2005). The O word: Why the Focus on Obesity Is Harmful to Community Health. *California Journal of Health Promotion, 3 (3),* 154–161.

Flegal, K., Graubard, B.I., Williamson, D.F., & Gail, M.H. (2005). Excess Deaths Associated with Underweight, Overweight, and Obesity. *JAMA: Journal of the American Medical Association, 293,* 1861–1867.

Fraser, L. (1997). *Losing It: America's Obsession with Weight and the Industry That Feeds on It.* New York: Dutton.

Friedman, J.M. (February 7, 2003). A War on Obesity, Not the Obese. *Science, 299,* 856–858.

Garner, D., & Wooley, S. (1991). Confronting the Failure of Behavioral and Dietary Treatments for Obesity. *Clinical Psychology Review, 11,* 729–780.

Gibbs, W. (2005). Obesity: An Overblown Epidemic? *Scientific American, 292 (6),* 70–77.

Gregg, E. Cheng, Y.J., Cadwell, B.L., Imperatore, G., Williams, D.E., Flegal, K.M., Venkat Narayan, K.M., & Williamson, D.F. (2005). Secular Trends in Cardiovascular Disease Risk Factors According to Body Mass Index in US Adults. *JAMA: Journal of the American Medical Association, 293,* 1868–1874.

Hall, D. (April 5, 1998). Fen-Phen Makers Fund Advocate Richard Atkinson, MD. *Wisconsin State Journal,* 1A, 3A.

Heshka, S., Anderson, J.W., Atkinson, R.L., Greenway, F.L., Hill, J.O., Phinney, S.D., Kolotkin, R.L., Miller-Kovach, K., & Pi-Sunyer, X. (2003). Weight Loss with Self-Help Compared with a Structured Commercial Program: A Randomized Trial. *JAMA: Journal of the American Medical Association, 289,* 1792–1798.

Hill, J.O. (June 2005). Is Obesity Bad? *Obesity Management, 1 (3),* 85–86.

Hirsch, J. (August 2, 2005). Carb-Makers Rejoice at Demise of Atkins Empire. *San Francisco Chronicle,* A3.

Ikeda, J., Lyons, P., Schwartzman, F., & Mitchell, R.A. (2004). Self-Reported Dieting Experiences of Women with Body Mass Index of 30 or More. *Journal of the American Dietetic Association, 104,* 972–974.

Johannes, L., & Stecklow, S. (February 9, 1998). Dire Warnings About Obesity Rely on a Slippery Statistic. *Wall Street Journal,* B1.

Kassirer, J., & Angell, M. (1998). Losing Weight: An Ill-Fated New Year's Resolution. *New England Journal of Medicine, 338,* 52–54

Kolata, G. (April 29, 2005). Still Counting on Calorie Counting. *New York Times,* C1.

Latner, J., & Stunkard, A. (2003). Getting Worse: The Stigmatization of Obese Children. *Obesity Research, 11,* 452–456.

Letters to the Editor. (April 16, 1998). *New England Journal of Medicine, 338 (16),* 1156–1158.

Lyons, P. (2003). Just Say No to the "War on Obesity." *National Women's Health Network News,* November–December, pp. 1, 5.

MacPherson, K., & Silverman, E. (February 17, 1997). Fat Pills, Fat Profits, Part 2. *Newark Star-Ledger,* 14.

McGinnis, J.M., & Foege, W.H. (1993). Actual Causes of Death in the United States. *JAMA: Journal of the American Medical Association, 270,* 2207–2212.

McKay, B. (July 23, 2002). Who You Calling Fat? *The Wall Street Journal,* B1.

Moore, T.J. (1993) *Lifespan: Who Lives Longer and Why?* New York: Simon and Schuster.

Moynihan, R. (2006). Expanding Definitions of Obesity May Harm Children: Obesity Task Force Linked to WHO Takes "Millions" from Drug Firms. *British Medical Journal, 332,* 1412.

Mundy, A. (2001). *Dispensing with the Truth: The Victims, the Drug Companies, and the Dramatic Story Behind the Battle over Fen-Phen*. New York: St. Martin's Press.

National Institutes of Health Technology Assessment Conference Panel. (1992). Methods for Voluntary Weight Loss and Control. *Annals of Internal Medicine, 116,* 942–949.

Oliver, E. (2006). *Fat Politics*. New York: Oxford University Press.

PR Newswire. (January 6, 1998). Dr. Koop and Leading Public Health Experts Challenge an Editorial in the *NEJM* Which "Trivializes" Obesity.

Reiling, J. (1999). National Expansion. *JAMA: Journal of the American Medical Association, 33,* 1108.

Robison, J. (2003). Health at Every Size: Antidote for the Obesity Epidemic. *Healthy Weight Journal, 17* (2), pp. 1, 16.

Schwartz, M., O'Neal Chambliss, H., Brownell, K.D., Blair, S.N., & Billington, C. (2003). Weight Bias Among Health Professionals Specializing in Obesity. *Obesity Research, 11 (9),* 1033–1039.

Seid, R. P. (1989). *Never Too Thin: Why Women Are at War with Their Bodies*. New York: Prentice Hall.

Stice, E., Cameron, R.P., Killen, J.D., Hayward, C., & Taylor, C.B. (1999). Naturalistic Weight-Reduction Efforts Prospectively Predict Growth in Relative Weight and Onset of Obesity Among Female Adolescents. *Journal of Consulting and Clinical Psychology, 67,* 967–974.

Stunkard, A., & Hume, M. (1959). The Results of Treatment for Obesity: A Review of the Literature and Report off a Series. *Archives of Internal Medicine, 103,* 79–85.

Tsai, A.G., & Wadden, T.A. (2005). Systematic Review: An Evaluation of Major Commercial Weight Loss Programs in the United States. *Annals of Internal Medicine, 142,* 56–66.

Wooley, S., & Garner, D. (1991). Obesity Treatment: The High Cost of False Hope. *Journal of the American Dietetic Association, 91,* 1248–1251.

Public Fat

Canadian Provincial Governments and Fat on the Web

Laura Jennings

Public policy approaches toward fat vary greatly from area to area. Annemarie Jutel (2001) examines major health policy documents of several nations, and her findings indicate a spectrum of approaches and attitudes toward fat and fat people. In general, the U.S. governmental approach emphasizes quantitative measures such as body mass index (BMI) and places "weight management before health management" (Jutel, 2001, p. 286). The national government of Canada falls at the other end of this spectrum, recognizing the shortcomings of BMI as a proxy for health and acknowledging the dangers of very low weights (Jutel, 2001).

In the United States, where powerful national health organizations spout warnings about an "obesity epidemic," many states view fat as an enemy. Some state leaders unquestioningly accept messages about the dangers of fat and magnify these messages as they pass them along to their constituents. In Arkansas, where Governor Huckabee recently lost a lot of weight, webpages portray fat as antithetical to health, and fat people as irresponsible and lazy. One page, describing the connections between physical activity and health, tells us that exercise helps prevent "obesity" and, therefore, heart attack and stroke. It asks: "Why don't people get moving? Some are discouraged by the 'no pain, no gain' philosophy once they get started. Some consider physical activity 'no fun.' The most common reason is 'not enough time.' But studies show that regular moderate physical activity can make a big difference in heart health. African Americans have much to gain by being active. More than four of 10 African-American adults have cardiovascular diseases (CVD) such as heart attack and stroke" (State of Arkansas, "Cardiovascular," 2006). This passage introduces race, leaving readers with the impression that being African American is tied either to a desire to be inactive or to ignorance regarding exercise and health issues. Both exacerbate existing racial stereotypes.

The Arkansas websites list explicit "causes" for fat. These include poor nutrition, lack of exercise, and hefty doses of individual failings. Arkansas state webpages present fat as both an economic and health problem, with causes and solutions that target fat and fat people, rather than health and social structures. A web letter from governor Mike Huckabee ends with this: "For many years our country put money and energy into treating disease and illness rather than dealing with avoiding disease through healthier lifestyles. We have staggering rates of heart attacks, high blood pressure and strokes simply because people opt not to take care of themselves" (State of Arkansas "Letter," 2006). This philosophy has lead to specific policies and recommendations, many stressing the individual's responsibility for health maintenance, and others invoking a kind of paternalistic government/business partnership aimed at ridding Arkansas of adipose tissue. In 2003, Arkansas passed Act 1220, creating the Child Health Advisory Committee; mandates of this group include removing junk food vending machines in schools, "requiring schools to include as part of each student's health report to parents an annual body mass index (BMI) percentile," and "requiring schools to annually provide parents an explanation of the possible health effects of body mass index, nutrition and physical activity" (State of Arkansas "Child Health," 2006).

Children aren't the only target of the Arkansas anti-fat campaign; an "Obesity" webpage encourages employers to post BMI charts in the workplace, because it "can be a great way to initiate conversation on weight management with employees" (State of Arkansas "Obesity," 2006). The document also suggests that employers "compile menus from local eateries and identify healthy items for employees to choose from" (State of Arkansas "Obesity," 2006).

Other states such as Illinois exercise more caution in their discussions of fat and in policies connected to fat. Even when fat is presented as a health problem, fat people are not demonized. Solutions suggested involve both personal effort (eat more fruits and veggies, increase exercise) and community or state effort (community gardens, education on nutrition, farmers market access for low-income people). Policy efforts in these states are directed at improving public health in general rather than singling out fat and fat people.

Just as individual U.S. states differ in their approaches to fat, so might Canadian provinces. On the other hand, Canada's commitment to universal health care for its citizens might result in a more comprehensive and unified approach to fat and fat-related policy. Do provinces share an understanding of whether fat constitutes a problem? If so, do they define and address the "problem" in similar ways? The exact language used and the nature of the claims made about fat illuminate underlying beliefs about people who are fat; these beliefs, when translated into policy, have significant effects on the people and groups targeted by health policy.

Methods

In this age of the internet, websites constitute the most public face of an organization; thus, to assess how Canadian provinces view and address fat, I examined the official websites of the four most populous provinces (Alberta, British Columbia, Quebec, and Ontario, which together account for 85% of Canada's population) and official documents linked to these sites. I took note of the exact wording used to discuss fat. For each province I asked: Is fat portrayed as a problem? If so, what type of problem, and do suggested solutions match the level at which the problem is conceptualized? I looked for documents or webpages that mention health benefits of proper nutrition or physical activity without also mentioning fat or weight loss. I examined the ways in which race, gender, age, and social class appear—or fail to appear—in discussions of fat and health on official provincial websites and documents. One limitation of this approach is that it entails much backtracking through the websites and links of the individual provinces, making it possible to miss relevant documents or pages.

Findings

Ontario

Many pages of the official Ontario website show both a strong anti-fat stance and a heavy reliance on positivist claims and measures. BMI is promoted repeatedly as a direct measure of health. Much of the information presented shows an unquestioning belief that fat is bad and weight loss good; even a page describing a study on the substantial dangers of yo-yo dieting concludes that "while many experts say the risks associated with yo-yo dieting shouldn't stop you from trying to lose weight if you are overweight, they do underscore the importance of finding a weight-loss plan that will help you not only lose the fat, but keep it off as well" (Province of Ontario "Are You," 2006).

In several places the language used is uncritical and vague, as if the authors themselves are uncomfortable with the information they provide (e.g., "They say" with no citation; Province of Ontario "5 Ways," 2006). An extensive section on "Childhood Obesity" speaks contemptuously of parents of fat children, painting them as fat, lazy, and guilty of "benign neglect." The page *Young Heavyweights* has a section called "Help Your Child Lose Weight," which maintains, "Getting your child to change his or her attitude towards the benefits of being healthy will be difficult if one parent pushes healthy nutrition and the other sits around and eats cookies every day" (Province of Ontario, "Young," 2006).

The Ontario website does have some health-related pages that do not stress the evils of fat or the virtues of weight loss. A few pages—those addressed to seniors and pregnant women—actually discourage weight loss. One page describing "Intuitive Eating" discourages dieting and encourages body acceptance (Province of Ontario "Intuitive," 2006). The author of this piece dilutes the positive message, however, by referring several times to intuitive eating as a means to weight loss.

A document called *Healthy Weights, Healthy Lives* discusses the variation in rates of "obesity" across Ontario (including rates among Native peoples that are twice that of other groups) and concludes that Toronto's lower rate is likely due to its higher proportion of non-Caucasians (Province of Ontario, "2004 Chief," 2006). This finding contrasts with the United States, where minority populations often have higher BMI levels. Unlike the United States, with its large Latino and Black populations, Ontario's biggest minority group is Asian—a group whose BMI level is usually lower than whites. This document acknowledges socio-structural factors influencing fat and offers solutions on a variety of levels, but much of the individual-level advice is unrealistic for those whose income levels are low (e.g., tips advising dieters to throw away half of any sweet food they feel they must eat) (Province of Ontario, "2004 Chief," 2006).

The assumption on Ontario's webpages is that fat and health cannot coexist. Ensuring that fat kids lose weight is not only a parental responsibility, but is required for good citizenship: "You'll not only be doing them a big favor, you'll also help ease the burden on the health care system as obesity threatens to become a national crisis" (Province of Ontario, "Waste Lines," 2006). *Healthy Weights, Healthy Lives* (Province of Ontario "2004 Chief," 2006) even has a section on how to determine if you live in an "obesogenic" environment.

According to a webpage titled *Preventing Illness, Promoting Wellness*, a major health focus of the province is to "reduce illnesses from smoking, obesity and environmental pollution" (Province of Ontario, "Preventing," 2006). The province has removed "junk" food from elementary school vending machines and is encouraging regular physical activity by enabling nonprofit groups to share school facilities. These community-level actions aim for improved health for all, rather than just targeting fat people.

Quebec

From the official homepage of the province of Quebec, it is easy to find several substantial documents on public health. In contrast to the Ontario site, Quebec's approach to health is more unified and less focused on fat, with health documents showing a public conscience and commitment to addressing health disparities. One of the major issues addressed in the document *National Report on the Health Status of the Population of Quebec: Producing Health* (Province of Quebec "National," 2006) is the effect of inequality on health, especially as it affects Native peoples. Environmental factors are stressed along with the psycho-social problems inherent in situations of inequality.

The authors of this document seem unsure of how seriously to take fat, and variously refer to it as "disease," "risk factor," or "determinant" of disease (Province of Quebec, "National," 2006). There are several sections, however, in which fat might have been mentioned and is not; when it is discussed, the tone is nonjudgmental and focuses on health rather than on "bad" actors. This document presents health problems as both individually and socially based and presses for solutions at both levels. One section specifically mentions that prejudice affects health and that Quebec's poorer and Native peoples suffer from worse environmental conditions and health outcomes than other groups.

A second document—*Quebec Public Health Program: 2003–2012* (hereafter QPHP) (Province of Quebec, "Public," 2006)—is similar in tone to the *Producing Health* document. There is clear recognition of the role of social structure in population health, and clear commitment to finding structural solutions (and determining the government's role in those solutions). Two sections of the paper—on major health problems and societal costs—discuss illness, injury, and death, including psycho-social issues. Environmental quality and the varying needs of different groups are mentioned; fat is not mentioned.

The *QPHP* document lays out six major areas for action. Only one of these mentions fat. Much of this section ties fat to health and to lifestyle factors, but social structure is not forgotten; the authors discuss the interaction between the ability to make healthy food choices and the social environment, including economic, physical, and legal conditions (Province of Quebec, "Public," 2006).

Another report, *Comparative Study on the Health of Quebec's Population and on the Performance of Its Health Care System: Highlights*, lists "obesity" after low birth weight, smoking, and sedentary lifestyle as a "risk factor for personal health" (Province of Quebec, "Comparative," 2002). This document briefly describes Quebec's status as second-thinnest province, refers to BMI as the determinant of healthy weight, and notes that "a higher proportion of women were underweight than men. Moreover, a higher proportion of women than men are of normal weight" (Province of Quebec, "Comparative," 2002). The social factors leading to gender differences in levels of fat are not mentioned, nor is there any acknowledgement of the risks of very low body weight or what this might mean for women's health.

Two final documents of interest from the Quebec website are *Main Quebec Health and Social Services Prevention and Promotion Initiatives* (Province of Quebec, "Main," 2004) and *Eat Your Way to Health: Fruits and Vegetables* (Province of Quebec, "Eat," 2006). The first references lifestyles, chronic diseases, unbalanced diet, and lack of exercise, but not fat. The second provides information about the health benefits of proper nutrition and exercise. One brief mention of "if you want to lose weight" is made (Province of Quebec, "Eat," 2006), but nothing is said about fat. The focus of these documents is on health promotion.

British Columbia

The British Columbia website sends mixed messages about fat. Numerous webpages address health issues (including nutrition and exercise) without mentioning fat or weight. The BC Ministry of Health's "BC Health Guide" site describes a program that has issued a 2010 challenge to BC residents: increase activity levels and consumption of fruits and vegetables, and decrease tobacco use, prevalence of fetal alcohol syndrome, and "obesity" (Province of British Columbia, "ActNow BC," 2006). Numerical targets are set for all except the fat reduction goal. Several programs are mentioned in conjunction with this challenge, and all target health in general rather than fat people.

"BC HealthGuide OnLine" (Province of British Columbia "Health," 2006) presents a lengthy list of possible topics, including "Obesity." The "Obesity" site is enormous and includes many links and subtopics. "Obesity" is defined as "an ongoing disease, not a cosmetic problem," and as a "complicated disease" that can be treated in many ways (Province of British Columbia, "Obesity," 2006). The website leaves little doubt that fat should be treated and encourages people who have regained lost weight to keep trying, with no mention of the dangers of yo-yo dieting. Sections addressing weight loss drugs and surgeries mention risks and side effects, but almost as an afterthought. No attempt is made to encourage internal—or external—dialogue about why eliminating fat is worth taking such risks or what role society plays in this (Province of British Columbia, "Obesity," 2006).

Unlike Quebec's site, the British Columbia website does not firmly connect social position to health. Although the "Obesity" pages give a brief nod to the role of structural factors in the fat "disease," all solutions presented there are individual-level. The programs described on the "ActNowBC" page, by contrast, do address such community-level issues as school nutrition, but race, class, and gender are not discussed.

Alberta

Alberta, too, sends mixed messages regarding fat. There are many instances in which fat could be mentioned and is not, whereas both nutrition and exercise are addressed. Following a link in "How Healthy Are We?" (Province of Alberta, "How," 2006) takes us to a long list of downloadable documents about health status in Alberta. Again, none refers in its title to fat, but one is titled *Self-Reported Body Mass Index and Its Correlates in Alberta: A Portrait from Survey and Administrative Data Sources* (Province of Alberta, "Self," 2005). This is a deeply flawed document. Through careful construction of BMI categories (such that the category they label "BMI > 40" is actually a combination of those with BMI > 40 and those with BMI > 35 who also have at least one chronic illness), the authors create the negative fat/health associations that they wish to find.

Throughout this report, verbal interpretations repeatedly downplay the health issues reported by those in the BMI < 18.5 category while highlighting what the authors say is progressively worsening health from "overweight" to "obese" to "morbidly obese" categories. Often the verbal interpretations are at odds with charts and graphs of the data, which in several instances clearly illustrate a U- or J-shaped relationship. Nowhere do they discuss the effects of category construction on their findings, nor is any attempt made to discuss effects of possible confounding factors such as social pressure for fat people to view themselves as unhealthy, or for doctors to view fat people as inherently sick and order more diagnostic tests than for thin people.

Another report, *Framework for a Healthy Alberta: Highlights* (Province of Alberta, "Framework," 2006), lays out health challenges and goals to be achieved by 2012. Fat is not mentioned, although a few references are made to the desirability of achieving "healthy weights" as defined by body mass index (it is not clear whether this includes raising the weights of very thin people). The emphasis is not on targeting fat but on promoting health. This document does not directly identify causes of health problems, but it does suggest solutions at both individual and structural levels. These include incentives to help people make healthy choices, building walking and cycling trails, and enacting regulations that limit access to tobacco and junk food.

A document titled *Alberta's Report on Comparable Health Indicators* (Province of Alberta, "Report," 2002) portrays being "underweight" as problematic in infancy.

Another chapter, however, discusses body mass index. Although the BMI category description includes "underweight," no mention is made of poor health outcomes for adults in this category, suggesting that by adult "healthy weight" the authors mean thin or "normal." The remainder of this document focuses on improving health and does not target fat or fat people.

The *Healthy Alberta Baseline Survey Quantitative Report* (Province of Alberta, "Healthy," 2002) is based on data from a 2002 survey conducted for the Ministry of Health and Wellness. Survey findings include gender differences (women are more likely to report self-perceptions of being "overweight") and a high percentage (98%) of respondents saying that they are responsible for their own health. The report plays up findings that support individual responsibility and downplays those that indicate structural factors influencing health.

The report *Keeping Albertans Healthy* (Province of Alberta, "Keeping," 2004) emphasizes individual responsibility for health and fat. Health solutions proposed in this report are largely individual, except for government-sponsored advertisements promoting individual solutions. An early mention that "some Albertans are dying from preventable causes, and not all groups enjoy optimal health . . . for example, First Nations communities are at greater risk of diabetes" indicates the structural nature of many health problems, but this is not followed by any mention of structural solutions (Province of Alberta, "Keeping," 2004, p. 2).

Discussion

The stance that a government takes on a public health issue depends on many things, including the nature of the issue itself. Is there clearly a problem, is there public/political support for a governmental role in addressing the problem, and is there a viable plan of action? Even when the answers are yes, cost is a factor, as is the relationship between those making the policy and those who will be most affected by it. If those in power do not identify with the people or groups most closely associated with a particular health issue, the issue is not likely to receive the same quality of attention that it would if such closeness existed. When a medical (or medicalized) issue is not so clear-cut, policy decisions become much more difficult. Fat is just such a case; although there seems to be a widespread view that fat is a problem, not everyone agrees or cares about it. Many in government, in the media, and in communities view fat as a problem of individual behavior. Those with this view are less likely to support expenditures of public time and monies for the fighting of fat. Such a battle, they contend, is better fought in the minds and kitchens of individual fat people.

Governments must decide whether fat is a problem worthy of policy attention. This decision cannot be divorced from public perceptions of groups thought most often to be fat. A province may decide that fat is problematic because it threatens the health of its citizens, or because fat citizens threaten the well-being (fiscal or otherwise) of the province. If levels of fat are higher in groups already perceived as threatening (i.e., racial minorities or the poor), then the latter view is more likely. In this case, individual-level solutions and appeals to civic duty—which increase stigmatization of fat people—are likely to influence decision makers. If, however, it is the group in power that is fattest, then governments that view fat as problematic are likely to be more concerned about it from a health standpoint. In this case, community- or state-level solutions requiring funding will appear more attractive, and stigmatization of fat people undesirable. For those rare states or provinces that do not readily identify fat as a problem, or which view it as one symptom of wider deficiencies in nutrition and physical activity, it is possible to take an approach that emphasizes access to healthy foods and exercise for all people, not just those who are fat.

The four provinces studied here vary considerably in their approaches to fat. Although Ontario, Alberta, and British Columbia clearly consider fat a dangerous killer of epidemic proportions, Quebec takes a less committal view. In terms of level of causation of health problems, Quebec repeatedly emphasizes socio-structural causes, whereas Ontario and British Columbia waiver somewhere on the individual-level side of the spectrum (at least on the subject of fat) and Alberta remains silent. Quebec matches its solution level to its level of causation by placing a strong emphasis on structural answers to health problems, in keeping with a view of citizenship as a guarantee of rights. Ontario, on the other hand, treats fat and citizenship as responsibilities, a philosophy in agreement with its largely individual-level solutions to the "problem" of fat. British Columbia stresses behavioral solutions, whereas Alberta hovers between behavioral and structural responses to fat. Although all four provinces recognize the individual's role in health and in fat, with the possible exception of Ontario each seems to recognize that policies targeting—and thereby further stigmatizing—fat people are not adequate solutions to the wider public health problems of nutrition and exercise deficiency.

REFERENCES

Jutel, A. (2001). Does Size Really Matter? Weight and Values in Public Health. Perspectives in Biology and Medicine, 44, 2, 283–296.

Province of Alberta. (2002, September). Alberta's Report on Comparable Health Indicators. Retrieved May 20, 2006, from http://www.health.alberta.ca/documents/Comparable-Health-Indicators-2002.pdf.

Province of Alberta (2003, November. Framework for a Healthy Alberta: Highlights. Retrieved May 20, 2006, from http://www.health.alberta.ca/documents/Framework-For-Health-HL-2003.pdf.

Province of Alberta. (2002, October). Healthy Alberta Baseline Survey Quantitative Report. Retrieved May 20, 2006, from http://www.health.alberta.ca/documents/Healthy-Alberta-survey-2002.pdf.

Province of Alberta. How Healthy Are We? Retrieved May 20, 2006, from http://www.health.alberta.ca/documents/Framework-For-Health-2003.pdf.

Province of Alberta. (2004, Fall). Keeping Albertans Healthy. Retrieved May 20, 2006, from http://www.health.alberta.ca/documents/Comparable-Keep-Healthy-2004.pdf.

Province of Alberta. (2005, April). Self-Reported Body Mass Index and Its Correlates in

Alberta: A Portrait from Survey and Administrative Data Sources. Retrieved May 20, 2006, from http://www.health.alberta.ca/documents/Body-Mass-Index-Report-2005.pdf.

Province of British Columbia. ActNow BC. Retrieved May 20, 2006, from http://www.actnowbc.ca/.

Province of British Columbia. BC Health Guide Online. Retrieved May 20, 2006, from http://www.bchealthguide.org/kbase/list/all/default.htm.

Province of British Columbia. Obesity. Retrieved May 20, 2006, from http://www.healthlinkbc.ca/kbase/topic/special/hw252864/sec1.htm.

Province of Ontario. Are You a Yo-Yo? Retrieved May 22, 2006, from http://www.healthyontario.com/FeatureDetails.aspx?feature_id=4035.

Province of Ontario. (2004). Chief Medical Officer of Health Report: Healthy Weights, Healthy Lives. Retrieved May 22, 2006, from http://www.mhp.gov.on.ca/english/health/healthy_weights_112404.pdf.

Province of Ontario. 5 Ways To Help Overweight Kids. Retrieved May 22, 2006, from http://www.healthyontario.com/Experts/Dr__Susan_Biali/5_Ways_To_Help_Overweight_Kids.htm.

Province of Ontario. Intuitive Eating. Retrieved May 22, 2006, from http://www.eatrightontario.ca/en/viewdocument.aspx?id=19.

Province of Ontario Preventing Illness, Promoting Wellness. Retrieved May 22, 2006, from http://www.gov.on.ca/ont/portal/!ut/p/.cmd/cs/.ce/7_0_A/.s/7_0_252/_s.7_0_A/7_0_252/_l/en?docid=012974.

Province of Ontario. Waste Lines. Retrieved May 22, 2006, from http://www.healthyontario.com/Features/Children_s_Health/Waste_Lines.htm.

Province of Ontario. Young Heavyweights. Retrieved May 22, 2006, from http://www.healthyontario.com/Features/Childhood_Obesity/Young_Heavyweights.htm.

Province of Quebec. (2002, September). Comparative Study on the Health of Quebec's Population and on the Performance of its Health Care System: Highlights. Retrieved May 23, 2006, from http://publications.msss.gouv.qc.ca/acrobat/f/documentation/2002/02-412-02A.pdf.

Province of Quebec. (2006, March). Eat Your Way to Health: Fruits and Vegetables. Retrieved May 23, 2006, from http://publications.msss.gouv.qc.ca/acrobat/f/documentation/2005/05-289-14A.pdf.

Province of Quebec. (2004). Main Quebec Health and Social Services Prevention and Promotion Initiatives. Retrieved May 23, 2006, from http://publications.msss.gouv.qc.ca/acrobat/f/documentation/2004/actprevention04a.pdf.

Province of Quebec. (2005). National Report on the Health Status of the Population of Quebec: Producing Health. Retrieved May 23, 2006, from http://publications.msss.gouv.qc.ca/acrobat/f/documentation/2005/05-228-02A.pdf.

Province of Quebec. (2003). Quebec Public Health Program: 2003–2012. Retrieved May 23, 2006, from http://publications.msss.gouv.qc.ca/acrobat/f/documentation/2003/03-216-02A.pdf.

State of Arkansas. Cardiovascular Health: Physical Activity. Retrieved May 5, 2006, from http://www.arkansashearthealth.com/physical_activities/physical_activities.html.

State of Arkansas. Child Health Advisory Committee. Retrieved May 5, 2006, from http://www.healthyarkansas.com/advisory_committee/advisory.html.

State of Arkansas. Letter from the Governor. Retrieved May 5, 2006, from http://www.arkansas.gov/ha/letter.html.

State of Arkansas. Obesity. Retrieved May 5, 2006, from http://www.arkansas.gov/ha/pdf/obesity.pdf.

‖‖‖

That Remains to Be Said
Disappeared Feminist Discourses on Fat in Dietetic Theory and Practice

Lucy Aphramor and Jacqui Gingras

Sometimes words are mere noise
ousting what needs to be revealed
and then the poem must hold out—
you must hold out the poem—
cold glass against the face of death
until something amorpheous condenses / taciturnly.

—Aphramor, *Craft* (2005a)

Introduction—Sometimes Words Are Mere Noise

In this chapter we, two feminist dietitian scholars, take a critical look at how our profession, although ideally situated to widen debate on fat and bodies, instead routinizes dominant understandings and eclipses alternative ways of telling and knowing fat. Dietetics recognizes knowledge as that which can be supported by dominant scientific literature developed around rigorous, quantifiable scientific methods. Such rational knowing has implications for how dietetics is taught and practiced (Liquori, 2001). Travers (1995) contends that professional nutrition discourse constructs nutrition and health inequities and contributes to public health problems. DeVault (1999) describes the professional training that dietetic students receive as a structure that produces isolation from families and communities; as a result, students learn to suppress emotions. All of this contributes to a gendered profession positioned in a way that doesn't acknowledge gender as positioning and doesn't acknowledge women's experiences as different from men's. Such omissions don't encourage practitioners or scientists to critique the source of knowledge as (likely) emerging from androcentric and western-centric epistemologies. That remains to be said.

But to uphold the rigor of the scientific convention limits engagement with meaning making: language is not a neutral tool but rather a powerfully charged political vector. The words that we use here influence our ability to generate possibilities (Lorde, 1984). Rather than locate our writing in the culture of positivism by choosing a relatively static scientific discourse, we have instead chosen to engage poetry as a way of "crafting a praxis-oriented culture" and troubling the status quo (Dorazio-Migliore, Migliore, & Anderson, 2005). In welcoming subordinated poetic voices, around which we have arranged our chapter, we deliberately reject the certainty of positivism (as well as the privilege that it affords us) and plump for a more unruly interface with our readers. We hope that this style presents dominant theories as indefinite, negotiable, situated, and open to query.

When dominant theories on, and ways of speaking about, food, eating, and fat do not sufficiently represent lived experiences, there exists an empathic rupture between practitioners' theories and Others' lives. Such a disparity, when viewed by the dietitian in terms of individuality and rational, autonomous client behavior, is seen as largely the responsibility of said client. Very often, the issue at stake is fatness, the large *body* seen as noncompliant, disobedient, and undisciplined, which could very well apply to the bodies of knowledge that dietitians automatically disappear in order to rely on a discourse that demonizes fat. This ideology is also a likely predicate for healthism.

In valuing feminist epistemologies the authors acknowledge, as Leahy writes, "that women's experiences and knowledge have often been marginalized or ignored, often at great cost" (Leahy, 2001, p. 39). Of course, in foregrounding gender we do not wish to obscure axes of ideological bias related to class, race, sexuality identity, age, or disability. Our hope is that this chapter encourages more dietetic theorists and practitioners to take up the notion of a socially integrated feminist science for dietitians, one that refuses to disappear feminist discourses on fat.

Contemporary Examples of Anti-fat Bias— Ousting What Needs to Be Revealed

Why do dietitians concern themselves with regulating fatness? The British Dietetic Association's (BDA) "Weight Wise Campaign" epitomizes dietetic health promotion activities (BDA, 2005). Fatness is framed as problematic because it would "increase the chances of having a heart attack, developing diabetes and having high blood pressure, and particularly important for teenagers, it can affect self-esteem . . . [and] also costs us all money." Here dietetics's healthist ideology endorses dominant and repressive views on fatness. It is naïve to link enhanced psychological well-being with assimilation. Teenagers of all sizes stand to benefit from health education that intrinsically teaches respect for all, regardless of appearance, along with a good dose of media literacy to help prevent eating disturbances, lookism (prejudice based on physical appearance), and fear of fat arising from misguided healthy-eating directives (Levine & Smolak, 1998). On the other hand, bullies and health practitioners who find it difficult to openly question the conflation of social fitness and health would likely benefit from raised social esteem. In homogenous, affluent societies, poverty and adiposity are strongly linked and gendered. A framing of financial liability, with implicit notions of guilt, blame, willfulness, and culpability, further derogates groups whose status is already eroded by society. Each of the Weight Wise statements arises from a masculinist science that purports to be impartial and, denying the interweaving of science with society, sustains dietetics as socially disintegrated and nonfeminist.

Unforgiving, Unfathomable Weight-Loss Practices

Adopting this particular fatness narrative, dietetics then upholds popular misconceptions about the evidence base for weight reduction and the efficacy of health interventions focused on behavioral change. A wide range of research has demonstrated that the latter only work for those in the upper and middle classes (Baumann, 1989). In choosing normative epistemologies that position the individual as an isolated physical unit making rational choices in a good-enough environment, such campaigns inadvertently perpetuate pseudo-medical justifications that amplify health inequalities and foreclose critical contextual inquiry. For instance, within the parameters of normative science, models linking caregiver burden, anger, and psychological risk factors, including racism, with health and body shape explicate the inter-factorial pathways among physiological deterioration, health habits, and socio-environmental context (Aphramor, 2005b). Yet, rather than integrating these findings, the dietetic project conserves a limited, consumerist, and decontextualized understanding of health and fatness in which issues of power, inequity, and gender remain peripheral and occluded.

This individualistic approach creates a theoretical desert where health/weight becomes something static and calculable to be manipulated. The energy balance metaphor might have its place as a tidy, if unsophisticated teaching aid, but as it ignores the cumulative dynamic of humans interacting with their environment from embryological development onward, it has little hope of manufacturing health.

Dietitian as Complicit—The Poem Must Hold Out

The true danger of the energy balance metaphor lies not in its failure to precisely explain metabolism but in the constricting hold that it has over the collective dietetic imagination. Atomistic reasoning endorses a non-relational orientation toward understanding health illness: the role of dietetics is to "find the behavioural equivalents of protease inhibitors" (Buchanan, 2000, p. 46). Operating within this framework, dietetics is destined to occlude the chaotic and contingent experience of social and physical reality in which health "is the expression of the extent to which the individual and social body maintain in readiness the resources required to meet the exigencies of the future" (Dubos, 1962, as quoted in Kelly, Davies, & Charlton, 1997, p. 356).

As Austin (1999, p. 246) notes, "nutritional public health has demonstrated little understanding of anything outside of traditional materialist ideology," resulting in a systematically overdefined bedrock for the profession, one that crucially maintains "nutritional science's incognizance of its relationship to experiences of eating, dieting, and body image" (p. 246)—and, we would add, fat prejudice. For the socially aware dietitian there is an experience of caughtness in her positioning. Recognizing anti-fat sentiment in ideological rationalizations and knowing that "the meaning of the female body never exists outside context even though the body is never just contextual" (Eisenstein, 1996, p. 46), she is charged with using highly abstract, individualistic, and morally loaded nutrition rules regarding fat. Gender ideology is rarely articulated, and yet gender matters: poor nutrition, food poverty, and fat prejudice are feminized; both the diet industry and the dietetics profession are highly gendered arenas. Weight loss infomercials stereotypically show (lean) male nutrition experts instructing fat female clients (Blaine & McElroy, 2002); dietitian practitioners stereotypically are women, who translate into practice the nutritional discourse produced by mostly male scientists (Liquori, 2001). Such a discrete separation between genders within dietetics's scientific pursuit further disappears fat discourse. A feminist dietetics problematizes reliance on the ideal of value-neutrality as it questions the mutually exclusive dualities and hierarchies of "hard fact" embedded in the profession's ideology (and amply reflected in the field's dearth of qualitative research) (Fade, 2003). It prompts a rethink of how dietetic attitudes toward fatness and gender play a role in legitimating and constructing science. Reproducing the everydayness of gender in(e/i)quity may render sexualized (and racialized) fat-phobia invisible, but the fact that dietetics may not declare its politics does not mean that no politics are present. More typically, there is little space for professional self-reflexiveness.

Objectionable Images into the Abyss—You Must Hold Out the Poem

The decision thus far not to engage with feminist perspectives means that the physiological and psychological sequelae of trauma—frequently a gendered phenomenon—on eating remain distanced from mainstream dietetics's fatness discourse. Knowing that trauma and abuse disturb the individual's ability to self-regulate eating (Herman, 1994; Reto, 2003) has enormous therapeutic potential. If the dietetic enterprise is to be seen as a rigorous venture, we need to consider why these insights have been overlooked. Why are we averse to engaging with feminist understandings of physicality and fatness? Is it because we are a relatively young and largely female profession still intent on proving the patriarchal worth of our ideological passport?

Consider an advertisement that appeared as an insert with the *Canadian Journal of Dietetic Practice and Research* in the summer of 2005. The flyer, intended to promote the profession, was created for Canadian dietitians by their professional association, Dietitians of Canada, and by the Dairy Farmers of Canada. Permission for the image to appear here was denied. The flyer features a slender woman sitting cross-legged on one end of a balanced seesaw, with the other end weighted by a colorful array of "healthy" foods. The center panel reads, "Registered Dietitians are an essential part of a balanced eating plan . . . just like the four food groups," and in small print, "You can trust Registered Dietitians to give you good advice on nutrition. Their university training has given them the technical knowledge needed to master this most complex science." Underpinned by a coercive appeal to the authoritative status of (a biased) science—and shored up by reassurances of explicitly male-identified academic expertise and a corollary ghost line that is inherently disempowering insofar as it seeds insecurity by casting suspicion on the value of existing forms of women's nutritional know-how—the message is that the untutored reader-eater should proceed to their next bite with caution.

Further, the lesson is that (thin, disciplined) dietitians are inseparable from "a balanced eating plan" and that good nutrition requires academia and technology without equally acknowledging the non-dietitian's role as an everyday eater. In its particular choices, the ad has airbrushed in an intangible aura of medical approval toward sizeist beauty norms and fed the current consumerist ideology to create both the morally responsible eater (who takes heed of its insistence regarding the "must-have" dietitian) and their less-responsible foil (who insubordinately ignores this advice and goes it alone). The recommended approach to nutrition yields "eating plans" necessarily devised with a particular type of scientized input, in which culturally sensitive understandings of food, empathy, and intuition carry little weight. This devaluing of non-legitimated nutritional beliefs embodies an ethnocentric prejudice. And, in that it catalyses and normalizes distrust of appetite and body signals, it feeds eating dysregulation (Reto, 2003). The polarization of responsibility for feeding and nurturing others, eating distress and abuse in society, and escalating food dread among many means that the culturally sanctioned disruption of appetite has very real, very gendered penalties.

Accepting the triumph of reason leaves contemporary western anxieties over fatness, femaleness, and the limits of the scientific project unexplored. Without transparency and constructive critique of agendas, dietetics simply promotes patriarchal norms. As women seeking entry into professional spheres, we acknowledge the lure of these qualities, but embodying masculinism is obviously not without consequence. Bordo (as quoted in Spanier, 1995) asks, "How is objectivity related to objectification?" (p. 48).

Performing Dietitian—Cold Glass Against the Face of Death

We have seen how dietitians, aligning themselves uncritically with positivistic views on fatness, work hard to promote weight loss and regulate the individual and professional dietetic body (Stephen, 2004). Becoming a dietitian enables such a dietitian performativity, where performativity is the stylized repetition of acts, continual citing of past practices, and reiteration of known customs (Butler, 1999). The appearance of "dietitian" as recognizable is "a performative accomplishment which the mundane social audience, including the [dietitians] themselves, come to believe and to perform in the mode of belief" (Butler, 1999, p. 179). Appropriating Butler, the dietitian as being/body is "a variable boundary, a surface whose permeability is politically regulated, a signifying practice within a cultural field of gender hierarchy and compulsory heterosexuality . . . [and] possessing a conditional history with limited possibilities"

(p. 177). To say "that the dietitian body, the gendered body is performative . . . suggests that she has no being apart from the various acts which constitute her dietitian reality. These acts create a deliberate illusion that is discursively maintained for the purposes of its own regulation" (Gingras, 2006, p. 122). Given an education in reductionistic discourses and a gendered positioning within a society that abhors corpulence, it is troubling, but not surprising, to find anti-fat bias and resistance to size acceptance philosophies among dietitians.

If the dietitian being/body is a gendered performative possessing conditional history with limited possibilities, what agency might exist in her attempts to embrace alternative (size acceptance) discourses on fat? Butler's earlier contributions do not imply much hope: "Precisely at the moment in which choice is impossible, the subject pursues subordination as the promise of existence. Subjection exploits the desire for existence, where existence is always conferred from elsewhere; it marks a primary vulnerability to the Other to be" (Butler, 1997, p. 21). Butler reminds us that as we continue to try to change the world, we remain deeply tied to the world as it is by desire and the need for recognition (Love, 2004, p. 18–19). What's more, we are not held to give an account of ourselves in our misuse and misunderstandings of power, discourse, and knowledge.

In its entrapment in historic ways of seeing, unaware of context and perspective, dietetics demonstrates mindlessness. Langer and Moldoveanu (2000) highlight the health and social benefits of the related concept of mindfulness, which they describe as "a process of drawing novel distinctions [which] can lead to . . . a greater sensitivity to one's environment, more openness to new information, the creation of new categories for structuring perception, and enhanced awareness of multiple perspectives in problem solving" (p. 2). The authors detail how mindfulness helps bridge the shortfall in algorithmic problem solving, thereby influencing our cognitive investment in stereotypes, how we are to be trusted (Gingras, 2005), the questions we ask, and the research avenues that we explore—in short, providing us new avenues for stimulating our interpersonal and professional development.

Poetics, Mindfulness, Imagination—Something Amorphous Condenses

Can we, by definition, add anything to our understanding of amorphous? When trying to define that which stands for "the indefinable," that which is beyond scientific reach and reason becomes quickly lost in translation. The added value of amorphous is its unintelligibility. In its evocation of poetic knowing, the observation that "mindfulness is not a cold cognitive process . . . the whole individual is involved" (Langer & Moldoveanu, 2000, p. 2) invites us to confront institutionalized limits on appropriate methods of coming to awareness. Ideas and templates for infringing this complicity already exist inside (Gingras, 2006) and outside dietetics (Dias, 2003; Midgeley, 2001).

In relation with these alternatives it behooves us to ask how dietitians and others theorizing on fatness might embody radical poetic discourses that can alter dietetic ways of listening/learning/speaking/doing—and hence of being fat. Because poetry involves all the faculties of perception (Skelton, 1978)—including the cerebral, emotional, instinctual, sensual, spiritual, and erotic, plus an above-usual element of participation in language—it encourages mindfulness. Poetry's drivers are complexity, uncertainty, and revision. It confounds science's valorized tenet of absolute truth by exposing the relativity of reality. In the words of the quantum physicist Danah Zohar (1991, p. 85), "Truth happens . . . That does not mean that something is rightly portrayed, but rather that in the revelation, that which is a whole attains to unconcealment." Consider, for instance, a verse from the poem "Leftovers" by Lucy Aphramor (2005c, p. 1): "'*What type of bread?*' and '*Do you spread?*' / It is torture to sit here and regurgitate again on the sterile / scoop of your skull. It's about a half-baked vision, fulsomeness. / The way you clean your teeth of me. / There is a type of violence." In continuing to disappear feminist discourses on fat, we enact a type of violence. Offering poetic discourse is what Lorde (1984) describes as deciding to do our work consciously, because "our erotic knowledge empowers us," poetic musings save our lives, and it "is a grave responsibility, projected from within each of us, not to settle for the convenient, the shoddy, the conventionally expected, nor the merely safe" (p. 57). It is a grave responsibility not to commit any type of violence. In speaking for poetry, Dunlop (2002, sec. 5, para. 1) suggests that "all art begins in the locations where certainty ends. Poetry begins here, deeply rooted in the ambiguities, blood rememberings, human obsessions and desires that . . . may be capable measures of truth."

Much Left to Say—(in)Taciturnly

Imagination nurtures dietetic theory and practice (Berenbaum, 2005), whereas an impoverished imagination glorifies the status quo by silencing and repressing vulnerable, feminist texts (Gingras, 2005b). Poetry is born of the imagination, instigates rather than routinizes, and illuminates alternative ways of telling, knowing, and being a dietitian. Poetics enlivens the emotional capacity of dietetic practice, which buttresses a feminist dietetic ethics because our work is at its core a fundamentally human endeavor. Our intention with this chapter is to bring forward contemporary examples within dietetics where anti-fat, healthist discourse enacts a type of violence; to integrate social feminist theories on the body and gender performativity with dietetic theory, practice, and agency; and finally to offer mindfulness and poetics as reconciliatory discourses whereby difference is not viewed as deviance, and complicity is rarely tolerated. Throughout the text we have transgressed dominant discourse with poetics, striving for congruence in our argument, which suggests that poetics has a place among traditionally privileged discourses (even feminist discourses). We hold hope for our complicated and disruptive text to remind and refresh about what it means to be deeply human, questionable, and responsible.

REFERENCES

Aphramor, L. (2005a). *An audience with uncertainty*. IAQS, (Directed by P. Allender) Ellen Terry Building, Coventry University. November 25.

Aphramor, L. (2005b). Is a weight-centred health framework salutogenic? some thoughts on unhinging certain dietary ideologies. *Social Theory and Health, 3*, 315–340.

Aphramor, L. (2005c). Leftovers. In *Who says size matters? weighty issues: representation, identity, and practice in the areas of eating disorders, obesity, and body management.* Conference Presentation, University of the West of England, Bristol, UK: British Psychological Society.

Austin, S.B. (1999). Fat, loathing, and public health: the complicity of science in a culture of disordered eating. *Culture, Medicine, and Psychiatry, 23*, 245–268.

Baumann, A. (1989). The epidemiology of inequity. In V. Brown (Ed.), *Proceedings of a sustainable healthy future.* Melbourne: La Trobe University.

Berenbaum, S. (2005). Imagination nourishes dietetic practice: 2005 Ryley-Jeffs Memorial Lecture. *Canadian Journal of Dietetic Practice and Research, 66*, 193–196.

Blaine, B. & McElroy, J. (2002). Selling stereotypes: weight loss infomercials, sexism and weightism. *Sex Roles, 46*, 351–357.

British Dietetic Association. (2005). *Weight Wise and Food First Campaigns.* Retrieved May 15, 2006, from http://www.barnsleyfoodnetwork.org.uk/Projects/Weight%20Wise/.

British Dietetic Association. (2006). Celiac disease advertisement. *Dietetics Today, 41*(3), 11.

Buchanan, D. (2000). *An ethic for health promotion: rethinking the sources of human wellbeing.* Oxford: Oxford University Press.

Butler, J. (1997). *The psychic life of power: theories in subjection.* Stanford, CA: Stanford University Press.

Butler, J. (1999). *Gender trouble: feminism and the subversion of identity.* New York: Routledge.

DeVault, M. (1999). Whose science of food and health: narratives of profession and activism from public-health nutrition. In A. E. Clarke & V. L. Olesen (Eds.), *Revisioning women, health, and healing: feminist, cultural, and technoscience perspectives* (pp. 166–183). New York: Routledge.

Dias, K. (2003). The Ana sanctuary: women's pro-anorexia narratives in cyberspace. *Journal of International Women's Studies, 4*, 31–45.

Dorazio-Migliore, M., Migliore, S., & Anderson, J. M. (2005). Crafting a praxis-oriented culture concept in the health disciplines: conundrums and possibilities. *Health: An Interdisciplinary Journal for the Social Study of Health, Illness, and Medicine, 9*(3), 339–360.

Dunlop, R. (2002). Who will be the throat of these hours . . . if not I, if not you? *Educational Insights.* Retrieved February 23, 2004, from http://www.csci.educ.ubc.ca/publication/insights/v07n02/contextualexplorations/dunlop/.

Eisenstein, Z. (1996). *Hatreds: racialized and sexualized conflicts in the 21st Century.* London: Routledge.

Fade, S. (2003). Communicating and judging the quality of qualitative research: the need for a new language. *Journal of Human Nutrition and Dietetics, 16*, 139–149.

Gingras, J.R. (2006). Unkept: promises, secrets, and perils within dietetic education and practice. Unpublished dissertation, Faculty of Education, University of British Columbia, Vancouver, BC.

Gingras, J.R. (2005a). Evoking trust in the nutrition counselor: why should we be trusted? *Journal of Agricultural and Environmental Ethics, 18*, 57–74.

Gingras, J.R. (2005b). The defeat of imagination: repressive codes governing our media. *Feminist Media Studies, 5*(2), 255–257.

Herman, J. (1994). *Trauma and recovery: from domestic abuse to political terror*. Glasgow: Pandora.

Kelly, M., Davies, J., & Charlton, B. (1997). Healthy cities: a modern problem or a post-modern solution. In M. Sidell, L. Jones, J. Katz, & A. Peberdy (Eds.), *Debates and dilemmas in promoting health: a reader* (pp. 353–362). New York: Palgrave Macmillan.

Langer, E.J., & Moldoveanu, M. (2000). The construct of mindfulness. *Journal of Social Issues, 56*, 1–9.

Leahy, T. (2001). Reflections of a feminist sports psychologist. In G. Tenenbaum (Ed.), *The practice of sports psychology* (pp. 37–47). Morgantown, WV: Fitness Information Technology.

Levine, M., & Smolak, L. (1998). The mass media and disordered eating. In W. Vandereycken & G. Noordenbos (Eds.), *Prevention of Eating Disorders* (pp. 23–56). London: Athlone Press.

Liquori, T. (2001). Food matters: changing dimensions of science and practice in the nutrition profession. *Journal of Nutrition Education, 33*, 234–246.

Lorde, A. (1984). Uses of the erotic: the erotic as power. In *Sister/outsider* (pp. 53–59). Freedom, CA: Crossing Press.

Love, H. (2004). Dwelling in ambivalence. *The Women's Review of Books, 22*(2), 18–19.

Midgeley, M. (2001). *Science and poetry*. London: Routledge.

Ministry of Education, Wellington. (2003). *For whose benefit? the politics of developing a health education curriculum*. Retrieved February 3, 2006, from http://tki.org.nz/r/health/curric_devt/tasker1_e.php.

Reto, C. (2003). Psychological aspects of delivering nursing care to the bariatric patient. *Critical Care Nursing Quarterly, 26*, 139–149.

Skelton, R. (1978). *Poetic truth*. London: Heinemann.

Spanier, B. (1995). *Im/partial science: gender ideology in molecular biology*. Bloomington: Indiana University Press.

Stephen, A. (2004). The challenges of obesity management. *Journal of Human Nutrition and Dietetics, 17*, 501–502.

Travers, K.D. (1995). "Do you teach them how to budget?" professional discourse in the construction of nutritional inequities. In D. Maurer & J. Sobal (Eds.), *Eating agendas: food and nutrition as social problems* (pp. 213–240). New York: Aldine de Gruyter.

Zohar, D. (1991). *The quantum self*. London: Flamingo.

Fatness (In)visible

Polycystic Ovarian Syndrome and the
Rhetoric of Normative Femininity

Christina Fisanick

It is estimated that 6 to 10 percent of all women have polycystic ovarian syndrome (PCOS), an endocrine disorder characterized by "obesity," male pattern hair growth and loss, irregular menstruation and infertility, and skin abnormalities such as skin tags, adult acne, and dark patches of skin under the armpits and between the thighs (Thatcher, 2000). Despite its prevalence, PCOS is often misdiagnosed or not diagnosed at all, leading Dr. Samuel Thatcher to dub it "the hidden epidemic" (p. 14). It is difficult to miss the irony (intended or not) in this designation. After all, in our image-obsessed culture, it would be hard to miss a three-hundred-pound, balding woman with a moustache. Reductive though this characterization is, it nonetheless represents a crucial way of thinking about PCOS and the bodies of women who have the syndrome. That is, women with PCOS have highly visible bodies but are coded by normative femininity as invisible.

On Be(com)ing a Woman: Negotiating Normative Femininity

To understand the ways in which women with PCOS both subscribe to and resist normative femininity, it is important to reiterate the current conversation surrounding femininity. Femininity is not a descriptor, but rather an ideological system in which all people participate. As Sandra Bartky (1997, p. 132) writes, "We are born male or female, but not masculine or feminine. Femininity is an artifice, an achievement, 'a mode of enacting and reenacting received gender norms which surface as so many styles of the flesh.'" The female body, then, is femininity's site for struggle and its vehicle for expression and coercion. Although corsets have long been banished from our everyday attire, we are faced with a more binding, more constrictive force than just strings and whalebone; we must struggle each day, each moment, within the bounds of an ideology that we can barely render visible, let alone easily resist. Femininity relies on a system of negation—no calluses, no bulges, no hair in the wrong places—and also a system of contradiction—produce children, but do not store enough fat to ovulate or have muscle tone; do not be strong, either. Coupled with its ability to conceal its own genesis and disguise its disciplinarians, femininity is a project doomed to failure.

It is in the arenas of negation and contradiction that the PCOS body excels. The PCOS body is at once a condition of excess—too much hair, too much fat, too much testosterone—and a condition of lack—too little hair, too little progesterone, too little ovulation. It is at once the body of the fertility goddess, the mother (large breasts, wide hips, round belly), and infertile. It has too much facial hair and not enough head hair. It is both male (excess testosterone) and female (genitalia). Is there a possibility, then, in this state of excess, of being both hyper-feminine and unfeminine—for women with PCOS and their bodies to subvert the dominant regime of normative femininity?

Subverting the System: Revealing the PCOS Body

The PCOS body—fat, irregular, infertile, and hairy—attempts to accomplish this subversion, but the body alone is not enough to alter the oppressive system of normative femininity, especially when the body is, as Charisse Goodman calls it, a "full-figured phantom," invisible in all ways that matter (1995, p. 25). Rather, it takes an actor to effect change by the way the acts are read and repeated.

Although there is no doubt that the fat female body and other so-called unfeminine bodies (hairy, disabled, disfigured) resist the norms of femininity by their very existence, I do not think that this resistance alone is enough to make a real difference in the larger project of demystifying and dismantling normative femininity. If demolishing femininity were as easy as simply getting fat, then, according to recent statistics, the problem of femininity would already be resolved, given that millions of American women are considered to be "overweight." Therefore, dismantling femininity must require much more than simply not looking the part. As Kathleen LeBesco notes, "We need some way of discerning which actions are truly disruptive of so-called normalcy, and which in fact help to maintain the status quo. . . . What performance in what context will help to destabilize naturalized identity categories?" (2001, p. 77). A look at the recent activities of the Polycystic Ovarian Syndrome Association (PCOSA) might reveal the distinction between acts that are actually transgressive and acts that simply appear to be so.

From its genesis as an Internet-based support group in 1995, PCOSA has evolved into an international nonprofit organization dedicated to educating the public, including patients, friends, and health-care providers, about the prevalence of the syndrome and its long-term health risks, such as heart disease and diabetes. As the organization has grown in membership and status, its efforts to increase awareness of PCOS have included yearly conferences, fund-raisers, and international publicity campaigns. Not all of the PCOSA efforts, however, have been successful in subverting conventional attitudes about PCOS and the women who have the syndrome. In 2004, PCOSA announced that it had found its spokeswoman—Tulin Reid, a well-known plus-size fashion model. Reid is a beautiful woman who, "despite" weighing about 160 pounds, conforms to many of the standards of femininity. She has full, shiny hair, no facial hair, smooth, clear skin, and well-proportioned hips and thighs. It was clear, however, that the woman that she was before "dealing with" the syndrome—when her "hair was falling out in handfuls, [she] had acne and [her] weight exploded from a fit 160 pounds to 250+ pounds in less than two months"—and the woman that she was after "a workout and eating plan" represented the before-and-after pictures that fat women are all too familiar with (PCOSA, 2004). In her "after" mode, Reid was not dangerous or disturbing or transgressive. She was a beautiful woman talking about the way she looked "before," when she was "unfit." As Le'a Kent (2001) notes about this before-and-after phenomenon, the fat person in this scenario does not exist. In essence, by choosing Tulin Reid as the spokeswoman for the syndrome, PCOSA effectively obeyed the rules of femininity, made the PCOS body invisible, erasing it out of existence. (In April 2005, Reid stepped down from her position as PCOSA spokesperson to devote her time to promoting her Web site, http://www.PCOSLiving.com. The position has not been refilled.)

I am not trying to belittle or demean Reid or PCOSA, but I am trying to illuminate the distinction between choosing a publicly acceptable body and choosing an "unacceptable" one to represent women who have a syndrome that makes their bodies unfeminine in so many ways. Reid represents the "after" picture—the possibilities of what you can look like if you beat the syndrome, which far too few women manage to do. And even those women who do manage to defeat PCOS usually find that the symptoms creep back over time. Reid was willing to tell the world about her struggles with a syndrome that defeminizes women, yet she did not have an unfeminine body. Perhaps some women found Reid inspiring, but to others she represented all that they wished, but would always fail, to be. I am not trying to essentialize the PCOS body, because it certainly can take many forms, including thin, clear-skinned, and thick-haired, but I am saying that PCOSA's chosen spokeswoman was not a representative with whom most women with PCOS could clearly identify.

Many questions arise from PCOSA's endeavors to make PCOS visible. Certainly, the organization desires to make the medical community and the general public aware of the syndrome, but at the same time, PCOSA wants the body that represents the PCOS body to be acceptable, to conform as much as possible to the standards of normative femininity. Is this attempt intended to make PCOSA and PCOS seem as credible as possible? After all, American culture sees fat women as silly, sloppy, lazy, and dishonest, among other negative qualities. On top of that, to have a fat, hairy, balding woman as a representative? Unseemly.

Then again, if these are truly the cultural interpretations of the PCOS body, could displaying such a body be transgressive? If PCOSA chose to use the body of an everyday woman with PCOS (and really, who would that be? what would she look like?) as its representative, would she be ignored, disregarded, not taken seriously because of the way her body is marked? Or could her very presence as a representative of the syndrome give her form credibility and thereby give credibility to the bodies of other women who have the syndrome?

The PCOS body has great potential to transgress the boundaries of normative femininity. In all of its hairy, balding fatness, the PCOS body represents a challenge to what is expected of the female body. The problem is that it lacks visibility. It is hidden within the matrix of cultural expectations, and attempts to make the PCOS body visible are regulated not only by society but by women with PCOS as well. Therefore, ways must be developed to put the PCOS body into the spotlight. Perhaps PCOSA could appoint a spokeswoman who occupies a more typical PCOS body to speak about and visibly represent women with the condition. Also, women with PCOS can become more involved in the activities of PCOSA, the National Association to Advance Fat Acceptance (NAAFA), and other organizations fighting for the acceptance of diversity in body type and kind. Finally, fat and thin allies can join together to raise awareness about this condition and to help women with PCOS move beyond the confines of normative femininity, thus benefiting not only women with the syndrome but all other women as well.

NOTE

Portions of this chapter were previously published as "Too fat, too hairy, too (in)visible: Polycystic Ovarian Syndrome and normative femininity," in *Gender Forum*, November 2005. © Christina Fisanick.

REFERENCES

Bartky, S. (1997). Foucault, femininity, and the modernization of patriarchal power. In K. Conboy, N. Medina, & S. Stanbury (Eds.), *Writing on the Body: Female Embodiment and Feminist Theory*. New York: Columbia University Press.

Goodman, W. C. (1995). *The Invisible Woman: Confronting Weight Prejudice in America*. Carlsbad, CA: Gurze Books.

Kent, L. (2001). Fighting abjection: Representing fat women. In J.E. Braziel & K. LeBesco (Eds.), *Bodies Out of Bounds: Fatness and Transgression*. Berkeley: University of California Press.

LeBesco, K. (2001). Queering fat bodies/politics. In J.E. Braziel & K. LeBesco (Eds.), *Bodies Out of Bounds: Fatness and Transgression*. Berkeley: University of California Press.

Polycystic Ovarian Syndrome Association (PCOSA). (2004, February 12). Tulin Reid named as national spokesperson for PCOSA. Retrieved February 19, 2007, from http://www.pco-support.org/spokesperson.php.

Thatcher, S. (2000). *PCOS, Polycystic Ovarian Syndrome: The Hidden Epidemic*. Indianapolis, IN: Perspectives Press.

Part III

Fatness as Social Inequality

Welcome to Part III of The Fat Studies Reader

Fatness as Social Inequality

These chapters address from a variety of perspectives the relationship between fatness and prejudice, discrimination, and other effects of social inequality. Attention is paid to the intersections of fatness with other characteristics, including youth, motherhood, gender, gender identity, and national origin.

After reading these chapters consider the following discussion questions:

Given the commonplace discourse of a "childhood obesity epidemic," what blame is placed on mothers and how does race factor into the discussion?

How does a cultural heritage of hostility toward fatness influence the bullying of fat youth?

Is bullying of fat youth and violence toward fat women a predictable consequence of current attitudes toward fatness? If so, what can be done about it?

Identify five strategies to make schools or family life safer for fat children.

What challenges exist within gay male culture for fat men and their admirers?

How does the viewer's perception of a person's sex or gender change the perception of fatness?

Why would what is "fat" for women differ from what is "fat" for men?

How does fat oppression affect women differently than others?

What similarities exist between struggles for equality between fat and transgender people using the legal system?

Should fat or transgender advocates focus on advancing the rights of the individual or the rights of the group if they cannot do both? What are the pros and cons of each position?

Describe the association between fatness and masculinity. Also describe the association between fatness and femininity.

Is there a way to fairly assign costs for airplane travel without treating fat people differently than other passengers?

What are the consequences for the lives of fat people of a policy that requires them to pay twice as much for travel as their thin peers? What are the implications for economic class and race?

Should airplanes, schools, and places of public accommodation be free to adjust seat size as they see fit?

How does stigma against fat people affect their ability to succeed in professions, including academia?

Fat Kids, Working Moms, and the "Epidemic of Obesity"
Race, Class, and Mother Blame

Natalie Boero

Introduction

The centrality of children to the "epidemic of obesity" has led to a search for the "causes" and "cures" of childhood fatness. In scientific and medical literature and the media, too much fast food, too much television, and too little exercise are seen as the main culprits (Boero, 2007). Yet one does not have to dig far below the surface to find a distinct trend of "mother blame" in common sense and professional understandings of both the causes of and interventions into this "epidemic of childhood obesity." As they are usually charged with the preparation, regulation, and purchase of food for their children, mothers—working mothers in particular—are held responsible for children's "poor" eating patterns and their assumed-related "obesity" (DeVault, 1991; Hochschild, 1989).

The weight of one's children has increasingly become a litmus test of good mothering. In her work, Sondra Solovay (2000) chronicles the dramatic cases of Christina Corrigan, a 680-pound thirteen-year-old whose mother was charged with felony child abuse/endangerment after Christina's tragic death, and "Zach Smuller," a young boy whose father threatened to fight his mother for custody of him because she could not or would not make him lose weight. The children's mothers were at the center of both the media attention to the cases (particularly the Corrigan case). Both the Corrigan and "Smuller" cases are chilling examples of the threats faced by fat children and their families amid the "obesity epidemic." Yet in this chapter I use examples from mainstream print media to argue that the mother blame associated with the size of children's bodies extends far beyond these "extreme" examples and has integrated itself into the everyday discourse and experience of mothering. I argue that as with other historic and contemporary examples of mother blame, evaluating the fitness of mothers based on the size of their children obscures larger structural issues of racism, economic inequality, fat phobia, and sexism among others.

Mother Blame

Mother blame is not new. Explaining social problems by pinpointing the failures of "bad" mothers has long been a part of popular and professional understandings of phenomena as widely divergent as homosexuality, crime, autism, depression, poverty, and birth defects. As Ladd-Taylor and Umansky (1998) suggest, however, this tendency to blame mothers has expanded and intensified in the past fifty years, exacerbating the social, economic, legal, and personal repercussions felt by those deemed "bad" mothers.

The blaming of mothers is intimately connected to cultural anxieties around the changing social roles of women (Singh, 2004; Vander Ven & Vander Ven, 2003). The cultural landscape is peppered with references to stereotypical "bad" moms—working mothers, welfare moms, teenage mothers, queer moms, and single mothers to name but a few. What all of these stereotypes share is that they highlight the normative conception of good mothering that assumes that good mothers are heterosexual, white, middle class, and do not work outside the home (Ladd-Taylor & Umansky, 1998). As Katha Pollitt (1998) points out, mother blame has now expanded into the womb with an increasing right-wing push for "fetal rights" and the increased surveillance of pregnant women. As I discuss below, this focus on the fetus is now front and center in the discourse of mother blame surrounding childhood "obesity."

Feminists have critiqued historical and contemporary mother blame as a patriarchal institution designed both to obscure the social conditions under which women mother and to naturalize the characteristics of those who fit into the social construct of the "good mother" (Anderson, George, & Nease, 2002; Garrey & Arendell, 1999). Indeed, in 1998 Ladd-Taylor and Umansky edited an entire volume on mother blame. In spite of this attention on the part of feminists, one particularly widespread and consequential form of mother blame has been all but left out of these critiques—the blaming of mothers for the fatness of their children.

Fatness and Mother Blame

Blaming mothers for the fatness of their children is not a new phenomenon. As early as the 1930s Dr. Hilde Bruch, in her work on eating disorders, suggested that mothers should be held responsible for having "overweight" children (Bruch, 1973). Bruch was especially critical of immigrant mothers whose fat children failed to fit the image of middle-class American citizenship (Saukko, 1999). This focus on the practices of minority and immigrant mothers resonates with current discussions of "childhood obesity" that point to African American and Hispanic populations as particularly problematic.

As with other forms of mother blame, the issue of "permissive" or "smothering" mothers was central to Bruch's theory. Bruch's writings on "obesity" are filled with examples of mothers who overfed their children to show affection, to reward, to placate, to assuage guilt, and to encourage dependency. Bruch (1973) also linked fatness in children, particularly boys, to effeminacy and homosexuality, thus intertwining mother blame, fatness, and homosexuality in a particularly potent way.

Others (Schwartz, 1986; Stearns, 1997) have also given historical examples of blaming mothers for having larger-than-average children. Hillel Schwartz suggests that the first American weight watchers were the health reformers of the early twentieth century, like Sylvester Graham and his disciples. For Graham, the battle against excesses in food would be fought "within the home, at table, by women" (Schwartz, 1986). Graham's focus on food simplicity reflected the moral reformism of the time and the need to defeat the evil of gluttony, yet none of these examples can compare with the hysteria and moralism seen in the more recent ratcheting up of mother blame in the context of the "obesity epidemic."

Mother Blame and the "Obesity Epidemic"

A culture of sloth and a sedentary lifestyle are popular targets in the media when looking for the origins of childhood obesity. Because children are constructed as more passive and vulnerable to the influences of advertising, those aspects of American culture and personal behavior that are individualized in discussions of adult obesity are not so individualized in discussions of childhood obesity. Implicit in this critique of American culture is a blame of working mothers for allowing their children to watch too much television, for not having their eating habits more closely monitored, and for relying on convenience foods for meals.

An article from the *New York Times* expresses this early concern: "In many households today, both parents work, so kids return to an empty house and settle in front of the television" (Williams, 1990, p. C1) This quote doesn't explicitly mention mothers, but when "both parents work," it is mothers, whose paid work is often seen as unnecessary, who are to blame for children being home alone (Hochschild, 1989; DeVault, 1991). In more recent article in the *San Francisco Chronicle*, a weight researcher places the onus on working parents, saying, "We have parents working so there is nobody home making a real meal and sitting down with the kids to eat. Kids are eating way too many carbs. They need not to be propped up in front of the TV or the computer" (Schevitz, 2003, p. A1). Working mothers have also been a target of weight researchers. In an article headlined "New Wake-Up Call: Study Ties Kids' Obesity to Mom's Job" (Lundstrom, 2002), the *Sacramento Bee* reports on a study titled "Maternal Employment and Overweight Children," which claims to have found that working mothers are more likely to have "overweight" children. Neither the article nor the study, however, discussed that possible correlations between the employment status of mothers and the size of children could be influenced by other factors, most notably socioeconomic status.

Beyond working mothers, families in general are often targets of blame in the "obesity epidemic" (Boero, 2007; Solovay, 2000). Shunting aside macro-structural issues, the same *Times* article reports, "Experts say they are now beginning to realize what sociologists and family therapists have long understood: that just about everything begins at home—in this case, health and fitness. Unfortunately, many noted, they also appear to end there" (Williams, 1990, p. C1). Similar to the individualizing concepts of control and willpower in explaining fatness in adults, explanations of fatness in children focus on culture generally and the family specifically, even as they avoid targeting children as individuals. Given their association with nature as well as their role in the transmission of culture, mothers come under fire from weight researchers. As children are held less personally responsible for their weight, mothers are viewed as passing on poor eating habits. As one researcher quoted in the *New York Times* said, "If the child learns to eat from their overweight parent, who learned from their overweight parent, and Mom buys the same way and does the same thing she did years ago, and now that kid isn't even running and jumping the way kids used to, that child is in trouble" (Lombardi, 1997, p. WC1). Mothers of color are particular targets in explaining high rates of "childhood obesity" among Hispanic and African Americans, and increasingly popular "community" programs designed to abate or prevent "obesity" in these populations focus on women and mothers as significant points of intervention. In a *New York Times* article on a program to prevent childhood obesity (Kolata, 2000), ethnic culture specifically emerges as a culprit, and "educating" mothers is seen as an appropriate intervention. This article tells the story of Maria Sanchez and her children, participants in an experimental weight loss program for Mexican American families at Stanford University. The article goes on to detail what the Sanchez family is "doing wrong": "The Stanford program, which labels foods red, yellow, or green, with meanings like a traffic signal's, deems Pan Dulce to be red" (Kolata, 2000, p. A1). Having discovered this, Mrs. Sanchez quickly switches from pan dulce (sweet baked goods) to cereal and nonfat milk for her family's breakfast.

The problem of culture here is larger than individual households, because these families also have to deal with other "social obstacles—like dinner at grandmother's house" (Kolata, 2000, p. A1); eating in extended families and community groups also runs counter to a more "modern" meal schedule, in which meals are eaten at home, prepared by mom, and thus more tightly controlled (DeVault 1991; Orbach 1978). In this sense, culture is ethnic, and eating standardized, low and nonfat "green light" foods prepared within the context of the nuclear family comes to be seen as the "natural" and "healthy" way to eat.

Another article in the *New York Times* (Marcus, 1998) details a similar "obesity prevention" program in a poor rural community in Alabama. According to the *Times*, program leaders are attempting to improve community health by "teaching women how to stay well by changing their behavior . . . and doing the unthinkable—banishing collard greens smothered in fatback and other traditional high-fat favorites in the rural South" (Marcus, 1998, p. 24). Like the above quote on fat parents passing "bad" eating habits on to their children, but with a slightly more nostalgic tone, program leaders suggest that they are "building on community talent with women who are cooking for their children and passing on behaviors to their children and their children's children" (p. 24). Thus, an analysis of macro-level social determinants of health is shunted aside in favor of a focus on "unhealthy" or ethic cultures.

As Katha Pollitt (1998) suggests, mother blame has now made its way into the womb, and the case of "childhood obesity" is no exception. In particular, pregnant fat women are warned that their own weight before and during pregnancy puts their fetus at risk for any number of things, including becoming a fat child. In 2004, the *Omaha World Herald* ran a story headlined "Campaign Highlights the Risk Obesity Poses to the Unborn" (Johnson, 2004). In the article, authors of a study on "obesity" and pregnancy suggest that fat women should try to lose weight before getting pregnant to avoid premature birth, cesarean section, gestational diabetes, and "obesity" in their unborn children. The article reports that even the March of Dimes has gotten involved and began distributing packets throughout the Nebraska "that describe steps to control obesity and other risks of early labor" (Johnson, 2004, p. 1B).

The main thrust of the mother blaming surrounding childhood "obesity" is that mothers of fat children just cannot win. In 2003, *USA Today* (Elias, 2003) published an article titled "Moms Often Unaware that Kids Are Overweight." The article reports that only two-thirds of mothers with children deemed "overweight" by current standards "correctly" classified their kids as such. The researchers were more concerned with the remaining third of mothers who labeled their "overweight" children "just right." Setting aside the issue of whether a child could be "overweight" *and* "just right," this article takes what I call the "maternal blindness" approach to children's weight. The researchers in this camp suggest that we need to educate mothers about how to determine whether their children weigh too much. Of course, mothers are also warned that if they "obsess" about weight—their own or that of their children—they run the risk that their children will too, and thus suffer from low self-esteem and possibly develop an eating disorder (Vander Ven & Vander Ven, 2003). Thus, moms again are left to navigate the increasingly "thin" line between "ignoring" their children's weight and overemphasizing it.

In the days of Hilde Bruch, the conventional wisdom has been that the mothers of fat children are too permissive and overindulge their children with "bad" food. This attitude continues today; an editorial in the *New York Times* suggests that "growing rates of childhood obesity in the United States may be tied, at least in part, to the fact that American children seem more out of control and ill-behaved than ever. And that that's because parents seem more ineffective and less likely to tell their children 'no' than ever" (Anon., 2003, p. 12). This quote not only encapsulates taken-for-granted assumptions about the parents of fat children, but it also illustrates prevailing fat-phobic understandings of fat children as out of control. These understandings only become more insidious as fat children become fat adults.

Although the image of the permissive or ignorant mother may predominate in discussions of fat children, recently much attention has been given to the possible relationship between strict parenting and "obesity" among children. A widely reported study from the Boston University School of Medicine suggests that although children of "permissive" parents are likely to be fat, children of strict parents are even more likely to have "weight problems" (Staff, 2006). The article quotes study authors as saying that parents should not force their children to exercise, as they may cause their kids to develop an aversion to exercise in the future. Ironically, those who would see "permissive" parenting as problematic would likely encourage a focus on exercise that the above researchers would see as too strict. The issue is not that one of these perspectives is correct; the issue is that, like so much of parenting advice, the "professional" knowledge around kids and "obesity" puts mothers in a situation where no matter what they do, they are putting their children at "risk."

Conclusion

Like other forms of mother blame, mother blaming in the context of the "obesity epidemic" is as much or more about social anxieties regarding the changing role of women, as well as the changing racial and ethnic composition of the nation, than it is about any real public health "crisis." Like the social construction of the "obesity epidemic" in general, the blaming of mothers for their kids' "excess" weight draws attention away from very real structural inequalities in health care, education, and employment that are often felt hardest by women and minorities.

The stakes around the issue of "childhood obesity" are high for parents and children. In an era when fat children can be taken from their parents under the guise of child "welfare," and when fat children and fat people in general continue to be discriminated against and subjected to risky and ineffective weight loss procedures, the critical analysis of the "obesity epidemic" becomes ever more urgent. The health of children is not served by the panic over childhood "obesity," and it is certainly not served by blaming mothers.

Given the function of the "obesity epidemic" to draw attention away from structural inequality, as well as the ways in which mother blame for childhood "obesity" ties in with other forms of mother blame, one would think that feminists would have taken up the issue of fat rights in the same way they have championed reproductive rights, the rights of working women, and the rights of children. I argue, however, that a general cultural acceptance of the "fat = unhealthy" equation, along with a larger societal fat phobia, in part explains why the "obesity epidemic" is only now beginning to be critically deconstructed by mainstream feminism and social science. This situation strongly makes the case for an interdisciplinary field of fat studies in which scholars and activists can consider the increasing intertwining of sexism, homophobia, racism, classism, and fat phobia, among other issues.

REFERENCES

Anonymous. (November 16, 2003). Eating well: Start them young. *New York Times*, p. 12.
Anderson, J., George, J., & Nease, J. (2002). Requirements, risks, and responsibility: Mothering and fathering in books about raising boys. *Analyses of Social Issues and Public Policy*, 2, 205–221.
Boero, N. (2007). All the news that's fat to print: The American "obesity epidemic" and the media. *Qualitative Sociology*, 2, 41–61.

Bruch, H. (1973). *Eating disorders: Obesity, and anorexia nervosa, and the person within.* New York: Basic Books.

DeVault, M. (1991). *Feeding the family: The social organization of caring as gendered work.* Chicago: University of Chicago Press.

Elias, M. (2003). New study confirms parents must lead the way in kids' weight loss. *USA Today*, p. D9.

Garrey, A., & Arendell, T. (1999). Children, work, and family: Some thoughts on "mother blame." Working Paper No. 4. Center for Working Families: University of California, Berkeley.

Hochschild, A. (1989). *The second shift: Working parents and the revolution at home.* New York: Viking Press.

Johnson, S. (July 1, 2004). Campaign highlights risk obesity poses to the unborn. *Omaha World Herald*, p. 1B.

Kolata, G. (October 19, 2000). When children grow fatter, experts search for solutions. *New York Times*, p. A1.

Ladd-Taylor, M., & Umansky, L. (1998). Introduction. In M. Ladd-Taylor & L. Umansky (Eds.), *"Bad" mothers: The politics of blame in twentieth-century America.* New York: New York University Press.

Lombardi, K.S. (July 20, 1997). Treating child obesity: From healthy eating to working out. *New York Times*, WC1.

Lundstrom, M. (November 21, 2002). New wake-up call: Study ties kids' obesity to mom's job. *Sacramento Bee*, A3.

Marcus, F.F. (June, 21, 1998). Why baked catfish holds lessons for their hearts. *New York Times*, p. 24.

Orbach, S. (1978). *Fat is a feminist issue.* New York: Berkley Books.

Pollitt, K. (1998). "Fetal rights": A new assault on feminism. In M. Ladd-Taylor & L. Umansky (Eds.), *"Bad" mothers: The politics of blame in twentieth-century America.* New York: New York University Press.

Saukko, P. (1999). Fat boys and goody girls: Hilde Bruch's work on eating disorders and the American anxiety about democracy, 1930–1960. In J. Sobal & D. Maurer (Eds.), *Weighty issues: Fatness and thinness as social problems.* New York: Aldine de Gruyter.

Schevitz, T. (August 4, 2003). Routine screening for obesity urged for kids; Body-mass index test should be tool, doctors' group says. *San Francisco Chronicle*, A1.

Schwartz, H. (1986). *Never satisfied: A cultural history of diets, fantasies, and fat.* London: Collier Macmillan.

Singh, I. (2004). Doing their jobs: Mothering with Ritalin in a culture of mother-blame. *Social Science and Medicine, 59*, 2, 1193–1205.

Solovay, S. (2000). *Tipping the scales of justice: Fighting weight based discrimination.* Amherst: Prometheus Books.

Staff. (June 5, 2006). Disciplinarian parents have fat kids—U.S. study. Reuters. Retrieved April 5, 2009, from http://www.redorbit.com/news/health/527070/disciplinarian_parents_have_fat_kidsus_study/index.html.

Stearns, P. (1997). *Fat history: Bodies and beauty in the modern west.* New York: New York University Press.

Vander Ven, T., & Vander Ven, M. (2003). Exploring patterns of mother-blaming in anorexia scholarship: A study in the sociology of knowledge. *Human Studies, 26*, 97–119.

Williams, L. (March 22, 1990). Growing up flabby in America. *New York Times*, C1.

Fat Youth as Common Targets for Bullying

Jacqueline Weinstock and Michelle Krehbiel

> Somehow I have managed to make it through high school, but it was
> a tough battle laced with thoughts of suicide and depression. I have
> had one serious boyfriend, but he always put me down, too . . . I am
> not completely through my journey. I still have issues, depression,
> and no self-esteem. I still get teased. (*Radiance*, 2004)

Are certain youth more likely than other youth to become victims of bullying? Although researchers debate this question, it is increasingly clear that being fat makes a youth an easy and common target for bullies. In this chapter, we explore the extent and impact of bullying on youth who are fat, identify the factors that likely contribute to the targeting of these youth, and reflect on strategies for intervening with and preventing this targeted bullying.

The Problem of Youth Bullying

Youth bullying is now recognized as a serious problem, one with both concurrent and long-term negative effects (Craig & Pepler, 2003; Rigby, 2003). Prevalence estimates range widely across studies, with 15–30% of youth reporting some type of involvement in bullying. Among those involved, 7–13% are bullies, 9–30% victims, and 1–13% both bullies and victims (or bully-victims) (see, e.g., Demaray & Malecki, 2003; Griffiths, Wolke, Page, & Horwood, 2005; Nansel, Overpeck, Pilla, Ruan, Simons-Morton, & Scheidt, 2001; Olweus, 1993). Garbarino and deLara (2002) argue that even the higher-range estimates likely underrepresent the full extent of the problem. Bullying has been identified among preschool children through to adolescents, and may reach its peak in the middle school years (Greenya, 2005; Nansel et al., 2001), with middle childhood being the time period when particular youth become regular targets/victims of bullying (Randall, 2001).

Definitions of bullying vary widely, yet there is increasing agreement among researchers that bullying "is a specific type of aggression in which (1) the behavior is intended to harm or disturb, (2) the behavior occurs repeatedly over time, and (3) there is an imbalance of power, with the more powerful person or group attacking a less powerful one" (Nansel et al., 2001, p. 2094). The power imbalance may be physical, psychological, or social; whatever the type, victims have a difficult time defending themselves.

Consequences of Youth Bullying

Despite popular myths that bullying toughens youth up, bullying clearly has negative concurrent and long-term consequences for bullies, victims, and bully-victims. Even bystanders—those who are aware of bullying but not directly involved—are negatively affected (Craig & Pepler, 2003). Direct victims of bullying are particularly harmed, experiencing a variety of psychosocial consequences including lower self-esteem; increased risk for depression, loneliness, anxiety, and behavior problems; feeling unhappy and unsafe at school; and being rejected by peers and lacking in friends or social support (see, e.g., Eisenberg & Aalsma, 2005; Griffiths et al., 2005; Nansel et al., 2001; Swearer, Grills, Haye, & Cary, 2004). Mishna and Alaggia (2005) go as far as to suggest that victimization may affect all areas of an individual's life. The negative effects have been associated with long-term problems such as difficulties with sexual relationships, physical health, and even cognitive dysfunctions of memory and attention (Randall, 2001). Like hate crimes, bullying sends a message to the victims—and to those who are (or believe they are) similar to these victims—that they are unacceptable, bad, wrong, inferior, and so forth. All too frequently, this message is internalized.

Bullying and Fat Youth

Only a few research studies have explicitly examined the relationship between bullying and weight. These studies suffer from many of the same challenges as other research on bullying—for example, heavy reliance on cross-sectional research designs and limited attention to whether identified patterns vary by a respondent's age, race, socioeconomic status, or sexual orientation. Yet the available literature indicates that the targeting of fat children is not only common but also commonly accepted.

Rates and Consequences of Victimization

Rates of bullying and the consequences of bullying based on weight vary according to the population studied and research questions asked, but in all available studies, reported rates have been quite high (see Puhl & Latner, 2007, for a recent review). For example, in Hayden-Wade, Stein, Ghaderi, Saelens, Zabinski, and Wilfrey's (2005) study of the prevalence of teasing experiences in a sample of seventy children categorized as overweight and eighty-six children not so categorized, the children in the overweight category reported significantly more teasing or criticism about some aspect of their appearance (78% vs. 37%). Further, of all the children who reported being teased, those in the overweight category reported significantly more teasing about their weight in particular (89% vs. 31%). The children in the overweight category also reported more frequent and longer-lasting teasing, and they reported being more upset by the teasing, than the children in the non-overweight category. Most significant, the degree of weight-related teasing was significantly positively correlated with concerns about weight, reported loneliness, and preference for solitary/sedentary activities, and negatively associated with physical appearance self-perception and enjoyment of active/ social activities. In another more recent and large-scale study, Geier and colleagues (2007) found that elementary schoolchildren who were classified as overweight were absent from school significantly more (for an average of almost two whole days) than their non–overweight classified peers. The authors suggest that children who are overweight may miss school to avoid peer ostracism, especially on days with gym class. Less likely in play are health-related factors, they argue, because the link between weight and health has not been shown to be as strong among children as among adults. In another study of ninety-two children and adolescents with a body mass index classified as overweight or at risk for overweight, researchers found that peer victimization was common and positively associated with self-reported symptoms of depression, loneliness, general anxiety, and social physique anxiety, while being negatively associated with physical activity (Storch, Milsom, DeBraganza, Lewin, Geffken, & Silverstein, 2007). Finally, in a large study of over 4,700 middle and high school youth, almost 25% reported being teased about their weight at least a few times a year, while 63% of girls and 58% of boys defined as "obese" reported experiencing some form of weight-based teasing (Eisenberg, Neumark-Sztainer, & Story, 2003; Neumark-Sztainer et al., 2002). Further, of those teased about their weight, 28.6% of girls and 16.1% of boys reported family members; 63% of girls and 24.7% of boys reported peers; and almost 15% of girls and 10% of boys reported both as sources of weight-based teasing. The available evidence clearly indicates that children and adolescents who are fat are often victimized, and the rates, sources, and consequences of bullying are startling and disturbing.

Causes of Weight-Based Bullying and Bullying Directed at Youth Who Are Fat

What are the causes of weight-based bullying and bullying directed at youth who are fat? Rather than address this important question, too many researchers focus on identifying the negative consequences to youth of *being* fat, and they do so with little attention to the context of fat discrimination and oppression. They note, for example, that fat children and adolescents are at increased risk for negative psychological outcomes such as poor self-esteem (U.S. Centers for Disease Control and Prevention, 2006). Or they note that both childhood and adolescent "obesity" may be associated with "being liked to a lesser extent by peers, being rejected by peers, and being the victims of various forms of peer aggression such as bullying" (Janssen, Craig, Boyce, & Pickett, 2004, p. 1187). One explanation offered by Janssen and colleagues (2004, p. 1193) for this association is "that overweight and obese youth have a poor self-concept because of their appearance and consequently interact less effectively with peers, resulting in rejection."

Such a proposed direction of effect, however, neither reflects a fat-positive perspective nor considers the impact of weight-based bullying and the context of fat oppression on peer relations and self-perceptions. Yet bullying research indicates that targeted children are more likely to be anxious, insecure, cautious, sensitive, quiet, withdrawn, and shy, and to be unhappy, feel lower in self-esteem, and hold negative self-beliefs that may lead them to blame themselves for their own victimization (see, e.g., Bollmer, Milich, Harris, & Maras, 2005; Olweus, 1993; Randall, 2001). Youth victimized by their peers also tend to have fewer friends (Eisenberg & Aalsma, 2005; Olweus, 1993) and lower overall friendship quality (Bollmer et al., 2005) than those who are not victimized.

Some researchers have found these individual and social characteristics both to precede being victimized by bullies and to "put children at risk for victimization because such behaviors convey to the bullies that these children are not assertive and are unlikely to defend themselves, which results in increased victimization over time" (Bollmer et al., 2005, p. 702; see also Olweus, 1993). These very characteristics, however, may develop in response to repeated weight-based bullying, being targeted on the basis of weight, and negotiating self-perceptions and peer and family relationships in a context of fat oppression. For example, Eisenberg, Neumark-Sztainer, and Story (2003, p. 733) found that weight-based teasing "was consistently associated with low body satisfaction, low self-esteem, high depressive symptoms, and thinking about and attempting suicide, even after controlling for actual body weight." Those teased by both peers and family evidenced especially high rates of negative emotional symptoms. These findings held for boys and girls, across racial and ethnic groups, and across weight groups.

Another contributing factor to weight-based bullying and other bullying of fat youth is that, as Myers and Rothblum (2004) emphasize, people freely express prejudice against fat people, and weight-based teasing is but one form of this expression. The willingness to express prejudice against fat people is itself influenced by the tendency for weight to be seen as controllable. This may be a particularly strong belief in the United States, which values self-discipline and thinness. Unfortunately, this view of weight as controllable leads many to blame those who are fat for being fat, and thus to treat fatness as an individual character flaw. Negative treatment is then viewed as deserved, making it very easy for those who bully fat people to "blame the victim."

This mistreatment—by peers, family members, institutional policies, and societal values—suggests that in contrast to Janssen Craig, Boyce, and Picket's (2004) proposed direction of effect noted earlier (that being fat leads to low self-concept and subsequently less effective peer relations), their alternative proposed direction of effect—"that overweight and obese youth are mistreated by peers because of their physical differences" (p. 1193)—is much more plausible. When being fat is treated as a cause of poor self-esteem, subsequently leading to poor peer relations and ultimately to being victimized by peers, the negative effects of fat oppression are only strengthened.

Conclusion and Future Directions: What Can We Do?

The available literature clearly indicates that bullying is associated with important psychological, social, and physical health problems for all directly involved in it. Additional research is needed that more explicitly identifies just what constitutes weight-based bullying (Eisenberg et al., 2003) and that examines the extent to which various external contexts and internal characteristics are associated with increased risk of victimization. Drawing on a developmental assets model (see, e.g., Benson, 1997; Orpinas & Horne, 2006), we know that those with fewer available internal (e.g., good self-esteem) and external (e.g., family support, positive school climate) assets are at greater risk for negative developmental outcomes. Children and adolescents who are fat clearly experience multiple risk factors at the individual, peer, and cultural levels, making them vulnerable to being targeted for bullying in general and, especially, for being targeted with weight-based bullying.

One recommended intervention/prevention strategy is to attend to and support the basic psychological need for acceptance among fat youth. For example, health-care providers, parents, and media representatives could actively counter unrealistic body norms and support fat youth in developing positive self-esteem and effective skills for dealing with both fat phobia and bullying. But this kind of strategy alone is inadequate. Efforts are also needed that focus on those who bully fat youth and the bystanders who passively accept this bullying. Puhl and Latner (2007) agree; they argue for the development and evaluation of fat stigma reduction programs that challenge negative stereotypes about fat children and adults. Such programs may do much to challenge bystanders' passive acceptance of bullying. We know that bystanders "play a central role in supporting bullying and promoting a culture of aggression," but "they also play an essential role—which must be supported—in intervening to stop bullying" (Craig & Pepler, 2003, p. 581). It is thus our view that multilevel prevention efforts directed at systemic change are needed (see also Olweus, 1993; Pepler, Smith, & Rigby, 2004), and that such efforts must address and challenge all forms of violence and oppression. At their core should be a valuation of diversity and respectful treatment of all youth, whatever their size, and an appreciation for the critical importance of acceptance to (and of) all youth (Benson, 1997; Garbarino & deLara, 2002).

Although many systems of oppression have been acknowledged and challenged in recent decades, societal acceptance of oppression on the basis of weight remains strong. Indeed, as Swearer and Espelage (2004, p. 3) argue, "Bullying does not occur in isolation. This phenomenon is encouraged and/or inhibited as a result of the complex relationships between the individual, family, peer group, school, community, and culture." As long as weight-based oppression remains acceptable, and acceptable body sizes remain narrowly defined, those youth who do not fit the norms will continue to be unfairly and repeatedly targeted.

REFERENCES

Benson, P.L. (1997). *All Kids Are Our Kids: What Communities Must Do to Raise Caring and Responsible Children and Adolescents*. San Francisco: Jossey-Bass.

Bollmer, J.M., Milich, R., Harris, M.J., & Maras, M.A. (2005). A friend in need: The role of friendship quality as a protective factor in peer victimization and bullying. *Journal of Interpersonal Violence*, 20, 701–712.

Craig, W.M., & Pepler, D.J. (2003). Identifying and targeting risk for involvement in bullying and victimization. *Canadian Journal of Psychiatry*, 48, 577–582.

Demaray, M.K., & Malecki, C.K. (2003). Perceptions of the frequency and importance of social support by students classified as victims, bullies, and bully/victims in an urban middle school. *School Psychology Review*, 32, 471–489.

Eisenberg, M.E., & Aalsma, M.C. (2005). Bullying and peer victimization: Position paper of the Society for Adolescent Medicine. *Journal of Adolescent Health*, 36, 88–91.

Eisenberg, M.E., Neumark-Sztainer, D., & Story, M. (2003). Association of weight-based teasing and emotional well-being among adolescents. *Archives of Pediatrics and Adolescent Medicine*, 157, 733–738.

Garbarino, J., & deLara, E. (2002). *And Words Can Hurt Forever: How To Protect Adolescents from Bullying, Harassment, and Emotional Violence*. New York: Free Press.

Geier, A.B., Foster, G.D., Womble, L.G., McLaughlin, J., Borradaile, K.E., Nachmani, J., Sherman, S., Kumanyika, S., & Shults, J. (2007). The relationship between relative weight and school attendance among elementary schoolchildren. *Obesity*, 15, 2157–2161.

Greenya, J. (2005, February 4). Bullying: Are schools doing enough to stop the problem? *The CQ Researcher*, 15(5), 101–103.

Griffiths, L.J., Wolke, D., Page, A.S., & Horwood, J.P. (2005). Obesity and bullying: Different effects for boys and girls. *Archives of Disease in Childhood*, 91, 121–125.

Hayden-Wade, H.A., Stein, R.I., Ghaderi, A., Saelens, B.E., Zabinski, M.F., & Wilfey, D.E. (2005). Prevalence, characteristics, and correlates of teasing experiences among overweight children vs. non-overweight peers. *Obesity Research*, 13, 1381–1392.

Janssen, I., Craig, W.M., Boyce, W.F., & Picket, W. (2004). Associations between overweight and obesity with bullying behaviors in school-aged children. *Pediatrics*, 113, 1187–1194.

Mishna, F., & Alaggia, R. (2005). Weighing the risks: A child's decision to disclose peer victimization. *Children & Schools*, 17, 217–226.

Myers, A.M., & Rothblum, E.D. (2004). Coping with prejudice and discrimination based on weight. In J. L. Chin (Ed.), *The Psychology of Prejudice and Discrimination*. Volume 4: *Combating Prejudice and All Forms of Discrimination*. New York: Praeger.

Nansel, T.R., Overpeck, M., Pilla, R.S., Ruan, J., Simons-Morton, B., & Scheidt, P. (2001). Bullying behaviors among US youth: Prevalence and association with psychosocial adjustment. *Journal of the American Medical Association*, 285, 2094–2100.

Neumark-Sztainer, D., Falkner, N., Story, M., Perry, C., Hanna, P.J., & Mulert, S. (2002). Weight-teasing among adolescents: Correlations with weight status and disordered eating behaviors. *International Journal of Obesity and Related Metabolic Disorders*, 26, 123–131.

Olweus, D. (1993). *Bullying at School: What We Know and What We Can Do*. Malden, MA: Blackwell.

Orpinas, P., & Horne, A.M. (2006). *Bullying Prevention: Creating a Positive School Climate and Developing Social Competence*. Washington, DC: American Psychological Association.

Pepler, D., Smith, P.K., & Rigby, K. (2004). Looking back and looking forward: Implications for making interventions work effectively. In P.K. Smith, D. Pepler, & K. Rigby (Eds.), *Bullying in Schools: How Successful Can Interventions Be?* New York: Cambridge University Press.

Puhl, R.M., & Latner, J.D. (2007). Stigma, obesity, and the health of the nation's children. *Psychological Bulletin, 133,* 557–580.

Radiance: The Magazine for Large Women Online. (2004). We get letters. Retrieved May 30, 2006, from http://www.radiancemagazine.com/letters/letters.html.

Randall, P. (2001). *Bullying in Adulthood: Assessing the Bullies and Their Victims.* New York: Brunner-Routledge.

Rigby, K. (2003). Consequences of bullying in schools. *Canadian Journal of Psychiatry, 48,* 583–590.

Storch, E.A., Milsom, V.A., DeBraganza, N., Lewin, A.B., Geffken, G.R., & Silverstein, J.H. (2007). Peer victimization, psychosocial adjustment, and physical activity in overweight and at-risk-for-overweight youth. *Journal of Pediatric Psychology, 32,* 80–89.

Swearer, S.M., & Espelage, D.L. (2004). Introduction: A social-ecological framework of bullying among youth. In D.L. Espelage & S.M. Swearer (Eds.), *Bullying in American Schools: A Social-Ecological Perspective on Prevention and Intervention.* Mahwah, NJ: Lawrence Erlbaum Associates.

Swearer, S.M., Grills, A.E., Haye, K.M., & Cary, P.T. (2004). Internalizing problems in students involved in bullying and victimization: Implications for intervention. In D.L. Espelage & S.M. Swearer (Eds.), *Bullying in American Schools: A Social-Ecological Perspective on Prevention and Intervention.* Mahwah, NJ: Lawrence Erlbaum Associates.

U.S. Centers for Disease Control and Prevention (2006). Body mass index: About BMI for children and teens. Retrieved April 24, 2006, from http://www.cdc.gov/nccdphp/dnpa/bmi/childrens_BMI/about_childrens_BMI.htm.

Bon Bon Fatty Girl

A Qualitative Exploration of Weight Bias in Singapore

Maho Isono, Patti Lou Watkins, and Lee Ee Lian

"You've put on weight, haven't you?" is a common entrée to conversation in Singapore, where casual remarks about body shape and size are widely accepted. This chapter explores how such remarks affect individuals, particularly young women in this culture. Results from a qualitative study are discussed in the context of the existing literature on weight bias in personal spheres. The discussion also speaks to Singapore's efforts to address eating disorders and forge a more adaptive approach to weight and health.

Since gaining independence in 1965, Singapore has seen dramatic economic development. This increase in wealth has coincided with an increase in weight among its people. Between the 1970s and 1990s, Singaporean males and females became 34.5% and 19.3% heavier, respectively (Jin-Jong, 1999). Meanwhile, "obesity in students from primary, secondary, and pre-university schools showed an almost three-fold increase from 5.4% in 1980 to 15.1% in 1991" (Toh, Chew, & Tan, 2002, p. 335). In 1992, the government conducted a national health survey of cardiovascular risk factors, using the widely accepted yet problematic criterion of body mass index (BMI) > 30 to define "obesity" (Prentice & Jebb, 2001). This survey revealed that 5.1% of Singaporean adults exceeded a BMI of 30. A 1998 follow-up survey showed that this rate had increased to 5.9% (Toh et al., 2002).

Interestingly, eating disorders have also increased considerably in recent decades, with a sixfold rise in documented cases between 1994 and 2002 (Ung, 2005). In contrast to "obesity," no national statistics have been gathered. Once unheard of, two case reports appeared in the early 1980s (Kua, Lee, & Chee, 1982; Ong, Tsoi, & Cheah, 1982). Over a decade passed before publication of a third study (Ung, Lee, & Kua, 1997). As presentations increased, health-care professionals garnered resources to treat these problems, establishing an eating disorders clinic at the Institute of Mental Health (IMH) in 1995. Lee, Lee, Pathy, and Chan (2005) recently published findings derived from 126 patients with anorexia nervosa who came there or to the Child Guidance Clinic. They appeared quite similar to anorexia nervosa sufferers in Western societies; most were females (91.3%), single (92.9%), and teenagers at the time of symptom onset. Subsequently, Ho, Tai, Lee, Cheng, and Liow (2006) analyzed questionnaire responses from 4,461 girls and women aged twelve to twenty-six years, recruited via random and convenience sampling. Results revealed a 7.4% prevalence rate of risk for developing eating disorders, again comparable to results from Western studies.

How did Singapore come to emulate Western cultures regarding rising rates of both "obesity" and eating disorders? Brown and Konner (1996) offer an anthropological explanation, noting that citizens' weights commonly increase in countries following industrialization. Further, as weight increases, fat bodies become stigmatized and thinness becomes the cultural ideal. According to Scheper-Hughes and Lock (1996), the body regulated by society is considered "correct" among the populace, and the "correct" body becomes associated with cultural meanings such as beauty, strength, and health. Over the past forty years, Singapore has transitioned from a relatively poor nation, in which body fat was desirable and plumpness was celebrated, to an economic power, in which body fat is abhorred and thinness is celebrated. Fung (2004, p. 34) states, "Not more than a few decades ago, the concept of beauty was a lady who would be, by today's anorexic standards, an overweight woman averaging more than 70 kilograms. These days, women larger than 40 kilograms may be considered too big." Support for these changing beauty standards comes from Wang, Ho, Anderson, and Sabry (1999), who found a strong preference for thinness among Singaporeans between the ages of seventeen and twenty-two. Nearly one-third of female respondents whose weights were deemed "borderline" to below "normal" expressed a desire to be even thinner. In that study, preference for thinness was significantly related to speaking English (vs. Chinese) at home. Wang and colleagues equated this language preference with rejection of traditional customs and subsequent adoption of Western mores.

One reflection of modern Singapore's disdain for fat is the burgeoning business of slimming centers and products (Ung & Lee, 1999). Lee and colleagues (2005) report that popular Singaporean magazines marketed to women contain approximately eight slimming ads per issue. The slimming industry explicitly links thinness with beauty and health. Paradoxically, the advertised procedures are quite questionable from both a health and weight loss perspective. Sadly, as illustrated in the well-publicized 2002 "Slim 10 Case," a twenty-seven-year-old woman who had taken a slimming product containing Fenfluramine experienced "drug-induced massive heptocellular necrosis with impending liver failure" (Singham, 2004, p. 57). Yee (2004, p. 184) laments that even after the Slim 10 saga, "the barrage of slimming advertisements does not seem to have abated," and citizens continue to consume these products despite warnings.

Although adults voluntarily avail themselves of slimming centers, since 1992 "overweight" children have been mandated to attend a school-based weight loss program. The government-sponsored Trim and Fit Program (TAF) was compulsory for all children between six and eight years of age who were overweight according to height and weight charts produced by the ministries of education and health. TAF's aim was to improve fitness and reduce weight through proper nutrition and physical activity, with schools rewarded based on students' weight reductions (Lee, 2003). Although health indices were emphasized, Lee (2003) also lists an aesthetic goal, looking better, as one of TAF's objectives. TAF was implemented by existing school personnel—that is, teachers who do not necessarily have expertise or prior training in health behavior. Sharma (2006) criticizes TAF on this account, as well as for the fact that it is based on no known theory of health behavior change. In terms of actual protocols, the Editorial Team (2004, p. 178) provides the following example of the "strict dieting regimen" that TAF entailed: No consumption of deep fried food, sweet products that consist of higher portions of simple sugar, preserved or canned food, or "tidbits." Participants must also reduce consumption of red meat while increasing consumption of fruits and vegetables. Soft drinks are to be replaced by daily consumption of eight to ten glasses of water. In addition to these dietary constraints, TAF involved mandatory physical activity, although it seems that schools had some leeway in creating their own exercise regimens. Lee (2003) lists jogging, calisthenics, and circuit training among the activities that might be included. The Editorial Team (2004) provides an example from a primary school at which ten minutes of rope skipping was required during the first ten minutes of recess before children were allowed to proceed to the canteen for food. In a recent broadcast critiquing TAF (Public Radio International [PRI], 2007), reporter Patrick Cox states, "It's lunch period at Rulang Elementary School in western Singapore. In the schoolyard, some 30 uniformed 6th-graders are about to begin a 20-minute aerobic workout. Afterwards, they'll scarf down a meal in the ten minutes that remain of their lunch break." Cox adds that TAF members have sometimes been segregated from other students in the cafeteria, and that, "in the early days of the program, heavyset children were even given calorie coupons to spend at the school cafeteria. The larger the child, the fewer coupons he could spend."

TAF was touted a great success as the percentage of "overweight" children decreased from 14.0% to 9.8% between 1992 and 2002 (Lee, 2003). It may have had deleterious side effects, however, perhaps more insidious than those associated with slimming programs. Although the idea behind TAF was to "make losing weight through increased physical activity as enjoyable as possible" while helping children to feel more confident, increase self-esteem, and reduce anxiety (Lee, 2003, p. 49), investigators began to question the psychological benevolence of this program. Ung and Lee (1999) suggested that some TAF instructors may be more punitive than inspirational, thus eroding students' confidence. Lee and colleagues (2005) found empirical support for this hypothesis. They asked participants with anorexia if they could identify a precipitating event for their symptoms. Most commonly cited (by 26.9% of the sample) were teasing and other weight-biased comments, many of which occurred within TAF.

Weight bias from family, friends, and others in one's immediate social sphere may have greater impact on psychological well-being, particularly body image, than broader cultural influences, such as the mass media (Thompson, Heinberg, Altabe, & Tantleff-Dunn, 2004). In fact, Thompson, Coovert, Richards, Johnson, and Cattarin (1995) found that, among heavier participants, only those who experienced weight-related teasing developed a negative body image. Neumark-Sztainer and Eisenberg (2005) describe other effects of weight-related teasing among teens in their large-scale study, including bingeing, skipping meals, and using laxatives and diet pills. These researchers suggest that participants may have been attempting to avoid further teasing by losing weight, but warn of the ineffectiveness and danger of resorting to such practices. In addition, teen victims of weight-related teasing reported greater depression, suicidal ideation, and suicide attempts than their peers who escaped such derision. Educational environments may constitute a setting in which children and teens are highly vulnerable to weight bias from peers as well as school personnel. Neumark-Sztainer and Eisenberg (2005) contend that the latter are susceptible to social biases regarding weight and may—however unintentionally—treat larger students differently according to these beliefs. These investigators specifically call for more qualitative research in this area so that the subjective meaning of weight bias and its consequences can be more fully understood.

Study Methodology

By employing a qualitative research design, this study provided an "insider's perspective" to weight bias in contemporary Singaporean society. Ethnography involving in-depth interviews with informants was the basis of this investigation. Such an approach aims to understand a way of life from the individuals' points of view. It entails learning *from* people rather than learning about people. Anthropologists employing this methodology reside among their informants during the research process to formulate the most germane interview questions. The first author lived in Singapore for three months, conducting her research through the IMH under the supervision of the third author, a psychiatrist heading the hospital's Eating Disorders Clinic. Informants recruited through this setting included sixteen individuals (95% female), aged fifteen to twenty-six (mean = twenty) years who had received diagnoses of anorexia, bulimia, or eating disorder of nonspecified type. Most were of Chinese descent (81%), reflecting the country's demographics. These persons constituted the target group. A control group of eight women with similar demographics but without eating disorders served a comparative purpose. The interviewer examined whether similar concerns were shared by target and control groups. Interviews lasting sixty to ninety minutes consisted of open-ended questions revolving around body image, eating behaviors, and interactions with significant others concerning the informants' physiques. Additional informants included teachers and mothers who were also in a position to reflect on weight bias in Singaporean society.

Study Results

Findings were striking; in both groups informants experienced weight bias from people close to them. They encountered stranger weight bias less often, but these exchanges still carried an emotional impact. For example, a target informant recollected a "frightening" event from primary school in which she was weighing herself at the side of a public pool. A man standing in line behind her exclaimed, "Your weight is so heavy! You need to slim down!" A control informant described an interaction with her landlady, who said, "I think you have put on weight. You are really fat now. Isn't that scary?" Many informants experienced bias in multiple social spheres, leading one twenty-one-year-old woman in the target group to remark, "I met so many people who teased me about my body. I hate my childhood because of it." Weight bias occurred in the form of teasing, advice, casual remarks, and outright censure. Informants typically construed this as harsh indictments of their worth and remained silent in the face of such comments; according to one respondent: "My cousin teased me about my body in a very funny way. I had no choice except laughing even though I was upset." This passive acceptance seemed to stem from the notion that such conversation is a "normal," albeit undesirable, aspect of Singaporean culture. Informants also seemed to accept weight bias because they viewed it as deserved. One informant explained that she did not defend herself against school ground taunts of "fat girl" because she believed them to be "true." Another said, "I thought it was my fault for being teased. Something was wrong with me." Although this study cannot ascertain a causal relationship between weight bias and psychological distress, many informants attributed their negative affect and eating-disordered behavior to these messages. After a childhood of weight-related criticism, one woman said that similar comments from coworkers instigated restrictive dieting and obsessive exercise regimens. Subsequently, she lost sixty pounds, became amenorrheic, and was diagnosed with anorexia.

Family

At family gatherings, Tracy, a control informant, was greeted with, "You are getting rounder! You are getting bigger now!" Melinda, diagnosed with anorexia and bulimia, remembered her uncle and aunt calling her "Ah Pui"—meaning "stupid, fat girl." Although upset by this moniker, she kept her feelings inside. Beth, diagnosed with bulimia, was called "fat girl" as a child by her father. Liou, a control informant who did however describe a period of restrictive dieting, reported her mother exclaiming, "Even if you went somewhere to advertise yourself for a husband, nobody will marry you because of the way you look." Wei-Chen, diagnosed with bulimia, vividly recounted her grandmother telling her as a child, "Your size is so huge. Your buttocks are getting bigger. You need to watch what you eat." Wei-Chen starved herself "to let them know I was unhappy and was destroying myself to express out all my miseries. I wanted to inflict guilt in them that their unfairness had caused physical damage in me, and behind the body there was a greater emotional damage." Jennifer, now recovered from anorexia and bulimia, explained that her maladaptive dieting was triggered by family members saying: "How come you have put on weight? Have you been exercising lately?" For Ai-Ling, diagnosed with bulimia, her family's query, "You've put on weight, haven't you?" was enough to spur her distress.

Friends and Partners

"Bon bon fatty girl" was a taunt that Sarah, a member of the target group, reported her childhood friends singing. "You look like a hamburger," Ming recalled a friend telling her. Liou admitted that, in sixth grade, a friend called her "fat" in Chinese every day. Although hating this label, she did not defend herself, as she deemed the description accurate. Beth described her secondary schoolmates teasing her in public, exclaiming, "She has so much fat on her stomach!" Melinda noted that even positive comments from her mother, such as, "You are natural," could not offset the impact of negative feedback from peers. Jennifer did not relate negative comments from peers, but she did note that friends admired her weight loss while she was anorexic. She also contended that having a boyfriend for the first time induced her to begin her eating-disordered behavior: "He did not say I must lose weight, but I remember he told me that girls should be below fifty kilograms. I think part of me started dieting because of him." Ai-Ling, who developed bulimia, similarly noted that a male friend had told her that thinner women were more attractive. Such indirect weight bias was not uncommon, particularly within a heterosexual dating context. For instance, Beth stated: "On campus, both men and women are watching others' appearances and commenting on girls' bodies. I think women do more than men do. Girls complain of their weight even if they are not overweight. Guys talk about girls' bodies. My guy friends asked me, 'Why do you even introduce those girls to us? They are not even pretty.' I am paranoid about guy's comments on girls' bodies. It stimulates me to purge." Liou confided that although friends tell her that she is "okay," they describe others' bodies akin to her own as "fat": "So, I indirectly feel that others think of me as fat."

School Personnel

Melinda described an incident in which a teacher drew a very round face on the board, identifying this as Melinda, who subsequently thought of herself as stupid, clumsy, and fat. A British schoolteacher who taught in Singapore provided the following account, witnessed by a colleague, of weight bias at the hands of school staff. During a group weigh-in of secondary schoolchildren, the nurse communicated to one girl that she was "so fat and lazy" and was "doing nothing to help herself": "The girl, by now close to tears, pleaded that she ran to school every day, but the nurse just wouldn't believe her. She just kept on. She told her that she would have to go see a doctor who would give her pills to make her lose weight. My friend, likewise, the boys in the class, heard every word. In the year following this incident, this girl lost so much weight, she was barely recognizable." The requisite school weigh-in has taken on greater importance in Singapore since results were used to channel children who exceed "normal" levels into the government-mandated TAF program. Liou related the significance of objectively being labeled "fat" by the school. Thus identified, she began an extreme diet, took slimming pills, and swam every day for three hours, eventually losing forty-four pounds. Liou reported relief that she was not involved with TAF, stating that she felt sorry for the participants because she had seen how they were negatively labeled.

The stigma of TAF was not lost on those children who failed to circumvent involvement. Furthermore, weight bias from TAF instructors seemed to contribute to psychological distress. Sung, a male in the target group, confided, "My friends were watching us while we ran during recess and they could play football instead. It was very embarrassing. Students did not want to be involved in this program because of it. The TAF affected my bulimia because it made me highly body conscious." Ying-Ping, a woman in the target group, declared that TAF was "humiliating since this program singled out heavy students. I was told, 'You would look better if you cut that weight' by my instructor." Likewise, Xia, a female control informant, said of TAF, "I hated it. It reminded me how fat I am." Manisha, a target informant, stated that TAF "hurt me." Wanting to avoid participation, she engaged in eating-disordered behavior that led to a twenty-four-pound weight loss. Although no longer required to participate, Manisha has been diagnosed with anorexia. Lisa, a control informant and five-year veteran of TAF, acknowledged, "There was a stigma associated with going. I used to hate telling people I was in it because they used to call it fat club in school. Think about it, TAF is the backwards of FAT. Not a nice acronym at all." She also described TAF instructors as "insensitive," relating remarks such as, "If you lose all that weight, you will be very pretty; if you don't lose weight, you cannot wear any kinds of clothes." When she began skipping TAF sessions, "I couldn't get away from teachers who would nag me about going all the time. I just felt really pressurized and really belittled. They were going around thinking and telling me that I was fat—too fat to be normal." The effect was that she "did not feel good at all. TAF automatically makes you think you are fat, slow, stupid, and lazy." She summarized, stating that TAF "was a waste of time. Nothing changed. It made me more conscious of my body and more aware of thinner people. It was really upsetting." Lisa's mother related that her daughter's involvement "negatively changed her perspective towards the government and school." Another mother of a TAF participant reported that "girls are made to feel in a way that it's a sin to be fat. Fat girls are rounded up to run and do sit ups and so on before school starts and also at recess after school. She is dieting and skips meals to try to stay out of the TAF program." Other mothers expressed that their children were embarrassed to exercise publicly and be singled out and rewarded for weight loss in front of other students. Finally, one teacher voiced qualms about TAF, stating: "It was very painful for me to see. Kids would cry. They don't look at how active a student is. Kids might be born with a bigger figure than others."

Discussion

This study gives voice to young Singaporeans' experiences with weight bias in personal settings, linking these events with affective distress, distorted body image, and a propensity for eating disorders. Even secondary or derivative weight discrimination, in which remarks were not directed at informants (Sobal, 2005), led to dieting, purging, and poor self-esteem. Some may dismiss the magnitude of weight-related teasing in childhood, viewing this as a harmless rite of passage, but research suggests otherwise. McLaren, Kuh, Hardy, and Gauvin (2004) surveyed nearly nine hundred middle-aged women about negative and positive body-related comments that they experienced when growing up, as well as those experienced currently from partners. They found a significant effect resulting from negative comments during childhood on current body esteem, independent of contemporary comments from partners. Positive comments in adulthood did not ameliorate the adverse impact of critical childhood comments, as was the case with one of the informants. Thus, weight bias has enduring effects forty to fifty years into the future.

Many informants experienced weight bias within the TAF program and came to view participation as shameful. Ironically, TAF appeared, in certain ways, detrimental rather than beneficial to students' well-being. Although it was "successful" in that it coincided with a drop in childhood "obesity" rates, some informants traced their negative affect and eating disorders to this experience. Sharma (2006, p. 164) warns that school-based interventions that single out overweight and obese children may produce stigmatization and cause psychosocial distress. Further, Putterman and Linden (2004) found that when weight loss is driven by appearance concerns—as it seemed to be based on informants' descriptions of TAF—female dieters reported greater use of unhealthy practices, greater body dissatisfaction, and lower self-esteem. In the PRI (2007) report, Cox states, "Education officials insist that no one set out to stigmatize overweight children. It's just turned out to be a by-product of the program—a by-product nonetheless tolerated by officials for 15 years." Cox interviewed physician Warren Lee, chairman of Singapore's Diabetic Society, who stated that TAF is "cruel to be kind," implying that such stigmatization early on is necessary to prevent children from experiencing it in later life, perhaps in the form of job discrimination, should they fail to lose weight. Cox also interviewed economist Barry Popkin, head of the obesity center at the University of North Carolina, who echoed this sentiment that some stigmatization is necessary for successful weight loss. Research exists, however, that contradicts these views. For instance, Bauer, Yang, and Austin (2004) found that weight bias in school settings may actually undermine health promotion efforts. In their study, both students and school staff identified bullying and teasing as barriers to participating in physical activity.

Clearly, school staff and parents must be educated about the seriousness of weight bias to avert further harm (Neumark-Sztainer & Eisenberg, 2005). News reports (e.g., PRI, 2007; Szwarc, 2007) suggest that TAF has been discontinued, or at least significantly altered, in light of such recognition. The Singapore Ministry of Education's Web site (http://www.moe.gov.sg/education/programmes/holistic-health-framework/) briefly addresses these changes. Under the heading, "Is the Trim and Fit (TAF) Programme scrapped?" the site states that the new "Holistic Health Framework" will "continue to assist overweight and underweight students with their weight management programmes as well as to provide for students with ideal weight to keep fit." Furthermore, schools are "encouraged to change the name of their weight management programmes from TAF to something more interesting to denote this change in focus." Regarding these changes, the PRI (2007) report indicates that although the "fitness clubs" are now open to all students regardless of weight classification, "overweight kids are still required to participate, and there's little evidence that other kids are choosing to join the clubs." The Ministry of Education's Web site also states that "the focus on managing weight and fitness levels have been broadened to include other areas in physical health as well as mental and social health." The site does not address eating disorders, however, or the potential of weight-biased treatment to instigate these and other forms of psychological distress. In fact, it poses a question, "What's wrong with being overweight?" with one of the answers, "Their friends will laugh at them and tease them," suggesting the inevitability of such treatment.

Singaporeans need to understand not only the devastating effects of weight bias, but also that individuals may be fat yet fit—-and that attempts to lose weight come with their own set of significant health consequences (Cogan & Ernsberger, 1999). Adults can then teach size acceptance to children at an early age as a means of primary prevention; resources for doing so are available through the Teaching Tolerance project (http://www.tolerance.org/teach/activities/activity.jsp?ar=825). Johnson (2005) connects her healing from lifelong weight bias to participation in organizations that campaign against this form of discrimination. Singapore has yet to engage in this sort of widespread activism. Although an International Alliance for Size Acceptance (http://www.size-acceptance.org) exists, the Philippines is Asia's only participating member.

Eating disorders have at least caught the attention of Singaporeans. In 2001, a public forum took place, and as a result the self-help group Support for Eating Disorders Singapore was born. In addition, the IMH Eating Disorders Clinic provides tertiary care to individuals diagnosed with these conditions. Perhaps future treatment might include assertiveness training to help clients combat the weight bias that they report encountering (Thompson et al., 2004). This strategy might be accompanied by cognitive therapy to address beliefs that excess weight is a personal failure, therefore warranting such mistreatment (Johnson, 2005). Lee (2004, p. 15) recently introduced these ideas to Singaporean physicians, asking them to examine their own attitudes about weight and to refrain from blaming their patients. She also encouraged them to help patients "accept their above-average body size and even celebrate their natural shapes." Nevertheless, a disconnect still seems to exist between eating disorders and weight-biased attitudes. Recently, an edited collection on the topic, *Slim Chance Fat Hope: Society's Obsession with Thinness*, was recently published in Singapore (Kian, 2004). Some chapters are consistent with the Health at Every Size perspective, presenting evidence for genetic limitations to weight loss and potential dangers of slimming products. Others are titled "Being Fat Can Be Beautiful Too!" and "Talents Matter More Than Size." One encouraging passage reads: "Singapore, with its love of campaigns, should consider a programme to promote a healthy body image among our young. Schools could include self-esteem courses; community health groups could conduct workshops on how to be healthy at one's weight, rather than thin at any cost" (Loh, 2004, p. 190). Regrettably, this book also contains messages to the contrary. Although the chapter on eating disorders alludes to the possibility that weight-related teasing instigated a case of anorexia, a passage in the same chapter, about a woman with bulimia, reads: "Her hands and legs were as big as an elephant's!

The only features that still looked pretty were the lush eyelashes and prominent double eyelids" (Ling, 2004, p. 143). Another chapter minimizes weight-biased teasing: "When friends joke about my body size, I laugh with them. These harmless banters would not make me lose any sweat. If they can really make me perspire and help me to slim down, I wish my friends could joke about me more!" (Kit, 2004, p. 194). Disappointingly, the book's final chapters advocate weight loss, emphasizing physical appearance as a motivation.

Like many other nations, Singapore has succumbed to panic over the "obesity epidemic" (Miller & Robison, 2006). Predictably, damage (in the form of eating disorders) has ensued. Singaporeans do appear, however, to be developing an awareness of eating disorders and their connection to the weight bias that permeates the country. Hopefully this newfound understanding will bring about involvement in the international size acceptance movement. Ultimately, Singaporeans must develop creative solutions to the problem of weight bias among its people.

REFERENCES

Bauer, K.W., Yang, Y.W., & Austin, S.B. (2004). "How can we stay healthy when you're throwing all this in front of us?" Findings from focus groups and interviews in middle schools on environmental influences on nutrition and physical activity. *Health Education and Behavior, 31*, 34–46.

Brown, P.J., & Konner, M. (1996). An anthropological perspective on obesity. In P.J. Brown (Ed.), *Understanding and Applying Medical Anthropology*. Mountain View, CA: Mayfield Publishing.

Cogan, J.C., & Ernsberger, P. (1999). Dieting, weight, and health: Reconceptualizing research and policy. *Journal of Social Issues, 55*, 187–205.

Editorial Team (2004). The Trim and Fit (TAF) programme: The route to physical fitness for school children. In C.T.S. Kian (Ed.), *Slim Chance Fat Hope: Society's Obsession with Thinness*. Singapore: World Scientific Printers.

Fung, D. (2004). Slim 10: Fat hopes? In C.T.S. Kian (Ed.), *Slim Chance Fat Hope: Society's Obsession with Thinness*. Singapore: World Scientific Printers.

Ho, T.F., Tai, B.C., Lee, E.L., Cheng, S., & Liow, P.H. (2006). Prevalence and profile of females at risk of eating disorders in Singapore. *Singapore Medical Journal, 47*, 499–503.

Jin-Jong, Q. (1999). Physical growth and development of adolescents. In A.C.S. Chang, S. Gopinathan, & W.K. Ho (Eds.), *Growing Up in Singapore: Research Perspectives on Adolescents*. Singapore: Simon and Schuster (Asia).

Johnson, C. A. (2005). Personal reflections on bias, stigma, discrimination, and obesity. In K.D. Brownell, R.M. Puhl, M.B. Schwartz, & L. Rudd (Eds.), *Weight Bias: Nature, Consequences, and Remedies*. New York: Guilford Press.

Kian, C.T.S. (Ed.) (2004). *Slim Chance Fat Hope: Society's Obsession with Thinness*. Singapore: World Scientific Printers.

Kit, L.W. (2004). To fight an ever losing battle: A personal account. In C.T.S. Kian (Ed.), *Slim Chance Fat Hope: Society's Obsession with Thinness*. Singapore: World Scientific Printers.

Kua, E.H., Lee, S.L., & Chee, K.T. (1982). Bulimia nervosa: A case report. *Singapore Medical Journal, 23*, 287–289.

Lee, E.L. (2004). Psychological aspects of obesity and body image. *The Singapore Family Physician, 31,* 15–16.

Lee, H.Y., Lee, E.L., Pathy, P., & Chan, Y.H. (2005). Anorexia nervosa in Singapore: An eight-year retrospective study. *Singapore Medical Journal, 46,* 275–281.

Lee, W. (2003). Fighting fat: With TAF in Singapore. *Diabetes Voice, 48,* 49–50.

Ling, C.M. (2004). Case studies of anorexic and bulimic patients. In C.T.S. Kian (Ed.), *Slim Chance Fat Hope: Society's Obsession with Thinness.* Singapore: World Scientific Printers.

Loh, S. (2004). Body image: A big deal. In C.T.S. Kian (Ed.), *Slim Chance Fat Hope: Society's Obsession with Thinness.* Singapore: World Scientific Printers.

McLaren, L., Kuh, D., Hardy, R., & Gauvin, L. (2004). Positive and negative body-related comments and their relationship with body dissatisfaction in middle-aged women. *Psychology and Health, 19,* 261–272.

Miller, W.C., & Robison, J. (2006). HAES around the world. *Health at Every Size, 19,* 193–194.

Neumark-Sztainer, D., & Eisenberg, M.E. (2005). Weight bias in a teen's world. In K.D. Brownell, R.M. Puhl, M.B. Schwartz, & L. Rudd (Eds.), *Weight Bias: Nature, Consequences, and Remedies.* New York: Guilford Press.

Ong, Y.L., Tsoi, W.F., & Cheah, J.S. (1982). A clinical and psychosocial study of seven cases of anorexia nervosa in Singapore. *Singapore Medical Journal, 23,* 255–261.

Prentice, A.M., & Jebb, S.A. (2001). Beyond body mass index. *Obesity Reviews, 2,* 141–147.

Public Radio International (2007). PRI's *The World*: Obesity series part III: Singapore. Retrieved on July 18, 2008, from http://www.theworld.org/?q=node/13906.

Putterman, E., & Linden, W. (2004). Appearance versus health: Does the reason for dieting affect dieting behavior. *Journal of Behavioral Medicine, 27,* 185–294

Scheper-Hughes, N., & Lock, M.M. (1996). The mindful body: A prolegomenon to future work in medical anthropology. In P.J. Brown (Ed.), *Understanding and Applying Medical Anthropology.* Mountain View, CA: Mayfield Publishing.

Sharma, M. (2006). International school-based interventions fro preventing obesity in children. *Obesity Reviews, 8,* 155–167.

Singham, R. (2004). The Slim 10 case. In C.T.S. Kian (Ed.), *Slim Chance Fat Hope: Society's Obsession with Thinness.* Singapore: World Scientific Printers.

Sobal, J. (2005). Social consequences of weight bias by partners, friends, and strangers. In K.D. Brownell, R.M. Puhl, M.B. Schwartz, and L. Rudd (Eds.), *Weight Bias: Nature, Consequences, and Remedies.* New York: Guilford Press.

Szwarc, S. (2007). Junkfood science. Retrieved on July 18, 2008, from http://junkfoodscience.blogspot.com/2007/03/definition-of-insanity.html.

Thompson, J.K., Coovert, M.D., Richards, K.J., Johnson, S., & Cattarin, J. (1995). Development of body image, eating disturbance, and general psychological functioning in female adolescents: Covariance structure modeling and longitudinal investigations. *International Journal of Eating Disorders, 18,* 221–236.

Thompson, J.K., Heinberg, L.J., Altabe, M., & Tantleff-Dunn, S. (2004). *Exacting Beauty: Theory, Assessment, and Treatment of Body Image Disturbance.* Washington, DC: American Psychological Association.

Toh, C.M., Chew, S.K., & Tan, C.C. (2002). Prevention and control of non-communicable diseases in Singapore: A review of national health promotion programs. *Singapore Medical Journal, 43,* 333–339.

Ung, E.K. (2005). Eating disorders in Singapore: Coming of age. *Singapore Medical Journal, 46,* 254–256.

Ung, E.K., & Lee, D.S.W. (1999). Thin desires and fat realities. *Singapore Medical Journal, 40,* 495–497.

Ung, E.K., Lee, S., & Kua, E.H. (1997). Anorexia nervosa and bulimia: A Singapore perspective. *Singapore Medical Journal, 38,* 332–335.

Wang, F.C., Ho, T.F., Anderson, J.N., & Sabry, Z.I. (1999). Preference for thinness in Singapore: A newly industrialized society. *Singapore Medical Journal, 40,* 502–507.

Yee, J.T.W. (2004). The slimming phenomenon in popular culture. In C.T.S. Kian (Ed.), *Slim Chance Fat Hope: Society's Obsession with Thinness.* Singapore: World Scientific Printers.

||||||||||||||||||||||||||||||||||||||||||||||||||||||||||||||||||||||||||

Part-Time Fatso

S. Bear Bergman

Sometimes I'm Fat, and Sometimes I'm Not

I look the same every day. I'm five feet nine inches tall, broad shouldered and white skinned, green eyed with short brown hair, roughly 275 pounds. I dress myself plainly—blue jeans and button-downs, boots or sandals. I wear glasses. All these things are true all the time, and yet even so I am only Fat in the normative, cultural, "Ew, gross, look at it jiggle" sense about a third of the time.

Whether I'm fat depends on whether the person or people looking at me believe me to be a man or a woman.

After the first reading of the above description, you got a mental picture of me, and it quite likely included a gender. But there are no gendered statements in that paragraph, in much the same way that (while I'm dressed, anyhow) there are no gendered statements on my body. You may be having the same dizzying gender experience that people have when they look at me on the street, in a restaurant, or on an airplane. If you are, then you already know what I'm about to say: whether the world thinks of me as fat depends entirely on how it interprets my gender.

I mean, certainly I am not a svelte specimen in any case. I'm broad beamed, and I have a comfortable belly (which I refer to affectionately as "the half-rack," my little pun on the "six-pack abs" phenomenon), ham-like thighs, and a general XXL-ness about me. Society, however, does not see all fat as being equal. A man can be much, much fatter than a woman and still be viewed as comfortably within the standard deviation; most department stores carry men's pants up to a size 42, which is the rough equivalent of a women's size 24—a size that a woman would have to visit a specialty big-girl store or "Women's" department to find. Men are comfortable on beaches with their beach-ball bellies hanging over their swimsuit waistbands, bronzing their fat in the sun, whereas my fat women friends struggle to find swimwear that does not feature a skirt.

So me, I'm transgendered. It means that the gender I present in the world is not congruent with the sex that I was assigned at birth; in practical terms, I mostly look like a man but have a body that some would consider physiologically female. Even though I don't identify as a man (I am a butch, which is its own gender), I am taken for a man about two-thirds of the time. And when I am taken for a man, I am not fat.

Photos by Coren Rau.

As a man, I'm a big dude, but not outside the norm for such things. I am just barely fat enough to shop at what I call The Big Fat Tall Guy Store, and can sometimes find my size in your usual boy-upholstery emporia. Major clothing labels, like Levi Strauss, make nice things in my size, and I am never forced to wear anything that appears to have been manufactured at Mendel the Tentmaker's House o' Fashion. (Although those things do exist for men, too. Those terrycloth shirts with the waistbands? Oy.) I can order extra salad dressing or ice cream or anything else in a restaurant and have it arrive without comment; I can eat it in public without anyone taking a bit of notice, even if I am shoving it into my mouth while walking down a crowded street and getting crumbs all over my chest in the process. I can run for a bus or train without anyone making a snide remark. As a big guy, I'm big enough to make miscreants or troublemakers decide to take their hostility elsewhere.

As a woman, I am revolting. I am not only unattractively mannish but also grossly fat. The clothes I can fit into at the local big-girl stores tend to fit around the neck and then get bigger as they go downward, which results in a festive butch-in-a-bag look—all the rage nowhere, ever. No matter how clearly I order a Coke in a restaurant I *must* be on a diet, and so I get a Diet Coke—usually with a lemon floating in it accusatorily, looking up at me as if to say, "This is as good as it's going to get, lardass." Wait staff develop selective amnesia about my side of fries or my request for butter, and G-d help me if I get caught eating (or even shopping) in public as a woman. Packs of boys follow me, mooing; women with aggressively coordinated outfits accost me in the grocery store to inform me that I *can* lose thirty pounds in thirty days and that they would *love* to help. There are pig calls ("Soooooooooieeeeeeeee!") and the particular piece of performance art that is someone shuddering every time I take a step (to signify the seismic reality of my enormous, ground-shaking bulk). The fat woman I am some days does not view a stroll down a dark street with anything but barely disguised fear.

Ironically, it's my fat for which I am sometimes most grateful when I want the world to see me as a man. My large frame and relative ease moving through the world in it are transgressive and unusual for women raised in this culture. I have a long stride, I hold my head up, and these factors alone sometimes tip the scales of perception over into the man category. My girth and breadth allow my smallish breasts to be read as "fat boy tits," and my broad-featured Ashkenazi face to look commanding and masculine instead of balabusta-with-a-head-cold. My fat-kid inability to sit with my legs crossed at the knee, and all the problems it caused during the years in which I was still being poured into dresses and skirts, created—through the miracle of adolescent rebellion—a lifetime habit of sitting with my legs crossed ankle over knee in the traditionally masculine, trouser-wearing style.

There are days that I see how much my fat serves my gender. As a butch, with a transmasculine (but not man) identity, I have chosen not to have any medical intervention for the moment—no hormones, no surgery. In part, this is an option for me because my natural physiognomy (mesomorphic musculature and masculine fat distribution) allows me to get read as a man anytime that I put even a bit of effort into it, and so there seems no pressing need to deal with all the sometimes difficult, always expensive medical processes that come along with medical (or transsexual) transition. Studies have proven that it takes four female cues to trump one male cue (Kessler & McKenna, 1978, p. 68), because male is the default in Western society. Queer theorists encourage us to think about something even as simple as how babies are gendered: "If it has a penis, it's a boy, and if not, it's a girl." How strange is it to our ears to reverse the statement, to say, "If it has a vagina it's a girl, and if not, it's a boy?" My large size, and the way that my fat lives on my body, becomes a male cue that not even my breasts *and* soft jawline *and* light voice can overwhelm in the eye of the theoretical beholder. So my fat body becomes a place of privilege, especially because it is not the case for so many transmasculine folks of my acquaintance. Some of them are pushed toward transition because of extreme gender dysphoria, some because of secondary sexual characteristics like large breasts or high voices that are difficult to overcome without a visit to the doctor. But some are moderately gender-nonspecific except for being short or slight—they may be read as women, or possibly as young boys, but not as men. My fat, taken together with my height and confidence in my body while I am out in the public view, say "man" in this culture, and give my gender identity just enough of a boost to negate other, more feminine cues.

So while the medical establishment is more than happy to sign off on me as "morbidly obese" on any given day, my actual experience as a fat person—or, rather, a Fat person: someone who is visibly deviant in the cultural gaze—varies minute-to-minute. Some moments I am being automatically handed extra peanuts on the airplane and asked whether I would please come move this heavy thing and generally living as though my soundtrack is Grana' Louise's brilliant blues cut "Big Fat Daddy." Less frequent, though always possible, are the moments in which I am handed another damn Diet Coke or a miraculous weight loss program flyer, hearing (or trying not to hear) the strains of NWA's "Fat Girl" instead. I'm a part-time fatso—Fat one minute and just a big boy the next. Jerked dizzyingly between genders, between ways of difference, I'm never sure whether I'm going to be acceptable or not. Even while I am working like crazy to make a world in which we're all acceptable no matter what size we are, I am sometimes, even still, reduced to asking for a Coke just to see for sure what gender someone thinks I am.

REFERENCES

Kessler, S., & McKenna, W. (1978). *Gender: An Ethnomethodological Approach.* New York: John Wiley and Sons.

Double Stigma: Fat Men and Their Male Admirers

Nathaniel C. Pyle and Michael I. Loewy

There is a thriving sub-sub-culture that very few people know about. Although there are many things that lesbian, gay, and bisexual people have in common with one another politically, there are actually many different queer communities (Collins, 2004). Within the greater queer population, various communities are marginalized; in response, they each form their own spaces in which to congregate (Boykin, 1996). Among these sub-cultures within a sub-culture are communities of fat gay men and their male admirers. These are men who either do not fit the dominant image of gay men, or are not attracted to it. The primary purpose of this chapter is to introduce a community of people who have been marginalized within the already marginalized queer communities: fat men and their male admirers.

First, we offer a brief history of big men's networks, including the Affiliated Big Men's Clubs (ABC) and the Girth and Mirth clubs. Then we explore the advent of many publications aimed at big men and their male admirers, as well as internet communities that connect chubby men and chubby-chasers worldwide. Finally we explore the curious growth of bear clubs and posit reasons for their rapid growth as compared to the older, smaller big men's clubs. Throughout, we try to paint a rich picture of the men who constitute this unique sub-culture while showing how they navigate a world that limits them due to their size.

Terminology

The term "chubby," usually reserved for children and babies, has been adopted by the gay big men's community as a term of endearment. Most of the web communities and publications directed at big gay men and their admirers use the term "chubby" as a positive descriptor (BCPI, 2006). The term for fat admirers embraced in the big men's community by most people is "chubby-chaser." The first reference of the term chubby-chaser in popular culture that we are aware of is in the play *The Ritz* by Terrence McNally (1976). Perhaps taking a lesson from their "coming out" experience as queer, the reclamation of a term that has hitherto been one of mockery is a way that many fat individuals move from self-shame to size-positivity.

Theory

Chubbies and chubby-chasers experience the ramifications of both heterosexism (the belief that heterosexuality is the norm and any sexual identity other than that is subordinate) and sizeism daily. Heterosexism and sizeism, in turn, are both firmly rooted in sexism. Therefore, the devaluing of both queer and of fat people is related to existent gender hierarchies and our cultural obsession with sexual inequality (Brown & Rothblum, 1989). Moreover, we all live in a homophobic (fear/aversion toward queered identities and queer people) and fat-phobic culture (Collins, 2004; Wann, 1998). The fear and hatred of both queer and fat people are often based on the belief that both groups (a) *choose* to be different and socially unacceptable, (b) could change if they really wanted to or tried harder, and, therefore, (c) deserve the discrimination that they experience (Boykin, 1996). Given the "ism" ideology coupled with the phobic feelings, prejudice against fat and queer people is then rooted in both the sense of entitlement and the privileges of the dominant group (Brown & Rothblum, 1989).

Furthermore, any person or group who threatens the sexist, racist, heterosexist, or sizeist social norms is subject to stigmatization. This means that even people who do not have stigmatized bodies (e.g., fat), but rather subvert the dominant paradigm by expressing attraction to those bodies, are subject to ridicule and prejudice. Because these social norms regarding body size exist not only in the dominant culture but also within queer communities, fat gay/bisexual men and their admirers are ostracized both by other gay/bisexual men as well as heterosexual society.

Sizeist, racist, and heterosexist attitudes can be activated just by thinking that someone is a member of the target group (Boykin, 1996). Because this prejudice is so ubiquitous and the consequences so damaging, the closet can be an attractive coping mechanism. Many sexual minorities (e.g., fat admirers, queer persons, etc.) will deny their very core because of social consequences. Chubby-chasers avoid many negative experiences and gain many privileges by staying in the closet, both as fat admirers and as gay/bisexual men. Passing as heterosexual is also a viable and attractive option for many chubbies who, as fat men, do not fit the dominant image of gay men. In addition to the personal psychological costs of passing, when large numbers of men choose to live in the closet there are also the social costs of group cohesion, size, and strength (Edgar, 1994).

History of Fat Marginalization in the Gay Community

After the 1969 Stonewall rebellion in New York (a riot outside a gay bar where the police were harassing and arresting patrons, which marks the beginning of the modern gay rights movement in the United States), there was an exodus of gay men from rural areas to large urban centers. These men were looking for places where they could be "out of the closet" or just meet other gay men. It was during this period that stereotypes about gay men became widespread, promoted by mainstream society, and internalized by gay men themselves.

The stereotype of gay men propagated by media is that of the thin or muscular young man (Levine, 1998). In fact, the pressure to be thin/muscular, young, and attractive by traditional standards is at least as strong among gay men as it is among heterosexual women. This similarity to the pressures that straight women feel has been attributed to the desire to be attractive to men. Men's sexual attractions are often based more on the visual stimulus of their object of attraction than those of women (Atkins, 1998). Like straight women who want to be attractive to men, gay men are aware that their appearance is crucial to finding a male mate.

Gay men, however, come in all races, shapes, sizes, and ages. Just as community centers and support groups began addressing the various needs of the queer communities, small sexual sub-cultures began to form within these greater communities in reaction to the rigid queer cultural norms. Among these sexual sub-cultures were leather clubs, bondage and domination clubs, clubs for older men and their admirers, and clubs for fat men and their admirers. The first clubs for big men and their male admirers were started in New York and San Francisco in the mid-1970s and were called Girth and Mirth (Suresha, 2002). These groups were havens for fat gay men who felt ostracized by the fat-phobic gay bar scene, which was, and still is, the main public arena for gay men.

As more clubs formed around the country, they began to organize at a national level, resulting in the Affiliated Big Men's Clubs (ABC) in 1985 (Textor, 1999). ABC is an umbrella organization that loosely links the twenty or more Girth and Mirth clubs around the country and coordinates the five or six national and regional gatherings each year. This has created a national network of big men and their admirers, who socialize together several times a year all over the world (Textor, 1999). The North American ABC event, dubbed Convergence, started in 1986 (Textor, 1999) and takes place in a different city in the United States or Canada each year. The presence of fat men and their male admirers is felt in the queer communities of these cities, as many bars and clubs sponsor events to attract convention dollars. The event is usually hosted at a major hotel or resort over Labor Day Weekend and attracts five hundred to one thousand men each year. Whether one spends the weekend having sex or catching up with old friends, Convergence offers a respite for a group that is doubly and triply stigmatized for their body size or attraction to a particular body size, sexual orientation, and, in some cases, race (Boykin, 1996; Collins, 2004). Unfortunately, in reporting on these groups, researchers tend to reinforce the stigma by endorsing the popular myth that fat people are obsessed with food. For example, in his 1999 report on the big men's movement, Textor focuses much of his attention on a very small minority within the big men's movement known as gainers and encouragers, individuals who fetishize weight gain through intentional overeating and overfeeding.

Evolution of the Community

Because many fat gay men live in rural areas or in regions that don't have an ABC club nearby, shortly after the formation of the first Girth and Mirth clubs, magazines aimed at big men and their male admirers began publication. Magazines like *Big Ad*,

Bulk Male, and *Heavy Duty* all started in the late 1980s and early 1990s (Textor, 1999). They featured pictures of big men (some X-rated), stories about relationships and sexual encounters between big men and their male admirers, and, most important, personal ads.

Personal ads in magazines have long been one of the few ways that members of small sub-communities of the U.S. population have been able to find one another (Bahdahdah, Tiemann, & Pyle, 2004; Phua & Kaufman, 2003). Many big gay men and their admirers met through personal ads in the 1970s through 1990s. These ads usually described their appearance, sexual or relationship status, and partner preferences. The magazines were largely supported by these personal ads, because it was quite difficult to find advertisers for such a small and stigmatized community. As we will discuss below, this stands in sharp contrast to the vast amounts of money being made through the commodification of the "bear" identity.

In the late 1990s, magazine personals gave way to the internet, and most of the magazines went out of publication. In their place emerged vast internet communities that soon became global. Several chat rooms emerged for large men and their admirers on America Online and other internet chat sites. Still in existence in 2006, Chubnet was the first web site developed for the sole purpose of connecting big men and their admirers (Textor, 1999). In recent years, more web sites have come online: BiggerCity, with an international focus and over one thousand ads; BiggerWorld, the European Chubnet; and even the old magazine *Bulk Male* is now Bulkmale.com. Internet technology has fostered growth in the movement; gatherings that used to draw fewer than one hundred men now draw several hundred. On the other hand, it is a fragile community, as evidenced by the aftermath of Hurricane Katrina. Convergence 2005 was scheduled for New Orleans; upon cancellation of the event, someone embezzled all the money that was to be returned to the people who had registered. As a result, attendance at the following year's convention in Houston was down to 150. In 2007, Convergence was hosted by the Twin Cities group and attendance was double the previous year, but still not up to the pre-Katrina numbers. The next two Convergences in 2008 and 2009 were in Washington DC and Las Vegas. Big men's web sites serve to connect members of the international big men's communities with local clubs and events all over the world. As a result, the movement is bigger and stronger than ever.

The Bears

Much bigger than any of the big men's networks, however, is the bear network. About ten years after the beginning of the big men's movement, a new identity emerged among queer communities: the "bear." The bears seemed to emerge from a combination of leather men, chubby men, and the aging of what Levine (1998) calls the homosexual clone. Clones were men who in the 1970s exuded a macho personality: they had a buff physique and usually wore jeans and T-shirts (possibly a flannel shirt), rejecting the femme qualities associated with gay men in favor of a hypermasculine gay image (Levine, 1998). As they got older, gay clones refined this image and merged into the bear sub-culture. Generally, bears are big, hairy men who exude a toughness and masculinity not necessarily associated with big men's clubs, although many bears attend events sponsored by big men's clubs and vice versa. Though bears are bigger and hairier than the gay stereotype, the emphasis is generally on the hirsute and stereotypically masculine qualities of the bear. This way, bears avoid the stigma of being fat, which is associated with laziness, self-indulgence, and stereotypically feminine traits like softness (Sedgwick & Moon, 1994). There is also an assumption in western culture that no fat person is even sexual, let alone sexually desirable. In this way fat men are excluded from sexual desire. The illusory correlation of fatness and femininity, or fatness and asexuality (Loewy, 1994), might be the reason that fat men's clubs, where fat rather than physical strength, hairiness, and other stereotypically masculine traits is the emphasis, have lagged behind in terms of membership numbers.

There was a very elaborate rating system developed to describe all the different qualities of the bear, officially called the "Natural Bear Classifications System" or "Bear Code" for short (Donohue & Stoner, 1996; see also table 16.1, below). This elaborate scale denotes a well-developed culture that, in a very short time, has evolved and grown a much larger constituency than the big men's groups from which it emerged. One indication of the scope of this development is the highly organized marketing of the culture. At bear events like International Bear Rendezvous in San Francisco each year, significant energy, space, and resources are devoted to selling and buying products of interest to bears and their admirers. Everything is available: internet chat sites; bear pornography; the full bear "uniform" of baseball caps, jeans, and flannel shirts; even beard conditioners are made available to eager consumers. All this promotes homogenization of a bear aesthetic. A trip to the vendor "maul" can outfit a bear for the weekend—if you have the money! The prominence of the vendor maul at the event is only the most obvious example of class exclusion within big men's and bear clubs. The gatherings of predominantly middle- and upper-middle-class, mostly white men almost always take place in a warm climate at a four-star resort. The posh locales, coupled with the dominance of the internet as the major method of communicating within the community, means that only people who can afford the travel and technology can access the benefits (Textor, 1999).

The Chasers

What attracts many of the big men to Girth and Mirth events are the men who are primarily or exclusively attracted to fat men. These "fat admirers" or "chubby-chasers" are members and leaders of the clubs around the country. Many have strong positive identities related to their sexual orientation as fat admirers. Similar to their chubby counterparts, however, some are deeply closeted (as gay, as a chaser, or both) and experience the Girth and Mirth events as a rare opportunity to interact in a positive and fun way with both the object(s) of their desire as well as others who share their extremely stigmatized orientation. Because most people travel to Convergence, there

TABLE 16.1
Excerpt from Bear Code

Code	Quality	Least	Most
B	Beard/Facial Hair	0 = No Beard	9 = ZZ Top
F	Fur/Body Hair	— = Totally Hairless	++ = The Werewolf
T	Tall/Height	— = Very Short	++ = Very Tall
W	Weight	— = Very Thin	++ = Very Fat
C	Cub/Younger (Acting)/also CD Hybrid	— = Somewhat Cubby	++ = Very Cubby
D	Daddy/Older (Acting)/also DC Hybrid	— = Somewhat Daddy	++ = Very Daddy
G	Groping/Likes to Be Touched	— = Don't Touch	++ = Anything Goes
K	Kink/Sexual Practices	— = Vanilla	++ = Anything Goes
S	Slut/Relationship Orientation	— = Monogamous	++ = Anything Goes
M	Muscles (No — for This Category)	+ = Some	++ = Arnold
E	Equipment (Size) (No — for This Category	+ = Wow!	++ = Ohmygod!
R	Rugged/Outdoorsy	— = Couch Potato	++ = Grizzly Adams
P	Peculiar/Odd (No — for This Category	+ = A Little	++ = A Lot
Q	Queer/Comfort with Being Out	— = Totally Closeted	++ = Fabulous

is an anonymity that allows those closeted individuals to be "out" in public places, at least for the duration of the event.

Just as sexual attraction does not always conform to mainstream notions of heterosexuality, neither does it always conform to mainstream notions of beauty. Some people are attracted to fat people even though fat is strongly stigmatized in our society. For a slender, conventionally attractive person to be sexually attracted to a fat person is beyond the comprehension of most people (Klein, 2001). Many people seem to have no compunction about telling chasers just how "weird" they are for "settling," or worse yet, *choosing*, to love or be attracted to someone so grotesque. Or they assume that the chaser loves his fat partner in spite of his size, rather than because of it. The truth is, there are a significant number of people, queer and straight, whose primary or exclusive sexual attraction is to fat individuals (NAAFA [National Association to Advance Fat Acceptance], 1998). Because fat people are stigmatized as unattractive and asexual, chubby-chasers are also stigmatized; fat chubby-chasers experience stigma both as fat people and as fat admirers.

Feelings of isolation that chasers often experience are alleviated by involvement in communities like Girth and Mirth or via internet chat. Though thin- to average-sized chasers make up only about 10–30% of the membership of these clubs, and attendance at these events and online communities consists mainly of chubbies, a chaser can still find individuals who share his tastes in men and participate in the age old tradition of "dishing" (talking about their shared attraction and collective identity). Talking about one's sexual orientation or object of affection with others who truly understand and share that orientation leads to behavioral validation and identity pride (Simon, 2004). Just as members of queer communities find strength in other queer people, chubby chasers find strength in connecting with one another and are able to do so through these clubs. In the 21st century, coming out is still a traumatic process for many queer individuals. The importance of having a slim or muscular body type, and being attracted to this same body type, is paramount in the gay men's community. In an era when mainstream television and movies feature queer characters and communities, discovering that one's sexual attraction is atypical, even among gay men, adds a level of complexity to the coming out process that is not addressed in any body of academic literature or by any of the psychological services available for young gay men.

Conclusion—Big Men's Networks and Size-Positivity

We do not want to represent the big men's network as an activist movement; far from it. Interestingly, it seems that there are many more politically, fiscally, and sometimes even socially conservative men in the big men's community than in many other queer communities. The groups are almost exclusively social in nature; there is no overt political or educational agenda. Although there may not be a gay liberation or fat liberation movement, there are definitely identity politics in play. A 1996 statement by San Francisco's Girth and Mirth board of directors said, "Gay and bisexual big men, and those who prefer big men, have cast off the shackles of hiding and insecurity and now revel in their proudly accepted identity" (Textor, 1999). Though the leadership and many of the members embrace a positive fat gay identity, a significant number of baby boomers married and had children before coming out of the closet, and some are still closeted. Identity politics and the closet makes for a group of men with a broad spectrum of attitudes ranging from self-loathing to self-affirming with regard to being fat, queer, or a chubby-chaser/fat admirer.

Few, if any, of these men would identify as fat activists or know anything about the fat activist movement. Nevertheless, the atmosphere at the events is very fat-friendly. Rarely do people talk about diets or efforts to lose weight. When people do, they are usually rebuked, made aware that the large body is desirable and that the self-loathing usually associated with being fat is not tolerated, let alone encouraged. Ultimately, those with more fat-positive attitudes begin to have an effect on those who are still internalizing the fat phobia and sizeism so prevalent in western culture. In a society where fat-positivity is seen as deviant, these men are successfully flaunting their radical, fat-positive identities and sexualities, thereby changing public perceptions of what it means to be fat, queer, or sexually attracted to fat men. Though few members of big men's clubs see themselves as social change agents, they have created infrastructures without which they could not find other men who appreciate them just the way they are, both as chubbies and as chubby-chasers. Regardless of whether they recognize it, these men are behaving in ways that facilitate social change toward a more size-positive way of seeing themselves and others.

REFERENCES

Atkins, D. (1998). Introduction: Looking queer. In D. Atkins (Ed.), *Looking Queer: Body Image and Identity in Lesbian, Bisexual, Gay, and Transgender Communities.* Binghamton, NY: Haworth Press.

Bahdahdah, A., Tiemann, K. & Pyle, N.C. (2004, April). *Mate Selection Among Muslims Living in America.* Paper presented at the annual meeting of the Midwest Sociological Society, Minneapolis, MN.

BCPI (1999–2006). Biggercity. Retrieved on April 16, 2006, from http://www.biggercity.com.

Boykin, K. (1996). *One More River to Cross: Black and Gay in America.* New York: Doubleday.

Brown, L.S., & Rothblum, E.D. (1989). *Overcoming Fear of Fat.* Binghamton, NY: Haworth Press.

Collins, P.H. (2004). *Black Sexual Politics.* New York: Routledge.

Donohue, B., & Stoner, J. (1996, May). The bear codes: The natural bears classification system (v1.1). *Resources for Bears.* Retrieved April 16, 2006, from http://resourcesforbears.com/nbcs.

Edgar, T. (1994). Self disclosure behaviors of the stigmatized: Strategies and outcomes for the revelation of sexual orientation. In R.J. Ringer (Ed.), *Queer Words, Queer Images: Communication and the Construction of Homosexuality.* New York: NYU Press.

Klein, R. (2001). Fat beauty. In J.E. Braziel & K. LeBesco (Eds.), *Bodies Out of Bounds: Fatness and Transgression.* Berkeley: University of California Press.

Levine, M.P. (1998). *Gay Macho: The Life and Death of the Homosexual Clone.* New York: NYU Press.

Loewy, M.I. (1994). *Size Bias by Mental Health Professionals: Use of the Illusory Correlation Paradigm.* Unpublished doctoral dissertation, University of California, Santa Barbara, CA.

McNally, T. (1976). *The Ritz.* Garden City, NY: Nelson Doubleday.

NAAFA Inc. (1998, August 13). NAAFA policy: Fat admirers. Retrieved on April 16, 2006, from http://www.naafaonline.com/dev2//about/Policies/FATADMIRERS.pdf.

Phua, V.C., & Kaufman, G. (2003). The crossroads of race and sexuality: Date selection among men in internet personal ads. *Journal of Family Issues 24*(8), 981–994.

Sedgwick, E.K, & Moon, M. (1994). Divinity: A dosier, a performance piece, a little-understood emotion. In E.K. Sedgwick (Ed.), *Tendencies.* Durham: Duke University Press.

Simon, B. (2004). *Identity in Modern Society: A Social Psychological Perspective.* Malden, MA: Blackwell Publishing.

Suresha, R. (2002). *Bears on Bears: Interviews and Discussions.* Los Angeles: Alyson Publications.

Textor, A. R. (1999). Organization, specialization, and desires in the big men's movement: Preliminary research in the study of subculture formation. *Journal of Gay, Lesbian, and Bisexual Identity, 4*(3), 217–239.

Wann, M. (1998). *Fat!So? Because You Don't Have to Apologize for Your Size!* Berkeley, CA: Ten Speed Press.

The Shape of Abuse
Fat Oppression as a Form of Violence Against Women

Tracy Royce

There is now a large body of scholarly work documenting the many ways in which fat people are stigmatized in contemporary U.S. society (see Wann, Burgard, this volume). Although fat men are certainly subject to prejudice and discrimination, anti-fat bias is particularly salient in the lives of fat women, who have to contend with unrealistic, ever-narrowing beauty standards and the considerable importance that society places on female appearance (Chen & Brown, 2005; Gailey & Prohaska, 2006; Schur, 1984; Wolf, 1991).

One area of special concern for fat women has gone relatively unexplored in the social science literature: the intersection of fat oppression and violence against women.[1] Since the advent of the anti-rape and anti–domestic violence movements, feminists have provided ample evidence of the pervasiveness and severity of various forms of violence against women (Brownmiller, 1975; Walker, 1979). Literature in this area increasingly embraces an intersectional approach, reflecting an understanding that a woman's race/ethnicity, class, sexuality, and other facets of identity shape not only the commission of violence, but also social and institutional responses to her victimization (Crenshaw, 1991; Renzetti, 1992; Waldron, 1996). Little has been established, however, about whether and how anti-fat bias may foster violence against the many women whose body size exceeds mainstream social acceptance. As a woman of size, antiviolence advocate, feminist, and survivor, I argue not only that violence affects fat women in ways specific to their size, but also that fat women are sometimes targeted for violence precisely because of their size. An increased understanding of the intersection of sizeism, sexism, and violence against women not only enhances the intellectual and political work of size acceptance proponents, antiviolence advocates, and feminists; it ultimately benefits fat women who already are or may become survivors of abuse.

The majority of the existing empirical studies that at least tangentially address the intersection of violence against women and body size document female fatness as a correlate of sexual abuse (Cloutier, Martin, & Poole, 2002; Felitti, 1991; Felitti 1993; Frayne, Skinner, Sullivan, & Freund, 2003). Clearly, research that establishes the traumatic consequences of childhood sexual abuse and sexual assault is important. But as

LeBesco and Braziel (2001) suggest, taken as a whole, this literature implicitly conflates the fat body and the traumatized body, suggesting that large body size is a pathology that emerges in the aftermath of male-perpetrated violence against women. Evoking additional unpleasant associations with fatness, authors of several works focusing on nonfamilial abductors of infants suggest that such offenders are likely to be female and fat (Baker, Burgess, & Rabun, 2002; Rabun, 2003).

With the tools to best illuminate connections between fat oppression and violence against women, feminist literature (Ansfield, 1998; Koppelman, 2003; Mabel-Lois & Aldebaran, 1983) helps fill the void in social science scholarship by providing theoretical and narrative accounts of fat women's victimization. Feminist literature is especially valuable in that it foregrounds the perspectives and experiences of oppressed people such as fat women, while demystifying structures of power, privilege, and hierarchies that contribute to fat women's marginalization. Incorporating this literature, I will first discuss how body size affects fat women's experience of partner abuse. Next, I will discuss verbal harassment perpetrated by intimates, authority figures, and strangers. Finally, I provide recommendations for future research and community activism to improve our understanding and response to size-related violence against women.

Abuse by a current or former partner is a leading cause of injury and death of women (Department of Justice, 2007). Feminists have theorized that partner abuse, at least in heterosexual contexts, is both a result of patriarchal domination on a societal level, and a means by which particular men exert power and control over "their" women (Jones, 2000). Historically, legal, religious, medical, and social institutions have been complicit in the abuse of battered women in a variety of ways, ultimately displacing blame for the abuse from perpetrators on to victims (Herman, 1997; Jones, 2000). Rather than stemming from individual batterers' pathologies, battering reflects the cultural devaluation of women; and institutionalized sexism perpetuates men's violent power and control over women: "Consider, for instance, a 1994 case in which a Maryland judge sentenced a defendant, a man who had killed his wife after he found her in bed with another man, to just eighteen months probation, stating that most men would have felt compelled to 'punish' their partners under such circumstances" (Curran & Renzetti, 2001, p. 221). Clearly, not all abusive relationships result in homicide. Abuse exists along a continuum, and abusers employ a variety of tactics to control their victims and impede their ability to leave the relationship. Because victims' experiences are not only shaped by their gender but also by their race/ethnicity, class, sexuality, and other aspects of identity (Crenshaw, 1991), batterers can exploit societal prejudice as an additional means of abuse. For example, a woman who batters her female lover can taunt her partner with the near certainty that if her partner tries to escape the abuse, her efforts to leave will be thwarted by institutionalized heterosexism and service providers' homophobic responses (Renzetti, 1992).

Similarly, batterers can wield societal fatphobia against their partners. Fat women in relationships with abusers are subject to their partners' fatphobic insults and verbal attacks on their desirability. Even for many people in non-abusive relationships, the fear of failing to find another partner is a compelling reason to stay in an unfulfilling relationship; having your partner repeatedly scream that you are a "fat, fucking ugly bitch" (Anonymous, 1991, p. 54) and that no one else could possibly want you can shatter self-esteem and make leaving virtually unthinkable. Anecdotal evidence suggests that abusers may also attempt to control their fat victims' dietary intake, or flaunt their interest in or affairs with thinner women.

Koppelman (2003) describes how such abuse both stems from and perpetuates fat women's marginalized position in society:

> In a society with a general penchant for punishing difference, and an excessively high regard for bodily appearances as cultural markers, it makes perfect sense that fat bodies will be abused in a variety of ways. In fact, it often does not matter if a woman is really fat; if she lives in a fat-fearing, fat-hating culture and she is in an intimate relationship with an abuser she is likely to be told she is fat, scolded and punished for being fat. This abuse is perhaps only that most literal expression of the punishment our culture imposes on bodies that dare to transgress from the socially prescribed norms. (Koppelman, 2003, p. 258)

And such punishment may not stop when a woman succeeds in extricating herself from an abusive relationship. She may then have little choice but to establish new abusive relationships, not with batterers, but with various service providers whose mission to help has been poisoned by anti-fat bias. Health-care professionals and mental health workers are infamous for anti-fat attitudes and mistreatment of fat people (Hassel, Amici, Thurston, & Gorsuch, 2001; Mabel-Lois & Aldebaran, 1983; Puhl & Brownell, 2001; Schwartz, Chambliss, Brownell, Blair, & Billington, 2003). Law enforcement officials, charged with upholding hard-won laws protecting women from physical and sexual violence, may revictimize rather than rescue fat women. In particular, fat women who have been sexually assaulted have disclosed that police officers have refused to take their reports and ridiculed them as insufficiently attractive to rape (Goodman, 1995; Mabel-Lois & Aldebaran, 1983). Such trivialization of harm, victim blaming, and other forms of secondary victimization may be experienced as more painful than the original abuse.

Further, although I would charge that all rhetoric that vilifies fat people is abusive, fat women's narratives suggest that heterosexual male partners routinely "critique" their fat partners' bodies, even in relationships that are not conventionally thought of as abusive (Doris K., 1983; Koppelman, 2003; Levy, 1983). But do such comments, in the absence of physical or sexual abuse, truly constitute "violence"? Gay (1997) argues that language "perpetuates the harm of a system of oppression" (p. 468), and can be deployed as a means of achieving dominance. Men's remarks about their female partners' bodies are sometimes made under the guise of "helpfulness"; other times they are overt in their cruelty (Doris K., 1983; Koppelman, 2003). In either case, these sizeist comments signify a gendered power differential between partners and evoke the sexist, fatphobic ideology that some batterers wield against their victims. The power of verbal abuse and shaming comments should not be underestimated. Emotional/verbal abuse and shame are associated with posttraumatic stress disorder (PTSD) symptomology (Street & Arias, 2001), and many battered women report that verbal abuse is the most damaging weapon in their batterers' arsenals (Walker, 1979). Additionally, men's criticisms of their partners' weight may develop into a pattern of haranguing and a struggle to control the shape and size of women's bodies. Again, sexism and anti-fat bias interact to undermine women's self-esteem and prevent them, literally and metaphorically, from taking up "too much" space (Koppelman, 2003).

Verbal assaults on the dignity and the bodily integrity of fat women are not confined to intimate relationships. Lenskyj's (1992) study investigating women's experiences with sexual harassment in university physical education and sports participation documents how female athletes who gain weight are tyrannized by coaches (often male) who mortify them publicly. Techniques of humiliation include public weigh-ins, insults, posted "fat lists" (Lenskyj, 1992), or "weekly 'Fat Pig' awards" (Maine, 2000, p. 248). This mistreatment can trigger eating disorders and extreme dieting in athletes eager not to be cut from teams. Lenskyj (1992) suggests that this form of harassment occurs at the intersection of sexism, sizeism, and homophobia, and that women athletes are not only policed with regard to their body size, but also incur negative consequences (such as being passed over for selection for a team or being forced to room with homophobic teammates) for triggering suspicions of lesbianism by failing to meet standards of conventional, thin, heterosexual femininity. Again, thinner athletes on such a team are also harmed by the intersection of these oppressions, as they must monitor their gender presentation and body size to avoid sanctions.

Perpetrators of verbal abuse of fat women need not have any prior relationship with their victims to dispense their vitriol. Fat women have disclosed their hurt, anger, and humiliation at being accosted, shamed, jeered at, yelled at from passing cars, preached to, poked, pinched, and offered unsolicited diet advice by strangers of both sexes (Ansfield, 1998; Goodman, 1995; Hannah, 1983; Wann, 1998). A few of the insults that fat women have endured include: "Are you fat enough?" (Ansfield, 1998, p. 18); "Slimfast, Slimfast, Jenny Craig, Jenny Craig" (Ansfield, 1998, p. 17); and, as stated by a first time acquaintance during a seminar exercise in which participants were encouraged to disclose something that they did not like about another participant, "I'd like to tell you that your body is repulsive, and it's especially repulsive to me because you have such a nice face" (Hannah, 1983, p. 136).

These are not caring or helpful comments, designed to alert fat women to the alleged health dangers of large body size. They are tangible evidence of some people's perceived entitlement to actively reinforce the marginalized position that fat women occupy in society. That some fatphobic people transgress norms of public courtesy so openly suggests that they see fat women as less than fully human and therefore undeserving of the treatment typically afforded to thinner strangers. Moreover, because such perpetrators have no previous relationship to those against whom they aggress, we can say with some confidence that this form of verbal violence specifically targets fat women because of their size. My personal experience as someone who has "weight cycled" over the years (cyclically gained and lost large amounts of weight) suggests that some male strangers are not only more likely to become verbally aggressive with a fat woman, but also to physically threaten and intimidate her, perhaps because they regard her as lacking sexual utility.

Social science literature provides ample evidence of the stigmatized position that fat people, particularly fat women, occupy in contemporary society. If we are to trust fat women's accounts of their own experiences (and we should), more empirical research documenting the intersection of fat oppression and violence against women is sorely needed. Qualitative research exploring fat women's experiences with battering, secondary victimization, sexual assault, stranger confrontation, and other forms of violence and abuse will not only fill a significant gap in the academy's knowledge, but can also amplify the voices of fat women. Quantitative research is also needed; there are currently no statistics quantifying the proportion of fat women who have been subjected to these and other forms of violence. Further, here I have privileged the intersection of gender and body size, but research investigating how women's race/ethnicity, class, and sexual orientation may differentially shape their experiences with fatphobic abuse should be conducted. My inventory of the realms in which fat oppression and violence against women intersect is incomplete at best, and should be expanded. For example, some women have proposed classifying bariatric surgeries as "crimes" (Kelly, 1983) or "mutilation" (Wolfe, 1983); it is worth increasing our understanding of women's experiences with and perceptions of these procedures. Finally, because of the pervasive silence surrounding violence against fat women, I have emphasized victimization rather than agency. The ways in which fat women cope with, resist, and organize against abuse also warrant investigation.

Research is no panacea, however, particularly if it is inaccessible (linguistically, theoretically, epistemologically, or otherwise) to advocates, activists, and stakeholders in the community who may not only apply the results to achieve social change, but who can also help create and shape studies in this area. Feminist participatory research, in which research participants have a vested interest in the study and collaborate with the investigator on its goals and design (Renzetti, 1992), is particularly well suited for this topic. Such research has the potential to produce not only academic results, but also consciousness-raising and advocacy, both of which are sorely needed in today's fatphobic climate. Increased reciprocity between researchers and community members not only enlivens research and increases its relevance for social change; it constitutes a form of activism in itself. Additionally, all community organizations focusing on battering, sexual assault, and other forms of violence against women should develop and integrate information on size oppression into their training curriculums. The problem of violence against fat women will not be quickly or easily solved. But elucidating this under-acknowledged form of oppression constitutes an essential step toward justice and equality.

NOTE

1. For a notable exception, see Gailey and Prohaska's (2006; and this volume) excellent work on "hogging"—heterosexual men's misogynist, anti-fat practice of hooking up with women they deem to be fat or unattractive for "laughs" or "sport."

REFERENCES

Anonymous. (1991). He only wants to help me. In B. Levy (Ed.), *Dating Violence: Young Women in Danger* (pp. 53–57). Seattle: Seal Press.

Ansfield, A. (1998). Rude remarks and right on rejoinders! *Radiance, 55,* 16–19.

Baker, T., Burgess, A.W., & Rabun, J.B. (2002). Abductor violence in nonfamily infant kidnapping. *Journal of Interpersonal Violence, 17*(11), 1218–1233.

Brownmiller, S. (1975). *Against Our Will: Men, Women, and Rape.* New York: Fawcett Columbine.

Chen, E.Y., & Brown, M. (2005). Obesity stigma in sexual relationships. *Obesity Research, 13*(8), 1393–1397.

Cloutier, S., Martin, S.L., & Poole, C. (2002). Sexual assault among North Carolina women: Prevalence and health risk factors. *Journal of Epidemiology and Community Health, 56,* 265–271.

Crenshaw, K. (1991). Mapping the margins: Intersectionality, identity politics, and violence against women of color. *Stanford Law Review, 43*(6), 1241–1299.

Curran, D.J, & Renzetti, C.M. (2001). *Theories of Crime* (2d ed.). Needham Heights, MA: Allyn and Bacon.

Department of Justice. (2007). Intimate partner violence in the U.S. Retrieved February 2, 2008, from http://www.ojp.gov/bjs/intimate/victims.htm.

Doris K. (1983). Ordinary hassles. In L. Schoenfielder & B. Wieser (Eds.), *Shadow on a Tightrope: Writings by Women on Fat Oppression* (pp. 113–117). San Francisco: Aunt Lute Books.

Felitti, V.J. (1991). Long-term medical consequences of incest, rape, and molestation. *Southern Medical Journal, 84*(3), 328–331.

Felitti, V.J. (1993) Childhood sexual abuse, depression, and family dysfunction in adult obese patients: A case control study. *Southern Medical Journal, 86*(7), 732–736.

Frayne, S.M., Skinner, K.M., Sullivan, L.M., & Freund, K.M. (2003). Sexual assault risk while in the military: Violence as a predictor of cardiac risk? *Violence and Victims, 18,* 219–225.

Gailey, J.A., & Prohaska, A. (2006). "Knocking off a fat girl": An exploration of hogging, male sexuality, and neutralizations. *Deviant Behavior, 27,* 31–49.

Gay, W.C. (1997). The reality of linguistic violence against women. In L. O'Toole & J. Schiffman (Eds.), *Gender Violence: Interdisciplinary Perspectives* (pp. 467–473). New York: New York University Press.

Goodman, W.C. (1995). *The Invisible Woman: Confronting Weight Prejudice in America.* Carlsbad, CA: Gurze Books.

Hannah, S.B. (1983). The human potential movement: Judging people's humanity by their looks. In L. Schoenfielder & B. Wieser (Eds.), *Shadow on a Tightrope: Writings by Women on Fat Oppression* (pp. 135–138). San Francisco: Aunt Lute Books.

Hassel, T.D., Amici, C.J., Thurston, N.S., & Gorsuch, R.L. (2001). Client weight as a barrier to non-biased clinical judgment. *Journal of Psychology and Christianity: Special Issue: Valuing Our Voices, 20,* 145–161.

Herman, Judith. 1997. *Trauma and Recovery: The Aftermath of Violence—from Domestic Abuse to Political Terror.* New York: Basic Books.

Jones, A. (2000). *Next Time She'll Be Dead: Battering and How to Stop It.* Boston: Beacon Press.

Kelly. (1983). Medical crimes. In L. Schoenfielder & B Wieser (Eds.), *Shadow on a Tightrope: Writings by Women on Fat Oppression* (pp. 185–186). San Francisco: Aunt Lute Books.

Koppelman, S. (2003). Afterword. In S. Koppelman (Ed.), *The Strange History of Suzanne LaFleshe, and Other Stories of Women and Fatness* (pp. 229–268). New York: The Feminist Press at City University of New York.

LeBesco, K., & Braziel, J.E. (2001). Editors' introduction. In J.E. Braziel & K. LeBesco (Eds.), *Bodies Out of Bounds: Fatness and Transgression* (pp. 1–15). Berkeley: University of California Press.

Lenskyj, H. (1992). Unsafe at home base: Women's experiences of sexual harassment in university sport and physical education. *Women in Sport and Physical Activity Journal, 1*, 19–24.

Levy, L. (1983). Outrages. In L. Schoenfielder & B. Wieser (Eds.), *Shadow on a Tightrope: Writings by Women on Fat Oppression* (pp. 79–81). San Francisco: Aunt Lute Books.

Mabel-Lois, L., & Aldebaran, (1983). Fat women and women's fear of fat. In L. Schoenfielder & B. Wieser (Eds.), *Shadow on a Tightrope: Writings by Women on Fat Oppression* (pp. 53–57). San Francisco: Aunt Lute Books.

Maine, M. (2000). *Body Wars: Making Peace with Women's Bodies: An Activist's Guide.* Carlsbad, CA: Gurze Books.

Puhl, R., & Brownell, K.D. (2001). Bias, discrimination, and obesity. *Obesity Research, 9*, 788–805.

Rabun, J.B. (2003). *For Healthcare Professionals: Guidelines on Prevention of and Response to Infant Abductions* (8th ed.). Alexandria, VA: National Center for Missing and Exploited Children. Retrieved August 26, 2006, from http://www.missingkids.com/missingkids/servlet/ResourceServlet?LanguageCountry=en_US&PageId=468.

Renzetti, C.M. (1992). *Violent Betrayal: Partner Abuse in Lesbian Relationships.* Newbury Park, CA: Sage Publications.

Schur, E. M. (1984). *Labeling Women Deviant: Gender, Stigma, and Social Control.* New York: Random House.

Schwartz, M.B., Chambliss, H.O., Brownell, K.D., Blair, S.N., & Billington, C. (2003). Weight bias among health professionals specializing in obesity. *Obesity Research, 11*, 1033–1039.

Street, A.E., and Arias, I. (2001). Psychological abuse and posttraumatic stress disorder in battered women: Examining the roles of shame and guilt. *Violence and Victims, 16*(1), 65–78.

Waldron, C.M. (1996). Lesbians of color and the domestic violence movement. *Journal of Gay and Lesbian Social Services, 4* (1), 43–52.

Walker, L. (1979). *The Battered Woman.* New York: Harper and Row.

Wann, M. (1998). *Fat!So? Because You Don't Have to Apologize for Your Size!* Berkeley, CA: Ten Speed Press.

Wolf, N. (1991). *The Beauty Myth: How Images of Beauty Are Used Against Women.* New York: William Morrow.

Wolfe, L. (1983). Weight loss surgery: Miracle cure or mutilation? In L. Schoenfielder & B. Wieser (Eds.), *Shadow on a Tightrope: Writings by Women on Fat Oppression* (pp. 162–166). San Francisco: Aunt Lute Books.

Fat Women as "Easy Targets"
Achieving Masculinity Through Hogging

Ariane Prohaska and Jeannine Gailey

"Hogging" is a practice in which men prey on women they deem fat or unattractive to satisfy sexual desires or compete with their peers. Hoggers, a self-imposed label, are groups of men who hang out at bars or parties and try to pick up fat women for sex or make bets with their friends about who can pick up the fattest or most unattractive woman (Gailey & Prohaska, 2006). The bets range from simply getting a phone number or dance to receiving some form of sexual gratification from the woman.

Hogging, as a scholarly topic, has largely been ignored until recently (Gailey & Prohaska, 2006), but has gained some attention in the news media. Self-proclaimed hoggers were interviewed for *Scene Magazine*, a local entertainment magazine in Cleveland, Ohio (Fenske, 2003). The men interviewed for the *Scene Magazine* article refer to women they pick up as "hogs" or "slump-busters" (Fenske 2003, p. 15), a phrase used by baseball player Mark Grace on the *Jim Rome Show* and by baseball player Jose Canseco in his 2005 autobiography, *Juiced* (Dowd, 2005). When one is looking for a slump-buster, a hog, or "road beef" (as Canseco puts it), he seeks out, as Grace mentioned, the "fattest gnarliest chick you can uncover" in order to try to break out of a slump (Dowd, 2005, p. 99). The implication of Grace's quote is that fat women are sexually easy and can help men out of a losing streak, either on the field or in the bedroom.

The present chapter focuses on how hogging is used as a tool whereby men create and maintain masculinity. The sociology of masculinities is a burgeoning field in the sociology of gender (see, e.g., Brannon, 1976; Connell, 1987; Kaufmann, 1994; Kimmel, 1998; 2006). Kimmel (2006) argues that there are multiple masculinities, with the dominant, hegemonic masculinity being the most rewarded in contemporary society. Men reward one another with power and prestige if they adhere to the hegemonic masculine ideal.

Robert Brannon (1976) discussed four aspects of the male gender role: (1) "No Sissy Stuff" (antifemininity); (2) "Be a Sturdy Oak" (inexpressiveness and independence); (3) "Give 'em Hell" (adventurousness and aggression); and (4) "Be a Big Wheel" (status and achievement). Men adhere to the masculine ideal in different ways: participating in sports, drinking heavily, or pursuing women for sexual purposes. One extreme way that men may attempt to adhere to normative masculinity is by hogging. We analyze the connection among achieving masculinity, women's size, and hogging by asking the following research questions: (1) Is sex the only goal of hogging, or is the goal to reaffirm one's threatened masculinity? and (2) Do men seek out fat women because they view them as "easy targets," or is hogging an excuse that men use because they had sex with fat or unattractive women?

Masculinities

The dominant form of masculinity in the United States is *hegemonic masculinity* (Connell, 1987). It is rooted in values such as control, dominance, competition, and aggression while devaluing emotional attachment. As mentioned, Brannon's (1976) four components of the male gender role do not exist within an individual man; masculinity must be achieved through social interactions. Masculinity, then, is a "homosocial enactment" (Kimmel, 2006, p. 140); men participate in activities that adhere to the hegemonic ideal so that other men will recognize their masculinity, thereby affirming that they are "real men" (Connell, 1987). Kaufmann (1994) argues that men who cannot be "big wheels" may find other ways to achieve masculinity (Gailey & Prohaska, 2006). Hogging may be an extreme case that resembles sexual aggression; showing one's power over women becomes a way to prove manhood and be a "big wheel."

Sexual conquest is an important part of hegemonic masculinity (Kimmel, 1998). One way for men to achieve status in their peer groups is by engaging in sexual acts with numerous women. Men who subscribe to hegemonic masculinity see alcohol as the easiest way to reduce women's inhibitions and gain access to sex (Kimmel, 1998). Once again, because society views this as normative behavior, men are rewarded by their peer groups and the consequences are often overlooked. Because hogging is an activity that often occurs in bars or at parties that serve alcohol, it is likely that this form of sexual predation is similar to other sexual acts pursued by men to prove their manhood.

It is important to note that most men are unable to live up to the ideal form of masculinity (Connell, 1987; Kaufmann, 1994; Kimmel, 2006). Hegemonic masculinity is most easily achieved by white, upper- and middle-class, heterosexual men; in other words, men in power who control access to scarce resources in society (Connell, 1987). Kimmel (2006) notes that this rigid construction of masculinity gives marginalized men—men of color, immigrant men, gay men, and working-class men, to name a few—a sense "that they are unmanly and will be exposed by other men" (p. 148). Men who do not fit into this category of normative masculinity may participate in "hypermasculine" behaviors to compensate for this feeling of "unmanliness."

Gender and Weight

Women in the United States are under considerable pressure to live up to normative beauty and thinness ideals. Research indicates that women who are in a "healthy weight range" often are obsessed with losing weight or report dissatisfaction with their figure (Germov & Williams, 1999). According to some scholars, the "beauty myth" and thin ideal sanctioned by the media are evidence of the patriarchal social control of women (see Bordo, 1993).

For women, "becoming an attractive object is a role obligation" (Schur, 1984, p. 66). The literature indicates that fat women are stigmatized more than fat men. Schur (1984) also contends that fatness is not just a physical state, but is often used as evidence of a character defect. Women who are fat are viewed as deviant, lazy, out of control, unattractive, and nonsexual (Austin, 1999; McKinley & Hyde, 1996; Schur, 1984). In turn, men then may not feel guilty for fulfilling hegemonic masculinity by victimizing women whom they view as deviant. In fact, hogging may serve as a form of social control over women's bodies.

Our previous research explored men's techniques of neutralization to reduce the stigma associated with hogging (Gailey & Prohaska, 2006). Our data indicated that men choose fat women as targets because they believe they are "easier" than women whom they consider physically attractive. Our previous study had two goals: first, to explore the behaviors, attitudes, and neutralization techniques of men who engaged in hogging; and second, to determine if men who were involved sexually with women who were fat were stigmatized or considered deviant by their peers. We found that this did occur. Men reported that it was common to make fun of a friend who had sexual encounters with women who were unattractive or fat. The current study on masculinity, weight, and hogging expands on this prior research by exploring whether hogging is a technique that men use to gain status with their peers and, therefore, affirm masculinity.

The Current Study

We employed two different methods to examine the relationship between masculinity and hogging: content analysis and semi-structured interviews (Prohaska & Gailey, n.d.). First, we performed a content analysis on the *Scene Magazine* article and relevant accounts from collegestories.com, an Internet website where college students write about their experiences with college life. Next, we interviewed the author of the *Scene Magazine* article, Sarah Fenske, to understand her experiences with interviewing men on this topic. She was able to provide us with information about both the socioeconomic characteristics of the men she interviewed and her recruitment techniques. Fenske's insight was especially helpful during the recruitment and interview-guide-construction portions of this project.

After performing the content analysis and interviewing Fenske, we conducted semi-structured interviews with thirteen college men, whose ages ranged from eighteen to forty-two, from a large, urban, Midwestern university (Prohaska and Gailey, n.d.). The sample was chosen mainly for convenience, but also because Fenske informed us that most of the men she interviewed had attended college. Additionally, because a portion of the data we collected was from collegestories.com, we felt that this population was appropriate for our exploratory study.

We constructed the interview guide from the content analysis, our interview with Fenske, and a review of the literature on masculinity, weight, and sexuality (Prohaska & Gailey, n.d.). The interviews began with basic questions, such as those regarding college major, expected date of graduation, and general dating behaviors. We hoped that this would help the men feel comfortable discussing their own or their friends' sexual and dating practices. We asked permission to tape-record the interviews and noted facial expressions and body language of the interviewees.

All data analysis was performed using QSR-NVivo (see Richards, 1999). Statements were coded based on Brannon's four components of masculinity (Prohaska & Gailey, n.d.). To review, Brannon conceptualized masculinity as involving four requirements: (1) Antifemininity: In their accounts, did the men make degrading comments about characteristics typically viewed as "feminine"? (2) Status and Achievement: Did the men discuss achieving a goal related to hegemonic masculinity? (3) Inexpressiveness and Independence: Did they talk about creating emotional distance between themselves and the women they were pursuing? and (4) Adventurousness and Aggression: Did they use alcohol to lower women's inhibitions? Here, we present all results briefly and expand on the results related to both masculinity and the weight of the women being pursued.

Results

Before we answer our research questions, it is useful to provide some basic background data. Nine of the men we interviewed had heard of hogging. Of these nine men, two admitted to participating in the sexual act, whereas the other seven reported on what they knew about hogging from friends or the media. The men who stated that they did not engage in sexual encounters often admitted to participating in the bets that facilitated hogging. Hogging was not the only concept mentioned when the act was described; when one interviewee was asked if he had heard of a practice where men preyed on fat women, he exclaimed, "It's dog's night baby and we're all gonna score!" Whatever name hogging was given, the men were describing the same actions (Prohaska & Gailey, n.d.).

Most of the men we interviewed described hogging as a way to achieve status with one's peers (forty times throughout the thirteen interviews), whether through winning the bet, entertaining others in the group, or through sexual gratification. Hogging was described as a way to mask insecurities about being rejected by "attractive" women, as an easy way to maintain emotional distance from women, and as a means of showing one's aggressiveness and adventurousness (Prohaska & Gailey, n.d.).

The content analysis yielded examples of men asserting their masculinity through inexpressiveness and independence (mentioned twenty-nine times), and adventurousness and aggression (mentioned eleven times), but gaining status in the group was the most frequently coded form of masculinity (mentioned thirty-four times) (Prohaska & Gailey, n.d.). For the purposes of this chapter, however, we discuss two ways that women's size became important to men who participated or knew about hogging. First, men saw fat women as "easy targets" whom they felt would put up little resistance to their sexual pursuits. Second, some of the men may be attracted to these women and use hogging as an "excuse" to avoid ridicule from their peers.

Fat Women as Easy Targets

Men interviewed by both Fenske and us largely agreed that the desired outcome of hogging was sex. After the bet, which provided entertainment, the purpose of hogging was, according to one interviewee, "sex, a blow job," "hot kinky sex," or "to see who could score that night." A common belief was that fat women were easy targets because they did not meet the societal ideal of physical attractiveness. One respondent noted, "It's common knowledge I think that most guys if you asked them, let's say, that maybe the less attractive of the heavier women were easier to do." Similarly, another interviewee stated, "[If] they want a quick, you know, quick sex fix, [they] might go up towards your, you know, heavier set or your uh, most people might consider your more ugly women to satisfy their sexual needs instead of going after someone that would be more attractive to you because they know they can get a one night stand out of this girl instead of, you know, trying to chase someone you know might already have a half dozen suitors." The above quote reveals two themes. First, men who participate in hogging pursue fat women because they are insecure about their abilities to court women whom they deem attractive. Additionally, statements such as these reflect Schur's (1984) conception of the beauty myth. If a woman is, from the pursuer's viewpoint, unattractive or fat, she is deviant. Accordingly, deviant women are viewed as deserving of negative treatment from others. Our previous research (Gailey & Prohaska, 2006) found that men who hogged often employed this neutralization technique. The men believed that the women either welcomed the attention or deserved it because they did not adhere to gender-based appearance norms. Men participate in hogging because they assume it is easier to receive sexual gratification from women who do not fit society's ideal of beauty or size; as a result, these men achieve status in their peer group by demeaning the woman and revealing the conquest.

The act must be divulged in order to gain status with friends. In most cases, sexual encounters that occurred because of hogging did not remain a secret. When asked if the encounter was discussed with the group, one respondent stated, "Oh yeah, oh yeah, you have to compare notes, you have to see who did what and what did who and how often it was done." One interviewee indicated that friends were in the room during intercourse: "We uh [laughing], this sounds kind of bad, we uh, have you ever heard of a rodeo? Usually on a night when a bet like that happens we do a rodeo. And we get pictures of it, usually the girl gets pretty pissed. But it's funny, we think it's funny." A rodeo, in this case, involves a group of men picking names out of a hat to see who will take home a fat woman for sexual purposes. The sexual act is watched, sometimes even photographed, by the man's peers. Flood (2008) discussed a rodeo in which the chosen man tied a woman to a bed in the middle of sexual intercourse while his friends hid in the closet. As the woman was restrained on her hands and knees, the man called to his friends to come out from their hiding places to watch as he attempted to stay on her back while she tried to free herself (Flood 2008, p. 351). In these cases, the men collectively participated in the sexual humiliation of the women, a situation that mimics gang rape not only because of the concurrent display of aggression and homosociality, but also because of the importance of recalling the behavior with peers later on (Sanday, 1990).

The above examples demonstrate that male participation, directly or vicariously, is a key component to hogging. At times, witnessing a friend leave with a fat or unattractive woman is not enough; "comparing notes" or watching intercourse take place is necessary to determine who wins the prize and, thus, who gains status in the group. Once again, the whole process, from the bet, to the sexual encounter, to the discussion of the event, contributes to group bonding. In the case of the "rodeo," hogging once again sparked laughter and provided entertainment. Interestingly, the man who reported watching the rodeo frequently discussed how he had "standards" that he would not "lower" just to have sex. But he still participated and was amused by the event. Hogging, then, is a homosocial activity in which all male participants have something to gain.

Hogging as an "Excuse"

At times, men would argue that they were hogging to justify their actions from the night before. It is unclear whether men are insecure about their abilities to pick up "thin" women, are justifying prior drunkenness, or are attracted to fat women. Using hogging as an excuse is another way to maintain status in the group; men do not want to be made fun of by their peers. A *Scene Magazine* interviewee summed up this idea: "It's hard to attribute all hogging to braggadocio and the fine art of B.S. Indeed, even some guys who've hogged insist it's no more than a way to justify drunken actions the morning after, 'Take a big girl home, and the next day, you say you went hogging . . . it's not like it's the plan. It's the backup plan'" (Fenske, 2003, p. 17). This defensiveness is echoed by Malamuth, Sockloskie, and Koss (1991) in their conception of "hostile masculinity." They argue that men who participate in violent behaviors toward women adhere to traditional gender roles. There are two components of hostile masculinity: (1) control and domination of women; and (2) insecurity, defensiveness, and distrust of women. Men may not feel that they are adhering to the hegemonic masculine ideal by having sex with a woman who is fat, but their peers accept "hogging" as a defense for their actions.

At times, it seems that the men are in adoration of the fat body, but they never proclaim this without the use of derogatory language. In fact, the men appear defensive. Men view hogging as a legitimate excuse for having sex with a fat woman, and it is difficult to tell if they are hiding their attraction to fat women to maintain status in their peer group. The passage below sums up this contradiction: "Rick runs through his Rolodex of hogging adventures with little prompting. There was his ex-girlfriend's sister: 'She was a little porker, and I violated her every way.' The secretary, with her big white breasts: 'She was a perfect hog. Beautiful face, big soft body'" (Fenske, 2003,

p. 15). Thus, in some instances, men may be interested in women who do not meet normative beauty standards and use hogging as an excuse to avoid ridicule from their friends or other men.

Conclusion

In this chapter, we discussed the act of hogging in terms of how men achieve masculinity by pursuing fat or unattractive women. We draw two conclusions from this exploratory study: (1) men view fat women as "easy targets" for sexual encounters, which gives men status in their peer groups; and (2) men use hogging as an "excuse" for either their insecurities about their ability to date "thin" women, their drunkenness, or their attraction to fat women. It is difficult, however, to tease out these relationships with these data. Most of the men we interviewed agreed that fat or unattractive women are undesirable to them; almost all of them had participated in hogging, however, by either encouraging their friends or by being the pursuer themselves. Thus, our data indicate that hogging allows a man to feel like a "real man"; that is, by participating in hogging, they are achieving normative masculinity.

There are a couple of limitations to the present study. One limitation involves the interview process. We are both women; therefore, the men we interviewed may have felt uncomfortable discussing hogging, which could be why the majority reported on friends' behaviors but not their own. They may have also toned down their language. We are aware that this is true for at least one interviewee who expressed his lack of comfort talking to women about sexual matters. Sarah Fenske reported a similar experience. The men she interviewed apologized for cursing around her, but not for referring to fat women in a derogatory manner. Fenske stated, "It was as if they viewed fat women differently than women who were not" (personal communication, April 4, 2004). Participants in Fenske's interviews, however, were interviewed in groups of two or more by a female journalist. Thus, her interviews were homosocial situations. The men may have been attempting to impress one another during the interview by embellishing their accounts of hogging. For these reasons alone, the complexity of the concept of masculinity necessitates that the interview setting and questions be carefully thought through.

The second limitation involves the sample. Our sample is relatively small and clearly cannot be considered representative of all college men. Given the clandestine nature of hogging and the exploratory aims of the present study, however, we feel that our sample, while not ideal, provides important insights into a behavior that has been largely ignored by the scholarly literature. Future research should use a larger, more diverse sample of men to improve the generalizability of the results. In addition, most of the men did not admit to hogging themselves, although many participated in the bets or were reportedly amused by the actions of their friends. Future studies should identify a larger sample of men who self identify as hoggers and discuss the behavior with them.

Despite the above limitations, recent research conducted by Michael Flood (2008) indicates that hogging is not unique to the United States and offers some validity to our findings. Flood's interviewees, from Australia, described events similar to the rodeo and numerous other instances where young men reportedly abused women whom they viewed as fat or unattractive.

Regardless of whether men are hogging because they view fat women as an easier conquest or because they are attracted to the fat body, it is obvious that the behavior exists partly because of normative beauty standards in the United States. As long as fat women are considered deviant, some men will continue to participate in this derogatory behavior. Additionally, as long as standards of masculinity are rigid and unachievable for most men, negative sexual consequences will exist for all women.

REFERENCES

Austin, S.B. (1999). Fat, loathing, and public health: The complicity of science in culture of disordered eating. *Culture, Medicine, and Psychiatry, 23,* 245–268.

Bordo, S. (1993). *Unbearable Weight: Feminism, Western Culture, and the Body.* Berkeley: University of California Press.

Brannon, R. (1976). The male sex role—and what it's done for us lately. In R. Brannon & D. David (Eds.). *The Forty-nine Percent Majority.* Reading, MA: Addison-Wesley.

Connell, R.W. (1987). *Gender and Power.* Stanford, CA: Stanford University Press.

Dowd, M. (February 20, 2005). Where's the road beef? *The New York Times,* 9.

Fenske, S. (2003). Big game hunters: They're men who chase chubbies for sport and pleasure: They call it hogging. *Scene Magazine, 34,* 15–18.

Flood, Michael. (2008). "Men, sex, and homosociality: How bonds between men shape their sexual relations with women." *Men and Masculinities, 10,* 339–360.

Gailey, J.A., & A. Prohaska. (2006). "Knocking off a fat girl": An exploration of hogging, male sexuality, and neutralizations. *Deviant Behavior, 27,* 31–49.

Germov, J., & L. Williams. (1999). Dieting women: Self-surveillance and the body panopticon. In J. Sobal & D. Maurer (Eds.). *Weighty Issues: Fatness and Thinness as Social Problems.* Hawthorne: New York.

Kaufmann, M. (1994). Men, feminism, and men's contradictory experiences of power. In H. Brod & M. Kaufman (Eds). *Theorizing Masculinities.* Thousand Oaks, CA: Sage Publications.

Kimmel, M.S. (1996). *Manhood in America: A Cultural History.* New York: Free Press.

Kimmel, M.S. (1998). Clarence, William, Iron Mike, Tailhook, Senator Packwood, The Spur Posse, Magic . . . and us. In M.E. Odem & J. Clay-Warner (Eds.). *Confronting Rape and Sexual Assault.* Wilmington, DE: Scholarly Resources.

Kimmel, M.S. (2006). Masculinity as homophobia: Fear, shame, and silence in the construction of gender identity. In T. Ore (Eds.). *The Social Construction of Difference and Inequality.* Boston: McGraw-Hill.

Malamuth, N.M., R.J. Sockloskie, & M.P. Koss. (1991). Characteristics of sexual aggressors against women: Testing a model using a national sample of college students. *Journal of Consulting and Clinical Psychology, 59,* 670–681.

McKinley, N.M., & J.S. Hyde. (1996). The objectified body consciousness scale. *Psychology of Women Quarterly*, 20, 181–215.

Prohaska, A., & J. Gailey. Achieving masculinity through sexual predation: The case of hogging. Unpublished manuscript.

Richards, L. (1999). *Using NVivo in Qualitative Research* (2d ed.). Bundoora, Australia: Qualitative Solutions and Research Pty.

Risman, B. (1998). *Gender Vertigo*. New Haven, CT: Yale University Press.

Sanday, P.R. (1990). *Fraternity Gang Rape: Sex, Brotherhood, and Privilege on Campus*. New York: New York University Press.

Schur, E.M. (1984). *Labeling Women Deviant: Gender, Stigma, and Social Control*. Philadelphia: Temple University Press.

No Apology

Shared Struggles in Fat and Transgender Law

Dylan Vade and Sondra Solovay

People who are transgender, fat, or both encounter significant obstacles to full participation in mainstream U.S. society. These obstacles include attitudinal, physical, and policy barriers that affect ordinary, daily activities like using bathrooms, going to school, and finding or maintaining employment. When attempting to overcome these barriers by using the legal system, not only are fat or transgender people expected to share a goal of assimilation, but they are coerced into reinforcing fat-phobic and transgender-phobic norms in to secure basic legal rights enjoyed by their non-fat and non-transgender peers. This is a cruel cycle: oppression necessitates the legal intervention, yet the person must participate in that very oppression to receive legal protection.

This ironic duality presents a dilemma for the targets of discrimination and also for the social justice–minded attorneys fighting to secure rights not only for the immediate client in current crisis, but also for the larger communities that will continue to exist over time. The authors of this chapter are not only attorneys but also members of, and allies to, the groups we are assisting—our own rights are also on the line. We are in a unique position: we want to reject strategies that further entrench prejudice against our communities; we know we are among the few who can help; and yet we know what "helping" entails. We cannot in good conscience turn our backs on abhorrent legal strategies when no alternatives exist and legal policy change is slow, arduous, and uncertain.

A little more than an hour's drive separates the California cities of Berkeley and Santa Cruz. A pair of weight discrimination cases demonstrate how even geographic neighbors may be judicial strangers depending on the legal tactics used.

Both John R. of Berkeley and Toni C. of Santa Cruz faced employment discrimination because they were fat. Toni applied for work at a grocery cooperative; John worked for an auto parts company. Toni was turned down for the position—the collective members told her that they thought her weight might interfere, citing the experience of a collective member who reported difficulties climbing ladders when she became heavier due to her pregnancy. Down the road in Berkeley, John, who weighed four hundred pounds and was fired after years of employment, learned from a fellow manager that his weight was the issue.

Both John and Toni sued for weight-based discrimination. John won $1,035,652 (Vogel, 1999). Toni, who took her case all the way to the California State Supreme Court, lost.

What is the difference between a million-dollar weight case award and a losing case? Like the difference between many winning and losing transgender cases, it's all about the attitude.

Does the claimant's attitude and experience about weight/gender reinforce or challenge dominant stereotypes? Winning cases generally adopt a legal posture that reinforces societal prejudices. Cases that challenge societal prejudices generally lose.

Both Toni and John encountered discrimination. Toni refused to locate the problem in, or on, her body, finding instead that the obstacle was the fat-phobic attitudes she faced (Cassista, 1999). Rejecting a medicalized view, she argued that she was perceived as disabled because of her weight, but that there was nothing "medically wrong" with her. Her argument is noteworthy because there were no apologies and nothing repentant in her tone.

John's approach was that his weight constituted a physiological disorder. He agreed that there was a problem with his body, that something was "wrong." He had tried fasting, hypnosis, and even having his jaws wired shut in his attempts to become a thin person (Vogel, 1999).

Toni was fiercely proud. She lost her case. John was apologetic. He won.

This is a recurrent theme in cases involving transgender or fat people. We lose our rights unless we apologize. And, keep in mind, we are not asking for anything extravagant. We just want basic civil rights, including the right to have a job, to use the bathroom at work, to keep custody of our children (in the absence of abuse or neglect), to adopt children if we can provide a safe and loving home, to get an education, to be free from involuntary commitment to institutions because of weight or gender expression, and to receive respectful care and assistance from medical providers, police, educators, attorneys, and other professionals. We are not asking for jobs where lower weights or non-transgender identities are genuine occupational qualifications. Those jobs are few and far between. The short list of such jobs might arguably include the type of firefighter likely to encounter weakened structures that require lower-weight workers, and medical educators who use their bodies to teach, for example, how to do a prostate exam on a transgender woman.

Our world, including our species, is blessed with biological diversity. It is normal for humans to enjoy a wealth of good, natural body sizes and genders, as well as more than two configurations of sexual and reproductive organs. People are different from each other in many ways. Despite this most obvious of facts, lawyers attempting to obtain justice for their fat or transgender clients must pretend that there is only one way to be male, only one way to be female, and only one acceptable body—thin. The courts demand support of the following, unspoken, false beliefs:

- There is exactly one good, natural, and healthy body size (thin).
- When a person behaves correctly, by consuming a reasonable amount of calories and exercising appropriately, a thin body will result.
- There are exactly two good, natural sexes/genders (female and male), which correspond in a direct and linear way to exactly two types of sexual organs (vagina and penis).
- When a person behaves correctly, a gender presentation that is obviously and exclusively female or male will result.

Attorneys representing transgender or fat clients and wishing to better their chances in court must present facts that confirm these unexamined societal "truths."

Law and Fat Bodies

Legal Options: Use Specific Statutes or Use Disability Law

Why are you fat? This should not be a particularly relevant legal inquiry, yet it is frequently the one on which a fat person's case will turn because most cases occur outside jurisdictions that have specific laws prohibiting weight discrimination.

Specific Statutes

In the United States there are only a small handful of locations where weight discrimination has specifically been made illegal by law; these locations include Washington, D.C.; the state of Michigan; Madison, Wisconsin; and the California cities of San Francisco and Santa Cruz (the Toni Cassista case is what inspired the creaton of the Santa Cruz law). Some of the laws cover weight specifically, like those of San Francisco and Michigan. Washington, D.C., takes a different approach, prohibiting discrimination based on appearance, which includes weight.

Disability Law

For a fat person outside those jurisdictions, the sole successful courtroom strategy used to date is disability law. A person who faces discrimination and cannot use disability law will have no legal recourse whatever. Whether the court will allow a fat person to use disability law is uncertain. Because there is no U.S. Supreme Court ruling, the use of disability law in a weight discrimination case depends on the individual's situation and on the jurisdiction's interpretation of the law.

The legal and lay definitions of disability differ. Federal and many similar state laws protect qualified people who are disabled. These complex laws generally cover people with a physical or mental impairment/condition that limits (or substantially limits) a major life activity like working or walking; people who have a *record* of such an impairment; and those who are *regarded as having* such an impairment, whether or not they actually do. A person who is denied a job because the employer believes that drug addicts are bad employees and wrongly perceives the applicant to be a drug addict would be protected under disability law. Nevertheless, courts are divided on whether a capable fat person who is perceived to be a bad employee due to weight-related stereotypes would be protected—several have said that there is no protection unless the fat person is *perceived* to have an *impairment that causes* the weight. Imagine that an employer believes that fat people do not have physical endurance and therefore refuses to hire them. If the employer believed that an applicant's weight was due to a thyroid problem, the employer's action would be *illegal* regardless of the actual cause of the body size; if the employer believed the weight resulted from overeating, the refusal to hire would be protected by the court. This result makes no sense.

The Equal Employment Opportunities Commission (EEOC) is normally persuasive, and courts eagerly follow their guidelines. The EEOC and similar guides have stated that when a person is one hundred pounds (or 100%) "overweight," they are good candidates for meeting the legal definition of disability. Recently the U.S. Court of Appeals for the Sixth Circuit ignored the EEOC, deciding that a fat person would not qualify as disabled without proving that an underlying disability was causing the weight. In other words, even a person weighing 1,200 pounds who is relatively immobile because of the weight will not receive protection under disability law should they be unlucky enough to live in the Sixth Circuit, unless they can prove an underlying medical cause for their weight—nearly impossible given the current state of medical science and the social blame associated with being fat. The Sixth Circuit and similar holdings are oddly inconsistent with legal precedent, because the *way* a person becomes disabled is irrelevant under disability law. Where weight is concerned, the court is clearly unwilling to provide protection to anyone seen as "eating" up to their body size (by voluntarily consuming an abnormal amount of calories); unquestionably, however, a drunk driver who crashes into a busload of children killing them all, and ends up using a wheelchair himself, *will* be protected by disability law in the Sixth Circuit. The manner of becoming disabled, and any immorality associated with it, is completely irrelevant to the court unless the claimant is a fat person. It should be noted that in late 2006, the Sixth Circuit was presented with an amicus curiae brief on this issue filed jointly by the National Organization for Women, the Southern Poverty Law Center, the Disability Rights Education and Defense Fund, and several other leading groups, including *all* the major fat-positive civil rights organizations headquartered in the United States. The court refused to read the brief. We are hard-pressed to think of many topics that, having gathered the support of such renowned organizations, would be so easily dismissed by the court.

It is also unusual to find a physical condition so demonized by the medical community and yet so distanced from disability law coverage. We are deeply uncomfortable with the fact that some portions of the medical community, who now stand against fat prejudice, come from a "love the fat person, hate the fat" perspective. We do not see this attitude as consistent with civil rights, just as "love the homosexual, hate the homosexuality" is inconsistent with queer rights.

Law and Transgender Bodies

Legal Options: Rely on Case Law, Use Statutes, and Use Disability Law

In comparison to the tiny handful of laws prohibiting weight discrimination, there are at least ninety-three laws specifically protecting transgender people from discrimination. Whereas the only state to outlaw weight discrimination is Michigan, thirteen states protect transgender people. Washington, D.C., protects both fat and transgender people (Transgender Law and Policy Institute, 2009).

Disability Law and Transgender Civil Rights

Distinct from enacting separate laws, or including gender identity and gender expression in existing civil rights law, a common recent route for protecting transgender people is through disability law (Enriquez v. W. Jersey Health Sys., 2001). (For more information, see the National Center for Lesbian Rights' website, http://www.nclrights.org). For example, in California, Cal. Government Code § 1296 (the Poppink Act) was enacted in 2000 and removed the exclusion of "transsexualism" from the disability protections of the Fair Employment and Housing Act. If a transgender Californian faces discrimination at work, such as coworkers using the wrong pronoun and name, she may sue using disability law. She would ask for the "reasonable accommodation" that her coworkers be required to use "she" and the correct name. And although we are grateful that in California transgender people have multiple legal options, including disability law, we are uncomfortable that a transgender recipient of harassment would need to demean herself by requesting that her harasser "accommodate" her. Calling someone by the wrong name consistently is plain rude. No one should have to ask for an "accommodation" to be treated respectfully and referred to accurately.

In disability law, it is frequently the claimant, be she transgender, deaf, or otherwise different, who is seen as having the problem. That person then requests to be "accommodated," if it's not too much trouble (not "unreasonable," in legal language). It is a significant imposition to ask the victim of discrimination to locate the problem on her own body.

This is not a criticism of the use of disability law, or the work that went into creating and enacting it. We understand the choices made and are deeply indebted to, and grateful for, those who have helped make our society more accessible. We recognize that disability rights activists use disability law with the utmost respect for people with disabilities. We are concerned, nonetheless, with the undertone of apology that the law may generate.

We are disturbed that disability law is not consistently applied. For instance, in California, transgender people are likely protected under disability law and fat people are likely not. We would like to see disability law applied equally to all people who logically fit under it and who choose to use it, which could include fat people. We would also like to see disability law rewritten to more strongly locate the "problem" in society, not on the body. We do not want anyone to have to apologize for being who they are.

Case Law and Statutory Law

Transgender people go to court for a variety of reasons: to keep their jobs, to keep their children, to have access to homeless shelters, or to have access to restrooms, just to name a few. No matter why a transgender person is in court, invariably a main point of inquiry will be, is this a man or is this a woman? Generally, only those transgender people who are deemed to be "true men" or "true women" have a chance of winning their case.

What does it take to be a "true woman" or "true man" in the eyes of the court? A person has to fit as many gender stereotypes as is humanly possible. Men must show that they played with trucks and, just as important, that they did not play with dolls (In re Estate of Gardiner, 2002; M.T. v. J.T, 1976; Frances B. v. Mark B., 1974). Women should wear skirts and, ideally, show that they are heterosexual and have "heterosexual intercourse." And all claimants should be prepared for the court to scrutinize genitals. For instance, in Michael Kantaras's custody case, the size and shape of his genitals was so important that the word "penis" was mentioned 273 times in the court's decision (Kantaras v. Kantaras, 2003).

Showing conformity with every female or male stereotype is quite a task even for a transgender person who identifies as female or male. It is virtually impossible for a transgender person who does not identify as either, as is the case with a significant portion of the transgender communities (Vade, 2005). When courts require transgender people to be, or to desire to be, hyper–gender normal to receive the basic civil rights generally afforded citizens, the court is asking transgender people to apologize for *being* transgender.

Curious Discussion

Why is it that courts have such a narrow view of gender when faced with a transgender person? It is true that gender stereotypes are alive and well and affect us all. Yet what courts are doing with transgender people seems excessive and out of step with the times. Our society is coming to the realization that not all men played with trucks when they were young, that some women are lesbians, that some men like to cook, and that many women wear pants. Why does this gender liberation disappear completely when courts are deciding transgender people's gender? Why do transgender people have to be more gender-conforming than anyone else? This is a curious phenomenon.

Fat and Transgender: Challenging Bodies

Transgender people are asked by the courts to be more gender normal than anyone else because transgender people, *by their very existence*, question the "societal truth" about gender. Even the most stereotypically female transgender women and the most stereotypically male transgender men defy existing gender norms by saying, loud and clear, that the gender we are assigned at birth is not necessarily our destiny. A female-to-male transgender person who is gay, wears nail polish, and chooses not to alter his body medically, challenges existing gender norms. And, regardless of identity, it is the happy and proud transgender person who says, "This is who I am, I am neither male nor female. I am different, and how I am is good," who challenges gender norms the most. This transgender person will likely lose in court.

The law requires the very people who question traditional gender norms to acknowledge, uphold, and glorify them in their quest for legal protection. This makes sense. If transgender people are seen as threatening, if transgender people make the judges and lawyers wonder about the solidity of their own gender, then what better way to gain reassurance that all is well, that gender is fixed, than to make transgender people testify that yes, gender is binary; yes, we all want to be either real women with clean-shaven legs and hairless upper lips or real men with big "packages"; yes, we are all heterosexual; yes, yes to every possible stereotype; yes, they are all true, and more than anything in the world we all want to glorify and embody those stereotypes—all of them. If transgender people worship gender stereotypes, they must be true—right?

Just as a transgender person who is proud of being transgender challenges gender norms, a fat person who does not want to lose weight challenges body norms. Some fat people arrive at the decision not to pursue weight loss because they believe that weight is largely immutable, that it is the exception rather than the rule when people have the power to control their weight to any significant, lasting degree. It is these fat people who are *especially* dangerous because they are challenging the value that society places on weight loss efforts and the belief that thin people have earned the benefits that they are accorded based on their body shape.

The law requires fat people to acknowledge, uphold, and glorify body norms. And this makes sense. Fat-affirmative attitudes are threatening. What better way to gain reassurance that the privileges enjoyed by the thin are deserved, that the billions of dollars and countless hours dedicated to weight loss are not mere vanity or a colossal, misguided, and selfish waste of resources, than to make *fat* people testify that yes, obviously thin is the goal; yes, we all want to be thin; yes, being fat is really bad, interfering with major life activities; yes, most fat people deserve their second-class-citizen status; yes, most could change if they had the discipline/restraint/morals/foresight; yes, I want to be thin because who would want to be ugly and unhealthy and stupid and asexual/hypersexual; yes, I would be thin but for some malfunction in my body; and yes, yes, YES to all those stereotypes. If even people with fat bodies worship and pursue the thin body, then our societal valuation system must be correct and there is no need to question it—right?

When fat people show that they want to be thin and that they have consistently tried to become thin, they reinscribe the societal truth of "thin is good/normal." If transgender people show that they hate being transgender and would like nothing more than to fit in and be the most gender-conforming man or woman that they can be, then gender norms (including the binary gender system) remain unchallenged.

Even if fat or transgender persons "failed" to transform themselves sufficiently to avoid discrimination, as long as they show a strong desire to conform to societal gender and body norms, the court will *consider* stepping in, using the force of law, to prevent the denial of basic civil rights. What matters more than the actual transformation is that the transgender or fat person states, in no uncertain terms, that gender and body norms are still in place, are still desired, and remain unquestionably true.

Your Authors

Personally, we elect not to erase our complexity or deny our difference. We choose not to apologize for our existence so that someone else can sleep in a gender illusion, or continue believing that their thin privilege is earned and that the disapproval and repulsion they feel toward fat, or the war that they have declared on fat, is justified.

Toward a New View: No Boxes, No Apologies

What if our laws and courts assumed this: Every person is different. We move differently, work differently, dress differently, express gender differently. What if difference were the given? And what if bodies were a given? We all have bodies. Our bodies come in different sizes, styles, and shapes.

We need to recognize there is no bright line dividing man from woman, fat from thin. Let's stop visualizing a continuum, with man at one end and woman at the other, or thin at one end and fat at the other. Dividing lines and continuum-style lines lead to the law of norms and make it far too easy for courts to threaten those who fall outside the norm with loss of children, employment, and opportunity—unless, or course, they support the norm, pray to the norm, and reinforce the norm.

Lines just do not work. One person's physical expression of their 180-pound weight will vary tremendously from someone else's, not only because of height, but due to measurements, proportions, stance, and attitude; each of these varies not only from person to person but also from moment to moment. A 180-pound woman who carries her weight in her belly and a 180-pound woman who carries her weight in her bosom and bottom occupy the same point linearly but completely different places in society. Context creates yet another variation: a 120-pound woman is "fat" for a fashion magazine; a 240-pound woman is "thin" at a National Association to Advance Fat Acceptance conference.

The linear conception also does not work for gender. Consider the masculinity expressed by a butch woman, a flamey fag, a nelly female-to-male transgender person, a third-gender boy-grrrl, a fierce femme, and a butch man. All six genders are all different. Try to order them on a line! Try to assign them to either side of the male/female divide. It is impossible. There are infinite ways to express gender. There are infinitely many different ways to be embodied.

No apologies. We must protect the civil rights of everyone, not just those who fit in boxes or fall to extremes on a faulty continuum. If we are going to survive as humans, we need to learn to be with our own difference, to learn to be with the difference around us, to learn from difference, to treasure—and cherish—difference.

NOTE

We wish to thank Alice Solovay, Christina Shin, Joe Samson, Susan Gonzales, Marilyn Wann, and Esther Rothblum for their insights and assistance. We also wish to thank the fierce attorneys and advocates fighting for the rights of fat, queer, transgender, and disabled people, without whom this piece could not have been written.

REFERENCES

Cassista, T. (1999) Personal interview with S. Solovay.

Enriquez v. W. Jersey Health Sys., 777 A.2d 365 (N.J. Super. Ct. App. Div. 2001), cert. denied, 785 A.2d 439 (N.J. 2001).

Frances B. v. Mark B., 355 N.Y.S.2d 712 (N.Y. Sup. Ct. 1974).

In re Estate of Gardiner, 42 P.3d 120 (Kan. 2002).

Kantaras v. Kantaras, No. 98–5375 (Fla. Cir. Ct. 2003).

M.T. v. J.T., 355 A.2d 204 (N.J. Super. Ct. App. Div. 1976).

Transgender Law and Policy Institute and National Gay and Lesbian Task Force (2009) Scope of explicitly transgender-inclusive anti-discrimination laws. Retrieved March 9, 2007, from http://www.transgenderlaw.org/ndlaws/ngltftlpichart.pdf.

Vade. D. (2005) Expanding gender and expanding the law: towards social and legal conceptualization of gender that is more inclusive of transgender people. *Michigan Journal of Gender and Law*, Volume II, Issue 2, 253–316.

Vogel, S. (1999) Why we get fat. *Discover*, Retrieved January 15, 2007, from http://discovermagazine.com/1999/apr/fat.

|||||||||||||||||||||||||||||||||||||||||||||||||||||||||||||||||||||||||||||||||||

20

Access to the Sky

Airplane Seats and Fat Bodies as Contested Spaces

Joyce L. Huff

As Michel Foucault (1979) has pointed out, since the eighteenth century Euro-American cultures have conceived of the body as adaptable, able to achieve and maintain socially prescribed standards. In the twenty-first-century United States, this body has come increasingly to be seen as capable of adapting itself to spaces constructed to meet the needs of corporations rather than those of individuals. For example, mass production, a process that accommodates manufacturers' desires to maintain high profit margins by producing goods quickly and cheaply, assumes that the consumer's body is mutable and will alter to fit into preconstructed spaces, such as off-the-rack, rather than tailor-made, clothing. In *Enforcing Normalcy*, Lennard J. Davis (1995) notes how easily the notion of the adaptable body, with its supposed ability to conform to norms, comes to serve as the basis for a social imperative that compels individuals to strive for normalcy. Although Davis articulates his critique of coercive social norms in relation to disability, his insights could just as easily apply to anyone whose body falls outside the parameters of today's narrowly defined notion of the "normal." In fact, the very notion that individual bodies are adaptable endorses a fiction of absolute corporeal control, when, in fact, our bodies resist our control in numerous ways.

Although it is frequently argued that niche markets are currently replacing mass markets, and that consequently products are now tailored to meet the needs of specific targeted groups rather than those of a hypothetical average individual, the notion of an adaptable body remains central to the manufacturer's vision of the consumer. Clothes marketed specifically to larger women, for instance, still come in standard sizes with fixed proportions to which individual bodies must adapt. In fact, such clothing is usually marketed along with products such as "foundation garments," which are designed to facilitate this adaptation.

The recent debate over Southwest Airlines's decision to enforce a long-standing policy requiring large passengers to pay higher fares highlights the ways in which the imperative to normalize may serve corporate interests at the expense of those of individuals. In June 2002, Southwest Airlines announced its intention to make passengers with hips spanning over seventeen inches pay for two airline seats. Southwest claimed that the policy was created in response to customer complaints: "Nine out of 10 customer complaints are from passengers who get squeezed in their seats by obese neighbors" (Nielson, 2002, p. E4). An anonymous ticket agent echoed this reason when she told the *San Francisco Chronicle*, "Probably 90 percent of the people who complain to us in writing are people who say they paid for a whole seat but didn't get it because the person next to them was so large" (St. John & Zamora, 2002, p. A17).

Southwest's decision sparked a national debate over the rights of fat passengers. In fact, when fat activist Sandie Sabo discussed the policy on the *Fight Back! Talk Back!* radio show hosted by consumer advocate David Horowitz (not to be confused with the conservative pundit of the same name), the issue prompted 407 posts to the show's online forum. Southwest defended its policy by proclaiming its dedication to serving its customers: "It is certainly not safe, comfortable, or fair for a person who has purchased a ticket to be left with only a portion of a seat or no seat" (Barrett, 2002). But fat activists challenged the sincerity of the airline's commitment to their customers—when the customers in question happen to be fat ones. For example, the National Association to Advance Fat Acceptance (NAAFA) took the airline to task for failing to meet the needs of fat passengers. "We feel that today's aircraft simply are not equipped to deal with larger passengers," said NAAFA spokesperson Jeanette De-Patie. "We at NAAFA don't want to take anyone else's space and don't believe anyone should have to be uncomfortable, but at 17" to 20", airline seats are very small" (Blickenstorfer, 2002). Southwest's reasoning obscures the fact that the limitations on the amount of space allotted to each airline passenger are artificially constructed by both the airlines themselves and their regulatory agencies to suit their own needs. Thus, far from being limited to a discussion of the safety, comfort, or rights of individual passengers, fat or thin, the ensuing controversy raised questions about the definition of the "normal" body in a world in which space is commodified.

In the debate, supporters of Southwest Airlines frequently employed a "minoritizing" discourse that cast limited space on airlines as a "fat people's issue." Here I am borrowing Eve Kosofsky Sedgwick's terminology. In *Epistemology of the Closet*, Sedgwick (1990) uses the terms "minoritizing" and "universalizing" to describe two opposing views of sexuality: one that represents sexual identity as "an issue of active importance primarily for a small, distinct, relatively fixed homosexual minority," and one that characterizes it as "an issue of continuing determinative importance in the lives of people across the spectrum of sexualities" (p. 1). These terms have since been appropriated by disability studies scholars, such as Rosemarie Garland Thomson (1997a), to discuss the ways in which the compulsory "norming" of bodies has been represented as a disabled person's problem (minoritizing), when such issues should be central to current discussions of identity politics (universalizing).

I employ Sedgwick's terms to discuss the way in which fat people are imagined as embodying the problems of corporeal identity in a twenty-first-century consumer culture. I find these words particularly useful in discussing the Southwest debate, because they emphasize the active nature of perception in structuring reality and thus implicate discursive and material practices, which are grounded in perception and the process of minoritization. To employ a minoritizing discourse is a political action, one that particularizes a societal issue and attempts to turn it into a private, individual problem, which then can, and should, be solved through individual, rather than social, action.

In the case of Southwest Airlines, minoritizing rhetoric classifies lack of space on airplanes as a fat person's problem, the implied solution to which is weight loss. Southwest represents the problem in terms of individual passengers fitting into individual seats—"an issue of active importance primarily for a small, distinct, relatively fixed" minority that does not fit their definition of the average customer. Most posters on *Fight Back*'s forum presumed that seats were designed to accommodate this hypothetical average customer, which they assumed represented the statistically average American. As L.A. Chung (2002) of San Francisco's *Mercury News* points out, Southwest has a "carefully cultivated image of being the airline for the average Joe." When the issue is represented in this way, it seems obvious that the solution should also be an individual one, adopted by the few who are directly affected by the problem. As one participant on the *Fight Back* forum, "malfunctionbob," states, "I think instead of taking the common American approach of making the world adjust to the few. [*sic*] Perhaps the few might adjust to the many" (2002b, p. 1). Such language makes it the responsibility of the individual to find ways of adapting to the policy or to pay for special accommodation.

Fat activists have countered the effort to minoritize the issue with a more universalizing discourse, one that presents airplane seating as a problem for the majority of individuals. They argue that airlines should be held accountable for creating seats that are uncomfortable for most passengers, be they fat or thin, tall or short, with physical disabilities or temporarily able-bodied. For example, on *Fight Back*, when a supporter of Southwest's policy employs the rhetoric of special needs, stating that larger seats for fat passengers would amount to "special accommodation that is subsidized by all," Sabo responds in a universalizing manner: "Why on earth should passengers larger than 17" across have to subsidize the airline's choice to use seating that is uncomfortable for almost all of the flying public?" (2002b, p. 1). The idea that some bodies' needs should be labeled "special" highlights what is really at stake in this debate: the definition of the normal, as opposed to the "special," body.

Similarly, lawyer and activist Sondra Solovay employs a universalizing discourse, this time one of universal human rights, when she argues, "It's an issue of fundamental civil rights when people are prevented from traveling because of their personal attributes" (Wastell, 2002, p. 18). Solovay echoes disability rights activists in focusing on the ways in which the culture is constructed to meet the needs of some individuals and not others: "There is nothing inherently limiting about blindness, deafness or wheelchair usage. These conditions are viewed by the court as limiting because they occur in the context of a society that has constructed structural and communication barriers that restrict people with these conditions from participating in daily activities" (2000, p. 148). She here implies that what is needed is a reconstruction of the physical and social environment to meet the needs of a greater number of people.

Sabo also universalizes, or at least, majorizes (if I may invent a term) the issue when she points out that since 55–60% of Americans have been deemed overweight by the National Institutes of Health, the fat customer has become statistically average, and that, therefore, there is nothing special about the accommodation sought in this case (*Fight*, 2002b, p. 1). Of course, in both fat and disability studies, it is now a commonplace that the idea of the "average" or "normal" individual represents not a statistical average, but rather a cultural ideal, which carries the weight of an ideological imperative. Davis's (1995) analysis of the development of the bell curve highlights the eugenicist ideology of human perfectibility that underpins the hegemony of such notions. Indeed, disability studies scholars have cited the current obsession with thinness in American culture as an example that unmasks the ideological nature of social norms in general. Thomson (1997b), for example, has reported that her female students' "struggle with the tyranny of slimness enables them to recognize that bodily aberration is relative to a cultural and historically specific standard that serves particular interests" (p. 302). It is not surprising, then, that the "average" customer, for whom Southwest presumably designs its seats, represents an ideological construct rather than a statistical average.

The underlying ideology that determines the size of the so-called average customer to whom Southwest supposedly caters is a capitalist one. Although airlines and their supporters may invoke average customers who represent cultural ideals, in fact seat sizing has a lot more to do with profit margins and maximizing the number of paying customers. After all, tallness is a trait that is culturally valued in the United States today, and airline seating does not accommodate the tall, as a lawsuit filed by the Tall Club of Silicon Valley in 2001 attests (Chung, 2002).

Southwest's press release presents airline seat size as absolute. "Our policy," they explain, "isn't about a person's weight . . . If a person occupies his/her *seat* and a portion or all of the adjoining *seat*, then that Customer will need to purchase the additional *seat* he/she is occupying" (italics mine) (Barrett, 2002). Here, the space taken up by passengers is quantified using the term "seats," as if this term designated a standard unit of measurement. It is passenger size, not seat size, Southwest implies, that is malleable.

But seat size is not immutable. Indeed, Sabo charges that when profit was the primary concern, Southwest itself has altered the size of its seats. She states, "There is no accident that Southwest Airlines is currently the only profitable airline, and the only airline that did not ask for federal bailout after 9/11. They did away with any options for larger seating, (business and first class), and made all their seating the smallest in the industry." And *Fight Back* poster Rosalie Prosser puts it more succinctly: "First they shrink the seats and then blame large people for not fitting" (2002a, p. 1). On their official website, Southwest responds to the question, "Why not make your seats wider or add a few wide seats on your aircraft?" by stating, "Our ongoing goal is to operate a low-fare, low cost airline, and the costs of reconfiguring our fleet would be staggering and would ultimately reflect in the form of higher fares for our customers" (2006). But, as Sabo notes, "this would all be academic if they would pull the price for 'lost' seats, or for supplying some real-sized seating, from their Executives' salaries" (*Fight*, 2002a, p. 1).

Cost-cutting measures that affect the distribution of space on airplanes, however, are not limited to the shrinking of seats. Fewer flights mean more crowded conditions as well. As journalist Carrie Levine (2006) states, "Since the number of available flights offered by troubled airlines has been shrinking, overcrowding is worsening the problem." And *USA Today*'s Chris Woodyard (2003) attributes the problem to Southwest's streamlined boarding policy, another cost-cutting tactic: "Sometimes the airline simply finds [fat passengers] a row that isn't expected to sell out . . . Southwest's problem appears to revolve around its policy of not reserving seats." In the case of Southwest's seating, then, it is corporate needs, rather than concerns for the comfort of any customer, average or not, that are accommodated when seating is designed. In fact, when a Southwest representative told members of the NAAFA at the 2002 conference that the policy was intended for the comfort and convenience of fat passengers, NAAFA members replied by asking, "Do you intend to also make using the restrooms more comfortable for large passengers?" (Blickenstorfer, 2002). The answer, not surprisingly, was no.

In a corporately constructed environment, space is not merely a limited resource, but also a purchasable resource, a commodity. As journalist Kathleen Parker (2002, p. 13A) concedes in her critique of Southwest, "Though space is less a tangible commodity than food, it is no less a 'product' if you happen to be in the airline business. Airlines sell space." Renee Wynne (2002, p. B5) writes a letter to the *Seattle Times* stating, "You use more space, you should pay more for it. Same thing with any other commodity." In this particular case, space on a plane is assigned a monetary value. The determining question revolves around the maximum number of bodies that can be placed into a mass produced airplane to maximize airline profit.

To define seat space as a commodity, however, is a misrepresentation that serves airline interests, according to Sabo. She asserts, "When you purchase an airline ticket you are purchasing a ticket for a trip, not a ticket for a seat." She goes on to explain, "The reason that the airline contracts with you for a trip (not a seat) is so that they have the legal right to change your seat (without your permission), bump you, over book flights (the key to their existence) or even cancel your flight." If the trip and not the space is indeed the true commodity, presumably fat customers should be provided with the space that they require to make their purchased trips: "If we are purchasing a ticket for a trip, then it seems to stand to reason that the airline is liable to provide that trip what ever it takes" (*Fight*, 2002a, p. 1).

In countering customer demands for larger and more comfortable seats, Southwest has responded that larger seats would mean fewer seats and fewer paying customers: "If we were to replace just three rows of three seats with two seats, each being one and a half times wider, we would have to significantly raise our fares to maintain our profit margin" (Barrett, 2002). But this logic denies the fact that, like seat size, fares are not fixed quantities—they vary according to customer demand—and, as specific flights are not always sold out, the overall profit margin on a flight is also constantly variable.

Southwest's policy assumes an audience accustomed to capitalist modes of thought, one that will endorse the premise that businesses need to continually increase profit margins, one that will believe that this need is sacrosanct to the degree that they will subordinate their own needs and desires to it. In fact, on the *Fight Back* forum, many respondents posted in defense of what one woman called "the needs and rights of a business to cater to the 'average' customer." According to this person, a 4'11" woman who labeled herself "The Short Poster," individuals can and must adapt themselves to suit corporate needs: "When I need to make an accommodation, I make it. If I don't fit in, I choose again, meaning I accommodate the need or go elsewhere. I don't demand that a riding stable have a saddle and stirrups short enough to fit me. I don't go to crowded museum exhibitions if it means I can't see over people to view the displays. The list is endless. So bloody what? I adapt . . . " (2002a, p. 2).

The Short Poster's response reveals the stigmatizing potential of minoritizing discourses. If individuals, or minority groups, are responsible for solutions to social problems, then it follows that they are also to blame when solutions are not found. For instance, Susan Nielson (2002) writes in the *Sunday Oregonian*, "We've outgrown our seats, and that's not Southwest's fault . . . let's not blame the airlines for size discrimination. Our appetites are insatiable, and our airplanes are only so big." Nielson claims that what is at is at stake is "why Americans got so big, and who's to blame" (p. E4). Here, the body visibly marked as unable or unwilling to adapt bears the responsibility for societal failures (in this case, airlines that fail to provide adequate seating), and is thus stigmatized. In his groundbreaking work on the subject, Erving Goffman (1963, p. 5) defines "stigma" as a negative attitude about a specific personal trait or "an undesired differentness from what we had anticipated." Southwest appears to have anticipated flying only customers with hips spanning seventeen inches or fewer when the seats were built; fat thus represents a differentness that they neither anticipated nor desired.

Indeed, many of the published responses to fat flyers seem to have less to do with space than with stigma. For instance, Jenn Cornall, quoted in the *New York Daily News*, says, "It was disgusting to have to share my seat with someone else's fat." Interviewer Lenore Skenazy responds that "whining flyers can complain about people with double chins in a way they could never complain about, say moms with lap children, because there is nothing immoral about motherhood. Can you imagine a business traveler moaning, 'Toddler flesh spilled into my seat'?" (2002, p. 33). In fact, one of the questions asked of Southwest representatives by NAAFA members at the 2002 convention was: "Do you intend to deal with other customer complaints in the same manner? Do you anticipate charging mothers with crying babies more? Or parents of children who kick the seat in front? How about loud people or those who use offensive language? Or those who talk too much or drink too much?" The Southwest representative replied that the NAAFA members were comparing "apples and oranges" (Blickenstorfer, 2002). Clearly, for NAAFA members, the comparison contrasted Southwest's differing treatment of a variety of customers who encroached on others, physically or audibly. For Southwest, however, what mattered were customer complaints, which were frequently grounded in stigma against fat people. NAAFA members did not demand that customers stop complaining or question the legitimacy of any complaint, including the ones about space; they merely pointed to the dissimilar ways in which complaints were handled by the airline when the grievance involved a stigmatized individual as opposed to a "normal" one.[1]

In effect, the airline expected the stigmatized group to be responsible for resolving the problem. Goffman states that in response to stigmatization, one might "make a direct attempt to correct what he [*sic*] sees as the objective basis of his failing" (1963, p. 9), as the Short Poster does when she accepts socially prescribed limits on her participation in the public sphere rather than challenge a corporation's right to construct public spaces to which she cannot adapt. Stigma can thus be exploited to shame minorities into compliance with dominant ideologies. In fact, for some supporters of Southwest's policy, the point was exactly that; Southwest's policy was lauded for providing a new way to humiliate those with bodily differences into compliance with the norm. Aptly named obesity expert Mike Lean, for example, states: "Someone who weighs 260lb hangs right over into the next seat. If that's the sort of penalty you're facing, it might persuade a few more people to be more thoughtful about their diet" (Timms, 2002, 4). But, as one poster on *Fight Back* points out, the policy is about body size, not about diet; "Hipster" states, "A policy that makes this distinction would only punish fast food eating couch potatoes larger than 17" and not the smaller fast food eating couch potatoes" (2002b, p. 1).

The tendency to defend, rather than to contest, the corporate right to allocate and commodify space can be seen in a discussion regarding passengers on the Washington, D.C., subway, or Metro. In this conversation, Southwest was invoked to make a distinction between publicly funded services and private businesses. The discussion began when passenger Lynn Wood wrote a letter to the *Washington Post* suggesting that fat Metro riders pay double fares. Metro spokesperson Lisa Farbstein responded by affirming the responsibility of public transportation to serve all members of the public. "Metro is a public transit authority" she begins. "That means that everybody has a right to use it, and it's subject to all the things people like and don't like about public spaces. The people who wrote in might not like sitting next to a larger person, but there are also folks who don't like sitting next to someone who wears perfume and scented products." She continues with a list of other inconveniences encountered in public spaces: "children who are squirming or screaming," "people who disturb the peace with inadequate headphones," and people who engage in "loud conversations, many on cell phones." She concludes, "Metro is not in the business of promoting prejudice and bigotry. People come in all sorts of different bodies, and they all have every right to ride Metro" (Shaffer, 2005). In response, some posters contrasted the rights of Metro riders with those of Southwest flyers. "Could I just suggest," says one poster, "that 'standards' for a public transportation system might be inclusive enough to allow any person to travel on its system for a fare; as opposed to a private airline which can set its own standards and price system as long as it doesn't unfairly discriminate?" (Shaffer, 2005).

Southwest employs the stigmatizing potential of minoritizing discourses when they frame the problem of limited space as one in which, according to a *Fight Back* poster, fat people crowd "NORMAL Sized [*sic*]" people (2002a, p. 7). Or, as David Stempler, president of the Air Travelers Association, puts it, "If passengers have supersized themselves and are encroaching on the space of others, fairness says you should be paying for the space" (St. John & Zamora, 2002, p. A17). Note that he uses supersized as a transitive verb, suggesting that the situation is caused by passengers and should be remedied by them.

Through stigmatizing rhetoric, the contested site becomes not the airline seat itself, but rather the body potentially occupying that seat. In making fat people the source of the problem—and thus responsible for its solution—Southwest has forestalled complaints from "normal" customers by displacing their aggression onto fat passengers. They have essentially attempted to erase the possibility of a scenario in which this aggression would be directed at airlines for failing to meet the general population's needs. Sabo goes so far as to state, "It is my allegation that SWA is pitting thin people against fat people . . . in a way to draw the attention away from their continuing attempts to jam as many passengers into an airline [*sic*] as they can. They are playing up the great disdain and prejudice that many thin Americans have against fat people" (*Fight*, 2002a, p. 1). An article in the *Sacramento Bee* even referred to the debate as a "mini-war between fat and thin passengers." The author, Anita Creamer (2002), goes further than Sabo, claiming that policies like Southwest's are an attempt to scapegoat fat people to forestall all sorts of complaints:

> Meanwhile, what a fine distraction all this has been from the fact that most of the annoyances of airline travel today have nothing to do with the overweight passenger sitting next to you. No, the airlines themselves are to blame for the lost kids and lost luggage, for frequent flyer miles that are all but impossible to redeem and for seats measuring only 18 inches across. And the airlines are to blame for overbooked flights, for delays and for ridiculous security policies that seem to require public officials to be searched nearly every time they fly. No matter how hard we try, we can't pin the bad business practices necessitating the $15 billion federal bailout of the airlines on fat people either.

Creamer concludes, "Trying to distract us by blaming even a small part of those inconveniences on fat people is an insult" (p. E1).

Such universalizing discourse prompts a search for more universal solutions. Parker (2002) humorously states, "Fat and Skinny Unite (FASU) and stop flying until the airlines give us bigger seats" (p. 13A). Solovay (2006), however, takes seriously the search for more universal solutions. She states, "This is an issue that affects most travelers, and it is important for travelers to stick together on this issue and hold airlines accountable for the space choices they make." It is important to note that neither Parker nor Solovay is suggesting that customers have no right to speak up when they feel that their rights or comfort have been infringed upon. Rather, while acknowledging that crowding on airplanes is a problem, they challenge the assumption that the cause necessarily lies in fat bodies and that the sole solution depends on the idea that individuals can and should adapt their bodies to meet the needs of corporations. Instead, they call for all consumers—fat and thin—to join together in demanding that the needs of *all* be met.

What activists are advocating amounts to a reconfiguration of the public sphere to allow the participation of a greater number of people. Sally Smith, editor in chief of *BBW* (Big Beautiful Woman) magazine, advocates such a universal solution when she asserts that "for most other things in this society, costs are amortized so that everyone can be included. It costs more to put wheelchair ramps on buildings, but we don't make people with disabilities subsidize the costs" (Payne, 2002, p. D1). And Sabo agrees: "Why wouldn't it be fair for everyone to share the cost of adding some larger seats for larger flyers? We share the cost for changing tables in restrooms, for handicapped parking, for ramps, and for all sorts of public assistance programs. The whole point of sharing the cost for accommodations between all members of society is specifically so those people needing those accommodations don't wind up forced out of society" (*Fight*, 2002a, p. 1). The rhetoric employed here presents the problem as not simply a problem of fat people and airline seats, but rather a universal one relating to how we wish to structure our society and who will be included in it.

And this, in the end, is the real question raised by the Southwest debates. The move from seat to body as contested site raises issues regarding how much space a body can inhabit in an environment constructed by twenty-first-century corporations. It is true that airlines have historically been considered bastions of size oppression because of weight restrictions on flight attendants; in fact, they have also been taken to task recently for perpetuating other forms of discrimination, such as banning female flyers who wear clothing considered promiscuous or gay couples who publicly display their affection for each other. But airlines are not the source of the problem; rather, their practices are symptomatic of the consequences that can result when the public sphere is designed in manner that excludes certain members of that public. What is needed in the case of fat bodies and airline seats is not simply larger seats but also an interrogation of the very notion of both the adaptable body and the corporate logic that deploys this concept in the distribution of public space.

The critique of bodily norms that is already taking place within disability studies is essential to this project. Southwest clearly saw their policy as a potential "disability issue" and were quick to point out on their website that "interstate airline travel is specifically excluded from Title II of the Americans with Disabilities Act" (Southwest, 2006). One commentator on *Fight Back* attempted to draw a distinction between "good" disabled people, who are supposedly willing to pay for their own accommodations, and "bad" fat people, who refuse to pull their own weight, so to speak. "Pay the money," "malfunctionbob" urges. "And before you go talking about disabled people and the like I'd like to say that they pay considerable expense adapting to the world of the many" (2002b, p. 1). This statement ignores current disability rights movements and wrongly casts people with disabilities as a "model minority." The strategy is to pit two relatively disempowered groups against each other, when a coalition would be beneficial to both groups, who share an interest in both the deconstruction of the notion of the normal body and the reallocation of public space.

NOTES

I would like to thank Robert McRuer, Abby Wilkerson, Pam Presser, Lisbeth Fuisz, Randy Kristensen, Nolana Yip, and Todd Ramlow for their feedback on early drafts of this chapter.

1. Solovay and Vade point to similarities in the treatment of fat individuals and members of other stigmatized groups in their chapter in this collection on fat and transgender individuals.

REFERENCES

Barrett, C. (2002). A Message from Southwest Airlines. Retrieved May 31, 2003, from http://web.archive.org/web/20020802161757/http://www.southwest.com/about_swa/press/additional_seat.html.

Blickenstorfer, C.H. (2002, August 9). NAAFA Think Tank: Airlines and Fat Passengers. Retrieved May 31, 2003, from http://web.archive.org/web/20021014025007/http://www.naafa.org/Convention2002/airlines.html.

Chung, L.A. (2002, June 25). Southwest's Policy Poses Big Questions. *The Mercury News*. Retrieved May 31, 2003, from http://www.accessmylibrary.com/coms2/summary_0286-6864223_ITM.

Creamer, A. (2002, July 1). Real Issues of Weight for Fliers. *Sacramento Bee*, E1.

Davis, L.J. (1995). *Enforcing Normalcy: Disability, Deafness, and the Body*. New York: Verso.

Fight Back! Feed Back! Forum. (2002a). 2 Seat Policy. Retrieved May 21, 2006, from http://forums.fightback.com/forumdisplay.php?f=3&page=2&sort=lastpost&order=desc&pp=25&daysprune=-1.

Fight Back! Feed Back! Forum. (2002b). Weight and Diet Dialogue Triggered by Airline Announcement. Retrieved May 21, 2006, http://forums.fightback.com/forumdisplay.php?f=3&page=2&sort=lastpost&order=desc&pp=25&daysprune=-1.

Foucault, M. (1979). *Discipline and Punish: The Birth of the Prison*. A. Sheridan (Trans.). New York: Vintage.

Goffman, E. (1963). *Stigma: Notes on the Management of Spoiled Identity*. New York: Simon and Schuster.

Levine, C. Man Has Weighty Problem with Airline. *Boston Bay Chronicles*. Retrieved May 22, 2006, from http://web.archive.org/web/20040909084415/http://eyetrack.morris.com/story_pages/5_a/03.shtml.

Nielson, S. (2002, June 23). This Battle of the Bulge Doesn't Fly. *Sunday Oregonian*, E4.

Parker, K. (2002, June 25). Skinny Seats the Real Culprits. *Milwaukee Journal Sentinel*, 13A.

Payne, M. (2002, June 22). Weigh More? You Pay More. *Sacramento Bee*, D1.

Sedgwick, E.K. (1990). *Epistemology of the Closet*. Berkeley: University of California Press.

Shaffer, R. (2005, September 26). Transcript: Dr. Gridlock. *Washington Post*. Retrieved May 22, 2006, http://www.washingtonpost.com/wp-dyn/content/discussion/2005/09/23/DI2005092301029.html

Skenazy, L. (2002, June 26). Extra Fares for Fat Folk are Flighty. *New York Daily News,* 33.

Solovay, S. Red Alert: Southwest Campaign. Retrieved May 21, 2006, from http://www.fat-shadow.com/SW.htm.

Solovay, S. (2000), *Tipping the Scales of Justice*. New York: Prometheus.

Southwest Airlines (2006). Customer of Size Q&A. Retrieved May 21, 2006, from http://www.southwest.com/travel_center/cos_qa.html.

St. John, K., & Zamora, J.H. (2002, June 20). Southwest to Make Overweight Buy 2 Seats. *San Francisco Chronicle*, A17.

Thomson, R G. (1997a). *Extraordinary Bodies: Figuring Physical Disability in American Literature and Culture*. New York: Columbia University.

Thomson, R.G. (1997b). Integrating Disability Studies into the Existing Curriculum. In L.J. Davis (Ed.), *The Disability Studies Reader*. New York: Routledge.

Timms, P. (2002, June 25). Paying for the Excess. *The Scotsman*, 4.

Wastell, D. (2002, June 23). Fatties Bite Back. *London Sunday Telegraph*, 18.

Woodyard, C. (2003, September 25). When It Comes to Weighty Flyers, Why Can't We All Just Get Along? *USA Today*. Retrieved May 22, 2006, from http://www.usatoday.com/travel/columnist/woodyard/2003-09-25-woodyard5_x.htm.

Wynne, R. (2002, June 22). Northwest Voices: A Sampling of Readers' Letters, Faxes, and E-mails. *Seattle Times*, B5.

21

Neoliberalism and the Constitution of Contemporary Bodies

Julie Guthman

A growing literature in social science uses terms such as "foodscape" or "toxic environment" as explanations for the so-called epidemic of obesity. The thrust of these arguments is that fast, junky food is everywhere, available all the time, which is the reason that North Americans, and to some extent their counterparts, the British, are becoming increasingly fat. I do not concede the factuality of the "obesity epidemic" as it has been constructed and represented, and I am troubled by the renewed stigmatization of fat people that this epidemic talk has produced. Yet it is important to take the foodscape argument seriously, both because it provides an alternative to rhetorics of personal responsibility and genetic determinism and because it ostensibly draws attention to broader political, economic, and cultural forces in understanding the constitution of contemporary bodies. In other words, it has some affinity with a public health perspective. In that regard, however, the foodscape discourse has several conceptual problems, not the least of which is that it begs the question of who is *not* fat or getting fat. This makes it a "thin" explanation both analytically and normatively. In other words, to employ these broad, macro analytics in understanding contemporary body sizes, thinness must be explained with the same richness as fatness.

The purpose of this essay, then, is to suggest what a richer explanation of contemporary fatness and thinness might look like. To do this, I turn to neoliberalism, arguably the leitmotif of the current era. I draw from scholarship that theorizes neoliberalism as both a political economic project and a mode of governmentality. The overarching argument is that the global political-economic contradictions of the neoliberal era are literally embodied, whereas the "problem" of "obesity" is implicated in how neoliberalism produces different sorts of subjects. Regarding the former I will argue that the material contradictions of neoliberal capitalism are not only resolved in the sphere of surplus distribution, but also in bodies, such that the double fix of eating and dieting produces a political economy of bulimia, as it were, but has differential effects on individuals (with strong correlations with class). Regarding the latter, I will note a culture of bulimia, where on one hand consuming is encouraged and on the other deservingness is performed by being thin no matter how that is accomplished. I will then discuss how the discourse of "obesity," including the foodscape argument, is an example of Foucauldian biopolitics. All of this is to suggest that epidemic talk itself has become a technique of neoliberal governmentality that not only disciplines people in relation to their bodies but also produces—and reflects— broader anxieties regarding citizenship, nation, and subjectivity.

At the outset, I wish to acknowledge that "obesity" is a medicalized term that does violence to fat people. Yet, because my argument rests in part on how "obesity" has become a powerful, disciplining discourse, I will use the term throughout the chapter in reference to the discourse, duly marked with scare quotes, but otherwise I will use less loaded terms when referring to body size. I trust the reader to recognize the difference. The primary arguments of the chapter will be developed in three different sections. First, however, I take a closer look at popular renditions of the foodscape argument and discuss its thinness.

Viewing the Foodscape

Amid the moral panic that pervades current discussions of an "obesity epidemic," some scholars and food writers are searching for more reasoned explanations that do not medicalize fatness or place inordinate blame on fat people. Aiming to shift responsibility for "obesity" to the public policy arena, many of these authors are looking to show how various aspects of the U.S. regulatory environment and economy have contributed to growth in girth. Most of these authors, however, steer clear of the substantive body of scholarship in the political economy of food, and instead resort to more simple arguments. Nevertheless, because most of the authors cited have so contributed to current discussions of "obesity," we must take their work seriously. In what follows I briefly describe four major variants.

The first of these variants points to productivist agriculture itself. In his book *Fat Land* (one of the more offensive of this genre), for example, Greg Critser (2003) cites a USDA report showing a 15 percent increase in the amount of food available in the United States from 1970 to 1994 (from 3,300 calories to 3,800 per capita) and a similar increase in calories consumed per capita during that same time period. Michael Pollan, in his recent book *The Omnivore's Dilemma* (2006), makes a similar argument when he points to U.S. agricultural policies that systematically create conditions of oversupply. In one section he suggests that the coevolution of corn and humans has been so successful that the many manifestations of industrial corn—from high-fructose corn syrup to highly processed snack foods—makes us "processed corn, walking" (p. 23). Wanting to give the "cause behind the causes," he says that the explanation for what he calls "a republic of fat . . . very simply, is this: When food is abundant and cheap, people will eat more of it and get fat" (p. 102).

A second variation looks toward the regulatory environment. In *Food Politics*, for instance, Marion Nestle (2002) does a great deal of work to show how food regulation and nutritional research has been captured by the industry that is their target. As a result, food labels are deliberately confusing to consumers, and educational devices, such as the food pyramid, do not give enough guidance for a healthy, nutritious diet.

In Brownell's (2004) explication of the "toxic environment," one of several concerns that he raises is pouring contracts (when beverage companies fund school programs in exchange for sole rights to have their sodas offered in the cafeteria) in the public schools and other ways in which unhealthy food makes its way into public spaces. The overall point is that neither the content of food nor the way that it is made available receives sufficient state oversight.

A third variant focuses on food marketing. Many have talked about the power of food advertising generally (including Brownell, 2004; Nestle, 2002). Critser (2003) and Schlosser (2001) have given particular focus to fast food marketing, including the advent of "super-sizing" and "value meals" in encouraging people to eat more food. Marion Nestle's recent book *What to Eat* (2006) complements the work of Canadian retail sociologist Anthony Winson (2004), whose research on "foodscapes" describes how the spatial layout of supermarkets encourages people to buy more than they intended, especially high-margin junk food. So here the problem is defined, albeit vaguely, as one of corporate power in making people eat what they otherwise would not.

A fourth variant considers the broader material landscape of food provision and urban development. This understanding of the "foodscape" has received less attention in the popular literature. Eric Schlosser's *Fast Food Nation* was unique in pointing to suburbanization and the proliferation of fast food strips as providing important revenue streams for cash-poor localities. The spread of box stores, which arguably encourage bulk purchases of highly processed food, also exemplify this trend. A new wave of research based in economic geography is addressing the effects of suburban expansion on exercise trends, particularly in regard to the dearth of walkable neighborhoods (Lopez, 2004; Wolch & Dreier, 2004). The implication here is that regional planning—or lack thereof—is contributing to fatness by reducing opportunities for exercise.

I am sympathetic to a project that that aims to understand how high caloric, nutritionally debilitated, and otherwise unhealthy food has been made too available, too cheap, and too profitable, or how urban design encourages driving. As explanations for "obesity," however, they are highly problematic. For one, this supply-side emphasis seems very facile, for it rests on the presumption that the increased availability (and cheapness) of high caloric food is a causal force in its increased consumption (people eat it because it is there). It then calls into play a second presumption, that food consumption and exercise are related to body size in a linear, regularized, and predictable way. Although nutritionist Marion Nestle states that the relationship between calories eaten and body fat stored is "simple," others, notably exercise physiologist Glenn Gaesser (2002), have contested this claim. Gard and Wright (2005) provide a particularly compelling and exhaustive review of "the science of obesity" that has failed to demonstrate a predictable relationship between food intake, exercise, and body size. Third, when all is said and done, the argument still places responsibility on the individual, as evidenced in Nestle's pervasive "eat less" message in *Food Politics*. Indeed, much of the new, popular food writing supposes that by imparting new knowledge about food, people will eat differently, and Nestle's particular emphasis on food labeling strongly suggests that with better information people will make "better choices." Yet, to paraphrase LeBesco (2004, p. 31), can one assume that knowledge of a product will change either one's attitude of love for it or one's long-term behavior of consuming it? Finally, if fast, junky food is everywhere, beckoning us all to eat it, the argument fails to explain why some people have remained or become thin during this time period where food has become so widely available. For that matter, the entire thesis of the "obesity epidemic" rests on the presumption that humans are naturally or have been historically thin.

Looking at fatness and thinness through a thicker political economy lens than that inherent to these arguments might shed more light on the constitution of contemporary body sizes. My use of neoliberalism as the central analytic, then, is not haphazard. Because the increase in the average body mass index (the standard, albeit highly contentious, measure of fatness) of Americans is concurrent to the neoliberal era, there might be clues to this change in the current political economy of capitalism. And the degree to which this increase has been both widely publicized and evoked rhetorics such as choice, personal responsibility, and citizenship says something about the proliferation of neoliberal govenmentalities.

The Political Economy of Neoliberalism and the Body as Spatial Fix

Neoliberalism, as Harvey (2005, p. 2) states, "Is in the first instance a theory of political economic practices that proposes that human well-being can best be advanced by liberating individual entrepreneurial freedoms and skills within an institutional framework characterized by strong private property rights, free markets, and free trade." As he and others have argued, neoliberalism as a political project emerged as a fix for the manifold crises in global capitalism that came home to roost in the 1970s (Harvey, 1989; McMichael, 2003). In the United States, the confluence of falling rates of profit under Fordist manufacture, high inflation, and the Vietnam War–created debt, among other things, gave rise to a high magnitude accumulation crisis—defined as a surplus of capital relative to profitable opportunities to invest. This historical conjuncture provided fodder for the emerging New Right and its desire to dismantle what existed of the welfare/regulatory state. As Harvey notes in *The Condition of Postmodernity* (1989), several possible fixes for the crisis existed in theory, but none was all too pretty. Devaluations (which did occur, notably in the rust belt) are always politically fraught; macro-economic regulation of the Keynesian sort was exactly what the right was out to dismantle, and temporal fixes of infrastructural development (which displace the problem into the future) would only add to the debt problem. This left the spatial fix—the absorption of excess capital and labor through geographic expansion—as the least rocky of the roads to take, paving the way to "globalization."

But in the neoliberal impulse to tear down what its adherents considered restraints to capital accumulation, new contradictions emerged. Today's worldwide recession is in large part a result of a lack of effective demand, as the middle class has eroded in the first world and "bloody Taylorism" has led to disarticulated capitalism abroad.

What has saved the U.S. middle class, and even U.S. capitalism writ large, is Wal-Mart producer-consumer relationships, which, it should be noted, have their counterparts in the fast-food industry. Cheap goods made by cheaper labor (including the super-exploitation of third world labor) prop up the declining wages of the middle class; their spending keeps the economy plodding along. In other words, contra Fordism, which had at its core a social wage that upheld demand for Fordist manufacture, the low-wage economy actively produced by McDonald's and its ilk makes people dependent on fast, cheap food. At the very least, disarticulated production-consumption relationships make super-sizing seem like a good deal.

Nevertheless, disarticulated accumulation is itself crisis-ridden, so that as many have remarked that neoliberalism's broader solution has become the "commodification of everything," not only making markets for things that were once held in common (the new enclosures), but also creating needs and desires where none previously existed. In that way, the expanded availability of food, which provides the mainstay of the supply-side explanation of "obesity," is the other side of the same coin as the attack on the social wage that gave rise to fast food. Fast food becomes a doubly good fix for capitalism; not only does it involve the super-exploitation of the labor force, but it also provides an outlet for surplus food. Insofar as this surplus manifests in more body mass, the contradiction is (temporarily) resolved in the body.

But what to do when what economists call the problem of inelastic demand kicks in—when one reaches an upper limit of food consumers' demand, because there is a limit on the total amount of food that any one person can eat—or when consumers otherwise want to thwart the weight-gaining effects of food? Neoliberalism's other fix is to create purchasable solutions to the problems that it generates. One solution, as others have noted, is to commodify dieting as well as eating (Austin, 1999; Fine, 1998; Fraser, 1998). Jenny Craig and Weight Watchers's frozen dinners, the thousands of diet books, and pay-as-you-go group weight loss therapy all demonstrate that diets can be sold and bought. A related solution is to design food products that do not act like food. Products like Simplesse, the substance used as fat in low-fat ice cream, or Splenda, the low-calorie sugar, break right through the problem of inelastic demand. As implied by the brand names, the commodity simply passes through, enabling it to be consumed with no weight-gaining effect. For that matter, some of the newer pharmaceuticals (e.g., Xenical) and nutritional supplements designed to reduce the body's absorption of fat (along with essential vitamins and minerals) fulfill a similar function. By thwarting the body's metabolizing functions, these products allow producers to sell much more of these products per person, ultimately speeding up the circulation of capital—another crisis fix. Finally, consumers can enroll in exercise programs, hire personal trainers, or obtain plastic surgery to attempt thinness (not that exercise programs are only engaged with the aim of thinness, as the Health at Every Size movement promotes). This double fix of eating and dieting, in other words, is not epiphenomenal; it has become a central piece of the U.S. economy. That these variant solutions tend to map onto social class, such that the relatively rich buy themselves weight loss while the relatively poor do not, helps explain both thinness and fatness but in no way controverts the overall point.

What these examples also suggest is that the material contradictions of neoliberal capitalism are not only resolved in the sphere of surplus distribution, but also in bodies. The neoliberal moment is key here precisely because it extends capital power into previously unoccupied lifeworlds and natures (Goldman, 2005) in a spatial fix of the body. For the body is not only a site through which capital circulates as labor power, but it is also a cite through which capital circulates as commodities (Harvey, 1998). So by accommodating a faster turnover of commodities, whether by fatness, disgorgement, or commodified dieting, the body becomes a place where capitalism's contradictions are temporarily resolved. To put this in a broader sense, neoliberalism's commodification of everything ensures that getting rid of food—whether in bodies, municipal, dumps, or food aid, for that matter, which has been shown to open up new markets—is as central to capitalist accumulation as is producing and eating it. Notwithstanding the laments of those who problematize the costs of "obesity," the dieting, health-care costs associated with excessive attempts at thinness, and waste management that accompany U.S. food surpluses are internal to the logic of neoliberal capital; they are not externalities. In other words, bulimia is not simply a way to read bodies; it is a way to read the neoliberal economy itself.

Neoliberal Governmentality and the Making of Eating/Dieting Subjects

At the same time that neoliberalism encourages a political economy of bulimia, it also reinforces what Susan Bordo (1993) has called a culture of bulimia. Yet, in contrast to Bordo's psychoanalytic reading of bulimia, which locates it in "the difficulty of finding homeostasis between the producer and consumer sides of the self . . . embod[ying] the unstable double bind of consumer capitalism" (p. 201), I draw on neo-Foucauldian notions of governmentality to understand the simultaneous production of both fatness and thinness. In *The History of Sexuality*, Foucault (1985) referred to governmentality as the conduct of conduct. Dean (1999), Rose (1996), and others have restated this to mean the principles, rationales, and principles by which individuals become self-governing. The notion of neoliberal governmentality suggests a particular mode of governance that dominates the present, which Rose has described as various attempts to enforce market logics through rationalities of competition, accountability, and consumer demand. According to Rose (p. 41), what also differentiates "advanced liberalism" from that associated with the welfare state is that advanced liberalism "does not seek to govern through 'society' but through the regulated choices of individual citizens, now construed as subjects of choices and aspirations to self actualization and fulfillment."

The rationale of consumer choice, and the idea that choice represents a sort of right, is thus key to neoliberal subject formation. According to Dean (1999, p. 155), the notion of "choice" emerged with the Thatcher-Reagan critique of excessive government. By exercising our choice, we are exercising our freedoms. Why, though, is it the project of today consumption for consumption's sake? In today's slippery-sloped economy, Americans have all but abandoned notions of citizenship as participation in the public sphere for a more individualist notion of self as the citizen-consumer whose contribution to society is mainly to purchase the products of global capitalism. Although the role of the U.S. consumer in the Fordist period was to work hard *and* to consume hard, in the neoliberal period of off-shoring production, only the consumption side is left to maintain American identity. Consumption has therefore become the way that middle-class Americans maintain a toehold on the map of the future. As Sklair (1995, p. 23) states, "The creation of a culture-ideology of consumerism, therefore, is bound up with the self-imposed necessity that capitalism must be ever-expanding on a global scale. This expansion crucially depends on selling more and more goods and services to people whose 'basic needs' (a somewhat ideological term) have already been comfortably met as well as to those whose 'basic needs' are unmet."

Insofar as eating, as Probyn (2000) argues, articulates who we are, it can be read in the same way: eating becomes the embodiment of that which today's society holds sacred: consumption. We buy and eat to be good subjects, to prop up a fragile capitalism. To argue from the obverse, can there be any doubt that neoliberalism was also a response to the "consume less" ideas that circulated in the 1970s crisis period? Although "eat less" messages are everywhere, they in some sense could be construed as a threat to capitalist growth, much like "drive less" (a concept that many consider to be laughable these days). At the very least, "eat less" must be combined with "consume more" in some other sphere, including dieting products.

At the same time, another rationale of neoliberal government is responsibilization. To exercise choice freely, one must be shaped, guided, and molded into one capable of exercising freedom (Dean, 1999, p. 155). The neoliberal critique of too much intervention returns improvement to the individual, who is expected to exercise choice and become responsible for his or her risks. In that way, neoliberalism also produces a hyper-vigilance about control and self-discipline. The pursuit of an often unexamined social value of "health" is, in that way, the sine qua non of neoliberal responsibilization (Crawford, 2006; Petersen & Lupton, 1996). Thinness, albeit a poor proxy for health, is thus viewed as a reflection of self-control and "personal responsibility" regardless of whether it is even consciously pursued.

In short, neoliberal governmentality produces contradictory impulses such that the neoliberal subject is compelled to participate in society as both an enthusiastic consumer and as a self-controlled subject. The perfect subject-citizen is able to achieve both eating and thinness, even if having it both ways entails eating non-foods of questionable health impact (Splenda) or throwing up the food that one does eat (the literal bulimic). Those who can achieve thinness amid this plenty are imbued with the rationality and self-discipline that those who are fat must logically lack. So, as thinness becomes a performance (and requisite) of success in a neoliberal world, it effectively becomes a criterion by which one is treated as a subject, a marker of deservingness in a political economy all too geared toward legitimizing such distinctions. Yet unlike the Puritan ethic, in which wanting less was a mark of salvation, the worthy neoliberal citizen must seem to want less while spending more. Spending money on becoming thin is the perfect solution for both neoliberal subjectivity and neoliberal capitalism more broadly.

Biopolitics and the Discourse of "Obesity"

Even though neoliberalism seems to produce two different subject positions—and two different embodiments of those positions—it still continues to pathologize "obesity." A remaining question is why "obesity" would be reelevated to a social problem when neoliberal discourse holds that there is no social, only the individual. The particular ways in which "obesity" is problematized, often through rhetorics attributing rising health-care costs, falling worker productivity, and even lax military readiness of fat people, suggest broad anxieties about citizenship and nation. These anxieties can be understood through Foucauldian notions of biopolitics.

In *History of Sexuality* (1985), Foucault describes how biopolitics emerged with the industrial revolution, which required able-bodied workers. Although it involved the penetration of social and self-disciplinary regimes into the most intimate domains of modern life, including the body, Foucault's point is that such practices were aimed at the level of "the population." The population, that is, became a thinkable unit of regulation and intervention, and government increasingly saw its purpose as intervening on behalf of improving biological vitality for the social. In doing so, the professing of norms and averages became powerful regularizing mechanisms, perhaps more so than even legal codes (Stoler, 1995), helping to create both citizenship and nationhood.

Clearly, biopolitics informs contemporary notions of public health. The field of public health relies heavily on epidemiological statistics (and hence correlation) to infer cause. Regardless of whether a causal relationship is established between, say, a bodily phenotype and increased health problems, the statistics nevertheless draw attention to an "at-risk" population (Petersen & Lupton, 1996). Thereafter, public health interventions are not directed primarily to those considered at risk; indeed, the purpose of such interventions is to change societal norms of behavior, to intervene at the level of the population (Rose, 1985). Indeed, the very idea of dividing populations into subgroups, some of whom are seen to retard the general welfare of population, is in some sense to prevent, contain, or eliminate the abnormal (Dean, 1999, p. 100).

And so it is with talk of an "obesity epidemic." We get the shocking statistics about inexorable roads toward fatness if current eating patterns continue. We are hounded with intense calculations of the nutritional constituents of all our favorite processed foods. In light of diet failure, we are told that "obesity" cannot be "cured," but rather only prevented (Germov & Williams, 1999; Sobal, 1999). We are directed to consider the "toxic environment" and the "foodscape" as ways to think about prevention, not "cure." Yet who are the consumers of these discourses? Who takes them seriously? Often, it appears, it is those who already feel righteous in their bodies and diets.

What I am suggesting, by way of a conclusion, is that the war on "obesity," including the "epidemic" talk, is most centrally about disciplining the so-called normal. In that way, "obesity" itself has become a technique of neoliberal governance. As Dean (1999, p. 146) notes, neoliberal responsibilization "identifies certain groups as without value and beyond improvement" in the service of governing the rest. The extent to which neoliberalism writ large actively produces economic and cultural Others indicates that "obesity" may be the trope of our times.

NOTE

This chapter is a revised and abridged version of an article originally published as "Embodying Neoliberalism: Economy, Culture, and the Politics of Fat" in *Environment and Planning D: Society and Space* 24(3). I wish to thank Pion Ltd. for permission to republish, as well as my original coauthor, Melanie DuPuis, who helped develop some of the ideas presented in this chapter. Any flaws remaining are my own, of course.

REFERENCES

Austin, S.B. (1999). Commodity knowledge in consumer culture: The role of nutritional health promotion in the making of the diet industry. In J. Sobal & D. Maurer (Eds.), *Weighty Issues: Fatness and Thinness as Social Problems*. New York: Aldine De Gruyter.

Bordo, S. (1993). *Unbearable Weight: Feminism, Western Culture, and the Body*. Berkeley: University of California Press.

Brownell, K.D. (2004). *Food Fight: The Inside Story of the Food Industry, America's Obesity Crisis, and What We Can Do About It*. New York: McGraw-Hill.

Crawford, R. (2006) Health as a meaningful social practice. *Health, 10*, 401–420.

Critser, G. (2003). *Fat Land: How Americans Became the Fattest People in the World*. Boston: Houghton Mifflin.

Dean, M. (1999). *Governmentality: Power and Rule in Modern Society*. Thousand Oaks, CA: Sage.

Fine, B. (1998). *The Political Economy of Diet, Health, and Food Policy*. London: Routledge.

Foucault, M. (1985). *History of Sexuality: An Introduction*. New York: Vintage.

Fraser, L. (1998). *Losing It: False Hopes and Fat Profits in the Diet Industry*. New York: Penguin.

Gaesser, G. (2002). *Big Fat Lies: The Truth About Your Weight and Your Health*. New York: Penguin.

Gard, M., & Wright, J. (2005). *The Obesity Epidemic: Science, Morality, and Ideology*. London: Routledge

Germov, J., & Williams, L. (1999). Dieting women: Self-surveillance and the body panopticon. In J. Sobal & D. Maurer (Eds.), *Weighty Issues: Fatness and Thinness as Social Problems*. New York: Aldine De Gruyter.

Goldman, M. (2005). *Imperial Nature: The World Bank and Struggles for Social Justice in an Age of Globalization*. New Haven, CT: Yale University Press.

Harvey, D. (1989). *The Condition of Postmodernity*. Cambridge, MA: Blackwell.

Harvey, D. (1998). The body as an accumulation strategy. *Environment and Planning D: Society and Space, 16*, 401–421.

Harvey, D. (2005). *A Brief History of Neoliberalism*. New York: Oxford University Press.

LeBesco, K. (2004). *Revolting Bodies? The Struggle to Redefine Fat Identity*. Amherst: University of Massachusetts.

Lopez, R. (2004). Urban sprawl and risk for being overweight or obese. *American Journal of Public Health, 94*, 1574–1579.

McMichael, P. (2003). *Development and Social Change: A Global Perspective*. Thousand Oaks, CA: Pine Forge Press.

Nestle, M. (2002). *Food Politics: How the Food Industry Influences Nutrition and Health*. Berkeley: University of California Press.

Nestle, M. (2006). *What to Eat*. New York: North Point Press.

Petersen, A., & Lupton, D. (1996). *The New Public Health: Health and Self in the Age of Risk*. Thousand Oaks, CA: Sage

Pollan, M. (2006). *The Omnivore's Dilemma: A Natural History of Four Meals*. New York: Penguin.

Probyn, E. (2000). *Carnal Appetites: FoodSexIdentities*. London: Routledge.

Rose, G. (1985). Sick individuals and sick populations. *International Journal of Epidemiology, 14*, 32–38.

Rose, N. (1996). Governing "advanced" liberal democracies. In A. Barry, T. Osborne, & N. Rose (Eds.), *Foucault and Political Reason: Liberalism, Neo-liberalism, and Rationalities of Government*. Chicago: University of Chicago Press.

Schlosser, E. (2001). *Fast Food Nation: The Dark Side of the American Meal*. Boston: Houghton Mifflin.

Sklair, L. (1995). *Sociology of the Global System*. Baltimore: Johns Hopkins University Press.

Sobal, J. (1999). The size acceptance movement and the social construction of body weight. In J. Sobal & D. Maurer (Eds.), *Weighty Issues: Fatness and Thinness as Social Problems*. Hawthorne, NY: Aldine de Gruyter.

Stoler, A. L. (1995). *Race and the Education of Desire*. Durham, NC: Duke University Press.

Winson, A. (2004). Bringing political economy into the debate on the obesity epidemic. *Agriculture and Human Values, 21*, 299–312.

Wolch, J., Pastor, M., Jr., & Dreier, P. (2004). *Up Against the Sprawl: Public Policy and the Making of Southern California*. Minneapolis: University of Minnesota Press.

|||||||||||||||||||||||||||||||||||||||||||||||||||||||||||||||||||||||||||||||||

22

Sitting Pretty

Fat Bodies, Classroom Desks, and Academic Excess

Ashley Hetrick and Derek Attig

Desks hurt us. Such an admission is an appropriate way to both begin this essay and explain the primary motivation behind our exploration of student bodies in classroom environments. It is through experiencing the physical pain and social shame of classroom desks that we first became interested in the issue of space and how it is distributed and policed in and through the homogenizing structures of desks. These desks are not, we argue, neutral and benign spaces; they are, rather, highly active material and discursive constructions that seek to both indoctrinate students' bodies and minds into the middle-class values of restraint and discipline, and inscribe these messages onto the bodies that sit in them. Classroom desks are one way that "discourses [are] deployed in order to contain fat bodies, fat people . . . [and] simultaneously construct and erase the fat body, attempting to expel it from representation at the very moment that defines it" (Braziel & LeBesco, 2001, p. 1). At the heart of desk design is the issue of containment, the protection of rigid spatial boundaries and uncompromising values that, paradoxically, both highlight and erase bodies that refuse to conform.

To sit in these desks—primarily in chairs attached to individual writing surfaces, or auditorium seating with hinged desks—our hips and stomachs must be pushed, shoved, and squeezed into unforgiving metal, wood, and plastic. The longer we sit in them, the more uncomfortable they become, biting into fleshy abundance and often resisting attempted release. Though we rely on these experiences of pain to ground and frame our examination, we also take care to resist what could be called the tyranny of experience. When the only or primary goal of an activist or academic project is making personal experience visible, Joan Scott writes, "analysis of the workings of this system and of its historicity" is prevented (1992, p. 25). Speaking specifically of those who identify as gay, she elaborates, "We know they exist, but not how they've been constructed; we know their existence offers a critique of normative practices, but not the extent of the critique" (p. 25). Cognizant of Scott's warning, we seek to use a consideration of our experiences as fat students as a way of approaching the description and scrutiny of the social, political, and educational conditions of those experiences.

We insist on understanding the fact of our physical discomfort not as an unfortunate side effect of our size or the desks' construction. Instead, we interpret our pain as a symptom of higher education's deliberate (if often unconscious) shaping of student minds and bodies. This reading is bolstered by the concept of the hidden curriculum, which "ha[s] been variously identified as the inculcation of values, political socialization, training in obedience and docility, the perpetuation of traditional class structure—functions that may be characterized generally as social control" (Vallance, 1973, p. 5). A hidden curriculum consists of those aspects of education that remain largely unarticulated and unexamined and which socialize students to specific ends. That it is called "hidden," however, is not to suggest that it is always invisible. "The hidden curriculum is not something that we must look behind or around in order to detect," Marina Gair and Guy Mullins write, for "in most cases it is plainly in sight, and functions effortlessly" (2001, p. 23). What is more visible to (and yet more unexamined by) students than the built environment of the college or university, "the physical set and setting . . . [which] function to convey socialization messages" (Costello, 2001, p. 44)? The desks and auditorium seating that represent and enable their very identities as students, for example, are visible but go unnoticed. That ignorance is not without cost. Desks designed for a specific type of body subtly—though often painfully—structure students' academic lives. They seek to restrain and reform those students who, for a want of restraint and docility and an excess of body, overflow the desks and the educational values embodied therein.

A primary function of classroom desks, we argue, is a paradoxical one: these aspects of the built environment make fat students visible in order to, eventually, make them invisible in a crowd of identically conforming bodies. "Society," Émile Durkheim wrote, "can survive only if there exists among its members a significant degree of homogeneity; education perpetuates and reinforces this homogeneity by fixing in the child, from the beginning, the essential similarities collective life demands" (Margolis et al., 2001, p. 6). The rigid design of the desk is an integral site at which higher education's homogenizing enterprise occurs, for contained within are messages that dictate, through pain and shame, how students should behave and appear. The desired embodiment (restrained and disciplined, manifested in thinness) and the docile, receptive attitude of students are clearly articulated and encouraged through molded seats and measured surfaces. Mass production is evident not only in desk design but also in its effects: in the classroom desk, there is a perhaps an unconscious attempt to shape student bodies in specifically classed, gendered, and racialized ways. That this intent is not always conscious—not always apparent or knowingly experienced—serves to naturalize its processes and effects, making it that much more insidious.

In the structure of classroom desks we read both an awareness and a neglect of fat student bodies, a simultaneous punishment and ignorance of fat existence in higher education's crafting of the ideal student body. Both of these potential motivations underlying desk construction actively and simultaneously participate in the erasure of fat student bodies. The unyielding wood and chafing plastic of desks, far from being small hassles of student life, benign in their pinching of flesh, are in fact part of the "disciplinary practices" (Bartky, 1991, p. 65) that reproduce bodies tailored to the academy's understanding of how a student should look, think, and act. From Sandra Lee Bartky's work on the construction of feminine bodies, we draw a connection between the disciplinary practices that seek to create the acceptable or recognizably feminine body and those that form the recognizable student. It is our desire to include classroom desks among those disciplinary practices that "aim to produce a body of a certain size and general configuration [and] those that bring forth from this body a specific repertoire of gestures, postures, and movements" (Bartky, 1991, p. 65).

The relationship between classroom desks and disciplinary practices that seek to form and control body "size and general configuration" is evident: the hard materials and unforgiving shapes of these desks punish student bodies that exceed their boundaries with pain and social shame. Some fat students are unable or unwilling to subject their bodies to the disciplinary powers of desks and must sit elsewhere. In these cases, desks can threaten fat students' very identities as students; if their bodies cannot fit into structures that signify their intellectually receptive status, then they are, symbolically at least, unable to learn. Homogenous thinness is rewarded with comfort and various other privileges accorded to those granted identification as both students and normal. In these ways, classroom desks control body size and thereby produce the ideal thin student.

Following again from Bartky, we can see that desks, as disciplinary practices, control student bodies through the cultivation or "bring[ing] forth" from these bodies "a specific repertoire of gestures, postures, and movements" (Bartky, 1991, p. 65). When we position Bartky's theories concerning the creation, control, and calling forth of bodies and bodily movement in conversation with the demands made by desks, we see that their sturdy materiality requires students to bend their bodies in and around the desks in specific ways to function both as students and as properly disciplined bodies. In other words, desks dictate not only the size and shape of student bodies, but also how these bodies move and interact with spaces in, on, and around desks. In this homogenizing environment of higher education, the ideal student body is called forth in and through her repetitive interactions with her standardized, individual allotment of what Christine Sleeter calls "the egg crate design" of college classrooms (Gair & Mullins, 2001, p. 31). Nowhere is her interaction with space more apparent than in the relationship between her body and her desk, particularly with the limited amount of space that she is assigned for writing, reading, and holding her materials. The thin, ideal student body conforms to the intended design of the desk; the gestures and movements required and thus performed are both witnesses to and creators of the recognizable student body. The bodies of fat students, however, compete with valuable writing surface for space, exceeding boundaries—oftentimes painfully—and violating desk design, thereby inhibiting exam- and note-taking. The disciplinary practices exhibited in and exercised through desks attempt to summon certain responses and movements from the fat student body, actions that would, with unconscious repetition, create the student form. With fat students, however, such attempts are met with fat's wild colonization of space. Fat student bodies quite literally overflow the molds of academia.

As we have seen, desks not only divide and police spatial boundaries, but they also teach students to police themselves, constraining their movements and, of course, their flesh inside the borders of the desk. Through the corporeal pain, as well as the fear and shame that it often promotes, the specifically racial and classed values of higher education are inscribed not only on the bodies of students, but also on their minds. This produces a panoptical effect (Foucault, 1991, pp. 195–228) wherein these students begin to carefully watch themselves and others, monitoring the lines of their bodies for conformity to the built environment. The gaze is thus used as a disciplinary tactic, and it is one that operates most successfully when enforced by students on their own and other bodies.

Many exercises of discipline, especially those practiced on the fat student body, are dependent on sight to exist and function; indeed, as Michel Foucault has written, discipline "presupposes a mechanism that coerces by means of observation; an apparatus in which the techniques that make it possible to see induce effects of power, and in which, conversely, the means of coercion make those on whom they are applied clearly visible" (1991, pp. 170–171). The act of seeing is itself an exercise in power. As such, there are certain instances in which calling attention to bodies and experiences can be more oppressive than empowering. The classrooms of higher education, bent on homogeneity, are sites in which sight—the disciplining gaze, with its acute awareness of dangerous difference—operates as an instrument of control and punishment. The experience of feeling so shamefully *seen* in the delicate process of squeezing into or out of a classroom desk is a singularly disciplining one. Indeed, it is the desk that most assists—even produces—the disciplinary gaze in its scrutiny (of self and others), comparison, and attempts at conformity. Desks make it possible to but briefly scan the room and immediately notice who fits and who does not; which students rest comfortably, with their legs perhaps crossed, and those wedged into every available inch of space, their legs, hips, and bellies reddening with the imprints of metal bars and plastic edges.

The disciplinary observation that occurs in these classrooms, around these desks, is not just directed at fat students but is also internalized by them. Some fat students, aware of their very visible difference and mindful of their disobedient flesh, attempt to hold their bodies in and around desks in such ways as to pretend that their fat does not exist. Rather than risk embarrassment by asking for or making alternative seating, these students accept the pain of nonconformity with silence and a desperate wish for no one to notice—to see—their fatness. The disciplinary effects of desks compel fat students to participate in their own erasure, prompting them to try to hide their bodies while simultaneously highlighting their impossibly concealable differences. The relationship between fat students and classroom desks is, indeed, an impossible one.

Desks seek to socialize student bodies and minds as docile, obedient, and restrained—a process and goal (not coincidentally) associated with middle-class whiteness. According to Richard Dyer, "the notion of whiteness" is inextricably and intimately linked to notions of "tightness, self-control, [and] mind over body" (1997, p. 6). Here we see that whiteness not only privileges the mind over the body, but also expects the former to rigidly restrain the latter as an ultimate, visible, and recurring testament of the invisible mind's power. Though whiteness abhors the body and its chaotic impulses, Dyer wrote, it must "reproduce [itself]" while continuing to "control and transcend . . . bodies. Only by (impossibly) doing both" is whiteness maintained (Dyer, 1997, p. 30). Reproduction here is explicitly referencing sexuality, though by expanding Dyer's conceptualization of whiteness and applying it to the disciplinary effects of desks, we can see the ways in which desks participate in the corporeal reproduction of the white, middle-class values of higher education. Using pain, shame, and the internalized disciplinary gaze, desk design subjects student bodies to normalizing, homogenizing assumptions concerning their size and shape. The white, middle-class, and educational appreciation for restraint and docility are inscribed on unruly flesh, and difference is both erased and emphasized. Thinness becomes the visible manifestation of the "control and transcend[ence]" of and over the loathed body.

Fatness in the popular imagination, write Jana Evans Braziel and Kathleen LeBesco, "equals reckless excess, prodigality, indulgence, lack of restraint, violation of order and space, transgression of boundary" (2001, p. 3). These qualities, as we have demonstrated, are those which the classroom desk punishes and seeks to erase from student bodies. But, we suggest, they also provide a starting point for imagining the possible resistance of fat bodies in the college classroom. Bodily excess can be painful for fat students, but it can also be productive of resistant classroom dynamics. By not fitting nicely (or attempting to fit at any cost) into confining classroom desks—by taking as much space as we please—fat students can work toward a reorganization of classroom space that does not privilege the slender or punish the plump.

First, however, it is necessary for students to *see* the desks as something other than natural parts of the classroom landscape. Even many of the fat students for whom sitting is painful often fail to see the desk as anything other than a sadly necessary anguish. The classroom desk is naturalized in such a way as to make it seem as though the fat body does not fit the desk—and not the other way around. The first step in a fat resistance to classroom desks, then, must be a project of denaturalization. Students must be made to see the desks as an influential part of their experiences of higher education.

In December, 2005, we undertook just such a project. We felt that although some people write on desks, most students do not often get a chance to talk back to the desks that they sit in almost every day. One night, we stole into a humanities building at Beloit College in which the classrooms are filled with particularly painful desks. On the desks' writing surfaces, we taped sheets of paper, each asking a different question: "Are you bored?" "Do you write on desks?" "Does this desk fit your body?" "How do you feel about this desk?" "How would you change this desk?" We left the sheets for four class days, checking each day to see various conversations develop and to replace any sheets that went mysteriously missing.

We were able to see, after removing the sheets and reading through them, the ways that students used the papers to converse anonymously with each other, ourselves, and the desks. Much of the student response was frivolous (or resolutely nonverbal—drawings of fish and Christmas trees and maps of Europe abounded), but even this got at the hierarchical environment of the classroom and the strange role that desks play in it. Although some students chided us for using so much paper to "make a silly point," many of the responses were interesting and illustrative. Some supported our hypothesis that we were not the only students for whom desks could be painful:

> "I'm too fat for this desk."
> "It's awful to get in & out of."
> "Too small for my womanly hips."
> "Tables are much better than tiny little uncomfortable desks!"
> "I wish it was bigger, but THAT's nothing new . . . "
> "I fits [sic], I guess . . . but it's uncomfortable as hell!"
> "Not really, my ass is too big."
> "It does not allow for some bodies. I can't see it to be comfortable to anyone."
> "I don't think this society fits my body."

These responses demonstrate the complicated and painful relationships some students have with their desks. These students also exhibit the beginnings of a critical examination of the ways that desks operate in higher education (and, as the last points out, its social contexts). Interestingly, many responses pointed to the variety of ways in which desks are uncomfortable and, through standardization, erase student difference. Left-handed, tall, and short students all variously declared their discomfort at the enforced normativity of classroom desks.

Several other responses criticized not the form of our project (we wasted too much paper) but the content. One student in particular illustrated perfectly the ways that fat students are blamed for desks' rigidity: "Yes [the desk fits my body], and if it didn't, I would need to exercise." To this righteously thin, properly disciplined student (and the one who wrote that fitting was not a problem because "I don't weigh 300 pounds"), the blame for any discomfort rests solely with fat students. The pain that desks cause, these students seem to believe, should make fat students desire changes in their bodies, not their surroundings. Another response also places blame on fat students and, in an attempt at humor, points to the idea that fat people are out of control, lacking restraint: "My name is Nick and I eat so much dessert that my ass is so fat I need to butter it up to slide it in the seat. Then I smell butter, get hungry, eat more, which then causes me to get fatter. It's an ongoing cycle." Although these responses confirmed some of our ideas about fat-negative thinking and classroom desks, they also showed at least some awareness of the materiality of the desk and its effect on fat students (however positively they thought of that effect).

One of the most interesting critical statements we received was also one that we puzzled over. Responding to the question regarding whether desks fit one's body, one student seemed to think that "suggesting [that] fat people can't fit in these [desks] . . . seems more insulting than building a chair too small." This statement illustrates a sentiment that we have noticed elsewhere in responses to activist projects. As long as it is repeated as truth and no one (at least publicly) disagrees, some people seem to believe that everyone is the same and there is no oppression in the world. In this approach, feminist or fat activism, for example, actually produces the subjugation that they claim to oppose. Perhaps such thinking makes sense in a society rhetorically obsessed with the idea of equality through the erasure of difference but utterly resistant to change. It is an interesting phenomenon and one that deserves more extensive analysis.

Another student asked us, through a sheet of paper, what we were going to do about it if the desk did not fit. Truthfully, in the short term, the answer was nothing tangible. This response does, however, offer us a chance to think about goals. The question of classroom desks and corporeal pain is not one that invites easy answers. If desks were simply made bigger, they would be enforcing only a slightly altered norm, one that would hurt some students as much as the current one does. Similarly, chairs without writing desks can be painful in a variety of ways as well. The purpose of the project was not to suggest specific plans for change but to insist that desks, as they are manufactured and used now, replicate damaging normative ideas about student bodies and collegiate learning. Overall, the project was a success. One of our questions prompted a student to remark, "It's a good question to ask, how do I feel about this desk, it's something I hadn't given thought to." We found similar responses on other sheets. By putting a small piece of paper on the writing surface and asking students to think about desks (particularly about desks and their bodies), we disrupted the normal, naturalized relationship between desk and student. We offer it as one example of resistance to the painful constraints of classroom desks.

Rose Robertson, a student at Beloit College, suggests through her actions a less circuitous route to resistance. A fat woman, Rose cannot sit comfortably in the desks that her school provides. When she enters a classroom where only desks are available, she unsubtly plunks herself down on the floor. This action often disrupts class and draws unapologetic attention to the desks' failure to fit her body. She participates in class but does so from the floor, forcing both professor and fellow students to crane their necks to see her and acknowledge both her difference as well as her blatant refusal to squeeze herself into the classroom desk and endure its attendant pain and discomfort.

Boundaries, both intellectual and physical, are policed with great zeal in higher education. Classroom desks are just one way that this occurs. We make a connection, especially appropriate given all our talk of "discipline," between rigid desks and the often unyielding structure of disciplines in higher education. Like fat students overflowing their desks, we envision fat studies (and other interdisciplinary endeavors) exploding simple disciplinary frameworks. Indeed, we would argue that academic excess is a vital part of fat studies, an enterprise too large and expansive to fit in standard structures. And just as fat student bodies have the potential to challenge the normalizing, physically painful shape forced on them, fat studies can be deployed to resist the similar, intellectually painful divisions called disciplines. Like Rose refusing to engage the painful form of the desk, scholars and students dedicated to interdisciplinarity must refuse to have their work cut down to size and forced into intellectually limiting boxes. They must, in their own way, sit on the floor.

Having squeezed ourselves into small desks, we often find upon attempting to get up that the desk remains briefly attached to our bodies. It is a fitting image for the ways that we carry cultural norms with us beyond their explicit enforcement. Along with the knowledge created in the classroom, we carry welts and marks on our hips and stomachs where discipline has been practiced on our bodies. Although we do not believe that higher education should be "above" or separate from its so-cial context, this pain pushes us to always be alert to "the social functions of higher education" (Margolis et al., 2001, p. 4). We should always work to be aware of the values-laden socialization that takes place in the college classroom. Although learn-ing should never be comfortable or complacent, educational discomfort should result from new ideas and challenging ways of thinking about problems, not wood, plastic, and metal.

REFERENCES

Bartky, S.L. (1991). *Femininity and Domination: Studies in the Phenomenology of Oppression.* New York: Routledge.

Braziel, J.E., & K. LeBesco. (2001). Editor's introduction. In J.E. Braziel & K. LeBesco, (Ed.), *Bodies Out of Bounds: Fatness and Transgression.* Berkeley: University of California Press.

Costello, C.Y. (2001). Schooled by the classroom: The (re)production of social stratification in professional school settings. In E. Margolis (Ed.), *The Hidden Curriculum in Higher Educa-tion.* New York: Routledge.

Dyer, R. (1997). *White.* New York: Routledge.

Foucault, M. (1991). *Discipline and Punish: The Birth of the Prison* (Alan Sheridan, Trans.). New York: Vintage. (Original work published 1975).

Gair, M., & G. Mullins. (2001). Hiding in plain sight. In E. Margolis (Ed.), *The Hidden Cur-riculum in Higher Education.* New York: Routledge.

Margolis, E., et al. (2001). Peekaboo: Hiding and outing the curriculum. In E. Margolis (Ed.), *The Hidden Curriculum in Higher Education.* New York: Routledge.

Scott, J.W. (1992). Experience. In J. Butler & J.W. Scott (Ed.), *Feminists Theorize the Political.* New York: Routledge.

Vallance, E. (1973). Hiding the hidden curriculum: An interpretation of the language of justi-fication in nineteenth-century educational reform. *Curriculum Theory Network, 4,* 5–21.

Stigma Threat and the Fat Professor
Reducing Student Prejudice in the Classroom

Elena Andrea Escalera

Weight Discrimination in Academia

Weight discrimination in the workplace has long been documented in many disciplines (Kristen, 2002; Roehling, 1999). This study looks at how fat discrimination plays out in a very specialized venue: the college classroom.

In academic settings, professors are not only evaluated by their colleagues, department chairs, and deans, but also by their students. Students, who have relatively less status in the system, have significant power in the evaluation of their professors. Rank and tenure committees use these evaluations to determine promotion and retention. Quite literally, a professor's job is on the line if student evaluations are low.

Student evaluations have been studied in relation to bias and discrimination, and many studies have found that these all important evaluations may not be the reliable form of teacher review that they are hoped to be. Sprague and Massoni (2005) found that student evaluations vary depending on how closely the teacher adhered to their expected gender role.

Discrimination in student evaluation extends to professors based on their appearance as well. Attractive professors received much higher evaluations than those who were rated less attractive by students (Hamermesh & Parker, 2005). Professors who dress in formal or stylish attire are also likely to receive better evaluations. Stylish clothing is often not available in larger sizes, resulting in an institutional barrier to large-sized faculty. In addition, fat is considered unattractive in this culture (Allon, 1982; Crandall, 1984). This being the case, a fat professor is going to be considered unattractive, and will likely see the impact of this cultural value in their evaluations.

In a recent course that I taught in Health Psychology, a student of mine made a comment that was much more subtle. The student said, "She talks too much about weight and disability, which have nothing to do with Health Psychology." Although I spent no more time on weight and disability than any other subject, and considerably less on the topic than on stress and cancer, this student was distressed that a fat disabled person was teaching about health. If this distress can be better understood, perhaps there are ways to diffuse student reactivity that can result in discriminatory behavior.

Stigma Threat and Anti-fat Bias

Anti-fat bias is not a new phenomenon (Allon, 1982). Because anti-fat bias is at its heart a bias, we can assume that the psychological processes involved are similar to other types of prejudice. People who have strong anti-fat bias have also been found to express more racism (in an overarching tendency toward intolerance for deviation from the norm). In a study using the Modern Racism Scale, Crandall (1994) found a correlation between anti-fat bias and racism, and demonstrated that the same processes were at work in anti-fat bias as in symbolic prejudice.

Stigma is not a characteristic of a person in the stigmatized group. It is a socially constructed phenomenon that shifts and changes over time. Stigma is the product of others' reactions to a person who is a member of a low-status or rejected group rather than anything essential to that person (Archer, 1985). Nevertheless, stigmatized people commonly blame themselves for the discrimination that they experience. In an experiment by Crocker, Cornwell, and Major (1993), women who experienced discrimination were more likely to blame their weight for the discrimination instead of blaming the person discriminating against them. This resulted in more negative emotional states and self-esteem problems than for other groups, which may put fat women at greater emotional and social risk.

Stigmas can cause *people who perceive* a stigmatized person to feel anxious and threatened. This idea, called *stigma threat* (Crocker, Major, & Steele, 1998), is especially relevant to classroom interactions because the presence of an instructor who is a member of a stigmatized group can create anxiety and distress in the students. A fat professor who is teaching a class about health has a stigma salient to the course material. A fat disabled professor teaching about health has multiple stigmas relevant to the subject matter. Having these kinds of "double whammy" collected stigmas creates an even greater risk for discrimination (Solovay, 2000).

Stigma threat can also interfere with the learning process and the professor's productivity and effectiveness (Hamermesh & Parker, 2005). Lower attractiveness (as defined by the students) of fat professors may actually be interfering with the learning process through the increased anxiety of the students. Subjects have been found to exhibit increased cardiovascular reactivity when in contact with people who have visible stigmas (Blascovich, Mendes, Hunter, Lickel, & Kowai-Bell, 2001). This study supports the idea that physiological reactivity increases with stigma threat but also interferes with task performance. The interference with task performance and memory is a characteristic of the threat response that carries risk not only for the professor, in terms of evaluation, but also for the student, in terms of learning and classroom performance.

Blascovich and colleagues (2001) discuss challenge and threat as motivational states. Threat is a situation where a person evaluates the demand of a given situation as being greater than their resources to perform. Challenge occurs when there is a demand for performance in a given situation but the person evaluates that situation as being within the range of their resources to perform. The presence of a fat person could increase a situation's uncertainty and unpredictability. The person interacting with the fat person would have to expend more effort to suppress automatic negative emotional responses or stereotypes (Devine, Evett, & Vasquez-Suson, 1996). Students may feel discomfort with their own emotional reactions to a fat person, their beliefs about fat people, and their uncertainty of how to respond to the professor without making offensive comments. If the student holds significant negative stereotypes about fat people, this could be an extremely stressful event, especially when weight becomes a salient factor in the subject matter of the course.

Reducing Bias in the Classroom

One approach to reducing anti-fat bias has been to educate students about the causes of fatness in order to dispel stereotypes. Puhl, Schwartz, and Brownell (2005) experimented with the use of perceived social consensus in reducing bias and changing attitudes toward fat people. When their subjects learned that others did not hold such biased views toward fat people, there was a decrease in negative stereotypes about fat people. This study also found that providing information about both the immutable and uncontrollable causes of fatness and the influence of heredity improved the explicit attitudes of their subjects. In another study that used education about fatness to decrease implicit bias, however, they found no significant change after the educational intervention (Teachman, Gapinski, Brownell, Rawlins, & Jeyaram, 2003).

The effectiveness of this approach depends to a large degree on how the student reacts to the source of the information. Stigma has a negative effect on the credibility of a communicator. Because people tend to perceive sincerity in those who argue against their own self-interest, students may see a fat professor as insincere and self-serving if they challenge common myths about the causes of fatness (Eagly, Wood, & Chaiken, 1978). In addition, attractiveness makes a person more persuasive (Chaiken, 1979), so if fat is seen as an unattractive trait, this could work against the fat professor as a communicator.

Measuring Stigma Threat in the Classroom

I decided to approach stigma threat in the classroom as anxiety. To reduce the students' anxiety from stigma threat, I used a classroom technique of assigning anonymous five-minute reaction papers at the end of each topic. This not only provides a qualitative measure of threat and challenge but also provides a way for students to express their anxiety, thus reducing physiological and psychological reactivity. Wilson (2004) notes that reflective writing can be an effective way to deal with anxiety. In addition, the reaction papers allow the students to shift their focus from me to their own attitude change processes.

I hoped to find a reduction in the anti-fat bias of the students over the course of the semester. To measure this effect, I used the IAT (Implicit Association Test)

(Greenwald, McGhee, & Schwartz, 1998). The IAT measures reaction time in word categorization tasks. It is a measure of the strength of a person's association between two concept categories. Because processing speed is not subject to conscious decision making, it is taken to index a person's implicit attitudes. This avoids the problems of self-report and self-presentation that occur in questionnaires or other conscious measures of attitudes and beliefs. Because people in the western world grow up and develop beliefs and stereotypes in cultures biased against fat people, they tend to have negative associations with fat (Allon, 1982). This means that the association between fat and negative traits should be strong. Testing conditions in which these stereotypes are active should show much faster reaction times.

Responses from the reaction papers fell into four categories suggested by the Stigma Threat Hypothesis. In neutral responses, students showed very little challenge to preexisting beliefs and did not show struggle or change in beliefs or attitudes. The neutral comments basically stated that they learned something new but did not evidence anxiety or uncertainty.

Example: "This week [guest speaker] talked to the class. I never knew how heavy people are discriminated against, especially in the health care system. The discussion that we had was very informative."

Challenge responses showed evidence that a belief was challenged. Most showed a change in attitude or belief. All the challenge comments suggested a way to resolve the issue or showed confidence that there could be a solution. These resolutions were primarily in terms of the students' ability to change their own behaviors and beliefs, a confidence in the ability of groups to change the social system, or their belief that education may effect change.

Example: "I think it was very interesting hearing [guest speaker] talk about the myths about being fat. I would say the thing that challenged a previous belief that I had was just how bad fat people are treated. I didn't think the views of fat people assumed so much and so many negative things about fat people. I thought our country was more open-minded than that, which is sad to see how much people assume. This became very evident in the myths she told us where clearly there is prejudice about being fat. Hopefully more people can receive such education to challenge the common stereotypes about being fat."

The threat expressive comments showed evidence that beliefs were being challenged. They were very similar to the challenge types of responses, except that they were less hopeful about there being a resolution. Many of these comments expressed a worry that the student would not be able to cope with the social demand of speaking with a stigmatized person without offending them.

Example: "This week I was challenged with the word *fat*. As I wrote in my journal, I always thought that I should use words like *heavy* or *overweight*. I think this frame of mind came from childhood and learning not to say *fat*. Also, it is a very uncommon word to use in a discussion with people in public. I now understand how much more hurtful the other words are [obese, overweight]. I don't know if I

FIGURE 23.1

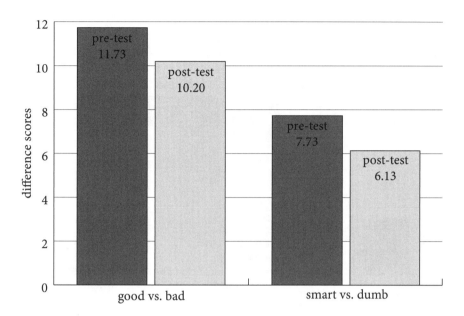

can use the word *fat* in the future, because even though I now understand the hurt of the other words, using the word *fat* is not really a socially common or acceptable thing to say."

Threat defensive comments occur when the person tries to reduce the anxiety and uncertainty of the situation by lashing out at the stigmatized person who is causing them to experience a negative state. Because the students were assigned to talk about their own beliefs, rather than give an evaluation of the professor, there are fewer threat defensive comments in my data than were observed by Hamermesh and Parker (2005). The threat defensive comments were directed at the speaker's appearance, however, which would be consistent with previous findings.

Example: "The belief that I had that was challenged was that there was a woman who was fat telling us that fat people are not what the stereotypes say—but—here we are looking at a woman who has a hem coming out in her skirt! It amazed me that if she was going to challenge beliefs she was not put together well enough not to be questioned herself. Now I wonder—why did she not perfect her appearance if she was speaking about appearance?!"

There was a significant difference in the type of responses (neutral, challenge, threat) made in each class topic (stigma salient vs. stigma non-salient). This suggests that stigma threat is increased during stigma-relevant class topics (p = 0.014, chi-square = 8.51, df = 2).

FIGURE 23.2

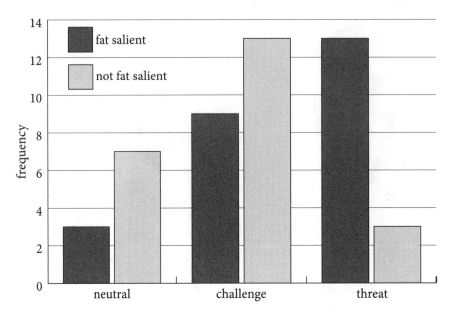

Each version of the IAT was analyzed with a paired t-test. The IAT pretest and posttest scores in the *good-bad* condition and the *smart-stupid* condition were significantly different. This shows a decrease in the implicit anti-fat bias between the beginning of the semester and the end of the semester (p = 0.040, p = 2.2632, df = 14, and p = 0.0165, t = 2.7214, df = 14).

Conclusions

Although the classroom is not a laboratory that can be controlled and manipulated without confounding variables, it is a very real crucible of social interaction that affects the lives of both students and professors. Not only does stigma threat endanger the professional safety and freedom of professors who belong to a stigmatized category, but it may actually interfere with the learning process itself.

The data from the reaction papers show that stigma threat is present in the classroom, especially when the stigma of the professor is made salient by the subject matter. The students in this study showed the same kind of perception of danger, uncertainty, and required effort that was found with subjects exposed to other stigmatized individuals (Blascovich et al., 2001). As Crandall (1994) suggests, the processes for anti-fat bias may be similar to those of racism. Students had anxiety reactions in other topic areas, but the anxiety was markedly threat related in fat-salient topics.

The IAT data show that there was a decrease in student anti-fat bias over the course of the semester. There was a change in the students' conceptual organization and association of concepts in memory. Although it is unclear whether it will affect their behavior, there is evidence of change in their stereotypes about fat people.

Only two of the scales of the IAT were significant, but they were the scales that suggest that stigma threat was reduced. The class curriculum addressed stereotypes about fat people in general, but only the scales based on *good* versus *bad* and *smart* versus *dumb* showed any significant change. If the curriculum was the determining factor in the reduction of implicit bias, one would expect the change to occur across all four scales. If the change was due to a reduction in stigma threat, however, then one would expect that the scales most relevant to student-professor relationship would be the most affected. *Good* versus *bad* and *smart* versus *stupid* would be categories specifically relevant to the academic setting.

Although cross-semester comparisons are confounded by cohort effects, the differences in the student evaluation means for Health Psychology present some interesting questions. The mean in the year previous to the intervention was 3.67 on a scale of 1 to 5. The mean for the year with the reaction papers was 4.33. The previous year, there were five written comments in total, two of which were discriminatory. The year in which the interventions took place, there were nine pages of comments, most of them positive, none of them discriminatory. Is it possible that allowing the students to focus on their own belief process reduced their stigma threat? It is impossible to say, but the difference is striking.

Fat professors do not always get such informative feedback, especially not from student evaluations. Professional risk is an assessment to be done by each individual professor. The demonstration that change can happen in the course of a semester, however, gives us hope that in the end, we really can make a difference in the lives of our students and their future patients and clients. It all depends on how professors see their own stigma. Is it a challenge or a threat?

REFERENCES

Allon, N. (1982) The stigma of overweight in everyday life. In B. Wolman (Ed.), *Psychological Aspects of Obesity: A Handbook* (pp. 130–174). New York: Van Nostrand Reinhold.

Archer, D. (1985). Social deviance. In G. Lindzey & E. Aronson (Eds.), *Handbook of Social Psychology* (pp. 743–804). New York: Random House.

Blascovich, J., Mendes, W.B., Hunter, S., Lickel, B., & Kowai-Bell, N. (2001). Perceiver threat in social interactions with stigmatized others. *Journal of Personality and Social Psychology, 80,* 253–267.

Chaiken, S. (1979). Communicator physical attractiveness and persuasion. *Journal of Personality and Social Psychology, 37,* 1387–1397.

Crandall, C. (1984). Social interest as a moderator of life stress. *Journal of Personality and Social Psychology, 47,* 164–174.

Crandall, C. (1994). Prejudice against fat people: Ideology and self-interest. *Journal of Personality and Social Psychology, 66,* 882–894.

Crocker, J., Cornwell, B., & Major, B. (1993). The stigma of overweight: Affective consequences of attributional ambiguity. *Journal of Personality and Social Psychology, 64,* no. 1, 60–70.

Crocker, J., Major, B., & Steele, C. (1998). Social stigma. In D.T. Gilbert, S.T. Fiske, & G. Lindzey. (Eds.), *The Handbook of Social Psychology* (4th ed., vol. 2, pp. 504–553). Boston: McGraw-Hill.

Devine, P.G., Evett, S.R., & Vasquez-Suson, K.A. (1996). Exploring the interpersonal dynamics of intergroup contact. In R.M. Sorrentino & E.T. Higgins (Eds.), *Handbook of Motivation and Cognition. Vol. 3: The Interpersonal Context* (pp. 423–464). New York: Guilford Press.

Eagly, A.H., Wood, W., & Chaiken, S. (1978). Casual inferences about communicators and their effect on opinion change. *Journal of Personality and Social Psychology, 36,* 424–435.

Greenwald, A.G., McGhee, D.E., & Schwartz, J.L.K. (1998). Measuring individual differences in implicit cognition: The implicit association test. *Journal of Personality and Social Psychology, 74,* 1464–1480.

Hamermesh, D., & Parker, A. (2005). Beauty in the classroom: Instructor's pulchritude and putative pedagogical productivity. *Economics of Education Review, 24,* 369–376.

Kristen, E. (2002). Addressing the problem of weight discrimination in employment. *California Law Review, 90,* 57.

Puhl, R., Schwartz, M., & Brownell, K. (2005). Impact of perceived consensus on stereotypes about obese people: A new approach for reducing bias. *Health Psychology, 24,* 517–525.

Roehling, M. (1999). Weight-based discrimination in employment: Psychological and legal aspects. *Personnel Psychology, 52,* 969

Solovay, S. (2000). *Tipping the Scales of Justice: Fighting Weight-Based Discrimination.* Amherst, NY: Prometheus.

Sprague, J., & Massoni, K. (2005). Student evaluations and gendered expectations: What we can't count can hurt us. *Sex Roles: A Journal of Research, 53,* 779.

Teachman, B., Gapinski, K., Brownell, K., Rawlins, M., & Jeyaram, S. (2003). Demonstrations of implicit anti-fat bias: The impact of providing causal information and evoking empathy. *Health Psychology, 22,* 68–78.

Wilson, T.D. (2004). Strangers to ourselves: Discovering the adaptive unconscious. In E. Aronson (Ed.), *Readings about the Social Animal* (9th ed.). New York: Worth Publishers.

|||||||||||||||||||||||||||||||||||||||||||||||||||||||||||||||||||||||

24

Fat Stories in the Classroom
What and How Are They Teaching About Us?

Susan Koppelman

Our thoughts, feelings, judgments, and understanding of reality are all shaped by and subject to the power of stories. Theoreticians and strategists, people in the helping professions, advertisers, and propagandists analyze how stories can influence people and policies; parents, preachers, and politicians have always recognized this power. So do revolutionaries. Liberation movement leaders encourage new stories told, sung, and danced in the voices of the oppressed. They pressure existing publications to include these voices, and they create new publications. Call it size acceptance, fat civil rights, body diversity, or fat liberation, our civil rights movement is committed to bringing about an end to the demonizing, dehumanizing, pathologizing, victimizing, stigmatizing, bullying, humiliating, oppression, scapegoating, and hatred of fat people. We are telling our stories through all the arts, publishing and performing them, we demand positive images of us in all media, and we now insist on their inclusion in pre-K through graduate school across the curriculum in ways that maximize their revolutionary, liberatory impact.

Are there already stories about fat people in the curriculum? Which stories? Which courses? And in what contexts are these stories being read? I queried six academic Listservs for information about short stories with significant fat characters. I examined the tables of contents of dozens of currently in-print short-story anthologies. Finally, I googled the title of the most frequently anthologized "fat" story—"The Fat Girl" by Andres Dubus—looking for syllabi that included that story. I analyzed those syllabi to garner some sense of what use was made (or was intended to be made) of that story

A syllabus published online is both a public document and a literary text. Regardless of whether or not the class "makes" (i.e., isn't cancelled), whether the author/teacher retains control in the classroom and adheres to the authored, published text describing expectations and intent, or whether the author/teacher changes direction in medias res, the public document remains online until removed, and can therefore be analyzed. Although what is printed on a syllabus is at best an approximation of what actually happens in a classroom, reading the syllabus can tell us much about the intentions and attitudes of its author; after all, a syllabus is a formulaic literary text expressing intentions, plans, expectations, and so forth. I analyzed syllabi as authored literary texts, statements of intent for a time bounded pedagogical endeavor that includes many elements: discussions, lectures, readings, attendance rules, accommodations for students with disabilities, grading, office hours, and the like. I consider specifically how the fictional fat person is positioned in the syllabi. The materials taught in conjunction with them are the most telling aspect of contextualization.

"The Fat Girl" by Andre Dubus was first published in his 1977 collection, *Adultery and Other Choices*. It was then included in *American Short Story Masterpieces* (Carver & Jenks, 1987), *The Vintage Book of Contemporary American Short Stories* (Wolff, 1994), *The Tyranny of the Normal* (Donley & Buckley, 1996), *College 101: A First-Year Reader* (Lawry, 1999), *What Are You Looking At? The First Fat Fiction Anthology* (Jarrell & Sukrungruang, 2003), *The Contemporary American Short Story* (Nguyen & Shreve, 2004), *An Introduction to Critical Reading* (McCraney, 2006), and the fifth edition of *Fiction: A Pocket Anthology* (Gwynn, 2007). These anthologies are expensive to produce (most of the stories are still protected by copyright, and consequently reprint costs are substantial), widely used in classrooms, profitable, and likely to remain in print. We can assume the continuing ubiquity of "The Fat Girl." So what is "The Fat Girl" about? And is it "good" for our cause?

I believe that "The Fat Girl" is a story of prolonged child abuse. In that place/space where a child should feel safest, most unconditionally loved and accepted, most nurtured—the family home—this girl child Louise is systematically and relentlessly deprived of food sufficient for her needs by her mother (who is systematically depriving herself as well), in concert with the passive collusion of her father. Being reminded at least twice a day at family meals that she is not acceptable, not "all right," not adequate, insufficient in the area of personal worth that evidently mattered most, Louise is not happy.

A fat activist might summarize the story as follows:

> Louise's mother, who has internalized fat hatred and yet has a predisposition to be fat, fearing that her daughter will become fat, begins to severely limit Louise's food when Louise is nine years old. Neither Louise's father nor her brother intervenes. In response to semi-starvation, Louise eats additional food in secret. The stricter the diets inflicted on her, the more weight Louise gains. She becomes socially isolated. Later, at college, her only friend offers to help Louise lose weight during their senior year. The nine months of semi-starvation result in a loss of almost one-third of her body weight. Louise returns to her parents' home, where her new slenderness is celebrated, marries a business associate of her father's, and lives the life her mother always wanted for her until, during pregnancy, Louise gains weight. After her child is born, she rejects a lifetime of continued semi-starvation. Her marriage ends because her husband shares the fat hatred of the general society. She welcomes the end of the pressure to be thin.

Most commentators on the story seem to agree with the summary prepared by Carol Donley, coeditor of *The Tyranny of the Normal*:

Fat Louise, with an eating disorder since she was nine, would diet in public and sneak candy and peanut butter sandwiches in private. Her parents pitied her and were embarrassed by her. Her college roommate caught her at the secret eating and offered to help her get control of her eating. The diet and exercise ritual, combined with smoking, brought her weight down 60 pounds and made her beautiful and eligible to be married. Her parents were proud. She got married. But often she felt "no one knew her"—that she really wasn't this slim 120 pound beauty.

Then during her pregnancy she lost the discipline and ate compulsively and secretly. After the baby was born she continued to eat—her husband disapproved and didn't want to touch her, her mother scolded. The marriage, based on appearances, started to fall apart; she looked forward to being alone with her child and able to eat anything she wanted without other people judging her. (Donley, 1997)

Donley concludes her subsequent commentary, however, with the following: "While the outside world may read the ending as a defeat, it may also be understood as Louise finding herself and accepting herself," thereby opening up a way to think about the story in a way more amenable to fat activists.

Excerpts from papers about the story for sale online generally echo Donley's summary—Louise has an eating disorder; her parents share similar attitudes toward her body size; her "successful" dieting in college rendered her "beautiful"; her "undisciplined" eating during pregnancy was compulsive (i.e., a resurfacing "eating disorder"); and she was "Fat Louise" rather than just Louise. They include no hint of a possible alternative reading such as that suggested by Donley's concluding sentence.

Because the story is taught so frequently, it behooves us to consider its impact on readers. Does reading the story make the readers nicer to fat people? Does it reinforce the idea that fat people are different from "normal" people? Does it make fat people feel that it's okay that they are fat? Does it support stereotypes? Does it encourage readers to believe that fatness is a sickness or a character flaw and, ultimately, for those who really try, a malleable condition? The representative chronological sampling of syllabi that follows allows us to speculate about whether this story has been used to promote acceptance of body diversity or to reinforce prejudices.

Joseph Hogan, University of Wisconsin, Whitewater, included "The Fat Girl" in his 2002 English 101 syllabus. On the day that students were to have read "The Fat Girl," the accompanying lecture was "Freud and Psychoanalysis." Within the context of classical Freudian psychoanalytic theory, there is likely no room for consideration of social stereotyping, fat liberation perspectives, or the oppression of those who are different. This use of the story would incline toward reinforcing prejudices, probably seeing the fat woman as an embodied exemplar of a certain kind of psychiatric disorder or fixation.

The University of California, Irvine, has pioneered a program in Medical Humanities and the Arts. During the program's third year, students take a course titled "The Patient's Voice: Humanities Component of the Family Medicine Third Year Clerkship," which is described as follows:

> The family medicine third year clerkship is a required longitudinal experience in
> which . . . students are assigned to the practice of a board-certified family physician
> . . . students are also expected to review 14 standard case vignettes with their preceptors
> (see below). These topics are also discussed at 5 didactic sessions. . . . Each case vignette
> has an accompanying literary reading. . . .
> Objectives:
> - To provide additional perspectives on the patient experience of illness for 14 com-
>   mon medical disorders seen in family practice settings
> - To encourage students to make concrete links between humanities and practical
>   clinical applications. (University of California, Irvine, 2002)

One of the fourteen "common medical disorders" is "obesity." Four readings are prescribed for this "common medical disorder," three by MDs and Andre Dubus's "The
Fat Girl." The fat person is here presented as medically disordered, pathological, a
patient to be treated, counseled, and perhaps "healed."

In the spring of 2004, Charlotte N. Markey assigned the Dubus story to her students in "The Psychology of Eating," a course taught at Rutgers University, Camden.
She describes the course as follows:

> This course focuses on understanding the psychological processes underlying humans'
> development of eating behaviors and the adoption of both healthy and maladaptive cog-
> nitions and behaviors concerning food, eating, and our bodies. Issues to be addressed
> include: food choice, the development of food preferences, motivation to eat, cultural
> influences on eating patterns, weight-regulation, body image, dieting behaviors, obesity,
> eating disorders, and treatment of unhealthy and clinical eating problems. The psychol-
> ogy (not physiological processes) of eating will be emphasized, and psychological prob-
> lems associated with eating will be thoroughly discussed. This class . . . will be taught
> . . . with a focus on comprehension and application of information about the Psychol-
> ogy of Eating to daily life. (Markey, 2004)

"The Fat Girl," read when the topic is "obesity," is co-assigned with the article "Etiology of Body Dissatisfaction and Weight Concerns Among 5-Year-Old Girls" (Davidson, Markey, & Birch, 2000). The story is presented in the context of "maladaptive
cognitions and behaviors concerning food, eating, and our bodies" (Markey, 2004).

The syllabus for "The Dismodern Body," taught in 2005 at the 100 level in the English department at Dickinson College by Joshua Kupetz, features a quotation from
Lennard J. Davis, respected pioneer disability studies scholar, at the top: "Difference
is what we all have in common" (2002, p. 239). The course focus is disability, and the
required readings indicate that the perspective on disability is social constructionist,
in which the persons with disabilities are the "I's," the subject voices. In other words,
the viewpoint is that being disabled is not a function of physical difference but of
the failure of society to accommodate difference. Kupetz explains: "This course examines the construction of 'body' and its (re)presentations, specifically bodies with
visible and non-visible impairments, as well as the social construction of 'disability.'

Additionally, it considers how contemporary thinking about the body might augur a 'dismodern' sensibility that reconfigures other areas of cultural inquiry" (Kupetz, 2005).

Dubus's "The Fat Girl" is to be read together with "Disability, Identity, and Representation," the introduction by Rosemarie Garland Thomson to her book *Extraordinary Bodies* (1997). The second class meeting features Raymond Carver's (1963) short story "Fat," which is the "fat story" that appears second-most frequently on course syllabi after "The Fat Girl." First published in *Harper's Bazaar* in September 1971, "Fat" is about a waitress's interaction with a fat customer she serves in a restaurant. Later in the course, the students watch the 1993 film *What's Eating Gilbert Grape?* and read Sander Gilman's "The Fat Detective: Obesity and Disability" (2002).

Kupetz's approach to teaching about fat people seems compatible with the fat liberation movement. It seems designed to present the fat body as one with socially imposed limitations rather than corporeally imposed limitations, one subject to oppression, stereotyping, and the consequent suffering of those impositions. But even in this syllabus, despite sociopolitical sophistication, we do not find the voice of the fat person speaking for her- or himself. If the perspective is that of the disability civil rights movement, Kupetz might remember one of the slogans of that movement: "Nothing about us without us." The voice of the victim of this socially constructed disability is missing here. Questioning the tendency to pathologize the fat body, however, is clearly done in good faith. Whether the fat person is a disabled person is much debated in the fat liberation movement. If stigmatization constitutes reason enough to include a category of individuals in the category "disabled," then all stigmatized categories would belong in the category "disabled." Because Kupetz includes fat people among those categorized "disabled," perhaps he tends to see the fat body as inherently a body disabled by more than stigma. In other words, the fat body is not okay if only the stigmatization ends.

Also in 2005, "The Fat Girl" appeared on the syllabus at the University of West Georgia for English 1102: Composition II. The professor, Paula Patch, describes her course as follows:

> This semester, we'll be studying the concept of "difference," particularly physical difference, as it is represented in literature. Each of us is unique only in the way we differ from others; that is, what makes me "me" is that I am not "you" or "him" or "her." In fact, in order for me to be "me" or for you to be "you," or even for us to be "us," there must exist an "other." Because this "other" exists, so too does a conflict exist—male versus female, black versus white, fat/thin, good/bad. It's these conflicts we will focus on, and how to resolve them, if at all. As you read, note the various conflicts the literature illuminates—within the text, between you and the text, and within society as a whole. (Patch, 2005)

Part of the semester is devoted to the short story. Dubus's "The Fat Girl" is one of several stories read in conjunction with Lennard Davis's "Bodies of Difference: Politics, Disability, and Representation" (2002). Once again, we see the fat body being considered in the context of disability studies. So, although surely these last two syllabi indicate through contextualization a greater understanding of the life circumstances of those who live in a fat body than is indicated by those who teach about fat bodies in the context of psychoanalytic disorders or diseased medical conditions, neither presents a fat liberation perspective. And, in fact, the final syllabus takes us back to the model of fatness as a diseased state.

In the spring of 2006, Susan Semoneta taught "The Fat Girl" in the short fiction course of the New York City Writing Project, English 231. The previous fall, she had adapted the story for the stage and produced it at the Fashion Institute of Technology, sponsored by the American Diabetes Association (there is no mention of diabetes in the story). This sponsorship gives reason to assume that the perspective on the fat body is a medicalized one.

Obviously the story lends itself to numerous interpretations and extraliterary "uses." Some see the ending of the story—in which Louise regains weight—as a fall from grace, an act of self-destruction, a manifestation of an eating disorder, a disordered personality, an escapist flight from social competition, or a retreat into self-hatred. Others see the ending as a triumphant dismissal of artificial social norms, an assertion of self, a reclamation of her true identity, or a celebration of inner-directedness. Still others see the ending as a fat body's resolve to regain and maintain what has become its set point after years of diets.

Are there legitimate ways of reading this story that differ markedly from the medicalized, defeated reading of the story that predominates in the course syllabi that we have examined here? And, if there are not, but we believe that this story authentically represents one of the kinds of experience that fat girls and women live out, can we find stories that will present other authentic experiences of fatness that do not reinforce stereotypes into the curriculum?

How will we get stories about fat people, told from the perspectives of fat activists, into the curriculum? What stories are available for us to consider? Which stories will be "good" for our cause? Assuming that the costs associated with replacing "The Fat Girl" in course readers and anthologies are prohibitive, what affordable stories might be taught in conjunction with it that would tell more liberatory stories of fat women's lives? I have edited *The Strange History of Suzanne LaFleshe, and Other Stories of Women and Fatness*, which includes twenty-five short stories by U.S. women writers first published between 1895 and 1997. I contacted half a dozen of the professors who use the book in their classes in either women's studies or English classes to see which stories were most preferred by their students. I was given the same two titles by four of them: "This Was Meant to Be" and the title story. "This Was Meant to Be" by Alberta Hughes Wahl was first published in 1946 in *Women's Home Companion*. The story recounts the success of "the tender little scheme" of a loving mother to rescue her daughter, Alison, from low self-esteem: "She's still in the awkward age and has no confidence in herself as a woman. . . . She's not at all pretty . . . but she's such a darling. . . . She only needs something, someone, to discover what she really is and then she will bloom. . . . She was short and . . . chubby" (Koppelman, 2003, p. 16). Without losing an ounce, Alison becomes a happy, confident, socially successful young woman. Only ten pages long, the story is a delightful antidote to "The Fat Girl," one that students are inspired and enlightened by. It is in the public domain and can be copied and used freely for teaching.

The second story that students respond to with enthusiasm is "The Strange History of Suzanne LaFleshe," Hollis Seamon's 1997 story about a woman, five feet eleven inches tall, who has dieted from 282 pounds to 145 pounds at Weight Watchers and discovered that she is not happy at that size. She writes, "Listen, every day you are being taught to hate and fear your own flesh. . . . You can hardly imagine, anymore, what it is to love your flesh for the pleasures it provides" (Koppelman, 2003, p. 215). She misses her self, her abundant flesh: "Please understand: I like my flesh. I like the way it moves and bounces; I like to see my breasts floating high, like islands in the bath. I like the sensation of my thighs squeezing together in stockings, caressing each other under one of my full flowered skirts" (p. 216). So she continues to show up at Weight Watchers to keep track of her regain of weight. She perplexes and then horrifies her counselor, Janet, who herself once weighed 207 pounds but who has held steady at 97 pounds for years now. Weight Watchers wants Suzanne gone! What a horrible example she is setting! Eventually Janet pairs her up with a young anorectic incest survivor, Theresa, and Suzanne helps Theresa begin to eat again. The story ends with them eating together, taking alternating bites from one shared plate.

How wonderful if the mother and daughter in "The Fat Girl" could read this story, watch the film *Hairspray*,[1] and then share a hearty meal, finally nurturing each other and themselves, loving and accepting each other and themselves. How wonderful it would be if these stories and this film were on those syllabi.

NOTE

Thanks to the following for careful readings and good suggestions for improving this chapter: Dennis Mills, Emily Toth, Alan L. Goldberg, and Mary Ray Worley.

1. In this film, mother and daughter working-class fat women struggle in different ways with prejudice. Edna Turnblad, the mother, has internalized fat hatred and given up on her dreams. High school student daughter Tracy has no prejudices and no inhibitions about pursuing both her dream to dance on a TV teenage dance party show and to end racial segregation in 1962 Baltimore.

REFERENCES

Carver, R. (1963). "Fat." In *Will You Please Be Quiet Please: Stories*. New York: McGraw-Hill.

Carver, R., & Jenks, T. (Eds.). (1987). *American Short Story Masterpieces*. New York: Delacorte Press.

Davidson, K.K., Markey, C.N., & Birch, L.L. (2000). "Etiology of Body Dissatisfaction and Weight Concerns Among 5-Year-Old Girls." *Appetite* 35: 143–51.

Davis, L.J. (2002). "Bodies of Difference: Politics, Disability, and Representation." In Brueggemann, B.J., Snyder, S., and Thomson, R.G. (Eds.), *Disability Studies: Enabling the Humanities*. New York: Modern Language Association.

Donley, C. (1997). Literature annotation for Dubus, Andre: "The Fat Girl." In Literature, Arts, and Medicine Database. Retrieved August 21, 2006, from http://web.archive.org/web/19970607052527/http://mchipoo.nyu.edu/lit-med/lit-med-db/webdocs/webdescrips/dubus874-des-.html.

Donley, C., & Buckley, S. (Eds.). (1996). *The Tyranny of the Normal.* Kent, OH: Kent State University Press.

Dubus, A. (1977). "The Fat Girl." In *Adultery and Other Choices.* Boston: D.R. Godine.

Gilman, S. (2002). "The Fat Detective: Obesity and Disability." In S.L. Snyder, B.J. Brueggemann, & R. Garland-Thomson (Eds.), *Disability Studies: Enabling the Humanities.* New York: Modern Language Association.

Gwynn, R.S. (Ed.). (2008). *Fiction: A Pocket Anthology,* 5th ed. New York: Longman.

Hogan, J. (2002). "English 101—Fall 2002 Syllabus." Retrieved August 21, 2006, from http://facstaff.uww.edu/hoganj/101syl02.html.

Jarrell, D., & Sukrungruang, I. (Eds.). (2003). *What Are You Looking At? The First Fat Fiction Anthology.* New York: Harvest Books.

Koppelman, S. (Ed.). (2003). *The Strange History of Suzanne LaFleshe, and Other Stories of Women and Fatness.* New York: Feminist Press of CUNY.

Kupetz, J. (2005). "The Dismodern Body: English 101, Spring 2005." Retrieved August 21, 2006, from http://www.dickinson.edu/~kupetzj/pdfs/engl101_sp2005_dismodern_syl.pdf.

Lawry, John D. (Ed.). (1999). *College 101: A First-Year Reader.* Burr Ridge, IL: McGraw-Hill.

Markey, C.N. (2004). "Rutgers University Psychology of Eating—830: Course Syllabus." Retrieved August 21, 2006, from http://www.crab.rutgers.edu/~chmarkey/psycofeatsyllabus.html.

McCraney, L. (Ed.). (2006). *An Introduction to Critical Reading,* 6th ed. Baltimore: Thomson-Wadsworth.

Nguyen, B.M., & Shreve, P. (Eds.). (2004). *The Contemporary American Short Story.* New York: Longman.

Patch, P. (2005). "English 1102: Composition II." Retrieved June 12, 2006, from http://www.westga.edu/~ppatch/1102%20Spring%202005/English%201102%20Spring%202005%20Syllabus%20MWF.htm#Attendance.

Sermoneta, S. (2006). "New York City Writing Project: FIT Short Fiction, Spring 2006." Retrieved August 22, 2006, from http://web.archive.org/web/20071106044417/http://www.nycwp.org/FITShortFiction/stories/storyReader$21.

Thomson, R.G. (1997). *Extraordinary Bodies: Figuring Physical Disability in American Culture and Literature.* New York: Columbia University Press.

University of California, Irvine. (2002). "College of Medicine, Program in Medical Humanities and Arts: Course Descriptions." Retrieved August 21, 2006, from http://web.archive.org/web/20020829153022/http://www.ucihs.uci.edu/com/medhum/courses/famcl.html.

Wolff, T. (Ed.). (1994). *The Vintage Book of Contemporary American Short Stories.* New York: Vintage.

|||||||||||||||||||||||||||||||||||||||||||||||||||||||||||||||||||||||||||||||

Part IV

Size-ism in Popular Culture and Literature

Welcome to Part IV of The Fat Studies Reader

Size-ism in Popular Culture and Literature

Our cultural context is rich in messages about what fat means for people, their worth, and their worthiness. Social attitudes are constantly informed by these messages. Popular culture and literature provide ample opportunities to reflect on the representation and construction of fatness and are especially active areas of fat studies scholarship.

After reading these chapters consider the following discussion questions:

How do members of fat and queer communities see themselves and construct their own erotic and political identities? How do these constructions differ from mainstream portrayals?

What roles are created in fiction for fat female characters and readers?

How are racial and ethnic representations of masculinity influenced by weight and food in literature?

In a culture where only thin women are "fit to be seen," what is the result of putting fat women center stage?

Why do so many women who make it to center stage pursue weight loss after achieving stardom?

What is the impact on fat spectators of famous fat people publically pursuing thinness?

What are the meanings and implications of thin actors dressing in "fat suits" in contemporary culture? Is this an acceptable practice? Why or why not?

‖‖‖

25

Fat Girls and Size Queens

Alternative Publications and the Visualizing of Fat and Queer Eroto-politics in Contemporary American Culture

Stefanie Snider

In the zines *FaT GiRL: A Zine for Fat Dykes and the Women Who Want Them* and *Size Queen: For Queen Size Queers and Our Loyal Subjects*, members of fat and queer pride movements produce textual and visual selves that center on their culturally contested bodies. Joining the personal and political in these activist objects, the zines simultaneously use and reject conventional ideas and ideals of deviant bodies to reinvent marginalized fat and queer identities. This is important for activist movements that work to find and infiltrate spaces within American culture to form self-representative and self-loving communities. An examination of these zines begins to tell us about how fatness, gender, and sexuality inform each other and are mapped onto bodily artifacts and politics in contemporary American (sub)cultures.

In her groundbreaking book *Revolting Bodies? The Struggle to Redefine Fat Identity*, fat studies scholar Kathleen LeBesco examines numerous discourses around fat bodies. She emphasizes the importance of communities that "are attempting to create and regulate a new social reality through the use of the written and spoken word" (LeBesco, 2004, p.4). She does so because of the value that she places on gender theorist Judith Butler's concept of "locutionary acts, which [when] repeated, become entrenched practices and, ultimately, institutions" (quoted in LeBesco, 2004, p. 4). Both LeBesco's and Butler's interest in linguistic repetition, or performativity, strongly informs my own work here on the visual self-representations produced in *FaT GiRL* and *Size Queen*. My project focuses on the centrality of visual imagery in the creation of the corporeal and discursive subcultural subjects that both embody the kinds of practices and form the institutions these theorists note as central to the production of the viable subject.

FaT GiRL: A Zine for Fat Dykes and the Women Who Want Them was created by a changing collective of self-identified fat dykes from the San Francisco Bay Area and published between 1994 and 1997. The zine contains images and text, including drawings, photographs, cartoons, poetry, prose, reviews, and transcribed roundtable discussions. *FaT GiRL* was printed on newsprint paper and circulated throughout the

United States and abroad. The cost was five dollars for each sixty- to seventy-page edition, printed at two thousand copies per issue.

Dealing with both queer and fat communities, dyke and fat pride, *FaT GiRL* is a complex object of visual culture that combines images and text to reformulate and define the multiplicities of fat dyke subcultures and their creative productions at a moment in history highlighted by greater visibility of queer communities and incipient size acceptance and fat pride activist movements. It exemplifies both a homemade and journalistic materiality. *FaT GiRL* is unique among symbols and communities of empowerment in terms of its use of explicit sexual imagery to define a politics of the erotic with and for fat lesbians.

Each of *FaT GiRL's* seven issues contain a variety of texts and images that contemplate and celebrate issues of being fat and lesbian, as well as related matters, such as race, class, S/M activities, food, advice about sex and dating and sexual accoutrements, personal ads, and notices for fat and queer positive stores and organizations. In the inaugural issue of *FaT GiRL*, from the summer of 1994, the frontispiece, located across from the mission statement and table of contents for the zine, exclaims that *FaT GiRL* is (among other things) "aggressive," "hungry," "in your face," "joyous," "kinky," "making room," "open minded," "smart," "unapologetic," "visual," and "XXXXXXXXXL" *(FaT GiRL* #1, n.p.). At quite literally the start of its run, *FaT GiRL* privileges visual and textual representation to advance its politics about being fat and queer. The words are represented in a variety of fonts, shapes, and sizes, much like the women visualized through the poetry, prose, drawings, and photographs within the zine. Multiple identities are proclaimed together, and although some might seem to be in contradiction with one another (such as butch and femme, charming and smutty, in your face and reflective), they are combined to enlighten the reader as to the panoply of available identities within and on top of the already proclaimed one of "fat dyke." In their mission statement, the *FaT GiRL* collective writes, "Fat Girl seeks to create a broad-based dialogue which both challenges and informs our notions of Fat-Dyke identity" *(FaT GiRL* #1, p. 1).

FaT GiRL emphasizes the conjunction between material and discursive productions of the body and social identities. By recognizing that discourse of and on the body, especially the multiply "deviant" body, is never natural or inherent, the collective members of *FaT GiRL* open up a space of representation in which they actively work to assert different modes of discourse about and around the fat lesbian body. At the same time, they textually and visually image fat lesbian bodies as corporeal sites through which eroticism, pride, and self-possession become embodied practices. The zine does not merely envision an alternative to the way in which fat dykes are theorized and discussed, but images alternatives to how they perform and create physical pleasure with and within their bodies as well.

The zine might be critiqued for its reliance on identitarian tactics to formulate its resistances to hegemonic bodily and sexual ideals. I do not believe, however, that such strategies are entirely and always problematic; rather, it seems indicative of the slippery slope of identity politics so often looked to in the late 1980s and 1990s. Although now widely disparaged, I would contend that some of these tactics produce

25.1. *FaT GiRL: A Zine for Fat Dykes and the Women Who Want Them* #1, 1994. Published with permission of Max Airborne.

25.2. *Size Queen: For Queen Size Queers and Our Loyal Subjects* #1, 2005. Published with permission of Max Airborne.

useful methods for inserting nonnormative communities into, and re-forming, the public sphere. The very reliance on shaping communities based on similar identifications can be understood as both problematic and hopeful. Although aligning oneself only along certain identity markers might in fact reinscribe exclusions that subcultural communities seek to transgress, forming multivalent communities, which include fat and queer categories in addition to other (e.g., classed, racialized, and gendered) identities, can locate individuals within more complex systems of culture and provide the beginnings of coalitional social structures. It is my contention, therefore, that *FaT GiRL* uses identitarian strategies as a fruitful starting point for fat and queer activism. As the *FaT GiRL* masthead proclaims, "FaT GiRL iS a PoLiTiCaL ACT" (*FaT GiRL* #1–#7), one that raises the stakes of living in fat and queer bodies within a culture that tends not to recognize either, and in fact actively makes them socially unintelligible within most media representation and publications.

A central way in which *FaT GiRL* visually formulates its political stance is through the photographs (either included as part of articles or on their own). These images are predominantly sexually explicit. Bondage and sadomasochistic themes dominate, though these are certainly not the only visuals explored within, as will be seen below. It is important here that many of the images can be seen as "inappropriate" and, in fact, depending on the viewer, perhaps "antifeminist." In this way, *FaT GiRL* flirts with all kinds of propriety—be it associated with the conventional and conservative or the critical and revolutionary. These kinds of photographs can be seen as bad and dangerous—dangerous to the people imaged and dangerous to society in general. But they are also emphatically active and often fun. They visualize fat and queer female subjects who have all too frequently been seen as passive, desexualized, and unworthy of sexual fantasizing by dominant cultural sexual ideals. And they do so by and through these fat and queer female subjects in order to simultaneously bring themselves pleasure, bring the zine's readers pleasure, and explode the boundaries of normative ideals of how fat women should behave sexually and politically. As described by several of the collective members, as well as in letters to the editorial collective in later issues, these kinds of explicit sex scenes featuring variously abled and sized queer women were previously almost unheard of.

A different kind of photo layout accompanies the first "*FaT GiRL* Roundtable," a transcribed discussion among several of the Fat Girl collective women. These images focus on food and eroticism, a theme that comes up frequently in several of the issues of *FaT GiRL*. No fewer than seventeen images are integrated with the text of the transcribed discussion and illustrate a number of the points made in the text. Food and bodies are offered by and to fat dykes for pleasurable and highly eroticized consumption. Whipped cream is licked from bellies, boots, and breasts; grapes are dangled above mouths; frozen popsicles are teasingly fellated. In this article and photo spread, collective member Barbara McDonald states, "Even within the dyke community, dykes see 'fat' first before they see 'dyke.' That's just one (of the many) reasons why we want to do *FaT GiRL*. And I wanted a feast of images, there just are not enough images of fat dykes. The ones out there are few and far between" ("FaT GiRL Roundtable," issue 1, p. 33). This article playfully provides McDonald with her feast of images portraying precisely that: fat dykes feasting on food and each other. These photographs attest to the taboo combination of fat, sex, queer female desire, and eating/food, each of which has been inscribed into normative culture as impossible and dreadful, particularly in any kind of relationship with any of the others. Fat, and really all, women are supposed to avoid luxurious and fattening foods—the pleasure here taken in sugary delights and each others' bodies exhibits what might be called reckless abandon by a culture determined to identify an "obesity epidemic" whose rhetoric depends on bodily shame and desire for a constructed thin ideal. In this photographic display, however, seemingly impossible desires and bodily formations take shape, exhibiting the viability of such lives and practices.

In fact, *FaT GiRL* delivers on McDonald's desire for a feast of fat dyke images throughout its run, picturing fully nude as well as variously dressed and accessorized fat dykes in autoerotic, group, and coupled sex scenes among their other photographs, drawings, and texts. As in this first issue, the collective places into visual representation images of actual fat queer female subjects engaged in erotic activities; they are shown enjoying themselves and other fat lesbian bodies in ways that defy stereotypes, in part due to the sheer number and variety of scenes and women depicted. The photographs published in *FaT GiRL* work to subvert conventional fat woman models by exploring in excess female-on-female sexual and gustatory pleasure; if fat queer women are shown as insatiable, it is in ways that claim fat women's bodies as deliciously corporeal.

Although *FaT GiRL* folded in 1997 after seven issues, the recent appearance of a new zine speaks to the continuing need for and interest in simultaneous fat and queer activism through the means of visual and material culture. Playing on the slang term for gay men who fetishize big cocks, *Size Queen: For Queen Size Queers and Our Loyal Subjects* was first released in July 2005. Produced by two former members of the Fat Girl collective, Max Airborne and Cherry Midnight, *Size Queen* is a glossy and colorful zine whose first issue includes articles by several now–widely known fat activists in the United States and Britain, including Nomy Lamm, Marilyn Wann, Sondra Solovay, and Charlotte Cooper. As its name suggests, *Size Queen* is a patently queer (though not always sexually) and at times cheeky visual and textual manifestation of contemporary fat and queer empowerment activism. Just as we saw in the first issue of *FaT GiRL*, *Size Queen* defines its creators and audiences through queerly terms inclusive of queer issues. On its cover, it lists is potential readers as "dykes, fags, trannies, queens, queers, kings, others, 3rd gender, no gender, fuck gender, ladies, lesbos, bears, cubs, allies, boys, girls, bois, grrrrls, [and] butches" (*Size Queen* #1, cover). According to the zine's masthead, "Size Queen is a movement, a collaboration between members of a community that have not yet all met, a project about visibility" (*Size Queen* #1, p. 1). *Size Queen* in many ways continues the objectives and visualizations manifested in *FaT GiRL* in terms of the kinds of images and texts of which it is made, including photographs of dykes having sex, community-focused articles, comics, and "trading cards." It is also a force in coalitional politics, as I earlier suggested of *FaT GiRL*. Individuals and groups with diverse identities and from multiple locations seem to come together under *Size Queen*'s rubric of revolution. It is evident here that collaboration—between and among its contributors and audience—is central to the empowering activism that it works to affect and represent.

Taking their basic mode of operation from the 1970s feminist motto, "The personal is political," these zines work to politicize issues about being fat and lesbian in contemporary culture. But they are not merely interested in producing publications that reflect their social standing. Rather, the zines and their collaborators are thinking critically about identities—not just replacing but also remaking representations in their own forms, as well as in the forms that they wish to see. *FaT GiRL* and *Size Queen* position themselves on the cusp of a highly charged conflict within identity politics movements. They can be seen to demand, and in fact realize, visibility for fat dyke communities within American culture. As performance theorist and historian Peggy Phelan (1993) has noted, visibility politics presents a sticky situation for subcultural communities that wish to be recognized but at the same time would like to refrain from being policed by cultural norms. *FaT GiRL* and *Size Queen*, by focusing their content and circulation on a target audience of whom the members of the collective are a part, reinforce an internal, subcultural community of fat dykes; it provides a space of representation for a specific, though not restrictive, community. At the same time, through their widespread circulation and interest in getting their words and images out to more mainstream media and publications, the creators of *FaT GiRL* and *Size Queen* might be recognized by American or Western culture broadly conceived as creating a space of identification and desire that stresses the "political as a way of seizing authority" (Duncombe, 1997, p. 30). Zine circulation occurs beyond academic borders and reaches past traditional forms of scholarship; at the same time, these zines very much embody such investigations and, as this chapter can attest, provoke such research.

The production and circulation of *FaT GiRL* and *Size Queen* contest the material and ideological conditions that render fatness and lesbianism deviant in contemporary culture. The images and texts therein put forth different ways of making and viewing the human body than has traditionally been realized. In eroticizing fat women eating food, taking pleasure in their fleshy bodies and those of other women, engaging in "perverse" and intellectual discussions on social justice, and imaging their selves as an intersection of identities that intervene in normative constructions of the body, these cultural representations assert the validity of their subjects in the face of social erasure and humiliation. From fat queer perspectives, they refuse the silence imposed on them from a society obsessed with keeping heterosexual and thin norms in place; they redefine the images and texts used by dominant culture to subjugate these identities under regimented power structures that maintain the dominant norms; and they create new ways of speaking and seeing contested bodily subjects. The images circulated in *FaT GiRL* and *Size Queen* create the rules of self-visualization and willingly (and joyfully) play with the danger of the fetishistic gaze against which Peggy Phelan warns. *FaT GiRL* and *Size Queen* generate rebellious and daring ways of seeing and interpreting fatness and queerness in contemporary culture.

NOTE

I would like to thank professors Richard Meyer and David Román at the University of Southern California for their support and criticism of this project. Without their generosity and insight, this chapter and my future work in fat studies and visual culture would not have been possible. I must also acknowledge my sincere appreciation of Jason Goldman's keen editorial eye and constant encouragement; and Max Airborne's art, humor, and permission to reproduce the covers of *FaT GiRL* #1 and *Size Queen* #1.

REFERENCES

Airborne, M., & Midnight, C. (Eds.). (2005). *Size Queen: For Queen Size Queers and Our Loyal Subjects #1*. San Francisco: Size Queen Publishing.

Duncombe, S. (1997). *Notes from the Underground: Zines and the Politics of Alternative Culture*. London: Verso.

FaT GiRL Collective. (1994–1997). *FaT GiRL: A Zine for Fat Dykes and the Women Who Want Them, #1–#7*. San Francisco: Fat Girl Publishing.

LeBesco, K. (2004). *Revolting Bodies? The Struggle to Redefine Fat Identity*. Amherst: University of Massachusetts Press.

McDonald, B. (1994). FaT GiRL Round Table. *FaT GiRL: A Zine for Fat Dykes and the Women Who Want Them #1*. San Francisco: Fat Girl Publishing.

Phelan, P. (1993). Broken Symmetries: Memory, Sight, Love. In *Unmarked: The Politics of Performance*. London: Routledge.

Fat Girls Need Fiction

Susan Stinson

> Here we see all the abilities of fancy, deftly woven together: its ability to endow a perceived form with rich and complex significance; its generous construction of the seen; its preference for wonder over pat solutions; its playful and surprising movements, delightful for their own sake; its tenderness; its eroticism; its awe before the fact of human mortality.
>
> —Martha Nussbaum, "The Literary Imagination in Public Life" (1991, p. 901)

Fat girls need fiction.

For this to be true does not require that fat girls need fiction more than anyone else, or that we need it because we are fat. Human beings are complex, and there is unlikely to be only one simple story about why we need anything.

I am a novelist, frankly biased, but I find it utterly compelling to think of bringing the qualities that Nussbaum attributes to fancy—a generous construction of the seen; preference for wonder over pat solutions; tenderness; eroticism; and awe before the fact of human mortality—to the contemplation of my fat body. The idea of the architects and disseminators of public health policy (or even, say, a nurse rolling up my sleeve to measure my blood pressure) considering fatness using such habits of mind represents the possibility of a very different world than the one where I live now. "Playful and surprising movements, delightful for their own sake" could be an appreciation not just of the workings of the imagination but also of fat in motion. I consider it a gift of many long, ardent, malleable hours of reading fiction that my mind makes that leap.

I originally read Fat Girl Dances with Rocks secretly over a period of weeks—the old Tower Records on Newbury Street in Boston had a copy, and I went back again and again and read it a few pages at a time, as this was pre-size-acceptance for me, and owing to my seemingly bottomless reserves of internalized fat hatred, I couldn't bring myself to take it to the counter and buy it. Like, in front of someone. WHOA. Never. I read it like really gruesome, really forbidden porn—it was simultaneously horrifying and exhilarating. I was disgusted with myself for wanting to read it but I couldn't stop.

I don't mean for this analogy to come across as disrespectful, but that's honestly how I was absorbing it.

One day I went in and the copy was gone. Someone must have bought it. I was devastated. That was telling.

When I did begin my own process of coming to love my body, I thought about that secret-reading experience a lot. I still do. (Lesley Kinzel, comment in the author's online journal, 2006)

Art critic Dave Hickey (1997) draws a distinction among those interested in any given art form between participants, who know that they need the art and actively engage in encouraging the conditions necessary for its creation in any way they can, and spectators, who simply pay the price of admission (or buy a book or whatever) and show up to passively consume a product. Participants bring life and fullness to art; spectators empty and kill it. When, nineteen years after I began writing my first novel, I read in my LiveJournal the description above of Lesley Kinzel's intense response to it, I was moved by her extremely high level of participation in the world of the book, despite her very mixed feelings and the fact that she never bought it. I knew Lesley as a very fat-positive online presence, and had met her briefly at community-related events, such as the huge Fat Girl Flea Market in New York City in 2005, and the Fat and the Academy conference at Smith College in 2006. She is clearly a participant in fat art and politics, which, along with lesbian writers groups and the once vibrant network of feminist presses, periodicals, and bookstores, are literally what brought my books into existence.

The edgy, risk-taking sensibilities of radical fat activists have permeated my work so that it can both lure and frighten a reader such as Lesley, who innocently happens upon it. Of my novels, *Fat Girl Dances with Rocks* (1994) is a coming-of-age story; *Martha Moody* (1995) is a magic realist historical romance (and meditation on writing using images of fat and butter as a metaphor for the creative process); and *Venus of Chalk* (2004) is a road book about a midlife crisis. All have fat lesbian protagonists and were published by small feminist presses.

Here is an excerpt from *Martha Moody* in which erotic exchange between lover and beloved, as well as writer and reader, are suffused with both fat and fancy:

I wrote about her nights after John had gone to sleep. I wrote her hand inside me, I wrote my body arching, I wrote her teeth on my nipples and her hair in my mouth. I told lies and made up stories and gave her special powers. I cupped her, formed her softness. She touched the tops of mountains with her languid double chin. She pressed her breasts against my bones. She lifted herself to find my slick tip with her nipple. She parted river waters so people carrying baskets could cross. She sank on me with her full weight, and I breathed shallow under her, caught by her substance and her wonder.

She flew. She spoke with angels. She played Jesus in the Bible. She carved a canyon with her tireless hands. She shook and brought forth waters. She sang whales into the ocean. She ploughed the ground with her knee while she rode a ridge and stroked her hands along the surfaces of grasses in the field.

I became the earth, her instrument—smoothed and dug and brought forth—but I wrote her powers into her and played her every night. The mornings were rushed and secret, bordered on all sides with commerce, but at night I made her stretch across me until we filled most open places I could imagine in this world. (p. 61)

Other authors of fiction that centers on fat characters and themes include Elana Dykewomon, Cathie Dunsford, Charlotte Cooper, Joan Drury, and Lynne Murray.

When I say that fat girls need fiction, I mean that we need to read and encourage the writing of a wide range of fiction about subjects both close to our various hearts and past the edges of our far-reaching imaginations. Beyond the desire to see our own lives and experiences reflected in fiction, we need those habits of mind and heart that deepen empathy with others and broaden our sense of both the just and the possible. Novelist Jeanette Winterson writes, "By remoulding the reality we assume to be objective, art releases to us realities otherwise hidden" (1995, p. 58).

In her brilliant short story "The Bunchgrass Edge of the World," Annie Proulx writes:

Ottaline had seen most of what there was to see around her with nothing new in sight. Brilliant events burst open not in the future but in the imagination. The room she had shared with Shan was a room within a room. In the unshaded moonlight her eyes shone oily white. The calfskin rug on the floor seemed to move, to hunch and crawl a fraction of an inch at a time. The dark frame of the mirror sank into the wall, a rectangular trench. From her bed she saw the moon-bleached grain elevator and behind it immeasurable range flecked with cows like small black seeds. She was no one but Ottaline in that peppery, disturbing light that made her want everything there was to want. The raw loneliness then, the silences of the day, the longing flesh led her to press her mouth into the crook of her own hot elbow. She pinched and pummeled her fat flanks, rolled on the bed, twisted, went to the window a dozen times, heels striking the floor until old Red in his pantry below called out, "What is it? You got a sailor up there?" (1999, p. 128)

Ottaline is a fat girl, "the family embarrassment" (p. 119), living on an isolated ranch with her parents and grandfather. The passage above seems to reach into the very belly of my fat girl yearnings; see, know, and evoke every one of those already heightened desires; and then use them to make a calfskin rug crawl with strange, agonizing slowness across the floor. I never imagined that those deeply private experiences of thwarted desire could be put to such use. It makes me understand a little more about their power.

Ottaline does enormous amounts of ranch work and, in her loneliness, entertains herself by listening to the conversations of strangers on the scanner. From wads of turnip greens to a treacherous John Deere 4030 tractor, the precision of observation in this hugely, pleasurably, emotionally complicated story is so heated as to be white hot. The simplest exchange pulses with decades of tension. Ottaline compares herself to her bodybuilding sister, Shan:

Ottaline studied Shan's photograph, said to her mother, "If it kills me I am goin a walk it off."

"Haven't I heard that before?" said Wauneta. "I know you." (p. 129)

The walks lead not to weight loss, but to a strange attempt at seduction by the rusting John Deere, which cajoles Ottaline as she marches past where it has been abandoned in a gravel pit. My love for the story is so great that just browsing through it makes my heart pound in a way that makes analysis difficult, as if I'm being wheedled by previously inanimate objects via the sheer beauty, nerve, and conviction of Proulx's literary skills. Although this is not a world in which good simply triumphs, Ottaline has a thoroughly satisfying fate, and if anyone forced me to choose just one story with which to prove why fat girls need fiction, this would be it.

Fat girls need stories of all kinds. We need to cultivate the ability to make skilled and daring imaginative leaps. We need empathy, emotional risk, and the evidence of the senses. Fat girls need fiction. Everyone else needs it, too.

NOTE

Thanks to Courtney Hudak for introducing me to the article by Nussbaum.

REFERENCES

Hickey, D. (1997). *Air Guitar: Essays on Art and Democracy.* Los Angeles: Art Issues Press.

Nussbaum, M. (1991). The Literary Imagination in Public Life. *New Literary History, 22 (4),* 877–910.

Proulx, A. (1999). *Close Range: Wyoming Stories.* New York: Scribner.

Stinson, S. (1994). *Fat Girl Dances with Rocks.* Denver, CO: Spinsters, Ink.

Stinson, S. (1995). *Martha Moody.* Denver, CO: Spinsters, Ink.

Stinson, S. (2004). *Venus of Chalk.* Ann Arbor, MI: Firebrand Books.

Winterson, J. (1995). *Art Objects: Essays on Ecstasy and Effrontery.* New York: Vintage Books.

Fat Heroines in Chick-Lit
Gateway to Acceptance in the Mainstream?

Lara Frater

There is one place in popular media where a fat woman gets a chance to star, and that is in novels of the Chick-Lit genre. Chick-Lit is defined by ChicklitBooks.com as a "genre comprised of books that are mainly written by women for women" (October 15, 2006). According to *Chick Lit: The New Women's Fiction*, edited by Suzanne Ferriss and Mallory Young (2006), the term was first used in 1995 in *Chick-Lit: Post-Feminist Fiction*, edited by Cris Mazza (1996). Chick-Lit differs from the Romance genre by giving us female characters who consider finding love to be less important than finding themselves. It became famous with the 1999 novel *Bridget Jones's Diary* by British author Helen Fielding (later made into a hit movie), which features the slightly "chubby" and neurotic Bridget Jones, who is keeping a diary in the hopes of curing herself of all vices, losing weight, and getting a better life.

Among Chick-Lit novels there is a popular subgenre that *Chick Lit Books* refers to as "Bigger Girl Lit." These novels feature a fat heroine not only looking for love and a better life but also peace with her body. In these books the fat girl is the leading lady and the thin girl plays the best friend. It was Jennifer Weiner's best seller *Good in Bed* (2001) that made it acceptable to have a fat lead character. The popularity of *Good in Bed* led to a string of similar books, including *Conversations with the Fat Girl* (Palmer, 2006), *The Way It Is* (Sanchez, 2003), and *Alternative Beauty* (Waggener, 2005). The protagonist of *Good in Bed*, Cannie, is fat, as opposed to Bridget Jones, who is closer to a socially acceptable weight. Both Bridget and Cannie suffer internal issues because they don't look like supermodels. For Cannie the pressure to conform is actually much worse. She has to deal with external issues linked to her weight, as evidenced through her receiving unwanted dieting advice, wading through poor family relationships, trouble finding clothes, dealing with frequent verbal abuse, and a trying to move up the ladder at her job.

Is the use of fatter characters in these novels positive or detrimental to the acceptance of fat bodies? Do the characters in the novels model acceptance or foster an obsession with weight? This chapter will examine five fat heroines in Chick-Lit novels: Cannie from *Good in Bed*, Ruby from *The Way It Is*, Ronnie from *Alternative Beauty*, Maggie from *Conversations with the Fat Girl*, and Serpentine from *All of Me*

(Berry, 2001). These picks come from recommended readings from the websites *Dangerously Curvy Novels* and *Chick Lit Books*. The chapter will focus on three themes found throughout these novels: obsession with weight loss, fear of being too fat, and size acceptance. Although the first two themes conflict with the third, I argue that Bigger Girl Lit ultimately reinforces fat acceptance in the mainstream media by demonstrating how such an outlook brings joy into the lives of the protagonists.

Despite the fact that the protagonists in these Bigger Girl Lit novels are fat, they are still often concerned with losing weight to some degree. This theme appears to undermine fat acceptance, reinforcing the idea that you should take the time to lose weight if you are fat, no matter what other problems are confronting you at the same time. For example, at the end of the Laura Palmer's *Conversations with the Fat Girl*, plus-size Maggie gets the guy, the job, and the great apartment. She is finally able to cast off her fat-turned-thin (and therefore ostensibly better) friend, Olivia. Despite all these strides, she still states with great pride that she has lost some weight: "This weekend was about a resurrection. This weekend was about Olivia and me making things right. This was supposed to be my show. How is this happening? I'm writing my food down now. I'm working out and I'm up to forty-five minutes on the StairMaster. I'm a size smaller. I'm a fucking size smaller" (Palmer, 2006, p. 277). A similar problem occurs in *All of Me* by Venise Berry. The main character Serpentine's size contributes to her trying to commit suicide. By the end of the novel, however, she begins to eat better and exercise. She remains large, but is less large than before, and importance is placed on the fact that she loses a dress size: "Serpentine's black sweater-and-skirt set, size 20, fit nicely. The major reason was her new exercise routine" (Berry, 2001, p. 256).

In *Alternative Beauty*, size 28 Ronnie wakes up in a world where fat is considered beautiful. During her time in the alternative universe, she becomes more interested in life, eats less, and loses weight. When she returns to her own world, she gets to keep her weight loss and continues to mention that she feels better as a thin person: "I remained a size ten. My appetite improved, but I became more active, and the extra calories were burned up by living, by happiness" (Waggener, 2005, p. 370). This unfortunately sets the notion that weight loss and maintenance can easily be attained by "getting a life."

In Chick-Lit, size 16 is a magical number. It is the maximum socially permitted size of a fat character. All but two of the characters I examined are size 16 or below. This bias isn't limited to the works investigated here: In *Losing It* by Lindsay Faith Rech (2003), you get the impression that the main character, Diana, is very fat, way above a size 16, as she seems like a stereotypical fat lady leading a lonely, sexless, clueless, friendless life. It turns out that Diana is only a size 16 and weighs 178 pounds: fat, but hardly the fat lady in the circus. In the 2004 fat-to-thin fantasy *Night Swimming* by Robin Schwarz, main character Charlotte weighs 253 pounds but happens to be a size 18, which is proportionally ridiculous, but it keeps the character below size 20. Only a few characters break the glass ceiling: Ruby in *The Way It Is* and Serpentine in *All of Me* hover around size 20 and remain there. Ronnie from *Alternative Beauty* is a size 28 but loses weight. Size 16 protects the character, the readers, and the author from the dreaded size 20, where the character has to shop (gasp) at Lane Bryant and won't find anything at the Gap. Once a character reaches size 20, it seems that they are past the point of self-acceptance and are now considered unhealthy. A perfect example is Ronnie, who feels that her large size is due to not being healthy: "So I stopped walking, which is part of the reason I reached 300 pounds" (Waggener, 2005, 290).

Although it is good to see mainstream and accepted characters from the size 9–16 range, as well as investigations of the issues that women of these sizes face (not thin enough to be "normal" but not big enough to be "fat"), it would be beneficial to see characters above size 16 and maybe even some that are super-sized (i.e., way above size 20 or 300 lbs). In all the books examined in this chapter, only Ronnie from *Alternative Beauty* is super-sized, but even she loses weight. Don't super-sized women want the career, the good life, a good man, and, most of all, acceptance? This appears to be yet another example of size prejudice at work, even in Bigger Girl Lit.

Despite the fact that many protagonists in these works actively seek to lose weight even after they learn to accept their bodies, and the fact that women bigger than size 20 are still vastly underrepresented, I will demonstrate that Bigger Girl Lit ultimately reinforces size acceptance and is therefore an important representative to fat acceptance in the mainstream media.

A perfect example of this theme is Ruby from *The Way It Is* by Patrick Sanchez. Ruby starts the story as an unhappy fat person recently divorced from a dull man who barely loved her. She is ashamed of eating, which is made worse by her constant bingeing and her bitter and mean mother. Due to financial woes, Ruby is forced to rent out her house to two women whom she quickly becomes jealous of: Simone, who is successful and thin, and the confident plus-size model Wanda. While dealing with all these issues, Ruby struggles to find happiness by dieting her way into a little black dress. When Ruby catches Simone wearing that same black dress, all the repressed rage from bingeing, and being teased and abused by her mother comes out. This allows her to begin down the road to size acceptance. She doesn't lose weight at all and is able to eat food freely. Her anger finally comes out and she nearly attacks Simone: "'Take it off!' Ruby demanded again and lunged toward Simone. Ruby screamed with such intensity that Simone, with real fear for her safety, reached for the zipper and began undoing the dress" (Sanchez, 2003, 283).

Releasing this repressed rage not only pushes Ruby to realize that changes need to happen in her life, but both Wanda and Simone (who are suffering from issues themselves) become privy to Ruby's feelings. With their help and her own inner strength, she begins down the road of size acceptance. She buys new clothes with the money she saved to buy thin clothes, asks out the man she pines over (and then dumps him when he turns out to be a jerk), and, most important, she doesn't lose weight at all and is able to eat food freely. Her acceptance leads to happiness: "She was accepting herself more and more every day, and forcing other people in her life to do the same. She no longer hated fat Ruby. In fact, she no longer thought in terms of Fat Ruby and Thin Ruby—she was just Ruby" (Sanchez, 2003, 329–330). Simone turns out to be a former fat woman who has an eating disorder due to her obsession with being thin.

At the end of the novel, Simone has become Ruby's antithesis: she is miserable trying to be thin, whereas Ruby is happy being fat.

Size acceptance also brings happiness to Cannie Shapiro in *Good in Bed*. In the beginning of the book Cannie learns that her ex-boyfriend Bruce is writing a column about their relationship and how she can't accept his love because she is fat. Cannie decides that the best way to deal with this is to lose weight and get back together with him. Neither idea works out: after a night of passion, Bruce doesn't want her and she ends up pregnant. After delivering a premature baby, Cannie walks the streets, unable to eat while she is apart from her daughter; consequently, she loses a lot of weight. Weiner makes it clear that Cannie's weight loss stems from her trauma, not from the discovery of the magic pill of weight loss: "The irony had not been lost on me. After a lifetime of obsession, of calorie counting, Weight watching, and StairMastering, I'd found a way to shed those unwanted pounds forever! To free myself of flan and cellulite! To get the body I'd always wanted! I should market this, I thought hysterically. The Placenta Abruptio Emergency Hysterectomy Premature and Possibly Brain-Damaged Baby Diet. I'd make a fortune" (Weiner, 2001, p. 341). When her daughter recovers with no negative long-term effects, Cannie begins regaining the weight and lives happily ever after as a fat chick: "I might be a big girl, I reasoned, but it wasn't the worst thing in the world. I was a safe harbor and a soft place to rest" (p. 359). Not only does she accept herself, but after the worry over her daughter she decides that there are more important things in life than weight: "And when my daughter was born almost two months too soon I learned there are worse things than not liking your thighs or your butt" (p. 365).

In Andrea Rains Waggener's *Alternative Beauty*, size 28 Ronnie, an aspiring clothes designer, has a bad day. She is threatened to be fired for being too fat at a plus size store, is verbally abused by her mother, and feels that she doesn't deserve her boyfriend Gilbert's love—all because she is fat. After a night of bingeing, she wishes that she could be in a more accepting world. When she wakes up the next morning, she gets her wish. She is now living in an alternative reality where fat is considered beautiful and skinny people are ostracized. At first Ronnie enjoys this new reality. She becomes the center of attention, the "belle of the ball." Her mother adores her. The same boss who wanted to fire her helps her get started as a fashion designer. Men worship her and constantly send flowers. She becomes involved with a sexy man who in her world would never have given her a second glance. This chances when she begins to lose weight rapidly. The sexy man no longer finds her attractive; the promising career ends. She ends up becoming an outcast again. She learns that true beauty comes in all sizes and that Gilbert loves her both at a size 10 and a size 28. Weight loss shows Ronnie the error of her ways; she is a wonderful, smart, and beautiful person no matter what her size or society's expectations: "Suddenly I got it. I saw the core of beauty. The pile on the floor wasn't perfect, not by any means. It was a jumble, the product of mindless rage. But it was beauty. Simple, unadorned beauty" (Waggener, 2005, 344).

In *Conversations with the Fat Girl*, Maggie is jealous of her best friend, Olivia, who for all intents and purposes abandons her in the fat acceptance fight by getting weight loss surgery. Olivia seems to have everything now that she is thin: the great job, the great fiancé, and of course the great figure. Maggie is made to feel less than human when she is with Olivia. It is only when Maggie stands up for herself after a waitress calls her a "gordita" that she takes the strides toward self-acceptance: "How many epiphanies is it going to take to finally get me to something. Now I have to decide if I want to continue to live like this. Not because of this bitch calling me out tonight, but because of the way I'm living my life. Or rather, not living it" (Palmer, 2006, p. 175). This gives her the confidence to get the dream internship, drop Olivia as a friend, and gain the courage to ask the object of her desire if he wants her (he does). Her acceptance of her weight allows her to no longer worry about what others think.

Serpentine in *All of Me* has a revelation similar to Maggie's, but for her, acceptance is far more difficult. Her lover's wandering eye (for his thin ex), combined with struggles at work (being told by her supervisor to lose weight or lose the promotion she's been working for) and a lifelong habit of unsuccessful dieting, eventually push her to attempt suicide. During her time in recovery she keeps a journal, rediscovers her spirituality, and finds that she is surrounded by women who love her. This is a turning point in her life; she dumps the flirtatious lover, fights to keep her job (by winning an award exposing the fact that fat-free products replace the fat with sugar), and, most important, stops dieting and obsessing about her weight. She learns to love herself no matter what her size because she believes that's what God wants: "It means people shouldn't judge each other the way they do and God's acceptance is all we need" (Berry, 2001, p. 268)

As I have demonstrated, Chick-Lit does not appear to uniformly reinforce body acceptance: characters obsess about weight loss and almost never go past the dreaded size 20. Nonetheless, Chick-Lit clearly displays that weight acceptance brings joy into the lives of larger women, freeing them from at least one serious problem—intense societal pressure to be thin. With the exception of Ronnie, every single main character, regardless of whether they lost weight, accepted that they are fat. Although Ronnie might be thin at the end of the novel, she resisted the social pressure of trying to stay fat in the alternative universe where fat is adored. In this sense, the positive change in self-image that each character undergoes as she works through her particular issues is something that any reader can apply to her own life.

Indeed, the mere presence of fat women in Bigger Girl Lit is important. Where else can you find bigger bodies in mainstream media? You aren't going to find them in films: when Jennifer Weiner's novel *In Her Shoes* was made into a film, a thin actress gained a mere twenty-five pounds to play the part of fat Rose. You aren't going to see them on television, where slightly chubby Kelly Osbourne is considered fat. You aren't going to find it in literature: fat characters in literature are often defined as suffering from psychological problems, such as Magdalena in Alice Walker's *By the Light of My Father's Smile* (1998), who is very fat and "eats herself to death," or Dolores in Wally Lamb's *She's Come Undone* (1996), who eats and becomes "disgustingly fat" (including poor habits such as not bathing) after being raped and loses weight after spending time in a mental institution (giving the message that good mental health means thinness). The anti-Chick-Lit anthology *This is Not Chick-Lit* (Merrick, 2006) features no stories where fat women are the center of attention. There is one story about a fat sad man and another story where some fat welfare moms appear in the background. Only in these Chick-Lit novels are we seeing fat bodies. These women reflect the real issues facing young women: trying to find their way in a world that celebrates thinness and calls fatness, any fatness, a disease. It's important that we do not dismiss the power of Chick-Lit as a gateway to fat acceptance in mainstream media. Despite the flaws of the size 20 glass ceiling and the celebration of weight loss, Chick-Lit is the biggest thing in the mainstream celebrating and accepting the fat body.

NOTE

With special thanks for Jonathan Frater and Michael Lutz.

REFERENCES

Berry, V. (2001). *All of Me: A Voluptuous Tale*. New York: New American Library.

Chick Lit Books. http://chicklitbooks.com.

Dangerously Curvy Novels. http://curvynovels.tripod.com.

Ferriss, S., & Young, M. (2006). *Chick Lit: The New Women's Fiction*. New York: Routledge.

Fielding, H. (1999). *Bridget Jones's Diary*. New York: Viking.

Lamb, W. (1996). *She Come Undone*. New York: Washington Square Press

Massa, C. (1996). *Chick-Lit: Post-feminist Fiction*, vol. 1. Normal, IL: Fiction Collective 2.

Merrick, E. (2006). *This Is Not Chick Lit*. New York: Random House.

Palmer, L. (2006). *Conversations with the Fat Girl: A Novel*. New York: Time Warner Books.

Rech, L.F. (2003). *Losing It: A Novel About Cynicism, Celibacy, and Stretch Marks*. Ontario, Canada: Red Dress Ink.

Sanchez, P. (2003). *The Way It Is*. New York: Kensington Publishing.

Schwarz, R. (2004). *Night Swimming*. New York: Warner Books.

Waggener, A.R. (2005) *Alternative Beauty: A Novel*. New York: Bantam.

Walker, A (1998). *By the Light of My Father's Smile*. New York: Random House.

Weiner, J. (2001). *Good in Bed*. New York: Pocket Books.

The Fat of the (Border)land

Food, Flesh, and Hispanic Masculinity in
Willa Cather's Death Comes for the Archbishop

Julia McCrossin

"There are nearly a thousand years of history in this soup," Bishop Latour proclaims as he complements his fellow French missionary Father Vaillant's culinary skills near the beginning of Willa Cather's *Death Comes for the Archbishop* (1990a, p. 299). Toward the end of the narrative, Latour urges his newest priests "to encourage the Mexicans to add fruit to their starchy diet" (p. 438). In the spaces between these two statements, spaces that span time and country and culinary habits, lies an undiscovered portion of the Southwest in *Death Comes for the Archbishop*. In this text these two Catholic priests often lament the state of indigenous diets in mid-nineteenth century New Mexico. This diet, a mix of European and Mesoamerican influences dating from the sixteenth century, is now one of the more popular modern cuisines in the United States. Although we do not get any lessons on creating the perfect corn tortilla in *Death Comes for the Archbishop*, we do get a cooking lesson of a different sort: a lesson on how food can serve as a secret language of history and nation forming, of masculinity and desire, and of how Cather's text mediates between larger historical discourses and the everyday lives of a heterogeneous population. Looking specifically at food (and the subsequent conflation of Hispanic men and fat) allows us to explicate some of the troubling characterizations that have adhered to the Hispanic subject since the beginning of American colonization. I use the descriptor "Hispanic," instead of "Latino" or "Chicano" or "Mexican American," to discuss Cather's characters because I feel that it most clearly describes the fact that some of the characters included in my analysis perceive themselves as Spanish, a belief that John M. Nieto-Phillips (2004) describes as "hispanidad"—a rhetorical move to help encourage acceptance of New Mexico into the union by stressing the "European" heritage of New Mexican residents.

One may be tempted to wonder why food in *Death Comes for the Archbishop* is an area worthy of such specialized attention. As Carole Counihan and Penny Van Esterik explain in the introduction to their text *Food and Culture: A Reader*, "Food marks social differences, boundaries, bonds, and contradictions. Eating is an endlessly evolving enactment of gender, family, and community relationships" (1997, p.

1). In much of the critical work on *Death Comes for the Archbishop*, those themes are discussed by ignoring food altogether or neglecting the pivotal role that Hispanics play in the text. As a consequence, crucial insights are overlooked, for food highlights the ways in which the Hispanic subject in the narrative is often marginalized. Such marginalization is not just the expected cultural biases of a bygone era, but is also symptomatic of something more. It speaks to Anglo-American fears of a hybridized "borderlands" Hispanic culture, and more specifically, an ambivalence over male Hispanic heterosexual desire and miscegenation. And although much of my argument pertains only to *Death Comes for the Archbishop*, the assumptions about Hispanic dietary practices continue to resonate in a culture that increasingly relies on dietary proscriptions to interpolate U.S. residents into "good" citizens. As Kathleen LeBesco argues, today's "failed citizen" is often a fat African American or Latina/o citizen, presumed through ignorance, poverty, and culture to be unable to make "healthy" food choices; thus, anti-fatness campaigns can be read as essentially eugenics campaigns (LeBesco, 2004).

The bountiful food motif in *Death Comes for the Archbishop* folds seamlessly into another key theme of the text, one that provides a way to analyze an oft-ignored area of body studies: the representation of the fat Hispanic male body. Critics have come to accept that the experiences of any individual are constructed by an interlocking and mutually constitutive range of identities, oftentimes identities linked to race, gender, class, sexuality, age, and ability; they are less likely to explore the particularities of how fat contributes to this formation. Scholars often dismiss fat as nothing more than a stereotype, or as incidental to cultural analysis. By failing to attend to the specificities of the fat subject, though, we also dismiss those subjects who actually inhabit the body of a fat minority. These failures are part of a practice that alienates any fat body from its racial, cultural, gendered, and sexualized identities. As *Death Comes for the Archbishop* illustrates, the proliferation of fat Hispanic male bodies in a canonical American text has specific things to say to us about nationality, race, gender, and sexuality. These bodies define what it means to be a U.S. citizen by their very real omission from discourses in cultural studies and literary criticism. Within the corpus of Willa Cather's fiction alone, there are many fat characters in need of a cultural studies analysis. Although the character of Fat Lizzie in *Sapphira and the Slave Girl* (Cather, 1990d) is a rote mammy stereotype, Cather on occasion offers more nuanced portrayals of fat people in her work. Although one would have to relegate the cold, devouring mother of the short story "The Sculptor's Funeral" (Cather, 1987) to the caricature category along with Fat Lizzie, Myra Henshawe from *My Mortal Enemy* (Cather, 1992), Captain Forrester from *A Lost Lady* (Cather, 1990b), and Clement Sebastian from *Lucy Gayheart* (Cather, 1990c) are less troublesome representations of corpulence in the novel. Two important things to note about these last three characters—they are all white and upper class, and the parameters of fat during Cather's time may not have even included them as fat enough to qualify as a stigmatizing identity. Obviously, the definition of fat is never constant throughout time and space.

The culinary instruction that Bishop Latour preaches in Cather's text echo some of the real practices undertaken in Mexico, where the evaluation of "good" and "bad" foods in the formation of a Mexican cuisine took on a significance far beyond any notions of health and taste. As food historian Jeffrey M. Pilcher argues:

> The significance of cuisine in Mexican history has extended far beyond the dinner table. In New Spain's hierarchical society, corn tortillas and wheat bread helped define ethnicity in the absence of clear racial boundaries. The colonial fiction of separate Indian and Hispanic republics disappeared with independence, but eating corn continued to denote lower-class status throughout the nineteenth century. Political elites, who believed that Native Americans must acquire European culture to qualify for Mexican citizenship, attacked corn as one cause of the country's backwardness. (1996, p. 214)

New Mexico was part of Mexico until the Treaty of Guadalupe Hildago in 1848, and New Mexico did not become the forty-seventh state until 1912. Although many Mexicans and New Mexicans of the nineteenth century claimed that their cuisine was of Spanish origin, the results of their culinary practices suggest a diet built on the foundation of Mesoamerican ingredients and cooking styles. As Mexico began to assert a national identity distinct from Spain, the country endeavored to erase most traces of indigenous origin from their gastronomy (Pilcher, 1998). It is from these hegemonic practices that the development of the discourses about the nutritional inferiority of corn, beans, and chiles came into being, and which inform the opinions that Bishop Latour (and Cather) express about the dietary practices of the Hispanic characters in *Death Comes for the Archbishop*.

It is tempting to read Cather's food themes in *Death Comes for the Archbishop* as merely a reflection of her own food preferences and nationality biases. Cather was known for her love of fine dining and French cuisine and culture (Stout, 2000). Instead of looking at Bishop Latour's opinions about the "starchy" Mexican diet as a reflection of Cather's own taste preferences, we should instead view the numerous criticisms of the Hispanic diet by the French priests as a reiteration of the procedures of nationality formation in Mexico that benefited those who renounced a diet with any trace of Mesoamerican originality. It is crucial to note, however, that although the nutritional dialogue in Mexico proclaimed the diet of corn, beans, squash, and tortillas "unhealthy," lacking in proteins and fruits, current nutritional research has shown that the vegetarian staples of this diet are nutritionally complete and healthy (Sanjur, 1995). These declarations of nutritional deficiencies in the more indigenous diets of Mexico were replicated in the United States as well. The *New York Times* published an article on June 20, 1880, about "The People of New Mexico: Their Modes of Life and Peculiar Traits." The reporter informs the reader that:

> Juan manages to live his unenergetic life because he is very ignorant, and his wants are few. His bill of fare consists in the main of a tortilla, or thin cake of flour or corn-meal and water, and a cup of coffee. Add to these some red or green peppers, with once in

a while a minute portion of mutton or goat's meat, and you have his general diet. In their seasons, in some parts of the Territory, he indulges in fruit-melons, pears, peaches, apples, and grapes—not as a rule of very good quality, for he knows and cares nothing of improving the stock of his orchard. (p. 10)

The claim in this article that "Juan" (as representative of all Hispanics in New Mexico) is unenergetic and ignorant is explicitly linked to his diet; thus the diet discrimination that Mexican elites were practicing against their lower-class compatriots was active in the United States, but against all people of Mexican heritage. Other governmental dietary pronouncements and procedures centered on the Hispanic subject over the past century in North America followed a path blazed in the early part of the twentieth century, when Mexican politicians used police inspectors to recruit recalcitrant corn eaters to public cooking classes (Pilcher, 1996). Marcia Chamberlain explains that by the 1950's, "Americanization programs taught Mexican American mothers to substitute white bread for tortillas, green lettuce for frijoles, and boiled meat for fried meat" (2001, p. 101). Ironically, recent studies have shown that the overall health of Latino/as suffer as they adapt to more "American" diets (Khan & Martorell, 1997). As Paul Campos (2004), Kathleen LeBesco (2004), and others have noted, the appetites and waistlines of Latino/a peoples are at the heart of our current moral panic over the "war on obesity."

Food in *Death Comes for the Archbishop* reifies nationalistic discourses in both Mexico and the United States that sought to quantify citizenship through cuisine. Turning our attention to fat, we are presented with questions not only of nationality, but also of race, gender, and sexuality. On the surface, the presentations of fat men in Cather's novel seem to be no more than a religious allegory of gluttony, but a closer look reveals that most of the fat men are signifiers for a consuming mestizo, or borderlands, culture that threatens the tight boundaries of racial subjectivity in U.S. culture. Further, linking this fearsome consumption to Hispanic men suggests an apprehension over the enactment of Hispanic masculinity. The narrative of *Death Comes for the Archbishop* describes the experiences of a real man, Archbishop Jean Baptiste Lamy, as he works to reestablish Roman Catholic principles in a region newly separated from Mexico and containing many priests who resent Lamy's authority. As many critics have noted, most of the priests other than Latour (Lamy) and Vaillant are portrayed as representations of the seven deadly sins, yet two of the priests (Baltazar and Lucero) are fat representatives of gluttony, and most of the Hispanic men (whether clergymen or not) are described by Cather as "full-figured." In the section titled "Legend of Fray Baltazar," the native Acomas kill Fray Baltazar as payback for years of abuse at the hands of this greedy priest. Baltazar's fatness and his obsessive attention to food suggest that his death is a deserved one. His Spanish heritage, however, illustrates, as Janis P. Stout has observed, that Cather "did not entertain a genuinely democratized or inclusive political vision, even for Americans of European stock. Some, in her view, were more equal than others" (Stout, 2000, p. 222). The paradox of this construction is that although Baltazar is punished for his attention to and enjoyment of fine dining, both Latour and Vaillant are valorized for their strenuous efforts to reproduce French cuisine in the Southwest. This conflict illustrates Stout's comment and implies that the threat of Hispanic masculinity is generated by their desires; although Fray Baltazar fathers no children, his symbolic progeny, Trinidad Lucero, personifies excessive desires of the flesh for food and for women. Looking primarily at Trinidad Lucero, the fat priest in training, helps to elucidate these assertions.

Hermione Lee's statement about the Fray Baltazar section is important to excavating the meanings that adhere to Trinidad Lucero's very fat body: "Appearances and actions are not deceptive; indeed, physical signs are insisted on with extreme emphasis, so that, in some of these 'parables,' an uncensored display of prejudices about bodies spills out over the requirements of the story" (1989, pp. 276–277). Lee's comment helps uncover the implications of Cather's fat Hispanic men as objects of disgust because of their ethnic/racial identity; the novel conflates repugnance for the desires of Hispanic men with the fat of their bodies. Cather's first description of Trinidad Lucero is a scene in which the sleeping man gets kicked in the chest by Padre Martinez; Cather tells us immediately before this kick that Lucero is "a very large man, very stout . . . and as he breathed his bulk rose and fell amazingly" (1990a, p. 363). A few pages later Kit Carson's wife reveals a tale that may be the only slapstick moment in all of Cather's novels: "He [Trinidad] tried to be like the Savior [during the Penitentes observances during Passion Week], and had himself crucified. Oh, not with nails! He was tied upon a cross with ropes, to hang there all night; they do that sometimes at Abiquiu, it is a very old-fashioned place. But he is so heavy that after he had hung there a few hours, the cross fell over with him, and he was very much humiliated" (p. 371). For many critics, these passages propose that Trinidad is nothing more than a string of adjectives without any real subjectivity; Hermione Lee calls him "repulsively fat, greedy, greasy, slothful, and imbecilic" (1989, p. 277). Cather herself delves into myriad details of how, in her words, Trinidad's "stupid" fat marks his body, and links Trinidad's fat body explicitly to desires out of control. Trinidad's undivided attention at the dinner table is on his food, which he "ate as if he were afraid of never seeing food again" (Cather, 1990a, p. 365). Only one thing can distract him from his meal: "When his attention left his plate for a moment, it was fixed in the same greedy way upon the girl who served the table-and who seemed to regard him with careless contempt" (p. 365). Food, fat, and lust are cleverly linked here to bolster my argument that Trinidad is the key to unlocking the secret discourse in *Death Comes for the Archbishop* that marks most Hispanic men as fat in order to express fears of hybrid culture and miscegenation.

As Manuel Broncano (2002) proposes, Trinidad's body, his grotesqueness, signifies an emasculation representative of a desire to contain the reproduction of a Latina/o culture. As Anglo-Americans began to settle in New Mexico, they concocted a feminized image of Mexican men, lounging in draping serapes and floppy sombreros (Pilcher, 2001); part of this feminizing discourse includes conceptualizing Mexican men as fat, because, as scholars have noted, the materiality of fat sculpts feminine curves onto many fat men. Fat, then, works to erase Hispanic masculinity in *Death Comes for the Archbishop* in order to arrest sexual practice and masculine power. A possible objection to this argument is represented in the many Hispanic families in the novel who feed, shelter, and donate resources to the French missionaries (exemplified by the phantom "Holy Family" legend toward the end of the narrative), and therefore belies the assertion that Cather's text abhors the reproduction of Hispanic families. Yet the fear is generated toward the creation and propagation of a hybrid *Mexican-Anglo* culture. We can look at the murder of Magdalena's three infants by her Anglo husband, Buck Scales, as but one example of this. This interpretation troubles some scholars' views that *Death Comes for the Archbishop*, unlike earlier Cather texts, like *O Pioneers!* celebrates intermarriage between ethnicities.

Gloria Anzaldua's concept of the mestiza and the borderlands provides a framework for viewing the threat that a hybrid culture poses to the hegemony of the United States. In *Borderlands/La Frontera: The New Mestiza*, she defines the borderlands subject as "cradled in one culture, sandwiched between two cultures, straddling all three cultures and their value systems, *la mestiza* undergoes a struggle of flesh, a struggle of borders, an inner war" (Anzaldua, 2001, p. 2215). Anzaldua's mestiza concept functions for men as well, and she identifies that the Chicano/a refusal to assimilate causes an alienating, multi-identified subjectivity, and that, for her in particular, "I have so internalized the borderland conflict that sometimes I feel like one cancels out the other and we are zero, nothing, no one" (2004, p. 1029). Looking at Cather's narrative, which takes place in a borderlands region adjacent to the one that Anzaldua identifies, the mestizo consciousness is under attack from containment strategies that elucidate her trepidation over a flourishing Hispanic culture in the United States. The fat Hispanic men in *Death Comes for the Archbishop* also evoke Judith Butler's extension of Mary Douglas's work, which positions a body with "unregulated permeability" as dangerous to the social system (Butler, 2001, p. 2493); the excesses of flesh and desire inscribed on their bodies upend any kind of stability and threaten the inflexible rules of race and citizenship in the Southwest U.S. territories. Not only through their race, but also in their fleshy materiality, the fat Hispanic men in Cather's text push at the boundaries of nationality, gender, race, sex, and culture, and although they may inhabit an inhospitable containment in this narrative, their consumption and bodily parameters suggest otherwise; these fat mestizo men propose an alternate view of identity, which encourages porous borders and indeterminate boundaries and celebrates a hybrid consciousness. Their fat bodies physically belie the possibility of nothingness.

Investigating the uses of food, consumption, and fat in Willa Cather's *Death Comes for the Archbishop* provides a counter-reading of the narrative that proposes a mestizo analysis of the discourses of nationality forming and inter-ethnic inclusiveness centered on the Hispanic subject. Cather's text implies a dread of hybrid, non-Anglo/ Gallic-identified ethnicities in the Southwest enacted in the fat, desiring bodies of Hispanic men. Gloria Anzaldua, however, uses similar themes of food and reproduction for a liberatory acceptance of this hybrid culture: "Indigenous like corn, like corn, the *mestiza* is a product of cross-breeding, designed for preservation under a variety of conditions. Like an ear of corn—a female seed bearing organ—the *mestiza* is tenacious, tightly wrapped in the husks of her culture. Like kernels she clings to the cob, with thick stalks and strong brace roots, she holds tight to the earth—she will survive the crossroads" (2001, p. 2215). Although Anzaldua is referring specifically to a female consciousness, her words are an affirmation for the entire Chicano/a culture. Despite two countries and multiple cultures' denial of the nutritional value of maize, the diet of corn (and beans) continues to offer sustenance to a growing, assertive Latino/a population in the United States and undermines the hegemonic discourse of European supremacy in *Death Comes for the Archbishop*.

REFERENCES

Anzaldua, G. (2001) Borderlands/La frontera. In V.B. Leitch (Ed.), *The Norton Anthology of Theory and Criticism*. New York: Norton.

Anzaldua, G. (2004). Borderlands/La frontera. In J. Rivkin & M. Ryan (Eds.), *Literary Theory: An Anthology*. 2nd ed. Malden, MA: Blackwell Publishing.

Broncano, M. (2002). Landscapes of the magical: Cather's and Anaya's explorations of the Southwest. In J.N. Swift & J.R. Urgo (Eds.), *Willa Cather and the American Southwest*. Lincoln: University of Nebraska Press.

Butler, J. (2001). Gender trouble. In V.B. Leitch (Ed.), *The Norton Anthology of Theory and Criticism*. New York: Norton.

Campos, P. (2004). *The Obesity Myth*. New York: Gotham Books.

Cather, W. (1987). The sculptor's funeral. In S. O'Brien (Ed.), *Cather: Early Novels and Stories*. New York: Library of America.

Cather, W. (1990a). *Death Comes for the Archbishop*. In S. O'Brien (Ed.), *Cather: Later Novels*. New York: Library of America.

Cather, W. (1990b). *A Lost Lady*. In S. O'Brien (Ed.), *Cather: Later Novels*. New York: Library of America.

Cather, W. (1990c). *Lucy Gayheart*. In S. O'Brien (Ed.), *Cather: Later Novels*. New York: Library of America.

Cather, W. (1990d). *Sapphira and the Slave Girl*. In S. O'Brien (Ed.), *Cather: Later Novels*. New York: Library of America.

Cather, W. (1992). *My Mortal Enemy*. In S. O'Brien (Ed.), *Cather: Stories, Poems, and Other Writings*. New York: Library of America.

Chamberlain, M. (2001). Oscar Zeta Acosta's *Autobiography of a Brown Buffalo*: A fat man's recipe for Chicano revolution. In K. LeBesco & J. E. Braziel (Eds.), *Bodies Out of Bounds: Fatness and Transgression*. Berkeley: University of California Press.

Counihan, C., & Van Esterik, P. (1997). Introduction. In C. Counihan & P. Van Esterik (Eds.), *Food and Culture: A Reader*. New York: Routledge.

Khan, L. K., & Martorell, R. (1997). Diet diversity in Mexican Americans, Cuban Americans, and Puerto Ricans. *Ecology of Food and Nutrition 36*, 401–415.

LeBesco, K. (2004). *Revolting Bodies: The Struggle to Redefine Fat Identity*. Amherst: University of Massachusetts Press.

Lee, H. (1989). *Willa Cather: Double Lives*. New York: Pantheon.

Nieto-Phillips, J.M. (2004). *The Language of Blood: The Making of Spanish-American Identity in New Mexico, 1880s–1930s*. Albuquerque: University of New Mexico Press.

The people of New Mexico: Their modes of life and peculiar traits. *New York Times*, 20 June 1880, 10.

Pilcher, J.M. (1996). Tamales or timbales: Cuisine and the formation of Mexican national identity, 1821–1911. *The Americas* 53.2, 193–216.

Pilcher, J.M. (1998). *Que Vivan Los Tamales! Food and the Making of Mexican Identity.* Albuquerque: University of New Mexico Press.

Pilcher, J.M. (2001). Tex-mex, cal-mex, new-mex, or whose mex? Notes on the historical geography of Southwestern cuisine. *Journal of the Southwest* 43.4, 659–679.

Sanjur, D. (1995). *Hispanic Foodways, Nutrition, and Health.* Boston: Allyn and Bacon.

Stout, J.P. (2000). *Willa Cather: The Writer and Her World.* Charlottesville: University of Virginia Press.

‖‖‖

Placing Fat Women on Center Stage

JuliaGrace Jester

As much as theatre is a form of expression, it is also a visual sphere in which norms of appearance are obeyed. According to Jill Dolan and others (1991; Feuer, 1999; Mulvey, 1975), theatre has been traditionally designed for the "male gaze," indicating both the (un)intended audience for theatre and the perspective from which much of theatre is presented. Under these conditions, it seems that there would be no place in theatre for fat women, who are neither objects of attraction nor traditionally considered beautiful (Callaghan, 1994). It is not that fat women have not had a place in theatre; it is merely that they have been relegated to the roles of the old, the ugly, or the comical. This also means that roles that do not specify the character's weight will rarely be given to fat women.

In mainstream theatre, women are often used exclusively in reference to others on stage (as mothers, wives, daughters) or they are sexualized in ways that cater to male fantasy (Dolan, 1998). Under this form of patriarchy, women can identify with the weak female (masochism), or identify with the male character and be complicit in their own objectification. Fat women are faced with slightly different options, as they can choose to either identify with the thin lead who will never really represent them, or they can choose to fight this misrepresentation of the "female."

The concept that thin is beautiful, and that fat is not, is not an innate aspect of human culture. As Richard Klein (2001) points out, in times of famine and food shortages, the desirable shape of a woman's body was large because a larger size indicated a position of wealth and power. Icons like Marilyn Monroe and Mae West, who were considered to be among the most beautiful and desirable women of their time, would be considered fat and undesirable by current standards of beauty and size (Risch, 2003).

Although the ideals of feminine beauty have changed over time, there is no doubt that in today's society being thin is the expected norm (Cramer & Steinwert, 1998). As Millman puts it, fat women are "stereotypically viewed as unfeminine, in flight from sexuality, antisocial, out of control, hostile, and aggressive" (1981, p. xi). So what does this mean for fat women who want to find a place to express themselves and be represented in the theatre?

Hartley says, "To the extent that the fat body has been vilified as marking a woman who refuses to accept the prescribed construction [of the female body], a place must be made in feminist scholarship for theorizing the fat body in ways that acknowledge the power of her refusal" (2001, p. 71). LeBesco (2001) agrees and suggests that the fat body be considered "revolting." Revolting has two relevant meanings, the first being a synonym for disgusting, and the second referring to something as being part of a revolution, an act for change. It is the transformation of that fat body from the former definition to the latter one that these authors are encouraging. LeBesco also encourages a performativity of fatness that both elicits and explodes the assumptions about the fat body by sexualizing and beautifying the fat form. The fat body should not be molded to a thin sensibility of beauty, but instead should enforce the ideal of fat as beautiful and sexual.

To address the representations of fat women and to begin understanding the theatricality of fat performance, we need to see how fat women are portrayed as leads, how fatness is performed and represented, and how plays can demonstrate the objectification of fat women. These representations of fat women, though they can be transformative and empowering, are complicated by the tendencies both to oversimplify the means of overcoming fat discrimination and to rely on comedy as a means for addressing what are difficult and serious issues for fat women. I will now turn to some specific plays that have fat women as lead characters.

Fat Women as Leads

Hairspray (Shaiman, O'Donnell, Meehan, & Wittman, 2002) is a musical based on the 1988 John Waters's movie by the same name. The musical follows the experiences of Tracy Turnblad, a pleasantly plump teenage girl, as she auditions for and gets onto a 1960's teen dance show despite the ways that other members of the show make fun of her size. There are two other fat women in the show, Tracy's mother, Edna Turnblad (generally played by a fat man cross-dressing as a fat woman), and Motormouth Maybelle, a black woman dealing with the double oppression of fat stigma and the racism of the time.

Over the course of the play, Tracy not only gets on the show but also fights for racial rights, wins a pageant, dates an Elvis-type crooner who had previously been dating a blond, skinny, manipulative girl, and helps her mother accept and love her big, fat self. This takes the tradition of the musical and rewrites it for a fat body, making it an example of the ways in which plays can examine and then implode the myths of the unlovable fat woman. Although this musical is comical and lighthearted, it also addresses the important issues of beauty ideals, discrimination, and sexuality. Unfortunately, as positive and powerful as *Hairspray* can be, it is not without its flaws. It gives unrealistic representations of the ease with which Tracy is both accepted by others and how she accepts herself. This does not necessarily resonate with the experiences of fat women who have grown up in a very anti-fat society (Myers & Rothblum, 2005).

The Most Massive Woman Wins (George, 1997), although still being comedic, seems better equipped to address both the difficulties of being a fat woman and the internalized self-hatred that can come with being the member of such a stigmatized group. This is a one-act, nonmusical play set in the waiting room of a liposuction clinic. The four characters, Carly, Cel, Sabine, and Rennie, are not necessarily all fat, but each represents the pressures place on women and women's bodies in our society. Throughout the play the women revert back to childhood memories that emphasize the early age at which girls are receiving pressures to be thin. The play also demonstrates the torments experienced by fat women through derisions such as "She's too fat for jump rope" (p. 274), "We'll never be so disgusting as her" (p. 276), and "She can't play dodge ball, she's ginormous" (p. 277)! This societal exclusion of and aversion to fat women is a form of stigmatization, which occurs when someone's "social identity, or membership in some social category, calls into question his or her full humanity—the person is devalued, spoiled or flawed in the eyes of others" (Crocker, Major, & Steele, 1998, p. 504).

In one scene Sabine is not taken seriously both because of who she is (a fat woman) and because she wrote her thesis on the media's influence on eating disorders, which is deemed to be an unworthy topic for scientific study by her committee members. Another scene demonstrates the difficulties that Carly has finding a job because of her size. The scenes are not maudlin and self-defeating; the play is meant to be a comedy and ridicules each of these acts of discrimination as an image of societal ignorance and cruelty.

The Most Massive Woman Wins does not merely reify the problems of fat women; it violates and reverses them. A monologue by Rennie epitomizes LeBesco's aforementioned idea of revolting: "Rennie: (referring to a photograph) Rennie . . . is not in her place at her mother's side because she is in the parish hall kitchen, devouring the three-foot-tall wedding cake meant to serve one hundred and eighty guests. . . . I ate and I ate and I ate it all up until there wasn't one crumb left, not a single frosted rosette, and I held that whole cake inside my body, I had it all to myself. And then I threw it all up on the kitchen floor and I walked out the backdoor into the night" (George, 1997, p. 289). This act by Rennie is both revolting, as in disgusting and unappealing, but is also a form of revolution against her lifelong hunger, her mother's constant pressures, and the stereotype of fat women as lacking self-control. Rennie didn't eat the cake because she lacked will power; she ate the cake to control the situation and violate everyone's ideas of right and wrong.

This play ends with all four women coming to accept themselves as who they are, which is symbolically represented by the removal of costumes, leaving them to stand in the triumphant glory of their underwear in front of the audience. This ending shows the women acknowledging and accepting their bodies and offers the audience the chance to "truly see" real women, women with fat and lumps and curves, defying society's usual cover-it-up-and-hide-it response to fat women. And though the women's bodies are on display, they are not really enacting the male gaze because their form violates the typical ideas of male desire and tries to reform what is considered "real" for women and their bodies. This ending, however, disconnects with the experiences of fat women in the real world because of the ease with which ingrained self-hatreds are apparently wiped out, to be replaced with quick self-acceptance.

Fat Pig by Neil LaBute (2005) addresses fat women as the objects of desire in a world that says that they should not be desirable. This play centers around Helen, a fat woman who meets Tom in a cafeteria. Helen has a wonderful wit that she often turns on herself, but in such a way as to point out the misconceptions that other people have about fat women. For instance, she says, "Big people are jolly, remember?" (p. 10) in response to Tom not realizing that she was joking about something. This both points out the stereotype of fat people as jolly and makes Tom realize that he has the preconceived notions about what fat women are like. As the play develops, Helen and Tom begin dating and we see Helen through Tom's eyes as a beautiful and sexy woman; but we also see her through the eyes of Tom's friends, who do not approve of Tom dating someone who is fat. Helen appears confident, intelligent, sweet, and honest; she is the most laudable individual in the play. Unfortunately, by the end of the play Tom caves into his fears of being judged by others and breaks up with Helen. Helen responds to this culminating rejection with quiet tears, as if resigned to such rejection rather than allying against it.

This play points out the pressures placed on fat women by society and the difficulty of overcoming the stereotypes and discrimination heaped on fat people. These plays cast fat women as representing beauty and goodness, criticize and attempt to deflate the negative messages sent to fat women about their bodies, and place fat women center stage. Though problems remain, such representations are improvements over previous caricatures and at least afford the opportunity for fat women to see characters with whom they can resonate and, hopefully, respect.

Fat as a Performance

We have much further to go in the reclaiming of the fat female as a sexual and valued being. Positive, realistic, and even sympathetic images of fat women are few and far between. Fat women are still vilified and mocked in popular culture and theatre, most often used as a source of humor or farce. In the musical *Do Black Patent Leather Shoes Really Reflect Up?* (Powers, Quinn, & Jans, 1988), Becky Bakowski starts out as a chubby little girl who loses a lot of weight one school year. It is this loss of weight that makes her attractive as the romantic lead. At the beginning of the play she is mocked by the other girls. She even sings a song asking if "God loves little fat girls, too?" But in order for this transformation from chubby little girl to svelte teen to occur, the performance must either be done by a skinny actress in a fat suit or by two separate actresses (one fat and one thin). Although the young fat Becky is seen as sweet and good, it is not until she is thin that she is truly valued by her peers. Unfortunately this just emphasizes the current societal bias toward thinness and prevents this play from changing the ways in which fat women are perceived.

Eve Ensler, well-known author of *The Vagina Monologues* (2000), also wrote *The Good Body* (2004), which focuses both on Eve's own relationship to her fattening body as well as on other women's relationships with their bodies. This play began as a one-woman show by Ensler, who is not particularly fat herself, but it tells stories of fatness from multiple character perspectives. Ideally this play would be as empowering for overall body image as *The Vagina Monologues* can be for women's freedom, sexual health, and well-being. Each of the stories, however, follows a woman who dislikes her body and explains ways to lose weight, change, or distort one's body. For example, "My body will be mine when I'm thin. I will eat a little at a time, small bites. I will vanquish ice cream . . . I will work not to feel full again. Always moving towards full, approaching full, but never really full. I will embrace my emptiness, I will ride it into holy zones. Let me be hungry. Let me starve. Please" (Ensler, 2004, p. 7). Despite this earlier plea, Ensler ends the play with the joyous eating of ice cream. This play makes fat something to avoid, to hate, to try to eliminate without any considerations for health. At one point the narrator points out how happy she was when she got really sick, could not eat, and therefore lost weight. Though this play discusses fatness and features fat characters, it is not about acceptance and appreciation for fat women (or women of any size), but instead focuses on change and the struggle for thinness.

Fat Women as Objects: An Example

Suzan-Lori Parks's 1997 play *Venus*, based on a true story, focuses on the Hottentot Venus, a voluptuous African woman who was taken from her home and turned into a sexualized sideshow attraction. This play gets its own section because it both performs fatness (the lead wears an extended posterior in order to have the exaggerated proportions indicated by the historical records surrounding the Hottentot Venus) and because it points out the concepts of normalized beauty that make large women a spectacle. Parks describes the Venus as follows: "Early in the 19th century a poor wretched woman was exhibited in England under the appellation of The Hottentot Venus. With an intensely ugly figure, distorted beyond all European notions of beauty, she was said to possess precisely the kind of shape which is most admired among her countrymen, the Hottentots" (1997, p. 159). The Venus in the play is treated alternately like a whore, an animal, a child, and an object. Her will and her desires are ignored by all around her. She is sexualized and dehumanized because of her shape, but also because of her status as an African woman. She is seen as exotic and savage, enabling other characters to take advantage of her. She is not human in their eyes and therefore deserves no consideration.

One cannot avoid being horrified at the treatment of the Hottentot Venus, but there is no parallel outrage to the ways in which fat women are treated today, both in society at large and within the microcosm of the theatre world. Though this play uses prosthetics to create fatness, it addresses the demoralization and objectification of any woman who does not fit the norm of beauty for body shape and size, addressing the ways in which fat women's sexuality and identity are constricted by the preconceptions of others.

Conclusion

Although fat women are not relegated solely to the crone roles in today's theatre, there is still much work needed to garner fat acceptance. There are plays that are affirming to fat women by showing them as sexual human beings, but there are also plays that deny the humanity of fat women and persist in sending the message that "only thin women get happy endings." A move toward a more consistently accepting theatre for fat women would need to address the following: the need for more plays that show fat women as strong, intelligent, and desirable; the continued critique of even well-meaning plays that reiterate and verify the fat-exclusive cultural standards of beauty; the need for fat women to be considered for roles not directly written for fat women; and an awareness of the ways in which expressing stereotypical ideas about fat women can be both beneficial (clarify the problem) and harmful (perpetuating the problem).

REFERENCES

Callaghan, K.A. (1994). *Ideals of Feminine Beauty: Philosophical, Social, and Cultural Dimensions*. Westport, Conn.: Greenwood Press.

Cramer, P., & Steinwert, T. (1998). Thin is good, fat is bad: How early does it begin? *Journal of Applied Developmental Psychology, 19*(3), 429–451.

Crocker, J., Major, B., & Steele, C. (1998). Social stigma. In D.T. Gilbert, S.T. Fiske, & G. Lindzey (Eds.), *The Handbook of Social Psychology* (pp. 504–553) (4th ed.). Boston: McGraw-Hill.

Dolan, J. (1991). *The Feminist Spectator as Critic*. Ann Arbor: University of Michigan Press.

Dolan, J. (1998). The discourse of feminisms: The spectator and representation. In L. Goodman & J. De Gay (Eds.), *The Routledge Reader in Gender and Performance* (pp. 288–294). New York: Routledge.

Ensler, E. (2004). *The Good Body*. NY: Villard.

Feuer, J. (1999). Averting the male gaze: Visual pleasure and images of fat women. In M.B. Haralovich & L. Rabinovitz (Eds.), *Television, History, and American Culture: Feminist Critical Essays* (pp. 181–200). Durham: Duke University Press.

George, M. (1997). *The Most Massive Woman Wins*. In E. Lane & N. Shengold (Eds.), *Plays for Actresses* (pp. 269–292). New York: Vintage Books.

Hartley, C. (2001). Letting ourselves go: Making room for the fat body in feminist scholarship. In J. E. Braziel & K. LeBesco (Eds.), *Bodies Out of Bounds: Fatness and Transgression* (pp. 60–73). Berkeley: University of California Press.

Klein, R. (2001). Fat beauty. In J. E. Braziel & K. LeBesco (Eds.), *Bodies Out of Bounds: Fatness and Transgression* (pp. 19–38). Berkeley: University of California Press.

LaBute, N. (2005). *Fat Pig*. New York: Faber and Faber.

LeBesco, K. (2001). Queering fat bodies/politics. In J. E. Braziel & K. LeBesco (Eds.), *Bodies Out of Bounds: Fatness and Transgression* (pp. 74–90). Berkeley: University of California Press.

Millman, M. (1981). *Such a Pretty Face: Being Fat in America*. New York: Berkley Books.

Mulvey, L. (1975). Visual pleasure and narrative cinema. *Screen 16*(3), 6–18.

Myers, A.M., & Rothblum, E.D. (2005). Coping with prejudice and discrimination based on weight. In J. L. Chin (Ed.), *The Psychology of Prejudice and Discrimination: Disability, Religion, Physique, and Other Traits*, vol. 4: *Race and Ethnicity in Psychology.* (pp. 112–134). Westport, Conn.: Praeger Publishers.

Parks, S.-L. (1997). *Venus.* New York: Theatre Communications Group.

Powers, J. R., Quinn, J., & Jans, A. (1988). *Do Black Patent Leather Shoes Really Reflect Up?* New York: S. French.

Risch, B.A. (2003). "Reforming the Fat Woman: The Narrative Encoding of Size in Contemporary Feature-Length Films." Dissertation Abstracts International, Section A: The Humanities and Social Sciences.

Shaiman, M., O'Donnell, M., Meehan, T., & Wittman, S. (2002). *Hairspray.* New York: Applause Theatre and Cinema Books.

"The White Man's Burden"

Female Sexuality, Tourist Postcards, and the Place of the Fat Woman in Early 20th-Century U.S. Culture

Amy Farrell

While doing research at the Alice Marshall Women's History Collection at Penn State, Harrisburg, I came across an entry reading "FAT WOMEN." Hoping to find information on dieting products and schemes, I had not expected such an explicit reference to my research on fat stigma. What I found were two huge notebooks that Marshall had meticulously filled with tourist postcards of fat women, dated from the 1910s through the 1940s, sent from beach destinations or national parks. Pictured on the cards are cartoon images of fat working women, of fat homemakers doing the laundry or getting dressed, of fat middle-class women traveling on trains and ships, and many, many of fat women sunbathing at the ocean.

These postcards reveal an important irony in the history of U.S. women. They mark the growth of tourism in the United States and of an increasingly mobile population, one that travels not only to follow work (which had been true for centuries) but now, with money and new opportunities, also for pleasure. Often written by women, these cards also provide evidence of the increased mobility and independence of women, particularly those who were white and middle class, enhanced by the strong feminist movement of the first decades of the century as well as the advent of car travel in the 1910s and 1920s (Scharff, 1991; Shaffer, 2001). (African American women still faced the danger and discrimination of Jim Crow laws; working-class women had less money available for leisure travel.) These cards, however, also reveal the decreased figurative and literal space available to any woman who did not toe the line of bodily control. The fat women in the postcards are all white, some middle-class consumers and tourists, some working-class or middle-class homemakers, some clearly "ethnic" and immigrant women; the images, however, mock all the women for their fatness. In other words, they demonstrate the establishment of the symbolic *place*—or rather, *no-place*—of the fat woman in the 20th century.

By the beginning of the 20th century, fatness for women became associated less with prosperity, healthful fertility, or attractive sensuality than with a body out of control. These postcards illuminate this shift in the cultural meaning of fat. Many of the postcards mock middle-class women, who have, according to these images, indulged too excessively in the growing consumer culture of both tourism and purchased goods. One shows a young fat woman on the beach, asking "Have I been places? See the labels on my trunk?" Instead of a suitcase with stickers, we see her bathing suit–clad body covered with labels, her stomach labeled "Danger Point, U.S.A.," her breasts labeled "Petter's Paradise, U.S.A.," and her round bottom marked "Lover's Seat, U.S.A." A typical saying on the postcards reads, "Travel Really 'Broadens' One"; in one, for instance, a small, dismayed man looks on as a fat woman bends over, trying to stuff herself into a too-small car. Her tiny feet accentuate the size of her bottom. The trunk is stuffed with suitcases, too full to close, suggesting that this woman both eats and buys too much. Another shows a fat woman dressed in furs and hat sitting astride a train, hanging on unsteadily. A skinny man, presumably the conductor, looks out at her with big eyes. The caption reads, "I expect you've treated yourself so well they'll have to put you on top of the train when you come home!" In another a well-dressed woman bends over, her huge bottom taking up nearly a quarter of the card. She points to a chair in a furniture store but tells the salesman, "It won't do, it's not large enough for my big sittin' room." We're supposed to laugh at the double entendre, referring both to her big buttocks and to her huge living room.

As scholars such as Hillel Schwartz (1986) and Joan Brumberg (1988) have argued in their histories of dieting, the late 19th and early 20th centuries in the United States were marked by significant cultural and social changes. As we moved from a primarily rural, farm-oriented nation to a primarily urban, consumer-oriented nation, many critics feared the loss of older habits of thrift and economy. These fears were exacerbated once again after the Depression, when new consumer options of buying on credit and spending beyond one's income became normative. It was within this context of concern over consumer excess, Schwartz and Brumberg argue, that both anorexia and the diet industries were born. Interestingly, what we see in the postcards are the ways that these fears over overconsumption were projected onto *women*. The men *looked on* but did not participate in the excess.

The work of philosopher Susan Bordo helps us to understand why the women in these postcards would be portrayed as fat and as the recipients of a judgmental and horrified male gaze. As Bordo reminds us in *Unbearable Weight* (1993), the 20th century inherited from the Enlightenment a dualistic and oppositional relationship of mind to body that continues to project the hatred of the body onto the female while associating the male with the rational. (This is not to say that men are not also concerned about their bodies or their weight, but that the force of the obsession and hatred falls particularly on women.) At the same time that females have been seen at most risk for exhibiting body and cultural excess, however, they have also, at least since the development of the cult of true womanhood in the 19th century, been expected to maintain civilization through their behavior, their clothing, and their relations with men and children. In terms of fatness, what this means is that women were considered more likely than men to exhibit "bodily excess" because their rational qualities were not sufficiently developed to control their bodies. Fatness also posed a bigger transgression for women than for men, however, because women were expected to maintain that line of civilized control.

In these postcards we see that women who did not toe this line of bodily control were presented as so comically excessive that they literally overcome the elements, blocking out the sun, stemming the tide, or causing tidal waves of their own. One shows a fat woman wearing a bathing suit at the edge of the ocean; a baby rests in the shade of her bottom as a thin male and female couple looks on. "Found a shady spot here! Take the sun a bit to get through this!" the caption reads. In another two dogs rest under the bottom of a woman bending over to pick up a beach ball. "Found the shadiest spot on the beach!" the card reads. Another features a male police officer lecturing a fat woman who lounges on the beach in her swimsuit and bathing cap: "Get up, Missus, and let the tide come in!" Certainly one can understand from these postcards that the fat female body is not supposed to enjoy the pleasures of the beach and sunbathing that were newly available to middle- and working-class Americans in the first half of the century. Moreover, they suggest that the fat female body is so gross (in both senses of the word—disgusting and huge) that it literally has the dangerous power of controlling natural forces of sun and sea. The fat female body is not welcome in *this* geographic space because it takes up too *much* geographic space.

The butt of many of the postcards' jokes—literally and figuratively—is women's voluminous buttocks. Sometimes the cards mock women's breasts or stomach, but the incessant focus is on the women's behinds. In postcard after postcard we see women bending down—to look for a shell, to do the laundry, to reach over the railing of a ship, to put on her stocking; we see the round cheeks of her bottom, often clad in some absurdly decorated and lacy undergarments. The poses of these women—bending down, buttocks on display— suggest the position of female animals in heat, who "present" themselves to interested males. More specifically, their huge buttocks are reminiscent of the early 19th-century representations of the African "Hottentot Venus," also known as Saartje Baartman. Baartman was the African woman brought to England in 1819 and exhibited in London and Paris for many years. Both physicians and the public incessantly commented on her buttocks and labia. Cartoons from the time showed men viewing Baartman from behind, with her buttocks exposed. To look or act like a "Hottentot," meant, in Anglo-American terms, that one was primitive, "Black," and overly sexual (Hall, 1997, p. 264).

The fat women in these postcards, then, not only take up too much geographic space; they also are portrayed as taking up excessive sexual space. Sometimes this overabundant sexuality seems to please the men in the postcards. Indeed, we often see the face of some amused—and presumably aroused—man spying on the woman. In a 1907 postcard, a tall thin man looks away from a fat woman who, while bending down, has split open her skirt; "This is enough to give a fellow palpitation," the caption reads. In a 1930s postcard we see a raggedy hobo sitting on railroad tracks, with a big blonde woman sitting on his lap, nearly knocking him over. "I'm on the right track—and everything is going along on schedule!" the caption reads. In one from the 1940s, we see a smiling plumber with a very large housewife sitting on his lap. "They told me to take care of the big tub in the kitchen!" the caption reads. One particularly interesting postcard shows a tropical island where a U.S. marine, grin on his face, grabbing a fat "native" girl, who looks shocked and worried: "The U.S. Marines Get Around A Lot! Leave the Heavy Work Up to Us!" In this one, the fat, the sexual, and the primitive are all clearly linked.

With the exception of the U.S. marine, whose exuberant manliness presumably excludes him from "civilized" behavior, the men in these postcards who look happy with fat women are either poor (the hobo), working class (the plumber), or silly (the comically small or thin). Most of these men in the "comic fat women" postcards look overcome by the fat women in their lives and on their laps. In one from 1909, a beleaguered man sits on a chair with a very fat, huge buttocked woman on his lap. "Our eyes have met Our lips not yet But O, You kid; I'll get You yet!" the caption reads as the woman presses forward toward the man's face. In a 1911 postcard a woman sits on a chair, her buttocks extending far beyond the edges of the seat. The man sits atop her, holding on tightly. "Just able to get around" the caption reads. In a 1930s postcard a fat woman embraces a thin balding man, who looks nervous and unhappy. "Don't worry about me. None of the guys up here can get around me," she says. Clearly this fat woman both threatens to crush the man *and* is oversexed, allowing numerous men to "try" to get their arms around her.

Medical and popular literature from the late 19th and early 20th centuries helps to make sense of the images in these postcards, particularly the ways that the fat women are portrayed as out of control and overly sexual. This literature also helps to explain why middle-class men would appear to abhor fat women, while working-class and poor men seem to enjoy them. Throughout the 19th century, political cartoons sometimes lampooned fat people, usually the "fat cat," the successful businessman or the rich politician. By the early 20th century, however, this was no longer the primary image. Indeed, by the late 19th and early 20th centuries, physicians and cultural thinkers linked "obesity" to lower levels of civilization and the primitive, and thinness to progress and civilization. In other words, thinness becomes associated with the middle class and the wealthy, whereas fatness becomes associated with the poor. These writings coincided with significant fields of study popular in the 19th century—phrenology, which classified "types" of people by their physical features; anthropology, which grouped racial and national "types" into hierarchical structures of civilization; and, finally, eugenics, the science of human breeding for "improvement." All three areas of study emerged during a period of widespread fear about the contamination threatened by the influx of immigrants to the United States and by the newly emancipated African Americans. Attempts to control the "contamination" often centered on issues of "hygiene and eugenics," particularly on matters relating to separating the "better" people from the "inferior" people (Brown, 2001, pp. 101–132).

Within the context of increased waves of immigration from Southern and Eastern Europe and migration from the South, nativist critics and health professionals argued that everything from health and fortitude to intelligence and character were inherited traits, in low supply among the immigrants and migrants, and in high supply among native-born Americans of Northern European stock. These professionals looked for signs that supposedly identified the "superior" versus the "inferior." Within this context, fatness became yet another signifier of inferiority, a line demarcating the divide between civilization and primitive cultures, whiteness and blackness, sexual restraint and sexual promiscuity, beauty and ugliness, progress and the past. In the early 20th century, an American physician, Dr. Leonard Williams, pointed to the supposed link between civilization and obesity: "It is to be admitted that there exists a settled belief among the uneducated, and even among many of the educated, that it is a man's duty to eat as much as he possibly can, in order to keep up his strength. This belief probably reaches back to the most primitive days when food was scarce and its enjoyment intermittent" (1926, p. 4). According to this theory, lower-class people harbor unconscious memories of times when worries about food supply shaped desire. According to many thinkers on fat and weight, the wealthy, the educated, the more civilized and advanced people literally had this tendency toward fatness "bred out" of them. They reasoned that "plumpness" would soon be solely a vestige of more primitive cultures. In *Girth Control*, a 1923 text published in both the United States and England, Henry Finck explains that beauty standards among the Africans, Polynesians, the Turkish, and the Aborigines of Australia valorized fatness; he described the ways that many of these cultures even encouraged their men and women to become fatter (pp. 2–3). He quickly reminds his British and American readers that "our standards of good looks are different from those of Hottentots, Moors and Turks" (p. 9). It is no surprise that Finck would use the Hottentots as examples here. Reminding his Anglo-American readers that they were not "Hottentots or Moors," but rather modern and British American citizens, Finck used fatness as a marker dividing the civilized from the primitive.

All this medical and popular literature, then, can be seen as cultural tools used to *teach* Americans to see fatness in women as a sign of primitive, out-of-control impulses. Yes, perhaps men do find fatness attractive, these discussions and images seem to note, but if the men are civilized, are middle class, are "white," then they shouldn't. Only the hobos among us would find a fat woman attractive. As Dr. Williams wrote in 1926, "Certain it is that in many savage tribes, and even among people who are by no means savage, the men prefer fat women." (p. 77). He argued, however, that "civilization" was changing men's "natural" sexual instinct. They were beginning to realize that they preferred thin women. And to accommodate this preference, he explained, women were taking part in slimming campaigns, fighting their natural—that is, primitive—"endocrinal" tendency to gain weight. As Williams approvingly noted, white women in "civilized countries" were beginning to realize (and presumably men were "learning" it too) that men preferred slim women. As Williams concluded, fat women were "repulsive sights, degrading alike to their sex and civilisation" (p. 67).

By the early 20th century, then, physicians and cultural commentators increasingly valorized the superiority of the thin body as one showing "correct" attitudes of control, both in terms of sexuality and appetites for food. According to this literature, the "thin ideal" needed to be taught to the "primitive," meaning immigrants, the working class, people of color, and women. Indeed, some of the postcards represent visually the same kind of rhetoric that the physicians were using at the turn of the century. They go beyond suggesting that middle-class men hold fat women in disdain, suggesting that it is men's responsibility to discipline fat women and their overabundant sexuality. In one of the postcards we see a big-bottomed young woman bending down to garden, her lacey underpants and stockings showing; a young man looks like he's about to paddle her with a board from the fence he's fixing. "Obey that impulse!" the postcard reads. "Come on down here and have a SMACKING good time!" In an earlier and more erudite card (from the clothing it looks like it was published in the 1910s) we see a photo of a white, well-dressed man sitting in a drawing room with a heavy woman on his lap. Under their feet is an animal skin rug, suggesting vacations to exotic locations. The caption reads, "THE WHITE MAN'S BURDEN." Evoking the title of Rudyard Kipling's 1899 poem, this postcard suggests that not only do more civilized white men abhor a fleshy and sexually exuberant woman, but also that it is his "responsibility" to tame her. In Kipling's poem, he urges the United States to bring colonial rule to the Philippines, as it is necessary for "the best ye breed" (white Americans) to control the "Folly" and "Sloth" of the Filipino people, whom he describes as heathens, "half-devil and half-child." Of course, just as the British imperialists, with whom Kipling grew up in India, enjoyed the privileges of their rule, the men in these postcards also seem to enjoy their "responsibility" to tame fat women. The first postcard promises a "smacking good time"; the second shows a man whose cheeks press into the woman's fleshy body and whose hands seem at any moment to reach for her breasts. Dr. Williams suggested in his treatises that civilized men were learning not to "enjoy" fleshy women; perhaps what they were learning instead, these postcards suggest, was to frame and express their conflicted enjoyment as a duty to discipline the "primitive."

In *Bodies Out of Bounds*, Jana Braziel and Kathleen LeBesco call for more work that "unravel[s]" the "discourses that have most intransigently defined and fixed fat bodies" (p. 1) and explores the ways that the meanings of fatness are linked to cultural ideas about race, gender, class, and sexuality (p. 12). This set of postcards from the first half of the 20th century, set in the context of the medical and popular literature from same period, begins to point to the deep historical roots of contemporary fat stigma and conflicting ideas associated with fatness. They suggest that as women gained more political and geographic freedom in the early 20th century, they were increasingly curtailed by a set of body disciplines that mocked and denigrated all those who did not seem to display proper modes of bodily control. The comic portrayal of white men both hating and longing for the enjoyments of fat women suggests a shifting culture whose conflicts are perhaps still at work, as the diet industry booms at the same time that there still exists a lively, if relatively underground, business of fat women's pornography. The body of the fat woman in these postcards represents the primitive, the excessive, the uncontrolled. We see similar representations of fat women today; indeed, recently I picked up a postcard, published in the late 1990s, that shows two white fat women, wearing bathing suits, looking out onto the ocean. The caption reads, "Having a whale of time." Like the early 20th-century postcards, this one represents fat women as animals, grotesque in size, too large to have the right to enjoy the pleasures of the beach. Like Dr. Williams, we are to understand that these fat women are a repulsive sight to women and to civilization. Such images permeate our culture. Scholars and cultural critics who study the machinations of the contemporary "obesity epidemic" and its "treatments," then, need to be cognizant of the strong historic threads that work their way through current popular discourse about fatness.

REFERENCES

Alice Marshall Women's History Collection. Pennsylvania State University, Harrisburg. Middletown, Pennsylvania.

Bordo, S. (1993). *Unbearable weight: Feminism, Western culture and the body.* Berkeley: University of California Press.

Braziel, J.E., & LeBesco, K. (Eds.). (2001). *Bodies out of bounds: Fatness and transgression.* Berkeley: University of California Press.

Brown, J. (2001). Purity and danger in colour: Notes on Germ Theory and the semantics of segregation, 1895–1915. In Gaudilliere, J.P. and Lowy, I. (Eds.), *Heredity and infection: The history of disease transmission.* New York: Routledge.

Brumberg, J.J. (1988*). Fasting girls: The history of anorexia nervosa.* New York: Penguin Books.

Finck, H. (1923). *Girth control: For womanly beauty, manly strength, health, and a long life for everybody.* New York: Harper and Brothers.

Hall, S. (1997). The spectacle of the other. In Hall, S. (Ed.), *Representation: Cultural representations and signifying practices.* London: Sage Publications.

Kipling, R. (1899). The white man's burden. *McClure's Magazine,* 4, 290–291.

Scharff, V. (1991). *Taking the wheel: Women and the coming of the motor age.* New York: Free Press.

Schwartz, H. (1986). *Never satisfied: A cultural history of diets, fantasies, and fat.* New York: Anchor Books.

Shaffer, M. (2001). *See America first: Tourism and national identity, 1880–1940.* Washington, DC: Smithsonian Institution Press.

Williams, L.L.B. (1926). *Obesity.* London: Humphrey Milford.

The Roseanne Benedict Arnolds

How Fat Women Are Betrayed by Their Celebrity Icons

Beth Bernstein and Matilda St. John

According to the latest federal guidelines, more than half the people in the United States are fat, but you would never know it by monitoring television and movie screens. Fat people—more specifically, fat women—are a majority group with few celebrities representing us in mainstream media. Housewives on Wisteria Lane may be desperate but they're not over a size 4. When given airtime, portrayals of fat women are rarely positive, often recycling hurtful and degrading stereotypes. For the fat viewer already feeling demonized for their size, it can be demoralizing never seeing anyone who resembles them portrayed as normal. To add insult to injury, many female celebrities who once picked up the torch for fat girl pride are putting it down. The Hollywood epidemic of gastric bypass surgeries is helping to fuel a string of celebrity defections from "fat and proud" to "thin and repentant."

The spectacle of Celebrity Wasting Syndrome—identified by Sondra Solovay and Marilyn Wann in Wann's 1998 book *FAT!SO?* (Wann, 1998, p. 56) as the infectious trend of celebrities losing weight as they achieve success— has gotten a hefty amount of press in recent years thanks to formerly skinny but now anorexic-looking ingénues such as Nicole Richie and Lindsay Lohan. Hysterical headlines fret, "Is Mary-Kate wasting away?" Yet the fat folks who fall victim to this syndrome don't receive the same anxious handwringing about the effects on their health, the assumption being that for them any downward shift in weight, regardless of how it was achieved, must be beneficial to their wellness.

We're living in a celebrity-obsessed culture that demands much of people who are, after all, just entertainers. For the modern celebrity, the line between personal life and professional life is blurry at best. Part of the trick of maintaining celebrity is remaining true to popular qualities while changing enough to hold the public's interest. With that in mind, we don't presume to intimate that change in itself constitutes betrayal, but rather the alignment with a marginalized group of people followed by a renouncement of that group as unhealthy and sick. The four celebrities discussed in this chapter specifically exploited their size to appeal to a perpetually underrepresented audience—fat women. Their subsequent frantic efforts to reduce their size, coupled with their pathologizing comments about weight, both negated their initial positive impact and left their fat fans feeling used, duped, and rejected.

Ricki Lake: Turncoat Turnblad

Given the scarcity of fat women in romantic leads, it was a great moment hearing, "Finally all of Baltimore knows: I'm big, blonde, and beautiful!" Fat girls everywhere thrilled to Tracy Turnblad, Ricki Lake's unforgettable character in John Waters's 1988 movie *Hairspray*: a round, rebellious teen who remained outrageously self-accepting in the face of fatphobes.

Magazine interviews with Lake continued this theme. When *Hairspray* was first released, she declared, "My plan is to redefine the fat-girl-as-heroine. I'm going to make fat fashionable again" (Svetky, 1988, p. 130). She scoffed that she wasn't "out to . . . lose 50 lbs. and be anorexic" (Allis, 1988, p. 81). Lake's upbeat presence was incredibly important; she didn't apologize for being fat and was willing to proclaim that if she got thin, it would be a sign of ill health.

Fast-forward to 1992: Lake had not had a hit in a couple of years. Suddenly, she reemerged in the press. Headlines proclaimed that she was "cutting herself down to size" (Rosen, 1992). Reporters swooned over Lake's smaller figure, and she effectively rewrote her story; from self-accepting rebel she became a miserable, unhealthy girl who had been unable to live a normal life. She whined that at her former weight she "could barely fit into a restaurant booth . . . it was hard to move. I'd walk up the stairs and be breathing heavy" (Rosen, 1992, p. 115). Even worse, Lake began giving out troubling details of how she lost weight: "I went through times when I would faint from not eating enough and working out too much" (Bandler & Ebron, 1994, p. 44). The media's response was largely positive and unquestioning, without noting that it might also be difficult to slide into a restaurant booth if one is unconscious.

Lake continued to betray her fat fan base with statements like, "I don't want to play fat girls anymore" (Rosen, 1992, p. 115). Her post–weight loss movie career includes only one leading role, the yawn-inspiring *Mrs. Winterbourne* (Benjamin, 1996). Since *Ricki Lake* (her television talk show) was cancelled in 2004, Lake's status on the celebrity food chain is in free-fall. Her sitcom pilot wasn't picked up, and the media barely covered her divorce, in which her ex-husband accused her of "ranting" as a result of weight-control drugs (Adkins, Wong, & Wren, 2004).

Just as Lake courted fat women only to betray them when her career stagnated, it appears that her "love yourself" message was also a gimmick. She stated in a 2002 interview, "I never set out to be a role model for large women. . . . My goal in life is to be loved and adored by everyone" (Sun, 2006). Her rebellious, take-that attitude gone, Ricki Lake is now too bland to resonate with an audience. For this reason, the sting of her turnabout is fleeting—we realize that the fat girl we loved had a Cyrano behind her (writer/director John Waters). We miss Tracy Turnblad, but Ricki Lake isn't worth missing.

Carnie Wilson: Poster Girl Available

Wilson, one-third of the 1990's pop group Wilson Phillips, is a formerly fat icon who has made a professional transition from fat singer to full-time weight loss advocate. The era of MTV image consciousness has brought increasingly restrictive standards for female beauty to pop music (in this world, when Mariah Carey or Beyoncé get up to a size 8 they're considered big). Fat on MTV is apparently only acceptable for male rappers (e.g., Notorious B.I.G., Bone Crusher). A girl group sporting a fat member was refreshing, even radical.

Amid snarky comments about her growing weight and music videos that highlighted the group's thinner members by concealing Wilson's body in shadows or, literally, positioning her behind a rock, Wilson found acceptance in the fat community. She gladly took on the mantle of spokesperson, appearing in size-positive publications. In 1996, she told *Radiance Magazine*: "I feel attractive, I present myself well . . . That image has been good for heavy people. I'm proud of that" (Ansfield, 1996). Wilson capitalized on this support by marketing an exercise video aimed at fat women (emphasizing the message that you can be fat, active, and healthy; see Lippman & Wilson, 1995), and in 1998 appeared at the National Association to Advance Fat Acceptance's rally, the Million Pound March.

Then, in August 1999, came the announcement that Wilson would not only be undergoing weight loss surgery (WLS), but that it would be streamed live on the internet (on a website co-owned by her manager). In interviews she now portrayed herself as unhappy and desperate: "I've been overweight since I was 4 years old and tried every weight loss method. I've struggled with it mentally and physically all these years and I've reached my limit" (Stern, 1999).

In an age of rampant fatphobia, Wilson's broadcast of her surgery is a modern-age stoning: log on and see the fat girl atone for her sin of gluttony. Three years earlier, Wilson said, "I feel like I was put on earth to help people like themselves more. I truly like myself" (Ansfield, 1996). In undertaking this drastic medical procedure, which forces a body to reduce its size (even her doctor referred to it as "induced starvation" (www.Spotlighthealth.com, 1999), it's difficult to see how Wilson is spreading a message of self-love or helping others like themselves more.

Post-surgery, Wilson devoted herself to pursuing both weight loss and publicity, advancing the message that fat is always, unequivocally, unhealthy. She doesn't portray her choices as idiosyncratic but proselytizes tirelessly: I was fat and unhealthy but I am here to save your fat soul with surgery, joyless exercise, and food restriction. Her transparent desperation for attention has found an audience of people grappling with fatphobia and weight obsession—in other words, former and future WLS patients. She brings to them the same bag of tricks that she offered the fat community; she led a 2005 Walk from Obesity (celebrating WLS) and is working on an exercise video for WLS patients (Wilson, 2005). Although she complains that she "doesn't want to be known as the gastric bypass girl" (Roberts, 2003), the creative work that originally brought her fame is now sparse at best. Even *People* magazine has referred to her as "famous weight loser Carnie Wilson" (Kelleher, 2003, p. 31).

In her book *Gut Feelings*, Wilson wrote of her stint as a fat star, "I found myself in the strange position of being an icon for a movement that I sincerely sympathized with, but that I never could really buy into for myself" (2001, p. 99). Lacking a critical analysis of cultural fatphobia, Wilson broadcasts her own oppressive beliefs as concrete, medicalized fact. Carnie Wilson's temporary stint as spokesperson speaks to the dearth of decent fat role models. She courted the fat vote because she had no other option; she might feel sorry for us but she apparently also felt disgusted to be in our midst. Once she discovered that medical science could engineer a new metabolism for her, she couldn't switch sides fast enough.

Oprah Winfrey: World's Most Powerful Yo-Yo Dieter

Ah, Oprah Winfrey: a beguiling yet relatively unhypocritical fat celebrity. Winfrey is unapologetically obsessed with her weight. She hates being fat, always has. Winfrey successfully transformed her battle with her body into a national obsession, spreading a message of self-hatred gussied up as self-empowerment and spiritual transformation. This powerful woman once proudly remarked that her ability to lose sixty-seven pounds on a liquid fast was "the single greatest achievement of my life" (People, 1991, p. 84). Never mind that she successfully broke the glass ceilings of race, class, and gender to become a bona fide media mogul—she stopped eating for four months!

It's been said that Winfrey succeeded despite being a (sometimes) fat woman of color, but we wonder if Winfrey's weight only enhances her appeal. Certainly her struggle with the scale makes her appear more human, fallible, and accessible than the average billionaire. Canny as ever, Winfrey seems to know this: "I wish I'd kept that weight off, but I do not feel like a failure. I feel like someone who has a weight problem. I feel like, oh, another 40 million Americans who are dealing with this in their lives" (People, 1991, p. 85).

After regaining the liquid-fast weight, Winfrey made small noises about accepting her lack of control over her size: "I've been dieting since 1977 and the reason I failed is that diets don't work. I tell people if you're underweight go on a diet and you'll gain everything plus more. That's why I say I will never diet again" (People, 1991, p. 82). She later attempted to make revisionist history on this statement in her 1996 diet book *Make the Connection*: "When I said that, I didn't mean I was going to give up losing weight. I just meant that I had to find something that worked. In the meantime, I was going to try to figure out how to be happy where I was" (Greene & Winfrey, 1996, pp. 18–19).

The media continues to track her ever-fluctuating weight, and Winfrey still refuses to make the cognitive connection that her body resists her efforts at dictating its size. In 2005, during a series of shows focused on weight-loss called "Oprah's Boot Camp," she wrote on her website, "With food, what works for me is treating refined and processed carbohydrates as though they are poison," and, "I still want to lose ten pounds, though, maybe 12." Incongruously, she writes in the same essay: "If I could add up the time I've spent worrying about what I ate and what I shouldn't have just eaten, feeling guilty about it, and getting down on myself about why I'm not where I want to be, it would probably be several years of my life. And you can't get those back" (Winfrey, 2005). Oprah Winfrey remains a powerful, expansive, and influential figure, yet she stands in thrall to the flummery that dieting as a lifestyle is her ticket out of body hatred and obsession. Imagine the personal and cultural transformation that could take place if Winfrey started appreciating her body as it is. Her enduring obsession with becoming physically diminutive stands out as a tragic waste of energy.

Roseanne Barr: The Mirror Has Two Faces (and a Double Chin)

Perhaps the most baffling celebrity turncoat is Roseanne Barr, who did more than anyone in Hollywood to normalize fat. Barr was everything that a Hollywood actress is not supposed to be: fat, loud, uncouth, hedonistic, unapologetic, and abrasive. No one before or since has dared to challenge so many facets of female Hollywood conformity.

Her long-running television show, *Rosanne* (Williams, 1988), centered around the lives of a fat couple, but their weight was, amazingly enough, never the punch line. When Barr spoke about fat in interviews, she went beyond the rhetoric of self-acceptance to a feminist analysis of fat. This was the first time that such statements were widely published, and the public reactions were strong on both sides of the issue.

In 1994, about the same time that she published a fat-positive autobiography (Barr, 1994), chinks began to appear in her fat-is-cool armor. Suddenly, Barr began to assert that fat (hers and everyone else's) was a symptom of pathology (in particular, childhood sexual abuse): "[Diets are] big ripoffs that exploit people in pain. Being fat is a symptom of a deeper psychological problem. . . . Overeating is just a way of protecting yourself from the pain of the truth. My weight loss is a symbol of me getting better" (Rosen et al., 1992, p. 74). Barr's insistence that fatness created safety was mystifying given that she would be the first to tell you how much it made her a target.

In mid-1998, around the time that her short-lived talk show went on the air, Barr quietly had elective weight-loss surgery. Sitting with an interviewer after having had her stomach reduced to the size of a fig, Barr was still vocal in her support of fat women: "We're done with the skinny little victim girl thing. We love fat chicks on our show. A lot of the chicks watching are fat, too" (Brown, 1998). Barr's betrayal hurts because she made an informed critique of the diet industry and continues to use her influence to support the fat community but cannot tolerate living in a marginalized body herself. That a cultural icon famous for standing her ground, however far it stood outside the mainstream, would make the choice to surgically alter her body to fit the iron maiden of Hollywood standards is the ultimate comment on the power of internalized fat oppression.

Post–weight loss, Barr is struggling to connect with an audience. She may be trying to play all sides, but the net effect is bizarre and disconcerting. We want to ask the real Roseanne Barr to please stand up, but we're a little afraid which one it would be.

Fat in the New Millennium: Prisoners of the "War on Obesity"

In this age of celebrity-as-spectacle and a government-sponsored war on obesity, Celebrity Wasting Syndrome is being played out in increasingly bizarre ways. A new wave of fatsploitation films has arrived (e.g. *Shallow Hal*, Farrelly & Farrelly, 2001; *Big Momma's House*, Gossnell, 2000): portrayals that ostensibly provide fat women with representation but in reality simply recycle damaging stereotypes (the big earth mother, the glutton, the funny fat girl who's everyone's best friend and no one's girlfriend, etc.). When a cheap laugh is called for, thin stars are happy to jump into fat suits and do a little dance, except now it's waddle n' gorge instead of shuck n' jive.

For a nanosecond, we thought that Kirstie Alley might have something interesting to say about becoming fat. When she finally spoke, however, she highlighted the compulsive overeating that led to her change in size, furthering the image of the lazy fat woman sitting on the couch eating an entire pie. Her television show *Fat Actress* (Alley & Brewster, 2005) had not even yet debuted when she began throatily accosting us with, "Hey! You're fat too!" in Jenny Craig commercials (Jenny Craig, 2005). The show, ostensibly a skewering of Hollywood's body obsession, was instead an uncomfortably clumsy and crass semi-improv fiasco showcasing Alley's vanity, racism, and desperation. The series lasted seven episodes and, having reinforced pretty much every negative stereotype about fat people, Alley crossed the border back into the land of the non-fat.

Star Jones Reynolds, who previously embraced her amplitude because, well, it was hers, remains coy about the "medical intervention" (Jones Reynolds, 2006, p. 80) that caused her body to deflate like a balloon after a birthday party. Anna Nicole Smith was another big gal that the new millennium offered us, storming the runway in her panties for Lane Bryant in 2002. She had a history of breaking size barriers in modeling, so imagine our chagrin when her reality show debuted (Ewing, Hayes, & McDermott, 2002). We tuned in ready to see a hot big girl and what we got was more insight than we ever wanted into how truly low-functioning she is: pouting, burbling, and rubbing up on things like a pornographic Baby Huey. Sweet Jesus, we thought, is this who's left? Must we loop Camryn Manheim's triumphant "This is for all the fat girls!" yell (from her 1998 Emmy acceptance speech) to remember what having a positive role model felt like?

How responsible should celebrities be to the people whose dollars and adoration give them the power and fame they seek? How much should we need Kathy Bates or Mo'Nique or Queen Latifah to stay thick and stay cool? Although we agree that it's not in their job description to be advocates for us, fat women in Hollywood are nevertheless such anomalies that, as tokens, whatever they say is conspicuous and amplified. When they act foolishly or make statements about weight, those of us who look anything like them are implicated by association. We know that ultimately the righteous fat-girl icon who provides us with inspiration and courage will have to be found in the mirror, but it's hard to resist falling for someone who models in public the wherewithal that's difficult to marshal in such a hostile environment.

Given that 95% of dieters regain their lost weight in one to five years (Grodstein, Levine, Spencer, Colditz, & Stampfer, 1996), we'll most likely be seeing more of these celebrities. Some degree of schadenfreude on our part is understandable should their hated fat return, because their herculean efforts to publicly distance themselves from us (both in body and ideology) revealed how disposable we are to them. Don't expect to see us holding "Welcome Back!" signs if and when they return to planet plush.

Rebound is a bitch, ladies.

REFERENCES

Adkins, G., Wong, M., & Wren, J. (December 6, 2004) Ricki's Sour Split. *People Weekly*, v62 n23 p22.

Alley, K., & Brewster, S. (Producers). (2005) Fat Actress [Television Series]. United States: Showtime.

Allis, T. (April 4, 1988). Not to be Taken Lightly, Ricki Lake Bounces Out of Hairspray with Body and Shine. *People Weekly*, v29 n13 pp81–82.

Ansfield, A. (Summer 1996). Meet Carnie Wilson: An Intimate Portrait. *Radiance Magazine*, v47, retrieved on July 23, 2006, from http://www.radiancemagazine.com/issues/1996/carnie.html.

Bandler, M., & Ebron, A. (June 28, 1994) How Ricki Lake Lost Over 100 Lbs. *Family Circle*, v107 n8 pp44–45.

Barr, R. (1994). My Lives. New York: Ballantine Books.

Benjamin, R. (Director). (1996). Mrs. Winterbourne [Motion Picture]. United States: TriStar Pictures.

Brown, C. (September 21, 1998). "Done With the Skinny Girl Thing": Putting Comedy Aside, Roseanne Tries Talk. *Newsweek,* v132 n12 p93.

Ewing, D., Hayes, K., & McDermott, M. (Producers). (2002). The Anna Nicole Show [Television Series]. United States: E! Entertainment Television.

Farrelly, B., & Farrelly, P. (Directors). (2001). Shallow Hal [Motion Picture]. United States: Conundrum Entertainment/Farrelly Brothers Productions/Shallow Hal Filmproduktion GmbH & Co. KG.

Gossnell, R. (Director). (2000). Big Momma's House [Motion Picture]. United States: 20th Century Fox/Regency Enterprises.

Greene, B., & Winfrey, O. (1996). Make the Connection: Ten Steps to a Better Body and a Better Life. New York: Hyperion Books.

Grodstein, F., Levine, R., Spencer, T., Colditz, G.A., & Stampfer, M.J. (1996). Three-Year Follow-Up of Participants in a Commercial Weight Loss Program: Can You Keep It Off? *Archives of Internal Medicine* 156 (12), 1302.

Jenny Craig Inc. (2005). Kirstie Alley Spokesperson Debut [Television Commercial].

Jones Reynolds, S. (January 16, 2006). Star Lite! With a New Book, a New Body and a Fab Guy, Star Jones Reynolds has Every Reason to Shine. *People Weekly*, v65 n2, p80.

Kelleher, T. (July 7, 2003). "Pics & Pans" (Review of television series *Fame*). *People Weekly*, v60 n1 p31.

Lippman, I., & Wilson, C. (1995). Great Changes [Exercise Video].

People Weekly (January 14, 1991). Big Gain, No Pain (Oprah Winfrey's Weight). *People Weekly*, v35 n1 pp82–84.

Roberts, D. (May 30, 2003). A Whole New Her: After Dropping 150 Pounds, Carnie Wilson is Taking on New Challenges. Retrieved on July 8, 2003, from http://www.abcnews.go.com/2020/story?id=123707.

Rosen, M. (November 16, 1992). Cutting Herself Down to Size. *People Weekly*, v38 n20 pp115–118.

Rosen, M., Gold, T., Stambler, L., McFarland, S., Huzinec, M., & Sporkin, E. (January 13, 1992). Hollywood Takes It Off. *People Weekly*, v37 n1 p72.

Stern, H. (November 17, 1999, original air date). The Howard Stern Show [Radio Series], episode 671.

Sun, L. (2006). [Biography for Ricki Lake.] Retrieved from on July 23, 2006,from http://www.imdb.com/name/nm0001442/bio.

Svetky, B. (December 1988). Lively, Loveable Ricki Lake. *Cosmopolitan*, v205 n6 p130.

Wann, M. (1998). FAT!SO?: Because You Don't Have to Apologize for Your Size. Berkeley: Ten Speed Press.

Waters, J. (Writer/Director). (1988). Hairspray [Motion Picture]. United States: New Line Cinema.

Williams, M. (Creator). (1988–1997). Roseanne [Television Series]. United States: ABC Television.

Wilson, C. (2001). Gut Feelings: From Fear and Despair to Health and Hope. Carlsbad, CA: Hay House.

Wilson, C. (January 4, 2005). Entry on Lite and Hope website. Retrieved on March 21, 2006, from http://www.liteandhope.com/carnie_wilson.php.

Winfrey, O. (2005). Oprah Makes the Commitment: From Oprah's Boot Camp. Retrieved on July 23, 2006, from http://www.oprah.com/article/health/commit_oprah/1.

www.spotlighthealth.com. (1999). Retrieved on May 23, 2000, from http://www.spotlighthealth.com.

‖‖‖

Jiggle in My Walk
The Iconic Power of the "Big Butt" in American Pop Culture

Wendy A. Burns-Ardolino

In 1978 the British rock band Queen proclaimed "Fat bottomed girls you make the rockin' world go round." This move to reappropriate the negative stereotypes of women's big butts and to revalue them as desirable, however, is conflicted and may be co-opted by the fluidity of cultural signs and meanings flowing freely in American popular culture. The image of the big butt continues to be a site of contestation in popular culture, as evidenced in music, fashion, and beauty cultures. Only thirteen years after Sir Mix-A-Lot argued, "So *Cosmo* says you're fat, well I ain't down with that" (1992), the Black Eyed Peas beg the question, "What you gon' do with all that junk, all that junk inside that trunk?" (2005). Not dissimilarly, advertising campaigns echo the multiple and mixed messages concerning the big butt. A 2006 Nike advertisement states, "My butt is big and that's just fine and those who might scorn it are invited to kiss it. Just do it." An advertisement for Sunsilk hair products, however, heralds the return of big hair and small derrieres with advertising copy that reads, "I wish my hair could borrow volume from my butt" (Sunsilk-Unilever 2006). These cultural signs, images, and representations signify the conflicted meanings of the big butt in American popular culture.

Although some may simply claim that women with big butts should either live their lives on the margins of society or get with the "ideal body" program and diet and exercise their behinds into submission, many women see this logic as problematic. In her seminal text *Fat Is a Feminist Issue*, Susie Orbach argues for the radical right of women to love their bodies whatever their shape or size. Orbach maintains: "For a woman to take pride in her body for herself, rather than as an instrument or as an object, is a radical act. For women to proclaim that comfort and pride at whatever size they may be creates a chink in the armor of a patriarchal order. Taking this stance is difficult and hard to do on our own. But as more women reject the stereotype of driven slimness and exhibit a pleasure in women's physical variety, individual women can draw on that collective strength to build acceptance and confidence" (1997, p. 206). When I read Orbach's mantra for the first time, I felt empowered to experience my body as a capacity for action rather than an object to be scrutinized. As I have read around in the fields of feminist theory, cultural studies, and body studies,

I have found more and more evidence to support the significance of this action as a radical act. Susan Bordo's *Unbearable Weight* (1993) supports Orbach's claim that women's bodies are the site of cultural battle for power, privilege, and dominance. Bordo notes, "As our bodily ideals have become firmer and more contained (we worship not merely slenderness but flablessness), any softness or bulge comes to be seen as unsightly—as disgusting, disorderly 'fat' which must be 'eliminated' or 'busted,' as popular exercise-equipment ads put it" (p. 57). The desire to be flabless, to eliminate our fat, is a manufactured desire.

This desire has been produced by a dominant culture that espouses Eurocentric body ideals—one can neither be "too rich or too thin." Hence it is not surprising that the desire to be thin, to eliminate fat, is a culturally produced desire—one that is attached to social class, race, and gender. The messages that circulate in popular culture in the form of privileged ideal bodies and denigrated fat bodies reinforce and codify the boundaries of desirable bodies. Angharad Valdivia discusses how class is signified by women's bodies in "The Secret of My Desire: Gender, Class, and Sexuality in Lingerie Catalogs." Valdivia compares the class significations evidenced by the postures, poses, and positioning of women's bodies in the catalogs of Frederick's of Hollywood and Victoria's Secret. She notes, "No study of women and advertising, especially one overlapping with the study of lingerie catalogs, would be complete without consideration of what has come to be known as 'the culture of slenderness.' It is nearly impossible not to notice that women as represented in popular culture have gotten thinner and thinner" (1997, p. 227). Further, Valdivia points out the significance of the class component of this thin ideal and suggests that fatness has come to be coded as a sign of lower class. She concludes, "This has implications in terms of appearance, with the result being that fat is a component of working-class representation, with Archie Bunker and Roseanne being the two most mentioned examples" (1997, p. 228).

Certainly the idea that fatness is a signifier of the working class is not revolutionary; it is important, however, to recognize the way that the female big butt becomes at once a symbol of empowerment and an object of ridicule as it is racialized, sexualized, and classified. This paradox is exemplified by the polyvalent meanings of Jennifer Lopez and Beyoncé Knowles—two pop culture icons known for their bootyliciousness (Destiny's Child, 2001). In *Black Sexual Politics: African Americans, Gender, and the New Racism*, Patricia Hill Collins argues that although bootyliciousness may be used as a selling point for JLo and Beyoncé, the sexualized spectacles of their commodified bodies give shape to racism, sexism, class exploitation, and heterosexism (2005, p. 27). Hence, Collins explains that even as these iconic women move in the circles of ideal beauty, the significations of their butts are co-opted by the hypersexualized image of the exotic other.

Magdalena Barrera's "Hottentot 2000: Jennifer Lopez and Her Butt" references a social class argument made by Laura Kipnis in her well-known critique of *Hustler* magazine titled "(Male) Desire and (Female) Disgust: Reading *Hustler*" (Barrera, 2002; Kipnis, 1992). This is most significant because Barrera brings race and class together in a critical analysis of the political power of the big butt. It is worth noting that race and class arguments are rarely aligned in a critique of dominant culture's representations of women's bodies, although clearly their convergence makes a stronger case against the interlocking systems of oppression named by bell hooks "white supremacist capitalist patriarchy" (1992a, p. 22). In this case, Barrera incorporates Kipnis's points about class into an argument concerning these interlocking systems of oppression. Kipnis argues that *Hustler*'s representations of women's bodies are transgressive in terms of social class and fly in the face of the classical body ideal. Kipnis states: "The very highness of high culture is structured through the obsessive banishment of the low, and through the labor of suppressing the grotesque body (which is, in fact, simply the material body, gross as that can be) in favor of what Bakhtin refers to as 'the classical body.' This classical body—a refined, orifice-less, laminated surface—is homologous to the forms of official high culture which legitimate their authority by reference to the values—the highness—inherent in this classical body" (1992, p. 376). Hence, Kipnis locates a space in popular culture, albeit in *Hustler*, for critiquing the ideal/classical/high (women's) body of the dominant culture.

Barrera takes Kipnis's analysis a step further, however, and articulates how race and class converge at the transgressive location of Jennifer Lopez's big butt. Barrera explains, "In Latino communities—especially Caribbean ones—butts are 'huge' both in terms of size and popularity. *Hustler* is not unique in highlighting the 'lower bodily stratum' as a sight of contestation—Latinos self-consciously do this on a daily basis" (2002, p. 409). In this way Barrera describes how Lopez's big butt—signifying race and class, Puerto Rican/Nuyorican (Guzman & Valdivia, 2004, p. 216), and working class—transgressively moves against Eurocentric/Anglo body ideals of thinness. A 2002 study of body size, body image, and self-esteem performed by Margaret Snooks and Sharon Hall support the notion that size and beauty standards vary according to ethnicity (2002, p. 465). This study reinforces the notion that the ethnic other is transgressive precisely because it stands outside of the dominant cultural norms, in this case the beauty standards for the size and shape of women's butts.

Barrera does not argue that this transgressive signification is fixed or absolute; rather, she concedes that the stereotype of the hypersexual Latina interferes with the transgressive impact of Lopez's big butt on the dominant culture. In fact, as the title of Barrera's article, "Hottentot 2000," suggests, Lopez maintains an affinity with Saartjie Baartman, who was dubbed the Hottentot Venus by settlers of South Africa and subjected to extreme racist objectification through exhibitions of her naked body on tour throughout Europe in the 1800s (Barrera, 2002, p. 410; Beltrán, 2002, p. 81; hooks, 1992b, p. 63; Willis & Williams, 2002, p. 59). Similarly, Mary Beltrán's "The Hollywood Latina Body as Site of Social Struggle: Media Constructions of Stardom and Jennifer Lopez's 'Cross-Over Butt'" argues that Lopez is the modern day equivalent of the Hottentot Venus (2002, p. 83). Although Barrera points out the difference between the conditions of objectification for Baartman, whose voice is silenced, and Lopez, who is heard, Barrera notes, "Lopez shares with Baartman the fact that no one needs to mention race, precisely because their butts are shorthand for 'otherness'" (2002, p. 408). Hence, the big butt immediately signifies otherness.

In spite of this seemingly simple system of symbolic othering where big butt equals other, it is important to recognize the complex system of classifying that continues to operate on the bodies of women with big butts. In "Brain, Brow, and Booty: Latina Iconicity in U.S. Popular Culture," Isabel Molina Guzman and Angharad Valdivia interrogate the classifying system of JLo's butt specifically, and Latina rear ends in general, within the signifying systems of racialization, sexualization, and exoticization. Guzman and Valdivia declare, "Recently popular representations of Latina booties as large, aberrant yet sexy, desirable and consumable contribute to the reification of racial dichotomies where Latinas occupy that in between space between the White booty (or the pre-adolescent invisible androgynous White booty) and the Black booty whose excess falls beyond the boundary of acceptability and desirability within U.S. popular culture" (2004, p. 218). In this way the Latina booty fits into a continuum where race, class, and gender are always already classed. In "Jennifer's Butt," film critic Frances Negrón-Mutaner simultaneously situates representations of the large, round, female Puerto Rican *culo* within an Afro-Caribbean context of humor and as a challenge to Anglo standards of beauty (1997, p. 189). Although the shape and size of the big butt logically make it stand out against the "ideal body" of dominant culture, the classifying components of racialization, sexualization, and exoticization may in fact co-opt the transgressive power of the big butt. Mary Beltrán argues that Lopez and her butt are precariously positioned between a transgressive symbol of alternate power and a co-opted representation of the exotic other (2002, p. 80).

This othering of the big booty, big butt, big *culo*, illustrates what critical race theorists have been saying for years—that race is classed. Patricia Hill Collins articulates the significance of this system of classification under the conditions of globalization. She notes: "Whites and Blacks thus represent two ends of a racial continuum, with one end populated by un-raced White *individuals*, and the other occupied by an intensely raced Black *group*. Latinos, Asians, and racial/ethnic immigrant groups jockey for a place between these two poles, forced to position themselves between the social meanings attached to White and Black—in this case, the beneficial treatment afforded individuals and the discrimination and stigma attached to Blacks as a derogated racial group" (2006, p. 179). This classification system of othering is articulated in the introduction to Sir Mix-A-Lot's rap song "Baby Got Back," where two Valley girls are talking: "Oh my god Becky, look at her butt. It's so big. She looks like one of those rap guy's girlfriends. Who understands those rap guys. They only talk to her because she looks like a total prostitute. I mean her butt. It's just so big. I can't believe it's so round. It's just out there. I mean, it's gross" (1992). The derogated object of the big butt stands in for all women with big butts—or does it? The last line of the introduction to "Baby Got Back" is, "Look, she's just so black" (1992), but I have never heard it played this way on the radio; it is always censored. This last line offends on a level that the rest of the introduction does not. The other lines of the introduction discuss the roundness (read fatness) of the big butt and the fetishism of the big butt in the context of the rapper's desire for a woman with a "healthy, juicy, double." The big butt is hypersexualized, but nonetheless desirable. The introduction to "Baby Got Back" is an articulation of the dominant culture's marginalization of the "other." The song itself is written against this "othering," but it is interesting that it takes a man's desire for the fatness of the big butt and all of its significations to bring women's big butts to the center of the discourse.

Certainly the line, "They only talk to her because she looks like a total prostitute," blurs the boundary between sexual empowerment and sexual objectification. The mention of prostitution is suggestive of class warfare; the Valley girls "other" the woman with a big butt by equating her with a tramp, a whore, a nymphomaniac, a hypersexualized other. These Valley girls suggest that the big butt signifies lower class in the form of looseness, wantonness, intense sexuality, and prostitution (as in "ass for cash"). Eric Hyman discusses the relationship between the ass and sexuality in an article from the *Journal of Popular Culture* titled "The Nonliteral, Non-gluteal, Semi-referential, Off-standard, Synecdochic, Supermetonymic, Paradoxical, Existential, Ever-lovin *Ass*" (1992). He states: "Most significant of all is that a woman's ass is one of the most important signals of sexual potential, if not availability—the human visual equivalent of other animals' olfactory pheromones. The ass's convexity gives it prominence; at least equally important is that this culture exploits that convexity to assign the ass a prominent sexual signaling function" (p. 207). Hence, the Valley girls and the dominant culture might assume that the more convex, the more round, the more protruding a woman's butt is, the more hypersexualized she becomes.

The assumption of hypersexuality is indeed problematic, but the last line of the introduction demonstrates pure racism. The white Valley girls are fearful, disgusted, and intimidated by the power of the racialized other. This last line underscores the classification of othering that goes beyond the shorthand of "big butt = other." The stigma of the big butt shares a metonymic relationship with the most intensely othered group. The big butt stands as the extremely raced, hypersexualized, and classified "other."

Guzman and Valdivia further critique this system of classification as it operates within a global economy of colonization, racialization, and exoticization. They note, "For this booty economy to retain its value, popular culture representations must continue to construct that mythical brown race that falls somewhere between Whiteness and Blackness and elides the dynamic hybridity of Latinidad that spans across the entire racial spectrum" (2004, p. 218). Although Guzman and Valdivia suggest that hybridity provides something of a way out for JLo and her big butt, Barrera concludes that Lopez has in fact become fetishized to the extent that she has become devoid of her own meaning and filled with the dominant culture's desire for the mythical, spicy, exotic other (2002, p. 416). In fact, American popular culture thrives on the consumption of this exotic other. bell hooks describes this process of commodification in her landmark essay "Eating the Other" (1992a), in which she explains, "Masses of young people dissatisfied by U.S. imperialism, unemployment, lack of economic opportunity, afflicted by the postmodern malaise of alienation, no sense of grounding, no redemptive identity, can be manipulated by cultural strategies that offer Otherness as appeasement, particularly through commodification" (p. 25). Although it is clear that hooks is referencing a racial other, it is not a stretch to apply this theory of eating the other to the consumption and commodification of the hypersexualized other, the lower-class other (as in slumming), or the big-butted other. Fetishism is not new, but its proliferation under the conditions of globalization has been intensified. Barrera sees Lopez's success as a product of intense fetishism, but warns us that the fetishism of JLo and her butt does not equal fetishism of all women with big butts. She notes, "How wonderful for Jennifer that she is shaking her booty all the way to the bank, but we must wonder how comforting this is for those Latina and Black women who are told that they are just plain old 'fat'" (2002, p. 416).

Female big butts, however, are not just plain old fat. There is the potential for transgression and resistance in the wiggle and jiggle of a woman's big butt. Erin Aubry describes the poetry in motion of her big butt in her essay, "The Butt: Its Politics, Its Profanity, Its Power" (2000), from the *Body Outlaws* anthology. Aubry writes,

> It was tricky, but I absorbed the better aspects of the butt stereotypes, especially the Tootsie-Roll walk—the wave, the undulation in spite of itself, the leisurely antithesis of the spring in the step. I liked the walk and how it defied that silly runway gait, with the hips thrust too far forward and the arms dangling back in the empty air. That is a pure apology for butts, a literal bending over backward to admonish the body for any bit of unruliness. Having a butt is more than unruly it's immoral—the modern-day equivalent of a woman eating a Ding Dong in public. (p. 28)

Aubry explains how she learned to appropriate the stereotypes of the big butt and use them to her advantage in her walk and her way of being in the world. She learns how to take up space, how to sit, stand, and lean with her hand on her hip in demonstrations of the physical power and prowess of her big butt. She comments early in the essay, "Every day, my butt wears me" (2000, p. 22). Her butt may wear her, but she manages it—no, she works it. Aubry transgresses the dominant culture's body ideals by boldly living in her body, by rolling with her butt. I read Aubry as a model for Orbach's radical act of empowerment, resistance, and transgression by taking pride in her body for herself.

Aubry notes that she finds some affirmation for this empowerment in popular music that celebrates women's big butts (2000, p. 30). Aubry's list includes "Baby Got Back," "Doin Da Butt," and "Rump Shaker," but music has celebrated women's big butts for years. A song titled "Big Fat Woman," originally recorded in 1938 by Blind Boy Fuller as "Meat Shakin' Woman," has been recorded more than twenty times and released more than forty times. The most recent rendition was recorded by Jerry Garcia for a group called Mother McCree's Uptown Jug Champions in 1998. While the writing credits are frequently given to Leadbelly, a blues singer, the song predates him (Grateful Dead Discography, 2006). The first verse of the song reads:

> I got a big fat woman, grease shakin' on her bone
> I say, hey, hey meat shakin' on her bone
> An' every time she shakes some man done left his home. (Blind Boy Fuller, 2001)

The fact that the song was re-recorded and re-released suggests its power, but clearly the woman in the song is desired, and indeed revered, for the shakin' of her meat— the jiggle of her flesh.

Seldom does the female big butt stand alone, however, without male desire. In Nike's 2006 "My Butt" advertising campaign, the copy reads:

> My Butt is big and round like the letter C
> And ten thousand lunges
> Have made it rounder
> But not smaller
> And that's just fine
> It's a space heater
> For my side of the bed
> It's my ambassador
> To those who walk behind me
> It's a border collie
> That herds skinny women
> Away from the best deals
> At clothing sales
> My butt is big
> And that's just fine
> And those who might scorn it
> Are invited to kiss it. Just do it.

In the advertisement, a woman's big, round butt stands alone. Valdivia (1997) would certainly critique it for its use of body cropping for it does objectify a woman's butt. It objectifies the female big butt in a powerful way, however, showing it as a symbol of pride, not something that should be hidden away. The round, protruding butt signifies beauty, power, poise, and physical strength. I have heard men comment that the text is too aggressive, that it puts them on edge, and that it is offensive to skinny women. I keep a copy of it on my office door, and I hope that it keeps the faint-hearted away. I sometimes read it like a mantra: "My butt is big and that's just fine and those who might scorn it are invited to kiss it." The ad does not rely on male desire to empower it. I cannot say whether it will sell a lot of Lycra sportswear for Nike, but it brings me hope.

I listen to pop music. I hear the Black Eyed Peas sing, "My hump, my hump, my lovely lady lumps . . . What you gon' do with all that junk? All that junk inside that trunk?" The answer in the song is, "I'ma get, get, get, get you drunk, get you love drunk off my hump." My answer is different. My answer is that the female big butt has been imbued with a cultural power, much of it reliant on the discourses of racialization, sexualization, and exoticization. The female big butt has been forced to carry the historical burdens of race, class, gender, and ethnicity. It has been down-trodden by interlocking systems of oppression that have sought to erase its meaning, its power, and its beauty, or at least to parse them away from their owners—those of us who wear big butts. Although the ridicule, stigma, hurt, and hate that have been projected onto the female big butt throughout the history of white supremacist capitalist patriarchy still surface in music, fashion, and beauty cultures, there are signs that beauty standards are opening up a bit—at least enough to let JLo and Beyoncé in. Although the rest of us who know we are not Beyoncé and JLo are still marginalized by beauty standards that tell us that we are just plain old fat, we can take our big butts out for a Tootsie Roll walk and explore our own curves, dips, and rolls knowing that there are plenty of us out here, struggling to resist the dominant culture's body ideals.

REFERENCES

Aubry, E.J. (2000). The butt: Its politics, its profanity, its power. In O. Edut (Ed.), *Body Outlaws: Young Women Write About Body Image and Identity*. Seattle: Seal Press.

Beltrán, M.C. (2002). The Hollywood Latina body as site of social struggle: Media constructions of stardom and Jennifer Lopez's cross-over butt. *Quarterly Review of Film and Video, 19*, 71–86.

Barrera, M. (2002). Hottentot 2000: Jennifer Lopez and her butt. In K. Phillips & B. Reay (Ed.), *Sexualities in History: A Reader*. New York: Routledge.

Bordo, S. (1993). *Unbearable Weight: Feminism, Western Culture, and the Body*. Berkeley: University of California Press.

Collins, P.H. (2005) *Black Sexual Politics: African Americans, Gender, and the New Racism*. New York: Routledge.

Collins, P.H. (2006). *From Black Power to Hip Hop: Racism, Nationalism, and Feminism*. Philadelphia: Temple University Press.

Grateful Dead Discography (October 23, 2006). *Big Fat Woman*. http://www.deaddisc.com/songs/Big_Fat_Woman.htm.

Guzman, I., & Valdivia, A.N. (2004). Brain, brow, and booty: Latina iconicity in U.S. popular culture. *The Communication Review, 7*, 205–221.

hooks, b. (1992a). Eating the other: Desire and resistance. In b. hooks (Ed.), *Black Looks: Race and Representation*. Boston: South End Press.

hooks, b. (1992b). Selling hot pussy: Representations of black female sexuality in the cultural marketplace. In b. hooks (Ed.), *Black Looks: Race and Representation*. Boston: South End Press.

Hyman, E. (1992) The nonliteral, non-gluteal, semi-referential, off-standard, synecdochic, supermetonymic, paradoxical, existential, ever-lovin *Ass. Journal of Popular Culture, 26*, 203–209.

Kipnis, L. (1992). (Male) desire and (female) disgust: Reading *Hustler*. In L. Grossberg, C. Nelson, & P. Treichler (Ed.), *Cultural Studies*. New York: Routledge.

Negron-Mutaner, F. (1997). Jennifer's butt. *Aztlán, 22*, 189.

Orbach, S. (1997). *Fat Is a Feminist Issue*. New York: Galahad Books.

Snooks, M.K. & Hall, S.K. (2002). Relationship of body size, body image, and self-esteem in African American, European American, and Mexican American middle-class women. *Health Care for Women International, 23*, 460–466.

Valdivia, A.N. (1997). The secret of my desire: Gender, class, and sexuality in lingerie catalogs. In K. Frith (Ed.), *Undressing the Ad: Reading Culture in Advertising*. New York: Peter Lang.

Willis, D., & Williams, C. (2002). *The Black Female Body: A Photographic History*. Philadelphia: Temple University Press.

ADVERTISEMENTS

Nike. (2006). My Butt. Advertisement. Online. http://commercial-archive.com/ooh/nike-gets-real-ads-women.

Sunsilk-Unilever. (September 2006) I wish my hair could borrow volume from my butt. Advertisement. *In Style*, 444.

MUSIC REFERENCES

Black Eyed Peas. (2005). My humps. *Monkey Business*. San Diego: A&M Records.

Blind Boy Fuller. (2001/1938). Meat shakin' woman. *The Essential* (original recording remastered). Atlanta: Classic Blues.

Destiny's Child. (2001). Bootylicious. *Survivor*. New York: Sony Records.

Mother McCree's Uptown jug champions. (1964). Big Fat Woman. *Mother McCree's Uptown Jug Champions*. Palo Alto, CA: Warner Bros.

Sir Mix-A-Lot. (1992). Baby got back. *Mack Daddy*. New York: Warner Bros.

Queen. (1978). Fat bottomed girls. *Jazz*. London: EMI, Elektra.

Seeing Through the Layers

Fat Suits and Thin Bodies in
The Nutty Professor *and* Shallow Hal

Katharina R. Mendoza

In November 2001, audiences flocked to theaters to see actress Gwyneth Paltrow's famously thin figure encased in a latex and foam fat costume in the romantic comedy *Shallow Hal*. Once novel, the fat suit is now just a regular part of the U.S. entertainment industry's repertoire of special effects. Calling this phenomenon the "new minstrel show," *Bitch* magazine writer Marisa Meltzer observes, "Fat people are now America's favorite celluloid punchlines" (2002, p. 19). The steadily growing list of film and television actors who have suited up in fake fat stretches from "Weird Al" Yankovic parodying Michael Jackson in the music video for "Fat" (1988) to John Travolta's sadly un-Divine Edna Turnblad in *Hairspray* (2007); from Courtney Cox in *Friends* (1995) to the entire cast of the sitcom *My Wife and Kids* (2001).

Hollywood's preoccupation with creating fat bodies for the big screen seems incongruous in a cultural climate that values thinness and feeds a billion-dollar weight loss industry. Drawing on drag, camp, and blackface, LeBesco has theorized the disruptive potential of fat suit performances. Just as drag can denaturalize essentialist gender identities, "the power and possibility of fat drag, it seems, comes in denaturalizing the thin 'original' body of the actor" (2005, p. 233). As yet this disruptive potential remains largely unrealized, and LeBesco, like other critics, finds that "whatever critical consciousness might emerge in the form of a 'size prejudice is bad' vibe of a *Shallow Hal* or *The Nutty Professor* ultimately finds itself sacrificed for cheap laughs at the expense of fat people" (2005, p. 237). Obviously there is more to the fat suit phenomenon than simply making mock, and so I extend reading fat suit performances to the narrative arcs that contain them, which I find undermine that potential critical consciousness in ways more insidious than cheap fat jokes. As cultural objects that create a visibility for transgressive bodies that only seems anomalous, fat suits in film are demonstrative and constitutive of normative discourses on fatness and weight loss.

This is particularly evident in the films *Shallow Hal* and Eddie Murphy's 1996 remake of *The Nutty Professor*, which I have singled out not because they use fat suits, but because they are movies that use fat suits to tell stories. Both films feature protagonists who are fat in their diegetic worlds; therefore "disguise" narratives, like Martin Lawrence's *Big Momma* movies (2000, 2006), or even films like Tyler Perry's *Diary of a Mad Black Woman* (2005), where the fat suit is used to enhance Perry's black matriarch drag, are outside the scope of this analysis. Meltzer (2002) points out that in many fat suit films the simple fact of a character's size passes for comedy—though I must point out that, on occasion, a film does require more, such as when *The Nutty Professor*'s Klump family members perform great feats of flatulence. But any discussion about the role of fatness in contemporary American culture is also a discussion about weight loss. By looking at how the fat suit is deployed in the service of a narrative—and not just to make a fat joke—we can see how such films are just the latest manifestations of the "inside every fat person is a thin person" trope so often found in weight loss discourse.

As in countless diet and exercise product advertisements featuring "before" and "after" photos, in most fat suit films the fat body does not appear by itself: its presence is always contingent on and shaped by the presence of its corresponding thin body. The fat suit enables a disorienting representation of a single character who either simultaneously inhabits two bodies at opposite ends of the size spectrum, as in *Shallow Hal*, or instantaneously morphs from one body into the other and then back again, as in *The Nutty Professor*. These coexistent bodies are presented as having an unequal relationship with each other in which the thin body, not surprisingly, dominates. These two films can be considered unusual in that they both feature fat romantic leads whose happy endings do not ultimately depend on makeovers or diets, as do so many "ugly duckling" narratives. This does not, however, prevent *Shallow Hal* and *The Nutty Professor* from enacting fantasies of weight loss: instantaneous and effortless in the former, fraught and effortful in the latter. Upon closer examination, the recuperation of fat characters in these films hinges on the presence of their thin personas—on the literal, diegetic, narrative demonstration that inside all that fat there is indeed a thin person just waiting to get out.

Rosemary

Shallow Hal, a modern-day parable about inner beauty, features Hal Larson (Jack Black), a great guy in every way, with one exception: he judges women on their looks and spends his time pursuing shallow relationships with "perfect 10s." But self-help guru Tony Robbins (playing himself) mystically alters Hal's perception so that he sees only "inner beauty." Hal then meets and falls in love with Rosemary Shanahan (Gwyneth Paltrow), with whom he has his first genuine relationship. Hal has no clue that the blonde bombshell he sees is only a fraction of her actual self. The audience, however, is in on the joke, having caught a glimpse of Rosemary in all her hefty glory, shopping for parachute-sized underwear. But Rosie, we are told, is a wonderful person, and the film literally depicts her inner beauty as Paltrow sans fat suit. For a time, the lovers enjoy each other, blissfully unaware that they each have very different ideas of what Rosie looks like. But eventually Hal's hypnosis lifts and causes a crisis in their relationship. Of course, true love wins in the end: Hal sees Rosemary's true form and realizes he still loves her, and they drive off into the sunset.

Surely the *fiction* of fat is a large part of what draws audiences to the box office. Images of fat are everywhere, from weight loss advertisements to humorous greeting cards, but the "obese" woman in *Shallow Hal* is unique because we know that somewhere inside that costume is Paltrow, size 0. LeBesco proposes that this knowledge, the awareness of a "safe distance" between actress Paltrow and character Rosie, *reassures* audiences that Paltrow is "in no danger of a slide into obesity" (2005, p. 238). Or could it be that moviegoers are paying for the fulfillment of a revenge fantasy, for the privilege of seeing a celebrity's idealized body buried, even temporarily, under folds of abject fat—in short, the opportunity to laugh at what is usually desired? Whether the audience gets satisfaction or relief at the juxtaposition of real Paltrow and fat suit Paltrow, the film itself contains a curious subtext of fantastical weight loss in which it is the illusory thin body that achieves the status of the real.

The plot seems promising enough at first glance; Rosemary neither apologizes for her size nor tries to change it. Unlike Sherman Klump's metamorphosis into Buddy Love, which I will discuss later, Rosemary does not literally become thin. Rather, Skinny Rosemary exists only in Hal's altered perception; what he "sees" is the physical embodiment of her inner beauty. Even so, the distinction between Fat Rosemary and Skinny Rosemary—Meltzer's nicknames for the character—is an important one. The film's central conflict is Hal's shallow nature, not Rosemary's fatness, but according to convention, her girth takes her out of the running as a valid love interest. Hal's infatuation with Skinny Rosie is therefore a necessary step toward true love and a happy ending for Hal and *Fat* Rosie. When, at film's end, Hal says to her, "You're beautiful," the audience is (mis)led to believe that Shallow Hal is shallow no more.

There is actually very little of Fat Rosie to be seen in this film; because Paltrow appears without the fat suit for most of it, the crux of the joke is that this apparently skinny girl affects the world around her with 350 pounds of force. We are invited to laugh as Skinny Rosie cannonballs into a swimming pool, causing a near tsunami. In this scene, a full body shot of a smiling, bikini-clad Skinny Rosie is preceded by visuals of a Fat Rosie shown only from the belly down; as she walks to the end of the diving board, the audience is invited to ponder the ample rolls spilling over her bikini bottom and the thighs bulging out from beneath it. It is Skinny Rosie, however, who executes the dive, her slight body breaking the surface of the water with a splash worthy of Shamu the killer whale. Skinny Rosie also breaks furniture on a regular basis; apparently, no chair is safe under her. As Skinny Rosie consumes mountains of nachos, pitchers of milkshakes, and giant wedges of cake, Hal watches in awe and asks, "Where does she put it all?" The audience, privy to Rosie's true girth, knows where.

Fat Rosie, when she *is* present, haunts her skinny self like a specter; the large reflection she casts walking by a plate glass window belies the slim woman that Hal sees. But as the film's conceit of "inner beauty" demands, Rosemary has to be made up of more than just her fat. By Hal's own account, she is "beautiful, caring, funny, intelligent"; kind to children and homeless people, she volunteers at the local hospital in between Peace Corps assignments. The film frames these nuances of character, however, as belonging more to Skinny Rosie than to Fat Rosie; it is the former whom the audience sees walking and talking, doing good deeds, and interacting with the other characters. The film *does* intermittently remind the audience of Fat Rosie's existence, but she is not a person in the sense that Skinny Rosie is; she is only pieces of a fat body, made available to viewers mostly in chopped up, fetishized chunks. The film indulges in numerous close-ups of cellulite-rippled arms, thighs, and buttocks, but it is not until after Hal's hypnosis is lifted that the audience ever sees Fat Rosie's face.

By the end of the film, all the nuances of character—even those behaviors coded as "fat"—have been vacated from Fat Rosie and assigned to her thin self; Fat Rosie has become superfluous. Broken into pieces, fat is removed from her body in an illusion of detachable weight; it is almost as if we were cracking open a false outer shell, revealing a whole, thin body fully invested with personality, movement, and agency, unburdened by fat. The film's happy ending is therefore suspect: if Hal had not been under the "inner beauty" hypnosis when he first met Rosie, he would never have fallen in love with her. One of the main issues in the film is whether Hal can—or should—love a fat woman. To Hal's best friend, Mauricio, such a thing would be a disaster; mainstream films typically do not place a fat woman in romantic and sexual contexts without turning it into a joke. There are moments in *Shallow Hal* when Fat Rosie approaches female romantic lead status; she may be large, but she's well-groomed and wears feminine clothing such as high heels and pretty skirts—no sweatpants or muumuus for this fat girl. As her relationship with Hal progresses, Rosie (both Fat and Skinny) starts wearing sexier clothes, appearing in a midriff top and short shorts, even a bikini. The film pulls back, however, at the last moment: the fat body is tellingly absent from the lighthearted striptease scene in which Skinny Rosie, and only Skinny Rosie, peels off a purple negligee set. The audience, we can only assume, heaves a collective sigh of relief at being spared the sight of Fat Rosie's naked body. Ultimately, the film's supposed endorsement of Rosemary as a valid love interest hinges on the thin, inner, real self inside her fat body.

The New Blackface?

In her article "Hollywood's Big New Minstrel Show," Meltzer compares fat suits to the blackface performances of the not-too-distant U.S. past. She opens the piece with an invocation of minstrelsy and closes with a description of the white actors in blackface shown in the end credits of Spike Lee's 2000 film *Bamboozled*, predicting, "Someday you'll see footage of Oscar winners Julia Roberts and Gwyneth Paltrow trundling along in their fat suits, and it'll be depressing and pathetic, but it won't be funny" (2002, p. 20).

Though not analogous, the politics of performance of blackface do resonate and, in the case of *The Nutty Professor*, intersect with the new fake fat. Eric Lott describes the central dynamic of this 19th-century theatrical practice as one of desire and disgust, "a dramatic spectacle based on an overriding investment in the body" (1993, p. 6). In Lott's analysis, the minstrel show functioned as a carnivalesque space that authorized the visibility of the black body, a space occupied by white working-class men who took on black bodies and accents to mock the emerging bourgeoisie class. Lott sees blackface as a site that mediated between black and white, the visible sign of the attraction and threat between the two, a "mixed erotic economy of celebration and exploitation" (1993, p. 6). Michael Rogin, on the other hand, cautions against such a celebratory reading and points out how the blackface mask was "grotesque, demeaning, [and] animalistic" (1996, p. 37). In minstrelsy, Rogin continues, the color line "was permeable in only one direction. Blackface took hold in the North, where blacks were free, not because it challenged racial subordination but because it replaced African American performance" (1997, p. 37). Although the desire/disgust dynamic described by Lott and Rogin can arguably be found in representations of most any marginalized group, what is interesting about the fat-body-as-grotesque is its potential, literalized by the fat *suit*, to become the thin body that it opposes and threatens. The composite body of actor and prosthetic costume represents the fat body in a way that exposes the interaction between desire and disgust while also driving home the point that only normative bodies are allowed to cross the boundary dividing fat and thin—as Sherman Klump discovers when he tries to cross over into thinness.

Sherman

In this remake of the 1963 Jerry Lewis classic, Sherman Klump is a fat, lonely chemistry professor whose life's work, both in and out of the lab, is the pursuit of thinness. Unable to diet, exercise, or Mega Shake his fat away, Sherman concocts a neon-blue DNA-restructuring potion that, when ingested, causes instantaneous—but temporary—weight loss. Sherman drinks the formula and loses half his girth, gaining a new body and a new persona, whom he names Buddy Love. Buddy is everything that Sherman isn't: confident, assertive, sexual, and, most important, thin. Ecstatic at first, Sherman soon realizes that his potion may be working a little too well—Buddy's elevated testosterone levels make him increasingly aggressive and difficult to control, and his destructive antics threaten to destroy Sherman's career and love life. As the film comes to its climax, Buddy tries to do away with Sherman himself, and a visually spectacular showdown ensues, with each persona battling for control over a single body. It's a close fight, but Sherman eventually emerges the victor; a fat man once again, he says, "I guess I'll just have to accept myself for who I am."

It is the sigh of resignation, the "I *guess*," that is the clearest sign that this is not, as Eddie Murphy said it would be, a film about "society's unfairness toward fat people" (Witt, 1999, p. 146). This is, rather, a tale about a fat man who has defined himself by his failure to be thin, and whose final, grudging self-acceptance is not sparked by any sort of epiphany, but rather by default—by the repeated demonstration of the biological inevitability of his fatness and the futility of trying to change his body. Sherman is doomed to fail from the very beginning, as we can tell by the way that he is marked, visually and verbally, as a fat man; he is introduced to the audience not as a whole person but as a jumble of fat body parts. The film opens with exercise guru Lance

Perkins on a television screen, punching and kicking his way through the Village People's "Macho Man"; from here, the camera pans to an anonymous round belly. Throughout this scene, the camera moves back and forth between full-body shots of Perkins and screen-filling close-ups of a fat belly, arms, and buttocks. From the outset, Sherman's ponderous, slow-moving body is presented in stark contrast to the frenetic Perkins, who periodically screeches to his exercise class, "Inside every one of you is a thin person just waiting to get out!" This first scene sets the tone for the rest of the film; long before the audience ever sees Sherman's smiling face, they have already explored the length and breadth of his substantial frame. Just in case anyone missed the point, Sherman marks himself as a fat man, perhaps sabotaging the very love interest that eventually pushes him to drastic weight loss measures; when he first meets the lovely Carla Purty (Jada Pinkett), a smitten Sherman stammers, "Why thank you—I'm fatter . . . I mean, I'm flattered!" Later, Buddy Love continues the fat-naming frenzy. Describing the weight loss potion to prospective financier Harlan Hartley, Buddy uses several hapless restaurant patrons as visual aids. In a flurry of "Jell-O arms," "turkey neck," "tank ass," and "saddlebag syndrome," he enumerates the undesirable body parts that the formula promises to banish. Sherman, far from being spared from this barrage, is its main victim; throughout the film Buddy taunts him with "fatso," "chunky butt," and "lard ass." That Buddy treats his long-suffering fat self so harshly makes either no sense or complete sense: given the amount of energy, time, and resources that Sherman has devoted to the pursuit of thinness, it is perhaps only logical that the normative body he finally achieves should retain the memory of the intense self-abjection through which it was produced.

Although Buddy seems the obvious counterpart to Sherman, the latter's identity as a fat man is actually defined by *two* thin characters. Before the arrival of Buddy Love, Sherman's self-definition is dependent on the image of Lance Perkins. To Sherman, the Caucasian Perkins represents the means to achieving a normative (thin, white) body; Perkins' image pervades Sherman's home not only by way of his almost-constant presence on the television but also via his smiling face on the labels of Sherman's cans of Lance Perkins Mega Shake and stacks of Lance Perkins Frozen Dinners. It soon becomes apparent, however, that nothing works; thwarted at every turn by ice cream, M&Ms, and his mother's fried chicken, Sherman is not a buff-body-in-the-making, but rather a fat failure. Turning to pseudo-scientific discourses about fatness, Sherman concocts his miraculous DNA-altering potion. Fat Sherman becomes a thing of the past, and Buddy Love the body of the present. But weight loss through DNA restructuring is no magic bullet—Sherman gets the thin body he desires, but only for a few hours at a time. Still, it's enough time for Buddy to begin plotting Sherman's permanent extermination. Note that the initial object of Sherman's aspirations, the white, effeminate Lance Perkins, has been replaced by the reality of the black, hypersexual Buddy Love. As the physical manifestation of all the ideologies about fatness that drive Sherman to transform himself, it makes narrative sense that Buddy's persona grows increasingly more unstable and destructive the longer he exists, and that when he turns his attentions to Sherman's love interest, Carla, she rejects his aggressive advances. Left to his own devices, Buddy could very well self-destruct; therefore, to preserve at least some semblance of an existence, the fat man must put down the thin usurper who is trying to take over his body, his career, and his woman. As underdogs often do in Hollywood, Sherman destroys Buddy and emerges as the authentic, victorious self. But in killing Buddy, has Sherman really managed to rid himself of the destructive ideologies about fatness that created Buddy in the first place? Sherman's coming to terms with himself is a consolation prize—"I *guess* I'll just have to accept myself for who I am"—an acceptance that hinges on a thin self who was more trouble than he was worth.

In *Professor*, fatness and weight loss are overtly raced and sexualized. Eddie Murphy stars in this film several times over: without the fat suit he is Buddy Love, and with the help of prosthetics and makeup effects, Murphy also plays Sherman, Papa, Mama, Grandma, and Eddie Klump. Witt finds that folded into this fat suit fest is a story about black gay male self-acceptance. By her account, Sherman is a man "caught between competing desires: for normative, public black heterosexuality, on the one hand, and for non-normative, closeted white orality, on the other" (1999, p. 146). Pointing to various clues in the film, Witt asserts that the fat, gluttonous Sherman represents white homosexuality, whereas the suave, svelte Buddy Love stands for virile black male heterosexuality, a difference that is driven home when Klump's white lab assistant, Jason (whom Witt positions as a potential love interest for the closeted professor), observes, "[Buddy's] testosterone levels were right off the charts. . . . He was so unlike you" (146).

The fat suit operates here as a link between black male homosexuality and black maternity; Sherman's breasts, belly, and ass echo those of his mother and symbolize her castrating love. Besides providing this literal point of contact between Sherman and Mama Klump, prosthetics and computer effects also make possible the film's climactic battle, in which Sherman and Buddy wrestle for control over one body. Throughout the film, and most extensively in this scene, the threat of mammification is literally visited on the virile black body: as the DNA-altering potion wears off, bits and pieces of fat Sherman disrupt Buddy's streamlined figure. Witt asserts, "The victory of Klump's breasts, ass, and belly over Love's crotch implies that sooner or later the truth of the maternal black body will out, at the expense of virile black masculinity" (p. 148). In a further twist, Witt wonders if it is actually Buddy who is eventually "outed" as the true homosexual in the film, which ends with the heterosexual pairing of Sherman and Carla Purty. This seems somewhat of a stretch, but in raising the possibility of Buddy's homosexuality Witt reminds me of another character: Murphy's often overlooked role as the Richard Simmons–esque Lance Perkins. Murphy plays not one but two exercise queens in this movie, and even as he literalizes the connection between Sherman and Mama Klump via the fat suit, he also concretizes, through whiteface, the link between the spandexed, aerobicized Buddy and the more obviously flaming white fitness guru/motivational speaker. Finally, it is interesting that both Lance Perkins and Buddy Love have size-normative bodies but exhibit nonnormative sexual behaviors. Sherman may inhabit a transgressively fat body, but he exhibits "correct" (hetero)sexual behaviors, in contrast to Lance's effeminacy and Buddy's overly aggressive sexuality. Though Sherman's fat body wins out in the end, it is bordered by these two thin men. On one side is Lance Perkins, the object of his aspirations; on the other, Buddy Love, the sculpted, hyper-phallic body that he momentarily got to touch but ultimately could not keep.

Inside Every Fat Person . . .

Before *Shallow Hal* was released in theaters, its producers and stars were very vocal about the film's message that inner beauty trumps outward appearance (Miller, 2001). Meanwhile, *The Nutty Professor*'s claim to progressiveness was that Murphy had agreed to star in the film on the condition that the film address society's ill treatment of the very fat (Witt, 1999), as when Sherman Klump morphs into Buddy Love, or when Skinny Rosemary Shanahan casts a fat reflection in a shop window. Even *Shallow Hal* bears this out, as Hal's acceptance of and love for Fat Rosie is enabled by his having already fallen for Skinny Rosie—who, according to the logic of the film, is Rosie's inner, and therefore real, self.

It is no coincidence that fat suits have become part of the entertainment repertoire at a time when people are experimenting with ever more aggressive and potentially dangerous weight loss protocols. Although the act of putting a thin actor in a fat suit in itself reinforces the unequal relationship between fat and thin, attention must also be paid to how these films' narrative trajectories defuse the disruptive potential of fat suit performance. Transforming a thin actor into a fat character is an investment involving hi-tech special effects and many hours in the makeup trailer. Significantly, this arduous behind-the-scenes process allows instantaneous on-screen transformations that effectively erase the effort and time that assumedly separates "Before" and "After." The point is not so much to create an authentic-looking fat person, but to create the convincing illusion of weight loss or weight gain; whatever happiness a fat character may have is always already contingent on the presence of her corresponding thinner self. Although fat suits are currently used in ways that exacerbate, rather than ameliorate, the problem of size prejudice, it is my hope that a better understanding of the dynamics at work in films like *Shallow Hal* and *The Nutty Professor* can help the size positive community as we work to reclaim our representations.

REFERENCES

Farrelly, P., & Farrelly, B. (Producers/Directors). (2001). *Shallow Hal* [Motion Picture]. United States: 20th Century Fox.

Grazer, B. (Producer), & Shadyac, T. (Director). (1996). *The Nutty Professor* [Motion Picture]. United States: Universal Pictures.

LeBesco, K. (2005). Situating fat suits: Blackface, drag, and the politics of performance. *Women and Performance*, 15:2, 231–242.

Lott, E. (1993*). Love and Theft: Blackface Minstrelsy and the American Working Class*. New York: Oxford University Press.

Meltzer, M. (2002). Hollywood's big new minstrel show. *Bitch: Feminist Response to Pop Culture*, 15, 19–20.

Miller, P. (2001, November Interview with Gwyneth Paltrow. *NY Rock*. Retrieved March 6, 2009, from http://www.nyrock.com/interviews/2001/paltrow_int.asp.

Rogin, M. (1996). *Blackface, White Noise: Jewish Immigrants in the Hollywood Melting Pot*. Berkeley: University of California Press.

Witt, D. (1999). *Black Hunger: Food and Politics of U.S. Identity*. New York: Oxford University Press.

Controlling the Body
Media Representations, Body Size, and Self-Discipline

Dina Giovanelli and Stephen Ostertag

We've all been in social settings where we've felt compelled to look and act certain ways. We might pause to ask why we feel this need to present ourselves in specific ways. The concept of panopticism provides one answer to this question. Panopticism refers to surveillance and social control where people alter their behavior because they feel as if others are constantly observing and judging them. With panopticism, power saturates the self and invades every minutia of existence. Initially, the term "panopticon" referred to either crime or sexuality (Foucault, 1977, 1978). More recently, it has evolved to encompass the mass media (Bartky, 1988; Ewen, 1988). We argue that "panopticism" has become so pervasive in contemporary societies that the mass media now engage in the surveillance and control of women's bodies.

We treat television as panopticon and examine fat female depictions. We focus specifically on women because the media panopticon is infused with patriarchal beliefs, and therefore women learn to see and judge themselves through men's eyes and according to men's criteria (Mulvey, 1975; Walter, 1995). We ask these questions because we are concerned with television's panoptic power and its implications for women's self-control. With this chapter we offer a small contribution to this complex relationship.

Media Representations and the Cosmetic Panopticon

Self-discipline and control through time and space reflect subjectivities thoroughly infused with patriarchy, where women's bodies confer a status in a hierarchy not of their own making; this hierarchy requires constant body surveillance and maintenance, often taking form in self-disciplining practices. Such control requires docile bodies (Foucault, 1977) and cannot be maintained without the internalization of patriarchy, saturating the soul through unremitting surveillance. The media contribute to women's self-control and self-discipline by serving as a panopticon (Bartky, 1988; Ewen, 1988), specifically a cosmetic panopticon (Gauchet, 2006). As a cosmetic panopticon, the media induce a state of permanent surveillance and judgment around concerns of physical appearance and standards of "beauty." Women's clothing, hair, body size, and movements are all shrouded in meaningful discourses and interpretive suggestions. Viewers are simultaneously reminded that violating expectations of physical appearance, perhaps by being fat and female, will be recognized and subject to gossip and discrimination. As such, the media tap daily into millions of women's sense of self and warn them of the horrors suffered by those who stray from established definitions of femininity.

Disciplining the Body

The construction of being "appropriately" female transgresses the physical body and incorporates other markers such as personality and movement. Accordingly, a woman must be smaller than a man, demure, and take up little space (Bartky, 1988). Fat women are, then, the antithesis of what it means to be appropriately feminine. Bartky (1988, p. 71) explains that women discipline themselves and their bodies to create what she terms "the ideal feminine body-subject," where control is directed at the body in the areas of time (through constant surveillance) and space (through women monitoring the space that their physical bodies occupy), and is practiced through diet, exercise, posture, and movement. Women are constantly reminded of "appropriate" looks and style, which are then expressed in self-evaluations, behavior, and self-control directed at diminishing size and restricting movement.

Although women may, and indeed do, work to resist social expectations, the cosmetic panopticon pressures all women to participate in creating the "ideal feminine body-subject." Women who refuse run the risk of being rejected by others and may develop a sense of shame and insecurity resulting in various formal and informal repercussions that pressure them to change their behavior. This is especially true for fat women, who frequently develop a sense of self-loathing as a direct reaction to their internalized social expectations and pressures (Goode, 1996). The ultimate result is that the demands on the body become so ingrained in the socialization process that women become, to themselves, their own jailers (Bordo, 2003, p. 63).

Creating the Docile Body: Symbolic Annihilation

The media's contribution to our understanding of the social world through representations happens in two distinct ways: the first is concerned with quantity and the second with quality. The quantitative focus pertains to frequency and asks *how often* social groups are represented in the media; the qualitative focus asks, When social groups are represented in the media, *how are they portrayed*? Therefore, the media serves to expose or conceal various social groups, serving an "out of sight, out of mind" function and equating to their numerical symbolic annihilation (Gerbner & Gross, 1976; Gross, 2001; Tuchman, 1978). The media also help inform our "public radar" by suggesting how viewers should interpret and understand media representations by providing the discourses (e.g., portrayals, stereotypes, and stigmas) within which they are represented. In both situations the media serve as a cosmetic panopticon by suggesting both the value of women's body size in the United States and how viewers are to feel and act according to body size. Women do indeed resist and reject these discourses, yet their ubiquitous and incessant nature creates an unyielding tide against which women must constantly swim.

Method

To investigate the symbolic annihilation of fat women, we conducted a content analysis of primetime programming (between 8:00 p.m. and 10:00 p.m., Monday through Saturday, and 7:00 p.m. to 10:00 p.m. on Sunday) on the major television networks (ABC, CBS, NBC, and Fox), during one week in March and October 2005. We concerned ourselves only with news programming, dramas, and sitcoms that have consistent fat female characters, which we defined according to our own subjective interpretations; we did not include sporting events. Programs that had fat females as "guest characters," like ABC's *Wife Swap*, were not included in our study. In our March 2005 pilot study, we assigned a sequential number for each half hour time slot of prime-time programming (hour-long programs were assigned two numbers, one for each half hour time slot) during our sample week (N = 30). We then used the internet site http://www.randomizer.org to sample 20 percent of prime-time television programming. Our sample yielded one program with a reoccurring fat female character, Katrina on Fox's *Stacked*. In October 2005 we subsequently sampled 100 percent of prime-time programming for our sample week, which yielded a second fat female television character, Berta on CBS's *Two and a Half Men*. By October 2005, Fox's *Stacked* had been removed from prime time. We then downloaded five episodes of *Stacked* and recorded five episodes of *Two and a Half Men* for further, in-depth analysis. Five episodes equates to approximately one month of programming, which we reasoned would provide enough data to generalize about the programs. We ground our discussion of fat female characters and media representations based on a careful examination of these two programs.

Findings

Of the two programs in our sample with fat female characters (Conchata Ferrell's character Berta on CBS's comedy *Two and a Half Men*, and Marissa Jaret Winokur's character Katrina from Fox's comedy *Stacked*), we found that their representations often revolved around sexuality and emphasized appearance (e.g., clothing) and behavior (e.g., dating and relationship interaction, and dialogue with other characters).

Two and a Half Men is a prime-time television sitcom that airs on CBS. According to the program's website, the characters include Charlie (Charlie Sheen), Charlie's brother, Alan (Jon Cryer), Alan's son, Jake (Angus T. Jones), Charlie and Alan's mother (Evelyn Harper), Alan's ex-wife (Judith Harper), Charlie and Alan's neighbor

Rose, Charlie's ex-girlfriend later turned Alan's wife, Kandi, and finally their fat female housekeeper, Berta (Conchata Ferrell).

Episodes of *Two and a Half Men* often began with Charlie courting a young, thin, and sexually attractive female, and with Alan, representing the moral conscience of the family, making comments about Charlie's behavior and the women he encounters. They both use Jake as a means for making various adult jokes, often revolving around sex in some form. Each episode is set up to imply that Charlie is having sex with a female guest character, who is always a thin woman and often wears revealing, sexually suggestive clothing.

Berta is a tough, no-frills woman with a "trucker's" mouth, exemplified in statements like, "What the hell happened to you?" (episode: *Hi, Mr. Horned One*), and "I hope you like the smell of pine-scented puke" (episode: *Something Salted and Twisted*). As a housekeeper, Berta often wears a grey or brown vest with a long-sleeve shirt, blue jeans, and work boots; she does not wear makeup, and has flat, straight, brown hair, all of which serve to illustrate her blue-collar persona. Berta's voice is powerful, deep, and loud rather than soft and sensual, and her movements are direct and lumbering rather than elegant and graceful. While in Berta's presence, Charlie and Alan often speak openly about their sexual desires, penises, and hormones. Berta's involvement in these discussions often includes supporting Charlie's sexual adventures and serves to reinforce his sexual appetite and desires. In fact, even female guest characters participate in this sexual activity and dialogue. Berta, however, never speaks of her own sexuality and romantic interests, and she says nothing to imply that she is sexually active or even interested. Overall, in a program seeped with sexual intimations and discourses, Berta's character lacks sexual desire and appetite.

Fox's *Stacked*, starring Pamela Anderson (a well-known sexual icon), is a sitcom involving five characters who either work at or frequent a local bookstore. Anderson's character, Skylar, joins Marissa Jaret Winokur's character, Katrina, as the two main female characters on the series. Skylar and Katrina work alongside two brothers, Stewart (Brian Scolaro) and Gavin (Elon Gold), who own the bookstore where most episodes take place. Finally, Harold, played by Christopher Lloyd, is a retired rocket scientist and the store's sole steady customer.

The physical differences between Skylar and Katrina are dramatic and easily observable. Katrina is the antithesis of Skylar: Skylar is tall and thin, with long legs and large breasts, whereas Katrina is dumpy, short, and dowdy. Additionally, Skylar's hair is long, wavy, full-bodied, and platinum blonde, whereas Katrina's hair is shorter, dark, and frizzy. Skylar wears revealing short skirts, high-heeled shoes, and low-cut tops; in fact, nearly everything she wears hugs her body and accentuates her sexuality. Katrina's style of dress, however, is more modest and conservative. Additionally, Skylar speaks with a soft effeminate voice, whereas Katrina's voice is loud and raspy. Most worthy of noting is that Skylar's nipples are often evident under her clothing, and when her low-cut tops are coupled with push-up bras, Skylar's cleavage becomes an important focal point of her character. Skylar's sex appeal is constantly promoted and reinforced through sexual innuendo and interaction with other characters. Katrina's sexuality, however, is often denigrated through those very same avenues.

Appearance aside, both women differ with respect to their romantic encounters and leisure activities. Skylar constantly references the dates that she's been on and the often wealthy, attractive, and successful men with whom she socializes. Katrina, on the other hand, is rarely portrayed as having any romantic interests, and when she does, it is done in a degrading and embarrassing way. For example, in the episode *Crazy Ray*, Katrina shows romantic interest in an unstable, homeless, and mentally ill person named "Crazy Ray," with whom she exchanges phone numbers. Eventually Katrina realizes that Crazy Ray is not going to call her and she expresses sadness and dejection. Katrina's desire for a relationship with Crazy Ray portrays her as romantically and sexually desperate enough to want attention from someone whom the other characters have vocally judged as flawed. Furthermore, Crazy Ray's refusal to call Katrina exemplifies him as the person who's rejecting her, demonstrating Katrina as the less valuable person in the interaction.

Additionally, other characters often make jokes about Skylar's sexual escapades, which include references to Skylar's high level of sexual expertise and her experiences as a "home wrecker." Furthermore, in the episode titled *The Two Faces of Eve*, Skylar is shown pulling hair during a fight with her female friend Eve, and the men on the show asserted that they found this behavior to be sexy and arousing. When Katrina engaged in the same behavior with Stewart during the same episode, however, the male characters framed the event as a turnoff and unappealing. These comments reinforce Skylar's position as a sexual being, whereas the absence of such comments and the presence of degrading comments directed toward Katrina reinforce her character as sexually and romantically undesirable and stigmatized.

The existence of only two fat female characters (Berta and Katrina), as well as their performances and personas, suggests that fat female television characters are both numerically annihilated (in that the major networks cast only two fat female characters for their prime-time television programming) and qualitatively annihilated (in that their characters' performances and persona are devoid of any sexual and romantic desirability or interest). In two programs saturated with sexual references and innuendos, Berta's character evades any suggestions that she is even interested in sex, let alone that she is sexually stimulating, and Katrina's lack of sexual and romantic desirability serves to reinforce and validate Skylar's dominant sexuality. Both women are denied their sexuality and at times are romantically humiliated in front of millions of viewers each week. We must now ask what these findings imply about the ways in which people perceive fat women, and how fat women perceive themselves.

The Fat Female and the Cosmetic Panopticon

Media representations are a major source of information about society, the world, and its inhabitants (Hall, 1979). As an institution that shapes and reflects values, norms, expectations, perceptions, and emotions, television functions as both a panopticon and a disciplining agent. It is upon these images that viewers actively develop "subjectivities" and understandings of one another (Hall, 1979). It is also upon these images that viewers ground their behavior and self-control.

Our sample of prime-time television suggests that fat female television characters are symbolically annihilated, both quantitatively and qualitatively: quantitatively in that they are present in only 1.7% of prime-time television viewing hours, despite the fact that fat women make up over 33% of the adult female population in the United States (Centers for Disease Control, 2006); and qualitatively because for those fat female characters that do exist, they are often romantically ignored or treated as sexually unappealing by surrounding characters. The few fat female television characters that do exist are consistently depicted in relation to thinner, highly sexualized female characters. In fact, fat women on prime-time television are used as props against which thinner women are compared, judged, and valued.

Stigma, Stigma Management, and Self-Control

Fat women's symbolic annihilation on television speaks to the media as cosmetic panopticon through its ability to pass judgment, stigmatize, and pressure people to manage their identity (Goffman, 1963; Goode, 1996). The cosmetic panopticon reflects a hierarchy of patriarchy, socially constructed so that simply being female is stigmatized and advances certain self-discipline practices (Bartky, 1988), and being a fat female is morally reprehensible and reason for extreme forms of body control. One of the most extreme forms can be seen in how people control their consumption. Such is the case for risky health behaviors like eating disorders (e.g., anorexia nervosa and bulimia) and the overuse of laxatives. The National Institute of Mental Health (2001) defines eating disorders as "serious disturbances in eating behavior, such as extreme and unhealthy reduction of food intake or severe overeating, as well as feelings of distress or extreme concern about body shape or weight." Exact estimates of the number of people with eating disorders are difficult to establish, but some suggest upward of eleven million people, with a ratio of women to men at ten to one (Anorexia Nervosa and Associated Disorders, 2006; National Eating Disorders Association, 2006). Recent trends, however, show that about 20–30% of younger people diagnosed with anorexia are males (Anorexia Nervosa and Associated Disorders, 2006).

These dangerous health behaviors often reflect cosmetic concerns like body image and are grounded on assumptions and expectations of being judged by others. In fact, a 2000 article in *Eating Disorders Review* (House Bill Aim to Raise Eating Disorders Awareness, 2000) reports that 42% of first- through third-grade girls and 81% of ten-year-old children think they are too fat. These numbers are even more startling given that people often begin to develop eating disorders during puberty and adolescence, perhaps partly explaining why a national study of college students found that almost 20% of them admitted to having an eating disorder, with most never seeking treatment (National Eating Disorders Association, 2006).

Eating disorders are often caused by, and symptomatic of, a number of interrelated psychological and social factors, and they pose numerous health risks, including cardiac failure, multiple organ dysfunctions, cardiovascular problems, abnormal adolescent development, and muscular atrophy (Anorexia Nervosa and Associated Disorders, 2006). We believe that the cosmetic panopticon is partly responsible for the roughly eleven million people diagnosed with eating disorders. Fat female television representations reflect a hierarchy of patriarchy that suggests to viewers how females should look and act if they wish to be viewed positively. Females who stray will be stigmatized, scorned, and constantly pressured and coerced to adhere to specific body expectations. For many women, achieving such body expectations requires exercising extreme control over their emotional, psychological, and physical self. The media as cosmetic panopticon likely contributes to this hierarchy of patriarchy through fat women's numerical and qualitative symbolic annihilation.

REFERENCES

Anorexia Nervosa and Associated Disorders. (2006). *General Information*. Retrieved November 11, 2006, from http://www.anad.org/22385/22406.html.

Bartky, S. L. (1988). Foucault, Femininity, and the Modernization of Patriarchal Power. In R. Weitz (Ed.), *The Politics of Women's Bodies: Sexuality, Appearance, and Behavior*. New York: Oxford University Press.

Bordo, S. (2003). *Unbearable Weight: Feminism, Western Culture, and the Body*. Los Angeles: University of California Press.

Centers for Disease Control and Prevention. (2006). Retrieved May 22, 2006, from http://www.cdc.gov/women/pubs/overwght.htm.

Ewen, S. (1988). *All Consuming Images: The Politics of Style in Contemporary Culture*. New York: Basic Books.

Foucault, M. (1977). *Discipline and Punish: The Birth of the Prison*. New York: Vintage Books.

Foucault, M. (1978). *The History of Sexuality: An Introduction*. New York: Vintage Books.

Gauchet, Gordon. (2006). Cosmetic Panopticon: Consumption and the Normative Gaze. Unpublished Manuscript. University of Connecticut.

Gerbner, G., & L. Gross. (1976). Living with Television: The Violence Profile. *Journal of Communication*. 26(2), 173–199.

Goffman, E. (1963). *Stigma: Notes on the Management of Spoiled Identity*. New York: Simon and Schuster.

Goode, E. (1996). The Stigma of Obesity. In Erich Goode (Ed.), *Social Deviance*. Boston: Allyn and Bacon.

Gross, L. (2001). Out of the Mainstream: Sexual Minorities and the Mass Media. In M.G. Durham & D.M. Kellner (Eds.), *Media and Cultural Studies: KeyWorks*. Malden, MA: Blackwell.

Hall, S. (1979). Culture, the Media and the "Ideological Effect." In J. Curran, M. Gurevitch, & J. Woollacott, (Eds.), *Mass Communication and Society*. London: Sage.

House Bill Aim to Raise Eating Disorders Awareness. (2000, May–June). *Eating Disorders Review*. 11(3), 1.

Mulvey, L. (1975). "Visual Pleasure and Narrative Cinema." *Screen.* 16(3): 6–18.

National Eating Disorder Association. (2006). National Eating Disorder Association Announces Results of Eating Disorders Poll on College Campuses Across the Nation. Retrieved November 11, 2006, from http://www.nationaleatingdisorders.org/nedaDir%255Cfil es%255Cdocuments%255CPressRoom%255CCollegePoll_9-28-06.doc.

National Institute of Mental Health. (2001). Eating Disorders: Facts About Eating Disorders and the Search for Solutions. Written by Melissa Spearing, Public Information and Communications Branch, NIH Publication No. 01–4901. Retrieved February 3, 2009, from http://www.pueblo.gsa.gov/cic_text/health/eatingdisorders/eatingdisorders.pdf.

Tuchman, G. (1978). Introduction. In G. Tuchman, A. Daniels, & J. Benet (Eds.), *Hearth and Home: Images of Women in the Mass Media.* New York: Oxford Press.

Walter, S.D. (1995). *Material Girls: Making Sense of Feminist Cultural Theory.* Los Angles: University of California Press.

Part V

Embodying and Embracing Fatness

Welcome to Part V of The Fat Studies Reader

Embodying and Embracing Fatness

This section addresses the challenges and successes of reclaiming the fat body in movement through exercise and dance. The essays in this section present the perspective of fat people who created either conceptual or physical space where they were encouraged to embrace their fat bodies.

After reading these chapters consider the following discussion questions:

What is the connection between physical embodiment, reclaiming the fat body in movement, and fat liberation politics?

Can one simultaneously effectively work for fat liberation while pursuing weight loss goals? Why or why not?

What assumptions attach to burlesque performance, as compared to other performance, and how do those assumptions change depending on the body size of the performer?

What motivates people to create space for fat embodiment?

What stereotypes attach to fat people exercising?

Do those stereotypes influence people of all sizes in the same way?

Using fat as a lens, consider the role of sexuality in creating personhood.

In addition to the activities discussed in these chapters, what other activities might support an individual's feeling of embodiment, whatever their weight?

What barriers exist that prevent or hinder fat people from enjoying physical activity?

Compare the impact on an individual of using exercise as a means of embracing and embodying fatness versus the practice of using exercise as a putative correction for fatness.

How do the essays address the tension between an individual's views of their own body and mainstream views of their bodies?

How do stereotypes about the fat body affect your choice, or the choices of your friends or loved ones, to engage in exercise or movement?

"I'm Allowed to Be a Sexual Being"
The Distinctive Social Conditions of the Fat Burlesque Stage

D. Lacy Asbill

The lights dim as jazz music fills the room. A voluptuous woman steps into the spotlight, wearing a man's suit and top hat. The woman begins to dance around the stage, lightly landing on the balls of her feet as she twirls, leaps, and spins to the music. She is amazingly graceful and fluid in her steps. As she moves, she begins to slowly strip out of her suit. First, she slips off her jacket. Then, in one quick motion, she drops her pants, revealing men's silk boxers! The audience roars with laughter. The dancer bats her eyelashes playfully in response, shimmying out of her boxers. Placing her foot on a chair, she rolls a stocking up her fleshy leg, hooking it into a garter belt. Next, she bends over and removes her hat; her voluminous red curls fly through the air as she flips her head back. She unbuttons her white shirt very slowly, teasing the audience. Electricity binds the dancer and the audience together; we hang on her every movement. Finally, she snaps open her shirt, ripping it off her body, and shakes her broad corseted chest to the audience's delight. As the song comes to a close, the dancer bends over, reaches into her corset, and releases her massive breasts. Wrapping a thick arm around her chest so as not to reveal her nipples, she lifts her other arm triumphantly into the air, winks at the audience and skips off stage— the perfect tease! The audience groans and shifts in their seats, clapping and shouting accolades at the stage. I hear a man behind me say, "Finally! We got to see something substantial!"

—Author's field notes, Peachy Plush (pseudonym) at Theatre Luxe, July 18, 2005

In modern burlesque performance, fat women's bodies are both *revealed* in their fleshy materiality and *revealing* of contemporary discourse about embodiment. Fat burlesque dancers use the performance space to present, define, and defend their sexualities, resisting a backdrop of medical and social discourses that inform their everyday lives. Although the fat body commonly represents a burgeoning public health epidemic, burlesque performance redefines the fat body as an object of sexual desire and as home to a desiring sexual subject. Through the sensuous art of strip-tease, these performers invoke, inhabit, and challenge limiting cultural conceptions about fat women's sexuality, purposefully creating social commentaries about their "abject" bodies. In this interdisciplinary, qualitative study, I use field observations and individual interviews to present a new vision of fat embodiment.

The social conditions of the burlesque stage offer resources to fat performers and audience members who want to experience their bodies in new and affirming ways. Burlesque is a form of erotic entertainment; therefore, fat women who step onto the eroticized context of the burlesque stage are immediately marked as sexual, without question or challenge. Brownie (pseudonym), a queer white woman in her twenties who has performed with the Corpulent Cuties and Bodacious Burlesque, explains that contemporary burlesque is "a way that women of unconventional beauty can display themselves and be sexual in public" (Interview, October 20, 2005). In a culture that rarely associates fat bodies with sexuality, publicly claiming sexual agency, desire, and desirability allows fat women to take pleasure in their bodies. For example, Tonsa Tush (pseudonym), a twenty-four-year-old bisexual African American women who has danced with Detroit Shimmy for three years, shares, "I like that in this setting, I'm allowed to be a sexual being. *I'm allowed to be a sexual being.* Yeah, I'm a big mamma, but you're going to like me anyway. In this place, it's allowed to think I'm beautiful. It's allowed to look at me and be like, 'Damn, she's hot.' After a performance, it's usually just like, 'You're amazing. Thank you.' And that's, that is just awesome that even I get that too" (Interview, November 6, 2005). Tonsa Tush explicitly contrasts the feelings and actions that are "allowed" in the burlesque scene with the possibilities of her everyday life. In burlesque, she is beautiful, hot, sexual, amazing. Her words "even I get that too," however, imply that people in other social settings fail to recognize her sexuality. Emphasizing that she is "allowed to be a sexual being" while on the burlesque stage, Tonsa Tush reports that this venue offers her a chance to engage her body's sexuality. On the burlesque stage, fat performers locate a particular set of social conditions that allow them to experience their bodies as desirable and affirming. The explicit sexuality of the burlesque stage, as well as the public nature of the performance, function to support a new, positive vision of fat sexual embodiment.

Although the burlesque stage offers dancers the opportunity to re-present their sexualities in public spaces and to inhabit their fat bodies in unique ways, these performances would not be sustainable if performed in empty theaters or to hateful crowds. In fact, the particular social rules that burlesque audiences enact are equally important in the successful creation of fat-positive performance spaces. The burlesque scene has its own patterns of interaction that become visible upon stepping into the space. Early in my fieldwork, I came to recognize the audience as a vital part of the show. The cheers of admiration from the crowd bolstered and energized the performers. One dancer shared with me, "A real burlesque audience knows that it's okay to clap and hoot and holler, and that we appreciate it, and that we like feed off each other's energy from that. So I appreciate that" (Brownie, Interview, October

35.1. The Chainsaw Chubbettes. Photo by Christine Woolner.

20, 2005). Although not every individual reacts this attentively, the audience is collectively responsive to the show. This helps to create a dynamic, cyclical relationship
between the audience and the performer: the audience responds enthusiastically to
the sensual nature of the performance while the performer reacts to the accolades
with increased confidence. This dialectic relationship provides a crucial interruption
from fat negativity, opening possibilities for pleasurable fat embodiment.

Ultimately, these raucous performances affect more than the dancers' sense of
self: they also make a celebratory statement about fat sexuality and body acceptance
to their audiences. Individual, face-to-face interactions after the shows reveal how
deeply the performances affect audience members. After nearly every performance
I observed, scores of women lined up to speak with the performers, sharing con-
gratulations, reflections, and revelations. The dancers I interviewed share that their
performances inspire strong individual reactions from their audiences. Brownie explains, "It really affects the audience. I mean, you get so many women coming up

35.2. Alotta Bouté. Photo by Don Spiro.

to you when you perform, and telling you how great it made them feel, and made them feel better about themselves, or seeing me up there made them realize that they maybe could feel better about themselves someday" (Interview, October 20, 2005). Brownie recognizes the particular impact that her performances have on women, inspiring them to construct new relationships with their bodies and sexualities. Peachy Plush (pseudonym), a queer white woman in her twenties who has danced with Bodacious Burlesque for three years, explains that her performances can have relevance for anyone:

> I love that it's not just, and this is an important thing, it's not just fat girls that I inspire. Like anyone watching the show can feel better about their bodies, because um, body images issues, everybody has ugly days. And for people to feel relief from that is a beautiful thing. And even more than relief, to have a positive self-image come from that, is a beautiful thing. I've heard everything from, "I'm going to go home and eat ice cream

and have sex!" [laughs] Which is excellent, that's a beautiful thing to inspire ice cream and sex. Yeah! Halleluiah! To um, to having people say it meant so much to me personally to see large people up there dancing and looking so sexy. And if they look good, then I can look good too, and look at that confidence, and it inspired and changed me. (Interview, January 3, 2006)

Peachy Plush's words demonstrate both playful and profound responses to her performances. Viewing fat burlesque can "inspire and change" audience members, creating the space necessary to occupy their bodies in affirming ways. Although some might view burlesque as a merely frivolous form of entertainment, the audience reactions that Peachy Plush and Brownie noted suggest that fat burlesque performers produce a new form of fat embodiment by inspiring their audiences to reconsider their own self-worth and desirability.

Fat burlesque performance is revealing on many counts. Contemporary burlesque's celebration of the fleshy materiality of the body allows fat women to experience their

35.3. Pussy Flambé. © 2005 by Dale Rio.

sexual embodiment in new and satisfying ways. This space also offers fat women the opportunity to invoke and respond to limiting cultural conceptions about their bodies and sexualities, re-framing and re-working what it means to be fat. Because fat burlesque dancers present confident, persuasive, and shameless erotic performances, both audience members and dancers can revel in the successful display of fat sexuality. These resistant performances have a broad impact, seeping into the everyday embodied realities of the performers and audience members, fortifying pleasurable "fat" identities. Although constructing the self is a lifelong process that evolves over time, the burlesque stage offers a set of unique social conditions that begin and support the work of positive identity formation for fat women.

Embodying Fat Liberation

Heather McAllister

As the founder and artistic director of Big Burlesque and the Fat-Bottom Revue, the world's first all-fat burlesque troupe, I've learned that fat liberation occurs only when we embody it physically as well as accepting it politically and theoretically.

Far from fat liberation community, I read Lisa Schoenfielder and Barb Wieser's *Shadow on a Tightrope* (1983). I stopped drinking diet soda and became a fat activist. My experience as a queer social justice activist dovetailed with my fat activism. Both of these identities—fat and queer—were crucial in the vision and structure of Big Burlesque. Regardless of the sexual orientation of the individual dancers, Big Burlesque was "queer" in every sense of the word.

When I started Big Burlesque, there were a couple of "bigger" burlesque performers on the neo-burlesque circuit, but they did not specifically advocate fat liberation. Fat dance is rare enough; fat exotic/erotic dance is pretty much unheard of outside of "fetish" acts that alienate rather than normalize fat bodies. Just being fat and positively sexual is radical in a culture thoroughly inculcated with sexism and anti-fat prejudice. In making this argument, I acknowledge that intentionally or not, New York–based performers like the Glamazon Girls, World-Famous Bob, and Dirty Martini pushed the envelope in the neo-burlesque scene. The NYC gals struck me as "just like everyone else, except bigger," which is certainly one good way to approach it; it reminded me, however, of assimilationist lesbians and gay men, who are "just like everyone else, except who we have sex with." I wanted something different.

The first performance of the Fat-Bottom Revue happened in 1999 at an alternative culture festival in the Nevada desert, Burning Man. For the following three years, I held workshops and performances sporadically until June 2002, when I contracted with Big Moves, the country's only organization dedicated to size diversity in dance, to produce a one-night-only show in San Francisco. The place was packed, and we received a long standing ovation. It was this positive reception and enthusiasm that spurred my decision to move to San Francisco and form a burlesque troupe made up *exclusively* of fat dancers.

Fat dancers are a rare enough breed, and even fewer are interested in burlesque as a form of self-expression. My outreach garnered me enthusiastic, talented, but, for the most part, untrained performers. Like many burlesque dancers, I had no formal experience as a choreographer and was not a professionally trained dancer myself; I was just a fat girl with a vision. But I took myself and my dancers seriously. It was a troupe requirement that everyone take an outside technique class in addition to rehearsal. I really wanted to bring *dance* to the burlesque stage. It was not about simply getting dolled up and taking it off; I was intent on giving our audience a quality show. As a member of several marginalized communities, I was unhappy with seeing below-par performance hailed as "great" simply because we are so desperate to see ourselves represented on stage that we accept anything.

Big Burlesque differed from "mainstream" burlesque in several significant ways. ALL of our dancers were fat, and my choice of the name Fat-Bottom Revue sent out a siren call. We had dancers of different gender identities, sizes, shapes, and abilities as part of our troupe, all with varying levels of comfort around striptease and nudity. I felt that it was important that dancers felt free to take off (down to pasties and g-string), or leave on, as much as was comfortable. This policy created an environment where fat dancers could explore erotic power and performance in a way that pushed boundaries but was still safe. Society dictates that certain bodies (thin, walking, etc.) are "normal," resulting in an exclusionary, limited standard in the performing arts. I insist that diversity of form is an advantage and a great opportunity for creative choreography and direction.

People were intrigued that we were a troupe; once they saw us parading full force onstage for a group piece, audiences everywhere went wild. Just the sheer visual

36.1. Courtesy of Kina Williams, http://KinaWilliams.com.

36.2. Courtesy of Kina Williams, http://KinaWilliams.com.

impact of anywhere from five to fifteen fatties taking off their clothes, on the same beat, perfectly timed with big hair and bigger smiles, was a knockout. We became something of a phenomenon. We did an East Coast tour and were featured on national and local television, courted by news media, documentary producers, even celebrities—all of whom were fascinated not only by the "burlesque renaissance," but specifically by an all-fat company. I used this to our best advantage—even if we were popular at first just because of the unique nature of the troupe, I made sure that the show itself merited the attention. We also caught the eye of accomplished fine arts photographer Leonard Nimoy (of *Star Trek* fame), who did two artfully nude photo shoots with the troupe. He was very receptive to our political message and used fat liberation language in his interviews and press releases. Again, we created a channel for a fat liberation message that was broadcast to people who would never otherwise have heard it.

Audience reaction to our shows was generally quite favorable. In fact, with one exception, I never heard a fatphobic comment or heckle directed at any of us while onstage. I was initially very selective in accepting performance opportunities because I felt that I had a personal and professional responsibility for the emotional safety of the troupe. As we gained experience and had ongoing positive reactions, I accepted more mainstream venues.

Reaction from other burlesque performers was, again with a few exceptions, enthusiastic and supportive. There were some people, however, who thought that the "openness" and "diversity" of the neo-burlesque scene was problematic precisely because it opened the door to "riffraff" like us. One writer opined that it was terrible that these fat people (us) should feel free to parade around. I often find this attitude

36.3. Courtesy of Kina Williams, http://KinaWilliams.com.

36.4. Courtesy of Kina Williams, http://KinaWilliams.com.

36.5. Courtesy of Kina Williams, http://KinaWilliams.com.

of resentment when fat people are, despite the odds, happy, fulfilled, sexy, talented, glamorous, and beautiful on their own terms. People say we are outrageous in daring to love and expose our bodies in the same way that thin people do.

Because we are at a point in our development as a movement where we are start-ing to see fat-positive (occasionally eroticized) images in various places, some fat feminists have questioned what they perceive to be too much of a focus on sexuality. But there is a big difference between debasing oneself because of a real or perceived lack of sexual opportunities, and empowering oneself and others to give fat people, particularly fat women, sexual currency. How she chooses to spend it is up to her, but I want a "level playing field"—where all bodies, including fat ones, can be seen as sexy and beautiful.

I've given size acceptance workshops in venues all over the United States and Canada. I can give the same information with or without a "burlesque" component. In a burlesque workshop, however, the participants have the chance to immediately embody the message of self-acceptance and sexiness in their bodies. I teach a few basic burlesque moves and set up the class so that each person has a chance to "show their stuff" in a way that they find comfortable. The transformations are revolution-ary. Women who were nervous about even attending the workshop come onstage and perform with me the same night.

This experience has proven to me that the fastest way to fat liberation is physical. We will never have our freedom if we live only "from the neck up," yet that is the way many fat people live, even, or especially, the activists and academics among us. Embodiment just *works*, and as a fat activist of nearly twenty years now, I want to use the most effective tools. Sex sells, and sexuality is a legitimate human right. I've used it for its very pleasure as well as to advance a political agenda. The oppression of anti-fat hatred is sited on the body, and it is in the body that those wounds can be healed. I hope that future ambitious adipositives will take what we've done and run with it, just as we built on the groundbreaking work of fat performers before us.

NOTE

Heather McAllister died on February 13, 2007, but her spirit and her belief that we can over-come fear and ignorance with love and knowledge lives on. She has often been described as revolutionary. Whether fighting racism, homophobia, classism, or fatphobia; whether in the streets or at the dinner table; whether for her own life, or for everyone's, Heather consciously worked toward improving herself and the world. Amid her own battle against ovarian cancer, she took her hard-won energy and time to write this chapter because she believed it was im-portant work . . . a life's work.

Not Jane Fonda
Aerobics for Fat Women Only

Jenny Ellison

Clad in high-cut leotards on the cover of her bestselling *Workout Book* and aerobics videos, Jane Fonda and her message of discipline as liberation are emblematic of the beauty and bodily norms of the 1980s (Kagan & Morse, 1988; Losano & Risch 2001).[1] Aerobics videos and classes, like Dancercise or Jazzercise, combine callisthenic exercise with dance moves and set them to music. By 1986 an estimated 21.9 million Americans were doing aerobics on a regular basis, most of them women (Kagan & Morse, 1988). Fonda was at the forefront of this trend. *Jane Fonda's Workout Book* (1981) sold over 1.8 million copies in its first two years of publication, and by 1987 her workout videos had sold 4 million copies (Hribar, 2001). Fonda represented the new ideal of femininity in the 1980s: she was athletic, slim, and sexy. Aerobics and aerobic clothing were popular signifiers of this new ideal, and images of women "working out" were used to sell films, food, and clothing in this era.

Though Fonda herself saw fitness as part of a pro-woman agenda and sought to "break the weaker sex mold" (Fonda 1981, p. 45), her body (and the aerobic body in general) has become a site of contestation about beauty and bodily norms in the late twentieth century. Feminist analyses of the phenomenon place aerobics on an "axis of continuity" (Bordo, 1988, p. 90) with a broader popular culture of the 1980s that idealized, disembodied, and demeaned women (Freedman, 2002; Kagan & Morse, 1988). Sports feminists believed that aerobics undermined the credibility of "real" female athletes because it focused more on keeping women slim than keeping women fit. Rosemary Dean argued that the very popularity of "keep-fit" classes stemmed from "women's anxiety over their body weight and appearance." Aerobics appears to have co-opted physical fitness for the purpose of selling slenderness and colorful leotards to women (Deem, 1987, p. 427). Participant observation and sociological studies of the aerobics phenomenon (Lloyd, 1996; Loland, 2000; MacNevin, 2002; Markula, 1995) similarly argued that aerobics classes were a site where "women . . . sculpt their bodies in line with dominant messages about femininity" (Maguire & Mansfield, 1998, p. 125). In this literature, aerobics, along with crash dieting and plastic surgery, is emblematic of the new normative femininity of the 1980s: the healthy body was a slender body. Sociological analyses of aerobics have problematized femininity, but they have failed to interrogate how women whose bodies lay outside the boundaries of the healthy ideal experienced aerobics.

For fat women, whose bodies have "failed to materialize" appropriately (LeBesco, 2004, p. 98), aerobics classes could be sites of oppression, embarrassment, and exclusion. Regardless of her fitness level, instructors often assumed that for health or aesthetic reasons fat women did not belong in an aerobics class. Some fat participants reported feeling out of place and awkward in aerobics classes designed for their "regular"-sized counterparts (Zatylny, A., personal interview, June 20, 2006; Laue, I., personal interview, October 3, 2005; White, S., personal interview, July 11, 2006). Despite cultural limitations faced by fat women who wanted to exercise, by 1990 an independent, fat women's only aerobics culture was thriving in Canada and the United States. What happened? Working against the notion that fatness was emblematic of a moral failing (laziness, overeating, or ignorance), self-identified fat women developed aerobics classes for other fat women. Often driven by the politics of the fat liberation and fat acceptance movements, these classes offered a space where fat women could explore their physicality with women they perceived to be like themselves. The phenomenon of aerobics classes created by fat women, for fat women, shows that the classes were a site for the (re)articulation of fat identities.

"Stop postponing your life until you lose weight and start living now" was the motto of Large as Life, an action group formed in Vancouver, Canada, to "promote increased self-acceptance in large women" (1981, p. 1). In September 1981 the group hired "a fitness instructor from the YMCA, a little skinny thing," who taught aerobics for fat women only (Partridge, K., personal interview, September 20, 2005). Few participated in these classes until Large as Life members obtained fitness leadership training. Once fat women themselves began to teach the classes, enrolment multiplied. By January 1984 the classes, exclusively for self-identified fat women, had expanded to thirteen Vancouver-area fitness centers (1984, p. 15). A few years later, former Large as Life member Suzanne Bell opened an entire fitness studio for fat women only (Bell, S., personal interview, October 4, 2005).

Large as Life members shared with other fat liberationists a critique of medicine and a belief that fat people could be fit. The group saw their aerobics classes as a "practical" (CKNW Radio, 1981) solution to the concerns of fat women who wanted "to get healthy, to start feeling better" about their bodies, and "to move around more" (Canadian Broadcasting Corporation, 1981). Whereas some women felt "ashamed" and ridiculed in aerobics classes, Large as Life provided a space where fat women felt "comfortable" exercising (Booth, E., personal interview, October 11, 2005; Laue, I., personal interview, October 3, 2005). Creating a fat-positive environment was also the motivation behind Women at Large, a private, for-profit chain of aerobics centers developed in 1983 in Yakima, Washington. As fat women, founders Sharlyne Powell and Sharon McConnell felt that they "never had any place to go" to "exercise without embarrassment or humiliation, or where . . . instructors had compassion" (Bartel, 1987, p. 6F). By 1988, Women at Large had twenty-nine franchises in the United States and Canada. Owners were required to weigh at least 175 pounds (Reardon, 1987).

Although Women at Large's broader agenda was to "rebuild self-esteem" (Downey, 1986, p. B1) and self-worth among its clientele, the company rejected the language and politics of fat liberation. Terms such as "fat" or "big" were avoided. Instead, Powell and McConnell insisted on referring to Women at Large members as "fluffy ladies" (Downey, 1986, p. B1), a term they believed lacked "demeaning connotation" (Bartel, 1987, p. 6F). Women at Large departs from Large as Life, who saw fat as both a personal and a political issue and provided classes at cost to members and nonmembers alike. In this respect, and despite a lack of communication or direct links with the United States, Large as Life shares with other pioneers of the women's fitness movement a belief that aerobics could be part of an activist agenda that challenged fat oppression in multiple social sites. *Radiance Magazine*, an immensely significant resource driving fat activism in the 1980s, popularized this approach to fat fitness.

Radiance started out as a newsletter for fat women in publisher Alice Ansfield's own aerobics class in the early 1980s (Ansfield, 1985). The magazine's special issues on fitness in 1985 and 1988 were milestones in the fat exercise movement. Through the pages of *Radiance*, fat women exercisers became visible to one another. An image of a fat woman in a white jumpsuit with matching headband appeared on the cover of the 1985 "Celebrate Your Body" issue. Inside, fat women were shown working out together in classes led by Bay Area fitness pioneers Deb Burgard of We Dance and Rosezella Canty-Letsome of Light on Your Feet. These stories seem to have inspired fat women in other cities to establish their own aerobics classes. Subsequent issues featured classified ads announcing the arrival of "low impact aerobics for BBWS with BBW instructors" in Illinois, New York, Texas, and Virginia (See "Heavy, Happy, and Healthy," 1991, p. 48; "In Chicago," 1988, p. 48; "Light on Your Feet Goes to Virginia," 1986, p. 30; "Smart Move—Finally," 1988, p. 48).

The notion that fat could be fit gained further momentum with the publication of *Great Shape: The First Exercise Guide for Large Women* in 1988. The book was coauthored by Pat Lyons and Deb Burgard, two women who connected through *Radiance*. *Great Shape* understands exercise as a pleasure that has been denied to fat women because of their body size. Echoing Large as Life, Lyons and Burgard (1988, p. 11) write, "Most of us have finally come to the conclusion that picking a number on a scale and postponing our lives until we reach that number is never going to work." As such, *Great Shape* offers women guidance on starting a fitness program, as well as an extensive appendix listing aerobics programs, fitness clothing, and exercise videos for large women. According to their listings, by 1988 there were at least twenty-seven aerobics programs for large women operating in ten different states (Lyons & Burgard, 1988).

Demand for fat-centered exercise programs was high, as the variety of aerobics classes available by the end of the 1980s attests. Fat women's participation in the activity should not be seen as simply a specialized form of aerobics. In the context of the fat liberation movement, aerobics were part of a wave of activism in the 1980s focused on improving the material, day-to-day experience of living fat. Exercise classes grew alongside other services developed by and for fat women, including plus-size clothing stores, clothing swaps, and personal development seminars. Aerobics were

37.1 Promotional shot of Suzanne Bell, c. 1986. Photo courtesy of Suzanne Bell Fitness and Fashion, Vancouver, BC.

part of an increasingly diverse and transnational approach to fat liberation in the 1980s. What the classes did share in common was that exercise became a framework for participants' own understanding of their fat bodies; participants' increasingly fat-positive view of their own embodiment made other explorations of their identity possible (Ellison, 2007).

When the first classes for fat women started in the 1980s, finding fashionable plus-size leotards, let alone having the courage to wear them, was a challenge for participants. Many women were tentative in their initial selection of aerobics wear. Rose-zella Canty-Letsome noted that her "students . . . started out hiding their bodies and wearing plain old sweatsuits," but eventually began "showing up in pink and purple leotards, looking gorgeous!" (Krynski, 1985, p. 13). As demand from fat women grew, manufacturers began to market a more colorful range of plus-size leotards. Smaller companies led by fat female entrepreneurs were at the vanguard of this trend. Responding to a dearth of available leotards in their area, entrepreneurs such as Suzanne Bell began to market their own lines. Bell customer and former Vancouver

Large as Life member Janet Walker described being "able to wear what other people were wearing" to aerobics classes as a "thrill" (personal interview, October 6, 2005). The success of clothing lines like Suzanne Bell's suggests that aerobics classes provided a safe environment where women could experiment with their embodied identity.

Like clothing, aerobics videos for fat women were developed by female entrepreneurs. Unable to find distribution through other channels, these videos tended to be marketed directly to consumers in the pages of *Radiance*, local newspapers, and women's directories. Jody Sandler, a former Large as Life instructor, released the first of two best-selling *In Grand Form* videos in 1986 (Sandler, J. personal interview, September 5, 2005). Other pioneers of the women's exercise movement, including Women at Large and Light on Your Feet, released videos in the late 1980s.

Critics of aerobics have tended to see tie-ins like clothing and videos as evidence that aerobics is an aesthetic rather than a health-promoting activity (Deem, 1987; Kagan & Morse, 1988; Losano & Risch, 2004; Theberge, 1987). Helen Lenskyj condemned the commercialization of aerobics in her pathbreaking book on women, sport, and sexuality, *Out of Bounds* (1986). Lenskyj argues that aerobics' "association with the cosmetic and fashion industries made it, in many instances, another arena for women to compete for male attention" (p. 129). Like the participant observation studies of aerobics cited above, this literature fails to consider the boundaries and tensions around (apparently) hegemonic feminine practices. Participation in a popular culture phenomenon like aerobics is not necessarily evidence that a woman is complicit with its message. It is also unlikely that aerobics participants had singular motivations that can easily be divided into good/pro-woman or bad/hegemonic reasons for exercising. Rather than a straightforward critique of femininity, fat women who worked out were inspired by a critique of, and a desire to take part in, aerobics culture. Fat women, and potentially many other women, participating in aerobics were critical and active consumers who created safe spaces to enjoy their bodies.

Aerobics continued to be a popular fitness activity for fat women into the 1990s. Since that time new ways for fat women to explore their physicality have become popular, such as the fat cheerleading and burlesque movements. In the context of fat history and fat studies, aerobics classes reveal that there were (and are) multiple fat identities. Efforts to reinscribe the fat body as capable, healthy, and desirable were driven by diverse and diffuse groups of women with differing political agendas. Ideas about fat fitness have also travelled: classes, along with videos, aerobics clothing manufacturers, and magazines, created informal networks among fat women in cities in Canada and the United States. The extent to which the notion that fat can be fit has actually permeated broader popular culture during this time is a subject for debate. Differences of ethnicity and class within fat acceptance movements are also issues that require further investigation. Who valued fitness and who had access to aerobics culture? Despite these limitations, looking beyond mainstream fitness culture allows us to see that aerobics classes were an activity particular to the 1980s that fat women used to explore their physicality, femininity, and identity. Aerobics classes allowed fat women spaces to talk back to feminine norms in this period; they became social sites in which to rearticulate the meaning of fat.

37.2 Jody Sandler's *In Grand Form Low Impact Aerobics,* 1986, http://www.
ingrandform.com.

NOTE

1. In newspaper stories from the 1980s, fat fitness instructors compared themselves, and were compared, to Jane Fonda. A *Canadian Press* story noted that Suzanne Bell was not trying to pass herself off as the "Jane Fonda of the Queen-sized set" (*Canadian Press*, 1986, p. D7). Using a similar metaphor, Jody Sandler of In Grand Form told the *Vancouver Sun*, "I'm not Jane Fonda. I don't live in L.A. . . . People are looking for a more down-to-earth approach" (Balcom, 1986, p. E4).

REFERENCES

Ansfield, A. (Spring 1985). From the Publisher. *Radiance*, 3.

Balcom, S. (20 November 1986). Here's a No-Frills Workout for Those Who'll Never Be a Fonda. *Vancouver Sun*, p. E4.

Bartel, P. (5 April 1987). Women at Large —Empathy Is Key to Helping "Fluffy Ladies" Regain Esteem. *St. Petersburg Times*, p. 6F.

Bordo, S. (1988). Anorexia Nervosa: Psychopathology as the Crystallization of Culture. In I. Diamond & L. Quinby (Eds.), *Feminism and Foucault: Reflections on Resistance* (pp. 87–117). Boston: Northeastern University Press.

Canadian Broadcasting Corporation. (15 September 1981). *CBC Radio Noon* [Radio Broadcast]. Vancouver: Canadian Broadcasting Corporation.

Canadian Press. (24 February 1986). Fitness Goes Over in a Big Way: Heavy Women Can Still Be Fit, Vancouver Instructor Preaches. *The Toronto Star*, p. D7.

CKNW Radio. (14 September 1981). *CKNW Call in Show with Gary Bannerman* [Radio Broadcast]. Vancouver: CKNW.

Deem, R. (1987). Unleisured Lives: Sport in the Context of Women's Leisure. *Women's Studies International Forum, 10*(4), 423–432.

Downey, M. (13 October 1986). "Women at Large" Helps Bodies and Self-Images. *Atlanta Constitution*, B1.

Ellison, J. (2007). "Stop Postponing Your Life Until You Lose Weight and Start Living Now": Vancouver's Large as Life Action Group, 1979–1985. *Journal of the Canadian Historical Association, 18*(1), 241–265.

Fonda, J. (1981). *Jane Fonda's Workout Book*. New York: Simon and Schuster.

Freedman, E.B. (2002). *No Turning Back: The History of Feminism and the Future of Women*. New York: Ballantine.

Heavy, Happy, and Healthy (Spring 1991). *Radiance*, p. 40

Hribar, A. (2001). "Consuming Lifestyles: Transforming the Body and the Self in Postfeminist America." Unpublished PhD diss., University of Illinois at Urbana-Champaign, Urbana.

In Chicago, Finally! (Spring 1988). *Radiance*, p. 48.

Kagan, E., & Morse, M. (1988). The Body Electronic: Aerobic Exercise on Video: Women's Search for Empowerment and Self-Transformation. *Drama Review: TDR, 32*(4), 164–180.

Krynski, S. (Spring 1985). Celebrate Your Body! *Radiance*, 12–14.

Large as Life. (August 1981). *Large as Life Newsletter*, 1.

Large as Life Action Group. (January 1984). New Classes to Start: Generous Jiggles. *The Bolster, 4*, 15.

LeBesco, K. (2004). *Revolting Bodies: The Struggle to Redefine Fat Identity*. Amherst: University of Massachusetts Press.

Lenskyj, H. (1986). *Out of Bounds: Women, Sport, and Sexuality*. Toronto: Women's Press.

Light on Your Feet Goes to Virginia! (Summer–Fall 1986). *Radiance*, p. 30.

Lloyd, M. (June 1996). Feminism, Aerobics, and the Politics of the Body. *Body and Society*, 2(2), 79–98.

Loland, N.W. (2000). The Art of Concealment in a Culture of Display: Aerobicizing Women's and Men's Experience and Use of Their Own Bodies. *Sociology of Sport Journal, 17*, 111–129.

Losano, A., & Risch, B.A. (2001). Resisting Venus: Negotiating Corpulence in Exercise Videos. In K. LeBesco & J.E. Braziel (Eds.), *Bodies Out of Bounds: Fatness and Transgression* (pp. 111–129). Berkeley: University of California Press.

Lyons, P., & Burgard, D. (1988). *Great Shape: The First Exercise Guide for Large Women*. New York: Arbor House–William Morrow.

MacNevin, A. (2002). Exercising Options: Holistic Health and Technical Beauty in Gendered Accounts of Bodywork. *Sociological Quarterly, 44*(2), 271–289.

Maguire, J., & Mansfield, L. (1998). "Nobody's Perfect": Women, Aerobics, and the Body Beautiful. *Sociology of Sport Journal, 15*, 109–137.

Markula, P. (1995). Firm but Shapely, Fit but Sexy, Strong but Thin: The Postmodern Aerobicizing Female Bodies, *Sociology of Sport Journal, 12*(4), 424–431, 434–453.

Reardon, L. (29 November 1987). Heavyweight Instructors Direct Health Clubs for Big Women. *The Omaha World-Herald*, p. E1.

Smart Move—Finally! (Spring 1988). *Radiance*, p. 48.

Theberge, N. (1987). Sport and Women's Empowerment. *Women's Studies International Forum, 10*(4), 387–393.

Exorcising the Exercise Myth
Creating Women of Substance

Dana Schuster and Lisa Tealer

"Fat 'n' Lazy"

The vision of fat women exercising, swimming, or working out rarely enters the mind of the average person in U.S. society. The Working-at-Being-Fat myth, held by most people, dictates that people get fat by choosing to avoid exercise in favor of sitting on the couch, eating donuts, and watching television; exercise is then the punishment, the penance, for this previous "bad" behavior. Like so many other assumptions made about fat people, the belief that they do not exercise is untrue. But what is the experience of working out as a fat person given these societal stereotypes, and how can that experience be made more equitable? Our culture—and particularly the fitness industry—has done a superlative job of making exercise safely accessible only to those whose bodies already fit within a narrow spectrum of shape and size. It has also promoted the "no-pain-no-gain-make-it-burn" approach that has turned childhood recess into a torturous obligation of adulthood. So how exactly might a fat person go about "exorcising" this myth so they might enjoy exercise?

The Dream

It began as a simple thought. A daydream in the shower, a vision while driving to work, that led to a semi-casual, "Wouldn't it be nice to have an entire health club that was weight-neutral?" during check-in at our San Francisco Bay Area Kaiser Permanente Great Shape movement class in mid-1996. What followed is the stuff of legends: the exuberant clamor of, "We'll help," and "You have to do it," gathered momentum and swept us up. So the dream became reality and Women of Substance Health Spa opened to offer all women—independent of their shape, size, or fitness level—the chance to discover the joy of physical movement and the accompanying health benefits, "because the measure of a woman has nothing to do with numbers!" Alas, even a dream-born health club was not to be easily free of body disparagement issues.

A Weight-Neutral Space

There are very real barriers to accessing exercise if you are fat. As we delved deeper into the specifics of creating a body judgment–free zone, we found that issues of equipment, space, instructional posters, artwork, and staffing loomed large as tangible deterrents for those of us who try to work out in fat bodies.

The traditional health club environment often has walls filled with images of ample-chested thin women leaning provocatively forward as they lift weights. Even the charts that illustrate how to use a specific piece of equipment or identify the various muscles of the body are generally presented with very little in the way of diversity, not only in terms of body size but also relative to race, culture, and age. Artwork tends to reinforce the "thin is where it's at" message that not so subtly lurks beneath the health club veneer. It became our mission to make sure that everything on display at Women of Substance Health Spa reflected the words from our brochures, so we took our own pictures for exercise charts and found artwork for our walls that celebrated variety in age, body type, and culture.

Anyone who has tried to balance a generous rear on one of those skinny little locker room benches or squeeze their wide shoulders into some confining upper-body strengthening machine might understand the challenge in finding accessible equipment. Every piece of equipment needed to be "pre-sized" by one or both of us and have documentation that it would accommodate bodies weighing up to four hundred pounds or more before it was purchased. Because there were none available, we needed to have custom-made sturdy benches built for our locker room and classes. Frequent discussions were held with manufacturers regarding modifications that would allow for safe and successful experiences across the spectrum of body shape and size. It was a marvelous educational adventure for us as well as for the many equipment vendors with whom we talked over the years.

Perhaps the most crucial step in creating a safe exercise space was to find staff and instructors who embodied diversity and could fully commit to our body-positive mission, which was no easy task in an industry that thrives on body dissatisfaction. We interviewed personal trainers who looked at us in disbelief as they proclaimed, "But how will anyone know they're making progress if we don't measure/weigh them?" We talked to instructors who could not let go of their own body judgment. We mistakenly hired staff who apparently sought out employment with us in an attempt to address their own eating disorders. What we learned in the process was to be crystal clear about the body judgment–free philosophy and require that each person sign a statement of commitment to uphold it in his or her words and actions. It was also essential to provide regular staff trainings that offered a safe venue for discussing personal body image issues as well practical techniques on effectively maintaining the weight-neutral and body-positive environment.

38.1 Members and guest enjoy a hula workshop at WOSHS. Photo by Lisa Tealer.

38.2 Fun with the "bunny hop" in a WOSHS class. Photo by Lisa Tealer.

No Scales

The doors officially opened in January 1997, the day after the Martin Luther King Jr. holiday. It seemed appropriate, because this was the birth of a movement of sorts: a movement of celebrating and moving one's body, whatever the size. And then one of our very first members came through the door and had a question: where was the scale? Lisa could not quite believe that after all the marketing via postcards, brochures, flyers, and the grand opening celebration the first person through the door would ask about a scale. Fortunately this member's desire to get in the pool was stronger then her no-scale dismay and she moved on to the locker room. The experience, however, confirmed how deeply ingrained is the quest for thinness and a "better" body; here was a woman who believed enough to join yet still sought out the traditional measurement of success—the numbers on a scale.

Along with a scale, gym locker rooms have always been a perfect set up for body disparagement. We became increasingly concerned over time about discussions in our locker room that brought into conflict (1) members who wanted to lose weight (via diets or surgery) and didn't feel supported—especially by the club owners; and (2) members who believed in the weight-neutral paradigm and did not want to listen to or engage in the "diet talk." The divisiveness of these perspectives began to leak out into classes, the pool, and social interactions, and threatened the core of our safe space. So we enlisted the assistance of a trusted therapist colleague and held a "town hall" meeting. We publicly acknowledged the issue, provided a venue for members and staff to bring their concerns out of the locker room, and created an opportunity to solidify the bottom line that "diet talk" (or any type of negative body talk) was not to be part of the gym environment. Expressing our support for personal choice around weight loss while clearly securing the unequivocal weight-neutrality of the club, was a fairly nerve-racking experience, but worthy nonetheless.

The Journey Continues

In late 1999 and early 2000 a plethora of dot-coms moved north up the peninsula to Redwood City, bringing with them increased housing prices and rental rates for both residential and commercial properties. Longtime residents saw this as the time to sell their homes and move out of the area; non–rent controlled tenants got hit with significant rent increases; and everyone with even the most basic reception or computer skills wanted to work for a start-up in the hopes of making their first million after a few months. Because we could not find anyone to hire as support staff, we worked more of the club hours and were unable to get out into the community and market the business. We lost a number of our senior members who sold their homes and moved, as well as members who were renters and no longer had "discretionary money" for a gym membership. The bottom line was that after three years of growth in our membership numbers, we hit a plateau in 2000 while our costs continued to rise.

Although these economic conditions resulted in the doors of Women of Substance Health Spa closing on April 30, 2001, the class that started it all continued. For thirteen-plus years, Great Shape, based on the work of Lyons and Burgard (2000), offered a movement class taught by, and designed especially for, large women. Aerobics, strengthening, and stretching components allowed members to either sit or stand, and the class was infused with positive affirmations and friendly reminders to be aware of body alignment, listen to body cues, drink water, and, most important, breathe and have fun. Great Shape was also a training ground for fitness professionals interested in acquiring experience in teaching to a size-diverse class, and along with Women of Substance Health Spa frequently served as a resource to the media (print and television) on topics including health, fitness, and body image.

The experience of being part of a Health at Every Size exercise environment that focused on self-care and body acceptance allowed women to internalize the value of health-promoting physical activity independent of their body size. The belief that health clubs and exercise classes need to be judgment-free and accessible to everyone has now permeated other fitness settings, as former members confidently request opportunities to enjoy movement and reject the traditional weight-centered gym perspective. For fat women, the experience of engaging in physically and emotionally safe "workouts" seemed to result in a sense of entitlement and commitment to demand nothing less than exercise equality.

Each woman who came through the doors of Women of Substance Health Spa over the years brought a gift of herself that contributed to and expanded the club's mission. Along with the members of Great Shape, these incredibly brave women of substance have continued to embody the Health at Every Size paradigm and are helping to move us all forward in the quest to exorcise the exercise myth.

NOTE

"Weight-neutral" and "body-positive" are concepts used with permission of http://www.bodypositive.com. Women of Substance Health Spa® and Kaiser Permanente® are registered trademarks.

REFERENCES

Lyons, P., & Burgard, D. (2000). *Great Shape: The First Fitness Guide for Large Women*. New York: iUniverse.com.

Part VI

||||||||||||||||||||||||||||||||||||||||||||||||||||||||||||||||||||||||||||||||||||

Starting the Revolution

Welcome to Part VI of The Fat Studies Reader

Starting the Revolution

There is a vast distance to go before achieving weight-based equality. These essays catalog the significant barriers to social change, but they also tap into a diverse and powerful grassroots movement that desires change. In these concluding chapters the focus is on where fat studies scholars and activists go from here.

After reading these chapters consider the following discussion questions:

What are the next questions that fat studies scholars should address?

Is fat prejudice a uniquely U.S. issue? Is fat studies a specifically U.S. field of inquiry? Why or why not?

Is the United States a unique source of mainstream attitudes about fatness, or have such attitudes arisen internationally?

In what ways do international cultural differences manifest in fat studies?

How does the U.S. government–sponsored and named "War on Obesity" affect fat adults in the United States and beyond? How does it affect children?

Given the World Health Organization's and the U.S. government's involvement in the "War on Obesity," what is their responsibility to that war's casualties?

What role does stigmatization play in fat discrimination?

When the government partners with weight-loss companies, can it be acting in the best interest of people of all sizes?

What are the kinds of resistance that an individual might encounter in starting to confront mainstream attitudes about fat, and how can an individual begin to overcome that resistance?

What are the barriers to fat organizing? Should they be overcome? If so, how can that be accomplished?

Is there one correct way to "throw weight around"? What options do individuals and groups have?

What is the difference between organizing by fat people as opposed to organizing for fat people?

How do mainstream attitudes affect people who do not identify as fat and who are not identified as fat?

What role should people who do not identify as fat play in challenging discrimination?

What stake do people who don't identify as fat have in addressing weight-based attitudes?

How does the assumption that weight is mutable affect organizing efforts by people of all sizes to create a more just society?

How does fat oppression serve as a seemingly non-racist way to oppress people based on race, ethnicity, and class?

What industries and groups would suffer, and to what degree would they be affected, if people accepted their body size?

Maybe It Should Be Called Fat American Studies

Charlotte Cooper

I am a fat activist and writer, I am British, I live in London, and I would like to discuss the way that U.S. identity is informing and influencing the direction of Fat Studies. Fat activists are not well connected in established networks outside the United States, and we are frequently isolated from one another. It seems to me that fat has come to be regarded as an issue sited specifically within the United States, and that nontraditional knowledge about fat, embodied in Fat Studies, remains locked inside that country.

I will suggest that although U.S. cultural dominance in the field is understandable, it is also problematic. I will propose that a truly expansive vision for this new academic territory should embrace a more cross-cultural position. I will be using my experiences as a fat activist and writer living in Britain but working with comrades in the United States to support my arguments, as well as testimonies from others working in the area both inside and outside the States. Please note that I am not an academic; my background is in activism and journalism, and my approach reflects this.

First, a handful of definitions: "America" is synonymous with the United States to people living in the United Kingdom. I am aware, however, that this blanket label is problematic regarding the many non-U.S. inhabitants of the American continent, so I will try and be careful with my usage of it in this chapter. Although I appreciate that there are subtle differences and overlaps among the groups, I use fat rights, Fat Studies, and fat activists almost interchangeably for the sake of easy reading. By "outsider" I mean those not living and working within the United States; conversely, "insider" refers to those Americans who are active within the U.S. fat rights movement.

How Fat Studies Came to Be Situated Within the United States

It is not surprising that Fat Studies could be thought of as an American discipline. Fat itself is regarded by the world's media as American, thus as the United States invented fast food and exported it to the rest of the world, so it bore the consequences of a poor dietary regime; as a result of the global fast food industry, the country has also exported its "obesity problem" to the rest of the world. The fat American is a well-known and well-worn stereotype around the globe.

This, of course, is a facile argument. Fat people are found in every culture; fatness is part of the fabric of humanity and is not the domain of one country to export to others. Nevertheless, the negative cliché of the fat American is a powerful one in the world's media, and the anti-fat rhetoric of the alleged global obesity epidemic continually locates its axis of evil within the United States. Moreover, in Britain fat activism itself is becoming the new export; the British media are fascinated by fat activists in the United States and usually focus on Stateside events and personalities rather than those in their own country.

Where the nationality of fat is regarded as American, it is inevitable that an intellectual and activist-based response to fat should also be believed to be located in the United States. British fat activist Simon Murphy states, "The world sees fat as American export, but America thinks this too" (personal conversation, 4 May 2006), and so the Americanization of fat continues to replicate itself. For example, recent books such as Greg Critser's *Fatland: How Americans Became the Fattest People in the World* (2004), Paul Campos's *The Obesity Myth: Why America's Obsession with Weight Is Hazardous to Your Health* (2004), and J. Eric Oliver's *Fat Politics: The Real Story Behind America's Obesity Epidemic* (2005) situate fat firmly within the United States and reinforce the notion that fat is an American subject. This is not just about the language used in the titles of these books; by locating and limiting the perceived problem in the States, and not expanding their scope to encompass a more global perspective, they effectively ignore the wider population, or make the assumption that people outside the United States have the same concerns, language, and perspectives as those within. If there were more works of this ilk, if these debates were being generated by other authors and applied cross-culturally, it would not matter that the focus was limited to the United States. But there are not more works like these; unfortunately, these are pioneering texts that stand on a relatively uncluttered subject shelf, and they all just happen to ignore the rest of the world.

Although the history of fat activism is sketchily and obscurely recorded, almost all the documentation and organizing that I have encountered, in nearly twenty years of activism, is based and circulated within the United States. Moreover, despite the existence of the U.S.-based International Size Acceptance Association (ISAA), most of the dominant fat activist organizations in the United States, like the National Association to Advance Fat Acceptance (NAAFA), are *national*, not international, affairs and are not well known beyond those national borders. Interestingly, the original title of NAAFA was the National Association to Aid Fat Americans! Indeed, this might still be a more appropriate name for the organization.

Furthermore, it's rare to find U.S.-based groups who have a systematic campaign of community outreach beyond the local milieu, despite possibilities offered by the internet. This keeps the membership and affiliates of such groups located within the United States. Similarly, events are effectively limited to those in the United States, or at least to those who can afford to take part, and are not restricted by disability or other access issues. Conferences and gatherings take place within the United States and are difficult for outsiders to access for lack of information or prohibitive travelling and conference costs. Membership may also be restricted to those who can

Americanize themselves (for example, by modifying language, accents, and cultural reference points) enough to establish communication and negotiate obstacles such as membership forms that assume a U.S. address and local payment details, or the difficulties of long-distance exchanges through various time zones and differing cultural perspectives.

The isolation of Fat Studies within the United States can be also contextualized within that country's geographical and cultural remoteness. The United States is a long-haul destination from any other continent, and leaving is a rare event for most people. Even without the limitations of too-narrow plane seats or financial restrictions, it is ironic—given a U.S. government fixated on aggressive foreign policy, and a media that dominates the global imagination—that such a small number of U.S. citizens, the richest population in the world, take the opportunity to visit alien cultures and learn from them.

During my travels around the United States, it's not uncommon to find people who have never left their home town or state. Sometimes people confuse my unmistakably English accent for Australian, French, or German—and, on one memorable occasion, somebody asked if I was from London, Kentucky. This never happens to me in other countries, and I consider this one more piece of evidence of an endemic parochialism, an ignorance of others, that colors many aspects of American life, including Fat Studies. The belief that "outside" is strange, mysterious, and unknowable prevents people from making international connections, and further ensures the limitation of ideas within U.S. borders.

Why the Americanization of Fat Studies Is a Problem

Although it is understandable why Fat Studies should have originated in the United States, its current isolation within that country is a problem in terms of the expansion, development, and growth of the discipline. Activists and scholars in other countries certainly have their own responsibility for creating and developing networks. Even while acknowledging that the movement is young, however, U.S. Fat Studies proponents currently have access to better resources, are comparatively organized, and are in a stronger position to encourage and support outsiders than are many within their own national boundaries. The United States should be spearheading attempts to broaden the scope of the subject around the world; although Fat Studies knowledge grows and develops within the United States, however, there is little impetus to spread it outward or engage with outsiders. This reluctance reinforces the belief that the discipline is a concept rooted in the United States, and that the American voice speaks the final word on the matter. Researcher Hannele Harjunen, from Finland, explains: "The problem is that the 'American sisters' do not always seem to be aware that Fat Studies really is very American influenced. They many times take it for granted. When they talk about fat and society, attitudes towards fat, the experiences of fat women and so forth, they are always inevitably talking about the American reality and experience" (personal e-mail, 3 May 2006).

Without an open-armed approach to the rest of the world, Fat Studies in the United States is in danger of becoming ever more cliquish, exclusive, and alienating—dominated by a handful of charismatic American personalities, with insiders and outsiders firmly separated. There is a systematic exclusion of potential participants from outside the United States. This exclusion might be unintentional, but it is there, even in the landmark Fat Studies book that you are holding right now: What is the ratio of U.S. to outsider contributors? Why is this? What is the effect of that ratio?

The lack of a multicultural perspective means that Fat Studies currently replicates and supports U.S. imperialism and reiterates tired models of western cultural dominance. As outsiders we modify ourselves in order to be understood by those in the United States, but we see little evidence of Americans behaving similarly for our benefit, even when visiting our countries. It seems as though the United States is assumed to be the norm and that everything else is "Other." This affects attitudes toward fat rights initiatives outside the United States, which, at worst, are exoticized, belittled, or unnoticed. It is my experience that those outsiders who do manage to break ranks are often faced with indifference and misunderstanding, even antipathy, when they speak up. Fat rights events that do not follow an American liberation model fail to show up on the U.S. radar: For example, Unskinny Bop (http://www.unskinnybop.co.uk) is a very socially mixed, queer, fat-friendly club in London that has been running since 2002 yet is virtually unknown in the United States. The organizers produce a chub-focused zine and actively welcome fat patrons. Despite being packed every month, this club remains unlauded in the United States and has not become a model for American fat activism.

In addition, the dependence on a Stateside perspective supports a limited view of how fat is regarded and experienced in the wider world. It creates a discipline that is believed to be the exclusive domain of the rich West rather than a subject relevant to everybody. Fat rights proponents are happy to trot out the cliché that "fat is okay in some cultures" without engaging in the complexity of what that truism really might mean, or creating a space where people from "some cultures" can express the reality of their lives. Furthermore, to date there have been no attempts to plot the global experience of fat, and thus wider cultural repercussions and debates are marginalized rather than examined.

Finally, the present isolation of the emergent Fat Studies movement that lies largely within the urban Northeast and West Coast is creating an insular environment. There is little networking among people, even within the United States and especially among minority groups, which has led to people working alone in ignorance of one another.

Embracing Cross-Cultural Perspectives

I am under no illusion that the Americocentrism that is such a big part of life in the United States is likely to evaporate soon, but I'd like to make a few suggestions as to how Fat Studies might widen its reach.

The work of making Fat Studies more inclusive must start with its proponents taking the time and effort to check their assumptions about who they are, who they believe Fat Studies stakeholders to be, and how best to reach those people.

The emphasis on identity and shared experience within Fat Studies, British fat activist Kay Hyatt points out, means that people's personal experience is sometimes presumed to be universal: "Some of the terms that I've heard Americans throwing about have little meaning in a UK context" (personal conversation, May 2006). This lack of meaning may be because some concepts do not translate into contexts where there is little visible fat community, or where community is informal, unstated, and "unpoliticized." A lack of presumption could be more helpful.

Finnish researcher Harjunen clarifies the need for increased cross-cultural understanding:

> I do realise that we non-American activists need to bring this issue up. For example the case of health care is very different in the Nordic countries and UK (I mean that it is universal, you are not denied access to medical care because of the weight as in the insurance-based systems), weight loss surgeries are almost non-existent here, but so are services for fat people, as well as the discussion about the politics of fat unfortunately. People believe in medicine, so-called health experts and public health campaigns almost blindly. My doctoral dissertation on fatness will be the first one in this country that comes from the field of social sciences not medicine or health sciences. (e-mail correspondence, 3 May 2006)

When the work being presented presumes universality, it would be useful to question whose universe is being represented. For example, at the 2006 Fat and the Academy student-led conference at Smith College in Northampton, Massachusetts, USA, all of the conference's speakers (and, I assume, attendees) were from the United States, yet there was, as far as I could see, no caveat to explain that this was an American event. The title alone—*the* Academy, not the *American* Academy—assumed its universality and did not accurately demarcate its scope. I am not questioning the efficacy of local initiatives, nor am I doubting the excellence of Fat and the Academy; instead I would like American Fat Studies supporters to embrace a greater understanding of the geographical location of knowledge, as well as a greater sensitivity toward their own perspectives and the interests being represented.

It would be wonderful if books and conferences and other Fat Studies activities were to become more international in scope, though there are many barriers to this. But when such events and resources are located purely in the United States, it would be useful for their authors and organizers to describe and acknowledge their cultural position; explain the reasons for it; endeavor to find ways, within their limited boundaries, to engage a more culturally diverse participation; and to consider how their focus might apply in different cultural contexts.

Beyond questioning, there are also practical ways to engender a more cross-cultural environment. For example: calls for submissions should reach institutions, organizations, and individuals across the world; Fat Studies supporters could initiate and engage in outreach and cultural exchange programs; and those groups could raise funds and make money available for outsiders to participate in Fat Studies within the United States, and for Americans to take part in outsider events.

I would also like to see Fat Studies becoming less dependent on the conference as a way of developing the discipline. At the moment, conference attendance is one of the prime ways that we can get recognition for our work. As U.S. activist and organizer Rebecca Widom explains: "Here's the thing: The only fat activists I know outside of the U.S. (including you), I met at conferences in the U.S." (personal exchange, 2006). Yet conferences are exclusive, available only to those who know how they work, who are already in the loop. They are also expensive and make regular attendance for outsiders untenable, especially for those who live far away or have a small income or must manage other commitments. But wherever conferences are held, let the organizers consider ways of developing long-distance involvement, perhaps by making conference materials available online as presentation texts, multimedia, discussion forums, and interactive content that solicits outsider participation.

If only a few of these suggestions were taken to heart and acted upon, the scope and reach of Fat Studies will have increased many times over. Small actions can help develop debates much farther than is currently possible given the Americanization of the subject; they can encourage a global connection with the issues, a reaching out rather than a closing off; create a greater understanding of the wider cultural implications of fatness; promote cultural sensitivity in a movement that recognizes and celebrates the differences among people; strengthen the discipline beyond its present limitations; encourage diverse voices to flourish throughout international as well as national and local organizations; and build an atmosphere of learning that is broad, complex, and gives space to people to speak their own truth—these small actions could even undermine the stereotype of the fat American.

With regard to this chapter, it is telling that I have deeper connections with Fat Studies thinkers in the United States than I do with those in my own country. If Fat Studies scholarship is in its infancy within the United States, it is practically fetal in the United Kingdom, but this may be changing. September 2007 heralds "Bodies of Evidence: Fat Across Disciplines," an interdisciplinary and international conference at the University of Cambridge's Centre for Research in the Arts, Social Sciences, and Humanities (CRASSH). This conference seeks to "examine the obese body as a case study of both the contested nature of evidence and as a site for the construction of interdisciplinary evidence and problem-solving" (2007). The conference is also organized with support from the Wellcome Trust, a biomedical research charity funded by the pharmaceuticals multinational GlaxoSmithKline, which has business interests in weight loss drug manufacture and retail. This raises questions as to the scope of the conference, yet Dr. Petra Jonvallen of Linkopings Universitet in Sweden will be presenting her paper "Obesity in the belly of Big Pharma: One example of how body fat is turned into a medical problem," which suggests that the ideas being presented might not necessarily be hobbled by anti-obesity and weight loss industry rhetoric. Indeed, the gathering is likely to offer new networking opportunities, an assessment of the current state of academic inquiry regarding Fat Studies in the United Kingdom, and possibilities for its development.

At present, as far as I know, there are a few organizations and individuals within the United States that consider how to engage with activists beyond their national boundaries. I am grateful to NoLose (the National Organization for Fat Dykes and Their Allies, http://www.nolose.org) for inviting me to give the keynote address at their 2005 conference. In a similar fashion, Paul McAleer of Big Fat Blog (http://www.bigfatblog.com) routinely includes non-U.S. features on the site with a warm-hearted spirit of inclusiveness and inquiry. The Fat Studies Yahoo! Group (http://groups.yahoo.com/group/fatstudies) has an international readership, as does Fatshionista (http://community.livejournal.com/fatshionista). There is some recognition of my own girl gang, The Chubsters (http://www.chubstergang.com), which has an international membership, and International No-Diet Day, which was originated by Mary Evans Young, a British woman, in 1992. Clearly there is more work to be done.

How likely is any of this to happen? When I posted a call for responses regarding the Americanization of Fat Studies on the Fat Studies Yahoo! Group, I was met with a massive silence that I interpreted as indifference or fear of speaking up about the subject. It's depressing to feel that I might be the only person discussing this issue in public. My Fat Studies comrades remain engrossed with identity, personal liberation, media representation, or health in a movement that continues to have difficulty in addressing its minority groups, as Devra Polack, a fat activist based in the United States and member of the NoLose board of directors, remarks: "It is important to reach out to people in other countries and also completely disenfranchised people within this country as well as beyond it. It is hard for me to separate these issues from global perspective, as I feel that the American Mainstream silences these voices as well" (personal e-mail, 10 April 2006). Others are too busy to connect with the issues of broadening the field because they are getting on with the hard, thankless slog of community organizing on minimal resources; or perhaps they are afraid of speaking up and putting themselves in the firing line of a load of angry Americans, or of appearing ignorant (as one outsider responded to me when I asked for comment for this chapter). Nevertheless, I hope this chapter helps bring about a change in attitude; I believe that Fat Studies cannot be limited by national boundaries, and I look forward to the day when its knowledge is being generated from far and wide.

REFERENCES

Campos, P. (2004) The Obesity Myth: Why America's Obsession with Weight Is Hazardous to Your Health. New York: Gotham.

CRASSH. (2007). Bodies of Evidence: Fat Across Disciplines. Retrieved 30 August 2007 from http://www.crassh.cam.ac.uk/events/2006–7/obesity.html.

Critser, G. (2004) Fatland: How Americans Became the Fattest People in the World. New York: Mariner Books.

Jonvallen, P. (2007). Obesity in the Belly of Big Pharma: One Example of How Body Fat Is Turned into a Medical Problem. In: CRASSH, Bodies of Evidence: Fat Across Disciplines.

Oliver, J.E. (2005) Fat Politics: The Real Story Behind America's Obesity Epidemic. New York: Oxford University Press.

Are We Ready to Throw Our Weight Around? Fat Studies and Political Activism

*Deb Burgard, Elana Dykewomon,
Esther Rothblum, and Pattie Thomas*

The authors of this volume are a force to be reckoned with. They constitute over fifty writers, researchers, and activists who are thoughtfully critiquing the status quo of fat-related practices. And they are just the tip of the iceberg. There are now over one hundred books written from a fat-affirmative perspective, including many autobiographical pieces and works of fiction for children, adolescents, and adults. They are stating that the so-called medical reality of weight is all smoke and mirrors.

We can imagine a world in which body size is not particularly salient. It would not be one of the dividing lines used to define beauty/ugliness, winning/losing, health/disease. In that world, "fat studies" might seem strange and irrelevant. But in our world, body size can determine one's quality of life. This is, in fact, the argument used by many of the people hawking weight loss: "Use our product/service so you can escape from the stigmatized group!" So how can we organize as fat activists, and what are the barriers?

The "War on Obesity"

The "War on Obesity," proclaimed by former U.S. surgeon general C. Everett Koop in 1996 (CNN, 1996), has become one of the most successful government campaigns. The micro-level battle is often fought between patient and doctor, client and insurance company, employee and employer, or student and school. But the fact that this battle is also fought in the national public policy context creates a perpetuation of this suffering and tends to solidify the construction of fatness as "bad," thereby leading to more suffering.

Stigmatization of fatness creates a catch-22 concerning health because stigma is known to damage the health of the stigmatized both directly, by creating mundane yet pervasive stress, and indirectly, through poor access to and execution of care. Understanding the role of stigmatization of fatness in this public policy debate suggests a deeper discussion beyond the politics of fatness. What needs to change is not only the stigma of fatness itself, but also the elimination of stigma as a basis for public policy and, perhaps, even public discourse.

It is not unusual for social problem constructions to rely on *stigmatization* to define the problem or to implement the solution. By tapping into existing cultural attitudes regarding easily identified groups, social problems can be "sold" to an audience. The "War on Obesity" relies on a social problems claim that Americans are getting fatter and that fatness is a public health issue; according to this logic, being fat is a disease called "obesity," or fat causes or contributes to a number of illnesses that could be made better through losing weight. Fat is defined as a problem that is solvable. BMI (the ratio of height to weight, or body mass index) has been constructed as a reliable indicator of both ill health and potential premature death. The specific solution is weight loss; according to this view, lowering BMI through weight loss lowers the risk factor for premature death and ill health.

Koop's lead in declaring the "War on Obesity" gave the campaign legitimacy not only because of his medical authority, but also because of his character and prior reputation as someone who did not let political agendas get in the way of science. Although Koop made this a public announcement at a press conference, he directed his remarks at physicians. Koop's "War on Obesity" speech was made in the service of the Shape Up America! campaign, founded two years earlier. According to a 1994 *New York Times* article, Shape Up America! began with one-million-dollar donations from several organizations, including Weight Watchers, the Campbell Soup Company, the Heinz Foundation, *Time* magazine, and the Kellogg Company (Burros, 1994). In addition, the website Integrity in Science reports that "other million-dollar original sponsors include: Jenny Craig, Slim*Fast, and a special project that was sponsored by the National Cattlemen's Beef Association" (information from Hill & Knowlton, which represents Dr. Koop, in phone call to M. Jacobson of the Center for Science in the Public Interest; CSPI, 2003). With such industry backers, the Shape Up America! campaign and its "War on Obesity" had specific economic interests from the start. No better illustration of these interests was the "*Time* Magazine and ABC News Summit on Obesity" that took place in June 2004. Backed by America's Milk Processors, Aetna, and the New Balance Foundation (funded by the makers of athletic shoes), this three-day gathering of researchers, authors, and the diet and fitness industries was a who's who of people who make a living from the "War on Obesity" (*Time*, 2004).

A subsequent surgeon general, Richard Carmona, led the charge for these economic interests by pushing the war metaphor of Koop into the new age of terrorism rhetoric. He is quoted on the "Summit on Obesity" homepage as saying: "As we look to the future and where childhood obesity will be in 20 years, it is every bit as threatening to us as is the terrorist threat we face today. It is the threat from within" (*Time*, 2004). The language of "war" and "terrorism" is meant to evoke specific and passionate responses so that, just like in times of war, resources are gathered and expended to address the perceived threat. Koop's war has escalated since his seemingly modest announcement of new BMI guidelines expanding the class of those considered overweight. This escalation is due, in part, to the strategy of addressing the claims of those who would and could make money from fighting this so-called war.

In every war there must be villains and victims. War is about defining who is "with us" and who is "against us." Defining these villains and victims in cultural discourse relies heavily on social stigma. Just wars are fought within the context of making something right that had been made wrong. But usually wars are fought through propaganda that demonizes specific groups of people, defining them as victimizing other groups of people.

To convince others that this is a social question, there must be some reason why the public should care about some people being fat. If fatness is simply a matter of personal habit, then little public issue can be taken. Thus, the construction often goes further, suggesting that the bad choices and lack of control are a drain on society as well as the person.

Joe McVoy, an eating disorders specialist and cofounder of the now-defunct Association for the Health Enrichment of Large People (AHELP), called the multibillion-dollar weight loss industry the "diet-pharmaceutical industrial complex" (Fraser, 1998, p. 224). The great success of the "War on Obesity" stems from the phenomenal growth of this diet-pharmaceutical industrial complex between 1996 and 2006.

So Why Haven't Fat People Organized More of a Resistance?

The existence of this book begs the question: Why haven't fat people responded to these attacks? Why haven't we had more impact when we have organized? Many social movements have drawn their most enthusiastic supporters from college campuses, even when those movements originated in nonacademic communities. Those progressive movements (anti-racism, women's and lesbian/gay/bisexual/transgender/queer liberation, disability rights) have created moral codes reflected in campus policies that attempt to prevent discrimination based on race, ethnicity, gender, religion, age, ability, and sexual orientation, among other categories. But we would be hard-pressed to find a campus anti-discrimination policy that addressed weight and appearance.

It is not because fatness is rare. Most people, especially women and girls, feel fat, regardless of their actual body weight. Far more people, especially women and girls, are fat compared to those who are lesbian or Jewish, for example. So why don't college campuses, to say nothing about communities in general, have lots of organizations dealing with weight discrimination? (This is not to say that being female or being Jewish makes life easy, even on progressive college campuses.)

As Estelle Freedman recently said to us, there is a difference in groups *for* oppressed people (e.g., organizations for the blind, for immigrants) versus groups *by* oppressed people. Using this theory, we argue that an oppressed group's progress can be measured by the ratio of organizations *for* versus *by* the group. It was not too long ago that organizations *for* "homosexuality" included psychiatric hospitals and prisons, whereas organizations *by* lesbians and gay men included a few mimeographed underground newsletters and gay bars that were threatened with police raids. When it comes to groups for fat people, the vast majority are still dieting centers and medical clinics, with just a handful of organizations by fat people for fat rights.

When we asked our friends and colleagues their opinions on why fat people have not organized, the majority stated that it is because fat people could lose weight if they tried. In contrast, they said, other oppressed groups have characteristics that cannot be changed (e.g., skin color, disability status). Maddox, Back, and Liederman (1968) asked people to indicate the degree to which different groups were responsible for their condition. Whereas only 2% of subjects felt that a blind person was responsible for his or her lack of sight, 76% felt that a "man with a flabby body" and 84% felt that "a woman needing a girdle" were responsible for their condition.

Yet it was not that long ago when lesbians and gay men were encouraged to undergo therapy to become heterosexual (bisexual people, presumably, were supposed to disregard same-sex fantasies and behaviors). Certainly there are people who change their religion to avoid oppression and make life easier for their children. People with brown skin die every year from overusing skin-lightening products that contain bleach. So weight is not the only characteristic perceived to be malleable.

Goffman (1963) has pointed out that the worst consequence of stigmatizing attitudes is that the stigmatized group comes to believe and accept the negative evaluations. Thus, fat people are not only stigmatized by Western society, but also come to believe that we are responsible for this oppression. Every institution in our culture—schools, health-care organizations, media, marketing—promotes a propaganda of weight control, so that it is nearly impossible for individuals not to believe that "fat is bad." Even when we can overcome this indoctrination, organizing around fat oppression is to open ourselves up to ridicule.

What's Really at Stake Here—Billions of Dollars

What would happen if fat people suddenly accepted our bodies? A number of industries would cease to exist—the multibillion-dollar dieting industry, the diet food industry, the diet cookbook industry, and the bariatric surgery industry. The health/exercise club industry and cosmetic surgery industry would lose millions of dollars. These industries (and many others that focus on appearance) depend on people, especially women, feeling dissatisfied with our bodies and buying into the myth of individual solutions instead of political action to change institutional bias. We are brainwashed into believing that our bodies are products and that these products can be standardized or shaped or changed at will, or that we can buy products that will change our bodies. The diet industry and pharmaceutical companies increasingly objectify our bodies so that everyone, from gender-questioning youth to senior citizens, is affected by this focus on the ideal appearance. Much more analysis and work needs to be done in this arena.

Because so many people are fat (and many more are thin but nevertheless internalize fat-phobic self-hatred), this is a group that cannot be allowed to organize. Its large size (no pun intended) threatens the very existence of the appearance-related corporate sector. And we must understand that to challenge entrenched financial interests requires an economic paradigm shift—an understanding that celebrating people of all sizes will provide a stronger basis for an economy than building industries on stigmatization.

Fat People Are Neither Rich nor Young

The prevalence of fatness is affected by socio-economic class, particularly for women. In Western societies, fat people tend to be poor whereas thin people tend to be wealthier. As Paul Ernsberger has described earlier in this book, the relationship between low social status and high body weight is particularly true for women.

Paul Campos (2004) has argued that discrimination based on weight is focused on poor people (because poorer people are fatter) and people of color (because people of color in the United States are often poor). In other words, fat oppression is a way to be racist and classist without appearing to target poor people of color directly.

Imagine if women could take back our bodies and feel comfortable and happy! Imagine if we were encouraged to love our bodies, no matter what. When fat people organize, we are saying that we own our bodies, that they are not for sale to the highest bidder. They are not malleable—they are fat bodies and will stay that way.

If women loved our bodies, *everything* would be different. Our culture is fixated on making women feel bad about our physical presentation, putting us in a constant state of performance anxiety. Men criticize women's bodies, knowing that it will make women feel terrible. But it is one thing to have a political understanding and another to have a personal one. Political understanding is a first step; the emotional step follows.

Facing the Dragon and Showing Up

Many of the people who took the first steps to speak out about fat oppression in the 1980s have gone on to become performers, models, entrepreneurs, artists, activists, writers, bloggers, and adorable loudmouths. They are not hiding themselves. They are not quietly going about their business. They are not ashamed to be themselves. They are out of the closet.

Those people are now the sandwich generation between the amazing pioneers of the Fat Underground and the younger activists, artists, and academics who seem to be bursting with energy in creating the next wave of challenges to the "Fat Is Bad" culture.

It strikes us at this moment in our history, as we look at all the chapters of this groundbreaking book, how breathtaking it is to witness members of a browbeaten group move out of hiding to express their experience. It may have been a long time coming, it may be a long struggle ahead, but we are witnessing a great healing when this happens and it is cause for celebration.

Consider how remarkable it is when people who have been repeatedly socially ostracized are somehow able to take the risk of being humiliated again, in the service of showing up as their real selves. In this act of taking our lives as the subject of scholarly inquiry—taking ourselves and our experiences seriously—don't we risk being humiliated all over again?

Well, yes, in fact, we are already experiencing the derisive reactions of dissertation advisers, medical experts, and mentors who tell us that focusing on Fat Studies would be a career-ending move. In a recent *New York Times* article, reporter Abby Ellin quotes psychologist professor Joseph Juhasz (2000, sec. 9, p. 6) as saying: "Certainly we have not reached a point where we can do away with queer studies or race studies or women's studies . . . But where do you draw the line? Is there going to be a department of man-boy-love studies? Do we need polygamy studies? At which point do you say, enough already?"

Somehow we have found each other and we like what we see. We have a drive to *show up.* We have been slowly creating an infrastructure for this changed attitude over the decades, and we have been encouraged by all the other courageous groups who have shown that there is a way out of oppression.

How do people transition from an almost universal self-blame for interpersonal pain to a more nuanced understanding of why others hurt them?

The stigma of being fat is similar to other traits that have been used to oppress, but it is also different. Is being fat more like being queer, in that you don't have a "community" growing up, you sense that it is an intimate part of your identity, and you might try hard to change it before you accept it? Is it more like being a member of a stigmatized ethnic group, because you cannot hide it from other people and it can be a reason you don't get a job? Is it more like being seen as disabled, because it can affect your mobility and access? Is it more like being a smoker, because it is supposed to be your own fault, you supposedly could change it if you tried hard enough, and maybe you do have the experience of changing it temporarily? Or is it more like being a woman, since so much of the stigma has to do with the despised (alleged) traits of femaleness (neediness, being out of control, and the overwhelming appetites of the female body)?

What about how fat people feel about other fat people? What makes us avoid one another and not know how varied and interesting we are? What allows us to push past that and begin to connect and challenge our own internal stereotypes? What happens when we meet people who seem to fulfill the fat stereotype? What happens when we meet people who bust the stereotype? How do our own stories change the visions that someone else develops for their life?

What does the transition away from oppression based on body size look like? What forms of art are created that capture both the suffering and liberation of fat people? In the end, Fat Studies is not just about oppression; it is about the experience of navigating a treacherous and heartbreakingly beautiful world in a body, one that can thrill or ache, be loved or despised, claimed or disowned. We are beginning to feel entitled to tell our stories, even knowing that there will be jeering. Too bad for them—they will miss the parade.

In her poem "Whole Cloth," Susan Stinson writes, "so much wild fatness, making its own song in motion, making a song in largeness" (p. 13). So much wild fatness!

In deciding to make the world we *do* live in a world that we *can* live in, fat people have taken up a long, arduous activism. We *are* organizing—but like all people in this militaristic time, it's not always easy to find the evidence of it. Take us seriously. Give the fat woman room. The songs she sings will challenge, surprise, and delight us.

NOTE

This title for this chapter is taken from the video *Throwing Our Weight Around: A Video About Fat Women's Lives* (1989), produced by Sandy Dwyer and released by Boston Area Fat Liberation.

REFERENCES

Burros, M. (1994, December 5). Former surgeon general begins push for Americans to slim down. *New York Times*, A20.

Campos, P. (2004). *The Obesity Myth: Why America's Obsession with Weight Is Hazardous to Your Health*. New York: Gotham Books.

CNN. (1996, October 29). Former surgeon general wages war on obesity. *CNN Interactive Health Story*. Retrieved August 28, 2006, from http://www.cnn.com/HEALTH/9610/29/nfm/obesity/index.html.

CSPI. (2003). Shape up America! *Integrity in Science*. Retrieved August 28, 2006, from http://www.cspinet.org/integrity/nonprofits/shape_up_america.html.

Ellin, Abby. Big people on campus. *New York Times*, November 26, 2006, section 9, pp. 1–2.

Fraser, L. (1998). *Losing It: False Hopes and Fast Profits in the Diet Industry*. New York: Penguin Plume.

Goffman, I. (1963). *Stigma: Notes on the Management of Spoiled Identity*. Englewood Cliffs, N.J.: Prentice Hall.

Maddox, G.L., Back, K., & Liederman, V. (1968). Overweight as social deviance and disability. *Journal of Health and Social Behavior, 9*, 287–298.

Stinson, S. (1993). *Belly Songs: In Celebration of Fat Women*. Northampton, MA: Orogeny Press.

Time. (2004). The *Time*/ABC news summit on obesity, June 2–4, 2004. *Time Online*. Retrieved August 28, 2006, from http://www.time.com/time/2004/obesity.

Appendix A
Fat Liberation Manifesto, November 1973

Judy Freespirit and Aldebaran

1. WE believe that fat people are fully entitled to human respect and recognition.

2. WE are angry at mistreatment by commercial and sexist interests. These have exploited our bodies as objects of ridicule, thereby creating an immensely profitable market selling the false promise of avoidance of, or relief from, that ridicule.

3. WE see our struggle as allied with the struggles of other oppressed groups against classism, racism, sexism, ageism, financial exploitation, imperialism and the like.

4. WE demand equal rights for fat people in all aspects of life, as promised in the Constitution of the United States. We demand equal access to goods and services in the public domain, and an end to discrimination against us in the areas of employment, education, public facilities and health services.

5. WE single out as our special enemies the so-called "reducing" industries. These include diet clubs, reducing salons, fat farms, diet doctors, diet books, diet foods and food supplements, surgical procedures, appetite suppressants, drugs and gadgetry such as wraps and "reducing machines."

   WE demand that they take responsibility for their false claims, acknowledge that their products are harmful to the public health, and publish long-term studies proving any statistical efficacy of their products. We make this demand knowing that over 99% of all weight loss programs, when evaluated over a five-year period, fail utterly, and also knowing the extreme proven harmfulness of frequent large changes in weight.

6. WE repudiate the mystified "science" which falsely claims that we are unfit. It has both caused and upheld discrimination against us, in collusion with the financial interests of insurance companies, the fashion and garment industries, reducing industries, the food and drug industries, and the medical and psychiatric establishment.

7. WE refuse to be subjugated to the interests of our enemies. We fully intend to reclaim power over our bodies and our lives. We commit ourselves to pursue these goals together.

FAT PEOPLE OF THE WORLD, UNITE! YOU HAVE NOTHING TO LOSE.

NOTE

Originally Published by the Fat Underground, Los Angeles, California. Also published in *Shadow on a Tightrope: Writings by Women on Fat Oppression*, edited by Lisa Schoenfielder and Barb Wieser, Aunt Lute Books, 1983.

Appendix B
Legal Briefs

This section provides a brief look at the actual legal language used to prohibit weight discrimination in sample jurisdictions. Laws prohibiting weight discrimination are known to exist in only a handful of places, including the following U.S. locations: the State of Michigan; Washington, D.C.; Madison, Wisconsin; and the California cities of Santa Cruz and San Francisco. Below are excerpts of the San Francisco and Michigan laws. In addition, the complete Compliance Guidelines for the San Francisco ordinance are included. The Guidelines themselves have the full force of law in the City and County of San Francisco. Pay particular attention to the definitions of height and weight used by the City and County of San Francisco (as provided in the Guidelines), which were crafted to avoid discrimination based, among many things, on the places where fat is located on the body.

1. Excerpt from San Francisco Municipal Code Chapter 12 A and B

SEC. 12A.1. FINDINGS.

The population of this City and County is composed of people of various racial, religious and ethnic groups. In this City and County the practice of discrimination on the actual or perceived grounds of race, religion, color, ancestry, age, sex, sexual orientation, gender identity, disability, weight, height or place of birth and the exploitation of prejudice related thereto adversely affects members of minority groups.

Such discriminatory practices are inimical to the public welfare and good order in that they: (a) impede social and economic progress for the entire citizenry by preventing members of minority groups from achieving full development of their individual potentialities and from contributing fully to the cultural and business life of the community; (b) constantly frustrate, degrade and embitter members of minority groups, thereby diminishing their initiative and interests in the community; and (c) tend to create intergroup hostilities and antisocial behavior.

The products of discrimination accumulate continuously, with the result that the social, economic and educational gaps between those suffering discrimination and the majority of the community constantly widen. As a result, mere prohibition of future and present discrimination, while essential, will not reduce the inequalities and disadvantages which a history of discrimination has produced. Accordingly, affirmative remedial action must be initiated, encouraged and coordinated.

Experiences of other urban centers throughout the nation have proved the need for and effectiveness of commissions empowered to study community race relations problems, to work with interested citizens to develop programs to ameliorate tensions and reduce cultural, social and economic disadvantages and to encourage and coordinate implementation of such programs consistent with the needs and rights of members of both the majority and the minority.

A substantial number of the aforementioned evils in this City and County are beyond the regulation of applicable State law, and insofar as State law is applicable, voluntary compliance therewith should be fostered by a local human relations commission.

(Amended by Ord. 75–77, App. 3/4/77; Ord. 433–94, App. 12/30/94; Ord. 255–99, File No. 991146, App. 10/8/99; Ord. 101–00, File No. 000476, App. 5/26/2000.) (Retrieved August 19, 2008, from http://www.municode.com/Resources/gateway. asp?pid=14131&sid=5.)

SEC. 12B.1. ALL CONTRACTS AND PROPERTY CONTRACTS TO INCLUDE NONDISCRIMINATION PROVISIONS; DEFINITIONS.

(a) All contracting agencies of the City, or any department thereof, acting for or on behalf of the City and County, shall include in all contracts and property contracts hereinafter executed or amended in any manner or as to any portion thereof, a provision obligating the contractor not to discriminate on the basis of the fact or perception of a person's race, color, creed, religion, national origin, ancestry, age, sex, sexual orientation, gender identity, domestic partner status, marital status, disability or Acquired Immune Deficiency Syndrome, HIV status (AIDS/HIV status), weight, height, association with members of classes protected under this chapter or in retaliation for opposition to any practices forbidden under this chapter against any employee of, any City employee working with, or applicant for employment with such contractor and shall require such contractor to include a similar provision in all subcontracts executed or amended thereunder.

(b) No contracting agency of the City, or any department thereof, acting for or on behalf of the City and County, shall execute or amend any contract or property contract with any contractor that discriminates in the provision of bereavement leave, family medical leave, health benefits, membership or membership discounts, moving expenses, pension and retirement benefits or travel benefits as well as any benefits other than bereavement leave, family medical leave, health benefits, membership or membership discounts, moving expenses, pension and retirement benefits or travel benefits between employees with domestic partners and employees with spouses, and/ or between the domestic partners and spouses of such employees, where the domestic partnership has been registered with a governmental entity pursuant to State or local law authorizing such registration, subject to the following conditions. In the event that the contractor's actual cost of providing a certain benefit for the domestic partner of an employee exceeds that of providing it for the spouse of an employee, or the contractor's actual cost of providing a certain benefit for the spouse of an employee exceeds that of providing it for the domestic partner of an employee, the contractor shall not be deemed to discriminate in the provision of benefits if the contractor conditions providing such benefit upon the employee agreeing to pay the excess costs. In addition, in the event a contractor is unable to provide a certain benefit, despite taking reasonable measures to do so, the contractor shall not be deemed to discriminate in the provision of benefits if the contractor provides the employee with a cash equivalent.

(Retrieved August 19, 2008, from http://www.municode.com/Resources/gateway. asp?pid=14131&sid=5.)

2. Complete Text of the San Francisco Compliance Guidelines to Prohibit Weight and Height Discrimination

San Francisco Administrative Code Chapters 12A, 12B and 12C and San Francisco Municipal/Police Code Article 33
CITY AND COUNTY OF SAN FRANCISCO
HUMAN RIGHTS COMMISSION
July 26, 2001
Table of Contents
INTENT
DEFINITIONS
   WEIGHT
   HEIGHT
   REASONABLE ACCOMMODATION
CONDUCT AND DEMEANOR
   POLICY IMPLEMENTATION AND PUBLICATION
   CONTINUING EDUCATION AND DIVERSITY TRAINING
   SUPERVISION
SERVICES AND ACCOMMODATIONS
   EQUITABLE ACCOMMODATIONS
   ACCESS AND EQUAL TREATMENT
   REASONABLE ACCOMMODATION
EMPLOYMENT
   NON-DISCRIMINATION
   HOSTILE ENVIRONMENT AND HARASSMENT
   STANDARDS
   PHYSICAL WORKPLACE
HOUSING
   NON-DISCRIMINATION
   ACCOMMODATIONS AND ALTERATIONS

I. INTENT

It is the intent of the Human Rights Commission that programs, services, and facilities are accessible to and functional for people of all weights and heights.

II. DEFINITIONS

The following definitions will apply in the construction and implementation of the guidelines described herein:

A. WEIGHT

Weight is a numerical measurement of total body weight, the ratio of a person's weight in relation to height or an individual's unique physical composition of weight through body size, shape, and proportions.

"Weight" encompasses, but is not limited to, an impression of a person as fat or thin regardless of the numerical measurement. An individual's body size, shape, proportions, and composition may make them appear fat or thin regardless of numerical weight.

B. HEIGHT

Height is a numerical measurement of total body height, an expression of a person's height in relation to weight, or an individual's unique physical composition of height through body size, shape, and proportions.

"Height" encompasses, but is not limited to an impression of a person as tall or short regardless of numerical measurement. The length of a person's limbs in proportion to the person's body may create an impression that the person is short, tall, or atypically proportioned, independent of numerical measurements of height.

C. REASONABLE ACCOMMODATION

An accommodation is a change in structure, policy, practice or procedure necessary to avoid discrimination. An accommodation is reasonable unless an entity can demonstrate that making the accommodation would fundamentally alter the nature of the service, program or activity or the accommodation constitutes an undue burden defined as a significant difficulty or expense, taking into account the entity's resources.

III. CONDUCT AND DEMEANOR

A. POLICY IMPLEMENTATION AND PUBLICATION

City contractors, subcontractors, agencies, business establishments, and organizations should implement and clearly communicate a non-discrimination policy regarding weight and height to all staff including managers. The non-discrimination policy should be communicated to customers, clients or third parties who propose a discriminatory practice. San Francisco employers and City contractors must post the Human Rights Commission's anti-discrimination notice in a location visible to all employees.

B. CONTINUING EDUCATION AND DIVERSITY TRAINING

The Human Rights Commission recommends that agencies, business establishments, and organizations require all staff including managers to receive continuing education in weight and height related discrimination issues. The Commission further recommends that weight and height be included in comprehensive diversity training programs.

C. SUPERVISION

An individual, employer, agency, landlord, or business establishment must prevent the use of disrespectful language or behavior related to weight or height by its staff, including managers, or by customers and clients at their place of business or while under their control. The person in charge must take corrective action to assure compliance such as telling the person making an offensive remark that the behavior is not allowed.

IV. SERVICES AND ACCOMMODATIONS

A. EQUITABLE ACCOMMODATIONS

Agencies, business establishments and organizations will provide appropriate and equitable accommodations, so all people, regardless of their weight or height, may share in the equal enjoyment of goods, services, facilities, privileges, and advantages of any place of public accommodation. In the event there is a surcharge to cover the cost of accommodation, this increase may be applied across the board but may not be passed on solely to the person or class of persons being accommodated. The following examples are meant to be illustrative, not exhaustive.

Example 1: Fixed seats are often too small for large or tall people. Businesses, such as theaters, with fixed seating will provide an adequate amount of seating without arms and with extra leg room. There must be an adequate supply of seats with various lines of sight and choices of admission prices.

Example 2: Swimming pools shall provide steps, handrails, or other appropriate entry and exit architecture to accommodate swimmers of all sizes.

Example 3: Hair salons, medical offices, and other organizations or establishments that provide dressing gowns or uniforms, will provide gowns or uniforms that fit. One size does not fit all.

B. ACCESS AND EQUAL TREATMENT

Agencies, business establishments and organizations will not obstruct access or deny participation in any service, facility, privilege, advantage, accommodation, or opportunity to individuals based on their weight or height, including but not limited to social services, health services, educational and training services, recreation services and programs. (Exceptions may apply only upon a showing of a bona fide need.)

Example: Medical providers shall have an adequate supply of large blood pressure cuffs and shall provide access to scales that accommodate a wide range of weights.

Medical providers must not deny treatment based on a person's weight or height. Further, medical providers must not make weight loss or weight gain related intervention a condition for treatment. People are often discouraged from seeking medical care because providers lecture them about weight loss rather than treating the condition they came in for. Medical providers may feel obligated to provide weight loss or gain information based on a belief that the information is medically necessary. At the same time, patients have the right to express disinterest in receiving that information and have the right to refuse treatment. The Commission urges medical providers to honor that choice.

C. REASONABLE ACCOMMODATION

A public accommodation shall make reasonable modifications in policies, practices and procedures when the modifications are necessary to avoid discrimination unless the organization can demonstrate that making the modification would fundamentally alter the nature of the service, program or activity. A modification is reasonable unless it constitutes an undue burden defined as a significant difficulty or expense on the organization, taking into account the organization's resources.

V. EMPLOYMENT

A. NON-DISCRIMINATION

Employers may not discriminate against any individual because of their weight or height in any aspect of employment, including but not limited to recruitment, selection, hiring, wages, uniforms, hours and conditions of employment, promotion, training, development, or benefits.

It is not an automatic defense to a charge of weight based employment discrimination that a person of the same weight was hired. For example, it is impermissible to reject a candidate because she carries her weight around her abdomen, in favor of a candidate of the same weight and height who is differently proportioned.

An employer may not exclude a person from a "front office" position or any other position because the employer believes the employee's weight is not in keeping with a professional appearance. The wishes, tastes or preferences of other employees or customers may not be asserted to justify discrimination.

B. HOSTILE ENVIRONMENT AND HARASSMENT

Employers must strive to maintain a respectful, non-hostile environment related to weight and height. Verbal or written harassment against an employee based on weight or height is prohibited. Unsolicited comments, advice, or literature recommending weight loss or gain are inappropriate. For example, a poster that proclaims "No Fat Cops" and encourages officers to seek help from the department about losing weight is inappropriate. However, it is appropriate to advocate increased health and fitness for people of all sizes. An employee must never be subjected to comments regarding weight or height once the employee has stated that such comments are unwelcome. An employee may not be retaliated against for expressing that prefer-ence or for insisting on the right to be free from weight and height-based discrimi-nation and harassment.

C. STANDARDS

Employment decisions must be based on merit or fitness for the position. Weight or height standards may not be used unless weight or height is a bona fide occupational qualification. Weight may not be used as a measure of health, fitness, endurance, flex-ibility, strength, character or self-control. Individuals of all sizes must be provided an equal opportunity to demonstrate their knowledge and ability. The employer advocat-ing the use of a weight or height standard bears the burden of proving the standard is a bona fide occupational qualification.

D. PHYSICAL WORKPLACE

Employers must undertake readily achievable modifications in the workplace includ-ing, but not limited to, accessible furnishings, workplace layout, and equipment. The employer shall give consideration to an employee seeking accommodation based on weight or height, unless the employer can demonstrate that another effective means exists or that the individual's expressed choice is not required. Employers shall ensure that common areas such as employee lounges, cafeterias, health units and exercise facilities are accessible to people of all sizes.

VI. HOUSING

A. NON-DISCRIMINATION

Homebuyers, rental applicants, tenants, and those utilizing housing-related services must not be discriminated against based on weight or height.

B. ACCOMMODATIONS AND ALTERATIONS

If a tenant needs and requests an accommodation because of weight or height, it must be made if it is readily achievable. Some examples of alterations that are usually readily achievable include: installing offset hinges to widen doorways, rearranging furnishings, lowering mirrors or replacing shower doors with shower curtains. The need or potential need to make an accommodation may not be considered as a factor in the decision to select a tenant.

A landlord shall not unreasonably withhold approval of alterations necessary to meet a tenant's needs related to weight and height.

For further assistance please call the Human Rights Commission at (415) 252–2500 (main number) or (415) 252–2550 (TTY/TTD).

(Retrieved August 19, 2008, from http://www.sfgov.org/site/sfhumanrights_page. asp?id=5911&mode=text.)

3. *Excerpt from the State of Michigan Law*

ELLIOTT- LARSEN CIVIL RIGHTS ACT

AN ACT to define civil rights; to prohibit discriminatory practices, policies, and customs in the exercise of those rights based upon religion, race, color, national origin, age, sex, height, weight, familial status, or marital status; to preserve the confidentiality of records regarding arrest, detention, or other disposition in which a conviction does not result; to prescribe the powers and duties of the civil rights commission and the department of civil rights; to provide remedies and penalties; to provide for fees; and to repeal certain acts and parts of acts.

The People of the State of Michigan enact:

ARTICLE I

Sec. 101. This act shall be known and may be cited as the "Elliott-Larsen Civil Rights Act."

Sec. 102. (1) The opportunity to obtain employment, housing and other real estate, and the full and equal utilization of public accommodations, public service, and educational facilities without discrimination because of religion, race, color, national origin, age, sex, height, weight, familial status, or marital status as prohibited by this act, is recognized and declared to be a civil right.

(Retrieved August 19, 2008, from http://www.michigan.gov/documents/act_453_elliott_larsen_8772_7.pdf.)

About the Contributors

LUCY APHRAMOR, BSc. Hons., RD, is a dietitian with a HAES-promoting cardiac re-habilitation team and holds a research post at Coventry University, United Kingdom.

D. LACY ASBILL received an MA in Human Sexuality Studies from San Francisco State University. She is the founding director of Girls Moving Forward, an education and empowerment service dedicated to ending the pervasive gender confidence gap in education.

DEREK ATTIG graduated from Beloit College in 2006 with majors in History and Women's Studies. Derek is now a PhD student in the Department of History at the University of Illinois at Urbana-Champaign.

S. BEAR BERGMAN (http://www.sbearbergman.com) is an author, a theater artist, and an instigator, as well as the author of *Butch Is a Noun* (Suspect Thoughts Press, 2006) and three award-winning solo performances.

BETH BERNSTEIN, MA, MFT, is a therapist in Oakland, California, and past host of the radio talk show *Body Language: The Show About How You Relate to Your Body.* Her writing has appeared in *Bitch, Bust,* the *Health at Every Size Journal,* and the an-thology *Bitchfest: 10 Years of Bitch Magazine.*

NATALIE BOERO, PhD, is on the sociology faculty at San Jose State University as an Assistant Professor, specializing in medical sociology, feminist theory, sociology of the body, and qualitative research methods.

DEB BURGARD, PhD, is a clinical psychologist, creator of the BodyPositive.com and ShowMeTheData (http://tech.groups.yahoo.com/group/ShowMeTheData/) websites, coauthor of *Great Shape: The First Fitness Guide for Large Women,* and columnist for the *Health at Every Size Journal.* She does research on the ways that everyday people across the weight spectrum integrate sustainable, self-nurturing practices into their lives.

WENDY A. BURNS-ARDOLINO, PhD, is Assistant Professor of Liberal Studies at Clayton State University, where she directs the Women's Studies Program and the Master of Arts Program in Liberal Studies. Her publications focus on feminist theory, body studies, globalization, and popular culture. Her most recent book, *Jiggle: (Re) shaping American Women*, was published in 2008. She continues to teach interdisciplinary courses that cut across the fields of cultural studies, women's studies, and media studies.

CHARLOTTE COOPER is author of *Fat and Proud: The Politics of Size* (The Women's Press, 1998) and *Cherry* (Diva, 2002). She lives and works in the United Kingdom and is the founding member of The Chubsters. More information can be found on http://www.charlottecooper.net.

ELANA DYKEWOMON has been a cultural worker and activist since the 1970s. Her books include *Riverfinger Woman, Nothing Will Be As Sweet As the Taste, Selected Poems*, the Jewish lesbian historical novel *Beyond the Pale* (which received the Lambda and Ferro-Grumley awards for lesbian fiction in 1998), and *Moon Creek Road*. She teaches at San Francisco State University, offers private creative writing classes for lesbians (see http://www.dykewomon.org), and is proud to live in Oakland, stirring up trouble whenever she can.

JENNY ELLISON is a doctoral student in history at York University in Toronto.

PAUL ERNSBERGER, PhD, is a biomedical scientist who is Associate Professor in the Department of Nutrition at Case Western Reserve University. His research focuses on the role of genetics in weight and the role of "yo-yo dieting" in cardiovascular disease. He is coeditor of the special issue of the *Journal of Social Issues* titled "Dying to Be Thin in the Name of Health: Shifting the Paradigm" and author of over one hundred peer-reviewed publications.

ELENA ESCALERA, PhD, is Assistant Professor of Psychology at St. Mary's College of California. She provided expert testimony before the San Francisco board of supervisors and the San Francisco Human Rights Commission during the passing of legislation adding weight and height to the San Francisco nondiscrimination ordinance.

AMY FARRELL, PhD, is Professor of American Studies and Women's Studies at Dickinson College in Carlisle, Pennsylvania. She is also the author of *Yours in Sisterhood: Ms. Magazine and the Promise of Popular Feminism* (University of North Carolina Press, 1998). She is currently finishing a book titled *Fat Shame: A Cultural History of Fat Stigma, Dieting, and the Fat Activist Movements*.

CHRISTINA FISANICK, PhD, is Assistant Professor of English at California University of Pennsylvania. Her research and teaching focus on issues of female embodiment in writing pedagogy, popular culture, social medicine, academic culture, and memoir. Her most recently published works include articles on polycystic ovarian syndrome and normative femininity, the role of the female professor's body in tenure and promotion decisions, and the fat professor's body in the classroom.

LAURA FRASER is a freelance writer and contributing editor to *More Magazine*. She is author of the book *Losing It: America's Obsession With Weight and the Industry That Feeds On It*. Her most recent book is *An Italian Affair* (Vintage).

LARA FRATER is a librarian, writer, feminist, and activist living in New York City. She is the author of *Fat Chicks Rule* and writes a blog and column at IGIGI by the same name. Find her at http://www.larafrater.com.

GLENN GAESSER, PhD, is the author of *Big Fat Lies: The Truth About Your Weight and Your Health* (Gurze Books, 2002). He is a professor in the Department of Exercise and Wellness, School of Applied Arts and Sciences, at Arizona State University in Mesa, Arizona.

JEANNINE A. GAILEY, PhD, is Assistant Professor of Criminal Justice at Texas Christian University. Her current research interests include organizational deviance, attributing responsibility for wrongdoing, and violence against women.

JACQUI GINGRAS, PhD, RD, is Assistant Professor at Ryerson University's School of Nutrition in Toronto, Ontario, Canada. Her research engages auto/ethnographic, narrative, and arts-informed methods as a means for situated and particular understandings of dietetic theory, education, and practice.

DINA GIOVANELLI is a fat doctoral student in Sociology at the University of Connecticut. Her research focuses on inequality, gender, and sociology of the body. Her dissertation will focus on the medicalization of fat bodies. Specifically, it will utilize an institutional ethnographic approach to investigate people's experiences with weight loss surgery.

JULIE GUTHMAN, PhD, is Associate Professor of Community Studies at the University of California at Santa Cruz, where she teaches and researches various aspects of the politics of agriculture, food, and, increasingly, bodies. She is the author of *Agrarian Dreams: The Paradox of Organic Farming in California* (University of California Press, 2004).

ASHLEY HETRICK graduated from Beloit College in 2007 with majors in Literary Studies and Women's and Gender Studies. Ashley is now a PhD student in the Department of English at the University of Illinois at Urbana-Champaign.

JOYCE L. HUFF, Ph.D., is Assistant Professor of English at Ball State University. She specializes in nineteenth-century British literature and culture, disability studies, and fat studies.

MAHO ISONO is a doctoral student in Cultural Anthropology at Waseda University in Tokyo.

LAURA JENNINGS, PhD, is an Assistant Professor at University of South Carolina Upstate. Her research interests include intersectional inequalities, medical sociology, and health policy.

JULIAGRACE JESTER received an interdisciplinary PhD from Miami University of Ohio in Social Psychology, Theatre, and Women's Studies. She is a researcher on the stigmatization of Women of Size and a practitioner of Theatre of the Oppressed. Her recent teaching experiences have included visiting professor positions at Wells College in Aurora, New York, and Ithaca College in Ithaca, New York.

SUSAN KOPPELMAN, PhD, is a writer, editor, and literary historian. She edited the anthology *The Strange History of Suzanne LaFleshe, and Other Stories of Women and Fatness* (The Feminist Press, 2003) and has edited eleven other books, including *The Other Woman: Stories of Two Women and a Man* (The Feminist Press, 1984), *Between Mothers and Daughters: Stories Across a Generation* (The Feminist Press, 1985, rev. ed. 2004), and *Women in the Trees: U.S. Women's Short Stories About Battering and Resistance, 1839–2000* (The Feminist Press, 2004).

MICHELLE KREHBIEL, PhD, is Assistant Professor of Integrated Professional Studies at the University of Vermont. Her research has focused on youth aggression.

KATHLEEN LEBESCO, PhD, is Professor and Chair of the Department of Communication Arts, Marymount Manhattan College. She is coeditor of *Bodies Out of Bounds: Fatness and Transgression* (University of California Press, 2001) and author of *Revolting Bodies? The Struggle to Redefine Fat Identity* (University of Massachusetts Press, 2004).

ELENA LEVY-NAVARRO, PhD, is an Associate Professor of English at the University of Wisconsin at Whitewater. She has published essays in the areas of fat studies, queer studies, and Renaissance studies. Her book *The Culture of Obesity in Early and Late Modernity: Body Image in Shakespeare, Jonson, Middleton, and Skelton* (Palgrave, 2008) uses history to envision alternatives to our modern pathologized category of obesity.

LEE EE LIAN is employed in the Department of Psychiatry at Singapore General Hospital where she is the director of the Eating Disorders Treatment Program.

MICHAEL I. LOEWY, PhD, is Associate Professor and Chair of the Department of Counseling at University of North Dakota.

PAT LYONS, RN, MA, is coauthor of *Great Shape: The First Fitness Guide for Large Women* and the project director for the UC Berkeley–based WomanCare Plus research and education project addressing weight bias and health disparities.

HEATHER MCALLISTER was the founder and director of Big Burlesque and Fat-Bottom Revue, the world's first all-fat burlesque troupe. She was a social justice activist on behalf of marginalized communities for over twenty years. Heather McAllister died on February 13, 2007. Amid her own battle against ovarian cancer, she took her hard-won energy and time to write this chapter because she believed it was important work . . . a life's work.

JULIA MCCROSSIN is a PhD candidate in English at George Washington University. Her current research interests include the re-signification of fat erotics, the intersectionality of fat and other identity constructs, the semiotics of fat, and how fat complicates contemporary discourses of nationality and citizenship across the globe.

KATHARINA R. MENDOZA is a doctoral student in the Women's Studies Department at the University of Iowa. She plans to return to her native Philippines as soon as local stores start selling quality plus-size clothing.

STEPHEN OSTERTAG is a professor of practice at Tulane University. He investigates how cultural readers use news media to construct and reinforce their social realities, and, somewhat separately, the collective behavior of community-based, volunteer-driven media organizations.

ARIANE PROHASKA is Assistant Professor of Sociology in the Department of Criminal Justice at the University of Alabama. Her research interests include gender, work, family, masculinities, public policy, and social inequality.

NATHANIEL C. PYLE is a doctoral student in Sociology at University of California, Santa Barbara, studying gender and sexuality. He is a proud chubby-chaser who is continuing to document the gay, big men's communities.

ESTHER ROTHBLUM, PhD, is Professor of Women's Studies at San Diego State University and has served on the National Advisory Board of the National Association to Advance Fat Acceptance. She conducts research on the stigma of women's weight and has edited over twenty books, including *Overcoming Fear of Fat*.

TRACY ROYCE is a doctoral student in the Department of Sociology at the University of California, Santa Barbara. Her research interests include gender and sexualities, violence against women, and weight-related prejudice and discrimination.

MATILDA ST. JOHN, MA, MFT, is a therapist in Oakland, California, and co–artistic director of Big Moves' West Coast Phat Fly Girls, a fat hip-hop and jazz dance troupe. Her writing has appeared in *Bitch, Bust*, the *Health at Every Size Journal*, and the anthology *Bitchfest: 10 Years of Bitch Magazine*.

DANA SCHUSTER is a fitness instructor and currently serves on the Board of ASDAH (Association for Size Diversity and Health). She also provides educational workshops on body image, self-esteem, size diversity, and health for students, teachers, and parents. She was the co-owner of Women of Substance Health Spa with Lisa Tealer.

STEFANIE SNIDER is a doctoral candidate in Art History at the University of Southern California. Her dissertation is focused on fat and lesbian visual representation in contemporary art.

SONDRA SOLOVAY, JD, is an attorney, Adjunct Professor of Law, content developer, and activist focusing on weight-related issues, diversity, and the law. She runs the Fat Legal Advocacy, Rights, and Education Project and is the author of *Tipping the Scales of Justice: Fighting Weight-Based Discrimination*.

SUSAN STINSON's novels are *Fat Girl Dances with Rocks*, *Martha Moody*, and *Venus of Chalk*, a Lambda Literary Award finalist. *Belly Songs: In Celebration of Fat Women* is her collection of poetry and lyric essays. She has been awarded support from the Barbara Deming/Money for Women Fund, the Vogelstein Foundation, and Norcroft, among others.

LISA TEALER is the diversity professional: a plus-size model, aerobics instructor, and a board member and Health at Every Size (HAES) chair of the National Association to Advance Fat Acceptance (NAAFA). She has written articles and conducted workshops on plus-size fitness, fat acceptance, and size diversity in the workplace. She was the co-owner of Women of Substance Health Spa with Dana Schuster.

PATTIE THOMAS, PhD, coauthor of *Taking Up Space: How Eating Well and Exercising Regularly Changed My Life* (Pearlsong Press 2005, with her husband, Carl Wilkerson, MBA), draws on her expertise as a medical sociologist to show the costs of stigma both in the particular and the general case. Among their ongoing projects, Pattie and Carl promote universal access in the travel industry through *The Ample Traveler* (http://theampletraveler.com). Pattie currently lives in Las Vegas, Nevada, where she and Carl own and operate SINdustry CITY Media Services, a multimedia project development firm.

DYLAN VADE, JD, PhD, is an attorney and cofounder of the Transgender Law Center in San Francisco, California. His most recent article is "Expanding Gender and Expanding the Law: Toward a Social and Legal Conceptualization That Is More Inclusive of Transgender People." He has spoken widely on transgender issues, including at the United Nations. Dylan is a queer transgender person, and he will not apologize for that, ever.

MARILYN WANN is founder of the *FAT!SO?* zine and author of *FAT!SO?: Because You Don't Have to Apologize for Your Size!* She is a diversity trainer and public commentator who has performed with the Padded Lilies (fat synchronized swim team featured on *The Tonight Show*), Big Moves modern dance, the Phat Fly Girls, and the Bod Squad. She also creates Yay! Scales, bathroom scales that display compliments instead of numbers.

PATTI LOU WATKINS received her PhD in clinical psychology and is Associate Professor at Oregon State University, where she teaches "Women, Weight, and Eating Disorders" as well as "Self-Esteem and Personal Power" and "Violence Against Women." She has recently edited the book *Handbook of Self-Help Therapies*.

JACQUELINE WEINSTOCK, PhD, is Associate Professor of Integrated Professional Studies at the University of Vermont. She has edited the books *Women in the Antarctic* (Haworth Press, 1998), *Lesbian Friendships: For Ourselves and Each Other* (New York University Press, 1996), and *Lesbian Ex-Lovers: The Really Long-Term Relationships* (Haworth Press, 2005).

BIANCA D. M. WILSON, PhD, is a community health psychologist and currently an Assistant Professor at California State University, Long Beach. She studies the relationships among culture, oppression, and sexual health within African American lesbian, gay, and bisexual communities.

Index

Academia. *See* University

Adiposity, 25; and mortality, 29

Adolescents: and body weight, 25; bullying of, xix, 120–126; and weight bias in Singapore, 127–138

Aerobics for fat women, 312–319; *In Grand Form* videos; 316, 317, 318n1; Great Shape, 320; Large as Life, 313–314, 316; Light on Your Feet, 316; Women at Large, 313–314

Affiliated Big Men's Clubs, 143, 145; convergence event, 145

African American: and Arkansas websites, 88; and bisexual, 54–64; and Black feminist theory, 56; and cardiovascular health, 58; and eugenics, 259; and fat, 54–64; and lesbian, 54–64; mother-blaming, 114, 116; women's communities, 60

Agar, Nicholas, 71–72

Airplane seats and fat bodies, xv, 176–186, 329; and Southwest Airlines, 176–186

Aldebaran (Sarah Fishman), 4

American Eugenics movement, 65–68

American Obesity Association, xvii, 80

Americans with Disabilities Act, 184

Americocentrism, 330

Anorexia nervosa, 48; among celebrities, 263, 294; in Singapore, 127, 129, 130, 131, 132, 133, 135

Ansfield, Alice, 314

Anti-fat prejudice. *See* Weight bias and discrimination

Anzaldua, Gloria, 246–247

Association for Size Diversity and Health, 4

Atkinson, Richard, 80

Australia, as fattest nation, 1

Baartman, Saartje, 258

Bacon, Linda, 84

Bariatric medicine, 75, 155; weight loss surgery, 265, 267

Bartky, Sandra Lee, 199

"Bear" culture for gay men, 143–150; Bear Code, 147–148

Behavioral Risk Factor Surveillance System Survey, 37, 39

Bell, Suzanne, 313, 315, 316

Big Fat Blog, 333

Bisexual men, and weight bias, 143–150

Bisexual women: and African American, 54–64; and fat, 54–64

Black. *See* African American

"Bodies of Evidence: Fat Across Disciplines" conference, 332

Body acceptance, on Ontario websites, 90

Body dissatisfaction, 60

Body Mass Index (BMI), xiv; on Alberta websites, 93; as arbitrary,49; Canada vs. U.S., 88; and HAES, 51; and mortality, 29; on Ontario websites, 90; as protective factor, 44; on report cards, 77

Body size diversity, 60–61

Bordo, Susan, 257, 272

Braziel, Jana Evans, xi, 15, 152, 201

Britain. *See* United Kingdom

Brookey, Robert, 69, 70

Brownell, Kelly, 189, 207

Bruch, Hilde, 114, 117

Brumberg, Joan, 257

Bulimia: among celebrities, 294; as "political economy," 187, 192, 193; in Singapore, 130, 131, 132, 133, 135

Bullying of fat children, xix, 120–126; causes of, 122–123; consequences of, 121; prevalence, 120; in Singapore, 134

Burgard, Deb, xii, xvii, 3, 314

Burlesque, 299–304, 305–311, 316; Big Burlesque, 305–311; Fat Bottom Revue, 305–311

Butch/femme: and masculinity, 174; and perceptions of weight, 139, 141; in zines, 224

Butler, Judith, 101, 102, 223

Buttocks: in popular culture, 271–279; of women in postcards, 256–262

Calories, foods low in, 26

Campos, Paul, xviii, 338

Canada: aerobics for fat women, 312–319; Alberta websites and fat, 93–94, 95; British Columbia websites and fat, 92–93, 95; convergence event for gay men; 145; Dieticians of Canada, 100; as fattest nation, 1; Native Canadians, 90, 91, 94; Ontario websites and fat, 90–91, 95; provincial government and fat, 88–96; Quebec websites and fat, 91–92, 95

Capitalism and bodies, 187–196

Carmona, Richard, 335

Cassista, Toni, 169

Cather, Willa, 241–248

Celebrities, 263–270; Allie, Kirstie, 268; Barr, Roseanne, 267; Celebrity Wasting Syndrome, 263, 268; Lake, Ricki, 264; Lopez, Jennifer, 272–276; Wilson, Carnie, 265–266; Winfrey, Oprah, 266–267

Centers for Disease Control (CDC), xiv, xvi, 80

Chick-Lit: Bigger Girl Lit, 235, 237, 239; and fat heroines, 235–240

Children: and adoption, 168; bias against fat children, 77; and body weight, 25–26; and bullying, 120–126; and custody, 168; focus of diet programs, xv; and mother blame, 113–119; and "obesity epidemic," xix, 81, 335; on Ontario websites, 90; removed from homes, 2; and weight bias in Singapore, 127–138

China, restrictions on adoption in, xix

The Chubsters, 333

Classrooms: and desk size, 197–204; and fat professors, 205–212; and fat content of syllabi, 213–220

College. *See* University

Collins, Patricia Hill, 56, 61, 272, 274

Conferences on fat studies, 3, 4; "Bodies of Evidence: Fat Across Disciplines" 332; Columbia University Teachers College conference, xi; "Fat and the Academy," Smith College xi, 4, 232, 331; Popular Culture/American Culture Association xi, 4; as U.S.-based, 328–329, 332

Cooper, Charlotte, 228, 233

Corrigan, Christine, 113

Council on Size and Weight Discrimination, xvi, xvii

Crandall, Christian, 206, 210

Custody, loss of, 113

Dancers, Burlesque, 299–304, 305–311

Davenport, Charles, 65–67

Davis, Angela, 59

Davis, Lennard, xxii, 176

Death Comes for the Archbishop, 241–248

Dieticians, 97–105; Dieticians of Canada, 100

Dieting. *See* Weight loss

Dietz, William, 79

Director, Sheana, xi

Disability: Americans with Disabilities Act, 1–84; law, 169–172; rights activists, 178; scholars, 71; studies, xxii, 179, 184, 216–218; theory, xxii

Dolan, Jill, 249

Donley, Carol, 214–215

Dubus, Andre, 213–220

Dyer, Richard, 200–201

Dykewomon, Elana, 233

Eating disorders, xii, 42, 47–48, 81, 113, 294–295; in Singapore, 127–138

Edelman, Lee, 17

Elliott, Cass, xviii

Employment, xix; and Compliance Guidelines for San Francisco, 343–349; and Fair Employment and Housing Act, 171; for fat college professors, 205–212; firing of fat employees, xx; health insurance, xx; hiring of fat applicants, xx; income, xix–xx; job applicants, xx; legal issues in discrimination, 167–168; mistreatment of fat workers, xix; relation to weight, 32

Ensler, Eve, 252–253

"Epidemic of obesity." *See* "Obesity epidemic"

Equal Employment Opportunities Commission (EEOC), 170

Eugenics, 65–74, 242, 259

Exercise: aerobics for fat women, 312–319; and African Americans, 57; barriers, 61; deaths due to lack of, xvi; and Health at Every Size, 43; school-based, 2; in Singapore, 127–138; and socioeconomic status, 26; Women of Substance Health Spa, 320–324

Fabrey, William, 4

Fagan, Reanne, 4

Fat: gene, 65–74; and violence against women, 151–157

"Fat and the Academy" Conference, Smith College, xi, 4, 232, 331

FaT GiRL: A Zine for Fat Dykes and The Women Who Want Them, 223–230

Fat Girl Dances With Rocks, 231–232

Fat Liberation Manifesto, 4, 341–342

Fat liberation movement, 149, 217, 311, 313, 314

Fat Lip Readers Theatre, xxvii, 83

Fat-phobic. *See* Weight bias and discrimination

Fat-positive perspective, 56

Fat pride community, x, xii

Fat suits, 252, 268, 280–288

Fat studies, ix–xxv, 1–2; at conferences, xi; courses, 3; definition of, ix; e-mail list, xi; as fat pride community, x; FatStudies Listserv, xxvii; in Great Britain, 327–333; and Health At Every Size, xii; and political activism, 334–340; scholars, xiii, 2; and social justice, x; and stakeholders, xv; as U.S.-based, 327–333; and weight-related beliefs, x

Fat Studies Yahoo! Group, 333

Fat Underground, x, xviii, 4, 84, 338, 342n1; Aldebaran (Sarah Fishman), 4; and Fat

Liberation Manifesto, 341–342; Fagan, Reanne, 4; Fonfa, Gudrun, 4; Fram, Sheri, 4; Freespirit, Judy, 4; Mabel-Lois, Lynn (Lynn McAfee), 4; Manow, Ariana, 4

Fatness, xxii, 4; "fat as unhealthy" stereotype, 49

Fatshionista, 333

FAT!SO? zine, xxii

Feminism: attention to mother blame, 113, 118; and dietetics, 97–105; and literature on violence against women, 152

Fenfluramine. *See* Phen-Fen

Fenske, Sarah, 160–161, 162, 164

Fiction. *See* Literature

Films: fat suits, 280–289; *Hairspray*, 219, 250, 280; *The Nutty Professor*, 280–289; *Shallow Hal*, 268, 280–289

Fishman, Sarah (Aldebaran), 4

Flegel, Katherine, xvi, xvii, 83

Foege, William, xvi, 82

Fonfa, Gudrun, 4

Food: in *Death Comes for the Archbishop*, 241–248; frequency, questionnaires, 39; processed, 26

Food and Drug Association (FDA), 78, 82

Foodscape, 187–188

Foucault, Michel, 70, 176; Foucauldian biopolitics, 188, 194

Fram, Sheri, 4

Freccero, Carla, 18

Freespirit, Judy, 4

Friedman, Jeffrey, 71, 82

Gay men: Affiliated Big Men's Clubs, 143; "Bear" culture, 143–150; *Big Ad* magazine, 145; BiggerWorld, 146; *Bulk Male* magazine/Bulkmale.com, 146; chat rooms for fat gay men, 146; Chubnet, 146; "chubby-chasers," 143–144, 148; cultural prejudice, 65; fat male admirers, 143–150; and the gay gene, 65–74; Girth and Mirth clubs, 143, 148; *Heavy Duty* magazine, 146; and weight, 143–150

Germany, as fattest nation, 1

Girth Control, 260

Girth and Mirth clubs, 143, 145, 148

"Globesity," xv
Goffman, Erwing, 182, 337
Goodman, Charisse, 107
Gortmaker, Steven, 27
Graham, Sylvester, 115
Great Britain. *See* United Kingdom
Great Shape movement, 320
Gurin, Joel, 84

Hairspray, 219, 250, 280; Ricki Lake, 264
Hamer, Dean, 68, 71
Harjunen, Hannele, 329, 331
Health: among fat African American women,
    55–57; among lesbians and bisexual
    women, 55–57; care, access to, 28; care
    providers, xx, xxi; disparities by race and
    sexuality, 54; -enhancing behaviors, 50;
    lack of relationship to weight, 27; mor-
    tality risks, 27; as problematic term, xii;
    without weight loss, 47
Health At Every Size (HAES), xii, xvii, 3, 18,
    42–53, 61, 76, 7–8, 83--85
Health care system, as anti-fat, 57
Health club for fat women, 320–324
Health insurance, xiv, xx, xxi, 58
Healthy Eating Index, 26
Height, and Compliance Guidelines for San
    Francisco, 343–349
Heterosexism, 58; in the health care system,
    59
Hill, James, 80
Hispanics. *See* Latinas/Latinos
History, 11–14; of diet industry, 76–77; of
    eugenics movement, 65–68; queer, 15–22;
    and tourist postcards, 256–262
"Hogging," 155, 158–166
Homosexuality. *See* Bisexual men; Bisexual
    women; Gay men; Lesbian
The Hottentot Venus (Saartje Baartman), 258,
    260, 272–273; *Venus* (the play), 253
Huckabee, Mike, 88
Hutchinson, Woods, 11

Implicit Association Test (IAT), 207–208,
    209–210, 211
In Grand Form videos, 316, 317, 318n1
Internalized fat oppression, xx, 337

International No Diet Day, 333
International Size Acceptance Association
    (ISAA), xxvii, 328
Internet sites: Big Fat Blog, 333; Bigger-
    World, 146; Bulkmale.com, 146; Cana-
    dian government, 88–96; Chat rooms for
    fat gay men, 1, 46; *Chick Lit Books*, 236;
    Chubnet for fat gay men, 146; The Chub-
    sters, 333; *Dangerously Curvy Novels*, 236;
    for fat gay men, 143; Fat Studies Yahoo!
    Group, xi, 333; Fatshionista, 333; for Poly-
    cystic Ovarian Syndrome, 107; university
    syllabi, 213–220

Jenny Craig program, 79, 268, 335
Jonson, Ben, 20–21

Kline, Wendy, 6–8
Koop, C. Everett, U.S. Surgeon General, 1,
    76, 79, 334–335
Koppelman, Susan, xi, 153

Lamm, Nomy, 228
Large as Life, 313
Latinas/Latinos: and blaming of mothers,
    114, 116; and buttocks, 273–274; and
    conceptions of fat, 16; and Hispanic
    masculinity in *Death Comes for the Arch-
    bishop*, 241–248
LeBesco, Kathleen, xi, 15, 107, 152, 190, 201,
    223, 242, 244, 250, 280, 282
Legal issues: California State Supreme Court,
    168; Compliance Guidelines for San
    Francisco, 343–349; and disability law,
    169–172; and employment discrimina-
    tion, 167; Equal Employment Opportuni-
    ties Commission (EEOC), 170; and fat,
    167–175; and language to prohibit weight
    discrimination, 343–350; and transgender,
    167–175
Lenskyj, Helen, 316
Lesbian(s): African American, 54–64; *FaT
    GiRL: A Zine for Fat Dykes and The
    Women Who Want Them*, 223–230; *Size
    Queen*, 223–230; women's communities,
    60
Lindstrom, Walter, xvii

Literature: Chick-Lit and fat heroines, 235–240; *Death Comes for the Archbishop* (Willa Cather), 241–24–8; *FaT GiRL*, 223–230; fiction for fat girls, 231–234; novels for fat girls, 231–234; short stories of fat people, 213–220; *Size Queen*, 223–230. *See also* Zines
Lyons, Pat, 314

Mabel-Lois, Lynn (Lynn McAfee), 4
Mackenzie, Margaret, x, 11
Magazines: *Big Ad*, 145; *Big Beautiful Woman* (BBW); 183; *Bulk Male*, 146; *Heavy Duty*, 146; *Radiance Magazine*, 265, 314, 316
Manow, Ariana, 4
Marriage and weight, 27, 31
Masculinity: Brannon, Robert, components of, 158, 161; in *Death Comes for the Archbishop*, 241–248; hegemonic, 159–160, 163; homosocial enactment of, 159; "hostile masculinity," concept of, 163
McAfee, Lynn, xvi, 4
McGinnis, J. Michael, 82
Medical: equipment size, xxi; professionals, 46; setting, xx, xxi
Medico-pharmaceutical industrial complex, ix
Mexican American. *See* Latinas/Latinos
"Morbidly obese," critique of term, xv
Mortality rates, xvi, 28; and adiposity, 29–30; life expectancy, 77; and weight, 44; and weight loss, 81
Mother blame, 113–119
Movies. *See* Films
Mundy, Alicia, 78
Music videos, 265
Myers, Anna, 123

NAAFA. *See* National Association to Advance Fat Acceptance
National Association to Advance Fat Acceptance x, xxvii, 4, 83, 109, 148, 174, 177, 180, 181, 265, 328; Declaration of Health Rights for Fat People, 4; Million Pound March, 265
National Health and Nutrition Examination Surveys, 37

National Institutes of Health, 75, 77–78, 79, 80, 84, 179, 294
National Weight Control Registry, 37–41
Native Americans, and adiposity, 30
Native Canadians: First Nations and diabetes, 94; on Ontario websites, 90; on Quebec websites, 91
Neoliberalism and bodies, 187–196
New England Journal of Medicine, open letter about false death rates, xvi
NoLose, 333
"Normal" weight, critique of term, xii
Nutrition: dietetics, 97–105; foods high in nutrients, 26; link to poverty, 26; in Singapore, 127–138

"Obesity": and biopolitics, 194; critique of term, xii, xiii–xiv; as cultural construction, 16; media focus, xvii; in popular culture, 2; prevalence of, xv, 37
"Obesity epidemic," 5, 15, 71, 75–87, 88, 113, 118, 136, 187–188, 190 194, 228, 262, 328
"Obesity, Inc.," 78, 79–82, 83
Ob(Lep) "obesity gene," 69, 81
Orbach, Susie, 271, 276
"Overweight:" critique of term, xii–xiv; deaths attributed to, xvi; prevalence of, xv

Pacific Island nations, xi; and adiposity, 30
Panopticism, 289–296
Pharmaceutical industry, 75, 337
Phen-Fen, 76, 78, 79, 80, 128
Physical activity. *See* Exercise
Physicians: appointments with, xxi; in the American Obesity Association, xvii; historical view of fat, 11–13; obstetric/gynecolists, xxi; views of fat patients, xx
Pi-Sunyer, Xavier, 80
Pollitt, Katha, 117
Polycystic Ovarian Syndrome, 106–109; Polycystic Ovarian Syndrome Association, 107
Popular Culture/American Culture Association, xi, 4
Poverty: link to fatness, 25–26; link to illness, 33
Proulx, Annie, 233–234

Public health policy, 75–87
Puritans, 13–14

Queer, xxii, 2; community and weight bias, 143–150; history, 15–22; politics and publications, 223–230; studies, 17; theory, 142; zine *FaT GiRL*: 223–230; zine *Size Queen*, 223–230

Racism, 5–8; and eugenics, 66; in the health care system, 59; and mother blame, 113–119
Radiance Magazine, 265, 314, 316
Redux, xvi, 76, 78, 79, 82
Reid, Tulin, 108
"Reproductive futurism," 17
Rothblum, Esther, x, 1, 123
Rudd Center on Food Policy and "Obesity," xvii, xx; mission statement, xvii

Sabo, Sandy, 177–179, 183, 184
Sandler, Jody, 316, 317
Schools: focus of dieting programs, xv; focus of exercise programs, 2
Schwartz, Hillel, 14n1, 16, 115, 257
Seamon, Hollis, 219
Seats: airplane, and fat bodies, 176–186, 329; classroom desk size, 197–204; Compliance Guidelines for San Francisco, 343–349; locker rooms, 321; and Southwest Airlines, 176–186
Sedgwick, Eve, 17, 177
Set point theory, 84
Sexism, 58; in the health care system, 59
Shadow on a Tightrope, 305
Shape Up America! (SUA!) campaign, 79, 82, 335
Singapore: "Holistic Health Framework," 134; Trim and Fat Program (TAF), 127–138; weight bias, 127–138
Size acceptance, x, 42, 83, 151, 213; and chick lit, 237–239; and dieticians, 102; and fat burlesque, 311; among gay men, 149; and HAES, 50; International Size Acceptance Association (ISAA), 328; in Singapore, 135
Size Queen, 223–230

Slim-Fast, 79
Smuller, Zach, 113
Social mobility, and weight, 27
Socioeconomic class (SES), 25–36; and mother blame, 113–119
Solovay, Sondra, xi, 1, 113, 178, 183, 228, 263
Southwest Airlines, 176–186
Stern, Judith, xvi
Stigma threat, 205–212, 294
Stinson, Susan, 340
The Strange History of Suzanne LaFleshe, And Other Stories of Women and Fatness, xi, 218–219
Stunkard, Albert, 77

Teasing of fat children, xix, 120–126; in Singapore, 129, 134, 136
Teenagers. *See* Adolescents
Television celebrities, 263–270; Allie, Kirstie, 268; Barr, Roseanne, 267; "Celebrity Wasting Syndrome" 263, 268; Lake, Ricki, 264; Wilson, Carnie, 265–266; Winfrey, Oprah, 266–267
Television portrayals of fat, 289–296; stacked, 291–293: *Two and a Half Men*, 291–293
Theatre: and fat characters, 249–255; and fat suits, 252; *Fat Pig*, 252; *The Good Body*, 252–253; *Hairspray*, 250; *The Most Massive Woman Wins*, 250–251; *Venus*, 253
Thomas, Patti, 18–19
Throwing Our Weight Around: A Video About Women's Lives, 340n1
Tourist postcards, 256–262
Transgender: and disability law, 171–172; and Fair Employment and Housing Act, 171; legal issues, 167–175; and perceptions of fat, 139–142; and resisting police brutality, x
Trim and Fit Program (TAF), Singapore, 127–138

"Underweight," xv; on Alberta websites, 93–94; deaths attributed to, xvi
United Kingdom: "Bodies of Evidence: Fat Across Disciplines" conference, 332; The Chubsers, 333; fat studies, 327–333; as

fattest nation, 1; refusal of in vitro fertilization, xix; Unskinny Bop, 330; "Weight Wise Campaign," 98

United States: Alabama "obesity" prevention program, 116; Arkansas Child Health Advisory Committee, –89; Arkansas websites on weight, 88–89; California Court of Appeal, xviii; California State Supreme Court, 16–8; Compliance Guidelines for San Francisco, 343–349; as fattest nation, 1; rural South, 116

University: applications by fat students, xix; and classroom desks, 197–204; completion related to weight, 27; courses on fat studies, 3; and fat content of syllabi, 213–220; and fat professors, 205–212; and ostracism of fat students, xix; as sites of political organizing, 336; and stigma threat, 205–212; student evaluation, xx

Unskinny Bop, 330

Valdivia, Angharad, 272, 275, 277

Victorian women, 14

Violence against fat women, 151–157; and "hogging," 155, 158–166

Wadden, Thomas, 78–79

Wahl, Roberta Hughes, 218

Wann, Marilyn, ix, 3, 228, 263

"War on Obesity," 1, 42, 51, 79, 82, 83, 268, 334–336

Websites. *See* Internet sites

Weight bias and discrimination, xiii, xviii, xxi, 43, 45, 51, 58, 76, 85; against college professors, 205–212; against fat children, 120–126; against fat students, xix; among gay men, 143–150; legal issues, 167–175; and mortality, xvi; as oppression, 1; reducing weight bias, 81; in Singapore, 127–138; and violence against women, 152–157

Weight cycling, 45, 47

Weight loss: advertisements, 17; challenging the practice, 46; fad diets, 77; failure of, 39, 75, 77–79; HAES as weight neutral, 49; liquid diets, 76, 266; long-term weight loss, 38; "permanent weight loss," 37; in Singapore, 127–138; surgery, 265

Weight loss industry, 75–87

Weight neutral approach, 44, 49

Weight Watchers: profits, 76; low success rate, 7–8; contribution to Koop, 79, 335

"Weight Wise Campaign," 98

Williams, Leonard, 260, 261

Winfrey, Oprah, 76, 266–267

Women at Large, 313

Women of Substance Health Spa, 320–324

World Health Organization, 1

Wooley, Susan, 82

Yo-yo dieting, 90, 93

Zines: *FaT GiRL: A Zine for Fat Dykes and The Women Who Want Them*, 223–230; *FAT!SO?*, xxii; *Size Queen: For Queen Size Queers and Our Loyal Subjects*, 223–230